Understanding Organizational Behavior

2ND EDITION

DEBRA L. NELSON
Oklahoma State University

JAMES CAMPBELL QUICK
The University of Texas at Arlington

THOMSON
SOUTH-WESTERN

Australia · Canada · Mexico · Singapore · Spain · United Kingdom · United States

THOMSON

SOUTH-WESTERN

Understanding Organizational Behavior, 2e
Debra L. Nelson & James Campbell Quick

VP/Editorial Director:
Jack W. Calhoun

VP/Editor-in-Chief:
Michael P. Roche

Publisher:
Melissa S. Acuña

Executive Editor:
John Szilagyi

Developmental Editor:
Leslie Kauffman, Litten Editing and Production, Inc.

Marketing Manager:
Jacquelyn Carrillo

Sr. Production Editor:
Elizabeth A. Shipp

Media Developmental Editor:
Kristen Meere

Media Production Editor:
Karen L. Schaffer

Manufacturing Coordinator:
Rhonda Utley

Production House:
Litten Editing and Production, Inc.

Compositor:
GGS Information Services, Inc.

Design Project Manager:
Anne Marie Rekow

Internal and Cover Designer:
Anne Marie Rekow

Cover Image:
Richard Cook

Printer:
Globus Printing, Inc.

To our students, who challenge us to be better than we are, who keep us in touch with reality, and who are the foundation of our careers.

CONTENTS IN BRIEF

CONTENTS

PART 3 INTERPERSONAL PROCESSES AND BEHAVIOR

PART 4   ORGANIZATIONAL PROCESSES AND STRUCTURE

PREFACE

Change was the overarching theme for the first edition of *Understanding Organizational Behavior*, and so it continues. For some people, change is experienced as a crisis. This is not necessarily bad when one understands that the Chinese symbol for crisis is a combination of the symbols for danger and opportunity. Yes, change may pose dangers for individuals and organizations. However, change also opens the door for new opportunities, new challenges, and new experiences. The early years of the twenty-first century have again seen the presence of world-changing events that have significant effects on organizations in all sectors of world economies. These changes also have significant effects on peoples' attitudes, feelings, and behavior at work. Organizational behavior is at the heart of productive business, and it is the basis for taking advantage of the opportunities that change offers us all.

Understanding Organizational Behavior, second edition, continues to reflect our core value of solid scholarly **foundations** on which the science of organizational behavior is built, our continuing interest in the **realities** of contemporary organizational life, and our belief that **challenges** are the pathway to taking advantage of the opportunities that change offers. The science of organizational behavior is anchored in broad, deep research roots in our discipline. Our book contains classic as well as leading-edge research in the field. Research and theory form the foundations of our knowledge. Organizational behavior is an applied discipline concerned with what is going on in organizations. Thus, we include examples from all types of organizations. Some of the examples show successes, while others show failures, of managers applying organizational behavior knowledge in the real world. Challenges are the opportunities we have to grow and develop both as individuals and organizations. In the book, they take the form of individual activities for proactive learning.

Organizational behavior is the study of individual behavior and group dynamics in organizational settings. It focuses on timeless topics like motivation, leadership, teamwork, and communication. Such issues have captured our attention for decades. Organizational behavior also encompasses contemporary issues in organizations. How do we encourage employees to engage in organizational citizenship behaviors, to go above and beyond the call of duty to exhibit exceptional performance? How do we restructure organizations in the face of increasing competition? What is the new psychological contract between employees and organizations? How have careers changed, and what can we expect in the future? How do we manage employee behavior in virtual organizations or teams? What happens when organizations with strong cultures and a need for constancy face the pressure to become current, competitive, and agile? *Understanding Organizational Behavior* thus engages both classic and emerging issues.

Our overarching theme of change is accompanied by four supporting subthemes: *globalization*, *diversity*, *technology*, and *ethics*. Each subtheme presents its own challenges and prods individuals to learn, grow, and adjust. This is especially true when it comes to ethics and the call from academicians, business people, and religious leaders for greater and stronger ethical leadership on the part of our business leaders. Personal integrity is a timeless value that is of continuing importance to all of us. Students and business leaders must learn about and wrestle with these important issues of character, just as did a Lockheed Martin software engineer asked to certify as good-to-go software of a USAF test aircraft just before a Christmans holiday. Because he was not given proper documentation, he chose to "not certify" even though it cost the company some real money to delay. However, he was unwilling to put the lives of USAF test pilots at risk. In addition to ethics and character, diversity can be a tremendous asset for organizations with the wealth of skills and knowledge that different people bring to work. To maximize the benefits of diversity, managers must build organizational cultures that view differences as assets.

New technologies call employees to learn new skills and abilities, and organizations expect all employees to learn continually. Our book rests on the assumption that learning involves not only acquiring knowledge but also developing skills. The rich theory and research in organizational behavior must be translated into application. Thus, the text presents the opportunity to know concepts, ideas, and theories, and to practice skills, abilities, and behaviors to enhance the management of human behavior at work. Both knowledge and skills are essential for our future managers. We hope the knowledge and skills presented here empower them to succeed in the changing world of work.

Chapter	Diversity	Globalization	Ethics	Technology
1	14, 16	14, 16	14, 16	14, 16
2	25, 27, 28, 29, 30, 31, 32, 33, 34, 35, 36, 47	25, 26, 27, 28, 29, 47	25, 26, 40, 41, 42, 43, 44, 45, 46, 47	25, 36, 37, 38, 39
3	65, 68, 70, 73	68, 73		
4	92, 93	82, 83, 86, 87, 92, 93	80, 81, 92, 93, 94, 95, 96, 97, 98, 99, 100, 101	
5	123	123		106
6				
7	161, 162	162, 163, 168, 170		171, 172, 173, 174
8	181, 186, 195, 196	196	179	
9	222, 223	213, 214, 223, 224	208, 226, 227	223, 224, 225, 226
10	243		233, 234, 235	
11	273, 275, 276	275, 276	276	
12	285, 297, 300, 302	285, 286, 300, 301, 302		
13		310, 320, 321, 322		326, 329
14	358	354, 355, 358		338, 339, 346, 347, 348, 355, 358
15	367, 378, 381, 384	378, 380, 381, 384	381, 382, 384	382, 384
16	388, 389	388, 389, 394, 402	389, 390, 410	389

SPECIAL FEATURES

Several special features of the book extend the *foundations, realities, and challenges* to specific applications. These features are designed to enhance the application of theory and research in practice, to stimulate student interest and discussion, and to facilitate cognitive as well as skill-based learning.

FOUNDATIONS

Each chapter includes leading-edge research studies related to the chapter's topic. The book is based on extensive classic and contemporary research literature. At the end of the textbook is a lengthy chapter-by-chapter reference list that students can refer to for in-depth treatments of the chapter topics.

REALITIES

Focus Companies The second edition features extensive examples from five key organizations: American Heart Association, Brinker International, Harley-Davidson, Hewlett-Packard, and Patagonia. These organizations represent manufacturing and service, profit and not-for-profit, and large and small organizations. By featuring these five key organizations throughout the book, students can familiarize themselves with the companies in greater depth than a single appearance would allow.

A host of relevant, recent examples are also included in each chapter. These examples spotlight contemporary organizational life. They are realities that reflect the themes of globalization, diversity, technology, and ethics. They include not only examples of successes but also examples of failures, which are opportunities for learning.

CHALLENGES

Challenge Exercises A Challenge is included in the body of each chapter. These are self-assessment exercises that provide the student with feedback on one aspect of the topic. Examples are the learning style inventory in Chapter 1, in which students discover their own learning preferences, and applying force field analysis inventory in Chapter 16, which helps students assess forces affecting change. Each Challenge is designed to enhance self-knowledge or to promote skill development in the subject matter. The student is able to use the results of the Challenge for self-discovery or behavioral change.

"You Be the Judge" Ethics Questions Ethics questions and dilemmas in the margins of each chapter provoke students to think about what is right and wrong as well as about the various ways to resolve ethical conflicts in organizations. Many of the ethical questions and dilemmas do not have a single answer; rather, they raise key issues for the students to think through.

Experiential Exercises A group-oriented Experiential Exercise is included at the end of each chapter. It is designed for students to work in teams to learn more about an important aspect of the chapter's topic. The exercises give students opportunities to develop interpersonal skills and to process their thinking within a teamwork setting. In the Chapter 15 exercise, "Contrasting Organizational Cultures," groups of students compare the cultures of two organizations and relate the dimensions of culture to the organizations' performance.

SOME DISTINCTIVE FEATURES STUDENTS LIKE

Understanding Organizational Behavior offers a number of distinctive, time-tested, and interesting features for students, as well as new and innovative features. Each chapter begins with a clear statement of learning objectives to provide students with expectations about what is to come. Graphics and tables enhance students' ease in grasping the topical material and involve students actively in the learning process.

Examples from diverse organizations (multinational, regional, non-profit, public) and industries (manufacturing, service, defense) are included. These examples are integrated throughout the text. A unique feature of the book is its focus on the five organizations mentioned earlier. These represent many different types of organizations—large and small, for profit and not-for-profit, product and service oriented. The purpose of this approach is to provide a sense of continuity and depth not achieved in single examples.

STUDY AIDS

To help you learn, understand, and apply the material in *Understanding Organizational Behavior*, the second edition provides unique and comprehensive study tools.

Web Site (http://nelson-quick.swlearning.com) A rich Web site at http://nelson-quick.swlearning.com complements the text, providing many extras for students. Resources include chapter glossaries, interactive quizzes, PowerPoint® slides, cases, related articles and activities, and links to other useful resources.

Experiencing Organizational Behavior An innovative product, *Experiencing Organizational Behavior* is a totally online collection of Web-based modules that uses the latest Flash technology in its animated scenarios, graphs, and models. Designed to reinforce key management principles in a dynamic learning environment, *Experiencing Organizational Behavior* maintains high motivation through the use of challenging problems. Try it by visiting http://www.experiencingob.com. *Experiencing Organizational Behavior* is available for purchase online by each individual module or as a collection of all 13 modules.

SOME DISTINCTIVE FEATURES INSTRUCTORS LIKE

Professors have demanding jobs. They should expect textbook authors and publishers to provide them with the support they need to do an excellent job for students. Among their expectations should be a well-integrated, complete ancillary package. *Understanding Organizational Behavior* has this package.

ANCILLARY PACKAGE

A comprehensive set of ancillaries supports the basic text: an instructor's resource manual with video guide, a test bank, Exam*View* (computerized testing software), PowerPoint® slides, a product support Web site, and a video program. The videos include a variety of short vignettes about real companies with which your students may already be familiar. Using video in the classroom will enhance the text presentation and reinforce its themes, adding continuity and integration to the overall understanding of organizational behavior.

Instructor's Manual with Video Guide (ISBN: 0-324-28233-8)
The instructor's manual with video guide for *Understanding Organizational Behavior* was prepared by David A. Foote (Middle Tennessee State University) and BJ Parker. Each chapter contains the following information:

- Chapter scan—a brief overview of the chapter.
- Suggested learning objectives that are presented in the textbook.
- Key terms—a list of key terms from the chapter.
- The chapter summarized—an extended outline with narratives under each major point to flesh out the discussion and offer alternative examples and issues to bring forward. The extended outlines are several pages long and incorporate many teaching suggestions.
- Assignment materials, including review questions and discussion and communication questions.
- Answer guidelines for assignment materials—detailed responses to the review questions, discussion and communication questions, and "You Be the Judge" ethics questions, with suggestions for keeping discussion on track in the classroom.
- Challenges—suggested answers for the Challenges.
- Experiential exercises—a brief description of each exercise as well as a detailed summary of anticipated results. Also included are alternative experiential exercises not found in the text. Discussion questions are provided with selected experiential exercises. Finally, a list of sources for still more may be found under "Extra Experiential Exercises."
- Cases—suggested answers for case discussion questions found on the product support Web site are provided in a detailed form.
- Integration of Myers-Briggs Type Indicator material (optional)—including full descriptions and exercises in communication, leadership, motivation, decision making, conflict resolution, power, stress

and time management, and managing change. For instructors unfamiliar with Myers-Briggs, a general introduction to this instrument is provided at the end of Chapter 3 of the instructor's manual. The introduction includes several good references for additional information about testing.

- Comprehensive video cases, including information on how to successfully incorporate the use of video in your lesson plan, are included for select chapters with accompanying video segments.
- Printouts of the PowerPoint® slides.

Test Bank (ISBN: 0-324-22454-0) The test bank, prepared by Jon G. Kalinowski (Minnesota State University, Mankato), has been thoroughly revised for this edition. The test bank contains more than 1,000 multiple-choice, true/false, matching, and essay questions. Each question has been coded according to Bloom's taxonomy, a widely known testing and measurement device used to classify questions according to level (easy, medium, or hard) and type (application, recall, or comprehension).

ExamView (ISBN: 0-324-22451-6) This supplement contains all of the questions in the printed test bank. This program is an easy-to-use test creation software compatible with Microsoft Windows. Instructors can add or edit questions, instructions, and answers, and select questions by previewing them on the screen, selecting them randomly, or selecting them by number. Instructors can also create and administer quizzes online, whether over the Internet, a local area network (LAN), or a wide area network (WAN).

PowerPoint® Slides Marilyn Bergmann and Donna Raleigh (University of Wisconsin, Eau Claire) have developed more than 250 PowerPoint® slides for this text. These slides feature figures from the text, lecture outlines, and innovative adaptations to enhance classroom presentation.

Instructor's Resource CD-ROM (ISBN: 0-324-22450-8) Key instructor ancillaries (instructor's manual, test bank, ExamView, and PowerPoint® slides) are provided on CD-ROM, giving instructors the ultimate tool for customizing lectures and presentations.

Web Site (http://nelson-quick.swlearning.com) *Understanding Organizational Behavior* has its own product support Web site at http://nelson-quick.swlearning.com. The full PowerPoint® presentation is available for you to download as lecture support for yourself as well as a study aid for your students. The instructor's manual and video guide are also available for download. A multiple-choice and true/false tutorial to help your students study for exams is also featured. Related articles and activities and a downloadable chapter on Stress and Well-Being at Work are provided.

Video Program (ISBN: 0-324-22452-4) An extensive updated video program has been developed especially for use with *Understanding*

Organizational Behavior. Video segments have been selected to support the themes of the book and to deepen students' understanding of the organizational behavior concepts presented throughout the text. Information on using the videos can be found in the instructor's manual. Companies profiled in the video series include Valassis Communications, Burke, Inc., JIAN Corporation, and Sunshine Cleaning Systems, among others.

CNN Video: Management and Organizations (ISBN: 0-324-15179-9) Forty-five minutes of short segments from CNN, the world's first 24-hour all-news network, are available on VHS cassette to use as lecture launchers, discussion starters, topical introductions, or directed inquiries.

OUR REVIEWERS ARE APPRECIATED

We would like to thank our professional peers and colleagues who reviewed the first edition and drafts of the manuscript to evaluate scholarly accuracy, writing style, and pedagogy. The many changes we made are based on their suggestions. We gratefully acknowledge the help of the following individuals:

David Adams, *Manhattanville College*

Terry R. Adler, *New Mexico State University*

Clarence Anderson, *Walla Walla College*

Talya Bauer, *Portland State University*

Joy Benson, *University of Illinois—Springfield*

Constant D. Beugré, *Kent State University, Tuscarawas Campus*

Deborah Ramirez Bishop, *Saginaw Valley State University*

William R. Blackerby, *Siena Heights University*

Katharine A. Bohley, *University of Indianapolis*

Cindy Brown, *South Plains College*

Beth Chung, *San Diego State University*

Jeanette A. Davy, *Wright State University*

David Drehmer, *DePaul University*

Sally Dresdow, *University of Wisconsin—Green Bay*

David A. Foote, *Middle Tennessee State University*

Jackie Gilbert, *Middle Tennessee State University*

Robert D. Goddard III, *Appalachian State University*

Andra Gumbus, *Sacred Heart University*

Nell Tabor Hartley, *Robert Morris College*

Fred Hughes, *Faulkner University*

Dong I. Jung, *San Diego State University*

John W. Lewis III, *Boston College*

John Mathieu, *University of Connecticut*

Jalane M. Meloun, *Kent State University*

Dorothy Perrin Moore, *The Citadel*

William D. Spangler, *SUNY—Binghamton*

Charlotte Sutton, *Auburn University*

William H. Turnley, *Kansas State University*

Kathleen Wilch, *Georgia Southwestern State University*

ACKNOWLEDGMENTS

The second edition of *Understanding Organizational Behavior* represents a true team effort, and we are grateful to our team members who made the process run smoothly. We are indebted to our editor, John Szilagyi, for his vision, guidance, and support, and for saying "yes" more often than "no." Leslie Kauffman, our developmental editor, made completing the second edition a pleasure by shepherding us and keeping us focused. Libby Shipp, our production editor, guided us with the utmost diligence and patience, and we are grateful for her contribution. With an eagle eye for the details, Malvine Litten did an excellent job of project management for the textbook. Lorretta Palagi did a wonderful job on our permissions.

Faye Cocchiara was wonderful in reviewing the most recent research and literature for many of the topics in the book, as well as ensuring the timeliness and accuracy of the information contained in the chapters. Her sensitivity to issues of workforce diversity, organizational cultures, and globalization enriched the perspectives we have on these important issues in organizational life and the workplace.

We are fortunate to have several colleagues who have made helpful contributions and supported our development through both editions of the textbook: Mike Hitt of Texas A&M University; Lisa Kennedy of Baylor College of Medicine; Raj Basu, Robert Dooley, Ken Eastman, and Mark Gavin, all of Oklahoma State University; Bret Simmons of North Dakota State University; David Gray, Dave Mack, Ken Price, and Jim Lavelle, all of the University of Texas at Arlington; and Joanne H. Gavin of Marist College.

Our families and friends have encouraged us throughout the development of the book. They have provided us with emotional support and examples for the book and have graciously allowed us the time to do the book justice. We are truly grateful for their support.

This book has been a labor of love for both of us. It has made us better teachers and also better learners. We hope it does the same for you.

Debra L. Nelson
James Campbell Quick

DEBRA L. NELSON

Dr. Debra L. Nelson is The CBA Associates Professor of Business Administration and Professor of Management at Oklahoma State University. She received her Ph.D. from the University of Texas at Arlington, where she was the recipient of the R. D. Irwin Dissertation Fellowship Award. Dr. Nelson is the author of over 70 journal articles focusing on organizational stress management, newcomer socialization, and management of technology. Her research has been published in the *Academy of Management Executive, Academy of Management Journal, Academy of Management Review, MIS Quarterly, Organizational Dynamics, Journal of Organizational Behavior*, and other journals. In addition, she is coauthor/coeditor of several books, including *Organizational Behavior: Foundations, Realities, and Challenges* (4th ed., South-Western/Thomson Learning, 2003), *Gender, Work Stress and Health* (American Psychological Association, 2002), *Advancing Women in Management* (Blackwell, 2002), and *Preventive Stress Management in Organizations* (American Psychological Association, 1997). Dr. Nelson has also served as a consultant to several organizations including AT&T, American Fidelity Assurance, Sonic, State Farm Insurance Companies, and Southwestern Bell. She has presented leadership and preventive stress management seminars in a host of organizations, including Blue Cross/Blue Shield, Conoco, Oklahoma Gas and Electric, Oklahoma Natural Gas, and Preview Network Systems. She was honored with the Greiner Graduate Teaching Award in 2001, the Chandler-Frates and Reitz Graduate Teaching Award in 1997, the Regents' Distinguished Teaching Award in 1994, and the Burlington Northern Faculty Achievement Award at OSU in 1991. Dr. Nelson also serves on the editorial review board of the *Academy of Management Executive*.

JAMES CAMPBELL QUICK

Dr. James Campbell (Jim) Quick is a Professor of Organizational Behavior at the University of Texas at Arlington, Director of the Doctoral Program in Business Administration, and a task force member for the creation of the Goolsby Leadership Academy in the College. Dr. Quick is a former Associate Editor of *The Academy of Management Executive*. He earned an A.B. with Honors from Colgate University, where he was awarded a Harvard Business School Association Internship. He earned an M.B.A. and a Ph.D. at the University of Houston. He completed post-graduate courses in behavioral medicine (Harvard Medical School) and combat stress (University of Texas Health Science Center at San Antonio).

Dr. Quick is a Fellow of the Society for Industrial and Organizational Psychology, the American Psychological Association, the American Psychological Society, and the American Institute of Stress. He was awarded a Presidential Citation by the American Psychological Association in 2001 and awarded the prestigious Harry and Miriam Levinson Award by the American Psychological Foundation in 2002.

Dr. Quick framed preventive stress management with his brother (Jonathan D. Quick, MD, MPH). He has received over $250,000 in funded support for research, scholarship, and intellectual contributions from the

Society for Human Resource Management, Hospital Corporation of America, the State of Texas, and the American Psychological Association. His articles have been published in leading journals such as the *Academy of Management Journal, Academy of Management Review*, and *Academy of Management Executive, Journal of Organizational Behavior, Air University Review, Stress Medicine*, and the *Journal of Medical Education*. He received the 1990 Distinguished Professional Publication Award for *Corporate Warfare: Preventing Combat Stress and Battle Fatigue,* coauthored with Debra L. Nelson and his brother for the American Management Association's *Organizational Dynamics*.

He is coauthor of *Preventive Stress Management in Organizations* (American Psychological Association, 1997), originally published in 1984 and released as *Unternehmen ohne Stress* in German. He is coauthor of *The Financial Times Guide to Executive Health* (Prentice Hall/Financial Times, 2002), released as *o Executivo em Harmonia* in Portuguese, and *Stress and Challenge at the Top: The Paradox of the Successful Executive* (John Wiley & Sons, 1990). He is coeditor of the *Handbook of Occupational Health Psychology* (APA, 2002), *The New Organizational Reality: Downsizing, Restructuring, and Revitalization* (APA, 1998), *Stress and Well-Being at Work* (APA, 1992), and *Work Stress: Health Care Systems in the Workplace* (Praeger Scientific, 1987), for which he received the 1987 Distinguished Service Award from the UTA College of Business. He is a member of Beta Gamma Sigma and Phi Beta Delta honor societies and the Great Southwest Rotary Club, where he is a Paul Harris Fellow.

Dr. Quick was the American Psychological Association's stress expert to the National Academy of Sciences on National Health Objectives for the Year 2000. Dr. Quick was a scientific exchange delegate to the People's Republic of China. He is an Editorial Board member of *Stress Medicine*.

Dr. Quick was recognized with the Texas Volunteer Recognition Award (American Heart Association, 1985), a listing in *Who's Who in the World*, 7th Edition (1984–85), *The Maroon Citation* (Colgate University Alumni Corporation, 1993), and two Minnie Stevens Piper Professorship Award nominations (1995/2001).

Colonel Quick, U.S. Air Force (Retired), was the Senior Individual Mobilization Augmentee at the San Antonio Air Logistics Center (AFMC), Kelly AFB, Texas, in his last assignment. He was twice Distinguished Visiting Professor of Psychology, 59th Medical Wing (1999/2004). His awards and decorations include *The Legion of Merit, Meritorious Service Medal*, and *National Defense Service Medal with Bronze Star*.

He is married to the former Sheri Grimes Schember.

PART 1

Introduction

1

Organizational Behavior in Changing Times

LEARNING OBJECTIVES

After reading this chapter, you should be able to do the following:

1. Define *organizational behavior*.

2. Identify six interdisciplinary contributions to the study of organizational behavior.

3. Identify the important system components of an organization.

4. Describe the formal and informal elements of an organization.

5. Understand the diversity of organizations in the economy, as exemplified by the five focus organizations.

6. Recognize the challenge of change for organizational behavior.

7. Demonstrate the value of objective knowledge and skill development in the study of organizational behavior.

HUMAN BEHAVIOR IN ORGANIZATIONS

Organizational behavior is individual behavior and group dynamics in organizations. The study of organizational behavior is primarily concerned with the psychosocial, interpersonal, and behavioral dynamics in organizations. However, organizational variables that affect human behavior at work are also relevant to the study of organizational behavior. These organizational variables include jobs, the design of work, communication, performance appraisal, organizational design, and organizational structure. Therefore, although individual behavior and group dynamics are the primary concerns in the study of organizational behavior, organizational variables are also important.

This chapter is an introduction to organizational behavior. The first section provides an overview of human behavior in organizations and its interdisciplinary origins. The second section presents an organizational context within which behavior occurs and briefly introduces five focus companies used selectively in the book. The third section highlights the importance of *change* and *challenge* for organizational behavior in these changing times. The fourth section addresses the ways people learn about organizational behavior and explains how the text's pedagogical features relate to the various ways of learning. The final section of the chapter presents the plan for the book.

Human behavior in organizations is complex and often difficult to understand. Organizations have been described as clockworks in which human behavior is logical and rational, but they often seem like snake pits to those who work in them.[1] The clockwork metaphor reflects an orderly, idealized view of organizational behavior devoid of conflict or dilemma because all the working parts (the people) mesh smoothly. The snake pit metaphor conveys the daily conflict, distress, and struggle in organizations. Each metaphor reflects reality from a different perspective—the organization's versus the individual's point of view. These metaphors reflect the complexity of human behavior, the dark side of which is seen in cases of air rage.

This section briefly contrasts two perspectives for understanding human behavior, the external and the internal perspectives. It then discusses the six scientific disciplines from which the study of organizational behavior has emerged. Each discipline has made a unique contribution to organizational behavior.

1. *Define* organizational behavior.

ORGANIZATIONAL BEHAVIOR
The study of individual behavior and group dynamics in organizations.

CHANGE
The transformation or modification of an organization and/or its stakeholders.

CHALLENGE
The call to competition, contest, or battle.

UNDERSTANDING HUMAN BEHAVIOR

The vast majority of theories and models of human behavior fall into one of two basic categories. One category has an internal perspective, and the other has an external perspective. The internal perspective considers factors inside the person to understand behavior. This view is psychodynamically oriented. People who subscribe to this view understand human behavior in terms of the thoughts, feelings, past experiences, and needs of the individual. The internal perspective explains people's actions and behavior in terms of their history and personal value systems. The internal processes of thinking, feeling, perceiving, and judging lead people to act in specific ways. The internal perspective has given rise to a wide range of motivational and leadership theories. This perspective implies that people are best understood from the inside and that people's behavior is best interpreted after understanding their thoughts and feelings.

The other category of theories and models of human behavior takes an external perspective. This perspective focuses on factors outside the person to understand behavior. People who subscribe to this view understand human behavior in terms of external events, consequences of behavior, and the environmental forces to which a person is subject. From the external perspective, a person's history, feelings, thoughts, and personal value systems are not very important in interpreting actions and behavior. This perspective has given rise to an alternative set of motivational and leadership theories. The external perspective implies that a person's behavior is best understood by examining the surrounding external events and environmental forces.

The internal and external perspectives offer alternative explanations for human behavior. For example, the internal perspective might say Mary is an outstanding employee because she has a high need for achievement, whereas the external perspective might say Mary is an outstanding employee because she is paid extremely well for her work. Kurt Lewin captured both perspectives in saying that behavior is a function of both the person and the environment.[2]

INTERDISCIPLINARY INFLUENCES

2. *Identify six interdisciplinary contributions to the study of organizational behavior.*

Organizational behavior is a blended discipline that has grown out of contributions from numerous earlier fields of study, only one of which is the psychological discipline from which Kurt Lewin came. These interdisciplinary influences are the roots for what is increasingly recognized as the independent discipline of organizational behavior. The sciences of psychology, sociology, engineering, anthropology, management, and medicine are the disciplines from which organizational behavior has emerged or by which it has been influenced. Each of these sciences has had its own important and unique influence on the discipline of organizational behavior.

PSYCHOLOGY
The science of human behavior.

Psychology is the science of human behavior and dates back to the closing decades of the nineteenth century. Psychology traces its own origins to philosophy and the science of physiology. One of the most prominent early psychologists, William James, actually held a degree in medicine (M.D.). Since its origin, psychology has itself become differentiated into a number of specialized fields, such as clinical, experimental, military, organizational, and social psychology. The topics in organizational psychology, which include work teams, work motivation, training and development, power and leadership, human resource planning, and workplace wellness, are very similar to the topics covered by organizational behavior.[3] An early leader in

---

YOU BE THE JUDGE

Which disciplines are important in understanding moral and ethical issues for organizations and management?

the field of psychology was Robert Yerkes, whose research efforts for the American military during World War I had later implications for sophisticated personnel selection methods used by corporations such as Johnson & Johnson, Valero Energy, and Chaparral Steel.[4]

Sociology, the science of society, has made important contributions to knowledge about group and intergroup dynamics in the study of organizational behavior. Because sociology takes the society rather than the individual as its point of departure, the sociologist is concerned with the variety of roles within a society or culture, the norms and standards of behavior that emerge within societies and groups, and the consequences of compliant and deviant behavior within social groups. For example, the concept of *role set* was a key contribution to role theory in 1957 by Robert Merton. The role set consisted of a person in a social role and all others who had expectations of that person. A team of Harvard educators used the concept to study the school superintendent role in Massachusetts.[5] More recently, the role set concept has been used to study the effects of codes of ethics in organizations.[6] These sociological contributions were the basis for subsequent studies of role conflict and ambiguity in companies such as Tenneco Automotive, Purex, and The Western Company of North America.

Engineering is the applied science of energy and matter. Engineering has made important contributions to our understanding of the design of work. By taking basic engineering ideas and applying them to human behavior in work organizations, Frederick Taylor had a profound influence on the early years of the study of organizational behavior.[7] Taylor's engineering background led him to place special emphasis on human productivity and efficiency in work behavior. His notions of performance standards and differential piece-rate systems contributed to a congressional investigation into scientific management at the behest of organized labor. Taylor was ahead of his times in many ways, and his ideas were often controversial during his lifetime. Nevertheless, applications of his original ideas are embedded in organizational goal-setting programs, such as those at Black & Decker, IBM, and Weyerhaeuser.[8] Even the notions of *stress* and *strain* have their origins in the lexicon of engineering.

Anthropology is the science of human learned behavior and is especially important to understanding organizational culture. Cultural anthropology focuses on the origins of culture and the patterns of behavior as culture is communicated symbolically. Current research in this tradition has examined the effects of efficient cultures on organization performance[9] and how pathological personalities may lead to dysfunctional organizational cultures.[10] Schwartz used a psychodynamic, anthropological mode of inquiry in exploring corporate decay at General Motors and NASA during the 1980s.[11]

Management, originally called administrative science, is a discipline concerned with the study of overseeing activities and supervising people in organizations. It emphasizes the design, implementation, and management of various administrative and organizational systems. March and Simon take

SOCIOLOGY
The science of society.

ENGINEERING
The applied science of energy and matter.

ANTHROPOLOGY
The science of the learned behavior of human beings.

MANAGEMENT
The study of overseeing activities and supervising people in organizations.

the human organization as their point of departure and concern themselves with the administrative practices that will enhance the effectiveness of the system.[12] Management is the first discipline to take the modern corporation as the unit of analysis, and this viewpoint distinguishes the discipline's contribution to the study of organizational behavior.

MEDICINE
The applied science of healing or treatment of diseases to enhance an individual's health and well-being.

Medicine is the applied science of healing or treatment of diseases to enhance an individual's health and well-being. Medicine embraces concern for both physical and psychological health, with the concern for industrial mental health dating back at least seventy years.[13] More recently, as the war against acute diseases is being won, medical attention has shifted from the acute diseases, such as influenza, to the more chronic, such as hypertension. Attention has also been directed to occupational health and well-being.[14] Individual behavior and lifestyle patterns play a more important role in treating chronic diseases than in treating acute diseases.[15] These trends have contributed to the growth of corporate wellness programs, such as Johnson & Johnson's "Live for Life Program" and Control Data Corporation's STAY-WELL program. Such programs have led to increasing attention to medicine in organizational behavior. The surge in health care costs over the past two decades has also contributed to increased organizational concern with medicine and health care in the workplace.[16]

THE ORGANIZATIONAL CONTEXT

A complete understanding of organizational behavior requires both an understanding of human behavior and an understanding of the organizational context within which human behavior is acted out. The organizational context is the specific setting within which organizational behavior is enacted. This section discusses several aspects of this organizational context and includes specific organizational examples. First, organizations are presented as systems. Second, the formal and informal organizations are discussed. Finally, five focus companies are presented as contemporary examples, which are drawn on throughout the text.

3. *Identify the important system components of an organization.*

ORGANIZATIONS AS OPEN SYSTEMS

Just as two different perspectives offer complementary explanations for human behavior, two other perspectives offer complementary explanations of organizations. Organizations are open systems of interacting components, which are people, tasks, technology, and structure. These internal components also interact with components in the organization's task environment. Organizations as open systems have people, technology, structure, and purpose, which interact with elements in the organization's environment.

What, exactly, is an organization? Today, the corporation is the dominant organizational form for much of the Western world, but other organizational forms have dominated other times and societies. Some societies have been dominated by religious organizations, such as the temple corporations of ancient Mesopotamia and the churches in colonial America.[17]

Other societies have been dominated by military organizations, such as the clans of the Scottish Highlands and the regional armies of the People's Republic of China.[18, 19] All of these societies are woven together by family organizations, which themselves may vary from nuclear and extended families to small, collective communities.[20, 21] The purpose and structure of the religious, military, and family organizational forms may vary, but people's behavior in these organizations may be very similar. In fact, early discoveries about power and leadership in work organizations were remarkably similar to findings about power and leadership within families.[22]

Organizations may manufacture products, such as aircraft components or steel, or deliver services, such as managing money or providing insurance protection. To understand how organizations do these things requires an understanding of the open system components of the organization and the components of its task environment.

Katz and Kahn and Leavitt set out open system frameworks for understanding organizations.[23] The four major internal components are task, people, technology, and structure. These four components, along with the organization's inputs, outputs, and key elements in the task environment, are depicted in Figure 1-1. The **task** of the organization is its mission, purpose, or goal for existing. The **people** are the human resources of the organization. The technology is the wide range of tools, knowledge, and/or techniques used to transform the inputs into outputs. The **structure** is how

TASK
An organization's mission, purpose, or goal for existing.

PEOPLE
The human resources of the organization.

STRUCTURE
The manner in which an organization's work is designed at the micro level, as well as how departments, divisions, and the overall organization are designed at the macro level.

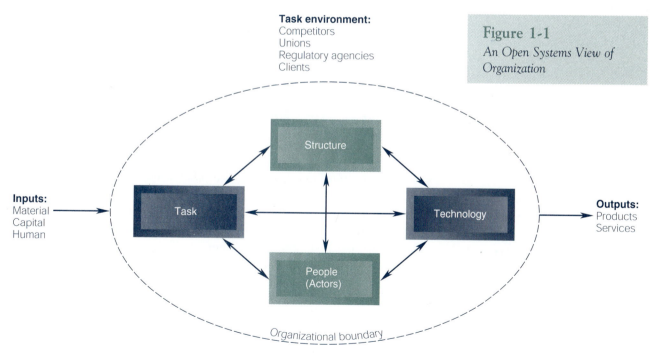

Task environment:
Competitors
Unions
Regulatory agencies
Clients

Figure 1-1
An Open Systems View of Organization

Inputs:
Material
Capital
Human

Structure

Task

Technology

People
(Actors)

Outputs:
Products
Services

Organizational boundary

Source: Based on Harold Leavitt, "Applied Organizational Change in Industry: Structural, Technological, and Humanistic Approaches," in J. G. March, ed., *Handbook of Organizations* (Chicago: Rand McNally, 1965), p. 1145. Reprinted by permission of James G. March.

work is designed at the micro level, as well as how departments, divisions, and the overall organization are designed at the macro level.

In addition to these major internal components, the organization as a system also has an external task environment. The task environment is composed of different constituents, such as suppliers, customers, and federal regulators. Thompson describes the task environment as that element of the environment related to the organization's degree of goal attainment; that is, the task environment is composed of those elements of the environment related to the organization's basic task.[24] For example, when steel was a major component in the production of cars, U.S. Steel was a major supplier for General Motors and Ford Motor Company—U.S. Steel was a major component of their task environments. As less steel and more aluminum was used to make cars, U.S. Steel became a less important supplier for General Motors and Ford—it was no longer a major component in their task environments.

The organization system works by taking inputs, converting them into throughputs, and delivering outputs to its task environment. Inputs consist of the human, informational, material, and financial resources used by the organization. Throughputs are the materials and resources as they are transformed by the organization's technology component. Once the transformation is complete, they become outputs for customers, consumers, and clients. The actions of suppliers, customers, regulators, and other elements of the task environment affect the organization and the behavior of people at work. For example, Onsite Engineering and Management experienced a threat to its survival in the mid-1980s by being totally dependent on one large utility for its outputs. By broadening its client base and improving the quality of its services (that is, its outputs) over the next several years, Onsite became a healthier, more successful small company. Transforming inputs into high-quality outputs is critical to an organization's success.

THE FORMAL AND INFORMAL ORGANIZATION

The open systems view of organization may lead one to view the design of an organization as a clockwork with a neat, precise, interrelated functioning. The *formal organization* is the official, legitimate, and most visible part that enables people to think of organizations in logical and rational ways. The snake pit organizational metaphor mentioned earlier has its roots in the study and examination of the *informal organization*, which is unofficial and less visible. The informal elements were first fully appreciated as a result of the *Hawthorne studies*, conducted during the 1920s and 1930s. It was during the interview study, the third of the four Hawthorne studies, that the researchers began to develop a fuller appreciation for the informal elements of the Hawthorne Works as an organization.[25] The formal and informal elements of the organization are depicted in Figure 1-2.

Potential conflict between the formal and informal organization makes an understanding of both important. Conflicts between these two elements erupted in many organizations during the early years of the twentieth

4. *Describe the formal and informal elements of an organization.*

FORMAL ORGANIZATION
The official, legitimate, and most visible part of the system.

INFORMAL ORGANIZATION
The unofficial and less visible part of the system.

HAWTHORNE STUDIES
Studies conducted during the 1920s and 1930s that discovered the existence of the informal organization.

Formal organization (overt)
Goals and objectives
Policies and procedures
Job descriptions
Financial resources
Authority structure
Communication channels
Products and services

Social surface

Informal organization (covert)
Beliefs and assumptions
Perceptions and attitudes
Values
Feelings, such as fear,
  joy, anger, trust, and hope
Group norms
Informal leaders

Figure 1-2
*Formal and Informal
Organization*

century and were embodied in the union–management strife of that era. The conflicts escalated into violence in a number of cases. For example, during the 1920s supervisors at the Homestead Works of U.S. Steel were issued pistols and boxes of ammunition "just in case" it became necessary to shoot unruly, dangerous steelworkers. Not all organizations are characterized by such potential formal–informal, management–labor conflict. During the same era, Eastman Kodak was very progressive. The company helped with financial backing for employees' neighborhood communities, such as Meadowbrook in Rochester, New York. Kodak's concern for employees and attention to informal issues made unions unnecessary within the company.

The informal elements of the organization are frequent points of diagnostic and intervention activities in organization development, though the formal elements must always be considered as well because they provide the context for the informal.[26] These informal elements are important because people's feelings, thoughts, and attitudes about their work do make a difference in their behavior and performance. Individual behavior plays out in the context of the formal and informal elements of the system, becoming organizational behavior. The uncovering of the informal elements in an organization was one of the major discoveries of the Hawthorne studies.

FIVE FOCUS ORGANIZATIONS

5. *Understand the diversity of organizations in the economy, as exemplified by the five focus organizations.*

Organizational behavior always occurs in the context of a specific organizational setting. Most attempts at explaining or predicting organizational behavior rely heavily on factors within the organization and give less weight to external environmental considerations.[27] Students can benefit from being sensitive to the industrial context of organizations and from developing an appreciation for each organization as a whole.[28]

The U.S. economy is the largest in the world, with a gross domestic product of more than $10.4 trillion in 2002. Figure 1-3 shows the major sectors of the economy. The largest sectors are service (44 percent), product manufacture of nondurable goods (21 percent), and fixed investments (11 percent). Taken together, the production of products and the delivery of services account for 73 percent of the U.S. economy. Government and fixed investments account for the remaining 27 percent. Large and small organizations operate in each sector of the economy shown in Figure 1-3.

The private sectors are an important part of the economy. The manufacturing sector includes the production of basic materials, such as steel, and the production of finished products, such as automobiles and electronic equipment. The service sector includes transportation, financial services, insurance, and retail sales. The government sectors, which provide essen-

Figure 1-3
U.S. Gross Domestic Product (Approximately $10.4 Trillion for 2002)

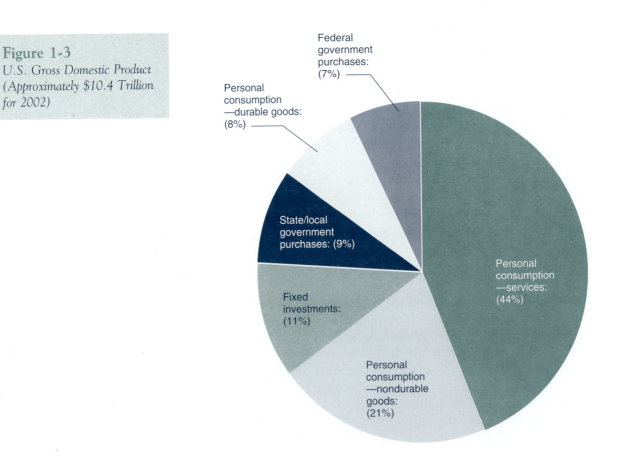

Federal government purchases: (7%)

Personal consumption—durable goods: (8%)

State/local government purchases: (9%)

Fixed investments: (11%)

Personal consumption—services: (44%)

Personal consumption—nondurable goods: (21%)

tial infrastructure, and nonprofit organizations are also important to our collective well-being because they meet needs not addressed in these economic sectors. We have chosen two manufacturing, one service, one retail, and one nonprofit organization to highlight throughout the text. These five organizations are Brinker International, Harley-Davidson, Hewlett-Packard, Patagonia, and the American Heart Association.

Each of these five organizations makes an important and unique contribution to the manufacturing or service sectors of the national economy and/or to our national well-being. These organizations are not alone, however. Hundreds of other small, medium, and large organizations are making valuable and significant contributions to the economic health and human welfare of the United States. Brief examples from many organizations are used throughout the book. We hope that by better understanding these organizations, you will have a greater appreciation for your own organization and others within the diverse world of private business enterprises and nonprofit organizations.

BRINKER INTERNATIONAL

Brinker International is a multiconcept casual dining restaurant company with more than 1,100 units in forty-seven states and twenty countries. The portfolio of restaurants includes Chili's Grill and Bar, Romano's Macaroni Grill, On the Border Mexican Grill and Cantina, Maggiano's Little Italy, Big Bowl, Cozymel's Coastal Mexican Grill, Corner Bakery Café, and Rockfish Seafood Grill. Norman Brinker is the dynamic leader who started his career in the restaurant business with Steak & Ale and Bennigan's before he bought Chili's. In May 1991, Chili's, Inc., was renamed Brinker International, based on Norman's name recognition and the fact that the name is easily recalled, to reflect the scope and diversity of the corporation's operations.[29]

By 1996, Brinker International was a billion-dollar company investing more than $200 million in capital expenditures annually and employing more than 60,000 people. From 25 restaurants in 1983, it had grown to eight chains of more than 500 restaurants serving more than 2,500,000 meals each week. In 2000, Norman Brinker became chairman emeritus of the company. By 2001, Brinker International had become a $3 billion business with a Charitable Committee contributing more than $1 million to a number of charities through the Brinker International Foundation. The company reflects the founder's values of achievement and concern for the human side of life.

HARLEY-DAVIDSON

In 1903, William Harley and Arthur Davidson made available to the public the first Harley-Davidson motorcycle. Harley-Davidson celebrated its 100th anniversary in 2003. By 1920, Harley-Davidson had more than 2,000 dealers in sixty-seven countries worldwide and was the world's largest motorcycle manufacturer. As a result of the company's licensing agreements with Sankyo Company of Japan, the Japanese motorcycle industry was founded in 1935. By the early 1980s, Harley-Davidson was in a pitched battle with the Japanese competition and fighting for its life. This competitive challenge spurred the company to make its celebrated financial turnaround in the late 1980s, leading to fifteen years of record revenues and earnings.[30]

By 2002, Harley-Davidson had net sales of about $4 billion and was selling more than 250,000 motorcycles per year. People are the company's only sustainable competitive advantage and its dealers are a key to the successful Harley business model. One of Harley-Davidson's most unique endeavors was the Harley Owners Group®, begun in 1983 and fondly referred to as H.O.G.® H.O.G. quickly became the largest factory-sponsored motorcycle club in the world and had reached a membership of 750,000 by 2002. In addition to manufacturing and selling heavyweight motorcycles, Harley-Davidson offers financial services through HDFS to its dealers and enthusiasts.

HEWLETT-PACKARD

Hewlett-Packard Company (HP) was one of five winners of the Ron Brown Award for Corporate Leadership in 2000. The company was founded in 1939 by Bill Hewlett and David Packard.[31] David Packard created the concept of "management by walking around" (MBWA) during the 1940s as a means to achieve a high involvement and open work culture. HP has been a leader in technology and in human resource management practices. As a technology leader, HP designed and produced the first handheld scientific calculator in 1972. As an innovator in management, HP introduced the radical notion of flexible work hours in 1967 and removed time clocks as a way to show respect for and trust in its employees. In 1999, HP named Carleton S. (Carly) Fiorina as president and chief executive officer of the company; she then became chairperson in 2000.

HP is a $72-billion-a-year business with seven major product lines and three service lines. HP products include computer desktops and workstations, mobile products, printing and digital imaging products, storage products, servers, networking products, and software. The company's services include e-services, personal services, and business services. HP has 141,000 employees and was one of the first companies to formalize telecommuting policies for its employees. The company has more than 540 sales and support offices and distributorships worldwide in 178 countries.

PATAGONIA

Established in the 1970s as a stepchild of Chouinard Equipment, the leading U.S. supplier of specialty climbing equipment, Patagonia recently celebrated its 25th anniversary as a privately held company. Patagonia is a subsidiary of Lost Arrow Corporation, a holding company. Patagonia's stated purpose is to inspire and implement solutions to the environmental crisis. The company manages the research and development, design, manufacturing, merchandising, and sale (retail, catalog, and Internet) of adult and children's outdoor products. Its products range from technical mountain biking wear to paddling gear, skiwear, fly-fishing outfits, hardgoods such as packs and travel bags, and, most recently, surfboards. Patagonia is renowned for its environmental consciousness and it is also a family-friendly company.[32]

Patagonia is a $220-million-a-year business with 950 employees, twenty-seven owned and operated retail stores, and a thriving Internet and catalog mail-order business. The company also sells to specialty retailers throughout the world. Since 1985, Patagonia has collected an annual "Earth Tax" that equals 1 percent of Patagonia's annual sales. The Earth Tax is earmarked for environmental causes that need financial support. The company receives more than 1,200 grant requests annually. To date, Patagonia has donated over $18 million to more than 1,000 organizations.

AMERICAN HEART ASSOCIATION

The American Heart Association was founded in 1924 by six cardiologists. The mission of the American Heart Association (AHA) is to reduce disability and death from cardiovascular diseases, including stroke. Cardiovascular disease has been the number one killer in the United States, for both men and women, for every year since 1900 except 1918. Since 1949, the AHA has given nearly $1.5 billion to heart and blood vessel research. The AHA provides vital information for men, women, children, and the elderly about the basic care, maintenance, and troubleshooting for their hearts.[33] During the 1980s, the AHA pursued an educational strategy for children, reasoning that heart-healthy habits established during childhood would be maintained in adulthood. More recently, the AHA has focused on workplace health promotion and formed a Heart at Work Committee at its national center.

The American Heart Association's millions of volunteers, corporate partners, and staff throughout the United States raised $532 million during 2001–2002. More than 25 percent of the AHA's yearly expenses are used to sponsor research. AHA-sponsored research has yielded important discoveries such as CPR, bypass surgery, and pacemakers. It is estimated that 61 million Americans—one in five men and women—have some form of cardiovascular disease, to include high blood pressure, stroke, and congenital defects.

THE CHALLENGE OF CHANGE

Changing times always pose a challenge for people and organizations. Global competition is a leading force driving change at work. Competition in the United States and world economies has increased significantly during the past couple of decades, especially in industries such as banking, finance, and air transportation. Corporate competition creates performance and cost pressures, which have a ripple effect on people and their behavior at work. The competition may lead to downsizing and restructuring, yet it provides the opportunity for revitalization as well.[34] Further, small companies are not necessarily the losers in this competitive environment. Scientech, a small power and energy company, found it had to enhance its

6. Recognize the challenge of change for organizational behavior.

managerial talent and service quality to meet the challenges of growth and big-company competitors. Product and service quality is one tool that can help companies become winners in a competitive environment. Problem-solving skills are another tool used by IBM, CDC, Northwest Airlines, and Southwest Airlines to help achieve high-quality products and services.

Too much change leads to chaos; too little change leads to stagnation. Terrence Murray is former chairman of FleetBoston Financial, a New England financial organization that grew dramatically in the late 1990s. As Mr. Murray says, "When there is change, morale is never going to be perfect."

INTERNATIONAL COMPETITION IN BUSINESS

Organizations in the United States are changing radically in response to increased international competition. According to noted economist Lester Thurow, the next several decades in business will be characterized by intense competition among the United States, Japan, and Europe in core industries.[35] Economic competition places pressure on all categories of employees to be productive and to add value to the firm. The uncertainty of unemployment resulting from corporate warfare and competition is an ongoing feature of organizational life for people in companies or industries that pursue cost-cutting strategies to achieve economic success. The international competition in the automotive industry among the Japanese, U.S., and European car companies embodies the intensity that can be expected in other industries in the future.

Some people feel that the future must be the focus in coming to grips with this international competition, whereas others believe we can deal with the future only by studying the past.[36] Global, economic, and organizational changes have dramatic effects on the study and management of organizational behavior.

FOUR THEMES RELATED TO CHANGE

Chapter 2 develops four themes related to change in contemporary organizations: globalization, technology, diversity, and ethics. These are four driving forces creating and shaping changes at work. Further, success in global competition requires organizations to be more responsive to ethnic, religious, and gender diversity in the workforce, in addition to responding positively to the competition in the international marketplace. Workforce demographic change and diversity are critical challenges in themselves for the study and management of organizational behavior.[37, 38] The theories of motivation, leadership, and group behavior based on research in a workforce of one composition may not be applicable in a workforce of a very different composition. This may be especially problematic if ethnic, gender, and/or religious differences lead to conflict between leaders and followers in organizations. For example, the former Soviet Union's military establishment found ethnic and religious conflicts between the officers and enlisted corps a real impediment to unit cohesion and performance during the 1980s.

CUSTOMER FOCUSED FOR HIGH QUALITY

Organizations are becoming more customer focused to meet changing product and service demands as well as customers' expectations of high quality. Quality has the potential for giving organizations in viable industries a competitive edge in meeting international competition.

Quality has become a rubric for products and services that are of high status. Total quality has been defined in many ways.[39] We define ***total quality management (TQM)*** as the total dedication to continuous improvement and to customers so that the customers' needs are met and their expectations exceeded. Quality is a customer-oriented philosophy of management with important implications for virtually all aspects of organizational behavior. Quality cannot be optimized, because customer needs and expectations are always changing. Quality is a cultural value embedded in highly successful organizations. Ford Motor Company's dramatic metamorphosis as an automotive leader is attributable to the decision to "make quality Job One" in all aspects of the design and manufacture of cars.

The pursuit of total quality improves the probability of organizational success in increasingly competitive industries. Quality is more than a fad; it is an enduring feature of an organization's culture and of the economic competition we face today. Quality is not an end in itself. It leads to competitive advantage through customer responsiveness, results acceleration, and resource effectiveness.[40] The three key questions in evaluating quality-improvement ideas for people at work are these: (1) Does the idea improve customer response? (2) Does the idea accelerate results? (3) Does the idea increase the effectiveness of resources? A "yes" answer means the idea should be implemented to improve total quality. Total quality is also dependent on how people behave at work.

BEHAVIOR AND QUALITY AT WORK

Whereas total quality may draw on reliability engineering or just-in-time management, total quality improvement can be successful only when employees have the skills and authority to respond to customer needs.[41] Total quality has direct and important effects on the behavior of employees at all levels in the organization, not just on employees working directly with customers. Chief executives can advance total quality by engaging in participative management, being willing to change everything, focusing quality efforts on customer service (not cost cutting), including quality as a criterion in reward systems, improving the flow of information regarding quality-improvement successes or failures, and being actively and personally involved in quality efforts. George Fisher, formerly chairman and CEO of Eastman Kodak, considers behavioral attributes such as leadership, cooperation, communication, and participation important elements in a total quality system.

Quality has become so important to our future competitiveness that the U.S. Department of Commerce now sponsors an annual award in the name

TOTAL QUALITY MANAGEMENT (TQM)
The total dedication to continuous improvement and to customers so that the customers' needs are met and their expectations exceeded.

of Malcolm Baldrige, former secretary of commerce in the Reagan administration, to recognize companies excelling in total quality management. The Malcolm Baldrige National Quality Award examination evaluates an organization in seven categories: leadership, information and analysis, strategic quality planning, human resource utilization, quality assurance of products and services, quality results, and customer satisfaction.

According to former president George H. W. Bush, "Quality management is not just a strategy. It must be a new style of working, even a new style of thinking. A dedication to quality and excellence is more than good business. It is a way of life, giving something back to society, offering your best to others."

Quality is one watchword for competitive success. Organizations that do not respond to customer needs find their customers choosing alternative product and service suppliers who are willing to exceed customer expectations. With this said, you should not conclude that total quality is a panacea for all organizations or that total quality guarantees qualified success.

MANAGING ORGANIZATIONAL BEHAVIOR IN CHANGING TIMES

Over and above the challenge of enhancing quality to meet international competition, managing organizational behavior during changing times is challenging for at least four reasons: (1) the increasing globalization of organizations' operating territory, (2) the increasing diversity of organizational workforces, (3) continuing technological innovation with its companion need for skill enhancement, and (4) the continuing demand for higher levels of moral and ethical behavior at work. These are the issues managers need to address in managing people at work.

Each of these four issues is explored in detail in Chapter 2 and highlighted throughout the text because they are intertwined in the contemporary practice of organizational behavior. For example, the issue of women in the workplace concerns workforce diversity and at the same time overlaps the globalization issue. Gender roles are often defined differently in various cultures and societies. In addition, sexual harassment is a frequent ethical problem for organizations in the United States, Europe, Israel, and South Africa as more women enter these workforces. The student of organizational behavior must appreciate and understand the importance of these issues.

YOU BE THE JUDGE

What are the most sensitive ethical issues in your business, industry, or organization today?

7. *Demonstrate the value of objective knowledge and skill development in the study of organizational behavior.*

LEARNING ABOUT ORGANIZATIONAL BEHAVIOR

Organizational behavior is neither a purely scientific area of inquiry nor a strictly intellectual endeavor. It involves the study of abstract ideas, such as valence and expectancy in motivation, as well as the study of concrete matters, such as observable behaviors and physiological symptoms of distress at work. Therefore, learning about organizational behavior is a multidimen-

Figure 1-4
Learning about Organizational Behavior

sional activity, as shown in Figure 1-4. First, it requires the mastery of a certain body of **objective knowledge**. Objective knowledge results from research and scholarly activities. Second, the study of organizational behavior requires **skill development** and the mastery of abilities essential to successful functioning in organizations. Third, it requires the integration of objective knowledge and skill development in order to apply both appropriately in specific organizational settings.

Researchers have found that increasing student diversity is best addressed through more diverse learning options for students and greater responsibility on the part of students as coproducers in the work of learning.[42] To gain a better understanding of yourself as a learner, so as to maximize your potential and develop strategies in specific learning environments, you need to evaluate the way you prefer to learn and process information. This chapter's Challenge (on page 18) offers you a short, quick way of assessing your learning style. If you are a visual learner, then use charts, maps, filmstrips, notes, or flash cards, and write things out for visual review. If you are an auditory learner, listen and take notes during lectures, but also consider taping them so you can fill in gaps later; review your notes frequently; and recite key concepts out loud. If you are a tactile learner, trace words as you are saying them, write down facts several times, and make study sheets.

OBJECTIVE KNOWLEDGE

Objective knowledge, in any field of study, is developed through basic and applied research. Research in organizational behavior has continued since early research on scientific management. Acquiring objective knowledge requires the cognitive mastery of theories, conceptual models, and research findings. In this book, the objective knowledge in each chapter is reflected in the notes that support the text material. Mastering the concepts and ideas that come from these notes enables you to intelligently discuss topics such as motivation, performance, leadership,[43] and executive stress.[44]

We encourage instructors and students of organizational behavior to think critically about the objective knowledge in organizational behavior. Only by engaging in critical thinking can one question or challenge the results of specific research and responsibly consider how to apply research results in a particular work setting. Rote memorization does not enable the student to appreciate the complexity of specific theories or the interrelationships among concepts, ideas, and topics. Good critical thinking, in contrast, enables the student to identify inconsistencies and limitations in the current body of objective knowledge.

OBJECTIVE KNOWLEDGE
Knowledge that results from research and scholarly activities.

SKILL DEVELOPMENT
The mastery of abilities essential to successful functioning in organizations.

Challenge

LEARNING STYLE INVENTORY

Directions: This twenty-four-item survey is not timed. Answer each question as honestly as you can. Place a check on the appropriate line after each statement.

	OFTEN	SOMETIMES	SELDOM
1. Can remember more about a subject through the lecture method with information, explanations, and discussion.			
2. Prefer information to be written on the chalkboard, with the use of visual aids and assigned readings.			
3. Like to write things down or to take notes for visual review.			
4. Prefer to use posters, models, or actual practice and some activities in class.			
5. Require explanations of diagrams, graphs, or visual directions.			
6. Enjoy working with my hands or making things.			
7. Am skillful with and enjoy developing and making graphs and charts.			
8. Can tell if sounds match when presented with pairs of sounds.			
9. Remember best by writing things down several times.			
10. Can understand and follow directions on maps.			
11. Do better at academic subjects by listening to lectures and tapes.			
12. Play with coins or keys in pockets.			
13. Learn to spell better by repeating the word out loud than by writing the word on paper.			
14. Can better understand a news development by reading about it in the paper than by listening to the radio.			
15. Chew gum, smoke, or snack during studies.			
16. Feel the best way to remember is to picture it in your head.			
17. Learn spelling by "finger spelling" words.			
18. Would rather listen to a good lecture or speech than read about the same material in a textbook.			
19. Am good at working and solving jigsaw puzzles and mazes.			
20. Grip objects in hands during learning period.			
21. Prefer listening to the news on the radio rather than reading about it in the newspaper.			
22. Obtain information on an interesting subject by reading relevant materials.			
23. Feel very comfortable touching others, hugging, hand-shaking, etc.			
24. Follow oral directions better than written ones.			

Scoring Procedures

Score 5 points for each OFTEN, 3 points for each SOMETIMES, and 1 point for each SELDOM.

Visual Preference Score = Points for questions 2 + 3 + 7 + 10 + 14 + 16 + 19 + 22 = _____

Auditory Preference Score = Points for questions 1 + 5 + 8 + 11 + 13 + 18 + 21 + 24 = _____

Tactile Preference Score = Points for questions 4 + 6 + 9 + 12 + 15 + 17 + 20 + 23 = _____

Source: Adapted from J. N. Gardner and A. J. Jewler, *Your College Experience: Strategies for Success, Third Concise Edition* (Belmont, Calif.: Wadsworth/ITP, 1998), pp. 62–63; and E. Jensen, *Student Success Secrets*, 4th ed. (Hauppauge, N.Y.: Barron's, 1996), pp. 33–36.

Critical thinking, based on knowledge and understanding of basic ideas, leads to inquisitive exploration and is a key to accepting the responsibility of coproducer in the learning process. A questioning, probing attitude is at the core of critical thinking. The student of organizational behavior should evolve into a critical consumer of knowledge related to organizational behavior—one who is able to intelligently question the latest research results and distinguish plausible, sound new approaches from fads that lack substance or adequate foundation. Ideally, the student of organizational behavior develops into a scientific professional manager who is knowledgeable in the art and science of organizational behavior.

SKILL DEVELOPMENT

Learning about organizational behavior requires doing as well as knowing. The development of skills and abilities requires that students be challenged, by the instructor or by themselves. Skill development is a very active component of the learning process.

The U.S. Department of Labor is concerned that people achieve the necessary skills to be successful in the workplace.[45] The essential skills identified by the Department of Labor are (1) resource management skills, such as time management; (2) information management skills, such as data interpretation; (3) personal interaction skills, such as teamwork; (4) systems behavior and performance skills, such as cause–effect relationships; and (5) technology utilization skills, such as troubleshooting. Many of these skills, such as decision making and information management, are directly related to the study of organizational behavior.[46]

Developing skills is different from acquiring objective knowledge in that it requires structured practice and feedback. A key function of experiential learning is to engage the student in individual or group activities that are systematically reviewed, leading to new skills and understandings. Objective knowledge acquisition and skill development are interrelated. The process for learning from structured or experiential activities is depicted in Figure 1-5 (on page 20). The student engages in an individual or group structured activity and systematically reviews that activity, which leads to new or modified knowledge and skills.

If skill development and structured learning occur in this way, there should be an inherently self-correcting element to learning because of the modification of the student's knowledge and skills over time.[47] To ensure that skill development does occur and that the learning is self-correcting as it occurs, three basic assumptions that underlie the previous model must be followed.

First, each student must accept responsibility for his or her own behavior, actions, and learning. This is a key to the coproducer role in the learning process. A group cannot learn for its members. Each member must accept responsibility for what he or she does and learns. Denial of responsibility helps no one, least of all the learner.

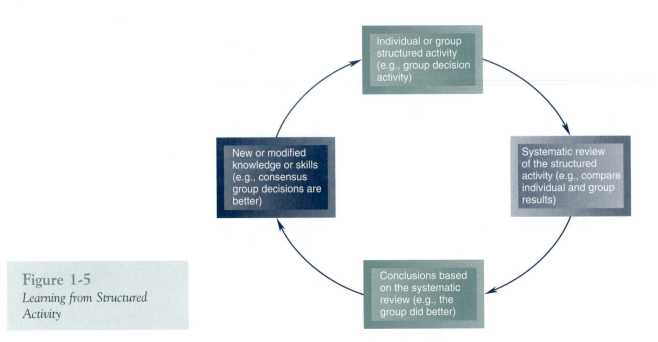

Figure 1-5
Learning from Structured Activity

Second, each student must actively participate in the individual or group structured learning activity. Structured learning is not passive; it is active. In group activities, everyone suffers if just one person adopts a passive attitude. Hence, all must actively participate.

Third, each student must be open to new information, new skills, new ideas, and experimentation. This does not mean that students should be indiscriminately open. It does mean that students should have a nondefensive, open attitude so that change is possible through the learning process.

APPLICATION OF KNOWLEDGE AND SKILLS

One of the advantages of structured, experiential learning is that a person can explore new behaviors and skills in a comparatively safe environment. Losing your temper in a classroom activity and learning about the potential adverse impact on other people will probably have dramatically different consequences from losing your temper with an important customer in a tense work situation. The ultimate objective of skill development and experiential learning is that one transfers the process employed in learning from structured activities in the classroom to learning from unstructured opportunities in the workplace.

Although organizational behavior is an applied discipline, a student is not "trained" in organizational behavior. Rather, one is "educated" in organizational behavior and is a coproducer in learning. The distinction between these two modes of learning is found in the degree of direct and immediate applicability of either knowledge or skills. As an activity, training more nearly ties direct objective knowledge or skill development to specific applications. By contrast, education enhances a person's residual pool of objective knowledge and skills that may then be selectively applied later—sometimes significantly later—when the opportunity presents itself. Hence, education is highly consistent with the concept of lifelong learning. Especially in a growing area of knowledge such as organizational behavior, the student can think of the first course as the outset of lifelong learning about the topics and subject.

PLAN FOR THE BOOK

Change and challenge are watchwords in organizations during these changing times. Managers and employees alike are challenged to meet change in the workplace: change in how work gets done, change in psychological and legal contracts between individuals and organizations, change in who is working in the organization, and change in the basis for organization. The four major challenges facing managers are the global environment, workplace diversity, technological innovation, and ethical issues at work. These four challenges, which are discussed in detail in Chapter 2, are shaping the changes occurring in organizations throughout the world. For example, the increasing globalization of business has led to intense international competition in core industries, and the changing demographics of the workplace have led to gender, age, racial, and ethnic diversity among working populations.

The first two chapters compose Part 1 of the book, the introduction. It is against the backdrop of the challenges discussed here that the specific content subjects in organizational behavior must be understood. In addition to the introduction, the text has three major parts. Part 2 addresses individual processes and behavior. Part 3 addresses interpersonal processes and behavior. Part 4 addresses organizational processes and structure.

The four chapters in Part 2 are designed to help the reader understand specific aspects of behavior. Chapter 3 discusses personality, perception, and attribution. Chapter 4 examines attitudes, values, and ethics. Finally, Chapters 5 and 6 address the broad range of motivational theories, learning, and performance management in organizations.

Part 3 is composed of six chapters designed to help the reader better understand interpersonal and group dynamics in organizations. Chapter 7 addresses communication in organizations. Chapter 8 focuses on an increasingly prominent feature of the workplace, teamwork and groups. Chapter 9 examines how individuals and groups make decisions. Chapter 10 is about power and politics, the bases of which shift as the organization shifts. Chapter 11 addresses the companion topics of leadership and followership. Finally, Chapter 12 examines conflict at work.

The four chapters in Part 4 are designed to help the reader better understand organizational processes and the organizational context of behavior at work. Chapter 13 examines traditional and contemporary approaches to job design.[48] Chapter 14 develops the topics of organizational design and structure, giving special attention to contemporary forces reshaping organizations and to emerging forms of organization. Chapter 15 addresses the culture of the organization. Finally, Chapter 16 brings closure to the text and the main theme of change by addressing the topic of managing change.

MANAGERIAL IMPLICATIONS: FOUNDATIONS FOR THE FUTURE

Managers must consider personal and environmental factors to understand fully how people behave in organizations and to help them grow to be all they can be. Human behavior is complex and at times confusing. Characteristics of the organizational system and formal–informal dynamics at work are important environmental factors that influence people's behavior. Managers should look for similarities and differences in manufacturing, service-oriented, nonprofit, and governmental organizations.

Change is a primary concern for contemporary managers. Changing customer demands for high-quality outputs challenge companies to meet the global competition. Globalization, workforce diversity, technology, and ethics are four themes related to change that are developed in Chapter 2. Another aspect of meeting the competition is learning. Managers must continually upgrade their knowledge about all aspects of their businesses, to include especially the human side of the enterprise. They must hone both their technical and their interpersonal skills, engaging in a lifelong educational process.

Several business trends and ongoing changes are affecting managers across the globe. These include continuing industrial restructuring, a dramatic increase in the amount and availability of information, a need to attract and retain the best employees, a need to understand a wide range of human and cultural differences, and a rapid shortening of response times in all aspects of business activities. Further, the old company towns are largely relics of the past, and managers are being called on to reintegrate their businesses with communities, cultures, and societies at a much broader level than has ever been required before. Trust, predictability, and a sense of security become important issues in this context. Reweaving the fabric of human relationships within, across, and outside the organization is a challenge for managers today.

Knowledge becomes power in tracking these trends and addressing these issues. Facts and information are two elements of knowledge in this context. Theories are a third element of a manager's knowledge base. Good theories are tools that help managers understand human and organizational behavior, help them make good business decisions, and inform them about actions to take or to refrain from taking. Managers always use theories, if not those generated from systematic research, then those evolved from the manager's implicit observation. Theories tell us how organizations, business, and people work—or do not work. Therefore, the student is challenged to master the theories in each topic area, then apply and test the theory in the real world of organizational life. The challenge for the student and the manager is to see what works and what does not work in their specific work context.

KEY TERMS

anthropology	informal organization	psychology
challenge	management	skill development
change	medicine	sociology
engineering	objective knowledge	structure
formal organization	organizational behavior	task
Hawthorne studies	people	total quality management (TQM)

Experiential Exercise

WHAT'S CHANGING AT WORK?

This exercise provides an opportunity to discuss changes occurring in your workplace and university. These changes may be for the better or the worse. However, rather than evaluating whether they are good or bad changes, begin by simply identifying the changes that are occurring. Later you can evaluate whether they are good or bad.

Step 1. The class forms into groups of approximately six members each. Each group elects a spokesperson and answers the following questions. The group should spend at least five minutes on each question. Make sure that each member of the group makes a contribution to each question. The spokesperson for each group should be ready to share the group's collective responses to these questions.

   a. *What are the changes occurring in your workplace and university?* Members should focus both on internal changes, such as reorganizations, and on external changes, such as new customers or competitors. Develop a list of the changes discussed in your group.

   b. *What are the forces that are driving the changes?* To answer this question, look for the causes of the changes members of the group are observing. For example, a reorganization may be

caused by new business opportunities, by new technologies, or by a combination of factors.

   c. *What signs of resistance to change do you see occurring?* Change is not always easy for people or organizations. Do you see signs of resistance, such as frustration, anger, increased absences, or other forms of discomfort with the changes you observe?

Step 2. Once you have answered the three questions in Step 1, your group needs to spend some time evaluating whether these changes are good or bad. Decide whether each change on the list developed in Step 1a is a good or bad change. In addition, answer the question "Why?" That is, why is this change good? Why is that change bad?

Step 3. Each group shares the results of its answers to the questions in Step 1 and its evaluation of the changes completed in Step 2. Cross-team questions and discussion follow.

Step 4. Your instructor may allow a few minutes at the end of the class period to comment on his or her perceptions of changes occurring within the university or businesses with which he or she is familiar.

2

Organizations and Managerial Challenges in the Twenty-First Century

LEARNING OBJECTIVES

After reading this chapter, you should be able to do the following:

1. Describe the dimensions of cultural differences in societies that affect work-related attitudes.

2. Explain the social and demographic changes that are producing diversity in organizations.

3. Describe actions managers can take to help their employees value diversity.

4. Understand the alternative work arrangements produced by technological advances.

5. Explain the ways managers can help employees adjust to technological change.

6. Discuss the assumptions of consequential, rule-based, and character ethical theories.

7. Explain six issues that pose ethical dilemmas for managers.

COMPETITION: THE CHALLENGES MANAGERS FACE

Hewlett-Packard (HP) is successful in meeting the competitive challenges of today's business environment. Most U.S. executives believe U.S. firms are encountering unprecedented global competition.[1] In the 1990s, the United States enjoyed its longest period of economic expansion since World War II while facing competition from other robust economies. Singapore, Finland, the Netherlands, and Switzerland all grew in competitiveness while Japan is losing ground. With competition increasing both at home and abroad, managers must find creative ways to deal with the competitive challenges they face at the beginning of the twenty-first century.

What major challenges must managers overcome in order to remain competitive? Chief executive officers of U.S. corporations cite four issues that are paramount: (1) globalizing the firm's operations to compete in global markets, (2) managing a diverse workforce, (3) keeping up with technological change and implementing technology in the workplace, and (4) managing ethical behavior.[2, 3]

Successful organizations manage all four challenges well. Companies like Harley-Davidson, Hewlett-Packard, and Patagonia owe their success to their ability to meet these challenges. You'll read about how they do this throughout the book and how other organizations tackle these challenges as well. In this chapter, we introduce you to these four challenges and the complexities of trying to manage them.

Globalization is a challenge that HP has handled well. HP was one of the few companies in the world to successfully marry the technologies of measurement, computing, and communication. The Internet along with rapid political and social changes have broken down old national barriers to competition. The world has become a global macroeconomic village with a boundaryless market in which all firms, large and small, must compete.[4]

Managing a diverse workforce is something organizations like Levi Strauss and Coors Brewing Company do extremely well. Both companies reap success from their efforts. The workforce of today is more diverse than ever before. Managers are challenged to bring together employees of different backgrounds in work teams. Often, this means having to deal with communication barriers, insensitivity, stereotypes, and ignorance of others' motivations and cultures.[5]

Technological change is one of the keys to strategic competitiveness. Imagine yourself as a small business owner of a package delivery firm. You'll be competing with FedEx, the proud owner of the most technologically advanced package tracking and delivery system in the world. Would you be able to compete? Technological change can be complex and risky. The boom and bust of 1999 and 2000 in the New Economy showed the risks for the dot.com companies of dealing with leading-edge technology.

Managing ethical behavior is a challenge that organizations like Johnson & Johnson are known for. The company's credo guides employee behavior and has helped employees do the right thing in some tough situations. Ethical behavior in business has been at the forefront of public consciousness for some time now. Insider trading scandals, influence peddling, and contract frauds are in the news daily, and the companies that are involved pay the price in terms of lost profits and loss of reputation.

Organizations must manage these four challenges well in order to remain competitive, or even to survive in today's turbulent environment. Throughout the book, we'll show you how organizational behavior can contribute to managing the challenges.

MANAGING IN A GLOBAL ENVIRONMENT

Only a few years ago, business conducted across national borders was referred to as "international" activity. The word *international* carries with it a connotation that the individual's or the organization's nationality is held strongly in consciousness.[6] *Globalization*, in contrast, implies that the world is free from national boundaries and that it is really a borderless world.[7] U.S. workers are now competing with workers in other countries. Organizations from other countries are locating subsidiaries in the United States, such as the U.S. manufacturing locations of Honda, Mazda, and Mercedes.

TRANSNATIONAL ORGANIZATION
An organization in which the global viewpoint supersedes national issues.

Similarly, what were once referred to as multinational organizations (organizations that did business in several countries) are now referred to as transnational companies. In **transnational organizations**, the global viewpoint supersedes national issues.[8] Transnational organizations operate over large global distances and are multicultural in terms of the people they employ. 3M, Dow Chemical, Coca-Cola, and other transnational organizations operate worldwide with diverse populations of employees.

CHANGES IN THE GLOBAL MARKETPLACE

Social and political upheavals have led organizations to change the way they conduct business and to encourage their members to think globally. The collapse of Eastern Europe was followed quickly by the demise of the Berlin Wall. East and West Germany were united into a single country. In the Soviet Union, perestroika led to the liberation of the satellite countries and the breaking away of the Soviet Union's member nations. Perestroika also brought about many opportunities for U.S. businesses, as witnessed by the press releases showing extremely long waiting lines at Moscow's first McDonald's restaurant.

GUANXI
The Chinese practice of building networks for social exchange.

Business ventures in China have become increasingly attractive to U.S. businesses. Coca-Cola has led the way. One challenge U.S. managers have tackled is attempting to understand the Chinese way of doing business. Chinese managers' business practices have been shaped by the Communist Party, socialism, feudalistic values, and *guanxi* (building networks for social exchange). Once *guanxi* is established, individuals can ask favors of each other with the expectation that the favor will be returned. The concept of *guanxi* is not unique to China. There are similar concepts in many other countries, including Russia and Haiti. It is a broad term that can mean anything from strongly loyal relationships to ceremonial gift-giving, sometimes seen as bribery. *Guanxi* is more common in societies with underdeveloped legal support for private businesses.[9]

To work with Chinese managers, Americans can learn to build their own *guanxi*; understand the Chinese chain of command; and negotiate slow, general agreements in order to interact effectively. Using the foreign government as the local franchisee may be effective in China. For example, KFC Corporation's operation in China is a joint venture between KFC (60 percent) and two Chinese government bodies (40 percent).[10]

In 1993, the European Union integrated fifteen nations into a single market by removing trade barriers. The member nations of the European Union are Belgium, Denmark, France, Germany, Greece, Ireland, Italy, Luxembourg, the Netherlands, Portugal, Spain, Austria, Finland, Sweden, and the United Kingdom. The integration of Europe provides many opportunities for U.S. organizations, including 350 million potential customers. Companies like Ford Motor Company and IBM, which entered the market early with wholly owned subsidiaries, will have a head start on these opportunities.[11] Competition within the European Union will increase, however, as will competition from Japan and the former Soviet nations.

The United States, Canada, and Mexico have dramatically reduced trade barriers in accordance with the North American Free Trade Agreement (NAFTA), which took effect in 1994. Organizations have found promising new markets for their products, and many companies have located plants in Mexico to take advantage of low labor costs. Daimler-Chrysler, for example, has a massive assembly plant in Saltillo. Prior to NAFTA, Mexico placed heavy tariffs on U.S. exports. The agreement immediately eliminated many of these tariffs and provided that the remaining tariffs be phased out over time.

All of these changes have brought about the need to think globally. Managers can benefit from global thinking by taking a long-term view. Entry into global markets requires long-term strategies.

UNDERSTANDING CULTURAL DIFFERENCES

One of the keys for any company competing in the global marketplace is to understand diverse cultures. Whether managing culturally diverse individuals within a single location or managing individuals at remote locations around the globe, an appreciation of the differences among cultures is crucial. Microcultural differences can play an important role in understanding the global work environment. Knowing cultural differences in symbols may even be important. Computer icons may not translate well in other cultures. The thumbs up sign, for example, means approval in the United States. In Australia, however, it is an obscene gesture. And manila file folders, like the icons used in Windows applications, aren't used in many European countries and therefore aren't recognized.[12]

1. *Describe the dimensions of cultural differences in societies that affect work-related attitudes.*

Do cultural differences translate into differences in work-related attitudes? The pioneering Dutch researcher Geert Hofstede focused on this question.[13] He and his colleagues surveyed 160,000 managers and employees of IBM who were working in sixty different countries.[14] In this way, the researchers were able to study individuals from the same company in the same jobs, but working in different countries. Hofstede's work is important, because his studies showed that national culture explains more differences in work-related attitudes than do age, gender, profession, or position within the organization. Thus, cultural differences do affect individuals' work-related attitudes. Hofstede found five dimensions of cultural differences that formed the basis for work-related attitudes. These dimensions are shown in Figure 2-1.

Individualism Versus Collectivism In cultures where **individualism** predominates, people belong to loose social frameworks, but their primary concern is for themselves and their families. People are responsible for taking care of their own interests. They believe that individuals should make decisions. Cultures characterized by **collectivism** are tightly knit social frameworks in which individual members depend strongly on extended families or clans. Group decisions are valued and accepted.

This dimension of cultural differences has workplace implications. Individualistic managers, as found in Great Britain and the Netherlands, emphasize and encourage individual achievement. In contrast, collectivistic managers, such as in Japan and Colombia, seek to fit harmoniously within the group. They also encourage these behaviors among their employees. There are also cultural differences within regions of the world. Arabs are more collectivist than Americans. Within the Arab culture, however, Egyptians are more individualistic than Arabs from the Gulf States (Saudi Arabia, Oman, Bahrain, Kuwait, Qatar, United Arab Emirates). This may be due to the fact that Egyptian businesspeople tend to have longer and more intense exposures to Western culture.[15]

Power Distance The second dimension of cultural differences examines the acceptance of unequal distribution of power. In countries with a high

INDIVIDUALISM
A cultural orientation in which people belong to loose social frameworks, and their primary concern is for themselves and their families.

COLLECTIVISM
A cultural orientation in which individuals belong to tightly knit social frameworks, and they depend strongly on large extended families or clans.

Figure 2-1
Hofstede's Dimensions of Cultural Differences

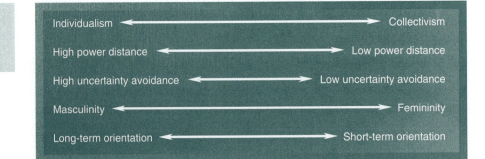

Source: Reprinted with permission of Academy of Management, PO Box 3020, Briar Cliff, N.Y. 10510-8020. *Cultural Constraints in Management Theories* (Figure). G. Hofstede, *Academy of Management Executive 7* (1993). Reproduced by permission of the publisher via Copyright Clearance Center, Inc.

power distance, bosses are afforded more power simply because they are the bosses. Titles are used, formality is the rule, and authority is seldom by-passed. Power holders are entitled to their privileges, and managers and employees see one another as fundamentally different kinds of people. India is a country with a high power distance, as are Venezuela and Mexico.

In countries with a low power distance, people believe that inequality in society should be minimized. People at various power levels are less threatened by, and more willing to trust, one another. Managers and employees see one another as similar. Managers are given power only if they have expertise. Employees frequently bypass the boss in order to get work done in countries with a low power distance, such as Denmark and Australia.

Uncertainty Avoidance Some cultures are quite comfortable with ambiguity and uncertainty, whereas others do not tolerate these conditions well. Cultures with high **uncertainty avoidance** are concerned with security and tend to avoid conflict. People have a need for consensus. The inherent uncertainty in life is a threat against which people in such cultures constantly struggle.

Cultures with low uncertainty avoidance are more tolerant of ambiguity. People are more willing to take risks and more tolerant of individual differences. Conflict is seen as constructive, and people accept dissenting viewpoints. Norway and Australia are characterized by low uncertainty avoidance, and this trait is seen in the value placed on job mobility. Japan and Italy are characterized by high uncertainty avoidance, so career stability is emphasized.

Masculinity Versus Femininity In cultures that are characterized by **masculinity**, assertiveness and materialism are valued. Men should be assertive, tough, and decisive, whereas women should be nurturing, modest, and tender.[16] Money and possessions are important, and performance is what counts. Achievement is admired. Cultures that are characterized by *femininity* emphasize relationships and concern for others. Men and women are expected to assume both assertive and nurturing roles. Quality of life is important, and people and the environment are emphasized.

Masculine societies, such as in Austria and Venezuela, define gender roles strictly. Feminine societies, in contrast, tend to blur gender roles. Women may be the providers, and men may stay home with the children. The Scandinavian countries of Norway, Sweden, and Denmark exemplify the feminine orientation.

Time Orientation Cultures also differ in **time orientation**; that is, whether the culture's values are oriented toward the future (long-term orientation) or toward the past and present (short-term orientation).[17] In China, a culture with a long-term orientation, values such as thrift and persistence, which focus on the future, are emphasized. In Russia, the orientation is short term. Values such as respect for tradition (past) and meeting social obligations (present) are emphasized.

POWER DISTANCE
The degree to which a culture accepts unequal distribution of power.

UNCERTAINTY AVOIDANCE
The degree to which a culture tolerates ambiguity and uncertainty.

MASCULINITY
The cultural orientation in which assertiveness and materialism are valued.

FEMININITY
The cultural orientation in which relationships and concern for others are valued.

TIME ORIENTATION
Whether a culture's values are oriented toward the future (long-term orientation) or toward the past and present (short-term orientation).

EXPATRIATE MANAGER
A manager who works in a country other than his or her home country.

U.S. Culture The position of the United States on these five dimensions is interesting. Hofstede found the United States to be the most individualistic country of any studied. On the power distance dimension, the United States ranked among the countries with weak power distance. Its rank on uncertainty avoidance indicated a tolerance of uncertainty. The United States also ranked as a masculine culture with a short-term orientation. These values have shaped U.S. management theory, so Hofstede's work casts doubt on the universal applicability of U.S. management theories.

Careers in management have taken on a global dimension. Working in transnational organizations may well give managers the opportunity to work in other countries. *Expatriate managers*, those who work in a country other than their home country, benefit from having as much knowledge as possible about cultural differences. Because managers are increasingly exposed to global work experiences, it is never too early to begin planning for this aspect of your career.

Understanding cultural differences becomes especially important for companies that are considering opening foreign offices, because workplace customs can vary widely from one country to another. Carefully searching out this information in advance can help companies successfully manage foreign operations. Consulate offices and companies operating within the foreign country are excellent sources of information about national customs and legal requirements.[18]

Another reality that can affect global business practices is the cost of layoffs in other countries. The practice of downsizing is not unique to the United States. Dismissing a forty-five-year-old middle manager with twenty years of service and a $50,000 annual salary can vary in cost from a low of $13,000 in Ireland to a high of $130,000 in Italy.[19] The cost of laying off this manager in the United States would be approximately $19,000. The wide variability in costs stems from the various legal protections that certain countries give workers.

DEVELOPING CROSS-CULTURAL SENSITIVITY

As organizations compete in the global marketplace, employees must learn to deal with individuals from diverse cultural backgrounds. Stereotypes may pervade employees' perceptions of other cultures. In addition, employees may be unaware of others' perceptions of the employees' national culture. A potentially valuable exercise is to ask members of various cultures to describe one another's cultures. This provides a lesson on the misinterpretation of culture.

Intel wants interns and employees to understand the company's culture, but more importantly, it wants to understand the employees' cultures. In an effort to increase diversity, Intel's proportion of ethnic minorities in managerial positions increased from 13 percent in 1993 to 19.5 percent in 2002, and is still climbing.[20] Many individuals feel their cultural heritage is important and may walk into uncomfortable situations at work. To prevent this, Intel's new workers are paired carefully with mentors, and mentors and protégés learn about each others' cultures.

Cultural sensitivity training is a popular method for helping employees recognize and appreciate cultural differences. Another way of developing sensitivity is to use cross-cultural task forces or teams. The Milwaukee-based GE Medical Systems Group (GEMS) has 19,000 employees working worldwide. GEMS has developed a vehicle for bringing managers from each of its three regions (the Americas, Europe, and Asia) together to work on a variety of business projects. Under the Global Leadership Program, several work groups made up of managers from various regions of the world are formed. The teams work on important projects, such as worldwide employee integration to increase the employees' sense of belonging throughout the GEMS international organization.[21]

Globalization is one challenge managers must meet in order to remain competitive in the changing world. Related to globalization is the challenge of managing an increasingly diverse workforce. Cultural differences contribute a great deal to the diversity of the workforce, but there are other forms of diversity as well.

MANAGING WORKFORCE DIVERSITY

Workforce diversity is an increasingly important issue for organizations. HP believes that diversity drives creativity and that creativity is at the heart of invention. The United States, as a melting pot nation, has always had a mix of individuals in its workforce. We once sought to be all alike, as in the melting pot, but we now recognize and appreciate individual differences. *Diversity* encompasses all forms of differences among individuals, including culture, gender, age, ability, religion, personality, social status, and sexual orientation.

DIVERSITY
All forms of individual differences, including culture, gender, age, ability, religion, personality, social status, and sexual orientation.

Attention to diversity has increased in recent years. This is largely because of the changing demographics of the working population. Managers feel that dealing with diversity successfully is a paramount concern for two reasons. First, managers need to know how to motivate diverse work groups. Second, managers need to know how to communicate effectively with employees who have different values and language skills.

Several demographic trends are affecting organizations. By the year 2020, the workforce will be more culturally diverse, more female, and older than ever. In addition, legislation and new technologies have brought more workers with disabilities into the workforce. Valuing diversity in organizations is an increasingly important issue, requiring the skill of learning to work together.[22]

CULTURAL DIVERSITY

Cultural diversity in the workplace is growing because of the globalization of business, as we discussed earlier. People of diverse national origins—Koreans, Bolivians, Pakistanis, Vietnamese, Swedes, Australians, and others—find themselves cooperating in teams to perform the work of the

2. *Explain the social and demographic changes that are producing diversity in organizations.*

organization. In addition, changing demographics within the United States significantly affect the cultural diversity in organizations. By 2020, minorities will constitute more than one-half of the new entrants to the U.S. workforce. The participation rates of African Americans and Hispanic Americans in the labor force increased dramatically in recent years. By 2020, white non-Hispanics will constitute 68 percent of the labor force (down from 83 percent in 2002); 14 percent of the workforce will be Hispanic (up from 12 percent); African Americans' share will remain at 11 percent, and 5 percent will be Asian.[23]

The jobs available in the future will require more skill than has been the case in the past. Often, minority workers have not had opportunities to develop leading-edge skills. Minority skill deficits are large, and the proportions of African Americans and Hispanic Americans who are qualified for higher level jobs are often much lower than the proportions of qualified whites and Asian Americans.[24] Minority workers are less likely to be prepared because they are less likely to have had satisfactory schooling and on-the-job training. Educational systems within the workplace are needed to supply minority workers the skills necessary for success. Companies such as Motorola are already recognizing and meeting this need by focusing on basic skills training.

GENDER DIVERSITY

The feminization of the workforce has increased substantially. The number of women in the labor force increased from 31.5 million in 1970 to 63 million in 2002. This increase accounts for almost 60 percent of the overall expansion of the entire labor force in the United States for this time period. In 2002, women made up almost 43 percent of the labor force, and by the year 2020, the labor force is predicted to be balanced with respect to gender. Women are also better prepared to contribute in organizations than ever before. Women now earn 32 percent of all doctorates, 52 percent of master's degrees, and 50 percent of all undergraduate degrees. Thus, women are better educated, and more are electing to work. In 2000, 54 percent of U.S. women were employed.[25]

Women's participation in the workforce is increasing, but their share of the rewards of participation is not increasing commensurately. Women hold only 12.5 percent of corporate officer positions in the *Fortune 500* companies.[26] Only 3.8 percent of the chairpersons and CEOs of *Fortune 500* firms are women.[27] HP CEO Carly Fiorina is still the exception, not the rule. Salaries for women persist at a level between 76 and 78 percent of their male counterparts' earnings.[28] Furthermore, because benefits are tied to compensation, women also receive lower levels of benefits.

In addition to lower earnings, women face other obstacles at work. The *glass ceiling* is a transparent barrier that keeps women from rising above a certain level in organizations. In the United States, it is rare to find women in positions above middle management in corporations.[29] The glass ceiling is not based on women's lack of ability to handle upper-level management

GLASS CEILING
A transparent barrier that keeps women from rising above a certain level in organizations.

positions. Instead, the barrier keeps women from advancing higher in an organization because they are women.

There is reason to believe that, on a global basis, the leadership picture for women is improving and will continue to improve. For example, the number of female political leaders around the world increased dramatically in recent decades. In addition, a large number of women have founded entrepreneurial businesses. Women now own one-third of all American businesses, and these women-owned businesses employ more people than the entire *Fortune 500* combined.[30]

Removing the glass ceiling and other obstacles to women's success represents a major challenge to organizations. Policies that promote equity in pay and benefits, encourage benefit programs of special interest to women, and provide equal starting salaries for jobs of equal value are needed in organizations. Corporations that shatter the glass ceiling have several practices in common. Upper managers clearly demonstrate support for the advancement of women, often with a statement of commitment issued by the CEO. Women are represented on standing committees that address strategic business issues of importance to the company. Women are targeted for participation in executive education programs, and systems are in place for identifying women with high potential for advancement.[31] Three of the best companies in terms of their advancement and development of women are Motorola, Deloitte & Touche, and the Bank of Montreal.[32]

AGE DIVERSITY

The graying of the U.S. workforce is another source of diversity in organizations. Aging baby boomers (those individuals born from 1946 through 1964) contributed to the rise of the median age in the United States to thirty-six in the year 2000—six years older than at any earlier time in history. This also means that the number of middle-aged Americans is rising dramatically. In the workforce, the number of younger workers is declining, as is the number of older workers (over age sixty-five). The net result will be a gain in workers aged thirty-five to fifty-four. By 2030, there will be seventy million older persons, more than twice their number in 1996. People over age sixty-five will comprise 13 percent of the population in 2010, and 20 percent of the population by 2030.[33]

This change in worker profile has profound implications for organizations. The job crunch among middle-aged workers will become more intense as companies seek flatter organizations and the elimination of middle-management jobs. Older workers are often higher paid, and companies that employ large numbers of aging baby boomers may find these pay scales a handicap to competitiveness.[34] However, a more experienced, stable, reliable, and healthy workforce can pay dividends to companies. The baby boomers are well trained and educated, and their knowledge can be a definite asset to organizations.

Another effect of the aging workforce is greater intergenerational contact in the workplace.[35] As organizations grow flatter, workers who were traditionally segregated by old corporate hierarchies (with older workers at the top and younger workers at the bottom) are working together. Four generations are cooperating: the silent generation (people born from 1930 through 1945), a small group that includes most organizations' top managers; the baby boomers, whose substantial numbers give them a strong influence; the baby bust generation, popularly known as Generation X (those born from 1965 through 1976); and the subsequent generation, tentatively called Generation Y or the baby boomlet.[36] Although there is certainly diversity within each generation, each generation differs in general ways from other generations.

ABILITY DIVERSITY

The workforce is full of individuals with different abilities, presenting another form of diversity. Individuals with disabilities are an underutilized human resource. An estimated 50 million individuals with disabilities live in the United States, and their unemployment rate is estimated to exceed 50 percent.[37] Nevertheless, the representation of individuals with disabilities in the workforce has increased because of the Americans with Disabilities Act, which went into effect in the summer of 1992. Under this law, employers are required to make reasonable accommodations to permit workers with disabilities to perform jobs. The act defines a person with a disability as "anyone possessing a physical or mental impairment that substantially limits one or more major life activities."[38] It protects individuals with temporary, as well as permanent, disabilities. The act's protection encompasses a broad range of illnesses that produce disabilities. Among these are acquired immune deficiency syndrome (AIDS), cancer, hypertension, anxiety disorders, dyslexia, blindness, and cerebral palsy, to name only a few.

Some companies recognized the value of employing workers with disabilities long before the legislation. Pizza Hut employs 3,000 workers with disabilities and plans to hire more. The turnover rate for Pizza Hut workers with disabilities is only one-fifth of the normal turnover rate.[39] McDonald's created McJobs, a program that has trained and hired more than 9,000 mentally and physically challenged individuals since 1981.[40] McJobs is a corporate plan to recruit, train, and retain individuals with disabilities. Its participants include workers with visual, hearing, or orthopedic impairments; learning disabilities; and mental retardation. Through classroom and on-site training, the McJobs program prepares individuals with disabilities for the work environment.

DIFFERENCES ARE ASSETS

Diversity involves much more than culture, gender, age, ability, or personality. It also encompasses religion, social status, and sexual orientation. The scope of diversity is broad and inclusive. All these types of diversity lend heterogeneity to the workforce.

The issue of sexual orientation as a form of diversity has received increasing attention from organizations. Approximately 1.5 million households in the United States are identified as homosexual domestic partnerships.[41] Sexual orientation is an emotionally charged issue. Often, heterosexual resistance to accepting gay, lesbian, or bisexual workers is caused by moral beliefs. Although organizations must respect these beliefs, they must also send a message that all people are valued. The threat of job discrimination leads many gay men and lesbians to keep their sexual orientation secret at work. This secrecy has a cost, however. Closeted gay workers report lower job satisfaction and organizational commitment, and more role conflict and conflict between work and home life issues than do openly gay workers or heterosexual workers.[42] People who work in organizations full of fear, distrust, stigmatization, and harassment are not likely to be able to perform well. A tolerant atmosphere can improve the productivity of heterosexual and homosexual workers alike. Some companies offer benefits to same-sex partners. Coors Brewing Company, the Walt Disney Company, and Lotus Development Corporation were among the first to extend these benefits.

Part of the challenge in managing diversity lies in attempting to combat prejudices and discrimination. Whereas prejudice is an attitude, discrimination is behavior. Both are detrimental to organizations that depend on productivity from every single worker. Often, in studies of ratings of promotion potential, minorities are rated lower than whites, and females are rated lower than males.[43] The disparity between the pay of women and minority-group members relative to white men increases with age.[44]

Digital Equipment Corporation (DEC—now part of Hewlett-Packard) faced a challenge in managing diversity in its Springfield, Massachusetts, plant, which employed predominantly African American workers. The task was to overcome the perception that the plant was separate from, different from, and not as good as DEC's predominantly white plants. DEC's Springfield employees tackled the issue by stressing empowerment (sharing power throughout the organization) and pushing for high-technology products that would give it a solid identity. The model used by the plant, called Valuing Differences, was based on two key ideas. First, people work best when they are valued and when diversity is taken into account. Second, when people feel valued, they build relationships and work together as a team.[45]

Managing diversity is one way a company can become more competitive. It is more than simply being a good corporate citizen or complying with affirmative action.[46] It is also more than assimilating women and minorities into a dominant male culture. Managing diversity includes a painful examination of hidden assumptions that employees hold. Biases and prejudices about people's differences must be uncovered and dealt with so that differences can be celebrated and exploited to their full advantage.

3. *Describe actions managers can take to help their employees value diversity.*

DIVERSITY'S BENEFITS AND PROBLEMS

Diversity can enhance organizational performance. Organizations can reap five main benefits from diversity. First, diversity management can help firms attract and retain the best available human talent. Second, diversity can enhance marketing efforts. Third, diversity promotes creativity and innovation. Fourth, diversity results in better problem solving. Fifth, diversity enhances organizational flexibility. These five benefits can add up to competitive advantage for a company that manages diversity well.

Lest we paint an overly rosy picture of diversity, we must recognize its potential problems. Five problems are particularly important: resistance to change, lack of cohesiveness, communication problems, conflicts, and decision making. People are more highly attracted to, and feel more comfortable with, others like themselves. It stands to reason that diversity efforts may be met with considerable resistance when individuals are forced to interact with others unlike themselves. Conflicts can also arise, and decision making may take more time.[47]

Whereas the struggle for equal employment opportunity is a battle against racism and prejudice, managing diversity is a battle to value the differences that individuals bring to the workplace. Organizations that manage diversity effectively can reap the rewards of increased productivity and improved organizational health.

MANAGING TECHNOLOGICAL INNOVATION

Another challenge that managers face is effectively managing technological innovation. *Technology* consists of the intellectual and mechanical processes used by an organization to transform inputs into products or services that meet organizational goals. Managers face the challenge of rapidly changing technology and of putting the technology to optimum use in organizations. The inability of managers to incorporate new technologies successfully into their organizations is a major factor that has limited economic growth in the United States.[48] Although the United States still leads the way in developing new technologies, it lags behind in making productive use of these new technologies in workplace settings.[49]

The Internet has radically changed the way organizations communicate and perform work. By integrating computer, cable, and telecommunications technologies, businesses have learned new ways to compete. In networked organizations, time, distance, and space become irrelevant. A networked organization can do business anytime and anywhere, which is essential in the global marketplace. And networking is essential for companies that want to provide quality service to customers. Del Monte Foods gets daily inventory reports electronically from grocers. When inventory falls to a certain level, the Del Monte network processes a restocking order. This allows retailers to drastically cut their investments in inventories. The World Wide Web has created a virtual commercial district. Customers can book air travel, buy compact discs, and "surf the Net" to conduct business around the globe.[50]

One fascinating technological change is the development of *expert systems*, computer-based applications that use a representation of human expertise in a specialized field of knowledge to solve problems. Expert systems can be used in many ways, including providing advice to nonexperts,

TECHNOLOGY
The intellectual and mechanical processes used by an organization to transform inputs into products or services that meet organizational goals.

EXPERT SYSTEM
A computer-based application that uses a representation of human expertise in a specialized field of knowledge to solve problems.

providing assistance to experts, replacing experts, and serving as a training and development tool in organizations.[51] They are used in medical decision making, diagnosis, and medical informatics.[52] Anheuser-Busch has used an expert system to assist managers in ensuring that personnel decisions comply with antidiscrimination laws.[53]

Robots, another technological innovation, were invented in the United States, and advanced research on **robotics** is still conducted here. However, Japan leads the world in the use of robotics in organizations. Organizations in the United States have fewer total robots than were added in 1989 alone in Japan.[54] Robots in Japan are treated like part of the family. They are even named after favorite celebrities, singers, and movie stars. Whereas Japanese workers are happy to let robots take over repetitive or dangerous work, Americans are more suspicious of labor-saving robots because employers often use them to cut jobs.[55] The main reason for the reluctance of U.S. organizations to use robots is their slow payout. Robotics represents a big investment that does not pay off in the short term. Japanese managers are more willing to use a long-term horizon to evaluate the effectiveness of robotics technology. Labor unions may also resist robotics because of the fear that robots will replace employees.

Some U.S. companies that experimented with robotics had bad experiences. Deere & Company originally used robots to paint its tractors, but the company scrapped them because programming the robots for the multitude of types of paint used took too long. Now Deere uses robots to torque cap screws on tractors, a repetitive job that once had a high degree of human error.

It is tempting to view technology from only the positive side; however, a little realism is in order. Some firms that have been disappointed with costly technologies are electing to *de*-engineer. And computer innovations often fail; 42 percent of information technology projects are abandoned before completion, and half of all technology projects fail to meet managers' expectations. Because some innovations fail to live up to expectations, and some simply fail, it is important to effectivly manage both revolutionary and evolutionary approaches to technological transitions.[56]

ROBOTICS
The use of robots in organizations.

YOU BE THE JUDGE

Suppose your company has the opportunity to install a marvelous new technology, but it will mean that 20 percent of the jobs in the company will be lost. As a manager, would you adopt the new technology? How would you make the decision?

ALTERNATIVE WORK ARRANGEMENTS

Technological advances have been responsible, to a large degree, for the advent of alternative work arrangements, the nontraditional work practices, settings, and locations that are now supplementing traditional workplaces. One alternative work arrangement is **telecommuting**, transmitting work from a home computer to the office using a modem. IBM, for example, was one of the first companies to experiment with the notion of installing computer terminals at employees' homes and having employees work at home. By telecommuting, employees gain flexibility, save the commute to work, and enjoy the comforts of being at home. Telecommuting also has disadvantages, however, including distractions, lack of opportunities to socialize with other workers, lack of interaction with supervisors, and decreased identification with the organization. Despite these disadvantages, telecommuters

4. *Understand the alternative work arrangements produced by technological advances.*

TELECOMMUTING
Transmitting work from a home computer to the office using a modem.

still feel "plugged in" to the communication system at the office. Studies show that telecommuters often report higher satisfaction with office communication than do workers in traditional office environments.[57]

There is a spectrum of other alternative work arrangements. *Hoteling* is a shared-office arrangement wherein employees have mobile file cabinets and lockers for personal storage, and "hotel" work spaces are furnished for them. These spaces must be reserved instead of being permanently assigned. *Satellite offices* comprise another alternative work arrangement. In such offices, large facilities are broken into a network of smaller workplaces that are located close to employees' homes. Satellites can save a company as much as 50 percent in real estate costs and can be quite attractive to employees. This can broaden the pool of potential employees, who can communicate with the home office via various technologies.[58] All of these alternative work arrangements signal a trend toward *virtual offices*, in which people work anytime, anywhere, and with anyone. The concept involves work being where people are, rather than people moving to where the work is.

THE CHANGING NATURE OF MANAGERIAL WORK

Technological innovation affects the very nature of the management job. Managers who once had to coax workers back to their desks from coffee breaks now find that they need to encourage workers mesmerized by new technology to take more frequent breaks.[59] Working with a computer can be stressful, both physically and psychologically. Eye strain, neck and back strain, and headaches can result from sitting at a computer terminal too long. In addition, workers can become accustomed to the fast response time of the computer and expect the same from their coworkers. When coworkers do not respond with the speed and accuracy of the computer, they may receive a harsh retort.

Computerized monitoring provides managers with a wealth of information about employee performance, but it also holds great potential for misuse. At Bell Canada, operators were evaluated on a system that tabulated average working time with customers. Operators found the practice highly stressful, and they sabotaged the system by giving callers wrong directory assistance numbers rather than taking the time to look up the correct ones. As a result, Bell Canada now uses average working time scores for entire offices rather than for individuals.[60]

New technologies and rapid innovation place a premium on a manager's technical skills. Managers today must develop technical competence in order to gain workers' respect, which does not come automatically. Computer-integrated manufacturing systems, for example, have been shown to require managers to use participative management styles, open communication, and greater technical expertise in order to be effective.[61] Technological change occurs so rapidly that turbulence characterizes most organizations. Workers must constantly learn and adapt to changing technology so that organizations can remain competitive. Managers must grapple with the challenge of helping workers adapt and make effective use of new technologies.

Helping Employees Adjust to Technological Change

Most workers are well aware of the benefits of modern technologies. The availability of skilled jobs and improved working conditions have been by-products of innovation in many organizations. Technology is also bringing disadvantaged individuals into the workforce. Microchips have dramatically increased opportunities for workers with visual impairments. Information can be decoded into speech using a speech synthesizer, into braille using a hard-copy printer, or into enlarged print visible on a computer monitor. Workers with visual impairments are no longer dependent on sighted persons to translate printed information for them, and this has opened new doors of opportunity.[62] Engineers at Carnegie-Mellon University have developed PizzaBot, a robot that individuals with disabilities can operate using a voice-recognition system. Despite these and other benefits of new technology in the workplace, however, employees may still resist change.

Technological innovations bring about changes in employees' work environments, and change has been described as the ultimate stressor. Many workers react negatively to change that they perceive as threatening to their work situation. Many of their fears center around loss—of freedom, of control, of the things they like about their jobs.[63] Employees may fear deterioration of their quality of work life and increased pressure at work. Further, employees may fear being replaced by technology or being displaced into jobs of lower skill levels.

Managers can take several actions to help employees adjust to changing technology. The workers' participation in early phases of the decision-making process regarding technological changes is important. Individuals who participate in planning for the implementation of new technology gain important information about the potential changes in their jobs; therefore, they are less resistant to the change. Workers are the users of the new technology. Their input in early stages can lead to a smoother transition into the new ways of performing work.

Providing effective training about ways to use the new technology is essential. Training helps employees perceive that they control the technology rather than being controlled by it. The training should be designed to match workers' needs, and it should increase the workers' sense of mastery of the new technology.

A related challenge is to encourage workers to invent new uses for technology already in place. *Reinvention* is the term for creatively applying new technology.[64] Innovators should be rewarded for their efforts. Individuals who explore the boundaries of a new technology can personalize the technology and adapt it to their own job needs, as well as share this information with others in the work group. In one large public utility, service representatives (without their supervisor's knowledge) developed a personal note-passing system that later became the basis of a formal communication system that improved the efficiency of their work group.

5. *Explain the ways managers can help employees adjust to technological change.*

REINVENTION
The creative application of new technology.

Managers face a substantial challenge in leading organizations to adopt new technologies more humanely and effectively. Technological changes are essential for earnings growth and for expanded employment opportunities. The adoption of new technologies is a critical determinant of U.S. competitiveness in the global marketplace.

MANAGING ETHICAL ISSUES AT WORK

In addition to the challenges of globalization, workforce diversity, and technology, managers frequently face ethical challenges and dilemmas in organizations. Some organizations manage ethical issues well. Johnson & Johnson employees operate under an organizational credo, presented later in this section. Another organization that manages ethical issues well is Merck & Company. This pharmaceutical company's emphasis on ethical behavior has earned it recognition as one of America's most admired companies in *Fortune*'s polls of CEOs.

Despite the positive way some organizations handle ethical issues, however, unethical conduct does sometimes occur. A few of the ethical problems that managers report as toughest to resolve include employee theft, environmental issues, comparable worth of employees, conflicts of interest, and sexual harassment.[65]

6. *Discuss the assumptions of consequential, rule-based, and character ethical theories.*

How can people in organizations rationally think through ethical decisions so that they make the "right" choices? Ethical theories help us understand, evaluate, and classify moral arguments; make decisions; and then defend conclusions about what is right and wrong. Ethical theories can be classified as consequential, rule based, or character.

CONSEQUENTIAL THEORY
An ethical theory that emphasizes the consequences or results of behavior.

Consequential theories of ethics emphasize the consequences or results of behavior. John Stuart Mills' utilitarianism, a well-known consequential theory, suggests that right and wrong are determined by the consequences of the action.[66] "Good" is the ultimate moral value, and we should maximize the most good for the greatest number of people. But do good ethics make for good business?[67] Right actions do not always produce good consequences, and good consequences do not always follow from right actions. And how do we determine the greatest good—in short-term or long-term consequences? Using the "greatest number" criterion can imply that minorities (less than 50 percent) might be excluded in evaluating the morality of actions. An issue that may be important for a minority but unimportant for the majority might be ignored. These are but a few of the dilemmas raised by utilitarianism.

RULE-BASED THEORY
An ethical theory that emphasizes the character of the act itself rather than its effects.

In contrast, *rule-based theories* of ethics emphasize the character of the act itself, not its effects, in arriving at universal moral rights and wrongs.[68] Moral rights, the basis for legal rights, are associated with such theories. In a theological context, the Bible, the Talmud, and the Koran are rule-based guides to ethical behavior. Immanuel Kant worked toward the ultimate moral principle in formulating his categorical imperative, a universal standard of behavior.[69] Kant argued that individuals should be treated with respect and dignity and that they should not be used as a means to an end. He argued that we should put ourselves in the other person's position and ask if we would make the same decision if we were in that person's situation.

Corporations and business enterprises are more prone to subscribe to consequential ethics than rule-based ethics, in part due to the persuasive arguments of the Scottish political economist and moral philosopher Adam Smith.[70] He believed that the self-interest of human beings is God's providence, not the government's. However, an alternative to those theories is offered through virtue-ethics.

Character theories of ethics emphasize the character of the individual and the intent of the actor, in contrast to either the character of the act itself or the consequences of the act. These theories emphasize virtue-ethics and are based on an Aristotelean approach to character. Robert Solomon is the best known advocate of this Aristotelean approach to business ethics.[71] He advocates a business ethics theory that centers on the individual within the corporation, thus emphasizing both corporate roles and personal virtues. The center of Aristotle's vision was on the inner character and virtuousness of the individual, not on the person's behavior or actions. Thus, the "good" person who acted out of virtuous and "right" intentions was one with integrity and ultimately good ethical standards. For Solomon, the six dimensions of virtue-ethics are community, excellence, role identity, integrity, judgment (phronesis), and holism. Further, "the virtues" are a shorthand way of summarizing the ideals that define good character. These include honesty, loyalty, sincerity, courage, reliability, trustworthiness, benevolence, sensitivity, helpfulness, cooperativeness, civility, decency, modesty, openness, and gracefulness, just to name a few.

Levi Strauss Company made a costly decision when its leadership decided not to do business in mainland China. That market alone could have doubled its revenues from international operations. But concerns about human rights violations, child labor, and the Chinese government's role in plant operations made the venture inconsistent with the company's basic values, ethics, and social responsibility. The company elected to forgo the opportunity rather than to follow cultural relativism.[72]

People need ethical theories to help them think through confusing, complex, difficult moral choices and ethical decisions. In contemporary organizations, people face ethical and moral dilemmas in many diverse areas. The key areas we address are employee rights, sexual harassment, romantic involvements, organizational justice, whistle-blowing, and social responsibility. We conclude with a discussion of professionalism and codes of ethics.

EMPLOYEE RIGHTS

Managing the rights of employees at work creates many ethical dilemmas in organizations. Some of these dilemmas are privacy issues related to technology. Computerized monitoring constitutes an invasion of privacy in the minds of some individuals. The use of employee data from computerized

CHARACTER THEORY
An ethical theory that emphasizes the character, personal virtues, and integrity of the individual.

7. *Explain six issues that pose ethical dilemmas for managers.*

information systems presents many ethical concerns. Safeguarding the employee's right to privacy and at the same time preserving access to the data for those who need it requires that the manager balance competing interests. Drug testing, free speech, downsizing and layoffs, and due process are but a few of the issues involving employee rights that managers face. Perhaps no issue generates as much need for managers to balance the interests of employees and the interests of the organization as the reality of AIDS in the workplace.

Laws exist that protect HIV-infected workers. As mentioned earlier, the Americans with Disabilities Act requires employees to treat HIV-infected workers as disabled individuals and to make reasonable accommodations for them. The ethical dilemmas involved with this situation, however, go far beyond the legal issues. How does a manager protect the dignity of the person with AIDS and preserve the morale and productivity of the work group when so much prejudice and ignorance surround this disease? Many organizations, such as Wells Fargo, believe the answer is education.[73] Wells Fargo has a written AIDS policy because of the special issues associated with the disease—such as confidentiality, employee socialization, coworker education, and counseling—that must be addressed. The Body Shop's employee education program consists of factual seminars combined with interactive theater workshops. The workshops depict a scenario in which an HIV-positive worker must make decisions, and the audience decides what the worker should do. This helps participants explore the emotional and social issues surrounding HIV.[74] Many fears arise because of a lack of knowledge about AIDS.

SEXUAL HARASSMENT

According to the Equal Employment Opportunity Commission, sexual harassment is unwelcome sexual attention, whether verbal or physical, that affects an employee's job conditions or creates a hostile working environment.[75] Court rulings, too, have broadened the definition of sexual harassment beyond job-related abuse to include acts that create a hostile work environment. In addition, Supreme Court rulings presume companies are to blame when managers create a sexually hostile working environment. Some organizations are more tolerant of sexual harassment. Complaints are not taken seriously, it is risky to complain, and perpetrators are unlikely to be punished. In these organizations, sexual harassment is more likely to occur. Sexual harassment is also more likely to occur in male-dominated workplaces.[76] Managers can defend themselves by demonstrating that they took action to eliminate workplace harassment and that the complaining employee did not take advantage of company procedures to deal with harassment. Even the best sexual harassment policy, however, will not absolve a company when harassment leads to firing, demotions, or undesirable working assignments.[77] How much do you know about sexual harassment? Complete this chapter's Challenge to get an idea.

There are three types of sexual harassment. *Gender harassment* includes crude comments or sexual jokes and behaviors that disparage someone's

YOU BE THE JUDGE

What are some of the concerns that a person with AIDS would have about his or her job? What are some of the fears that coworkers would have? How can a manager balance these two sets of concerns?

Challenge

HOW MUCH DO YOU KNOW ABOUT SEXUAL HARASSMENT?

Indicate whether you believe each statement below is true (T) or false (F).

_____ 1. Sexual harassment is unprofessional behavior.

_____ 2. Sexual harassment is against the law in all fifty states.

_____ 3. Sexual advances are a form of sexual harassment.

_____ 4. A request for sexual activity is a form of sexual harassment.

_____ 5. Verbal or physical conduct of a sexual nature may be sexual harassment.

_____ 6. Sexual harassment occurs when submission to sex acts is a condition of employment.

_____ 7. Sexual harassment occurs when submission to or rejection of sexual acts is a basis for performance evaluation.

_____ 8. Sexual harassment occurs when such behavior interferes with an employee's performance or creates an intimidating, hostile, and offensive environment.

_____ 9. Sexual harassment includes physical contact of a sexual nature, such as touching.

_____ 10. Sexual harassment requires that a person have the intent to harass, harm, or intimidate.

All of the items are true except item 10, which is false. While somewhat ambiguous, sexual harassment is defined in the eyes of the beholder. Give yourself 1 point for each correct answer. This score reflects how much you know about sexual harassment. Scores can range from 0 (poorly informed about sexual harassment) to 10 (well informed about sexual harassment). If your score was less than 5, you need to learn more about sexual harassment.

See W. O'Donohue, ed., *Sexual Harassment* (Boston: Allyn and Bacon, 1997) for theory, research and treatment. See http://www.eeoc.gov/stats/harass.html for the latest statistics.

gender or convey hostility toward a particular gender. *Unwanted sexual attention* involves unwanted touching or repeated unwanted pressures for dates. *Sexual coercion* consists of implicit or explicit demands for sexual favors by threatening negative job-related consequences or promising job-related rewards.[78] Recent theory has focused attention on the aggressive behavior of sexual harassers.[79]

Sexual harassment costs the typical *Fortune 500* company $6.7 million per year in absenteeism, turnover, and loss of productivity. ICN Pharmaceuticals has paid out millions to settle four sexual harassment complaints against former CEO Milan Panic. Plaintiffs may now sue not only for back pay, but also for compensatory and punitive damages. And these costs do not take into account the negative publicity that firms may encounter from sexual harassment cases, which can cost untold millions. Sexual harassment can have strong negative effects on victims. Victims are less satisfied with their work, supervisors, and coworkers and may psychologically withdraw at work. They may suffer poorer mental health and even exhibit symptoms of post-traumatic stress disorder in conjunction with the harassment experience. Some victims report alcohol abuse, depression, headaches, and nausea.[80]

Several companies have created comprehensive sexual harassment programs that seem to work. Atlantic Richfield (ARCO), owned by British Petroleum and a player in the male-dominated energy industry, has a handbook on preventing sexual harassment that includes phone numbers of state agencies where employees can file complaints. In essence, it gives employees a road map to the courthouse, and the openness seems to work.

ROMANTIC INVOLVEMENTS

Hugging, sexual innuendos, and repeated requests for dates may constitute sexual harassment for some, but they are a prelude to romance for others. This situation carries with it a different set of ethical dilemmas for organizations.

A recent fax poll indicated that three-fourths of the respondents felt it was okay to date a coworker, while three-fourths disapproved of dating a superior or subordinate. In *Meritor vs. Vinson*, the Supreme Court ruled that the agency principle applies to supervisor–subordinate relationships. Employers are liable for acts of their agents (supervisors) and can thus be held liable for sexual harassment. Other employees might claim that the subordinate who is romantically involved with the supervisor gets preferential treatment. Dating between coworkers poses less liability for the company because the agency principle does not apply. Policing coworker dating can also backfire: Wal-Mart lost a lawsuit when it tried to forbid coworkers from dating. Though most managers realize that workplace romance cannot be eliminated through rules and policies, they believe that intervention is a must when romance constitutes a serious threat to productivity or workplace morale.[81]

ORGANIZATIONAL JUSTICE

Another area in which moral and ethical dilemmas may arise for people at work concerns organizational justice, both distributive and procedural. *Distributive justice* concerns the fairness of outcomes individuals receive. For example, the salaries and bonuses of U.S. corporate executives became a central issue with Japanese executives when President George H. W. Bush and American CEOs in key industries visited Japan in 1992. The Japanese CEOs questioned the distributive justice in keeping the American CEOs' salaries at high levels at a time when so many companies were in difficulty and laying off workers.

Procedural justice concerns the fairness of the process by which outcomes are allocated. The ethical questions here do not concern the just or unjust distribution of organizational resources. Rather, the ethical questions in procedural justice concern the process. Has the organization used the correct procedures in allocating resources? Have the right considerations, such as competence and skill, been brought to bear in the decision process? And have the wrong considerations, such as race and gender, been excluded from the decision process? Some research has shown cultural differences in the effects of distributive and procedural justice, such as between Hong Kong and the United States.[82]

DISTRIBUTIVE JUSTICE
The fairness of the outcomes that individuals receive in an organization.

PROCEDURAL JUSTICE
The fairness of the process by which outcomes are allocated in an organization.

WHISTLE-BLOWING

Whistle-blowers are employees who inform authorities of wrongdoings by their companies or coworkers. Whistle-blowers can be perceived as either heroes or "vile wretches" depending on the circumstances of the situation. For a whistle-blower to be considered a public hero, the gravity of the situation that the whistle-blower reports to authorities must be of such magnitude and quality as to be perceived as abhorrent by others.[83] In contrast, the whistle-blower is considered a vile wretch if others see the act of whistle-blowing as more offensive than the situation the whistle-blower reports to authorities.

Whistle-blowing is important in the United States because committed organizational members sometimes engage in unethical behavior in an intense desire to succeed. Organizations can manage whistle-blowing by communicating the conditions that are appropriate for the disclosure of wrongdoing. Clearly delineating wrongful behavior and the appropriate ways to respond are important organizational actions.

WHISTLE-BLOWER
An employee who informs authorities of the wrongdoings of his or her company or coworkers.

SOCIAL RESPONSIBILITY

Corporate *social responsibility* is the obligation of an organization to behave in ethical ways in the social environment in which it operates. Ethical conduct at the individual level can translate into social responsibility at the organizational level. When Malden Mills, the maker of Polartec, burned down in 1995, the company's president, Aaron Feuerstein, paid workers during the months it took to rebuild the company. Although doing so cost the company a lot of money and was not required by law, Feuerstein said his own values caused him to do the socially responsible thing. Firms that are seen as socially responsible have a competitive advantage in attracting applicants.[84]

SOCIAL RESPONSIBILITY
The obligation of an organization to behave in ethical ways.

CODES OF ETHICS

One of the characteristics of mature professions is the existence of a code of ethics to which the practitioners adhere in their actions and behavior. An example is the Hippocratic oath in medicine. Although some of the individual differences we address in Chapter 4 produce ethical or unethical orientations in specific people, a profession's code of ethics becomes a standard against which members can measure themselves in the absence of internalized standards.

No universal code of ethics or oath exists for business as it does for medicine. However, Paul Harris and four business colleagues, who founded Rotary International in 1905, made an effort to address ethical and moral behavior right from the beginning. They developed the four-way test, shown in Figure 2-2 (on page 46), which is now used in more than 166 nations throughout the world by the 1.2 million Rotarians in more than 30,000 Rotary clubs.

Beyond the individual and professional level, corporate culture is another excellent starting point for addressing ethics and morality. In Chapter 15 we examine how corporate culture and leader behavior trickle down the company,

The Four-Way Test
OF WHAT WE THINK, SAY, OR DO

1. Is it the TRUTH?

2. Is it FAIR to all concerned?

3. Will it build GOODWILL and better friendships?

4. Will it be BENEFICIAL to all concerned?

Figure 2-2
The Four-Way Test

setting a standard for all below. In some cases, the corporate ethics may be captured in a regulation. For example, the Joint Ethics Regulation (DOD 5500.7-R, August 1993) specifies the ethical standards to which all U.S. military personnel are to adhere. In other cases, the corporate ethics may be in the form of a credo. Johnson & Johnson's credo, shown in Figure 2-3, helped hundreds of employees ethically address the criminal tampering with Tylenol products. In its 1986 centennial annual report, J & J attributed its success in this crisis, as well as its long-term business growth (a compound sales rate of 11.6 percent for 100 years), to "our unique form of decentralized management, our adherence to the ethical principles embodied in our credo, and our emphasis on managing the business for the long term."

Figure 2-3
The Johnson & Johnson Credo

We believe our first responsibility is to the doctors, nurses and patients,
to mothers and fathers and all others who use our products and services.
In meeting their needs everything we do must be of high quality.
We must constantly strive to reduce our costs
in order to maintain reasonable prices.
Customers' orders must be serviced promptly and accurately.
Our suppliers and distributors must have an opportunity
to make a fair profit.

We are responsible to our employees,
the men and women who work with us throughout the world.
Everyone must be considered as an individual.
We must respect their dignity and recognize their merit.
They must have a sense of security in their jobs.
Compensation must be fair and adequate,
and working conditions clean, orderly and safe.
We must be mindful of ways to help our employees fulfill
their family responsibilities.
Employees must feel free to make suggestions and complaints.
There must be equal opportunity for employment, development
and advancement for those qualified.
We must provide competent management,
and their actions must be just and ethical.

We are responsible to the communities in which we live and work
and to the world community as well.
We must be good citizens—support good works and charities
and bear our fair share of taxes.
We must encourage civic improvements and better health and education.
We must maintain in good order
the property we are privileged to use,
protecting the environment and natural resources.

Our final responsibility is to our stockholders.
Business must make a sound profit.
We must experiment with new ideas.
Research must be carried on, innovative programs developed
and mistakes paid for.
New equipment must be purchased, new facilities provided
and new products launched.
Reserves must be created to provide for adverse times.
When we operate according to these principles,
the stockholders should realize a fair return.

Source: Reprinted with permission from Johnson & Johnson.

Individual codes of ethics, professional oaths, and organizational credos all must be anchored in a moral, ethical framework. They are always open to question and continuous improvement using ethical theories as a tool for reexamining the soundness of the current standard. Although a universal right and wrong may exist, it would be hard to argue that there is only one code of ethics to which all individuals, professions, and organizations can subscribe.

MANAGERIAL IMPLICATIONS: FACING THE CHALLENGES

The success of organizations in the new millennium will depend on managers' ability to address the challenges of globalization, diversity, technology, and ethics. Failure to address the challenges can be costly. Think about Pepsi's losses to Coke in the global cola wars. Coke is winning the battle and capitalizing on the huge opportunities and profits from global markets. A racial discrimination lawsuit against Texaco not only cost the company millions in a settlement, but also damaged the company's reputation. Mitsubishi suffered a similar fate in a sexual harassment scandal. Failure to address these challenges can mean costly losses, damage to reputations, and ultimately an organization's demise.

These four challenges are also important because the way managers handle them shapes employee behavior. Developing global mind-sets among employees expands their worldview and puts competition on a larger scale. Knowing that diversity is valued and differences are assets causes employees to think twice about engaging in behaviors that are discriminatory. Valuing technological change leads employees to experiment with new technologies and develop innovative ways to perform their jobs. Sending a message that unethical behavior is not tolerated lets employees know that doing the right thing pays off.

These four challenges are recurring themes that you will see throughout this book. We will show you how companies are tackling these challenges and how organizational behavior can be used to do this effectively, which is a must if organizations are to remain competitive.

KEY TERMS

character theory	glass ceiling	rule-based theory
collectivism	*guanxi*	social responsibility
consequential theory	individualism	technology
distributive justice	masculinity	telecommuting
diversity	power distance	time orientation
expatriate manager	procedural justice	transnational organization
expert system	reinvention	uncertainty avoidance
femininity	robotics	whistle-blower

Experiential Exercise

ETHICAL DILEMMAS

Divide the class into five groups. Each group should choose one of the following scenarios and agree on a course of action.

1. Sam works for you. He is technically capable and a good worker, but he does not get along well with others in the work group. When Sam has an opportunity to transfer, you encourage him to take it. What would you say to Sam's potential supervisor when he asks about Sam?

2. Your boss has told you that you must reduce your work group by 30 percent. Which of the following criteria would you use to lay off workers?

   a. Lay off older, higher paid employees.

   b. Lay off younger, lower paid employees.

   c. Lay off workers based on seniority only.

   d. Lay off workers based on performance only.

3. You are an engineer, but you are not working on your company's Department of Transportation (DOT) project. One day you overhear a conversation in the cafeteria between the program manager and the project engineer that makes you reasonably sure a large contract will soon be given to the ABC Company to develop and manufacture a key DOT subsystem. ABC is a small firm, and its stock is traded over the counter. You feel sure that the stock will rise from its present $2.25 per share as soon as news of the DOT contract gets out. Would you go out and buy ABC's stock?

4. You are the project engineer working on the development of a small liquid rocket engine. You know that if you could achieve a throttling ratio greater than 8 to 1, your system would be considered a success and continue to receive funding

support. To date, the best you have achieved is a 4 to 1 ratio. You have an unproven idea that you feel has a 50 percent chance of being successful. Your project is currently being reviewed to determine if it should be continued. You would like to continue it. How optimistically should you present the test results?

5. Imagine that you are the president of a company in a highly competitive industry. You learn that a competitor has made an important scientific discovery that is not patentable and will give that company an advantage that will substantially reduce the profits of your company for about a year. There is some hope of hiring one of the competitor's employees who knows the details of the discovery. Would you try to hire this person?

Each group should present its scenario and chosen course of action to the class. The class should then evaluate the ethics of the course of action, using the following questions to guide discussion:

1. Are you following rules that are understood and accepted?

2. Are you comfortable discussing and defending your action?

3. Would you want someone to do this to you?

4. What if everyone acted this way?

5. Are there alternatives that rest on firmer ethical ground?

Scenarios adapted from R. A. DiBattista, "Providing a Rationale for Ethical Conduct from Alternatives Taken in Ethical Dilemmas," *Journal of General Psychology* 116 (1989): 207–214; discussion questions adapted with the permission of The Free Press, a Division of Simon & Schuster, Inc. from *The Manager as Negotiator: Bargaining for Cooperation and Competitive Gain* by David A. Lax and James K. Sebenius 0-02-918770-2. Copyright © 1986 by David A. Lax and James K. Sebenius. All rights reserved.

PART 2

Individual Processes and Behavior

3

Personality, Perception, and Attribution

LEARNING OBJECTIVES

After reading this chapter, you should be able to do the following:

1. Describe individual differences and their importance in understanding behavior.

2. Define *personality*.

3. Explain four theories of personality.

4. Identify several personality characteristics and their influences on behavior in organizations.

5. Explain how personality is measured.

6. Discuss Carl Jung's contribution to our understanding of individual differences, and explain how his theory is used in the Myers-Briggs Type Indicator.

7. Define *social perception* and explain how characteristics of the perceiver, the target, and the situation affect it.

8. Identify five common barriers to social perception.

9. Explain the attribution process and how attributions affect managerial behavior.

INDIVIDUAL DIFFERENCES AND ORGANIZATIONAL BEHAVIOR

In this chapter and continuing in Chapter 4, we explore the concept of *individual differences*. Individuals are unique in terms of their skills, abilities, personalities, perceptions, attitudes, values, and ethics. These are just a few of the ways individuals may be similar to or different from one another. Individual differences represent the essence of the challenge of management, because no two individuals are completely alike. Managers face the challenge of working with people who possess a multitude of individual characteristics, so the more managers understand individual differences, the better they can work with others. Figure 3-1 illustrates how individual differences affect human behavior.

The basis for understanding individual differences stems from Lewin's early contention that behavior is a function of the person and the environment.[1] Lewin expressed this idea in an equation: $B = f(P, E)$, where B = behavior, P = person, and E = environment. This idea has been developed by the *interactional psychology* approach.[2] Basically, this approach says that in order to understand human behavior, we must know something about the person and something about the situation. There are four basic propositions of interactional psychology:

1. Behavior is a function of a continuous, multidirectional interaction between the person and the situation.

2. The person is active in this process and is both changed by situations and changes situations.

3. People vary in many characteristics, including cognitive, affective, motivational, and ability factors.

1. *Describe individual differences and their importance in understanding behavior.*

INDIVIDUAL DIFFERENCES
The way in which factors such as skills, abilities, personalities, perceptions, attitudes, values, and ethics differ from one individual to another.

INTERACTIONAL PSYCHOLOGY
The psychological approach that emphasizes that in order to understand human behavior, we must know something about the person and about the situation.

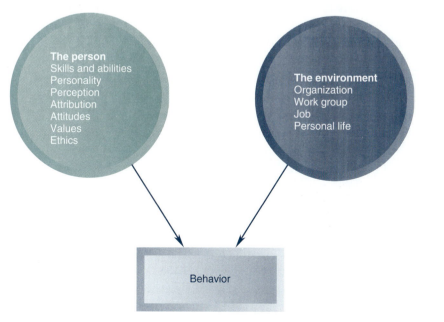

The person
Skills and abilities
Personality
Perception
Attribution
Attitudes
Values
Ethics

The environment
Organization
Work group
Job
Personal life

Behavior

Figure 3-1
Variables Influencing Individual Behavior

4. Two interpretations of situations are important: the objective situation and the person's subjective view of the situation.[3]

The interactional psychology approach points out the need to study both persons and situations. We will focus on personal and situational factors throughout the text. The person consists of individual differences such as those we emphasize in this chapter and Chapter 4: personality, perception, attribution, attitudes, values, and ethics. The situation consists of the environment the person operates in, and it can include things like the organization, work group, personal life situation, job characteristics, and many other environmental influences. One important and fascinating individual difference is personality.

PERSONALITY

2. *Define* personality.

PERSONALITY
A relatively stable set of characteristics that influence an individual's behavior.

What makes an individual behave in consistent ways in a variety of situations? Personality is an individual difference that lends consistency to a person's behavior. *Personality* is defined as a relatively stable set of characteristics that influence an individual's behavior. Although there is debate about the determinants of personality, we conclude that there are several origins. One determinant is heredity, and some interesting studies have supported this position. Identical twins who are separated at birth and raised apart in very different situations have been found to share personality traits and job preferences. For example, about half of the variation in traits like extraversion, impulsiveness, and flexibility was found to be genetically determined; that is, identical twins who grew up in different environments shared these traits.[4] In addition, the twins held similar jobs.[5] Thus, there does appear to be a genetic influence on personality.

Another determinant of personality is the environment a person is exposed to. Family influences, cultural influences, educational influences, and other environmental forces shape personality. Personality is therefore shaped by both heredity and environment.

PERSONALITY THEORIES

3. *Explain four theories of personality.*

Four major theories of personality are the trait theory, psychodynamic theory, humanistic theory, and the integrative approach. Each theory has influenced the study of personality in organizations.

TRAIT THEORY
The personality theory that states that in order to understand individuals, we must break down behavior patterns into a series of observable traits.

Trait Theory Some early personality researchers believed that to understand individuals, we must break down behavior patterns into a series of observable traits. According to *trait theory*, combining these traits into a group forms an individual's personality. Gordon Allport, a leading trait theorist, saw traits as broad, general guides that lend consistency to behavior.[6] Thousands of traits have been identified over the years. Raymond Cattell, another prominent trait theorist, identified sixteen traits that formed the basis for differences in individual behavior. He described traits in bipolar adjective combinations such as self-assured/apprehensive, reserved/outgoing, and submissive/dominant.[7]

More recently, researchers have argued that all traits can be reduced to five basic factors. The "Big Five" traits include extraversion, agreeableness, conscientiousness, emotional stability, and openness to experience.[8] Descriptions of the "Big Five" are shown in Table 3-1. The "Big Five" are broad, global traits that are associated with behaviors at work.

From preliminary research, we know that introverted and conscientious employees are less likely to be absent from work.[9] In making peer evaluations, individuals with high agreeableness tend to rate others more leniently, while individuals with high conscientiousness tend to be tougher as raters.[10] Extraverts tend to have higher salaries, receive more promotions, and are more satisfied with their careers.[11] Across lots of occupations, people who are conscientious are high performers. When you view more specific occupations, however, different patterns of the Big Five factors are related to high performance. For customer service jobs, individuals high in emotional stability, agreeableness, and openness to experience perform best. For managers, emotional stability and extraversion are traits of top performers.[12]

The trait approach has been the subject of considerable criticism. Some theorists argue that simply identifying traits is not enough; instead, personality is dynamic and not completely stable. Further, early trait theorists tended to ignore the influence of situations.[13]

Psychodynamic Theory Based on the work of Sigmund Freud, ***psychodynamic theory*** emphasizes the unconscious determinants of behavior.[14] Freud saw personality as the interaction among three elements of personality: the id, ego, and superego. The id is the most primitive element, the source of drives and impulses that operate in an uncensored manner. The superego, similar to what we know as conscience, contains values and the "shoulds and should nots" of the personality. There is an ongoing conflict between the id and the superego. The ego serves to manage the conflict between the id and the superego. In this role, the ego compromises, and the

PSYCHODYNAMIC THEORY
The personality theory that emphasizes the unconscious determinants of behavior.

Extraversion	The person is gregarious, assertive, and sociable (as opposed to reserved, timid, and quiet).
Agreeableness	The person is cooperative, warm, and agreeable (rather than cold, disagreeable, and antagonistic).
Conscientiousness	The person is hardworking, organized, and dependable (as opposed to lazy, disorganized, and unreliable).
Emotional stability	The person is calm, self-confident, and cool (as opposed to insecure, anxious, and depressed).
Openness to experience	The person is creative, curious, and cultured (rather than practical with narrow interests).

Table 3-1
The "Big Five" Personality Traits

Sources: P. T. Costa and R. R. McCrae, *The NEO-PI Personality Inventory* (Odessa, Fla.: Psychological Assessment Resources, 1992); J. F. Salgado, "The Five Factor Model of Personality and Job Performance in the European Community," *Journal of Applied Psychology* 82 (1997): 30–43.

result is the individual's use of defense mechanisms such as denial of reality. The contribution of psychodynamic theory to our understanding of personality is its focus on unconscious influences on behavior.

Humanistic Theory Carl Rogers believed that all people have a basic drive toward self-actualization, which is the quest to be all you can be.[15] The **humanistic theory** focuses on individual growth and improvement. It is distinctly people centered and also emphasizes the individual's view of the world. The humanistic approach contributes an understanding of the self to personality theory and contends that the self-concept is the most important part of an individual's personality.

HUMANISTIC THEORY
The personality theory that emphasizes individual growth and improvement.

Integrative Approach Recently, researchers have taken a broader, more **integrative approach** to the study of personality.[16] To capture its influence on behavior, personality is described as a composite of the individual's psychological processes. Personality dispositions include emotions, cognitions, attitudes, expectancies, and fantasies.[17] *Dispositions*, in this approach, simply mean the tendencies of individuals to respond to situations in consistent ways. Influenced by both genetics and experiences, dispositions can be modified. The integrative approach focuses on both person (dispositions) and situational variables as combined predictors of behavior.

INTEGRATIVE APPROACH
The broad theory that describes personality as a composite of an individual's psychological processes.

PERSONALITY CHARACTERISTICS IN ORGANIZATIONS

Managers should learn as much as possible about personality in order to understand their employees. Hundreds of personality characteristics have been identified. We have selected five characteristics because of their particular influences on individual behavior in organizations: locus of control, self-efficacy, self-esteem, self-monitoring, and positive/negative affect. Because these characteristics affect performance at work, managers need to have a working knowledge of them.

4. *Identify several personality characteristics and their influences on behavior in organizations.*

Locus of Control An individual's generalized belief about internal (self) versus external (situation or others) control is called **locus of control**. People who believe they control what happens to them are said to have an internal locus of control, whereas people who believe that circumstances or other people control their fate have an external locus of control.[18] Research on locus of control has strong implications for organizations. Internals (those with an internal locus of control) have been found to have higher job satisfaction and performance, to be more likely to assume managerial positions, and to prefer participative management styles.[19]

Internals and externals have similar positive reactions to being promoted, which include high job satisfaction, job involvement, and organizational commitment. The difference between the two is that internals continue to be happy long after the promotion, whereas externals' joy over the promotion is short lived. This might occur because externals do not believe their own performance led to the promotion.[20]

LOCUS OF CONTROL
An individual's generalized belief about internal control (self-control) versus external control (control by the situation or by others).

Knowing about locus of control can prove valuable to managers. Because internals believe they control what happens to them, they will want to exercise control in their work environment. Allowing internals considerable voice in how work is performed is important. Internals will not react well to being closely supervised. Externals, in contrast, may prefer a more structured work setting, and they may be more reluctant to participate in decision making.

Self-Efficacy **Generalized self-efficacy** is a general belief about one's own capabilities to deal with the events and challenges that make life demanding. Employees with high generalized self-efficacy have more confidence in their job-related abilities and other personal resources (i.e., energy, influence over others, etc.) that help them function effectively on the job. People with low generalized self-efficacy often feel ineffective at work and may express doubts about performing a new task well. Previous success or performance is one of the most important determinants of self-efficacy. People who have positive beliefs about their efficacy for performance are more likely to attempt difficult tasks, to persist in overcoming obstacles, and to experience less anxiety when faced with adversity.[21]

Generalized self-efficacy is often confused with locus of control; however, they are distinctly different. Self-efficacy means possessing the skills required to execute courses of action that will result in a desired outcome. Locus of control refers to whether or not a person believes that the consequences of his efforts are controlled by others. For example, a salesman with high self-efficacy may have confidence in his ability to meet customer expectations, but does not necessarily blame himself for all lost sales.[22] There is another form of self-efficacy, called task-specific self-efficacy, which we will cover in Chapter 6.

> **GENERALIZED SELF-EFFICACY**
> An individual's beliefs and expectations about his or her ability to accomplish a specific task effectively.

Self-Esteem **Self-esteem** is an individual's general feeling of self-worth. Individuals with high self-esteem have positive feelings about themselves, perceive themselves to have strengths as well as weaknesses, and believe their strengths are more important than their weaknesses.[23] Individuals with low self-esteem view themselves negatively. They are more strongly affected by what other people think of them, and they compliment individuals who give them positive feedback while cutting down people who give them negative feedback.[24]

Evaluations from other people affect our self-esteem. For example, you might be liked for who you are or you might be liked for your achievements. Being liked for who you are is more stable, and people who have this type of self-esteem are less defensive and more honest with themselves. Being liked for your achievement is more unstable; it waxes and wanes depending on how high your achievements are.[25]

A person's self-esteem affects a host of other attitudes and has important implications for behavior in organizations. People with high self-esteem perform better and are more satisfied with their jobs.[26] When they

> **SELF-ESTEEM**
> An individual's general feeling of self-worth.

are involved in a job search, they seek out higher status jobs.[27] A work team made up of individuals with high self-esteem is more likely to be successful than a team with lower average self-esteem.[28]

Very high self-esteem may be too much of a good thing. When people with high self-esteem find themselves in stressful situations, they may brag inappropriately.[29] This may be viewed negatively by others, who see spontaneous boasting as egotistical. Very high self-esteem may also lead to overconfidence, and to relationship conflicts with others who may not evaluate this behavior favorably.[30] Individuals with high self-esteem may shift their social identities to protect themselves when they do not live up to some standard. Take two students, Denise and Teresa, for example. If Denise outperforms Teresa on a statistics exam, Teresa may convince herself that Denise is not really a good person to compare against because Denise is an engineering major and Teresa is a physical education major. Teresa's high self-esteem is protecting her from this unfavorable comparison.[31]

Self-esteem may be strongly affected by situations. Success tends to raise self-esteem, whereas failure tends to lower it. Given that high self-esteem is generally a positive characteristic, managers should encourage employees to raise their self-esteem by giving them appropriate challenges and opportunities for success.

SELF-MONITORING
The extent to which people base their behavior on cues from other people and situations.

Self-Monitoring A characteristic with great potential for affecting behavior in organizations is ***self-monitoring***—the extent to which people base their behavior on cues from other people and situations.[32] High self-monitors pay attention to what is appropriate in particular situations and to the behavior of other people, and they behave accordingly. Low self-monitors, in contrast, are not as vigilant to situational cues and act from internal states rather than paying attention to the situation. As a result, the behavior of low self-monitors is consistent across situations. High self-monitors, because their behavior varies with the situation, appear to be more unpredictable and less consistent. You can use this chapter's Challenge to assess your own self-monitoring tendencies.

Research is currently focusing on the effects of self-monitoring in organizations. In one study, the authors tracked the careers of 139 MBAs for five years to see whether high self-monitors were more likely to be promoted, change employers, or make a job-related geographic move. The results were "yes" to each question. High self-monitors get promoted because they accomplish tasks through meeting the expectations of others and because they seek out central positions in social networks.[33] They are also more likely to use self-promotion to make others aware of their skills and accomplishments.[34] However, the high self-monitor's flexibility may not be suited for every job, and the tendency to move may not fit every organization.[35] Because high self-monitors base their behavior on cues from others and from the situation, they demonstrate higher levels of managerial self-awareness. This means that, as managers, they assess their own workplace behavior accurately.[36]

Challenge

ARE YOU A HIGH OR LOW SELF-MONITOR?

For the following items, circle T (true) if the statement is characteristic of your behavior. Circle F (false) if the statement does not reflect your behavior.

1. I find it hard to imitate the behavior of other people. T F
2. At parties and social gatherings, I do not attempt to do or say things that others will like. T F
3. I can only argue for ideas that I already believe. T F
4. I can make impromptu speeches even on topics about which I have almost no information. T F
5. I guess I put on a show to impress or entertain others. T F
6. I would probably make a good actor. T F
7. In a group of people, I am rarely the center of attention. T F
8. In different situations and with different people, I often act like very different persons. T F
9. I am not particularly good at making other people like me. T F
10. I am not always the person I appear to be. T F
11. I would not change my opinions (or the way I do things) in order to please others or win their favor. T F
12. I have considered being an entertainer. T F
13. I have never been good at games like charades or at improvisational acting. T F
14. I have trouble changing my behavior to suit different people and different situations. T F
15. At a party, I let others keep the jokes and stories going. T F
16. I feel a bit awkward in company and do not show up quite as well as I should. T F
17. I can look anyone in the eye and tell a lie with a straight face (if it is for a good cause). T F
18. I may deceive people by being friendly when I really dislike them. T F

Scoring:

To score this questionnaire, give yourself 1 point for each of the following items that you answered T (true): 4, 5, 6, 8, 10, 12, 17, and 18. Now give yourself 1 point for each of the following items that you answered F (false): 1, 2, 3, 7, 9, 11, 13, 14, 15, and 16. Add both subtotals to find your overall score. If you scored 11 or above, you are probably a *high self-monitor*. If you scored 10 or under, you are probably a *low self-monitor*.

Source: From *Public Appearances, Private Realities: The Psychology of Self-Monitoring* by M. Snyder. Copyright © 1987 by W. H. Freeman and Company.

Although research on self-monitoring in organizations is in its early stages, we can speculate that high self-monitors respond more readily to work group norms, organizational culture, and supervisory feedback than do low self-monitors, who adhere more to internal guidelines for behavior ("I am who I am"). In addition, high self-monitors may be enthusiastic participants in the trend toward work teams because of their ability to assume flexible roles.

Positive/Negative Affect Recently, researchers have explored the effects of persistent mood dispositions at work. Individuals who focus on the positive aspects of themselves, other people, and the world in general are said

POSITIVE AFFECT
An individual's tendency to accentuate the positive aspects of himself or herself, other people, and the world in general.

NEGATIVE AFFECT
An individual's tendency to accentuate the negative aspects of himself or herself, other people, and the world in general.

STRONG SITUATION
A situation that overwhelms the effects of individual personalities by providing strong cues for appropriate behavior.

to have **positive affect**.[37] In contrast, those who accentuate the negative in themselves, others, and the world are said to possess **negative affect** (also referred to as negative affectivity).[38] Interviewers who exhibit positive affect evaluate job candidates more favorably than do interviewers whose affect is neutral.[39] Employees with positive affect are absent from work less often.[40] Individuals with negative affect report more work stress.[41] Individual affect also influences the work group. Positive individual affect produces positive team affect, and this leads to more cooperation and less conflict within the team.[42]

Positive affect is a definite asset in work settings. Managers can do several things to promote positive affect, including allowing participative decision making and providing pleasant working conditions. We need to know more about inducing positive affect in the workplace.

The characteristics previously described are but a few of the personality characteristics that affect behavior and performance in organizations. Can managers predict the behavior of their employees by knowing their personalities? Not completely. You may recall that the interactional psychology model (Figure 3-1) requires both person and situation variables to predict behavior. Another idea to remember in predicting behavior is the strength of situational influences. Some situations are **strong situations** in that they overwhelm the effects of individual personalities. These situations are interpreted in the same way by different individuals, evoke agreement on the appropriate behavior in the situation, and provide cues to appropriate behavior. A performance appraisal session is an example of a strong situation. Employees know to listen to their boss and to contribute when asked to do so.

A weak situation, in contrast, is one that is open to many interpretations. It provides few cues to appropriate behavior and no obvious rewards for one behavior over another. Thus, individual personalities have a stronger influence in weak situations than in strong situations. An informal meeting without an agenda can be seen as a weak situation.

Organizations present combinations of strong and weak situations; therefore, personality has a stronger effect on behavior in some situations than in others.[43]

MEASURING PERSONALITY

Several methods can be used to assess personality. These include projective tests, behavioral measures, and self-report questionnaires.

The **projective test** is one method used to measure personality. In these tests, individuals are shown a picture, abstract image, or photo and are asked to describe what they see or to tell a story about what they see. The rationale behind projective tests is that each individual responds to the stimulus in a way that reflects his or her unique personality. The Rorschach ink blot test is a projective test commonly used to assess personality.[44] Like other projective tests, however, it has low reliability. The individual being assessed may look at the same picture and see different things at different

5. *Explain how personality is measured.*

PROJECTIVE TEST
A personality test that elicits an individual's response to abstract stimuli.

times. Also, the assessor may apply his or her own biases in interpreting the information about the individual's personality.

There are *behavioral measures* of personality as well. Measuring behavior involves observing an individual's behavior in a controlled situation. We might assess a person's sociability, for example, by counting the number of times he or she approaches strangers at a party. The behavior is scored in some manner to produce an index of personality. Some potential problems with behavioral measures include the observer's ability to stay focused and the way the observer interprets the behavior. In addition, some people behave differently when they know they are being observed.

The most common method of assessing personality is the *self-report questionnaire*. Individuals respond to a series of questions, usually in an agree/disagree or true/false format. One of the more widely recognized questionnaires is the Minnesota Multiphasic Personality Inventory (MMPI). The MMPI is comprehensive and assesses a variety of traits, as well as various neurotic or psychotic disorders. Used extensively in psychological counseling to identify disorders, the MMPI is a long questionnaire. The Big Five traits we discussed earlier are measured by another self-report questionnaire, the NEO Personality Inventory. Self-report questionnaires also suffer from potential biases. It is difficult to be objective about your own personality. People often answer the questionnaires in terms of how they want to be seen, rather than as they really are.

Another popular self-report questionnaire is the Myers-Briggs Type Indicator (MBTI). In the next section, we will introduce the Jungian theory of personality. The MBTI is an instrument that has been developed to measure Jung's ideas about individual differences. Many organizations use the MBTI, and we will focus on it as an example of how some organizations use personality concepts to help employees appreciate diversity.

BEHAVIORAL MEASURES
Personality assessments that involve observing an individual's behavior in a controlled situation.

SELF-REPORT QUESTIONNAIRE
A common personality assessment that involves an individual's responses to a series of questions.

YOU BE THE JUDGE

What are the ethical uses of personality tests? What are the unethical uses?

A POPULAR APPLICATION OF PERSONALITY THEORY IN ORGANIZATIONS: THE MYERS-BRIGGS TYPE INDICATOR

One approach to applying personality theory in organizations is the Jungian approach and its measurement tool, the MBTI.

Swiss psychiatrist Carl Jung built his work on the notion that people are fundamentally different, but also fundamentally alike. His classic treatise, *Psychological Types*, proposed that the population was made up of two basic types—extraverted and introverted.[45] He went on to identify two types of perception (sensing and intuiting) and two types of judgment (thinking and feeling). Perception (how we gather information) and judgment (how we make decisions) represent the basic mental functions that everyone uses.

Jung suggested that human similarities and differences could be understood by combining preferences. We prefer and choose one way of doing things over another. We are not exclusively one way or another; rather, we

6. *Discuss Carl Jung's contribution to our understanding of individual differences, and explain how his theory is used in the Myers-Briggs Type Indicator.*

have a preference for extraversion or introversion, just as we have a preference for right-handedness or left-handedness. We may use each hand equally well, but when a ball is thrown at us by surprise, we will reach to catch it with our preferred hand. Jung's type theory argues that no preferences are better than others. Differences are to be understood, celebrated, and appreciated.

During the 1940s, a mother–daughter team became fascinated with individual differences among people and with the work of Carl Jung. Katharine Briggs and her daughter, Isabel Briggs Myers, developed the *Myers-Briggs Type Indicator* to put Jung's type theory into practical use. The MBTI is used extensively in organizations as a basis for understanding individual differences. More than 3 million people complete the instrument per year in the United States.[46] The MBTI has been used in career counseling, team building, conflict management, and understanding management styles.[47]

THE PREFERENCES

There are four basic preferences in type theory and two possible choices for each of the four preferences. Table 3-2 shows these preferences. The combination of these preferences makes up an individual's psychological type.

Extraversion/Introversion The *extraversion/introversion* preference represents where you get your energy. The extravert (E) is energized by interaction with other people. The introvert (I) is energized by time alone. Extraverts typically have a wide social network, whereas introverts have a more narrow range of relationships. As articulated by Jung, this preference has nothing to do with social skills. Many introverts have excellent social skills but prefer the internal world of ideas, thoughts, and concepts. Extraverts represent approximately 70 percent of the U.S. population.[48] Our culture rewards extraversion and nurtures it. Jung contended that the extraversion/introversion preference reflects the most important distinction between individuals.

MYERS-BRIGGS TYPE INDICATOR (MBTI)
An instrument developed to measure Carl Jung's theory of individual differences.

EXTRAVERSION
A preference indicating that an individual is energized by interaction with other people.

INTROVERSION
A preference indicating that an individual is energized by time alone.

Table 3-2
Type Theory Preferences and Descriptions

EXTRAVERSION	INTROVERSION	THINKING	FEELING
Outgoing	Quiet	Analytical	Subjective
Publicly expressive	Reserved	Clarity	Harmony
Interacting	Concentrating	Head	Heart
Speaks, then thinks	Thinks, then speaks	Justice	Mercy
Gregarious	Reflective	Rules	Circumstances
SENSING	**INTUITING**	**JUDGING**	**PERCEIVING**
Practical	General	Structured	Flexible
Specific	Abstract	Time oriented	Open ended
Feet on the ground	Head in the clouds	Decisive	Exploring
Details	Possibilities	Makes lists/uses them	Makes lists/loses them
Concrete	Theoretical	Organized	Spontaneous

In work settings, extraverts prefer variety, and they do not mind the interruptions of the phone or visits from coworkers. They communicate freely but may say things that they regret later. Introverts prefer quiet for concentration, and they like to think things through in private. They do not mind working on a project for a long time and are careful with details. Introverts dislike telephone interruptions, and they may have trouble recalling names and faces.

Sensing/Intuiting   The *sensing/intuiting* preference represents perception or how we prefer to gather information. In essence this preference reflects what we pay attention to. The sensor (S) pays attention to information gathered through the five senses and to what actually exists. The intuitor (N) pays attention to a "sixth sense" and to what could be rather than to what actually exists.[49] Approximately 70 percent of people in the United States are sensors.[50]

> **SENSING**
> Gathering information through the five senses.
>
> **INTUITING**
> Gathering information through "sixth sense" and focusing on what could be rather than what actually exists.

At work, sensors prefer specific answers to questions and can become frustrated with vague instructions. They like jobs that yield tangible results, and they enjoy using established skills more than learning new ones. Intuitors like solving new problems and are impatient with routine details. They enjoy learning new skills more than actually using them. Intuitors tend to think about several things at once, and they may be seen by others as absentminded. They like figuring out how things work just for the fun of it.

Thinking/Feeling   The *thinking/feeling* preference represents the way we prefer to make decisions. The thinker (T) makes decisions in a logical, objective fashion, whereas the feeler (F) makes decisions in a personal, value-oriented way. The general U.S. population is divided 50/50 on the thinking/feeling preference, but it is interesting that two-thirds of all males are thinkers, whereas two-thirds of all females are feelers. It is the one preference in type theory that has a strong gender difference. Thinkers tend to analyze decisions, whereas feelers sympathize. Thinkers try to be impersonal, whereas feelers base their decisions on how the outcome will affect the people involved.

> **THINKING**
> Making decisions in a logical, objective fashion.
>
> **FEELING**
> Making decisions in a personal, value-oriented way.

In work settings, thinkers do not show much emotion, and they may become uncomfortable with people who do. They respond more readily to other people's thoughts. They are firm minded and like putting things into a logical framework. Feelers, in contrast, are more comfortable with emotion in the workplace. They enjoy pleasing people and need a lot of praise and encouragement.

Judging/Perceiving   The *judging/perceiving* preference reflects one's orientation to the outer world. The judger (J) loves closure. Judgers prefer to lead a planned, organized life and like making decisions. The perceiver (P), in contrast, prefers a more flexible and spontaneous life and wants to keep options open. Imagine a J and a P going out for dinner. The J asks the P to choose a restaurant, and the P suggests ten alternatives. The J just wants to decide and get on with it, whereas the P wants to explore all the options.

> **JUDGING**
> Preferring closure and completion in making decisions.
>
> **PERCEIVING**
> Preferring to explore many alternatives and flexibility.

For judgers in all arenas of life, and especially at work, there is a right and a wrong way to do everything. They love getting things accomplished and delight in marking off the completed items on their calendars. Perceivers tend to adopt a wait-and-see attitude and to collect new information rather than draw conclusions. Perceivers are curious and welcome new information. They may start too many projects and not finish them.

The Sixteen Types

The preferences combine to form sixteen distinct types, as shown in Table 3-3. For example, let's examine ESTJ. This type is extraverted, sensing, thinking, and judging. ESTJs see the world as it is (S); make decisions objectively (T); and like structure, schedules, and order (J). Combining these qualities with their preference for interacting with others makes them natural managers. ESTJs are seen by others as dependable, practical, and

Table 3-3
Characteristics Frequently Associated with Each Type

	Sensing Types		Intuitive Types	
Introverts	**ISTJ** Quiet, serious, earn success by thoroughness and dependability. Practical, matter-of-fact, realistic, and responsible. Decide logically what should be done and work toward it steadily, regardless of distractions. Take pleasure in making everything orderly and organized—their work, their home, their life. Value traditions and loyalty.	**ISFJ** Quiet, friendly, responsible, and conscientious. Committed and steady in meeting their obligations. Thorough, painstaking and accurate. Loyal, considerate, notice and remember specifics about people who are important to them, concerned with how others feel. Strive to create an orderly and harmonious environment at work and at home.	**INFJ** Seek meaning and connection in ideas, relationships, and material possessions. Want to understand what motivates people and are insightful about others. Conscientious and committed to their firm values. Develop a clear vision about how best to serve the common good. Organized and decisive in implementing their vision.	**INTJ** Have original minds and great drive for implementing their ideas and achieving their goals. Quickly see patterns in external events and develop long-range explanatory perspectives. When committed, organize a job and carry it through. Skeptical and independent, have high standards of competence and performance for themselves and others.
	ISTP Tolerant and flexible, quiet observers until a problem appears, then act quickly to find workable solutions. Analyze what makes things work and readily get through large amounts of data to isolate the core of practical problems. Interested in cause and effect, organize facts using logical principles, value efficiency.	**ISFP** Quiet, friendly, sensitive, and kind. Enjoy the present moment, what's going on around them. Like to have their own space and to work within their own time frame. Loyal and committed to their values and to people who are important to them. Dislike disagreements and conflicts, do not force their opinions or values on others.	**INFP** Idealistic, loyal to their values and to people who are important to them. Want an external life that is congruent with their values. Curious, quick to see possibilities, can be catalysts for implementing ideas. Seek to understand people and to help them fulfill their potential. Adaptable, flexible, and accepting unless a value is threatened.	**INTP** Seek to develop logical explanations for everything that interests them. Theoretical and abstract, interested more in ideas than in social interaction. Quiet, contained, flexible, and adaptable. Have unusual ability to focus in depth to solve problems in their area of interest. Skeptical, sometimes critical, always analytical.

Note: I = introvert; E = extravert; S = sensor; N = intuitor; T = thinker; F = feeler; J = judger; and P = perceiver.

(*continued*)

able to get any job done. They are conscious of the chain of command and see work as a series of goals to be reached by following rules and regulations. They may have little tolerance for disorganization and have a high need for control. Research results from the *MBTI Atlas* show that most of the 7,463 managers studied were ESTJs.[51]

There are no good and bad types, and each type has its own strengths and weaknesses. There is a growing volume of research on type theory. The MBTI has been found to have good reliability and validity as a measurement instrument for identifying type.[52, 53] Type has been found to be related to learning style, teaching style, and choice of occupation. For example, the MBTI types of engineering students at Georgia Tech were studied in order to see who was attracted to engineering and who was likely to leave the

Table 3-3
Concluded

Sensing Types		Intuitive Types	
ESTP	**ESFP**	**ENFP**	**ENTP**
Flexible and tolerant, they take a pragmatic approach focused on immediate results. Theories and conceptual explanations bore them—they want to act energetically to solve the problem. Focus on the here-and-now, spontaneous, enjoy each moment that they can be active with others. Enjoy material comforts and style. Learn best through doing.	Outgoing, friendly, and accepting. Exuberant lovers of life, people, and material comforts. Enjoy working with others to make things happen. Bring common sense and a realistic approach to their work and make work fun. Flexible and spontaneous, adapt readily to new people and environments. Learn best by trying a new skill with other people.	Warmly enthusiastic and imaginative. See life as full of possibilities. Make connections between events and information very quickly, and confidently proceed based on the patterns they see. Want a lot of affirmation from others, and readily give appreciation and support. Spontaneous and flexible, often rely on their ability to improvise and their verbal fluency.	Quick, ingenious, stimulating, alert, and outspoken. Resourceful in solving new and challenging problems. Adept at generating conceptual possibilities and then analyzing them strategically. Good at reading other people. Bored by routine, will seldom do the same thing the same way, apt to turn to one new interest after another.
ESTJ	**ESFJ**	**ENFJ**	**ENTJ**
Practical, realistic, matter-of-fact. Decisive, quickly move to implement decisions. Organize projects and people to get things done, focus on getting results in the most efficient way possible. Take care of routine details. Have a clear set of logical standards, systematically follow them and want others to also. Forceful in implementing their plans.	Warmhearted, conscientious, and cooperative. Want harmony in their environment, work with determination to establish it. Like to work with others to complete tasks accurately and on time. Loyal, follow through even in small matters. Notice what others need in their day-by-day lives and try to provide it. Want to be appreciated for who they are and for what they contribute.	Warm, empathetic, responsive, and responsible. Highly attuned to the emotions, needs, and motivations of others. Find potential in everyone, want to help others fulfill their potential. May act as catalysts for individual and group growth. Loyal, responsive to praise and criticism. Sociable, facilitate others in a group, and provide inspiring leadership.	Frank, decisive, assume leadership readily. Quickly see logical and inefficient procedures and policies, develop and implement comprehensive systems to solve organizational problems. Enjoy long-term planning and goal setting. Usually well informed, well read, enjoy expanding their knowledge and passing it on to others. Forceful in presenting their ideas.

Extraverts label appears vertically alongside both rows.

major. STs and NTs were more attracted to engineering. Es and Fs were more likely to withdraw from engineering courses.[54] Type has also been used to determine an individual's decision-making style and management style.

Recent studies have begun to focus on the relationship between type and specific managerial behaviors. The introvert (I) and the feeler (F), for example, have been shown to be more effective at participative management than their counterparts, the extravert and the thinker.[55] Companies like AT&T, ExxonMobil, and Honeywell use the MBTI in their management development programs to help employees understand the different viewpoints of others in the organization. The MBTI can also be used for team building. Hewlett-Packard and Armstrong World Industries use the MBTI to help teams realize that diversity and differences lead to successful performance.

Type theory is valued by managers for its simplicity and accuracy in depicting personalities. It is a useful tool for helping managers develop interpersonal skills. Managers also use type theory to build teams that capitalize on individuals' strengths and to help individual team members appreciate differences.

It should be recognized that there is the potential for individuals to misuse the information from the MBTI in organizational settings. Some inappropriate uses include labeling one another, providing a convenient excuse that they simply can't work with someone else, and avoiding responsibility for their own personal development with respect to working with others and becoming more flexible. One's type is not an excuse for inappropriate behavior.

We turn now to another psychological process that forms the basis for individual differences. Perception shapes the way we view the world, and it varies greatly among individuals.

SOCIAL PERCEPTION

7. *Define social perception and explain how characteristics of the perceiver, the target, and the situation affect it.*

SOCIAL PERCEPTION
The process of interpreting information about another person.

Perception involves the way we view the world around us. It adds meaning to information gathered via the five senses of touch, smell, hearing, vision, and taste. Perception is the primary vehicle through which we come to understand ourselves and our surroundings. *Social perception* is the process of interpreting information about another person. Virtually all management activities rely on perception. In appraising performance, managers use their perceptions of an employee's behavior as a basis for the evaluation.

One work situation that highlights the importance of perception is the selection interview. The consequences of a bad match between an individual and the organization are devastating for both parties, so it is essential that the data gathered be accurate. Typical first interviews are brief, and the candidate is usually one of many seen by an interviewer during a day. How long does it take for the interviewer to reach a decision about a candidate? In the first four to five minutes, the interviewer often makes an accept or reject decision based on his or her perception of the candidate.[56]

Perception is also culturally determined. Based on our cultural backgrounds, we tend to perceive things in certain ways. Read the following sentence:

Finished files are the result of years of scientific study combined with the experience of years.

Now quickly count the number of Fs in the sentence. Individuals for whom English is their second language see all six Fs. Most native English speakers report that there are three Fs. Because of cultural conditioning, *of* is not an important word and is ignored.[57] Culture affects our interpretation of the data we gather, as well as the way we add meaning to it.

Valuing diversity, including cultural diversity, has been recognized as the key to international competitiveness.[58] This challenge and others make social perception skills essential to managerial success.

Three major categories of factors influence our perception of another person: characteristics of ourselves, as perceivers; characteristics of the target person we are perceiving; and characteristics of the situation in which the interaction takes place. Figure 3-2 shows a model of social perception.

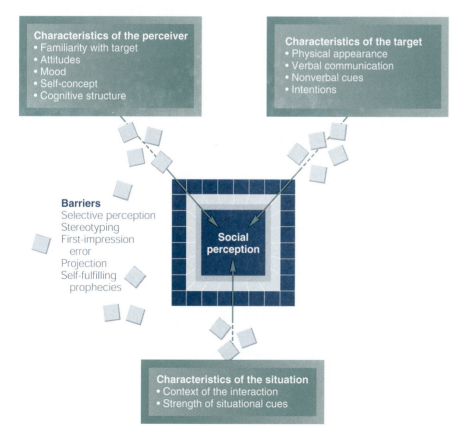

Characteristics of the perceiver
• Familiarity with target
• Attitudes
• Mood
• Self-concept
• Cognitive structure

Characteristics of the target
• Physical appearance
• Verbal communication
• Nonverbal cues
• Intentions

Barriers
Selective perception
Stereotyping
First-impression error
Projection
Self-fulfilling prophecies

Social perception

Characteristics of the situation
• Context of the interaction
• Strength of situational cues

Figure 3-2
A Model for Social Perception

CHARACTERISTICS OF THE PERCEIVER

Several characteristics of the perceiver can affect social perception. One such characteristic is *familiarity* with the target (the person being perceived). When we are familiar with a person, we have multiple observations on which to base our impression of him or her. If the information we have gathered during these observations is accurate, we may have an accurate perception of the other person. Familiarity does not always mean accuracy, however. Sometimes, when we know a person well, we tend to screen out information that is inconsistent with what we believe the person is like. This is a particular danger in performance appraisals where the rater is familiar with the person being rated.

The perceiver's *attitudes* also affect social perception. Suppose you are interviewing candidates for a very important position in your organization— a position that requires negotiating contracts with suppliers, most of whom are male. You may feel that women are not capable of holding their own in tough negotiations. This attitude will doubtless affect your perceptions of the female candidates you interview.

Mood can have a strong influence on the way we perceive someone.[59] We think differently when we are happy than we do when we are depressed. In addition, we remember information that is consistent with our mood state better than information that is inconsistent with our mood state. When in a positive mood, we form more positive impressions of others. When in a negative mood, we tend to evaluate others unfavorably.

Another factor that can affect social perception is the perceiver's *self-concept*. An individual with a positive self-concept tends to notice positive attributes in another person. In contrast, a negative self-concept can lead a perceiver to pick out negative traits in another person. Greater understanding of self allows us to have more accurate perceptions of others.

Cognitive structure, an individual's pattern of thinking, also affects social perception. Some people have a tendency to perceive physical traits, such as height, weight, and appearance, more readily. Others tend to focus more on central traits, or personality dispositions. Cognitive complexity allows a person to perceive multiple characteristics of another person rather than attending to just a few traits.

CHARACTERISTICS OF THE TARGET

Characteristics of the target, who is the person being perceived, influence social perception. *Physical appearance* plays a big role in our perception of others. The perceiver will notice the target's physical features like height, weight, estimated age, race, and gender. Clothing says a great deal about a person. Blue pin-striped suits, for example, are decoded to mean banking or Wall Street. Perceivers tend to notice physical appearance characteristics that contrast with the norm, that are intense, or that are new or unusual.[60] A loud person, one who dresses outlandishly, a very tall person, or a hyperactive child will be noticed because he or she provides a contrast to what is commonly encountered. In addition, people who are novel can attract attention. Newcomers or minorities in the organization are examples of novel individuals.

Physical attractiveness often colors our entire impression of another person. Interviewers rate attractive candidates more favorably, and attractive candidates are awarded higher starting salaries.[61, 62] People who are perceived as physically attractive face stereotypes as well. We will discuss these and other stereotypes later in this chapter.

Verbal communication from targets also affects our perception of them. We listen to the topics they speak about, their voice tone, and their accent and make judgments based on this input.

Nonverbal communication conveys a great deal of information about the target. Eye contact, facial expressions, body movements, and posture all are deciphered by the perceiver in an attempt to form an impression of the target. It is interesting that some nonverbal signals mean very different things in different cultures. The "okay" sign in the United States (forming a circle with the thumb and forefinger) is an insult in South America. Facial expressions, however, seem to have universal meanings. Individuals from different cultures are able to recognize and decipher expressions the same way.[63]

The *intentions* of the target are inferred by the perceiver, who observes the target's behavior. We may see our boss appear in our office doorway and think, "Oh no! She's going to give me more work to do." Or we may perceive that her intention is to congratulate us on a recent success. In any case, the perceiver's interpretation of the target's intentions affects the way the perceiver views the target.

CHARACTERISTICS OF THE SITUATION

The situation in which the interaction between the perceiver and the target takes place also influences the perceiver's impression of the target. The *social context* of the interaction is a major influence. Meeting a professor in his or her office affects your impression in a certain way that may contrast with the impression you would form had you met the professor in a local restaurant. In Japan, social context is very important. Business conversations after working hours or at lunch are taboo. If you try to talk business during these times, you may be perceived as rude.[64]

The *strength of situational cues* also affects social perception. As we discussed earlier in the chapter, some situations provide strong cues as to appropriate behavior. In these situations, we assume that the individual's behavior can be accounted for by the situation, and that it may not reflect the individual's disposition. This is the **discounting principle** in social perception.[65] For example, you may encounter an automobile salesperson who has a warm and personable manner, asks about your work and hobbies, and seems genuinely interested in your taste in cars. Can you assume that this behavior reflects the salesperson's personality? You probably cannot, because of the influence of the situation. This person is trying to sell you a car, and

DISCOUNTING PRINCIPLE
The assumption that an individual's behavior is accounted for by the situation.

in this particular situation he or she probably treats all customers in this manner.

You can see that characteristics of the perceiver, the target, and the situation all affect social perception. It would be wonderful if all of us had accurate social perception skills. Unfortunately, barriers often prevent us from perceiving another person accurately.

BARRIERS TO SOCIAL PERCEPTION

8. *Identify five common barriers to social perception.*

Several factors lead us to form inaccurate impressions of others. Five of these barriers to social perception are selective perception, stereotyping, first-impression error, projection, and self-fulfilling prophecies.

We receive a vast amount of information. *Selective perception* is our tendency to choose information that supports our viewpoints. Individuals often ignore information that makes them feel uncomfortable or threatens their viewpoints. Suppose, for example, that a sales manager is evaluating the performance of his employees. One employee does not get along well with colleagues and rarely completes sales reports on time. This employee, however, generates the most new sales contracts in the office. The sales manager may ignore the negative information, choosing to evaluate the salesperson only on the contracts generated. The manager is exercising selective perception.

SELECTIVE PERCEPTION
The process of selecting information that supports our individual viewpoints while discounting information that threatens our viewpoints.

A *stereotype* is a generalization about a group of people. Stereotypes reduce information about other people to a workable level, and they are efficient for compiling and using information. Stereotypes become even stronger when they are shared with and validated by others.[66] Stereotypes can be accurate, and when they are accurate, they can be useful perceptual guidelines. Most of the time, however, stereotypes are inaccurate. They harm individuals when inaccurate impressions of them are inferred and are never tested or changed.[67] Information technology careers, for example, have been stereotyped such that fewer young people are entering the field. The stereotype of these careers is outdated and inaccurate.

STEREOTYPE
A generalization about a group of people.

Suppose that a white male manager passes the coffee area and notices two African American men talking there. He becomes irritated at them for wasting time. Later in the day, he sees two women talking in the coffee area. He thinks they should do their gossiping on their own time. The next morning, the same manager sees two white men talking in the coffee area. He thinks nothing of it; he is sure they are discussing business. The manager may hold a stereotype that women and minorities do not work hard unless closely supervised.

In multicultural work teams, members often stereotype foreign coworkers rather than getting to know them before forming an impression. Team members from less developed countries are often assumed to have less knowledge simply because their homeland is economically or technologically less developed.[68] Stereotypes like these can deflate the productivity of the work team, as well as create low morale.

Attractiveness is a powerful stereotype. We assume that attractive individuals are also warm, kind, sensitive, poised, sociable, outgoing, independent, and strong. Are attractive people really like this? Certainly, all of them are not. A study of romantic relationships showed that most attractive individuals do not fit the stereotype, except for possessing good social skills and being popular.[69]

Some individuals may seem to us to fit the stereotype of attractiveness because our behavior elicits from them behavior that confirms the stereotype. Consider, for example, a situation in which you meet an attractive fellow student. Chances are that you respond positively to this person, because you assume he or she is warm, sociable, and so on. Even though the person may not possess these traits, your positive response may bring out these behaviors in the person. The interaction between the two of you may be channeled such that the stereotype confirms itself.[70] Another stereotype that people often hold involves sex roles. Sometimes we hold strong beliefs about what men and women are like, and what their roles should be.

First impressions are lasting impressions, so the saying goes. Individuals place a good deal of importance on first impressions, and for good reason. We tend to remember what we perceive first about a person, and sometimes we are quite reluctant to change our initial impressions.[71] *First-impression error* occurs when we observe a very brief bit of a person's behavior in our first encounter and infer that this behavior reflects what the person is really like. Primacy effects can be particularly dangerous in interviews, given that we form first impressions quickly and that these impressions may be the basis for long-term employment relationships.

Projection, also known as the false-consensus effect, is a cause of inaccurate perceptions of others. It is the misperception of the commonness of our own beliefs, values, and behaviors such that we overestimate the number of others who share these things. We assume that others are similar to us, and that our own values and beliefs are appropriate. People who are different are viewed as unusual and even deviant. Projection occurs most often when you surround yourself with others similar to you. You may overlook important information about others when you assume we are all alike and in agreement.[72]

Self-fulfilling prophecies are also barriers to social perception. Sometimes our expectations affect the way we interact with others such that we get what we wish for. Self-fulfilling prophecy is also known as the Pygmalion effect, named for the sculptor in Greek mythology who prayed that a statue of a woman he had carved would come to life, a wish that was granted by the gods.

Early studies of self-fulfilling prophecy were conducted in elementary school classrooms. Teachers were given bogus information that some of their pupils had high intellectual potential. These pupils were chosen randomly; there were really no differences among the students. Eight months later, the "gifted" pupils scored significantly higher on an IQ test. The teachers' expectations had elicited growth from these students, and the teachers had given them tougher assignments and more feedback on their performance.[73] Self-fulfilling prophecy has been studied in many settings, including at sea. The Israeli Defense Forces told one group of naval cadets that they

FIRST-IMPRESSION ERROR
The tendency to form lasting opinions about an individual based on initial perceptions.

PROJECTION
Overestimating the number of people who share our own beliefs, values, and behaviors.

SELF-FULFILLING PROPHECY
The situation in which our expectations about people affect our interaction with them in such a way that our expectations are fulfilled.

probably wouldn't experience seasickness, and even if they did, it wouldn't affect their performance. The self-fulfilling prophecy worked! These cadets were rated better performers than other groups, and they also had less seasickness. The information improved the cadets' self-efficacy—they believed they could perform well even if they became seasick.[74]

The Pygmalion effect has been observed in work organizations as well.[75] A manager's expectations of an individual affect both the manager's behavior toward the individual and the individual's response. For example, suppose your initial impression is that an employee has the potential to move up within the organization. Chances are you will spend a great deal of time coaching and counseling the employee, providing challenging assignments, and grooming the individual for success.

Managers can harness the power of the Pygmalion effect to improve productivity in the organization. It appears that high expectations of individuals come true. Can a manager extend these high expectations to an entire group and have similar positive results? The answer is yes. When a manager expects positive things from a group, the group delivers.[76]

IMPRESSION MANAGEMENT

Most people want to make favorable impressions on others. This is particularly true in organizations, where individuals compete for jobs, favorable performance evaluations, and salary increases. The process by which individuals try to control the impressions others have of them is called *impression management*. Individuals use several techniques to control others' impressions of them.[77]

IMPRESSION MANAGEMENT
The process by which individuals try to control the impressions others have of them.

Some impression management techniques are self-enhancing. These techniques focus on enhancing others' impressions of the person using the technique. Name-dropping, which involves mentioning an association with important people in the hopes of improving one's image, is often used. Managing one's appearance is another technique for impression management. Individuals dress carefully for interviews because they want to "look the part" in order to get the job. Self-descriptions, or statements about one's characteristics, are used to manage impressions as well.

Another group of impression management techniques are *other-enhancing*. The aim of these techniques is to focus on the individual whose impression is to be managed. Flattery is a common other-enhancing technique whereby compliments are given to an individual in order to win his or her approval. Favors are also used to gain the approval of others. Agreement with someone's opinion is a technique often used to gain a positive impression. People with disabilities, for example, often use other-enhancing techniques. They may feel that they must take it upon themselves to make others comfortable interacting with them. Impression management techniques are used by individuals with disabilities as a way of dealing with potential avoidance by others.[78]

Are impression management techniques effective? Most of the research has focused on employment interviews, and the results indicate that candidates who engage in impression management by self-promoting performed better in interviews, were more likely to obtain site visits with potential employers, and were more likely to get hired.[79, 80] In addition, employees who engage in impression management are rated more favorably in performance appraisals than those who do not.[81]

Impression management seems to have an impact on others' impressions. As long as the impressions conveyed are accurate, this process can be a beneficial one in organizations. If the impressions are found to be false, however, a strongly negative overall impression may result. Furthermore, excessive impression management can lead to the perception that the user is manipulative or insincere.[82] We have discussed the influences on social perception, the potential barriers to perceiving another person, and impression management. Another psychological process that managers should understand is attribution.

ATTRIBUTION IN ORGANIZATIONS

As human beings, we are innately curious. We are not content merely to observe the behavior of others; rather, we want to know *why* they behave the way they do. We also seek to understand and explain our own behavior. **Attribution theory** explains how we pinpoint the causes of our own behavior and that of other people.[83]

The attributions, or inferred causes, we provide for behavior have important implications in organizations. In explaining the causes of our performance, good or bad, we are asked to explain the behavior that was the basis for the performance.

INTERNAL AND EXTERNAL ATTRIBUTIONS

Attributions can be made to an internal source of responsibility (something within the individual's control) or an external source (something outside the individual's control). Suppose you perform well on an exam in this course. You might say you aced the test because you are smart or because you studied hard. If you attribute your success to ability or effort, you are making an internal attribution.

Alternatively, you might make an external attribution for your performance. You might say it was an easy test (you would attribute your success to degree of task difficulty) or that you had good luck. In this case, you are attributing your performance to sources beyond your control, or external sources. You can see that internal attributions include such causes as ability and effort, whereas external attributions include causes like task difficulty or luck.

Attribution patterns differ among individuals.[84] Achievement-oriented individuals attribute their success to ability and their failures to lack of effort, both internal causes. Failure-oriented individuals attribute their failures to lack of ability, and they may develop feelings of incompetence as a result of their attributional pattern. Evidence indicates that this

ATTRIBUTION THEORY
A theory that explains how individuals pinpoint the causes of their own behavior and that of others.

9. *Explain the attribution process and how attributions affect managerial behavior.*

attributional pattern also leads to depression.[85] Women managers, in contrast to men managers, are less likely to attribute their success to their own ability. This may be because they are adhering to social norms that compel women to be more modest about their accomplishments, or because they believe that success has less to do with ability than with hard work.[86]

Attribution theory has many applications in the workplace. The way you explain your own behavior affects your motivation. For example, suppose you must give an important presentation to your executive management group. You believe you have performed well, and your boss tells you that you've done a good job. To what do you attribute your success? If you believe careful preparation and rehearsal led to your success, you're likely to take credit for the performance and to have a sense of self-efficacy about future presentations. If, however, you believe that you were just lucky, you may not be motivated to repeat the performance because you believe you had little influence on the outcome.

One situation in which a lot of attributions are made is the employment interview. Candidates are often asked to explain the causes of previous performance (Why did you perform poorly in math classes?) to interviewers. In addition, candidates often feel they should justify why they should be hired (I work well with people, so I'm looking for a managerial job). Research shows that successful and unsuccessful candidates differ in the way they make attributions for negative outcomes. Successful candidates are less defensive and make internal attributions for negative events. Unsuccessful candidates attribute negative outcomes to things beyond their control (external attributions), which gives interviewers the impression that the candidate failed to learn from the event. In addition, interviewers fear that the individuals would be likely to blame others when something goes wrong in the workplace.[87]

ATTRIBUTIONAL BIASES

The attribution process may be affected by two very common errors: the fundamental attribution error and the self-serving bias. The tendency to make attributions to internal causes when focusing on someone else's behavior is known as the *fundamental attribution error*.[88] The other error, *self-serving bias*, occurs when focusing on one's own behavior. Individuals tend to make internal attributions for their own successes and external attributions for their own failures.[89] In other words, when we succeed, we take credit for it; when we fail, we blame the situation on other people.

Both of these biases were illustrated in a study of health care managers who were asked to cite the causes of their employees' poor performance.[90] The managers claimed that internal causes (their employees' lack of effort or lack of ability) were the basis for their employees' poor performance. This is an example of the fundamental attribution error. When the employees were asked to pinpoint the cause of their own performance problems, they blamed a lack of support from the managers (an external cause), which illustrates self-serving bias.

FUNDAMENTAL ATTRIBUTION ERROR
The tendency to make attributions to internal causes when focusing on someone else's behavior.

SELF-SERVING BIAS
The tendency to attribute one's own successes to internal causes and one's failures to external causes.

There are cultural differences in these two attribution errors. As described above, these biases apply to people from the United States. In more fatalistic cultures, such as India's, people tend to believe that fate is responsible for much that happens. People in such cultures tend to emphasize external causes of behavior.[91]

In China, people are taught that hard work is the route to accomplishment. When faced with either a success or a failure, Chinese individuals first introspect about whether they tried hard enough or whether their attitude was correct. In a study of attributions for performance in sports, Chinese athletes attributed both their successes and failures to internal causes. Even when the cause of poor athletic performance was clearly external, such as bad weather, the Chinese participants made internal attributions. In terms of the Chinese culture, this attributional pattern is a reflection of moral values that are used to evaluate behavior. The socialistic value of selfless morality dictates that individual striving must serve collective interests. Mao Ze-dong stressed that external causes function only through internal causes; therefore, the main cause of results lies within oneself. Chinese are taught this from childhood and form a corresponding attributional tendency. In analyzing a cause, they first look to their own effort.[92]

The way individuals interpret the events around them has a strong influence on their behavior. People try to understand the causes of behavior in order to gain predictability and control over future behavior. Managers use attributions in all aspects of their jobs. In evaluating performance and rewarding employees, managers must determine the causes of behavior and a perceived source of responsibility. One tough call managers often make is whether allegations of sexual harassment actually resulted from sexual conduct and, if harassment did occur, what should be done about it. To make such tough calls, managers use attributions.

Attribution theory can explain how performance evaluation judgments can lead to differential rewards. A supervisor attributing an employee's good performance to internal causes, such as effort or ability, may give a larger raise than a supervisor attributing the good performance to external causes, such as help from others or good training. Managers are often called on to explain their own actions as well, and in doing so they make attributions about the causes of their own behavior. We continue our discussion of attributions in Chapter 6 in terms of how attributions are used in managing employee performance.

MANAGERIAL IMPLICATIONS: USING PERSONALITY, PERCEPTION, AND ATTRIBUTION AT WORK

Managers need to know as much as possible about individual differences in order to understand themselves and those with whom they work. An understanding of personality characteristics can help a manager appreciate

YOU BE THE JUDGE

Suppose a manager makes a misattribution of an employee's poor performance. What are the ethical consequences of this?

differences in employees. With the increased diversity of the workforce, tools like the MBTI can be used to help employees see someone else's point of view. These tools can also help make communication among diverse employees more effective.

Managers use social perception constantly on the job. Knowledge of the forces that affect perception and the barriers to accuracy can help the manager form more accurate impressions of others.

Determining the causes of job performance is a major task for the manager, and attribution theory can be used to explain how managers go about determining causality. In addition, knowledge of the fundamental attribution error and self-serving bias can help a manager guard against these biases in the processes of looking for causes of behavior on the job.

In this chapter, we have explored the psychological processes of personality, perception, and attribution as individual differences. In the next chapter, we will continue our discussion of individual differences in terms of attitudes, values, and ethics.

KEY TERMS

attribution theory

behavioral measures

discounting principle

extraversion

feeling

first-impression error

fundamental attribution error

generalized self-efficacy

humanistic theory

impression management

individual differences

integrative approach

interactional psychology

introversion

intuiting

judging

locus of control

Myers-Briggs Type Indicator (MBTI)

negative affect

perceiving

personality

positive affect

projection

projective test

psychodynamic theory

selective perception

self-esteem

self-fulfilling prophecy

self-monitoring

self-report questionnaire

self-serving bias

sensing

social perception

stereotype

strong situation

thinking

trait theory

Experiential Exercise

MBTI TYPES AND MANAGEMENT STYLES

Part I. This questionnaire will help you determine your preferences. For each item, circle either a or b. If you feel both a and b are true, decide which one is more like you, even if it is only slightly more true.

1. I would rather
   a. Solve a new and complicated problem.
   b. Work on something I have done before.

2. I like to
   a. Work alone in a quiet place.
   b. Be where the action is.

3. I want a boss who
   a. Establishes and applies criteria in decisions.
   b. Considers individual needs and makes exceptions.

4. When I work on a project, I
   a. Like to finish it and get some closure.
   b. Often leave it open for possible changes.

5. When making a decision, the most important considerations are
   a. Rational thoughts, ideas, and data.
   b. People's feelings and values.

6. On a project, I tend to
   a. Think it over and over before deciding how to proceed.
   b. Start working on it right away, thinking about it as I go along.

7. When working on a project, I prefer to
   a. Maintain as much control as possible.
   b. Explore various options.

8. In my work, I prefer to
   a. Work on several projects at a time, and learn as much as possible about each one.
   b. Have one project that is challenging and keeps me busy.

9. I often
   a. Make lists and plans whenever I start something and may hate to seriously alter my plans.
   b. Avoid plans and just let things progress as I work on them.

10. When discussing a problem with colleagues, it is easy for me to
    a. See "the big picture."
    b. Grasp the specifics of the situation.

11. When the phone rings in my office or at home, I usually
    a. Consider it an interruption.
    b. Do not mind answering it.

12. Which word describes you better?
    a. Analytical.
    b. Empathetic.

13. When I am working on an assignment, I tend to
    a. Work steadily and consistently.

    b. Work in bursts of energy with "down time" in between.

14. When I listen to someone talk on a subject, I usually try to
    a. Relate it to my own experience and see if it fits.
    b. Assess and analyze the message.

15. When I come up with new ideas, I generally
    a. "Go for it."
    b. Like to contemplate the ideas some more.

16. When working on a project, I prefer to
    a. Narrow the scope so it is clearly defined.
    b. Broaden the scope to include related aspects.

17. When I read something, I usually
    a. Confine my thoughts to what is written there.
    b. Read between the lines and relate the words to other ideas.

18. When I have to make a decision in a hurry, I often
    a. Feel uncomfortable and wish I had more information.
    b. Am able to do so with available data.

19. In a meeting, I tend to
    a. Continue formulating my ideas as I talk about them.
    b. Only speak out after I have carefully thought the issue through.

20. In work, I prefer spending a great deal of time on issues of
    a. Ideas.
    b. People.

21. In meetings, I am most often annoyed with people who
    a. Come up with many sketchy ideas.
    b. Lengthen meetings with many practical details.

22. I am a
    a. Morning person.
    b. Night owl.

23. What is your style in preparing for a meeting?
    a.   I am willing to go in and be responsive.
    b.   I like to be fully prepared and usually sketch an outline of the meeting.

24. In a meeting, I would prefer for people to
    a.   Display a fuller range of emotions.
    b.   Be more task oriented.

25. I would rather work for an organization where
    a.   My job was intellectually stimulating.
    b.   I was committed to its goals and mission.

26. On weekends, I tend to
    a.   Plan what I will do.
    b.   Just see what happens and decide as I go along.

27. I am more
    a.   Outgoing.
    b.   Contemplative.

28. I would rather work for a boss who is
    a.   Full of new ideas.
    b.   Practical.

In the following, choose the word in each pair that appeals to you more:

29. a.   Social.
    b.   Theoretical.

30. a.   Ingenuity.
    b.   Practicality.

31. a.   Organized.
    b.   Adaptable.

32. a.   Active.
    b.   Concentration.

SCORING KEY

Count one point for each item listed below that you have circled in the inventory.

Score for I	Score for E	Score for S	Score for N	Score for T	Score for F	Score for J	Score for P
2a	2b	1b	1a	3a	3b	4a	4b
6a	6b	10b	10a	5a	5b	7a	7b
11a	11b	13a	13b	12a	12b	8b	8a
15b	15a	16a	16b	14b	14a	9a	9b
19b	19a	17a	17b	20a	20b	18b	18a
22a	22b	21a	21b	24b	24a	23b	23a
27b	27a	28b	28a	25a	25b	26a	26b
32b	32a	30b	30a	29b	29a	31a	31b

Total

Circle the one with more points—I or E.   Circle the one with more points—S or N.   Circle the one with more points—T or F.   Circle the one with more points—J or P.

Your score is

I or E _____   T or F _____

S or N _____   J or P _____

Part II. The purpose of this part of the exercise is to give you experience in understanding some of the individual differences that were proposed by Carl Jung and are measured by the MBTI.

Step 1. Your instructor will assign you to a group.

Step 2. Your group is a team of individuals who want to start a business. You are to develop a mission statement and a name for your business.

Step 3. After you have completed Step 2, analyze the decision process that occurred within the group.

How did you decide on your company's name and mission?

Step 4. Your instructor will have each group report to the class the name and mission of the company, and then the decision process used. Your instructor will also give you some additional information about the exercise and provide some interesting insights about your management style.

Source: "MBTI Types and Management Styles" from D. Marcic and P. Nutt, "Personality Inventory," in D. Marcic, ed., *Organizational Behavior: Experiences and Cases* (St. Paul: West, 1989), 9–16. Reprinted by permission.

4

Attitudes, Values, and Ethics

LEARNING OBJECTIVES

After reading this chapter, you should be able to do the following:

1. Explain the ABC model of an attitude.

2. Describe how attitudes are formed.

3. Define *job satisfaction* and *organizational commitment* and discuss the importance of these two work attitudes.

4. Identify the characteristics of the source, target, and message that affect persuasion.

5. Distinguish between instrumental and terminal values.

6. Explain how managers can deal with the diverse value systems that characterize the global environment.

7. Describe a model of individual and organizational influences on ethical behavior.

8. Discuss how value systems, locus of control, Machiavellianism, and cognitive moral development affect ethical behavior.

In this chapter, we continue the discussion of individual differences we began in Chapter 3 with personality, perception, and attribution. Persons and situations jointly influence behavior, and individual differences help us to better understand the influence of the person. Our focus now is on three other individual difference factors: attitudes, values, and ethics.

ATTITUDES

An *attitude* is a psychological tendency that is expressed by evaluating a particular entity with some degree of favor or disfavor.[1] We respond favorably or unfavorably toward many things: animals, coworkers, our own appearance, politics.

Attitudes are important because of their links to behavior. Attitudes are also an integral part of the world of work. Managers speak of workers who have "bad attitudes" and conduct "attitude adjustment" talks with employees. Often, poor performance attributed to bad attitudes really stems from lack of motivation, minimal feedback, lack of trust in management, or other problems. These are areas that managers must explore.

It is important for managers to understand the antecedents to attitudes as well as their consequences. Managers also need to understand the different components of attitudes, how attitudes are formed, the major attitudes that affect work behavior, and how to use persuasion to change attitudes.

THE ABC MODEL

Attitudes develop on the basis of evaluative responding. An individual does not have an attitude until he or she responds to an entity (person, object, situation, issue) on an affective, cognitive, or behavioral basis. To understand the complexity of an attitude, we can break it down into three components, as depicted in Table 4-1 (on page 80).

These components—affect, behavioral intentions, and cognition—compose what we call the ABC model of an attitude.[2] *Affect* is the emotional component of an attitude. It refers to an individual's feeling about something or someone. Statements such as "I like this" or "I prefer that" reflect the affective component of an attitude. Affect is measured by physiological indicators such as galvanic skin response (changes in electrical resistance of skin that indicate emotional arousal) and blood pressure. These indicators show changes in emotions by measuring physiological arousal. An individual's attempt to hide his or her feelings might be shown by a change in arousal.

The second component is the intention to behave in a certain way toward an object or person. Our attitudes toward women in management, for example, may be inferred from observing the way we behave toward a female supervisor. We may be supportive, passive, or hostile, depending on our attitude. The behavioral component of an attitude is measured by observing behavior or by asking a person about behavior or intentions. The statement "If I were asked to speak at commencement, I'd be willing to try to do so, even though I'd be nervous" reflects a behavioral intention.

ATTITUDE
A psychological tendency expressed by evaluating an entity with some degree of favor or disfavor.

1. *Explain the ABC model of an attitude.*

AFFECT
The emotional component of an attitude.

	Component	Measured By	Example
A	Affect	Physiological indicators Verbal statements about feelings	I don't like my boss.
B	Behavioral intentions	Observed behavior Verbal statements about intentions	I want to transfer to another department.
C	Cognition	Attitude scales Verbal statements about beliefs	I believe my boss plays favorites at work.

Table 4-1

The ABC Model of an Attitude

Source: Adapted from M. J. Rosenberg and C. I. Hovland, "Cognitive, Affective, and Behavioral Components of Attitude," in M. J. Rosenberg, C. I. Hovland, W. J. McGuire, R. P. Abelson, and J. H. Brehm, *Attitude Organization and Change* (New Haven, Conn.: Yale University Press, 1960). Copyright 1960 Yale University Press. Used with permission.

The third component of an attitude, cognition (thought), reflects a person's perceptions or beliefs. Cognitive elements are evaluative beliefs and are measured by attitude scales or by asking about thoughts. The statement "I believe Japanese workers are industrious" reflects the cognitive component of an attitude.

The ABC model shows that to thoroughly understand an attitude, we must assess all three components. Suppose, for example, you want to evaluate your employees' attitudes toward flextime (flexible work scheduling). You would want to determine how they feel about flextime (affect), whether they would use flextime (behavioral intention), and what they think about the policy (cognition). The most common method of attitude measurement, the attitude scale, measures only the cognitive component.

As rational beings, individuals try to be consistent in everything they believe in and do. They prefer consistency (consonance) between their attitudes and behavior. Anything that disrupts this consistency causes tension (dissonance), which motivates individuals to change either their attitudes or their behavior to return to a state of consistency. The tension produced when there is a conflict between attitudes and behavior is *cognitive dissonance*.[3]

Suppose, for example, a salesperson is required to sell damaged televisions for the full retail price, without revealing the damage to customers. She believes, however, that doing so constitutes unethical behavior. This creates a conflict between her attitude (concealing information from customers is unethical) and her behavior (selling defective TVs without informing customers about the damage).

The salesperson, experiencing the discomfort from dissonance, will try to resolve the conflict. She might change her behavior by refusing to sell the defective TV sets. Alternatively, she might rationalize that the defects are minor and that the customers will not be harmed by not knowing about them. These are attempts by the salesperson to restore equilibrium between

COGNITIVE DISSONANCE
A state of tension that is produced when an individual experiences conflict between attitudes and behavior.

her attitudes and behavior, thereby eliminating the tension from cognitive dissonance.

Managers need to understand cognitive dissonance because employees often find themselves in situations in which their attitudes conflict with their behavior. They manage the tension by changing their attitudes or behavior. Employees who display sudden shifts in behavior may be attempting to reduce dissonance. Some employees find the conflicts between strongly held attitudes and required work behavior so uncomfortable that they leave the organization to escape the dissonance.

ATTITUDE FORMATION

Attitudes are learned. Our responses to people and issues evolve over time. Two major influences on attitudes are direct experience and social learning.

Direct experience with an object or person is a powerful influence on attitudes. How do you know that you like biology or dislike math? You have probably formed these attitudes from experience in studying the subjects. Research has shown that attitudes that are derived from direct experience are stronger, held more confidently, and more resistant to change than attitudes formed through indirect experience.[4] One reason attitudes derived from direct experience are so powerful is their availability. This means that the attitudes are easily accessed and are active in our cognitive processes.[5] When attitudes are available, we can call them quickly into consciousness. Attitudes that are not learned from direct experience are not as available, so we do not recall them as easily.

In *social learning*, the family, peer groups, religious organizations, and culture shape an individual's attitudes in an indirect manner.[6] Children learn to adopt certain attitudes by the reinforcement they are given by their parents when they display behaviors that reflect an appropriate attitude. This is evident when very young children express political preferences similar to their parents'. Peer pressure molds attitudes through group acceptance of individuals who express popular attitudes and through sanctions, such as exclusion from the group, placed on individuals who espouse unpopular attitudes.

Substantial social learning occurs through *modeling*, in which individuals acquire attitudes by merely observing others. After overhearing other individuals expressing an opinion or watching them engaging in a behavior that reflects an attitude, the observer adopts the attitude.

For an individual to learn from observing a model, four processes must take place:

1. The learner must focus attention on the model.

2. The learner must retain what was observed from the model. Retention is accomplished in two basic ways. In one, the learner "stamps in" what was observed by forming a verbal code for it. The other way is through symbolic rehearsal, by which the learner forms a mental image of himself or herself behaving like the model.

2. *Describe how attitudes are formed.*

SOCIAL LEARNING
The process of deriving attitudes from family, peer groups, religious organizations, and culture.

3. Behavioral reproduction must occur; that is, the learner must practice the behavior.

4. The learner must be motivated to learn from the model.

Culture also plays a definitive role in attitude development. Consider, for example, the contrast in the North American and European attitudes toward vacation and leisure. The typical vacation in the United States is two weeks, and some workers do not use all of their vacation time. In Europe, the norm is longer vacations; and in some countries, *holiday* means everyone taking a month off. The European attitude is that an investment in longer vacations is important to health and performance.

ATTITUDES AND BEHAVIOR

If you have a favorable attitude toward participative management, will your management style be participative? As managers, if we know an employee's attitude, to what extent can we predict the person's behavior? These questions illustrate the fundamental issue of attitude–behavior correspondence, that is, the degree to which an attitude predicts behavior.

This correspondence has concerned organizational behaviorists and social psychologists for quite some time. Can attitudes predict behaviors like being absent from work or quitting your job? Some studies suggested that attitudes and behavior are closely linked, while others found no relationship at all or a weak relationship at best. Attention then became focused on when attitudes predict behavior and when they do not. Attitude–behavior correspondence depends on five things: attitude specificity, attitude relevance, timing of measurement, personality factors, and social constraints.

Individuals possess both general and specific attitudes. You may favor women's right to reproductive freedom (a general attitude) and prefer pro-choice political candidates (a specific attitude), but not attend pro-choice rallies or send money to Planned Parenthood. That you don't perform these behaviors may make the link between your attitude and behavior on this issue seem rather weak. However, given a choice between a pro-choice and an anti-abortion political candidate you will probably vote for the pro-choice candidate. In this case, your attitude seems quite predictive of your behavior. The point is that the greater the attitude specificity, the stronger its link to behavior.[7]

Another factor that affects the attitude–behavior link is relevance.[8] Attitudes that address an issue in which we have some self-interest are more relevant for us, and our subsequent behavior is consistent with our expressed attitude. Suppose there is a proposal to raise income taxes for those who earn $150,000 or more. If you are a student, you may not find the issue of great personal relevance. Individuals in that income bracket, however, might find it highly relevant; their attitude toward the issue would be strongly predictive of whether they would vote for the tax increase.

The timing of the measurement also affects attitude–behavior correspondence. The shorter the time between the attitude measurement and the observed behavior, the stronger the relationship. For example, voter preference polls taken close to an election are more accurate than earlier polls.

Personality factors also influence the attitude–behavior link. One personality disposition that affects the consistency between attitudes and behavior is self-monitoring. Recall from Chapter 3 that low self-monitors rely on their internal states when making decisions about behavior, while high self-monitors are more responsive to situational cues. Low self-monitors therefore display greater correspondence between their attitudes and behaviors.[9] High self-monitors may display little correspondence between their attitudes and behavior because they behave according to signals from others and from the environment.

Finally, social constraints affect the relationship between attitudes and behavior.[10] The social context provides information about acceptable attitudes and behaviors.[11, 12] New employees in an organization, for example, are exposed to the attitudes of their work group. Suppose a newcomer from Afghanistan holds a negative attitude toward women in management because in his country the prevailing attitude is that women should not be in positions of power. He sees, however, that his work group members respond positively to their female supervisor. His own behavior may therefore be compliant because of social constraints. This behavior is inconsistent with his attitude and cultural belief system.

WORK ATTITUDES

Attitudes at work are important because, directly or indirectly, they affect work behavior. This was dramatically illustrated in a comparison of the product quality of air conditioners manufactured in the United States versus those made in Japan.[13] In general, there is a perception that Japanese products are of higher quality. When air conditioners from nine U.S. plants and seven Japanese plants were compared, the results were bad news for the U.S. plants. The Japanese products had significantly fewer defects than the U.S. products.

The researchers continued their study by asking managers in both countries' plants about their attitudes toward various goals. Japanese supervisors reported that their companies had strong attitudes favoring high-quality products, while U.S. supervisors reported quality goals to be less important. U.S. supervisors reported strong attitudes favoring the achievement of production scheduling goals, while Japanese supervisors indicated that schedules were less important. The researchers concluded that the attitudes of U.S. managers toward quality were at least partly responsible for lower-quality products.

Although many work attitudes are important, two attitudes in particular have been emphasized. Job satisfaction and organizational commitment are key attitudes of interest to managers and researchers.

Job Satisfaction   Most of us believe that work should be a positive experience. **Job satisfaction** is a pleasurable or positive emotional state resulting from the appraisal of one's job or job experiences.[14] It has been treated

3. *Define job satisfaction and organizational commitment and discuss the importance of these two work attitudes.*

JOB SATISFACTION
A pleasurable or positive emotional state resulting from the appraisal of one's job or job experiences.

Challenge

ASSESS YOUR JOB SATISFACTION

Think of the job you have now or a job you've had in the past. Indicate how satisfied you are with each aspect of your job below, using the following scale:

    1 = Extremely dissatisfied
    2 = Dissatisfied
    3 = Slightly dissatisfied
    4 = Neutral
    5 = Slightly satisfied
    6 = Satisfied
    7 = Extremely satisfied

1. The amount of job security I have.
2. The amount of pay and fringe benefits I receive.
3. The amount of personal growth and development I get in doing my job.
4. The people I talk to and work with on my job.
5. The degree of respect and fair treatment I receive from my boss.
6. The feeling of worthwhile accomplishment I get from doing my job.
7. The chance to get to know other people while on the job.
8. The amount of support and guidance I receive from my supervisor.
9. The degree to which I am fairly paid for what I contribute to this organization.
10. The amount of independent thought and action I can exercise in my job.
11. How secure things look for me in the future in this organization.
12. The chance to help other people while at work.
13. The amount of challenge in my job.
14. The overall quality of the supervision I receive on my work.

Now, compute your scores for the facets of job satisfaction.

Pay satisfaction:

    Q2 ___ + Q9 ___ = ___   Divided by 2: ___

Security satisfaction:

    Q1 ___ + Q11 = ___   Divided by 2: ___

Social satisfaction:

    Q4 ___ + Q7 ___ + Q12 ___ = ___   Divided by 3: ___

Supervisory satisfaction:

    Q5 ___ + Q8 ___ + Q14 ___ = ___   Divided by 3: ___

Growth satisfaction:

    Q3 ___ + Q6 ___ + Q10 ___ + Q13 ___ = ___   Divided by 4: ___

Scores on the facets range from 1 to 7. (Scores lower than 4 suggest there is room for change.)

This questionnaire is an abbreviated version of the Job Diagnostic Survey, a widely used tool for assessing individuals' attitudes about their jobs. Compare your scores on each facet to the following norms for a large sample of managers.

Pay satisfaction:	4.6
Security satisfaction:	5.2
Social satisfaction:	5.6
Supervisory satisfaction:	5.2
Growth satisfaction:	5.3

How do your scores compare? Are there actions you can take to improve your job satisfaction?

Source: R. Hackman/G. Oldham, *Work Redesign* (pp. 284 & 317), © 1980. Reprinted by permission of Prentice-Hall, Inc., Upper Saddle River, N.J.

both as a general attitude and as satisfaction with five specific dimensions of the job: pay, the work itself, promotion opportunities, supervision, and coworkers.[15] You can assess your own job satisfaction by completing this chapter's Challenge.

An individual may hold different attitudes toward various aspects of the job. For example, an employee may like her job responsibilities but be dissatisfied with the opportunities for promotion. Characteristics of individuals also affect job satisfaction. Those with high negative affectivity are more likely to be dissatisfied with their jobs. Challenging work, valued rewards, opportunities for advancement, competent supervision, and supportive coworkers are dimensions of the job that can lead to satisfaction.

There are several measures of job satisfaction. One of the most widely used measures comes from the Job Descriptive Index (JDI). This index measures the specific facets of satisfaction by asking employees to respond yes, no, or cannot decide to a series of statements describing their jobs. Another popular measure is the Minnesota Satisfaction Questionnaire (MSQ).[16] This survey also asks employees to respond to statements about their jobs, using a five-point scale that ranges from very dissatisfied to very satisfied.

Are satisfied workers more productive? Or, are more productive workers more satisfied? The link between satisfaction and performance has been widely explored. One view holds that satisfaction causes good performance. If this were true, then the manager's job would simply be to keep workers happy. Although this may be the case for certain individuals, job satisfaction for most people is one of several causes of good performance.

Another view holds that good performance causes satisfaction. If this were true, managers would need to help employees perform well, and satisfaction would follow. However, some employees who are high performers are not satisfied with their jobs.

The research shows modest support for both views, but no simple, direct relationship between satisfaction and performance has been found.[17] One reason for these results may be the difficulty of demonstrating the attitude–behavior links we described earlier in this chapter. Future studies using specific, relevant attitudes and measuring personality variables and behavioral intentions may be able to demonstrate a link between job satisfaction and performance.

Another reason for the lack of a clear relationship between satisfaction and performance is the intervening role of rewards. Employees who receive valued rewards are more satisfied. In addition, employees who receive rewards that are contingent on performance (the higher the performance, the larger the reward) tend to perform better. Rewards thus influence both satisfaction and performance. The key to influencing both satisfaction and performance through rewards is that the rewards are valued by employees and are tied directly to performance.

Job satisfaction has been shown to be related to many other important personal and organizational outcomes. Job satisfaction is related to *organizational citizenship behavior*—behavior that is above and beyond the call of duty. Satisfied employees are more likely to help their coworkers, make positive comments about the company, and refrain from complaining when things at work do not go well.[18] Going beyond the call of duty is especially important to organizations using teams to get work done. Employees depend on extra help from each other to get things accomplished.

ORGANIZATIONAL CITIZENSHIP BEHAVIOR
Behavior that is above and beyond the call of duty.

Satisfied workers are more likely to want to give something back to the organization because they want to reciprocate their positive experiences.[19] Often, employees may feel that citizenship behaviors are not recognized because they occur outside the confines of normal job responsibilities. Organizational citizenship behaviors (OCBs) do, however, influence performance evaluations. Employees who exhibit behaviors such as helping others, making suggestions for innovations, and developing their skills receive higher performance ratings.[20]

There are differences in the conditions that encourage organizational citizenship behaviors among younger versus older workers. For workers younger than thirty-five, being satisfied with their jobs, committed to the organization, and trusting in management produced more OCB. For older workers, their own moral judgment predicted OCB.[21]

Although researchers have had a tough time demonstrating the link between job satisfaction and individual performance, this has not been the case for the link between job satisfaction and organizational performance. Companies with satisfied workers have better performance than companies with dissatisfied workers.[22] This may be due to the more intangible elements of performance, like organizational citizenship behavior, that contribute to organizational effectiveness but aren't necessarily captured by just measuring individual job performance.

Job satisfaction is related to some other important outcomes. People who are dissatisfied with their jobs are absent more frequently. The type of dissatisfaction that most often leads employees to miss work is dissatisfaction with the work itself. In addition, dissatisfied workers are more likely to quit their jobs, and turnover at work can be very costly to organizations. Dissatisfied workers also report more psychological and medical problems than do satisfied employees.[23]

Like all attitudes, job satisfaction is influenced by culture. One study found that Japanese workers reported significantly lower job satisfaction than did U.S. workers.[24] Interestingly, the study showed that job satisfaction in both Japan and the United States could be improved by participative techniques such as quality circles and social activities sponsored by the company. Research also has shown that executives in less industrialized countries have lower levels of job satisfaction.[25]

Culture may also affect the factors that lead to job satisfaction. In a comparison of employees in the United States and India, the factors differed substantially. Leadership style, pay, and security influenced job satisfaction for the Americans. For the employees in India, however, recognition, innovation, and the absence of conflict led to job satisfaction.[26]

Because organizations face the challenge of operating in the global environment, managers must understand that job satisfaction is significantly affected by culture. Employees from different cultures may have differing expectations of their jobs; thus, there may be no single prescription for increasing the job satisfaction of a multicultural workforce.

Organizational Commitment The strength of an individual's identification with an organization is known as ***organizational commitment***. There are three kinds of organizational commitment: affective, continuance, and normative. **Affective commitment** is an employee's intention to remain in an organization because of a strong desire to do so. It consists of three factors:

- A belief in the goals and values of the organization
- A willingness to put forth effort on behalf of the organization
- A desire to remain a member of the organization.[27]

Affective commitment encompasses loyalty, but it is also a deep concern for the organization's welfare.

Continuance commitment is an employee's tendency to remain in an organization because the person cannot afford to leave.[28] Sometimes, employees believe that if they leave, they will lose a great deal of their investments in time, effort, and benefits and that they cannot replace these investments.

Normative commitment is a perceived obligation to remain with the organization. Individuals who experience normative commitment stay with the organization because they feel that they should.[29]

Certain organizational conditions encourage commitment. Participation in decision making and job security are two such conditions. Certain job characteristics also positively affect commitment. These include autonomy, responsibility, and interesting work.[30]

Affective and normative commitments are related to lower rates of absenteeism, higher quality of work, increased productivity, and several different types of performance.[31] Managers should encourage affective commitment because committed individuals expend more task-related effort and are less likely than others to leave the organization.[32]

Managers can increase affective commitment by communicating that they value employees' contributions, and that they care about employees' well-being. Affective commitment also increases when the organization and employees share the same values, and when the organization emphasizes values like moral integrity, fairness, creativity, and openness.[33]

Several researchers have examined organizational commitment in different countries. One study of workers in Saudi Arabia found that Asians working there were more committed to the organization than were Westerners and Arab workers.[34] Another study revealed that American workers displayed higher affective commitment than did Korean and Japanese workers.[35] The reasons for these differences need to be explored.

Job satisfaction and organizational commitment are two important work attitudes that managers can strive to improve among their employees. And these two attitudes are strongly related. Both affective and normative commitment are related to job satisfaction. Increasing job satisfaction is likely to increase commitment as well. To begin with, managers can use attitude surveys to reveal employees' satisfaction or dissatisfaction with specific

ORGANIZATIONAL COMMITMENT
The strength of an individual's identification with an organization.

AFFECTIVE COMMITMENT
The type of organizational commitment that is based on an individual's desire to remain in an organization.

CONTINUANCE COMMITMENT
The type of organizational commitment that is based on the fact that an individual cannot afford to leave.

NORMATIVE COMMITMENT
The type of organizational commitment that is based on an individual's perceived obligation to remain with an organization.

facets of their jobs. Then they can take action to make the deficient aspects of the job more satisfying. Work attitudes are also important because they influence business outcomes. Job satisfaction and organizational citizenship behavior are linked to customer satisfaction and company profitability.[36]

PERSUASION AND ATTITUDE CHANGE

4. *Identify the characteristics of the source, target, and message that affect persuasion.*

To understand how attitudes can change, it is necessary to understand the process of persuasion. Through persuasion, one individual (the source) tries to change the attitude of another person (the target). Certain characteristics of the source, the target, and the message affect the persuasion process. There are also two cognitive routes to persuasion.

Source Characteristics Three major characteristics of the source affect persuasion: expertise, trustworthiness, and attractiveness.[37] A source who is perceived as an expert is particularly persuasive. Trustworthiness is also important. Lew Platt, former chairman of Hewlett-Packard, began changing attitudes toward women and work long ago. Then general manager, he found that HP was a white male haven, and the assumption was that any problems women had in the workforce were of their own making. His own attitude changed when his wife died, and he was forced to play the roles of breadwinner, child caretaker, and housekeeper. His own experience of multiple roles gave him "expertise," and he was a trusted manager. He persuaded others to join him in developing flexible work schedules, work at home as an option, and job sharing in order to accommodate women's needs, and made HP among the first companies to institute these innovations. He reminded male colleagues that most women are married to men who also work, but two-thirds of male managers have stay-at-home wives.[38] Finally, attractiveness and likability play a role in persuasion. Attractive communicators have long been used in advertising to persuade consumers to buy certain products. As a source of persuasion, managers who are perceived as being experts, who are trustworthy, or who are attractive or likable will have an edge in changing employee attitudes.

Target Characteristics Some people are more easily persuaded than others. Individuals with low self-esteem are more likely to change their attitudes in response to persuasion than are individuals with high self-esteem. Individuals who hold very extreme attitudes are more resistant to persuasion, and people who are in a good mood are easier to persuade.[39] Undoubtedly, individuals differ widely in their susceptibility to persuasion. Managers must recognize these differences and realize that their attempts to change attitudes may not receive universal acceptance.

Message Characteristics Suppose you must implement an unpopular policy at work. You want to persuade your employees that the policy is a positive change. Should you present one side of the issue or both sides? Given that your employees are already negatively inclined toward the policy, you will have more success in changing their attitudes if you present both sides. This shows support for one side of the issue while acknowledging that another side does exist. Moreover, refuting the other side makes it more difficult for the targets to hang on to their negative attitudes.

Messages that are obviously designed to change the target's attitude may be met with considerable negative reaction. In fact, undisguised deliberate attempts at changing attitudes may cause attitude change in the opposite direction! This is most likely to occur when the target of the persuasive communication feels her or his freedom is threatened.[40] Less threatening approaches are less likely to elicit negative reactions.

Cognitive Routes to Persuasion When are message characteristics more important, and when are other characteristics more important in persuasion? The elaboration likelihood model of persuasion, presented in Figure 4-1, proposes that persuasion occurs over two routes: the central route and the peripheral route.[41] The routes are differentiated by the amount of elaboration, or scrutiny, the target is motivated to give the message.

The *central route* to persuasion involves direct cognitive processing of the message's content. When an issue is personally relevant, the individual is motivated to think carefully about it. In the central route, the content of the message is very important. If the arguments presented are logical and convincing, attitude change will follow.

In the *peripheral route* to persuasion, the individual is not motivated to pay much attention to the message's content. This is because the message may not be perceived as personally relevant, or the individual may

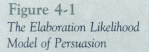

Figure 4-1
The Elaboration Likelihood Model of Persuasion

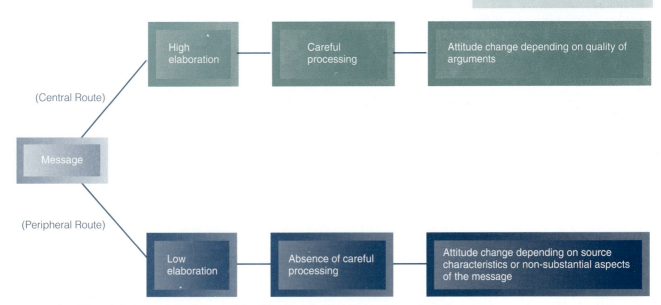

Source: Adapted from R. E. Petty and J. T. Cacioppo, "The Elaboration Likelihood Model of Persuasion," in L. Berkowitz, ed., *Advances in Experimental Social Psychology*, vol. 19 (New York: Academic Press, 1986), 123–205, with permission from Elsevier.

be distracted. Instead, the individual is persuaded by characteristics of the persuader—for example, expertise, trustworthiness, and attractiveness. In addition, the individual may be persuaded by statistics, the number of arguments presented, or the method of presentation—all of which are nonsubstantial aspects of the message.

The elaboration likelihood model shows that the target's level of involvement with the issue is important. That involvement also determines which route to persuasion will be more effective. In some cases, attitude change comes about through both the central and the peripheral routes. To cover all of the bases, managers should structure the content of their messages carefully, develop their own attributes that will help them be more persuasive, and choose a method of presentation that will be attractive to the audience.[42]

We have seen that the process of persuading individuals to change their attitudes is affected by the source, the target, the message, and the route. When all is said and done, however, managers are important catalysts for encouraging attitude change.

VALUES

VALUES
Enduring beliefs that a specific mode of conduct or end state of existence is personally or socially preferable to an opposite or converse mode of conduct or end state of existence.

Another source of individual differences is values. Values exist at a deeper level than attitudes and are more general and basic in nature. We use them to evaluate our own behavior and that of others. As such, they vary widely among individuals. *Values* are enduring beliefs that a specific mode of conduct or end state of existence is personally or socially preferable to an opposite or converse mode of conduct or end state of existence.[43] This definition was proposed by Rokeach, an early scholar of human values. Values give us a sense of right and wrong, good and bad.

As individuals grow and mature, they learn values, which may change over the life span as an individual develops a sense of self. Cultures, societies, and organizations shape values. Parents and others who are respected by the individual play crucial roles in value development by providing guidance about what is right and wrong. Values come to the forefront of an individual's development during adolescence, and many individuals stabilize their value systems during this life stage.

Businesses have shown increasing interest in values over recent years. This interest goes along with the emphasis on ethics in organizations that we described in Chapter 2. Because values are general beliefs about right and wrong, they form the basis for ethical behavior. Liz Claiborne, Inc., a leading seller of women's clothing and accessories, thrives on a unique value system called "Liz Claiborne Priorities." At the heart of its Priorities is the development of each employee's enthusiasm, vitality, commitment, and individual dignity. Relationships with suppliers and customers are based on trust, fairness, and mutual respect. These values inherent in the Priorities ensure ethical behavior.[44] We will focus on the importance of shared values in the organization in Chapter 15. Our emphasis in this chapter is on values as sources of variation among individuals.

INSTRUMENTAL AND TERMINAL VALUES

Rokeach distinguished between two types of values: instrumental and terminal. *Instrumental values* reflect the means to achieving goals; that is, they represent the acceptable behaviors to be used in achieving some end state. Instrumental values identified by Rokeach include ambition, honesty, self-sufficiency, and courage. *Terminal values*, in contrast, represent the goals to be achieved or the end states of existence. Rokeach identified happiness, love, pleasure, self-respect, and freedom among the terminal values. A complete list of instrumental and terminal values is presented in Table 4-2. Terminal and instrumental values work in concert to provide individuals with goals to strive for and acceptable ways to achieve the goals.

Americans' rankings of instrumental and terminal values have shown remarkable stability over time.[45] Rokeach studied their rankings in four national samples from 1968, 1971, 1974, and 1981. There was considerable stability in the rankings across the studies, which spanned a thirteen-year period. Most of the values shifted only one position in the rankings over this time span. The highest ranked instrumental values were honesty, ambition, responsibility, forgiving nature, open-mindedness, and courage. The highest ranked terminal values were world peace, family security, freedom, happiness, self-respect, and wisdom.

Although the values of Americans as a group have been stable, individuals vary widely in their value systems. For example, social respect is one terminal value that people differ on. Some people desire respect from others and work diligently to achieve it, and other people place little importance

5. *Distinguish between instrumental and terminal values.*

INSTRUMENTAL VALUES
Values that represent the acceptable behaviors to be used in achieving some end state.

TERMINAL VALUES
Values that represent the goals to be achieved or the end states of existence.

INSTRUMENTAL VALUES		
Honesty	Ambition	Responsibility
Forgiving nature	Open-mindedness	Courage
Helpfulness	Cleanliness	Competence
Self-control	Affection/love	Cheerfulness
Independence	Politeness	Intelligence
Obedience	Rationality	Imagination
TERMINAL VALUES		
World peace	Family security	Freedom
Happiness	Self-respect	Wisdom
Equality	Salvation	Prosperity
Achievement	Friendship	National security
Inner peace	Mature love	Social respect
Beauty in art and nature	Pleasure	Exciting, active life

Table 4-2
Instrumental and Terminal Values

Source: Table adapted with the permission of The Free Press, a Division of Simon & Schuster, Inc., from *The Nature of Human Values* by Milton Rokeach. Copyright © 1973 by The Free Press. All rights reserved.

on what others think of them. Individuals may agree that achievement is an important terminal value but may disagree on how to attain that goal.

Age also affects values. Baby boomers' values contrast with those of the baby busters, who are beginning to enter the workforce. The baby busters value family life and time off from work and prefer a balance between work and home life. This contrasts with the more driven, work-oriented value system of the boomers. The United States is not the only nation affected by age differences in values. Many European nations have found that values of young workers differ from those of older generations. Younger generations place more emphasis on personal development at work and on good pay as compared with previous generations.

WORK VALUES

Work values are important because they affect how individuals behave on their jobs in terms of what is right and wrong.[46] Four work values relevant to individuals are achievement, concern for others, honesty, and fairness.[47] Achievement is a concern for the advancement of one's career. This is shown in such behaviors as working hard and seeking opportunities to develop new skills. Concern for others is shown in caring, compassionate behaviors such as encouraging other employees or helping others work on difficult tasks. These behaviors constitute organizational citizenship, as we discussed earlier. Honesty is providing accurate information and refusing to mislead others for personal gain. Fairness emphasizes impartiality and recognizes different points of view. Individuals can rank-order these values in terms of their importance in their work lives.[48]

Although individuals' value systems differ, when they share similar values at work, the results are positive. Employees who share their supervisor's values are more satisfied with their jobs and more committed to the organization.[49] Values also have profound effects on the choice of jobs. Traditionally, pay and advancement potential have been the strongest influences on job choice decisions. One study, however, found that three other work values—achievement, concern for others, and fairness—exerted more influence on job choice decisions than did pay and promotion opportunities.[50]

This means that organizations recruiting job candidates should pay careful attention to individuals' values and to the messages that organizations send about company values. At Prudential Financial, the key value is integrity; it is Prudential's "rock" in guiding relationships among employees, customers, and regulatory agencies.[51]

CULTURAL DIFFERENCES IN VALUES

As organizations face the challenges of an increasingly diverse workforce and a global marketplace, it becomes more important than ever for them to understand the influence of culture on values. Doing business in a global marketplace often means that managers encounter a clash of values between different cultures. Take the value of loyalty, for example. In Japan, loyalty means "compassionate overtime." Even though you have no work to do, you should stay late to give moral support to your peers who are working late.[52] In contrast, Koreans value loyalty to the person for whom one works.[53] In the United States, family and other personal loyalties are more highly valued than is loyalty to the company or one's supervisor.

Cultures differ in what they value in terms of an individual's contributions to work. Collectivist cultures such as China and Mexico value a person's contributions to relationships in the work team. In contrast, individualist cultures (the United States, the Netherlands) value a person's contribution to task accomplishment. Both collectivist and individualist cultures value rewards based on individual performance.[54]

Values also affect individuals' views of what constitutes authority. French managers value authority as a right of office and rank. Their behavior reflects this value, as they tend to use power based on their position in the organization. In contrast, managers from the Netherlands and Scandinavia value group inputs to decisions and expect their decisions to be challenged and discussed by employees.[55]

As a global company, Levi Strauss has considerable experience dealing with value conflicts. When the company learned that its contractors in Bangladesh were employing children under fourteen years old, the company was alarmed. This practice violates International Labor Organization standards and Levi Strauss's own ethics code. Yet managers discovered that the children were the sole breadwinners for their families. Levi Strauss came up with a creative solution. The company asked the contractors to send the children back to school, yet continue to pay them full wages while they were in school—and then rehire them after age fourteen. Levi Strauss funded the child's education, including books, uniforms, and tuition.[56]

Value differences between cultures must be acknowledged in today's global economy. We may be prone to judging the value systems of others, but we should resist the temptation to do so. Tolerating diversity in values can help us understand other cultures. Value systems of other nations are not necessarily right or wrong—they are merely different. The following suggestions can help managers understand and work with the diverse values that characterize the global environment[57]:

1. Learn more about and recognize the values of other peoples. They view their values and customs as moral, traditional, and practical.

2. Avoid prejudging the business customs of others as immoral or corrupt. Assume they are legitimate unless proved otherwise.

3. Find legitimate ways to operate within others' ethical points of view—do not demand that they operate within your value system.

4. Avoid rationalizing "borderline" actions with excuses such as the following:

   • "This isn't really illegal or immoral."
   • "This is in the organization's best interest."
   • "No one will find out about this."
   • "The organization will back me up on this."

6. *Explain how managers can deal with the diverse value systems that characterize the global environment.*

5. Refuse to do business when stakeholder actions violate or compromise laws or fundamental organizational values.

6. Conduct relationships as openly and as aboveboard as possible.

As business becomes more global, we may see values evolve and change in some cultures. Korea's *segyewha*, or globalization, has led to considerable economic restructuring and to the adoption of what is called the "new human resource management," which is similar to American high-involvement HRM strategies like teamwork, empowerment, and performance-based pay. The Korean companies that have adopted the new HRM see people as a source of competitive advantage and have experienced better performance as a result of the changes.[58]

Values are important because they provide guidance for behavior. They are intertwined with the concept of ethics, the next dimension of individual differences to be examined.

ETHICAL BEHAVIOR

ETHICAL BEHAVIOR
Acting in ways consistent with one's personal values and the commonly held values of the organization and society.

Ethics is the study of moral values and moral behavior. **Ethical behavior** is acting in ways consistent with one's personal values and the commonly held values of the organization and society.[59] As we saw in Chapter 2, ethical issues are a major concern in organizations. There is evidence that paying attention to ethical issues pays off for companies. In the early 1990s, James Burke, then the CEO of Johnson & Johnson, put together a list of companies that devoted a great deal of attention to ethics. The group included Johnson & Johnson, Coca-Cola, Gerber, Kodak, 3M, and Pitney Bowes. Over a forty-year period, the market value of these organizations grew at an annual rate of 11.3 percent, as compared to 6.2 percent for the Dow Jones industrials as a whole.[60] Doing the right thing can have a positive effect on an organization's performance.

Failure to handle situations in an ethical manner can cost companies. Employees who are laid off or terminated are very concerned about the quality of treatment they receive. Honestly explaining the reasons for the dismissal and preserving the dignity of the employee will reduce the likelihood that the employee will initiate a claim against the company. One study showed that less than 1 percent of employees who felt the company was being honest filed a claim; more than 17 percent of those who felt the company was being less than honest filed claims.[61]

Unethical behavior by employees can affect individuals, work teams, and even the organization. Organizations thus depend on individuals to act ethically. One company recognized for its comprehensive efforts to encourage ethical behavior is General Dynamics. Several years ago, the company launched a program to integrate its ethical standards into everyday business conduct.[62] It developed a booklet of ethical standards, distributed it to all employees, and undertook a massive training effort to express to all employees the importance of ethical behavior. The company also

YOU BE THE JUDGE

Suppose a coworker is engaging in behavior that you find personally unethical, but the behavior is not prohibited by the company's ethical standards. How would you handle the issue?

appointed employees throughout the corporation to serve as ethics directors. The directors answer employees' questions about ethical problems and screen allegations about potential violations of General Dynamics' code of conduct. Many of the directors maintain hotlines for employees to use.

In the first two years after the hotlines were established, General Dynamics employees contacted ethics directors more than 30,000 times. Although most employee calls were requests for information or advice, some calls were more serious. Ethics contacts resulted in 1,400 sanctions, the most common being warnings. Time-reporting violations, in which employees overstated the number of hours they worked, were the most frequent reasons for warnings.

Today's high-intensity business environment makes it more important than ever to have a strong ethics program in place. In a survey of more than 4,000 employees conducted by the Washington, D.C.–based Ethics Resource Center, one-third of the employees said that they had witnessed ethical misconduct in the past year. If that many employees actually saw unethical acts, imagine how many unethical behaviors occurred behind closed doors! The most common unethical deeds witnessed were lying to supervisors (56 percent), lying on reports or falsifying records (41 percent,) stealing or theft (35 percent), sexual harassment (35 percent), drug or alcohol abuse (31 percent), and conflicts of interest (31 percent).[63]

One of the toughest challenges managers face is aligning the ideal of ethical behavior with the reality of everyday business practices. Violations of the public's trust are costly. Since Jack in the Box restaurants' *E. coli* crisis, the company has faced image and financial problems. Studies show that firms experience lower accounting returns and slow sales growth for as long as five years after being convicted of a corporate illegality.[64]

The ethical issues that individuals face at work are complex. A review of articles appearing in *The Wall Street Journal* during just one week revealed more than sixty articles dealing with ethical issues in business.[65] As Table 4-3 (on page 96) shows, the themes appearing throughout the articles were distilled into twelve major ethical issues. You can see that few of these issues are clear-cut. All of them depend on the specifics of the situation, and their interpretation depends on the characteristics of the individuals examining them. For example, look at issue 2: lying. We all know that "white lies" are told in business. Is this acceptable? The answer to this question varies from person to person. Thus, the perception of what constitutes ethical versus unethical behavior in organizations varies among individuals. When people lose money, they look for someone to blame.

Ethical behavior is influenced by two major categories of factors: individual characteristics and organizational factors.[66] Our purpose in this section is to look at the individual influences on ethical behavior. We examine organizational influences throughout the remainder of the book—particularly in Chapter 15, where we focus on creating an organizational culture that reinforces ethical behavior.

1. **Stealing:** Taking things that don't belong to you.
2. **Lying:** Saying things you know aren't true.
3. **Fraud and deceit:** Creating or perpetuating false impressions.
4. **Conflict of interest and influence buying:** Bribes, payoffs, and kickbacks.
5. **Hiding versus divulging information:** Concealing information that another party has a right to know, or failing to protect personal or proprietary information.
6. **Cheating:** Taking unfair advantage of a situation.
7. **Personal decadence:** Aiming below excellence in terms of work performance (e.g., careless or sloppy work).
8. **Interpersonal abuse:** Behaviors that are abusive of others (e.g., sexism, racism, emotional abuse).
9. **Organizational abuse:** Organizational practices that abuse members (e.g., inequitable compensation, misuses of power).
10. **Rule violations:** Breaking organizational rules.
11. **Accessory to unethical acts:** Knowing about unethical behavior and failing to report it.
12. **Ethical dilemmas:** Choosing between two equally desirable or undesirable options.

Table 4-3

Ethical Issues from One Week in The Wall Street Journal

Source: Adapted from J. O. Cherrington and D. J. Cherrington, "A Menu of Moral Issues: One Week in the Life of *The Wall Street Journal*," *Journal of Business Ethics* 11 (1992): 255–265. Reprinted by permission of Kluwer Academic Publishers.

7. *Describe a model of individual and organizational influences on ethical behavior.*

The model that guides our discussion of individual influences on ethical behavior is presented in Figure 4-2. It shows both individual and organizational influences.

Making ethical decisions is part of each manager's job. It has been suggested that ethical decision making requires three qualities of individuals[67]:

1. The competence to identify ethical issues and evaluate the consequences of alternative courses of action

2. The self-confidence to seek out different opinions about the issue and decide what is right in terms of a particular situation

3. Toughmindedness—the willingness to make decisions when all that needs to be known cannot be known and when the ethical issue has no established, unambiguous solution.

What are the individual characteristics that lead to these qualities? Our model presents four major individual differences that affect ethical behavior: value systems, locus of control, Machiavellianism, and cognitive moral development.

VALUE SYSTEMS

Values are systems of beliefs that affect what the individual defines as right, good, and fair. Ethics reflects the way the values are acted out. Ethical behavior, as noted earlier, is acting in ways consistent with

YOU BE THE JUDGE

Some people have argued that the biggest deficiency of business school graduates is that they have no sense of ethics. What do you think?

8. *Discuss how value systems, locus of control, Machiavellianism, and cognitive moral development affect ethical behavior.*

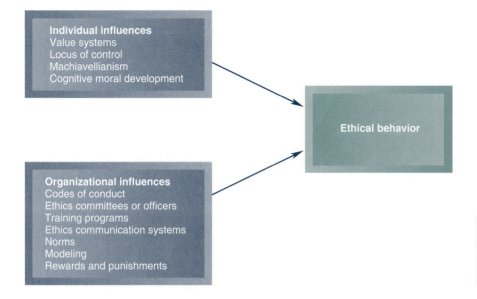

Figure 4-2
Individual/Organizational Model of Ethical Behavior

one's personal values and the commonly held values of the organization and society.

Employees are exposed to multiple value systems: their own, their supervisor's, the company's, the customers', and others'. In most cases, the individual's greatest allegiance will be to personal values. When the value system conflicts with the behavior the person feels must be exhibited, the person experiences a value conflict. Suppose, for example, that an individual believes honesty is important in all endeavors. Yet this individual sees that those who get ahead in business fudge their numbers and deceive other people. Why should the individual be honest if honesty doesn't pay? It is the individual's values, a basic sense of what is right and wrong, that override the temptation to be dishonest.[68]

American Century Cos., a mutual funds company, is one of *Fortune*'s 100 best companies to work for. Values play a big role in the company, and one of the values is the importance of family. The founders of the company, headquartered in Kansas City, are benefactors to many charities, and American Century's employees follow suit by performing 4,500 hours of community service per year. "Family" at this company means more than just nuclear family or people within the company. The benefits also reflect this value: Domestic partner benefits are offered that permit the employee to choose who is "family" in terms of receiving medical coverage. Some have chosen a younger brother or sister, an in-law, or a significant other.[69]

LOCUS OF CONTROL

Another individual influence on ethical behavior is locus of control. In Chapter 3, we introduced locus of control as a personality variable that affects individual behavior. Recall that individuals with an internal locus of control believe that they control events in their lives and that they are responsible for what happens to them. In contrast, individuals with an external locus of control believe that outside forces such as fate, chance, or other people control what happens to them.[70]

Internals are more likely than externals to take personal responsibility for the consequences of their ethical or unethical behavior. Externals are more apt to believe that external forces caused their ethical or unethical behavior. Research has shown that internals make more ethical decisions than do externals.[71] Internals also are more resistant to social pressure and are less willing to hurt another person, even if ordered to do so by an authority figure.[72]

MACHIAVELLIANISM

MACHIAVELLIANISM

A personality characteristic indicating one's willingness to do whatever it takes to get one's own way.

Another individual difference that affects ethical behavior is Machiavellianism. Niccolò Machiavelli was a sixteenth-century Italian statesman. He wrote *The Prince*, a guide for acquiring and using power.[73] The primary method for achieving power that he suggested was manipulation of others. *Machiavellianism*, then, is a personality characteristic indicating one's willingness to do whatever it takes to get one's own way.

A high-Mach individual behaves in accordance with Machiavelli's ideas, which include the notion that it is better to be feared than loved. High-Machs tend to use deceit in relationships, have a cynical view of human nature, and have little concern for conventional notions of right and wrong.[74] They are skilled manipulators of other people, relying on their persuasive abilities. Low-Machs, in contrast, value loyalty and relationships. They are less willing to manipulate others for personal gain and are concerned with others' opinions.

High-Machs believe that the desired ends justify any means. They believe that manipulation of others is fine if it helps achieve a goal. Thus, high-Machs are likely to justify their manipulative behavior as ethical.[75] They are emotionally detached from other people and are oriented toward objective aspects of situations. And high-Machs are likelier than low-Machs to engage in behavior that is ethically questionable.[76] Employees can counter Machiavellian individuals by focusing on teamwork instead of on one-on-one relationships, where high-Machs have the upper hand. It is also beneficial to make interpersonal agreements public and thus less susceptible to manipulation by high-Machs.

COGNITIVE MORAL DEVELOPMENT

COGNITIVE MORAL DEVELOPMENT

The process of moving through stages of maturity in terms of making ethical decisions.

An individual's level of **cognitive moral development** also affects ethical behavior. Psychologist Lawrence Kohlberg proposed that as individuals mature, they move through a series of six stages of moral development.[77] With each successive stage, they become less dependent on other people's opinions of right and wrong and less self-centered (acting in one's own interest). At higher levels of moral development, individuals are concerned with broad principles of justice and with their self-chosen ethical principles. Kohlberg's model focuses on the decision-making process and on how individuals justify ethical decisions. His model is a cognitive developmental theory about how people think about what is right and wrong and how the decision-making process changes through interaction with peers and the environment.

Cognitive moral development occurs at three levels, and each level consists of two stages. In Level I, called the premoral level, the person's ethical decisions are based on rewards, punishments, and self-interest. In Stage 1, the individual obeys rules to avoid punishment. In Stage 2, the individual follows the rules only if it is in his or her immediate interest to do so.

In Level II, the conventional level, the focus is on the expectations of others (parents, peers) or society. In Stage 3, individuals try to live up to the expectations of people close to them. In Stage 4, they broaden their perspective to include the laws of the larger society. They fulfill duties and obligations and want to contribute to society.

In Level III, the principled level, what is "right" is determined by universal values. The individual sees beyond laws, rules, and the expectations of other people. In Stage 5, individuals are aware that people have diverse value systems. They uphold their own values despite what others think. For a person to be classified as being in Stage 5, decisions must be based on principles of justice and rights. For example, a person who decides to picket an abortion clinic just because his religion says abortion is wrong is not a Stage 5 individual. A person who arrives at the same decision through a complex decision process based on justice and rights may be a Stage 5 individual. The key is the process rather than the decision itself. In Stage 6, the individual follows self-selected ethical principles. If there is a conflict between a law and a self-selected ethical principle, the individual acts according to the principle.

As individuals mature, their moral development passes through these stages in an irreversible sequence. Research suggests that most adults are in Stage 3 or 4. Most adults thus never reach the principled level of development (Stages 5 and 6).

Since it was proposed, more than thirty years ago, Kohlberg's model of cognitive moral development has received a great deal of research support. Individuals at higher stages of development are less likely to cheat,[78] more likely to engage in whistle-blowing,[79] and more likely to make ethical business decisions.[80, 81]

Kohlberg's model has also been criticized. Gilligan, for example, has argued that the model does not take gender differences into account. Kohlberg's model was developed from a twenty-year study of eighty-four boys.[82] Gilligan contends that women's moral development follows a different pattern—one that is based not on individual rights and rules but on responsibility and relationships. Women and men face the same moral dilemmas but approach them from different perspectives—men from the perspective of equal respect and women from the perspective of compassion and care. Researchers who reviewed the research on these gender differences concluded that the differences may not be as strong as originally stated by Gilligan. Some men use care reasoning, and some women may use justice reasoning, when making moral judgments.[83]

There is evidence to support the idea that men and women view ethics differently. A large-scale review of sixty-six studies found that women were more likely than men to perceive certain business practices as unethical. Young women were more likely to see breaking the rules and acting on insider information as unethical. Both sexes agreed that collusion, conflicts of interest, and stealing are unethical. It takes about twenty-one years for the gender gap to disappear. Men seem to become more ethical with more work experience; the longer they are in the workforce, the more their attitudes become similar to those held by women. There is an age/experience effect for both sexes: Experienced workers are more likely to think lying, bribing, stealing, and colluding are unethical.[84]

Individual differences in values, locus of control, Machiavellianism, and cognitive moral development are important influences on ethical behavior in organizations. Given that these influences vary widely from person to person, how can organizations use this knowledge to increase ethical behavior? One action would be to hire individuals who share the organization's values. Another would be to hire only internals, low-Machs, and individuals at higher stages of cognitive moral development. This strategy obviously presents practical and legal problems.

There is evidence that cognitive moral development can be increased through training.[85] Organizations could help individuals move to higher stages of moral development by providing educational seminars. However, values, locus of control, Machiavellianism, and cognitive moral development are fairly stable in adults.

The best way to use the knowledge of individual differences may be to recognize that they help explain why ethical behavior differs among individuals and to focus managerial efforts on creating a work situation that supports ethical behavior.

Most adults are susceptible to external influences; they do not act as independent ethical agents. Instead, they look to others and to the organization for guidance. Managers can offer such guidance by encouraging ethical behavior through codes of conduct, ethics committees, ethics communication systems, training, norms, modeling, and rewards and punishments, as shown in Figure 4-2. We discuss these areas further in Chapter 15.

MANAGERIAL IMPLICATIONS: ATTITUDES, VALUES, AND ETHICS AT WORK

Managers must understand attitudes because of their effects on work behavior. By understanding how attitudes are formed and how they can be changed, managers can shape employee attitudes. Attitudes are learned through observation of other employees and by the way they are reinforced. Job satisfaction and organizational commitment are important attitudes to encourage among employees, and participative management is an excellent tool for doing so.

Values affect work behavior because they affect employees' views of what constitutes right and wrong. The diversity of the workforce makes it imperative that managers understand differences in value systems. Shared values within an organization can provide the foundation for cooperative efforts toward achieving organizational goals.

Ethical behavior at work is affected by individual and organizational influences. A knowledge of individual differences in value systems, locus of control, Machiavellianism, and cognitive moral development helps managers understand why individuals have diverse views about what constitutes ethical behavior.

This chapter concludes our discussion of individual differences that affect behavior in organizations. Attitudes, values, and ethics combine with personality, perception, and attribution to make individuals unique. Individual uniqueness is a major managerial challenge, and it is one reason there is no single best way to manage people.

KEY TERMS

affect	ethical behavior	organizational citizenship behavior
affective commitment	instrumental values	organizational commitment
attitude	job satisfaction	social learning
cognitive dissonance	Machiavellianism	terminal values
cognitive moral development	normative commitment	values
continuance commitment		

Experiential Exercise

IS THIS BEHAVIOR ETHICAL?

The purpose of this exercise is to explore your opinions about ethical issues faced in organizations. The class should be divided into twelve groups. Each group will randomly be assigned one of the following issues, which reflect the twelve ethical themes found in *The Wall Street Journal* study shown in Table 4-3.

1. Is it ethical to take office supplies from work for home use? Make personal long-distance calls from the office? Use company time for personal business? Or do these behaviors constitute stealing?

2. If you exaggerate your credentials in an interview, is it lying? Is lying in order to protect a coworker acceptable?

3. If you pretend to be more successful than you are in order to impress your boss, are you being deceitful?

4. How do you differentiate between a bribe and a gift?

5. If there are slight defects in a product you are selling, are you obligated to tell the buyer? If an advertised "sale" price is really the everyday price, should you divulge the information to the customer?

6. Suppose you have a friend who works at the ticket office for the convention center where Dave

Matthews Band will be appearing. Is it cheating if you ask the friend to get you tickets so that you won't have to fight the crowd to get them? Is buying merchandise for your family at your company's cost cheating?

7. Is it immoral to do less than your best in terms of work performance? Is it immoral to accept workers' compensation when you are fully capable of working?

8. What behaviors constitute emotional abuse at work? What would you consider an abuse of one's position power?

9. Are high-stress jobs a breach of ethics? What about transfers that break up families?

10. Are all rule violations equally important? Do employees have an ethical obligation to follow company rules?

11. To what extent are you responsible for the ethical behavior of your coworkers? If you witness unethical behavior and don't report it, are you an accessory?

12. Is it ethical to help one work group at the expense of another group? For instance, suppose one group has excellent performance and you want to reward its members with an afternoon off. The other work group will have to pick up the slack and work harder if you do this. Is this ethical?

Once your group has been assigned its issue, you have two tasks:

1. First, formulate your group's answer to the ethical dilemmas.

2. After you have formulated your group's position, discuss the individual differences that may have contributed to your position. You will want to discuss the individual differences presented in this chapter as well as any others that you feel affected your position on the ethical dilemma.

Your instructor will lead the class in a discussion of how individual differences may have influenced your positions on these ethical dilemmas.

Source: Issues adapted from J. O. Cherrington and D. J. Cherrington, "A Menu of Moral Issues: One Week in the Life of *The Wall Street Journal*," *Journal of Business Ethics* 11 (1992): 255–265. Reprinted by permission of Kluwer Academic Publishers.

5

Motivation at Work

LEARNING OBJECTIVES

After reading this chapter, you should be able to do the following:

1. Define *motivation*.

2. Explain how Theory X and Theory Y relate to Maslow's hierarchy of needs.

3. Discuss the needs for achievement, power, and affiliation.

4. Describe the two-factor theory of motivation.

5. Describe how inequity influences individual motivation and behavior.

6. Explain seven different strategies for resolving inequity.

7. Describe the expectancy theory of motivation.

8. Describe the cultural differences in motivation.

This is the first of two chapters about motivation, behavior, and performance at work. A comprehensive approach to understanding motivation, behavior, and performance must consider three elements of the work situation—the individual, the job, and the work environment—and how these elements interact.[1] This chapter emphasizes internal and process theories of motivation. It begins with individual need theories of motivation; turns to the two-factor theory of motivation, which foreshadows theories of job design discussed in Chapter 13; and finishes by examining two individual–environment interaction or process theories of motivation. The next chapter (Chapter 6) emphasizes external theories of motivation and focuses on factors in the environment to help understand good or bad performance.

MOTIVATION AND WORK BEHAVIOR

1. *Define motivation.*

MOTIVATION
The process of arousing and sustaining goal-directed behavior.

Motivation is the process of arousing and sustaining goal-directed behavior. Motivation is one of the more complex topics in organizational behavior. *Motivation* comes from the Latin root word *movere*, which means "to move."

Motivation theories attempt to explain and predict observable behavior. The wide range and variety of motivation theories result from the great diversity of people and complexity of their behavior in organizations. Early attempts were made to develop universal theories of motivation, but more recent research recognizes the limitations as well as the power of the various theories and classes of theories. Motivation theories may be broadly classified into internal, process, and external theories of motivation. Internal theories of motivation give primary consideration to variables within the individual that give rise to motivation and behavior. The hierarchy of needs theory exemplifies the internal theories. Process theories of motivation emphasize the nature of the interaction between the individual and the environment. Expectancy theory exemplifies the process theories. External theories of motivation focus on the elements in the environment, including the consequences of behavior, as the basis for understanding and explaining people's behavior at work. Any single motivation theory explains only a small portion of the variance in human behavior. Therefore, alternative theories have developed over time in an effort to account for the unexplained portions of the variance in behavior.

INTERNAL NEEDS

Philosophers and scholars have theorized for centuries about human needs and motives. During the past century, attention narrowed to understanding motivation in businesses and other organizations.[2] Max Weber, an early German organizational scholar, argued that the meaning of work lay not in the work itself but in its deeper potential for contributing to a person's ultimate salvation.[3] From this Calvinistic perspective, the Protestant ethic was the fuel for human industriousness. The Protestant ethic said people should work hard because those who prospered at work were more likely to find a place in heaven. Although Weber, and later Blood, both used the term *Protestant ethic*, many see the value elements of this work ethic in the broader Judeo-Christian tradition. We concur.

A more complex motivation theory was proposed by Sigmund Freud. For him, a person's organizational life was founded on the compulsion to work and the power of love.[4] He saw much of human motivation as unconscious by nature. **Psychoanalysis** was Freud's method for delving into the unconscious mind to better understand a person's motives and needs. Freud's psychodynamic theory offers explanations for irrational and self-destructive behavior, such as suicide or workplace violence. The motives underlying such traumatic work events may be understood by analyzing a person's unconscious needs and motives. Freud's theorizing is important as the basis for subsequent need theories of motivation. Recent research suggests that people's deeper feelings may transcend culture, with most people caring deeply about the same few things.[5]

Internal needs and external incentives both play an important role in motivation. Although extrinsic motivation is important, so too is intrinsic motivation, which varies by the individual.[6] Therefore, it is important for managers to consider both internal needs and external incentives when attempting to motivate their employees. Further, managers who are more supportive and less controlling appear to elicit more intrinsic motivation from their employees.

EXTERNAL INCENTIVES

Early organizational scholars made economic assumptions about human motivation and developed corresponding differential piece rate systems of pay that emphasized external incentives. These organizational scholars assumed that people were motivated by self-interest and economic gain. The Hawthorne studies confirmed the beneficial effects of pay incentives on productivity but also found that social and interpersonal motives in behavior were important.[7]

Those who made economic assumptions about human motivation emphasized financial incentives for behavior. The Scottish political economist and moral philosopher Adam Smith argued that a person's **self-interest** was God's providence, not the government's.[8] Gordon Forward, a member of the non-executive board of Texas Industries (TXI), believes people are motivated by "enlightened" self-interest. Self-interest is what is in the best interest and benefit to the individual; enlightened self-interest additionally recognizes the self-interest of other people. Adam Smith laid the cornerstone for the free enterprise system of economics when he formulated the "invisible hand" and the free market to explain the motivation for individual behavior. The "invisible hand" refers to the unseen forces of a free market system that shape the most efficient use of people, money, and resources for productive ends. His theory of political economy subsequently explained collective economic behavior. Smith's basic assumption was that people are

PSYCHOANALYSIS
Sigmund Freud's method for delving into the unconscious mind to better understand a person's motives and needs.

SELF-INTEREST
What is in the best interest and benefit to an individual.

motivated by self-interest for economic gain to provide the necessities and conveniences of life. This implies that financial and economic incentives to work are the most important considerations in understanding human behavior. Further, employees are most productive when motivated by self-interest.

Technology is an important concept in Smith's view, because he believed that a nation's wealth is determined by two circumstances: (1) the skill, dexterity, and judgment with which labor is applied and (2) the proportion of the nation's population employed in useful labor versus the proportion not so employed. He considered the first circumstance to be more important. The more efficient and effective labor is, the greater the abundance of the nation. Technology is important as a force multiplier for the productivity of labor in creating products or delivering services.

Frederick Taylor, the founder of scientific management, was also concerned with labor efficiency and effectiveness.[9] His central concern was to change the relationship between management and labor from one of conflict to one of cooperation.[10] Taylor believed the basis of their conflict was the division of the profits within the company. Instead of continuing this conflict over how to divide the profits, labor and management should form a cooperative relationship aimed at enlarging the total profits.

MASLOW'S NEED HIERARCHY

Abraham Maslow, a psychologist, proposed a need theory of motivation emphasizing psychological and interpersonal needs in addition to physical needs and economic necessity. His theory was based on a need hierarchy later applied through Theory X and Theory Y, two sets of assumptions about people at work. In addition, his need hierarchy was reformulated in an ERG theory of motivation using a revised classification scheme for basic human needs.

THE HIERARCHY OF NEEDS

The core of Maslow's theory of human motivation is a hierarchy of five need categories.[11] Although he recognized that there were factors other than one's needs (for example, culture) that were determinants of behavior, he focused his theoretical attention on specifying people's internal needs. Maslow labeled the five hierarchical categories as physiological needs, safety and security needs, love (social) needs, esteem needs, and the need for self-actualization. Maslow's *need hierarchy* is depicted in Figure 5-1, which also shows how the needs relate to Douglas McGregor's assumptions about people, which will be discussed next.

Maslow conceptually derived the five need categories from the early thoughts of William James[12] and John Dewey,[13] coupled with the psychodynamic thinking of Sigmund Freud and Alfred Adler.[14] Maslow's need theory was later tested in research with working populations. For example, one study reported that middle managers and lower level managers had different perceptions of their need deficiencies and the importance of their needs.[15] More recently, Motorola adapted motivational techniques aimed

NEED HIERARCHY
The theory that behavior is determined by a progression of physical, social, and psychological needs by higher order needs.

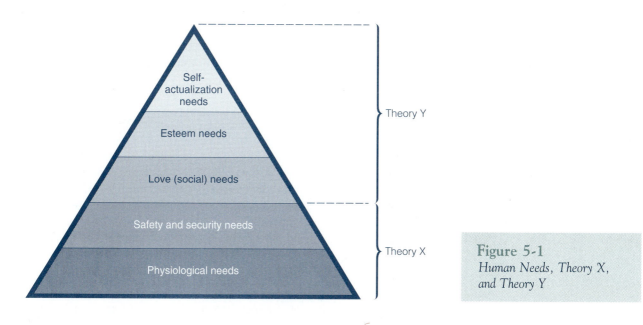

Figure 5-1
Human Needs, Theory X, and Theory Y

at social and interpersonal needs for its teamwork from its Penang operations in Malaysia to its factory in Florida. One distinguishing feature of Maslow's need hierarchy is the following progression hypothesis. Although some research has challenged the assumption, the theory says that only ungratified needs motivate behavior.[16] Further, it is the lowest level of ungratified needs in the hierarchy that motivates behavior. As one level of need is met, a person progresses to the next higher level of need as a source of motivation. Hence, people progress up the hierarchy as they successively gratify each level of need. For example, an employee may satisfy security needs by obtaining two big promotions and then be motivated by developing good working relationships with coworkers. The problem with the progression hypothesis is that it leaves no way to move down the hierarchy, which could occur, for example, if a person at the esteem level lost a job and was now worried about security.

THEORY X AND THEORY Y

One important organizational implication of the need hierarchy concerns how to manage people at work (see Figure 5-1). Douglas McGregor understood people's motivation using Maslow's need theory. He grouped the physiological and safety needs as "lower order" needs and the social, esteem, and self-actualization needs as "upper order" needs. McGregor proposed two alternative sets of assumptions about people at work based on which set of needs were the motivators.[17] He labeled these sets of assumptions **Theory X** and **Theory Y**. They are included in Table 5-1 (on page 108). Regardless of people's motivation to work, McGregor saw the responsibility of management as being the same. Specifically, "management is responsible for organizing the elements of productive enterprise—money, materials, equipment, people—in the interest of economic ends."[18]

2. *Explain how Theory X and Theory Y relate to Maslow's hierarchy of needs.*

THEORY X
A set of assumptions of how to manage individuals who are motivated by lower order needs.

THEORY Y
A set of assumptions of how to manage individuals who are motivated by higher order needs.

THEORY X	THEORY Y
■ People are by nature indolent. That is, they work as little as possible. ■ People lack ambition, dislike responsibility, and prefer to be led. ■ People are inherently self-centered and indifferent to organizational needs. ■ People are by nature resistant to change. ■ People are gullible and not very bright, the ready dupes of the charlatan and the demagogue.	■ People are not by nature passive or resistant to organizational needs. They have become so as a result of experience in organizations. ■ The motivation, the potential for development, the capacity for assuming responsibility, and the readiness to direct behavior toward organizational goals are all present in people. Management does not put them there. It is a responsibility of management to make it possible for people to recognize and develop these human characteristics for themselves. ■ The essential task of management is to arrange conditions and methods of operation so that people can achieve their own goals best by directing their own efforts toward organizational objectives.

Table 5-1

McGregor's Assumptions about People

According to McGregor, people should be treated differently depending on whether they are motivated by lower order or higher order needs. Specifically, McGregor believed that Theory X assumptions are appropriate for employees motivated by lower order needs. Theory Y assumptions, in contrast, are appropriate for employees motivated by higher order needs, and Theory X assumptions are then inappropriate. In addition, McGregor believed that in the 1950s, when he was writing, the majority of American workers had satisfied their lower order needs and were therefore motivated by higher order needs.

Employee participation programs are one consequence of McGregor's Theory Y assumptions. Ford Motor Company's first step in revitalizing its workforce through an employee involvement (EI) program was based on Theory Y assumptions about human nature.[19] Southwest Airlines is another company that uses Theory Y concepts in its management.

Gordon Forward, a member of the non-executive board of Texas Industries (TXI), considers the assumptions made about people central to motivation and management.[20] He views employees as resources to be developed, not labor costs to be charged off. A future-thinking, enlightened executive, Forward has fun at work and at play. Using Maslow's need hierarchy and Theory Y assumptions about people, he cultivated and developed a productive, loyal workforce in TXI's Chaparral Steel unit.

ERG THEORY

Clayton Alderfer, while recognizing the value of Maslow's contribution to understanding motivation, believed that the original need hierarchy was not quite accurate in identifying and categorizing human needs.[21] As an evolutionary development of the need hierarchy, Alderfer proposed the ERG

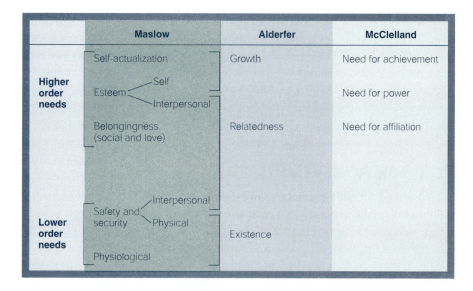

Figure 5-2
Three Need Theories of Motivation

theory of motivation, which grouped human needs into only three basic categories: existence, relatedness, and growth.[22] Alderfer classified Maslow's physiological and physical safety needs in an existence need category; Maslow's interpersonal safety, love, and interpersonal esteem needs in a relatedness need category; and Maslow's self-actualization and self-esteem needs in a growth need category.

In addition to the differences in categorizing human needs, ERG theory added a regression hypothesis to go along with the progression hypothesis originally proposed by Maslow. Alderfer's regression hypothesis helped explain people's behavior when frustrated at meeting needs at the next higher level in the hierarchy. Specifically, the regression hypothesis states that people regress to the next lower category of needs and intensify their desire to gratify these needs. Hence, ERG theory explains both progressive need and gratification up the hierarchy and regression when people are faced with frustration. Figure 5-2 shows the relationship between Maslow's hierarchy of needs and Alderfer's ERG theory.

McCLELLAND'S NEED THEORY

A second major need theory of motivation focuses on personality and learned needs. Henry Murray developed a long list of motives and manifest needs in his early studies of personality.[23] David McClelland, a psychologist, was inspired by Murray's early work.[24] McClelland identified three learned or acquired needs he called manifest needs. These manifest needs were the needs for achievement, for power, and for affiliation. Individuals and national cultures differ in their levels of these needs. Some individuals have a high need for achievement, whereas others have a moderate or low need for achievement. The same is true for the other two needs. Hence, it

3. *Discuss the needs for achievement, power, and affiliation.*

is important to emphasize that different needs are dominant in different people. For example, a manager may have a strong need for power, a moderate need for achievement, and a weak need for affiliation. Each need has quite different implications for people's behavior. The Murray Thematic Apperception Test (TAT) was used as an early measure of the achievement motive and was further developed, both qualitatively and quantitatively, by McClelland and his associates.[25] The TAT is a projective test, and projective tests were discussed in Chapter 3.

NEED FOR ACHIEVEMENT

NEED FOR ACHIEVEMENT
A manifest (easily perceived) need that concerns individuals' issues of excellence, competition, challenging goals, persistence, and overcoming difficulties.

The *need for achievement* concerns issues of excellence, competition, challenging goals, persistence, and overcoming difficulties.[26] A person with a high need for achievement seeks excellence in performance, enjoys difficult and challenging goals, and is persevering and competitive in work activities. Questions that address the need for achievement are ones like these: Do you enjoy difficult, challenging work activities? Do you strive to exceed your performance objectives? Do you seek out new ways to overcome difficulties?

McClelland found that people with a high need for achievement perform better than those with a moderate or low need for achievement, and he has noted national differences in achievement motivation. Individuals with a high need for achievement have three unique characteristics. First, they set goals that are moderately difficult yet achievable, because they want both challenge and a good chance for success. Second, they like to receive feedback on their progress toward these goals. Because success is important to them, they like to know how they are doing. Third, they do not like having external events or other people interfere with their progress toward the goals. They are most comfortable working on individual tasks and activities that they control.

High achievers often hope and plan for success. They may be quite content to work alone or with other people—whichever is more appropriate to their task. High achievers like being very good at what they do, and they develop expertise and competence in their chosen endeavors. An example of a person with a high need for achievement is an information systems engineer who declines supervisory or managerial responsibility and devotes her energy to being the very best information systems engineer she can be.

Recent research shows that need for achievement generalizes well across countries with adults who are employed full-time.[27] In addition, international differences in the tendency for achievement have been found in global research on achievement. Specifically, achievement tendencies are highest for the United States, an individualistic culture, and lowest for Japan and Hungary, collectivistic societies.[28]

NEED FOR POWER

YOU BE THE JUDGE

Is it ethical for you to pursue your own needs first at work? Are your needs in conflict with what is fair and equitable for others at work? Do you consider the thoughts and feelings of other people at work?

NEED FOR POWER
A manifest (easily perceived) need that concerns an individual's need to make an impact on others, influence others, change people or events, and make a difference in life.

The *need for power* is concerned with making an impact on others, the desire to influence others, the urge to change people or events, and the desire to make a difference in life. The need for power is interpersonal, be-cause it involves influence attempts directed at other people. People with a high need for power like to be in control of people and events. McClel-land makes an important distinction between socialized power, which is used for the social benefit of many, and personalized power, which is used for the personal gain of the individual. The former is a constructive force in orga-nizations, whereas the latter may be a very disruptive, destructive force in organizations.

A high need for power was one distinguishing characteristic of man-agers rated the "best" in McClelland's research. Specifically, the best man-agers had a very high need for socialized power, used for the collective well-being of the group, as opposed to personalized power.[29] These man-agers are concerned for others; have an interest in the organization's larger goals; and have a desire to be useful to the larger group, organization, and society.

Social and hierarchical status are important considerations for people with a high need for power. The more they are able to rise to the top of their organizations, the greater is their ability to exercise power, influence, and control so as to make an impact. Successful managers have the greatest up-ward velocity in an organization; they rise to higher managerial levels more quickly than their contemporaries.[30] These successful managers benefit their organizations most if they have a high socialized power need. The need for power is discussed further in Chapter 10, on power and politics.

NEED FOR AFFILIATION

The *need for affiliation* is concerned with establishing and maintain-ing warm, close, intimate relationships with other people.[31] People with a high need for affiliation are motivated to express their emotions and feel-ings to others while expecting other people to do the same in return. They find conflicts and complications in their relationships disturbing and are strongly motivated to work through any such barriers to closeness. The re-lationships they have with others are therefore close and personal, empha-sizing friendship and companionship.

People who have moderate to low needs for affiliation are more likely to feel comfortable working alone for extended periods of time. Modest or low levels of interaction with others are likely to satisfy these people's af-filiation needs, allowing them to focus their attention on other needs and activities. People with a high need for affiliation, in contrast, always hope to be included in a range of interpersonal activities, in or away from work. They may play important integrative roles in group or intergroup activities because they work to achieve harmony and closeness in all relationships.

Over and above these three needs, Murray's manifest needs theory in-cluded the need for autonomy. This is the desire for independence and free-dom from any constraints. People with a high need for autonomy like to work alone and to control the pace of their work. They dislike bureaucratic rules, regulations, and procedures. Figure 5-2 is a summary chart of the three

NEED FOR AFFILIATION
A manifest (easily perceived) need that concerns an individual's need to establish and maintain warm, close, intimate relationships with other people.

need theories of motivation just discussed; it shows the parallel relationships between the needs in each of the theories. While Maslow and Alderfer would refer to higher and lower order needs, McClelland does not make a similar distinction.

HERZBERG'S TWO-FACTOR THEORY

4. *Describe the two-factor theory of motivation.*

Frederick Herzberg departed from the need theories of motivation and examined the experiences that satisfied or dissatisfied people at work. This motivation theory became known as the two-factor theory.[32] Herzberg's original study included 200 engineers and accountants in western Pennsylvania during the 1950s. Herzberg asked these people to describe two important incidents at their jobs: one that was very satisfying and made them feel exceptionally good at work, and another that was very dissatisfying and made them feel exceptionally bad at work.

Herzberg and his colleagues believed that people had two sets of needs—one related to the animalistic avoidance of pain and one related to the humanistic desire for psychological growth. Conditions in the work environment would affect one or the other of these needs. Work conditions related to satisfaction of the need for psychological growth were labeled *motivation factors*. Work conditions related to dissatisfaction caused by discomfort or pain were labeled *hygiene factors*. Each set of factors related to one aspect of what Herzberg identified as the human being's dual nature regarding the work environment. Thus, motivation factors relate to job satisfaction, and hygiene factors relate to job dissatisfaction.[33] These two independent factors are depicted in Figure 5-3.

MOTIVATION FACTOR
A work condition related to satisfaction of the need for psychological growth.

HYGIENE FACTOR
A work condition related to dissatisfaction caused by discomfort or pain.

MOTIVATION FACTORS

Job satisfaction is produced by building motivation factors into a job, according to Herzberg. This process is known as job enrichment. In the original research, the motivation factors were identified as responsibility, achievement, recognition, advancement, and the work itself. These factors relate to the content of the job and what the employee actually does on the job. When these factors are present, they lead to superior performance and effort on the part of job incumbents. These factors directly influence the way people feel about their work. Figure 5-3 also shows that salary is a motivational factor in some studies. Many organizational reward systems now include other financial benefits, such as stock options, as part of an employee's compensation package. Research has found job satisfaction positively linked to earnings and changes in earning, as well as voluntary turnover.

Motivation factors lead to positive mental health and challenge people to grow, contribute to the work environment, and invest themselves in the organization. During the 1980s, recognition was used as an important motivation factor at the former Perpetual Financial Corporation, which hosted a company-wide "Salute to Associates" to thank employees. However, pro-

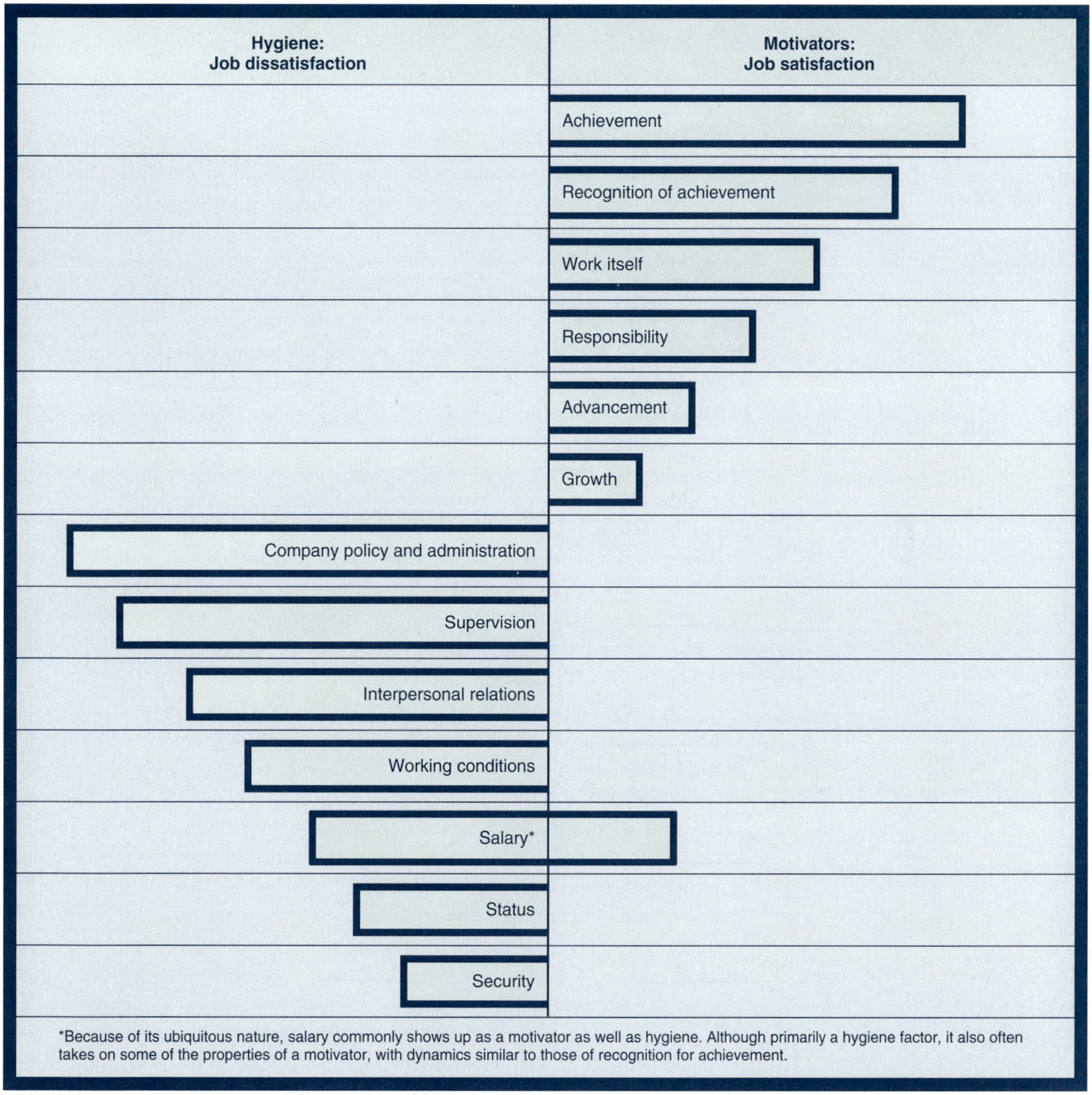

Hygiene: Job dissatisfaction	Motivators: Job satisfaction
	Achievement
	Recognition of achievement
	Work itself
	Responsibility
	Advancement
	Growth
Company policy and administration	
Supervision	
Interpersonal relations	
Working conditions	
Salary*	
Status	
Security	

*Because of its ubiquitous nature, salary commonly shows up as a motivator as well as hygiene. Although primarily a hygiene factor, it also often takes on some of the properties of a motivator, with dynamics similar to those of recognition for achievement.

Source: Reprinted from Frederick Herzberg, *The Managerial Choice: To Be Efficient or to Be Human* (Salt Lake City: Olympus, 1982). Reprinted by permission.

Figure 5-3
The Motivation–Hygiene Theory of Motivation

grams like this one require constant supervision and do not eliminate the need for other rewards.

According to the theory and Herzberg's original results, the absence of these factors does not lead to dissatisfaction. Rather, it leads to the lack of satisfaction. The motivation factors are the more important of the two sets of factors, because they directly affect a person's motivational drive to do a good job. When they are absent, the person will be demotivated to perform well and achieve excellence. The hygiene factors are a completely distinct set of factors unrelated to the motivation to achieve and do excellent work.

HYGIENE FACTORS

Job dissatisfaction occurs when the hygiene factors are either not present or not sufficient. In the original research, the hygiene factors were company policy and administration, technical supervision, interpersonal relations with one's supervisor, working conditions, salary, status, and security. These factors relate to the context of the job and may be considered support factors. They do not directly affect a person's motivation to work but influence the extent of the person's discontent. These factors cannot stimulate psychological growth or human development. They may be thought of as maintenance factors, because they contribute to an individual's basic needs. Excellent hygiene factors result in employees' being *not dissatisfied* and contribute to the absence of complaints about these contextual considerations.

When these hygiene factors are poor or absent, the person complains about "poor supervision," "poor medical benefits," or whatever hygiene factor is poor. Employees experience a deficit and are dissatisfied when the hygiene factors are not present. Even in the absence of good hygiene factors, employees may still be very motivated to perform their jobs well if the motivation factors are present. Although this may appear to be a paradox, it is not, because the motivation and hygiene factors are independent of each other.

The combination of motivation and hygiene factors can result in one of four possible job conditions. First, a job high in both motivation and hygiene factors leads to high motivation and few complaints among employees. In this job condition, employees are motivated to perform well and are contented with the conditions of their work environment. Second, a job low in both factors leads to low motivation and many complaints among employees. Under such conditions, employees are not only demotivated to perform well but are also discontented with the conditions of their work environment. Third, a job high in motivation factors and low in hygiene factors leads to high employee motivation to perform coupled with complaints about aspects of the work environment. Discontented employees may still be able to do an excellent job if they take pride in the product or service. Fourth, a job low in motivation factors and high in hygiene factors leads to low employee motivation to excel but few complaints about the work environment. These complacent employees have little motivation to do an outstanding job.

Two conclusions can be drawn at this point. First, hygiene factors are of some importance up to a threshold level, but beyond the threshold there is little value in improving the hygiene factors. Second, the presence of motivation factors is essential to enhancing employee motivation to excel at work. This chapter's Challenge asks you to rank a set of ten job reward factors in terms of their importance to the average employee, to supervisors, and to you.

Challenge

WHAT'S IMPORTANT TO EMPLOYEES?

There are many possible job rewards that employees may receive. Listed below are ten possible job reward factors. Rank these factors three times. First, rank them as you think the average employee would rank them. Second, rank them as you think the average employee's supervisor would rank them for the employee. Finally, rank them according to what you consider important.

Your instructor has normative data for 1,000 employees and their supervisors that will help you interpret your results and place the results in the context of Maslow's need hierarchy and Herzberg's two-factor theory of motivation.

Employee	Supervisor	You
4	1	4
6	2	1
5	3	5
3	4	3
1	5	2
2	6	6
10	7	9
9	8	10
8	9	8
7	10	7

1. job security *LO/Hy*
2. full appreciation of work done *HO /MO*
3. promotion and growth in the organization */MO*
4. good wages */Hy*
5. interesting work */MO*
6. good working conditions */Hy*
7. tactful discipline */Hy*
8. sympathetic help with personal problems *HO/MO*
9. personal loyalty to employees *HO/Hy*
10. a feeling of being in on things */MO*

CRITIQUE OF THE TWO-FACTOR THEORY

Herzberg's two-factor theory has been criticized. One criticism concerns the classification of motivation and hygiene factors. Data have not shown a clear dichotomization of incidents into hygiene and motivator factors. For example, employees almost equally classify pay as a hygiene factor and as a motivation factor. A second criticism is the absence of individual differences in the theory. Specifically, individual differences such as age, sex, social status, education, or occupational level may influence the classification of factors as motivation or hygiene. A third criticism is that intrinsic job factors, such as the work flow process, may be more important in determining satisfaction or dissatisfaction on the job. Finally, almost all of the supporting data for the theory come from Herzberg and his students using his peculiar type of critical-incident storytelling technique. These criticisms challenge and qualify, yet do not invalidate, the theory. Recent research has found his theory valid in a government research and development environment.[34] Herzberg's two-factor theory has important implications for job enrichment and the design of work, as discussed in Chapter 13.

SOCIAL EXCHANGE AND EQUITY THEORY

Equity theory is a social exchange process theory of motivation that focuses on the individual–environment interaction. In contrast to internal needs theories of motivation, equity theory is concerned with the social processes that influence motivation and behavior. Peter Blau suggests that power and exchange are important considerations in understanding human behavior.[35] In the same vein, Amitai Etzioni developed three categories of exchange relationships or involvements people have with organizations: committed, calculated, and alienated involvements.[36] The implications of these involvements for power are discussed in detail in Chapter 10. Etzioni characterized committed involvements as moral relationships of high positive intensity, calculated involvements as ones of low positive or low negative intensity, and alienated involvements as ones of high negative intensity. Committed involvements may characterize a person's relationship with a religious group, and alienated involvements may characterize a person's relationship with a prison system. Social exchange theory may be the best way to understand effort–reward relationships and the sense of fairness at work as seen in a Dutch study.[37]

DEMANDS AND CONTRIBUTIONS

Calculated involvements are based on the notion of social exchange in which each party in the relationship demands certain things of the other and contributes accordingly to the exchange. Business partnerships and commercial deals are excellent examples of calculated involvements. When they work well and both parties to the exchange benefit, the relationship has a positive orientation. When losses occur or conflicts arise, the relationship has a negative orientation. A model for examining these calculated exchange relationships is set out in Figure 5-4. We use this model to examine the nature of the relationship between a person and his or her employing organization.[38] The same basic model can be used to examine the relationship between two individuals or two organizations.

Demands Each party to the exchange makes demands upon the other. These demands express the expectations that each party has of the other in the relationship. The organization expresses its demands on the individual in the form of goal or mission statements, job expectations, performance objectives, and performance feedback. These are among the primary and formal mechanisms through which people learn about the organization's demands and expectations of them.

The organization is not alone in making demands of the relationship. The individual has needs to be satisfied as well, as we have previously discussed. These needs form the basis for the expectations or demands placed on the organization by the individual. These needs may be conceptualized from the perspective of Maslow, Alderfer, Herzberg, or McClelland. Different individuals have different needs.

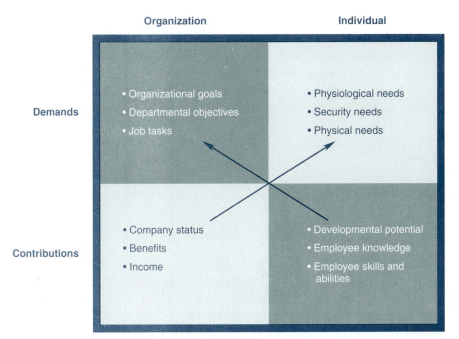

Organization | Individual

Demands
- Organizational goals
- Departmental objectives
- Job tasks

- Physiological needs
- Security needs
- Physical needs

Contributions
- Company status
- Benefits
- Income

- Developmental potential
- Employee knowledge
- Employee skills and abilities

Figure 5-4
The Individual–Organizational Exchange Relationship

Source: Reproduced with permission from McGraw-Hill, Inc. J.P. Campbell, M.D. Dunnette, E.E. Lawler III, and K.E. Weick, Jr., *Managerial Behavior, Performance and Effectiveness.* (New York: McGraw-Hill, Inc., 1970).

Contributions Just as each party to the exchange makes demands upon the other, each also has contributions to make to the relationship. These contributions are the basis for satisfying the demands expressed by the other party in the relationship. Employees are able to satisfy organizational demands through a range of contributions, including their skills, abilities, knowledge, energy, professional contacts, and native talents. As people grow and develop over time, they are able to increasingly satisfy the range of demands and expectations placed upon them by the organization.

In a similar fashion, organizations have a range of contributions available to the exchange relationship to meet individual needs. These contributions include salary, benefits, advancement opportunities, security, status, and social affiliation. Some organizations are richer in resources and better able to meet employee needs than other organizations. Thus, one of the concerns that individuals and organizations alike have is whether the relationship is a fair deal or an equitable arrangement for both members of the relationship.

ADAMS'S THEORY OF INEQUITY

Blau's and Etzioni's ideas about social process and exchange provide a context for understanding fairness, equity, and inequity in work relationships. Stacy Adams explicitly developed the idea that *inequity* in the social exchange process is an important motivator. Adams's theory of inequity suggests that people are motivated when they find themselves in situations

5. *Describe how inequity influences individual motivation and behavior.*

INEQUITY
The situation in which a person perceives he or she is receiving less than he or she is giving, or is giving less than he or she is receiving.

of inequity or unfairness.[39] Inequity occurs when a person receives more, or less, than the person believes is deserved based on effort and/or contribution. Inequity leads to the experience of tension, and tension motivates a person to act in a manner to resolve the inequity.

When does a person know that the situation is inequitable or unfair? Adams suggests that people examine the contribution portion of the exchange relationship just discussed. Specifically, people consider their inputs (their own contributions to the relationship) and their outcomes (the organization's contributions to the relationship). People then calculate an input/outcome ratio, which they compare with that of a generalized or comparison other. Figure 5-5 shows one equity situation and two inequity situations, one negative and one positive. For example, inequity in (b) could occur if the comparison other earned a higher salary, and inequity in (c) could occur if the person had more vacation time, in both cases all else being equal. Although not illustrated in the example, nontangible inputs, like emotional investment, and nontangible outcomes, like job satisfaction, may well enter into a person's equity equation.

Pay inequity has been a particularly thorny issue for women in some professions and companies. Eastman Kodak and other companies have made real progress in addressing this inequity through pay equity.[40] As organizations become increasingly international, it may be difficult to determine pay and benefit equity/inequity across national borders.

Adams would consider the inequity in Figure 5-5(b) to be a first level of inequity. A more severe, second level of inequity would occur if the comparison other's inputs were lower than the person's. Inequalities in one (inputs or outcomes) coupled with equality in the other (inputs or outcomes) are experienced as a less severe inequity than inequalities in both inputs and outcomes. Adams's theory, however, does not provide a way of determining if some inputs (such as effort or experience) or some outcomes are more important or weighted more than others, such as a degree or certification.

Figure 5-5
Equity and Inequity at Work

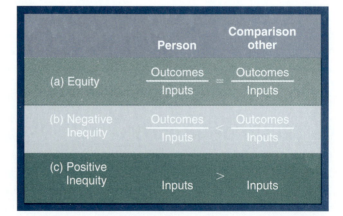

THE RESOLUTION OF INEQUITY

Once a person establishes the existence of an inequity, a number of strategies can be used to restore equity to the situation. Adams's theory provides seven basic strategies to restore equity for the person: (1) alter the person's outcomes, (2) alter the person's inputs, (3) alter the comparison other's outcomes, (4) alter the comparison other's inputs, (5) change who is used as a comparison other, (6) rationalize the inequity, and (7) leave the organizational situation.

Within each of the first four strategies, a wide variety of tactics can be employed. For example, if an employee has a strategy to increase his or her income by $11,000 per year to restore equity, the tactic might be a meeting between the employee and his or her manager concerning the issue of salary equity. The person would present relevant data on the issue. Another tactic would be for the person to work with the company's compensation specialists. A third tactic would be for the person to bring the matter before an equity committee in the company. A fourth tactic would be for the person to seek advice from the legal department.

The selection of a strategy and a set of tactics is a sensitive issue with possible long-term consequences. In this example, a strategy aimed at reducing the comparison other's outcomes may have the desired short-term effect of restoring equity while having adverse long-term consequences in terms of morale and productivity. Similarly, the choice of legal tactics may result in equity but have the long-term consequence of damaged relationships in the workplace. Therefore, as a person formulates the strategy and tactics to restore equity, the range of consequences of alternative actions must be taken into account. Hence, not all strategies or tactics are equally preferred. The equity theory does not include a hierarchy predicting which inequity reduction strategy a person will or should choose.

Field studies on equity theory suggest that it may help explain important organizational behaviors. For example, one study found that workers who perceived compensation decisions as equitable displayed greater job satisfaction and organizational commitment.[41] In addition, equity theory may play an important role in labor–management relationships with regard to union-negotiated benefits.

NEW PERSPECTIVES ON EQUITY THEORY

Since the original formulation of the theory of inequity, now usually referred to as equity theory, a number of revisions have been made in light of new theories and research. One important theoretical revision proposes three types of individuals based on preferences for equity.[42] *Equity sensitives* are those people who prefer equity based on the originally formed theory. Equity sensitivity contributes significantly to variation in free time spent working.[43] *Benevolents* are people who are comfortable with an equity ratio less than that of their comparison other, as exhibited in the Calvinistic

6. *Explain seven different strategies for resolving inequity.*

YOU BE THE JUDGE

Assume you know an employee who is being underpaid because the company believes it can save money and the employee will not complain. Is this unethical? Should you tell the employee about the underpayment condition?

EQUITY SENSITIVE
An individual who prefers an equity ratio equal to that of his or her comparison other.

BENEVOLENT
An individual who is comfortable with an equity ratio less than that of his or her comparison other.

ENTITLED
An individual who is comfortable with an equity ratio greater than that of his or her comparison other.

heritage of the Dutch.[44] These people may be thought of as givers. **Entitleds** are people who are comfortable with an equity ratio greater than that of their comparison other, as exhibited by some offspring of the affluent who want and expect more.[45] These people may be thought of as takers.

Research suggests that a person's organizational position influences self-imposed performance expectations.[46] Specifically, a two-level move up in an organization with no additional pay creates a higher self-imposed performance expectation than a one-level move up with modest additional pay. Similarly, a two-level move down in an organization with no reduction in pay creates a lower self-imposed performance expectation than a one-level move down with a modest decrease in pay. This suggests that organizational position may be more important than pay in determining the level of a person's performance expectations. Some limitations of equity theory are its heavy emphasis on pay as an outcome, the difficulty in controlling the choices of a comparison other, and the difficulty the theory has had in explaining the overpayment condition.

Although most studies of equity theory take a short-term perspective, equity comparisons over the long term should be considered as well. Increasing, decreasing, or constant experiences of inequity over time may have very different consequences for people.[47] For example, do increasing experiences of inequity have a debilitating effect on people? In addition, equity theory may help companies implement two-tiered wage structures, such as the one used by American Airlines in the early 1990s. In a two-tiered system, one group of employees receives different pay and benefits than another group of employees. A study of 1,935 rank-and-file members in one retail chain using a two-tiered wage structure confirmed the predictions of equity theory.[48] The researchers suggest that unions and management may want to consider work location and employment status (part-time versus full-time) prior to the implementation of a two-tiered system.

EXPECTANCY THEORY OF MOTIVATION

7. *Describe the expectancy theory of motivation.*

VALENCE
The value or importance one places on a particular reward.

EXPECTANCY
The belief that effort leads to performance.

INSTRUMENTALITY
The belief that performance is related to rewards.

Whereas equity theory focuses on a social exchange process, Vroom's expectancy theory of motivation focuses on personal perceptions of the performance process. His theory is founded on the basic notions that people desire certain outcomes of behavior and performance, which may be thought of as rewards or consequences of behavior, and that they believe there are relationships between the effort they put forth, the performance they achieve, and the outcomes they receive. Expectancy theory is a cognitive process theory of motivation.

The key constructs in the expectancy theory of motivation are the *valence* of an outcome, *expectancy*, and *instrumentality*.[49] Valence is the value or importance one places on a particular reward. Expectancy is the belief that effort leads to performance (for example, "If I try harder, I can do better"). Instrumentality is the belief that performance is related to re-

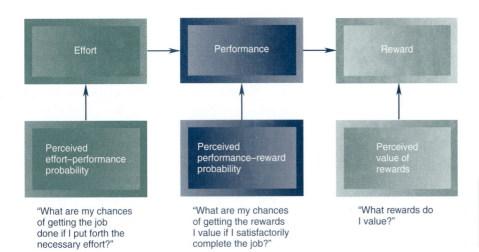

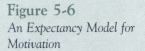

Figure 5-6
An Expectancy Model for Motivation

wards (for example, "If I perform better, I will get more pay"). A model for the expectancy theory notions of effort, performance, and rewards is depicted in Figure 5-6.

Valence, expectancy, and instrumentality are all important to a person's motivation. Expectancy and instrumentality concern a person's beliefs about how effort, performance, and rewards are related. For example, a person may firmly believe that an increase in effort has a direct, positive effect on performance and that a reduced amount of effort results in a commensurate reduction in performance. Another person may have a very different set of beliefs about the effort–performance link. The person might believe that regardless of the amount of additional effort put forth, no improvement in performance is possible. Therefore, the perceived relationship between effort and performance varies from person to person and from activity to activity.

In a similar fashion, people's beliefs about the performance–reward link vary. One person may believe that an improvement in performance has a direct, positive effect on the rewards received, whereas another person may believe that an improvement in performance has no effect on the rewards received. Again, the perceived relationship between performance and rewards varies from person to person and from situation to situation. From a motivation perspective, it is the person's belief about the relationships between these constructs that is important, not the actual nature of the relationship. During volatile times in business, the performance–reward linkage may be confusing. Some CEOs work to manage expectations during these periods in order to help and to motivate employees.

Expectancy theory has been used by managers and companies to design motivation programs,[50] such as Tenneco's PP&E (Performance Planning and Evaluation) system in the 1970s. In Tenneco's case, the PP&E system was designed to enhance a person's belief that effort would lead to better performance and that better performance would lead to merit pay increases and other rewards. Valence and expectancy are particularly important in establishing priorities for people pursuing multiple goals.[51]

A person's motivation increases along with his or her belief that effort leads to performance and that performance leads to rewards, assuming the person wants the rewards. This is the third key idea within the expectancy theory of motivation. It is the idea that the valence, or value, that people place on various rewards varies. One person prefers salary to benefits, whereas another person prefers just the reverse. All people do not place the same value on each reward. Expectancy theory has been used in a wide variety of contexts, including test-taking motivation among students.[52]

MOTIVATIONAL PROBLEMS

Within the expectancy theory framework, motivational problems stem from three basic causes. These causes are a disbelief in a relationship between effort and performance, a disbelief in a relationship between performance and rewards, and lack of desire for the rewards offered.

If the motivational problem is related to the person's belief that effort will not result in performance, the solution lies in altering this belief. The person can be shown how an increase in effort or an alteration in the kind of effort put forth can be converted into improved performance. For example, the textbook salesperson who does not believe more calls (effort) will result in greater sales (performance) might be shown how to distinguish departments with high-probability sales opportunities from those with low-probability sales opportunities. Hence, more calls (effort) can be converted into greater sales (performance).

If the motivational problem is related to the person's belief that performance will not result in rewards, the solution lies in altering this belief. The person can be shown how an increase in performance or a somewhat altered form of performance will be converted into rewards. For example, the textbook salesperson who does not believe greater sales (performance) will result in overall higher commissions (rewards) might be shown computationally or graphically that a direct relationship does exist. Hence, greater sales (performance) are directly converted into higher commissions (rewards).

If the motivational problem is related to the value the person places on, or the preference the person has for, certain rewards, the solution lies in influencing the value placed on the rewards or altering the rewards themselves. For example, the textbook salesperson may not particularly want higher commissions, given the small incremental gain he would receive at his tax level. In this case, the company might establish a mechanism for sheltering commissions from being taxed or alternative mechanisms for deferred compensation.

Research results on expectancy theory have been mixed.[53] The theory has been shown to predict job satisfaction accurately.[54] However, the theory's complexity makes it difficult to test the full model, and the measures of instrumentality, valence, and expectancy have only weak validity.[55] In addition, measuring the expectancy constructs is time consuming, and the values for each construct change over time for an individual. Finally, a theory assumes the individual is totally rational and acts as a minicomputer, calculating probabilities and values. In reality, the theory may be more complex than people as they typically function.

MOTIVATION AND MORAL MATURITY

Expectancy theory would predict that people work to maximize their personal outcomes. This is consistent with Adam Smith's ideas of working for one's own self-interest. Ultimately, Adam Smith and expectancy theories believe that people work to benefit themselves alone. Expectancy theory would not explain altruistic behavior for the benefit of others. Therefore, it may be necessary to consider an individual's *moral maturity* in order to better understand altruistic, fair, and equitable behavior. Moral maturity is the measure of a person's cognitive moral development, which was discussed in Chapter 4. Morally mature people act and behave based on universal ethical principles, whereas morally immature people act and behave based on egocentric motivations.[56]

MORAL MATURITY
The measure of a person's cognitive moral development.

CULTURAL DIFFERENCES IN MOTIVATION

Most motivation theories in use today have been developed by Americans in the United States and are about Americans.[57] When researchers have examined the universality of these theories, they have found cultural differences, at least with regard to Maslow's, McClelland's, Herzberg's, and Vroom's theories. For example, while self-actualization may be the pinnacle need for Americans in Maslow's need hierarchy, security may be the most important need for people in cultures such as Greece and Japan who have a high need to avoid uncertainty.[58] Although achievement is an important need for Americans, research noted earlier in the chapter suggested that other cultures do not value achievement as much as Americans do.

8. *Describe the cultural differences in motivation.*

The two-factor theory has been tested in other countries as well. Results in New Zealand did not replicate the results found in the United States; supervision and interpersonal relationships were important motivators in New Zealand rather than hygienic factors as in America.[59] Finally, expectancy theory may hold up very nicely in cultures that value individualism but break down in more collectivist cultures that value cooperative efforts. In collectivist cultures, rewards are more closely tied to group and team efforts, thus rendering unnecessary the utility of expectancy theory.

MANAGERIAL IMPLICATIONS: MANY WAYS TO MOTIVATE PEOPLE

Managers must realize that all motivation theories are not equally good or equally useful. The later motivation theories, such as the equity and expectancy theories, may be more scientifically sound than earlier theories, such as the two-factor theory. Nevertheless, the older theories of motivation have conceptual value, show us the importance of human needs, and provide a basis for the later theories. The individual, internal theories of motivation and the individual–environment interaction process theories uniquely contribute to our overall understanding of human behavior and motivation at work.

Managers cannot assume they understand employees' needs. They should recognize the variety of needs that motivate employee behavior and ask employees to better understand their needs. Individual employees differ in their needs, and managers should be sensitive to ethnic, national, gender, and age differences in this regard. Employees with high needs for power must be given opportunities to exercise influence, and employees with high needs for achievement must be allowed to excel at work.

Managers can increase employee motivation by training (increased perceptions of success because of increased ability), coaching (increased confidence), and task assignments (increased perceptions of success because of more experience). Managers should ensure that rewards are contingent on good performance and that valued rewards, such as time off or flexible work schedules, are available. Managers must understand what their employees want.

Finally, managers should be aware that morally mature employees are more likely to be sensitive to inequities at work. At the same time, these employees are less likely to be selfish or self-centered and more likely to be concerned about equity issues for all employees. Morally mature employees will act ethically for the common good of all employees and the organization.

KEY TERMS

benevolent	moral maturity	need hierarchy
entitled	motivation	psychoanalysis
equity sensitive	motivation factor	self-interest
expectancy	need for achievement	Theory X
hygiene factor	need for affiliation	Theory Y
inequity	need for power	valence
instrumentality		

Experiential Exercise

WHAT TO DO?

According to Stacy Adams, the experience of inequity or social injustice is a motivating force for human behavior. This exercise provides you and your group with a brief scenario of an inequity at work. Your task is to consider feasible actions for redress of this inequity.

John and Mary are full professors in the same medical school department of a large private university.

As a private institution, neither the school nor the university makes the salaries and benefits of its faculty a matter of public record. Mary has pursued a long-term (fourteen years) career in the medical school, rising through the academic ranks while married to a successful businessman with whom she has raised three children. Her research and teaching *contributions have been broad ranging and award winning. John joined the medical school within the last three years and was recruited for his leading-edge contribution to a novel line of research on a new procedure. Mary thought he was probably attracted with a comprehensive compensation package, yet she had no details until an administrative assistant gave her some information about salary and benefits a month ago. Mary learned that John's base contract salary is 16 percent higher than hers ($250,000 versus $215,000), that he was awarded an incentive pay component for the commercialization of his new procedure, and that he was given an annual discretionary travel budget of $35,000 and a membership in an exclusive private club. Mary is in a quandary about what to do. Given pressures from the board of trustees to hold down costs associated with public and private pressure to keep tuition increases low, Mary wonders how to begin to close this $70,000 + inequity gap.*

Step 1. Working in groups of six, discuss the equity issues in this medical school department situation using the text material on social exchange and equity theory. Do the outcome differences here appear to be gender based, age based, performance based, or marital status based? Do you need more information? If so, what additional information do you need?

Step 2. Consider each of the seven strategies for the resolution of inequity as portrayed in this situation. Which ones are feasible to pursue based on what you know? Which ones are not feasible? Why? What are the likely consequences of each strategy or course of action? What would you advise Mary to do?

Step 3. Once your group has identified feasible resolution strategies, choose the best strategy. Next, develop a specific plan of action for Mary to follow in attempting to resolve the inequity so that she can achieve the experience and the reality of fair treatment at work.

Step 4 (Optional). Your group may be asked to share its preferred strategy for this situation and your rationale for the strategy.

6

Learning and Performance Management

LEARNING OBJECTIVES

After reading this chapter, you should be able to do the following:

1. Define *learning*, *reinforcement*, *punishment*, *extinction*, and *goal setting*.

2. Distinguish between classical and operant conditioning.

3. Explain the use of positive and negative consequences of behavior in strategies of reinforcement and punishment.

4. Identify the purposes of goal setting and five characteristics of effective goals.

5. Describe effective strategies for giving and receiving performance feedback.

6. Compare individual and team-oriented reward systems.

7. Describe strategies for correcting poor performance.

This is the second of two chapters addressing motivation and behavior. Chapter 5 emphasized internal and process theories of motivation. This chapter focuses on external theories of motivation and factors in the work environment that influence good and bad performance. The first section addresses learning theory and the use of reinforcement, punishment, and extinction at work. It also touches on Bandura's social learning theory and Jung's personality approach to learning. The second section presents theory, research, and practice related to goal setting in organizations. The third section addresses the definition and measurement of performance. The fourth section is concerned with rewarding performance. The fifth and concluding section addresses how to correct poor performance.

LEARNING IN ORGANIZATIONS

Learning is a change in behavior acquired through experience. Learning may begin with the cognitive activity of developing knowledge about a subject, which then leads to a change in behavior. Alternatively, the behaviorist approach to learning assumes that observable behavior is a function of its consequences. According to the behaviorists, learning has its basis in classical and operant conditioning. Learning helps guide and direct motivated behavior.

1. Define *learning, reinforcement, punishment, extinction,* and *goal setting.*

LEARNING
A change in behavior acquired through experience.

CLASSICAL CONDITIONING

Classical conditioning is the process of modifying behavior so that a conditioned stimulus is paired with an unconditioned stimulus and elicits an unconditioned response. It is largely the result of the research on animals (primarily dogs) by the Russian physiologist Ivan Pavlov.[1] Pavlov's professional exchanges with Walter B. Cannon and other American researchers during the early 1900s led to the application of his ideas in the United States.[2] Classical conditioning builds on the natural consequence of an unconditioned response to an unconditioned stimulus. In dogs, this might be the natural production of saliva (unconditioned response) in response to the presentation of meat (unconditioned stimulus). By presenting a conditioned stimulus (for example, a bell) simultaneously with the unconditioned stimulus (the meat), the researcher caused the dog to develop a conditioned response (salivation in response to the bell).

Classical conditioning may occur in a similar fashion in humans.[3] For example, a person working at a computer terminal may get lower back tension (unconditioned response) as a result of poor posture (unconditioned stimulus). If the person becomes aware of that tension only when the manager enters the work area (conditioned stimulus), then the person may develop a conditioned response (lower back tension) to the appearance of the manager.

Although this example is logical, classical conditioning has real limitations in its applicability to human behavior in organizations—for at least three reasons. First, humans are more complex than dogs and less amenable to simple cause-and-effect conditioning. Second, the behavioral environments

2. Distinguish between classical and operant conditioning.

CLASSICAL CONDITIONING
Modifying behavior so that a conditioned stimulus is paired with an unconditioned stimulus and elicits an unconditioned response.

in organizations are complex and not very amenable to single stimulus–response manipulations. Third, complex human decision making makes it possible to override simple conditioning.

OPERANT CONDITIONING

OPERANT CONDITIONING
Modifying behavior through the use of positive or negative consequences following specific behaviors.

Operant conditioning is the process of modifying behavior through the use of positive or negative consequences following specific behaviors. It is based on the notion that behavior is a function of its consequences,[4] which may be either positive or negative. The consequences of behavior are used to influence, or shape, behavior through three strategies: reinforcement, punishment, and extinction.

Organizational behavior modification (O.B. Mod., commonly known as OBM) is a form of operant conditioning used successfully in a variety of organizations to shape behavior by Luthans and his colleagues.[5] The three types of consequences used in OBM to influence behavior are financial reinforcement, nonfinancial reinforcement, and social reinforcement. A major review of the research on the influence of OBM in organizations found that it had significant and positive influence on task performance in both manufacturing and service organizations, but that the effects were most powerful in manufacturing organizations.[6] Recent research showed that money based (financial) reinforcement improved performance more than routine pay for performance, social recognition, and performance feedback.[7]

THE STRATEGIES OF REINFORCEMENT, PUNISHMENT, AND EXTINCTION

3. *Explain the use of positive and negative consequences of behavior in strategies of reinforcement and punishment.*

Reinforcement is used to enhance desirable behavior, and punishment and extinction are used to diminish undesirable behavior. The application of reinforcement theory is central to the design and administration of organizational reward systems. Well-designed reward systems help attract and retain the very best employees. Strategic rewards help motivate behavior, actions, and accomplishments, which advance the organization toward specific business goals.[8] Strategic rewards go beyond cash to include training and educational opportunities, stock options, and recognition awards such as travel. Strategic rewards are important positive consequences of people's work behavior.

POSITIVE CONSEQUENCES
Results of a behavior that a person finds attractive or pleasurable.

NEGATIVE CONSEQUENCES
Results of a behavior that a person finds unattractive or aversive.

Reinforcement and punishment are administered through the management of positive and negative consequences of behavior. *Positive consequences* are the results of a person's behavior that the person finds attractive or pleasurable. They might include a pay increase, a bonus, a promotion, a transfer to a more desirable geographic location, or praise from a supervisor. *Negative consequences* are the results of a person's behavior that the person finds unattractive or aversive. They might include disciplinary action, an undesirable transfer, a demotion, or harsh criticism from a supervisor. Positive and negative consequences must be defined for the person receiving them. Therefore, individual, gender, and cultural differences may be important in their classification.

The use of positive and negative consequences following a specific behavior either reinforces or punishes that behavior.[9] Thorndike's law of effect states that behaviors followed by positive consequences are more likely to recur and behaviors followed by negative consequences are less likely to recur.[10] Figure 6-1 shows how positive and negative consequences may be applied or withheld in the strategies of reinforcement and punishment.

Reinforcement **Reinforcement** is the attempt to develop or strengthen desirable behavior by either bestowing positive consequences or withholding negative consequences. Positive reinforcement results from the application of a positive consequence following a desirable behavior. Bonuses paid at the end of successful business years are an example of positive reinforcement. Marriott International provides positive reinforcement by honoring fifteen to twenty employees each year with its J. Willard Marriott Award of Excellence. Each awardee receives a medallion engraved with the words that express the basic values of the company: dedication, achievement, character, ideals, effort, and perseverance.

Negative reinforcement results from withholding a negative consequence when a desirable behavior occurs. For example, a manager who reduces an employee's pay (negative consequence) if the employee comes to work late (undesirable behavior) and refrains from doing so when the employee is on time (desirable behavior) has negatively reinforced the employee's on-time behavior. The employee avoids the negative consequence (a reduction in pay) by exhibiting the desirable behavior (being on time to work).

Either continuous or intermittent schedules of reinforcement may be used. These reinforcement schedules are described in Table 6-1 (on page 130). When managers design organizational reward systems, they consider not only the type of reinforcement but also how often the reinforcement should be provided.

Punishment **Punishment** is the attempt to eliminate or weaken undesirable behavior. It is used in two ways. One way to punish a person is to

REINFORCEMENT
The attempt to develop or strengthen desirable behavior by either bestowing positive consequences or withholding negative consequences.

PUNISHMENT
The attempt to eliminate or weaken undesirable behavior by either bestowing negative consequences or withholding positive consequences.

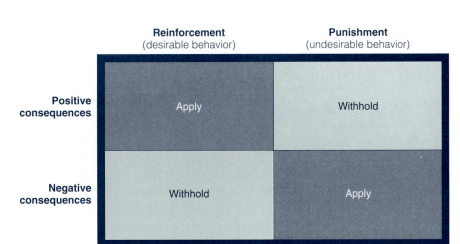

Figure 6-1
Reinforcement and Punishment Strategies

	Reinforcement (desirable behavior)	Punishment (undesirable behavior)
Positive consequences	Apply	Withhold
Negative consequences	Withhold	Apply

Schedule	Description	Effects on Responding
Continuous		
	Reinforcer follows every response	1. Steady high rate of performance as long as reinforcement follows every response 2. High frequency of reinforcement may lead to early satiation 3. Behavior weakens rapidly (undergoes extinction) when reinforcers are withheld 4. Appropriate for newly emitted, unstable, low-frequency responses
Intermittent		
	Reinforcer does not follow every response	1. Capable of producing high frequencies of responding 2. Low frequency of reinforcement precludes early satiation 3. Appropriate for stable or high-frequency responses
Fixed Ratio	A fixed number of responses must be emitted before reinforcement occurs	1. A fixed ratio of 1:1 (reinforcement occurs after every response) is the same as a continuous schedule 2. Tends to produce a high rate of response that is vigorous and steady
Variable Ratio	A varying or random number of responses must be emitted before reinforcement occurs	Capable of producing a high rate of response that is vigorous, steady, and resistant to extinction
Fixed Interval	The first response after a specific period of time has elasped is reinforced	Produces an uneven response pattern varying from a very slow, unenergetic response immediately following reinforcement to a very fast, vigorous response immediately preceding reinforcement
Variable Interval	The first response after varying or random periods of time have elapsed is reinforced	Tends to produce a high rate of response that is vigorous, steady, and resistant to extinction

Table 6-1
Schedules of Reinforcement

Source: Table from *Organizational Behavior Modification* by Fred Luthans and Robert Kreitner. Copyright © 1985, p. 58, by Scott Foresman and Company and the authors. Reprinted by permission of the authors.

apply a negative consequence following an undesirable behavior. For example, a professional athlete who is excessively offensive to an official (undesirable behavior) may be ejected from a game (negative consequence). The other way to punish a person is to withhold a positive consequence following an undesirable behavior. For example, a salesperson who makes few visits to companies (undesirable behavior) and whose sales are well below the quota (undesirable behavior) is likely to receive a very small commission check (positive consequence) at the end of the month.

One problem with punishment is that it may have unintended results. Because punishment is discomforting to the individual being punished, the experience of punishment may result in negative psychological, emotional, performance, or behavioral consequences. For example, the person being punished may become angry, hostile, depressed, or despondent. From an organizational standpoint, this result becomes important when the punished person translates negative emotional and psychological responses into negative actions. A General Motors employee who had been disciplined pulled an emergency cord and shut down an entire assembly line. A hardware store owner was killed by a man he had fired for poor performance. Work slowdowns, sabotage, and subversive behavior are all unintended negative consequences of punishment.

Extinction   An alternative to punishing undesirable behavior is ***extinction***—the attempt to weaken a behavior by attaching no consequences (either positive or negative) to it. It is equivalent to ignoring the behavior. The rationale for using extinction is that a behavior not followed by any consequence is weakened. Some patience and time may be needed for extinction to be effective, however.

Extinction may be practiced, for example, by not responding (no consequence) to the sarcasm (behavior) of a colleague. Extinction may be most effective when used in conjunction with the positive reinforcement of desirable behaviors. Therefore, in the example, the best approach might be to compliment the sarcastic colleague for constructive comments (reinforcing desirable behavior) while ignoring sarcastic comments (extinguishing undesirable behavior).

Extinction is not always the best strategy, however. In cases of dangerous behavior, punishment might be preferable to deliver a swift, clear lesson. It might also be preferable in cases of seriously undesirable behavior, such as employee embezzlement and other illegal or unethical behavior.

BANDURA'S SOCIAL LEARNING THEORY

A social learning theory proposed by Albert Bandura is an alternative and complement to the behavioristic approaches of Pavlov and Skinner.[11] Bandura believes learning occurs through the observation of other people and the modeling of their behavior. Executives might teach their subordinates a wide range of behaviors, such as leader–follower interactions and stress management, by exhibiting these behaviors. Since employees look to their supervisors for acceptable norms of behavior, they are likely to pattern their own responses on the supervisor's.

Central to Bandura's social learning theory is the notion of ***task-specific self-efficacy***, an individual's beliefs and expectancies about his or her ability to perform a specific task effectively. (Generalized self-efficacy was discussed in Chapter 3.) Individuals with high self-efficacy believe that they have the ability to get things done, that they are capable of putting forth the effort to accomplish the task, and that they can overcome any obstacles to their success. Employees with low task-specific self-efficacy quit trying prematurely and may even fail at a task. There are four sources of task-specific self-efficacy: prior experiences, behavior models (witnessing the

EXTINCTION
The attempt to weaken a behavior by attaching no consequences to it.

TASK-SPECIFIC SELF-EFFICACY
An individual's beliefs and expectancies about his or her ability to perform a specific task effectively.

success of others), persuasion from other people, and assessment of current physical and emotional capabilities.[12] Believing in one's own capability to get something done is an important facilitator of success. There is strong evidence that self-efficacy leads to high performance on a wide variety of physical and mental tasks.[13] High self-efficacy has also led to success in breaking addictions, increasing pain tolerance, and recovering from illnesses. Conversely, success can enhance one's self-efficacy. For example, women who trained in physical self-defense increased their self-efficacy, both for specific defense skills and for coping in new situations.[14]

Alexander Stajkovic and Fred Luthans draw on Bandura's ideas of self-efficacy and social learning in expanding their original work in behavioral management and OBM into a more comprehensive framework for performance management.[15] Bandura saw the power of social reinforcement, recognizing that financial and material rewards often occur following or in conjunction with the approval of others, whereas undesirable experiences often follow social disapproval. Thus, self-efficacy and social reinforcement can be powerful influences over behavior and performance at work. A comprehensive review of 114 studies found that self-efficacy is positively and strongly related to work performance, especially for tasks that are not too complex.[16] Stajkovic and Luthans suggest that managers and supervisors can be confident that employees with high self-efficacy are going to perform well. The challenge managers face is how to select and develop employees so that they achieve high self-efficacy.

Managers can help employees develop self-efficacy. The strongest way for an employee to develop self-efficacy is to succeed at a challenging task. Managers can help by providing job challenges, coaching and counseling for improved performance, and rewarding employees' achievements. Empowerment, or sharing power with employees, can be accomplished by interventions that help employees increase their self-esteem and self-efficacy. Given the increasing diversity of the workforce, managers may want to target their efforts toward women and minorities in particular. Research has indicated that women and minorities tend to have lower than average self-efficacy.[17]

LEARNING AND PERSONALITY DIFFERENCES

The cognitive approach to learning mentioned at the beginning of the chapter is based on the *Gestalt* school of thought and draws on Jung's theory of personality differences (discussed in Chapter 3). Two elements of Jung's theory have important implications for learning and subsequent behavior.

The first element is the distinction between introverted and extraverted people. Introverts need quiet time to study, concentrate, and reflect on what they are learning. They think best when they are alone. Extraverts need to interact with other people, learning through the process of expressing and exchanging ideas with others. They think best in groups and while they are talking.

The second element is the personality functions of intuition, sensing, thinking, and feeling. These functions are listed in Table 6-2, along with

Personality Preference	Implications for Learning by Individuals
Information Gathering	
Intuitors	Prefer theoretical frameworks.
	Look for the meaning in material.
	Attempt to understand the grand scheme.
	Look for possibilities and interrelations.
Sensors	Prefer specific, empirical data.
	Look for practical applications.
	Attempt to master details of a subject.
	Look for what is realistic and doable.
Decision Making	
Thinkers	Prefer analysis of data and information.
	Work to be fairminded and evenhanded.
	Seek logical, just conclusions.
	Do not like to be too personally involved.
Feelers	Prefer interpersonal involvement.
	Work to be tenderhearted and harmonious.
	Seek subjective, merciful results.
	Do not like objective, factual analysis.

Table 6-2
Personality Functions and Learning

Source: O. Kroeger and J. M. Thuesen, *Type Talk: The 16 Personality Types That Determine How We Live, Love, and Work* (New York: Dell Publishing Co., 1989).

their implications for learning by individuals. The functions of intuition and sensing determine the individual's preference for information gathering. The functions of thinking and feeling determine how the individual evaluates and makes decisions about newly acquired information.[18] Each person has a preferred mode of gathering information and a preferred mode of evaluating and making decisions about that information. For example, an intuitive thinker may want to skim research reports about implementing total quality programs and then, based on hunches, decide how to apply the research findings to the organization. A sensing feeler may prefer viewing videotaped interviews with people in companies that implemented total quality programs and then identify people in the organization most likely to be receptive to the approaches presented.

GOAL SETTING AT WORK

Goal setting is the process of establishing desired results that guide and direct behavior. Goal-setting theory is based on laboratory studies, field research experiments, and comparative investigations by Edwin Locke, Gary Latham, John M. Ivancevich, and others.[19] Goals help crystallize the sense of purpose and mission that is essential to success at work. Priorities,

4. *Identify the purposes of goal setting and five characteristics of effective goals.*

GOAL SETTING
The process of establishing desired results that guide and direct behavior.

purpose, and goals are important sources of motivation for people at work, often leading to collective achievement, even in difficult times.

CHARACTERISTICS OF EFFECTIVE GOALS

Various organizations define the characteristics of effective goals differently. For the former Sanger-Harris, a retail organization, the acronym SMART communicated the approach to effective goals. SMART stands for Specific, Measurable, Attainable, Realistic, and Time-bound. Five commonly accepted characteristics of effective goals are specific, challenging, measurable, time-bound, and prioritized.

Specific and challenging goals serve to cue or focus the person's attention on exactly what is to be accomplished and to arouse the person to peak performance. In a wide range of occupations, people who set specific, challenging goals consistently outperform people who have easy or unspecified goals, as Figure 6-2 shows.

Measureable, quantitative goals are useful as a basis for feedback about goal progress. Qualitative goals are also valuable. The Western Company of North America (now part of BJ Services Company) allowed about 15 percent of a manager's goals to be of a qualitative nature.[20] A qualitative goal might be to improve relationships with customers. Further work might convert the qualitative goal into quantitative measures such as number of complaints or frequency of complimentary letters. In this case, however, the qualitative goal may well be sufficient and most meaningful.

Time-bound goals enhance measurability. The time limit may be implicit in the goal, or it may need to be made explicit. For example, without the six-month time limit, an insurance salesperson might think the sales goal is for the whole year rather than for six months. Many organizations work on standardized cycles, such as quarters or years, where very explicit time limits are assumed. If there is any uncertainty about the time period of the goal effort, the time limit should be explicitly stated.

Figure 6-2
Goal Level and Task Performance

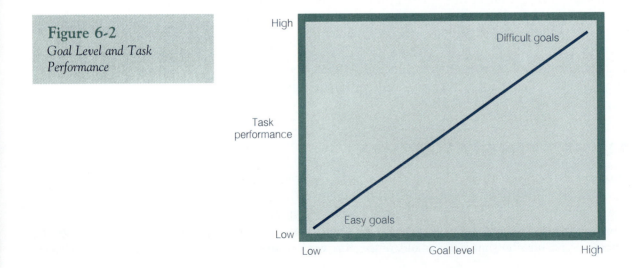

The priority ordering of goals allows for effective decision making about resource allocation.[21] As time, energy, or other resources become available, a person can move down the list of goals in descending order. The key concern is with achieving the top-priority goals. Priority helps direct a person's efforts and behavior. Although these characteristics help increase motivation and performance, that is not the only function of goal setting in organizations.

Goal setting serves one or more of three functions. First, it can increase work motivation and task performance.[22] Second, it can reduce the role stress that is associated with conflicting or confusing expectations.[23] Third, it can improve the accuracy and validity of performance evaluation.[24]

INCREASING WORK MOTIVATION AND TASK PERFORMANCE

Goals are often used to increase employee effort and motivation, which in turn improve task performance. The higher the goal, the better the performance; that is, people work harder to reach difficult goals. The positive relationship between goal difficulty and task performance is depicted in Figure 6-2.

Three important behavioral aspects of enhancing performance motivation through goal setting are employee participation, supervisory commitment, and useful performance feedback. Employee participation in goal setting leads to goal acceptance by employees. Goal acceptance is thought to lead to goal commitment and then to goal accomplishment. Special attention has been given to factors that influence commitment to difficult goals, such as participation in the process of setting the difficult goals.[25] Even in the case of assigned goals, goal acceptance and commitment are considered essential prerequisites to goal accomplishment.

Supervisory goal commitment is a reflection of the organization's commitment to goal setting. Organizational commitment is a prerequisite for successful goal-setting programs, such as management by objectives (MBO) programs.[26] The organization must be committed to the program, and the employee and supervisors must be committed to specific work goals as well as to the program. (MBO is discussed in more detail later in the chapter.)

The supervisor plays a second important role by providing employees with interim performance feedback on progress toward goals. Performance feedback is most useful when the goals are specific, and specific goals improve performance most when interim feedback is given.[27] When done correctly, negative performance feedback can lead to performance improvement.[28] For example, assume an insurance salesperson has a goal of selling $500,000 worth of insurance in six months but has sold only $200,000 after three months. During an interim performance feedback session, the supervisor may help the salesperson identify his problem—that he is not focusing his calls on the likeliest prospects. This useful feedback coupled with the specific goal helps the salesperson better focus his efforts to achieve the goal. Feedback is most helpful when it is useful (helping the salesperson

YOU BE THE JUDGE

Suppose a team of behavioral scientists was asked to enhance the motivation of military personnel to kill their enemy. Is this request ethical? Is it socially desirable? Should the team accept the assignment? Explain.

identify high-probability prospects) and timely (halfway through the performance period).

REDUCING ROLE STRESS OF CONFLICTING AND CONFUSING EXPECTATIONS

A second function of goal setting is to reduce the role stress associated with conflicting and confusing expectations. This is done by clarifying the task–role expectations communicated to employees. Supervisors, coworkers, and employees are all important sources of task-related information. A fourteen-month evaluation of goal setting in reducing role stress found that conflict, confusion, and absenteeism were all reduced through the use of goal setting.[29]

The improved role clarity resulting from goal setting may be attributable to improved communication between managers and employees. An early study of the MBO goal-setting program at Ford Motor Company found an initial 25 percent lack of agreement between managers and their bosses concerning the definition of the managers' jobs. Through effective goal-setting activities, this lack of agreement was reduced to about 5 percent.[30] At FedEx, managers are encouraged to include communication-related targets in their annual MBO goal-setting process.[31]

IMPROVING THE ACCURACY AND VALIDITY OF PERFORMANCE EVALUATION

The third major function of goal setting is improving the accuracy and validity of performance evaluation. One of the best methods of doing so is to use *management by objectives (MBO)*—a goal-setting program based on interaction and negotiation between employees and managers. MBO programs have been pervasive in organizations for nearly thirty years.[32]

MANAGEMENT BY OBJECTIVES (MBO)
A goal-setting program based on interaction and negotiation between employees and managers.

According to Peter Drucker, who originated the concept, the objectives-setting process begins with the employee writing an "employee's letter" to the manager. The letter explains the employee's general understanding of the scope of the manager's job, as well as the scope of the employee's own job, and lays out a set of specific objectives to be pursued over the next six months or year. After some discussion and negotiation, the manager and the employee finalize these items into a performance plan.

Drucker considers MBO a participative and interactive process. This does not mean that goal setting begins at the bottom of the organization. It means that goal setting is applicable to all employees, with lower level organizational members and professional staff having a clear influence over the goal-setting process.[33] (The performance aspect of goal setting is discussed in the next section of the chapter.)

Goal-setting programs have operated under a variety of names, including goals and controls at Purex (now part of Dial Corporation), work planning and review at Black & Decker and General Electric, and performance planning and evaluation at the former Tenneco, Inc., and IBM. Most of these programs are designed to enhance performance,[34] especially when incentives are associated with goal achievement.

The two central ingredients in goal-setting programs are planning and evaluation. The planning component consists of organizational and individual goal setting. Organizational goal setting is an essential prerequisite to individual goal setting; the two must be closely linked for the success of both.[35] At FedEx, all individual objectives must be tied to the overall corporate objectives of people, service, and profit.

In planning, discretionary control is usually given to individuals and departments to develop operational and tactical plans to support the corporate objectives. The emphasis is on formulating a clear, consistent, measurable, and ordered set of goals to articulate *what* to do. It is also assumed that operational support planning helps determine *how* to do it. The concept of intention is used to encompass both the goal (*what*) and the set of pathways that lead to goal attainment (*how*), thus recognizing the importance of both what and how.[36]

The evaluation component consists of interim reviews of goal progress, conducted by managers and employees, and formal performance evaluation. The reviews are mid-term assessments designed to help employees take self-corrective action. They are not designed as final or formal performance evaluations. The formal performance evaluation occurs at the close of a reporting period, usually once a year. Tenneco's program in the 1970s was an example of a goal-setting program that systematically incorporated planning and evaluation components.[37]

Because goal-setting programs are somewhat mechanical by nature, they are most easily implemented in stable, predictable industrial settings. Although most programs allow for some flexibility and change, they are less useful in organizations where high levels of unpredictability exist, as in basic research and development, or where the organization requires substantial adaptation or adjustment. Finally, individual, gender, and cultural differences do not appear to threaten the success of goal-setting programs.[38] Thus, goal-setting programs may be widely applied and effective in a diverse workforce.

PERFORMANCE: A KEY CONSTRUCT

Goal setting is designed to improve work performance, an important organizational behavior directly related to the production of goods or the delivery of services. Performance is most often thought of as task accomplishment, the term *task* coming from Taylor's early notion of a worker's required activity.[39] Some early management research found performance standards and differential piece-rate pay to be key ingredients in achieving high levels of performance, while other early research found stress helpful in improving performance up to an optimum point.[40] Hence, outcomes and effort are both important for good performance. This section focuses on task-oriented performance.

One company that elicits high levels of performance from its people is FedEx. Chairman, president, and CEO Frederick W. Smith emphasizes

People-Service-Profit (P-S-P) and the importance of performance feedback and performance-based rewards in ensuring sustained high levels of performance.

DEFINING PERFORMANCE

Performance must be clearly defined and understood by the employees who are expected to perform well at work. Performance in most lines of work is multidimensional. For example, a sales executive's performance may require administrative and financial skills along with the interpersonal skills needed to motivate a sales force. Or a medical doctor's performance may demand the positive interpersonal skills of a bedside manner to complement the necessary technical diagnostic and treatment skills for enhancing the healing process. Each specific job in an organization requires the definition of skills and behaviors essential to excellent performance. Defining performance is a prerequisite to measuring and evaluating performance on the job.

Although different jobs require different skills and behaviors, organizational citizenship behavior (OCB) is one dimension of individual performance that spans many jobs. OCB was defined in Chapter 4 as behavior that is above and beyond the call of duty. OCB involves individual discretionary behavior that promotes the organization and is not explicitly rewarded; it includes helping behavior, sportsmanship, and civic virtue. According to supervisors, OCB is enhanced most through employee involvement programs aimed at engaging employees in the work organization rather than through employee involvement in employment decisions in nonunion operations.[41] OCB emphasizes collective performance in contrast to individual performance or achievement. OCB is just one of a number of performance dimensions to consider when defining performance for a specific job within an organization.

PERFORMANCE APPRAISAL
The evaluation of a person's performance.

Performance appraisal is the evaluation of a person's performance once it is well defined. Accurate appraisals help supervisors fulfill their dual roles as evaluators and coaches. As a coach, a supervisor is responsible for encouraging employee growth and development. As an evaluator, a supervisor is responsible for making judgments that influence employees' roles in the organization. The procedural justice of a performance appraisal system has often been considered a one-dimensional concept.

The major purposes of performance appraisals are to give employees feedback on performance, to identify the employees' developmental needs, to make promotion and reward decisions, to make demotion and termination decisions, and to develop information about the organization's selection and placement decisions. For example, a review of 57,775 performance appraisals found higher ratings on appraisals done for administrative reasons and lower ratings on appraisals done for research or for employee development.[42]

MEASURING PERFORMANCE

Ideally, actual performance and measured performance are the same. Practically, this is seldom the case. Measuring operational performance is easier than measuring managerial performance because of the availability of quantifiable data. Measuring production performance is easier than measuring research and development performance because of the reliability of the measures. Recent research has focused on measuring motivation for task performance and has found that wording and context may influence the validity of direct self-reports.[43]

Performance appraisal systems are intended to improve the accuracy of measured performance and increase its agreement with actual performance. The extent of agreement is called the true assessment, as Figure 6-3 shows. The figure also identifies the performance measurement problems that contribute to inaccuracy. These include deficiency, unreliability, and invalidity. Deficiency results from overlooking important aspects of a person's actual performance. Unreliability results from poor-quality performance measures. Invalidity results from inaccurate definition of the expected job performance.

Early performance appraisal systems were often quite biased. See, for example, Table 6-3 (on page 140), which is a sample of officer effectiveness reports from an infantry company in the early 1800s. Even contemporary executive appraisals have a dark side, arousing managers' and executives' defenses. Addressing emotions and defenses is important to making appraisal sessions developmental.[44] Some performance review systems lead to forced rankings of employees, which may be controversial.

Performance-monitoring systems using modern electronic technology are sometimes used to measure the performance of vehicle operators, computer technicians, and customer service representatives. For example, such systems might record the rate of keystrokes or the total number of keystrokes

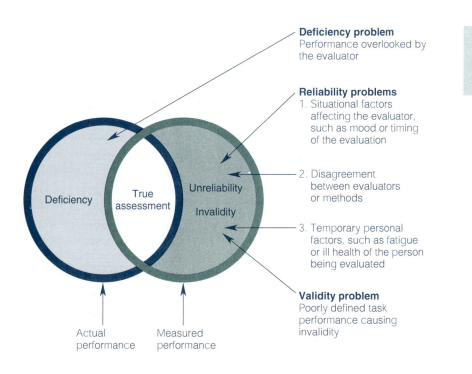

Deficiency problem
Performance overlooked by the evaluator

Reliability problems
1. Situational factors affecting the evaluator, such as mood or timing of the evaluation

2. Disagreement between evaluators or methods

3. Temporary personal factors, such as fatigue or ill health of the person being evaluated

Validity problem
Poorly defined task performance causing invalidity

Deficiency · True assessment · Unreliability · Invalidity

Actual performance · Measured performance

Figure 6-3
Actual and Measured Performance

Table 6-3

Officer Effectiveness Reports, circa 1813

Alexander Brown—Lt. Col., Comdg.—A good natured man.
Clark Crowell—first Major—A good man, but no officer.
Jess B. Wordsworth—2nd Major—An excellent officer.
Captain Shaw—A man of whom all unite in speaking ill. A knave despised by all.
Captain Thomas Lord—Indifferent, but promises well.
Captain Rockwell—An officer of capacity, but imprudent and a man of violent passions.
1st Lt. Jas. Kearns—Merely good, nothing promising.
1st Lt. Robert Cross—Willing enough—has much to learn—with small capacity.
2nd Lt. Stewart Berry—An ignorant unoffending fellow.
Ensign North—A good young man who does well.

Source: Table from *The Air Officer's Guide*, 6th ed., Copyright © 1952 Stackpole Books. Used with permission.

for a computer technician. The people subject to this type of monitoring are in some cases unaware that their performance is being measured. What is appropriate performance monitoring? What constitutes inappropriate electronic spying on the employee? Are people entitled to know when their performance is being measured? The ethics of monitoring performance may differ by culture. The United States and Sweden, for example, respect individual freedom more than Japan and China do. The overriding issue, however, is how far organizations should go in using modern technology to measure human performance.

Goal setting and MBO are results-oriented methods of performance appraisal that do not necessarily rely on modern technology. Like performance-monitoring systems, they shift the emphasis from subjective, judgmental performance dimensions to observable, verifiable results. Goals established in the planning phase of goal setting become the standard against which to measure subsequent performance. However, rigid adherence to a results-oriented approach may risk overlooking performance opportunities.

Another method for improving the accuracy of performance appraisal is to have multiple evaluators contribute to the final appraisal. Superiors, peers, employees, and clients all contribute something unique because each group has a different vantage point. Most traditional evaluations are completed by superiors. Peer and employee evaluations may add a new dimension by covering such areas as cooperation and supervisory style. For example, one mid-level executive behaved very differently in dealing with superiors, peers, and employees. With superiors, he was positive, compliant, and deferential. With peers, he was largely indifferent, often ignoring them. With employees, he was tough and demanding, bordering on cruel and abusive. Without each of these perspectives, the executive's performance would not have been accurately assessed.

FedEx has incorporated a novel and challenging approach to evaluation in its blueprint for service quality. All managers at FedEx are evaluated by their employees through a survey-feedback-action system. Employees evaluate their managers using a five-point scale on twenty-nine standard statements and ten local option ones. Low ratings suggest problem areas requiring management attention. For example, the following statement received low ratings from employees in 1990: Upper management pays attention to ideas and suggestions from people at my level. CEO Fred Smith became directly involved in addressing this problem area. One of the actions he took to correct the problem was the development of a biweekly employee newsletter.

PERFORMANCE FEEDBACK: A COMMUNICATION CHALLENGE

Once clearly defined and accurate performance measures are developed, there is still the challenge of performance feedback. Feedback sessions are among the more stressful events for supervisors and employees. Early research at General Electric found employees responded constructively to positive feedback and were defensive over half the time in response to critical or negative feedback. Typical responses to negative feedback included shifting responsibility for the shortcoming or behavior, denying it outright, or providing a wide range of excuses for it.[45]

5. Describe effective strategies for giving and receiving performance feedback.

Both parties to a performance feedback session should try to make it a constructive learning experience, since positive and negative performance feedback has long-term implications for the employee's performance and for the working relationship. American Airlines follows three guidelines in providing evaluative feedback so that the experience is constructive for supervisor and employee alike.[46] First, refer to specific, verbatim statements and specific, observable behaviors displayed by the person receiving the feedback. This enhances the acceptance of the feedback while reducing the chances of denial. Second, focus on changeable behaviors, as opposed to intrinsic or personality-based attributes. People are often more defensive about who they are than about what they do. Third, plan and organize for the session ahead of time. Be sure to notify the person who will receive the feedback. Both the leader and the follower should be ready.

In addition to these ideas, many companies recommend beginning coaching and counseling sessions with something positive. The intent is to reduce defensiveness and enhance useful communication. There is almost always at least one positive element to emphasize. Once the session is under way and rapport is established, then the evaluator can introduce more difficult and negative material. Because people are not perfect, there is always an opportunity for them to learn and to grow through performance feedback sessions. Critical feedback is the basis for improvement and is essential to a performance feedback session.

Self-evaluations are increasingly used for performance feedback, and there is evidence they lead to more satisfying, constructive evaluation interviews and less defensiveness concerning the evaluation process.[47] On the other hand, a key criticism of self-evaluations is their low level of agreement with supervisory evaluations.[48] High levels of agreement may not necessarily be desirable, however, if the intent of the overall evaluation process is to provide a full picture of the person's performance. The 360-degree feedback method can be an effective way of providing a well-rounded view of performance.[49]

DEVELOPING PEOPLE AND ENHANCING CAREERS

A key function of a good performance appraisal system is to develop people and enhance careers. Developmentally, performance appraisals should emphasize individual growth needs and future performance. If the supervisor is to coach and develop employees effectively, there must be mutual trust. The supervisor must be vulnerable and open to challenge from the subordinate while maintaining a position of responsibility for what is in the subordinate's best interests.[50] The supervisor must also be a skilled, empathetic listener who encourages the employee to talk about hopes and aspirations.[51]

The employee must be able to take active responsibility for future development and growth. This might mean challenging the supervisor's ideas about future development as well as expressing individual preferences and goals. Passive, compliant employees are unable to accept responsibility for themselves or to achieve full emotional development. Individual responsibility is a key characteristic of the culture of the Chaparral Steel Company (part of Texas Industries). The company joke is that the company manages by "adultry" (pun intended). Chaparral Steel treats people like adults and expects adult behavior from them.

KEY CHARACTERISTICS OF AN EFFECTIVE APPRAISAL SYSTEM

An effective performance appraisal system has five key characteristics: validity, reliability, responsiveness, flexibility, and equitability. Its validity comes from capturing multiple dimensions of a person's job performance. Its reliability comes from capturing evaluations from multiple sources and at different times over the course of the evaluation period. Its responsiveness allows the person being evaluated some input into the final outcome. Its flexibility leaves it open to modification based on new information, such as federal requirements. Its equitability results in fair evaluations against established performance criteria, regardless of individual differences.

REWARDING PERFORMANCE

One function of a performance appraisal system is to provide input for reward decisions. If an organization wants good performance, then it must reward good performance. If it does not want bad performance, then it must not reward bad performance. If companies talk "teamwork," "values," and "customer focus," then they need to reward behaviors related to these ideas. Although this idea is conceptually simple, it can become very complicated in practice. Reward decisions are among the most difficult and complicated decisions made in organizations, and among the most important decisions. When leaders confront decisions about pay every day, they should know that it is a myth that people work for money.[52] While pay and rewards for performance have value, so too do trust, fun, and meaningful work.

A KEY ORGANIZATIONAL DECISION PROCESS

Reward and punishment decisions in organizations affect many people throughout the system, not just the persons being rewarded or punished. Reward allocation involves sequential decisions about which people to reward, how to reward them, and when to reward them. Taken together, these decisions shape the behavior of everyone in the organization, because of the vicarious learning that occurs as people watch what happens to others, especially when new programs or initiatives are implemented. People carefully watch what happens to peers who make mistakes or have problems with the new system; then they gauge their own behavior accordingly.

INDIVIDUAL VERSUS TEAM REWARD SYSTEMS

One of the distinguishing characteristics of Americans is the value they place on individualism. Systems that reward individuals are common in organizations in the United States. One of the strengths of these systems is that they foster autonomous and independent behavior that may lead to creativity, to novel solutions to old problems, and to distinctive contributions to the organization. Individual reward systems directly affect individual behavior and may encourage competitive striving within a work team. Although motivation and reward techniques in the United States are individually focused, they are often group focused outside the United States.[53]

Too much competition within a work environment, however, may be dysfunctional. At the Western Company of North America (now part of BJ Services Company), individual success in the MBO program was tied too tightly to rewards, and individual managers became divisively competitive. For example, some managers took last-minute interdepartmental financial actions in a quarter to meet their objectives, but by doing so, they caused other managers to miss their objectives. These actions raise ethical questions about how far individual managers should go in serving their own self-interest at the expense of their peers.

Team reward systems solve the problems caused by individual competitive behavior. These systems emphasize cooperation, joint efforts, and the sharing of information, knowledge, and expertise. The Japanese and Chinese cultures, with their collectivist orientations, place greater emphasis than Americans on the individual as an element of the team, not a member apart from the team. Digital Equipment Corporation (now part of Hewlett-Packard) used a partnership approach to performance appraisals. Self-managed work group members participated in their own appraisal process. Such an approach emphasizes teamwork and responsibility.

Some organizations have experimented with individual and group alternative reward systems.[54] At the individual level, these include skill-based

6. *Compare individual and team-oriented reward systems.*

YOU BE THE JUDGE

Suppose your company announced that it would pay bonuses to employees who met a certain performance standard. The company did not realize, however, that many employees would be able to reach the standard with hard work and that the bonuses would cost the company much more than expected. Is it fair to lower the bonus rate? Is it fair to increase the performance standard for bonuses after the fact? Explain.

and pay-for-knowledge systems. Each emphasizes skills or knowledge possessed by an employee over and above the requirements for the basic job. At the group level, gain-sharing plans emphasize collective cost reduction and allow workers to share in the gains achieved by reducing production or other operating costs. In such plans, everyone shares equally in the collective gain. Marshall Industries found that collective profit sharing improved performance.

The Power of Earning

The purpose behind both individual and team reward systems is to shape productive behavior. Effective performance management can be the lever of change that boosts individual and team achievements in an organization. So, if one wants the rewards available in the organization, then one should work to earn them. Performance management and reward systems assume a demonstrable connection between performance and rewards. Organizations get the performance they reward, not the performance they say they want.[55] Further, when there is no apparent link between performance and rewards, people may begin to believe they are entitled to rewards regardless of how they perform. The concept of entitlement is very different from the concept of earning, which assumes a performance–reward link.

The notion of entitlement at work is counterproductive when taken to the extreme because it counteracts the power of earning.[56] People who believe they are entitled to rewards regardless of their behavior or performance are not motivated to behave constructively. Merit raises in some organizations, for example, have come to be viewed as entitlements, thus reducing their positive value in the organizational reward system. People believe they have a right to be taken care of by someone, whether that is the organization or a specific person. Entitlement engenders passive, irresponsible behavior, whereas earning engenders active, responsible, adult behavior. If rewards depend on performance, then people must perform responsibly to receive them. The power of earning rests on a direct link between performance and rewards.

CORRECTING POOR PERFORMANCE

7. Describe strategies for correcting poor performance.

Often a complicated, difficult challenge for supervisors, correcting poor performance is a three-step process. First, the cause or primary responsibility for the poor performance must be identified. Second, if the primary responsibility is a person's, then the source of the personal problem must be determined. Third, a plan of action to correct the poor performance must be developed. This chapter's Challenge gives you an opportunity to examine a poor performance you have experienced.

Poor performance may result from a variety of causes, the more important being poorly designed work systems, poor selection processes, inadequate training and skills development, lack of personal motivation, and

Challenge

CORRECTING POOR PERFORMANCE

At one time or another, each of us has had a poor performance of some kind. It may have been a poor test result in school, a poor presentation at work, or a poor performance in an athletic event. Think of a poor performance event that you have experienced and work through the following three steps.

Step 1. Briefly describe the specific event in some detail. Include why you label it a poor performance (bad score? someone else's evaluation?).

Step 2. Analyze the Poor Performance

a. List all the possible contributing causes to the poor performance. Be specific, such as the room was too hot, you did not get enough sleep, you were not told how to perform the task, etc. You might ask other people for possible ideas, too.

1. _____
2. _____
3. _____
4. _____
5. _____
6. _____
7. _____

b. Is there a primary cause for the poor performance? What is it?

Step 3. Plan to Correct the Poor Performance

Develop a step-by-step plan of action that specifies what you can change or do differently to improve your performance the next time you have an opportunity. Include seeking help if it is needed. Once your plan is developed, look for an opportunity to execute it.

personal problems intruding on the work environment. Not all poor performance is self-motivated; some is induced by the work system. Therefore, a good diagnosis should precede corrective action. For example, it may be that an employee is subject to a work design or selection system that does not allow the person to exhibit good performance. Identifying the cause of the poor performance comes first and should be done in communication with the employee. If the problem is with the system and the supervisor can fix it, then everyone wins as a result.

If the poor performance is not attributable to work design or organizational process problems, then attention should be focused on the employee. At least three possible causes of poor performance can be attributed to the employee. The problem may lie in (1) some aspect of the person's relationship to the organization or supervisor, (2) some area of the employee's personal life, or (3) a training or developmental deficiency. In the latter two cases, poor performance may be treated as a symptom as opposed to a motivated consequence. In such cases, identifying financial problems, family difficulties, or health disorders may enable the supervisor to help the employee solve problems before they become too extensive. Employee assistance programs (EAPs) can be helpful to employees managing personal problems.

Poor performance may also be motivated by an employee's displaced anger or conflict with the organization or supervisor. In such cases, the employee may or may not be aware of the internal reactions causing the problem. In either event, sabotage, work slowdowns, work stoppages, and similar forms of poor performance may result from such motivated behavior. The supervisor may attribute the cause of the problem to the employee, and the employee may attribute it to the supervisor or organization. To solve motivated performance problems requires treating the poor performance as a symptom with a deeper cause. Resolving the underlying anger or conflict results in the disappearance of the symptom (poor performance).

ATTRIBUTION AND PERFORMANCE MANAGEMENT

According to attribution theory, managers make attributions (inferences) concerning employees' behavior and performance.[57] The attributions may not always be accurate. For example, a former ABC executive who had a very positive relationship with his boss was not held responsible for profit problems in his district. The boss attributed the problem to the economy instead. Supervisors and employees who share perceptions and attitudes, as in the ABC situation, tend to evaluate each other highly.[58] Supervisors and employees who do not share perceptions and attitudes are more likely to blame each other for performance problems.

Harold Kelley's attribution theory aims to help us explain the behavior of other people. He also extended attribution theory by trying to identify the antecedents of internal and external attributions. Kelley proposed that individuals make attributions based on information gathered in the form of three informational cues: consensus, distinctiveness, and consistency.[59, 60] We observe an individual's behavior and then seek out information in the form of these three cues. *Consensus* is the extent to which peers in the same situation behave the same way. *Distinctiveness* is the degree to which the person behaves the same way in other situations. *Consistency* refers to the frequency of a particular behavior over time.

We form attributions based on whether these cues are low or high. Figure 6-4 shows how the combination of these cues helps us form internal or external attributions. Suppose you have received several complaints from customers regarding one of your customer service representatives, John. You have not received complaints about your other service representatives (low consensus). Upon reviewing John's records, you note that he also received customer complaints during his previous job as a sales clerk (low distinctiveness). The complaints have been coming in steadily for about three months (high consistency). In this case, you would most likely make an internal attribution and conclude that the complaints must stem from John's behavior. The combination of low consensus, low distinctiveness, and high consistency leads to internal attributions.

Other combinations of these cues, however, produce external attributions. High consensus, high distinctiveness, and low consistency, for example, produce external attributions. Suppose one of your employees, Mary, is performing poorly on collecting overdue accounts. You find that the behavior is widespread within your work team (high consensus) and that Mary is performing poorly only on this aspect of the job (high distinctiveness), and that most of the time she handles this aspect of the job well (low con-

CONSENSUS
An informational cue indicating the extent to which peers in the same situation behave in a similar fashion.

DISTINCTIVENESS
An informational cue indicating the degree to which an individual behaves the same way in other situations.

CONSISTENCY
An informational cue indicating the frequency of behavior over time.

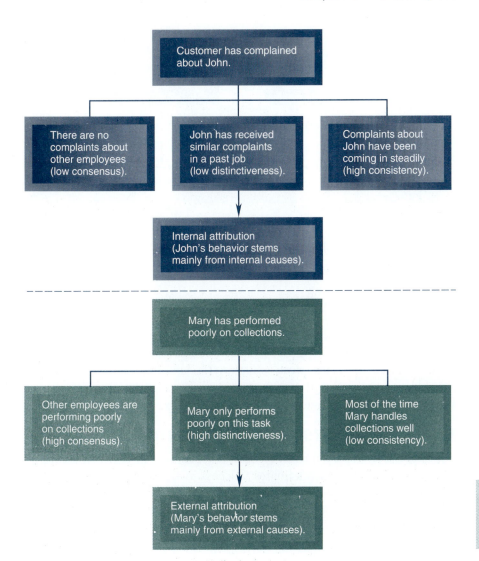

Customer has complained about John.

There are no complaints about other employees (low consensus).

John has received similar complaints in a past job (low distinctiveness).

Complaints about John have been coming in steadily (high consistency).

Internal attribution (John's behavior stems mainly from internal causes).

Mary has performed poorly on collections.

Other employees are performing poorly on collections (high consensus).

Mary only performs poorly on this task (high distinctiveness).

Most of the time Mary handles collections well (low consistency).

External attribution (Mary's behavior stems mainly from external causes).

Figure 6-4
Informational Cues and Attributions

sistency). You will probably decide that something about the work situation caused the poor performance—perhaps work overload or an unfair deadline.

Consensus, distinctiveness, and consistency are the cues used to determine whether the cause of behavior is internal or external. The process of determining the cause of a behavior may not be simple and clear-cut, however, because of some biases that occur in forming attributions.

Figure 6-5 (on page 148) presents an attribution model that specifically addresses how supervisors respond to poor performance. A supervisor who observes poor performance seeks cues about the employee's behavior in the three forms discussed above: consensus, consistency, and distinctiveness.

On the basis of this information, the supervisor makes either an internal (personal) attribution or an external (situational) attribution. Internal attributions might include low effort, lack of commitment, or lack of ability. External attributions are outside the employee's control and might

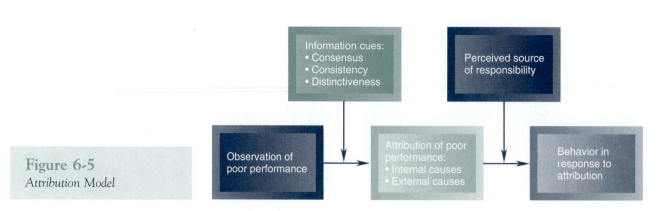

Figure 6-5
Attribution Model

include equipment failure or unrealistic goals. The supervisor then determines the source of responsibility for the performance problem and tries to correct the problem.

Supervisors may choose from a wide range of responses. They can, for example, express personal concern, reprimand the employee, or provide training. Supervisors who attribute the cause of poor performance to a person (an internal cause) will respond more harshly than supervisors who attribute the cause to the work situation (an external cause). Supervisors should try not to make either of the two common attribution errors discussed in Chapter 3: the fundamental attribution error and the self-serving bias.

COACHING, COUNSELING, AND MENTORING

Supervisors have important coaching, counseling, and mentoring responsibilities to their subordinates. Success in the mentoring relationship hinges on the presence of openness and trust.[61] This relationship may be one where performance-based deficiencies are addressed or one where personal problems that diminish employee performance, such as depression, are addressed.[62] In either case, the supervisors can play a helpful role in employee problem-solving activities without accepting responsibility for the employees' problems. One important form of help is to refer the employee to trained professionals.

Coaching and counseling are among the career and psychosocial functions of a mentoring relationship.[63] ***Mentoring*** is a work relationship that encourages development and career enhancement for people moving through the career cycle. Mentoring relationships typically go through four phases: initiation, cultivation, separation, and redefinition. The relationship can significantly enhance the early development of a newcomer and the mid-career development of an experienced employee. One study found that good performance by newcomers resulted in leaders giving more delegation.[64] Career development can be enhanced through peer relationships as an alternative to traditional mentoring relationships.[65] Executive coaching is increasingly being used as a way of outsourcing the business mentoring functions.[66] Informational, collegial, and special peers aid the individual's development through information sharing, career strategizing,

MENTORING
A work relationship that encourages development and career enhancement for people moving through the career cycle.

job-related feedback, emotional support, and friendship. Hence, mentors and peers may both play constructive roles in correcting an employee's poor performance and in enhancing overall career development.

MANAGERIAL IMPLICATIONS: PERFORMANCE MANAGEMENT IS A KEY TASK

People in organizations learn from the consequences of their actions. Therefore, managers must exercise care in applying positive and negative consequences to ensure that they are connected to the behaviors the managers intend to reward or punish. Managers should also be judicious in the use of punishment and should consider extinction coupled with positive reinforcement as an alternative to punishment for shaping employee behavior. The strategic use of training and educational opportunities, stock options, and recognition awards is instrumental to successful organizational reward systems. Managers can serve as positive role models for employees' vicarious learning about ethical behavior and high-quality performance.

Goal-setting activities may be valuable to managers in bringing out the best performance from employees. Managers can use challenging, specific goals for this purpose and must be prepared to provide employees with timely, useful feedback on goal progress so that employees will know how they are doing. Goal-setting activities that are misused may create dysfunctional competition in an organization and lead to lower performance.

Good performance evaluation systems are a valuable tool for providing employees with clear feedback on their actions. Managers who rely on valid and reliable performance measures may use them in employee development and to correct poor performance. Managers who use high-technology performance monitoring systems must remember that employees are humans, not machines. Managers are responsible for creating a positive learning atmosphere in performance feedback sessions, and employees are responsible for learning from these sessions.

Finally, managers can use rewards as one of the most powerful positive consequences for shaping employee behavior. If rewards are to improve performance, managers must make a clear connection between specific performance and the rewards. Employees should be expected to earn the rewards they receive; they should expect rewards to be related to performance quality and skill development.

KEY TERMS

classical conditioning	extinction	mentoring	positive consequences
consensus	goal setting	negative consequences	punishment
consistency	learning	operant conditioning	reinforcement
distinctiveness	management by objectives (MBO)	performance appraisal	task-specific self-efficacy

Experiential Exercise

POSITIVE AND NEGATIVE REINFORCEMENT

Purpose: To examine the effects of positive and negative reinforcement on behavior change.

1. Two or three volunteers are selected to receive reinforcement from the class while performing a particular task. The volunteers leave the room.

2. The instructor identifies an object for the student volunteers to locate when they return to the room. (The object should be unobtrusive but clearly visible to the class. Some that have worked well are a small triangular piece of paper that was left behind when a notice was torn off a classroom bulletin board, a smudge on the chalkboard, and a chip in the plaster of a classroom wall.)

3. The instructor specifies the reinforcement contingencies that will be in effect when the volunteers return to the room. For negative reinforcement, students should hiss, boo, and throw things (although you should not throw anything harmful) when the first volunteer is moving away from the object; cheer and applaud when the second volunteer is getting closer to the object; and, if a third volunteer is used, use both negative and positive reinforcement.

4. The instructor should assign a student to keep a record of the time it takes each of the volunteers to locate the object.

5. Volunteer number 1 is brought back into the room and is instructed: "Your task is to locate and touch a particular object in the room, and the class has agreed to help you. You may begin."

6. Volunteer number 1 continues to look for the object until it is found while the class assists by giving negative reinforcement.

7. Volunteer number 2 is brought back into the room and is instructed: "Your task is to locate and touch a particular object in the room, and the class has agreed to help you. You may begin."

8. Volunteer number 2 continues to look for the object until it is found while the class assists by giving positive reinforcement.

9. Volunteer number 3 is brought back into the room and is instructed: "Your task is to locate and touch a particular object in the room, and the class has agreed to help you. You may begin."

10. Volunteer number 3 continues to look for the object until it is found while the class assists by giving both positive and negative reinforcement.

11. In a class discussion, answer the following questions:

    a. How did the behavior of the volunteers differ when different kinds of reinforcement (positive, negative, or both) were used?

    b. What were the emotional reactions of the volunteers to the different kinds of reinforcement?

    c. Which type of reinforcement—positive or negative—is most common in organizations? What effect do you think this has on motivation and productivity?

PART 3

Interpersonal Processes and Behavior

7

Communication

LEARNING OBJECTIVES

After reading this chapter, you should be able to do the following:

1. Understand the roles of the communicator, the receiver, perceptual screens, and the message in interpersonal communication.

2. Practice good reflective skills.

3. Describe the five communication skills of effective supervisors.

4. Explain five barriers to communication and how to overcome them.

5. Distinguish between defensive and nondefensive communication.

6. Describe contemporary information technologies used by managers.

Communication is the evoking of a shared or common meaning in another person. *Interpersonal communication* is communication that occurs between two or more people in an organization. Reading, listening, managing and interpreting information, and serving clients are among the interpersonal communication skills identified by the Department of Labor as being necessary for successful functioning in the workplace.[1]

This chapter addresses the interpersonal and technological dimensions of communication in organizations. The first section presents an interpersonal communication model and a reflective listening technique intended to improve communication. The next section of the chapter addresses the five communication skills that characterize effective supervisors. The third section examines five barriers to effective communication and gives suggestions for overcoming them. The fourth section compares defensive and nondefensive communication. The fifth section discusses kinds of nonverbal communication. The final section gives an overview of the latest technologies for information management in organizations.

COMMUNICATION
The evoking of a shared or common meaning in another person.

INTERPERSONAL COMMUNICATION
Communication between two or more people in an organization.

INTERPERSONAL COMMUNICATION

Interpersonal communication is important in building and sustaining human relationships at work. Interpersonal communication cannot be replaced by the advances in information technology and data management that have taken place during the past several decades. The model in this section of the chapter provides a basis for understanding the key elements of interpersonal communication. These elements are the communicator, the receiver, the perceptual screens, and the message. Reflective listening is a valuable tool for improving interpersonal communication.

1. *Understand the roles of the communicator, the receiver, perceptual screens, and the message in interpersonal communication.*

AN INTERPERSONAL COMMUNICATION MODEL

Figure 7-1 (on page 154) presents an interpersonal communication model as a basis for the discussion of communication. The model has four basic elements: the communicator, the receiver, perceptual screens, and the message. The *communicator* is the person originating the message. The *receiver* is the person receiving the message. The receiver must interpret and understand the message. *Perceptual screens* are the windows through which we interact with people in the world. The communicator's and the receiver's perceptual screens influence the quality, accuracy, and clarity of the message. The screens influence whether the message sent and the message received are the same or whether distortion occurs in the message. Perceptual screens are composed of the personal factors each person brings to interpersonal communication, such as age, gender, values, beliefs, past experiences, cultural influences, and individual needs. The extent to which these screens are open or closed significantly influences both the sent and received messages.

The *message* contains the thoughts and feelings that the communicator intends to evoke in the receiver. The message has two primary components. The thought or conceptual component of the message (its content) is contained in the words, ideas, symbols, and concepts chosen to relay the

COMMUNICATOR
The person originating a message.

RECEIVER
The person receiving a message.

PERCEPTUAL SCREEN
A window through which we interact with people that influences the quality, accuracy, and clarity of the communication.

MESSAGE
The thoughts and feelings that the communicator is attempting to elicit in the receiver.

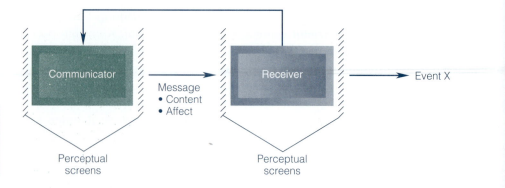

Figure 7-1

A Basic Interpersonal Communication Model

Message
• Content
• Affect

Communicator

Receiver

Event X

Perceptual screens

Perceptual screens

message. The feeling or emotional component of the message (its affect) is contained in the intensity, force, demeanor, and sometimes the gestures of the communicator. This component of the message adds to the conceptual component the emotional overtones, such as joy or anger, fear, or pain. This addition often enriches and clarifies the message. The feeling component gives the message its full meaning.

The *feedback loop* may or may not be activated in the model. Feedback occurs when the receiver provides the communicator with a response to the message.

The *language* of the message is increasingly important because of the multinational nature of many organizations. Language is the words, their pronunciation, and the methods of combining them used by a community of people. Language will be addressed as a possible barrier to communication. For example, special language barriers arise for non-Japanese-speaking Americans who work with Japanese workers and for non-Spanish-speaking Canadians who work with Spanish-speaking workers.

Data are the uninterpreted, unanalyzed elements of a message. *Information* is data with meaning to some person who has interpreted or analyzed them. Messages are conveyed through a medium, such as a telephone or face-to-face discussion. Messages differ in *richness*, the ability of the medium to convey the meaning.[2] Table 7-1 compares different media with regard to data capacity and information richness.

FEEDBACK LOOP
The pathway that completes two-way communication.

LANGUAGE
The words, their pronunciation, and the methods of combining them used and understood by a group of people.

DATA
Uninterpreted and unanalyzed facts.

INFORMATION
Data that have been interpreted, analyzed, and have meaning to some user.

RICHNESS
The ability of a medium or channel to elicit or evoke meaning in the receiver.

Table 7-1

Communication Media: Information Richness and Data Capacity

Medium	Information Richness	Data Capacity
Face-to-face discussion	Highest	Lowest
Telephone	High	Low
Electronic mail	Moderate	Moderate
Individualized letter	Moderate	Moderate
Personalized note or memo	Moderate	Moderate
Formal written report	Low	High
Flyer or bulletin	Low	High
Formal numeric report	Lowest	Highest

Source: Table created from information in Edwin A. Gerloff, *Organizational Theory and Design: A Strategic Approach for Management.* New York: McGraw-Hill Book Company, 1985, pp. 295–296. Reprinted with permission from the author.

REFLECTIVE LISTENING

Reflective listening is the skill of carefully listening to another person and repeating back to the speaker the heard message to correct any inaccuracies or misunderstandings. This kind of listening emphasizes the role of the receiver or audience in interpersonal communication. Managers use it to understand other people and help them solve problems at work.[3] Reflective listening enables the listener to understand the communicator's meaning, reduce perceptual distortions, and overcome interpersonal barriers that lead to communication failures. Reflective listening ensures that the meanings of the sent and received messages are the same. Reflecting back the message helps the communicator clarify and sharpen the intended meaning. It is especially useful in problem solving.

Reflective listening can be characterized as personal, feeling oriented, and responsive.[4] First, reflective listening emphasizes the personal elements of the communication process, not the impersonal or abstract elements of the message. The reflective listener demonstrates empathy and concern for the communicator as a person, not an inanimate object. Second, reflective listening emphasizes the feelings communicated in the message. Thoughts and ideas are often the primary focus of a receiver's response, but that is not the case in reflective listening. The receiver should pay special attention to the feeling component of the message. Third, reflective listening emphasizes responding to the communicator, not leading the communicator. Receivers should distinguish their own feelings and thoughts from those of the speaker so as not to confuse the two. The focus must be on the speaker's feelings and thoughts in order to respond to them. A good reflective listener does not lead the speaker according to the listener's own thoughts and feelings.

Four levels of verbal response by the receiver are part of active reflective listening: affirming contact, paraphrasing expressed thoughts and feelings, clarifying implicit thoughts and feelings, and reflecting "core" feelings not fully expressed. Nonverbal behaviors also are useful in reflective listening. Specifically, silence and eye contact are responses that enhance reflective listening.

Each reflective response is illustrated through the case of a software engineer and her supervisor. The engineer has just discovered a major problem, which is not yet fully defined, in a large information system she is building for a very difficult customer.

Affirming Contact The receiver affirms contact with the communicator by using simple statements such as "I see," "Uh-huh," and "Yes, I understand." The purpose of an affirmation response is to communicate attentiveness, not necessarily agreement. In the case of the software engineer, the supervisor might most appropriately use several affirming statements as the engineer begins to talk through the problem. Affirming contact is especially reassuring to a speaker in the early stages of expressing thoughts and feelings about a problem, especially when there may be some associated anxiety or discomfort. As the problem is more fully explored

2. *Practice good reflective skills.*

REFLECTIVE LISTENING
A skill intended to help the receiver and communicator clearly and fully understand the message sent.

and expressed, it is increasingly useful for the receiver to use additional reflective responses.

Paraphrasing the Expressed After an appropriate time, the receiver might paraphrase the expressed thoughts and feelings of the speaker. Paraphrasing is useful because it reflects back to the speaker the thoughts and feelings as the receiver heard them. This verbal response enables the receiver to build greater empathy, openness, and acceptance into the relationship while ensuring the accuracy of the communication process.

In the case of the software engineer, the supervisor may find paraphrasing the engineer's expressed thoughts and feelings particularly useful for both of them in developing a clearer understanding of the system problem. For example, the supervisor might say, "I hear you saying that you are very upset about this problem and that you are not yet clear about what is causing it." It is difficult to solve a problem until it is clearly understood.

Clarifying the Implicit People often communicate implicit thoughts and feelings about a problem in addition to their explicitly expressed thoughts and feelings. Implicit thoughts and feelings are not clearly or fully expressed. The receiver may or may not assume that the implicit thoughts and feelings are within the awareness of the speaker. For example, the software engineer may be anxious about how to talk with a difficult customer concerning the system problem. This may be implicit in her discussion with her supervisor because of the previous discussions about this customer. If her anxiety feelings are not expressed, the supervisor may want to clarify them. For example, the supervisor might say, "I hear that you are feeling very upset about the problem and may be worried about the customer's reaction when you inform him." This would help the engineer shift the focus of her attention from the main problem, which is in the software, to the important and related issue of discussing the matter with the customer.

Reflecting "Core" Feelings Next, the receiver should go beyond the explicit or implicit thoughts and feelings that the speaker is expressing. The receiver, in reflecting the core feelings that the speaker may be experiencing, is reaching beyond the immediate awareness level of the speaker. "Core" feelings are the deepest and most important ones from the speaker's perspective. For example, if the software engineer had not been aware of any anxiety in her relationship with the difficult customer, her supervisor's ability to sense the tension and bring it to the engineer's awareness would exemplify reflecting core feelings.

The receiver runs a risk of overreaching in reflecting core feelings if a secure, empathetic relationship with the speaker does not already exist or if strongly repressed feelings are reflected back. Even if the receiver is correct, the speaker may not want those feelings brought to awareness. Therefore, it is important to exercise caution and care in reflecting core feelings to a speaker.

Silence Long, extended periods of silence may cause discomfort and be a sign or source of embarrassment, but silence can help both speaker and listener in reflective listening. From the speaker's perspective, silence may be useful in moments of thought or confusion about how to express difficult ideas or feelings. The software engineer may need some patient, silent response as she thinks through what to say next. Listeners can use brief periods of silence to sort out their own thoughts and feelings from those of the speaker. Reflective listening focuses only on the latter. In the case of the software engineer's supervisor, any personal, angry feelings toward the difficult customer should not intrude on the engineer's immediate problem. Silence provides time to identify and isolate the listener's personal responses and exclude them from the dialogue.

Eye Contact Eye contact is a nonverbal behavior that may help open up a relationship and improve communication between two people. The absence of any direct eye contact during an exchange tends to close communication. Cultural and individual differences influence what constitutes appropriate eye contact. For example, some cultures, such as in India, place restrictions on direct eye contact initiated by women or children. Too much direct eye contact, regardless of the individual or culture, has an intimidating effect.

Moderate direct eye contact, therefore, communicates openness and affirmation without causing either speaker or listener to feel intimidated. Periodic aversion of the eyes allows for a sense of privacy and control, even in intense interpersonal communication.

One-Way versus Two-Way Communication Reflective listening encourages two-way communication. **Two-way communication** is an interactive form of communication in which there is an exchange of thoughts, feelings, or both and through which shared meaning often occurs. Problem solving and decision making are often examples of two-way communication. **One-way communication** occurs when a person sends a message to another person and no feedback, questions, or interaction follow. Giving instructions or giving directions are examples of one-way communication. One-way communication occurs whenever a person sends a one-directional message to a receiver with no reflective listening or feedback in the communication.

One-way communication is faster, although how much faster depends on the amount and complexity of information communicated and the medium chosen. Even though it is faster, one-way communication is often less accurate than two-way communication. This is especially true for complex tasks where clarifications and iterations may be required for task completion. Where time and accuracy are both important to the successful completion of a task, such as in combat or emergency situations, extensive training prior to execution enhances accuracy and efficiency of execution without two-way communication.[5] Firefighters and military combat personnel engage extensively

TWO-WAY COMMUNICATION
A form of communication in which the communicator and receiver interact.

ONE-WAY COMMUNICATION
Communication in which a person sends a message to another person and no feedback, questions, or interaction follow.

in such training to minimize the need for communication during emergencies. These highly trained professionals rely on fast, abbreviated, one-way communication as a shorthand for more complex information. However, this communication only works within the range of situations for which the professionals are specifically trained.

It is difficult to draw general conclusions about people's satisfaction with one-way versus two-way communication. For example, communicators with a stronger need for feedback or who are not uncomfortable with conflicting or confusing questions may find two-way communication more satisfying. In contrast, receivers who believe that a message is very straightforward may be satisfied with one-way communication and dissatisfied with two-way communication because of its lengthy, drawn-out nature.

FIVE KEYS TO EFFECTIVE SUPERVISORY COMMUNICATION

3. *Describe the five communication skills of effective supervisors.*

Interpersonal communication, especially between managers and employees, is a critical foundation for effective performance in organizations as well as health and well-being.[6] Language and power are intertwined in the communication that occurs between managers and their employees.[7] One large study of managers in a variety of jobs and industries found that managers with the most effective work units engaged in routine communication within their units, whereas the managers with the highest promotion rates engaged in networking activities with superiors.[8] Another study of male and female banking managers suggested that higher performing managers are better and less apprehensive communicators than lower performing managers.[9] Oral communication and voice behavior are important contextual performance skills that enhance the psychosocial quality of the work environment.

A review of the research on manager–employee communication identified five communication skills that distinguish "good" from "bad" supervisors.[10] These skills include being expressive speakers, empathetic listeners, persuasive leaders, sensitive people, and informative managers. Some supervisors are good and effective without possessing each of these skills, and some organizations value one or another skill over the others. Thus, dyadic relationships are at the core of much organization-based communication.[11]

EXPRESSIVE SPEAKERS

Better supervisors express their thoughts, ideas, and feelings and speak up in meetings. They are comfortable expressing themselves. They tend toward extroversion. Supervisors who are not talkative or who tend toward introversion may at times leave their employees wondering what their supervisors are thinking or how they feel about certain issues. Supervisors who speak out let the people they work with know where they stand, what they believe, and how they feel.

Challenge

ARE YOU A GOOD LISTENER?

Reflective listening is a skill that you can practice and learn. Here are ten tips to help you become a better listener.

1. Stop talking. You cannot listen if your mouth is moving.
2. Put the speaker at ease. Break the ice to help the speaker relax. Smile!
3. Show the speaker you want to listen. Put away your work. Do not look at your watch. Maintain good eye contact.
4. Remove distractions. Close your door. Do not answer the telephone.
5. Empathize with the speaker. Put yourself in the speaker's shoes.
6. Be patient. Not everyone delivers messages at the same pace.
7. Hold your temper. Do not fly off the handle.
8. Go easy on criticism. Criticizing the speaker can stifle communication.
9. Ask questions. Paraphrase and clarify the speaker's message.
10. Stop talking. By this stage, you are probably very tempted to start talking, but do not. Be sure the speaker has finished.

Think of the last time you had a difficult communication with someone at work or school. Evalute yourself in that situation against each of the ten items. Which one(s) do you need to improve on the most?

EMPATHETIC LISTENERS

In addition to being expressive speakers, the better supervisors are willing, empathetic listeners. They use reflective listening skills; they are patient with, and responsive to, problems that employees, peers, and others bring to them about their work. They respond to and engage the concerns of other people. For example, the president of a health care operating company estimated that he spent 70 percent of his interpersonal time at work listening to others.[12] He listens empathetically to some personal, as well as work, dilemmas without taking responsibility for others' problems or concerns. Empathetic listeners are able to hear the feelings and emotional dimensions of the messages people send them, as well as the content of the ideas and issues. Better supervisors are approachable and willing to listen to suggestions and complaints. This chapter's Challenge gives you an opportunity to evaluate how good a listener you are.

PERSUASIVE LEADERS (AND SOME EXCEPTIONS)

Better supervisors are persuasive leaders rather than directive, autocratic ones. All supervisors and managers must exercise power and influence in organizations if they are to ensure performance and achieve results. These better supervisors are distinguished by their use of persuasive communication when influencing others. Specifically, they encourage others to achieve results instead of telling others what to do. They are not highly directive or manipulative in their influence attempts.

The exceptions to this pattern of communication occur in emergency or high-risk situations, such as life-threatening traumas in medical emergency rooms or in oil rig firefighting. In these cases, the supervisor must be directive and assertive.

SENSITIVE TO FEELINGS

Better supervisors are also sensitive to the feelings, self-image, and psychological defenses of their employees. Although the supervisor is capable of giving criticism and negative feedback to employees, he or she does it confidentially and constructively. Care is taken to avoid giving critical feedback or reprimanding employees in public. Those settings are reserved for the praise of employees' accomplishments, honors, and achievements. In this manner, the better supervisors are sensitive to the self-esteem of others. They work to enhance that self-esteem as appropriate to the person's real talents, abilities, and achievements.

INFORMATIVE MANAGERS

Finally, better supervisors keep those who work for them well informed and are skilled at appropriately and selectively disseminating information. This role involves receiving large volumes of information, through a wide range of written and verbal communication media, and then filtering through the information before distributing it appropriately. The failure to filter and disseminate information selectively to employees can lead to either information overload for the employees or a lack of sufficient information for performance and task accomplishment. Better supervisors favor giving advance notice of organizational changes and explaining the rationale for organizational policies.

A person may become a good supervisor even in the absence of one of these communication skills. For example, a person with special talents in planning and organizing or in decision making may compensate for a shortcoming in expressiveness or sensitivity. Further, when supervisors and employees engage in overt behaviors of communication and forward planning, they have a greater number of agreements about the employee's performance and behavior.[13] Overall, interpersonal communication is a key foundation for human relationships.

4. *Explain five barriers to communication and how to overcome them.*

BARRIERS TO COMMUNICATION
Aspects such as physical separation, status differences, gender differences, cultural diversity, and language that can impair effective communication in a workplace.

BARRIERS TO COMMUNICATION

Barriers to communication are factors that block or significantly distort successful communication. About 20 percent of communication problems that cause organizational problems and drain profitability can be prevented or solved by communication policy guidelines.[14] Further, effective managerial communication skills help overcome some other, but not all, barriers to and problems with communication in organizations. These barriers to communication in organizations may be temporary and can be overcome. Awareness and recognition are the first steps in formulating ways to overcome the barriers. Five communication barriers are physical separation, status differences, gender differences, cultural diversity, and language. The discussion of each concludes with one or two ways to overcome the barrier.

PHYSICAL SEPARATION

The physical separation of people in the work environment poses a barrier to communication. Telephones and technology, such as electronic mail, often help bridge the physical gap. We address a variety of new technologies in the closing section of the chapter. Although telephones and technology can be helpful, they are not as information rich as face-to-face communication (see Table 7-1).

Periodic face-to-face interactions help overcome physical separation problems, because the communication is much richer, largely because of nonverbal cues. The richer the communication, the less the potential for confusion or misunderstandings. Another way to overcome the barrier of physical separation is through regularly scheduled meetings for people who are organizationally interrelated.

STATUS DIFFERENCES

Status differences related to power and the organizational hierarchy pose another barrier to communication among people at work, especially within manager–employee pairs.[15] Because the employee is dependent on the manager as the primary link to the organization, the employee is more likely to distort upward communication than either horizontal or downward communication.

Effective supervisory skills, discussed at the beginning of the chapter, make the supervisor more approachable and help reduce the risk of problems related to status differences. In addition, when employees feel secure, they are more likely to be straightforward in upward communication. The absence of status, power, and hierarchical differences, however, is not a cure-all. New information technologies provide another way to overcome status-difference barriers, because they encourage the formation of nonhierarchical working relationships.[16]

GENDER DIFFERENCES

Communication barriers can be explained in part by differences in conversational styles.[17] Thus, when people of different ethnic or class backgrounds talk to one another, what the receiver understands may not be the same as what the speaker meant. In a similar way, men and women have different conversational styles, which may pose a communication barrier between those of opposite sexes. For example, women prefer to converse face to face, whereas men are comfortable sitting side by side and concentrating on some focal point in front of them. Hence, conversation style differences may result in a failure to communicate between men and women. Again, what is said by one may be understood to have an entirely different meaning by the other. Male–female conversation is really cross-cultural communication. In a work context, one study found that female employees sent less information to their supervisors and experienced less information overload than did male employees.[18]

An important first step to overcoming the gender barrier to communication is developing an awareness of gender-specific differences in conversational style. These differences can enrich organizational communication and empower professional relationships.[19] A second step is to seek clarification of the person's meaning rather than freely interpreting meaning from one's own frame of reference.

CULTURAL DIVERSITY

Cultural values and patterns of behavior can be very confusing barriers to communication. Important international differences in work-related values exist between people in the United States, Germany, the United Kingdom, Japan, and other nations.[20] These value differences have implications for motivation, leadership, and teamwork in work organizations.[21] Habitual patterns of interaction within a culture often substitute for communication. Outsiders working in a culture foreign to them often find these habitual patterns confusing and at times bizarre. For example, the German culture places greater value on authority and hierarchical differences. It is therefore more difficult for German workers to engage in direct, open communication with their supervisors than it is for U.S. workers.[22]

These types of cultural stereotypes can be confusing and misleading in cross-cultural communications. When people from one culture view those in another culture through the lens of stereotypes, they in effect are discounting the individual differences within the other culture. For example, an Asian stereotype of Americans may be that they are aggressive and arrogant and, thus, insensitive and unapproachable. Or, an American stereotype of Chinese and Japanese may be that they are meek and subservient, unable to be appropriately strong and assertive. Individuals who depend on the accuracy of these forms of cultural stereotypes may be badly misled in communicating with those in other cultures.

A first step to overcoming cultural diversity as a communication barrier is increasing awareness and sensitivity. In addition, companies can provide seminars for expatriate managers as part of their training for overseas assignments. Bernard Isautier, chairman and CEO of PetroKazakstan, believes that understanding and communication are two keys to success with workplace diversity, which is an essential ingredient for success in international markets.[23] A second step is developing or acquiring a guide, map, or beacon for understanding and interacting with members of other cultures. One approach to doing this is to describe a nation in terms of a suitable and complex metaphor.[24] For example, Irish conversations, the Spanish bullfight, and American football are consensually derived metaphors that can enable those outside the culture to understand members within the culture.

LANGUAGE

Language is a central element in communication. It may pose a barrier if its use obscures meaning and distorts intent. Although English is the international language of aviation, it is not the international language of business. Where the native languages of supervisors and employees differ, the risk of barriers to communication exists. However, increasing numbers of business men and women are bilingual or multilingual. For example, former Honeywell CEO Michael Bonsignore's ability to speak four languages helped him conduct business around the world more fluently. Less obvious are subtle distinctions in dialects within the same language, which may cause confusion and miscommunication. For example, the word *lift* means an elevator in Great Britain and a ride in the United States. In a different vein, language barriers are created across disciplines and professional boundaries by technical terminology. Acronyms may be very useful to those on the inside of a profession or discipline as means of shorthand communication. Technical terms can convey precise meaning between professionals. However, acronyms and technical terms may only serve to confuse, obscure, and derail any attempt at clear understanding for people unfamiliar with their meaning and usage. For example, clinical depression has meaning to a professional psychologist and may have a wide range of meanings to a layperson. Use simple, direct, declarative language. Speak in brief sentences and use terms or words you have heard from your audience. As much as possible, speak in the language of the listener. Do not use jargon or technical language except with those who clearly understand it.

DEFENSIVE AND NONDEFENSIVE COMMUNICATION

Defensive communication in organizations also can create barriers between people, whereas nondefensive communication helps open up relationships.[25] *Defensive communication* includes both aggressive, attacking, angry communication and passive, withdrawing communication. **Nondefensive communication** is an assertive, direct, powerful form of communication. It is an alternative to defensive communication. Although aggressiveness and passiveness are both forms of defensive communication, assertiveness is nondefensive communication. Organizations are increasingly engaged in courtroom battles and media exchanges, which are especially fertile settings for defensive communication. Catherine Crier had extensive experience as a trial lawyer and judge in dealing with defensive people. She carried this knowledge over into her position as a news anchor for CNN, ABC, Fox News, and currently on Court TV as the host of "Catherine Crier Live." Her four basic rules are (1) define the situation, (2) clarify the person's position, (3) acknowledge the person's feelings, and (4) bring the focus back to the facts.

Defensive communication in organizations leads to a wide range of problems, including injured feelings, communication breakdowns, alienation in

5. *Distinguish between defensive and nondefensive communication.*

DEFENSIVE COMMUNICATION
Communication that can be aggressive, attacking, and angry, or passive and withdrawing.

NONDEFENSIVE COMMUNICATION
Communication that is assertive, direct, and powerful.

working relationships, destructive and retaliatory behaviors, nonproductive efforts, and problem-solving failures. When such problems arise in organizations, everyone is prone to blame everyone else for what is not working.[26] The defensive responses of counterattack or sheepish withdrawal derail communication. Such responses tend to lend heat, not light, to the communication. An examination of eight defensive tactics follows the discussion of the two basic patterns of defensiveness in the next section.

Nondefensive communication, in contrast, provides a basis for asserting and defending oneself when attacked, without being defensive. There are appropriate ways to defend oneself against aggression, attack, or abuse. An assertive, nondefensive style restores order, balance, and effectiveness in working relationships. A discussion of nondefensive communication follows the discussion of defensive communication.

DEFENSIVE COMMUNICATION AT WORK

Defensive communication often elicits defensive communication in response. The two basic patterns of defensiveness are dominant defensiveness and subordinate defensiveness. One must be able to recognize various forms of defensive communication before learning to engage in constructive, nondefensive communication.

Subordinate Defensiveness Subordinate defensiveness is characterized by passive, submissive, withdrawing behavior. The psychological attitude of the subordinately defensive person is "You are right, and I am wrong." People with low self-esteem may be prone to this form of defensive behavior, as well as people at lower organizational levels. When people at lower organizational levels fear sending bad news up the organization, information that is sensitive and critical to organizational performance may be lost.[27] People who are subordinately defensive do not adequately assert their thoughts and feelings in the workplace. Passive-aggressive behavior is a form of defensiveness that begins as subordinate defensiveness and ends up as dominant defensiveness. It is behavior that appears very passive but, in fact, masks underlying aggression and hostility.

Dominant Defensiveness Dominant defensiveness is characterized by active, aggressive, attacking behavior. It is offensive in nature: "The best defense is a good offense." The psychological attitude of the dominantly defensive person is "I am right, and you are wrong." People who compensate for low self-esteem may exhibit this pattern of behavior, as well as people who are in higher level positions within the organizational hierarchy.

Junior officers in a regional banking organization described such behavior in the bank chairman, euphemistically called "The Finger." When giving orders or admonishing someone, he would point his index finger in a domineering, intimidating, emphatic manner that caused defensiveness on the part of the recipient.

DEFENSIVE TACTICS

Unfortunately, defensive tactics are all too common in work organizations. Eight major defensive tactics are summarized in Table 7-2. They might be best understood in the context of a work situation: Joe is in the process of completing a critical report for his boss, and the report's deadline is drawing near. Mary, one of Joe's peers at work, is to provide him with some input for the report, and the department secretary is to prepare a final copy of the report. Each work example in the table is related to this situation.

Until defensiveness and defensive tactics are recognized for what they are, it is difficult either to change them or to respond to them in nondefensive ways. Defensive tactics are how defensive communication is acted out. In many cases, such tactics raise ethical dilemmas and issues for those involved. For example, is it ethical to raise doubts about another person's values, beliefs, or sexuality? At what point does simple defensiveness become unethical behavior?

Power plays are used by people to control and manipulate others through the use of choice definition (defining the choice another person is allowed to make), either/or conditions, and overt aggression. The underlying dynamic in power plays is that of domination and control.

A put-down is an effort by the speaker to gain the upper hand in the relationship. Intentionally ignoring another person or pointing out his or her mistakes in a meeting are kinds of put-downs.

Labeling is often used to portray another person as abnormal or deficient. Psychological labels are often used out of context for this purpose, such as calling a person "paranoid," a word that has a specific, clinical meaning.

Defensive Tactic	Speaker	Work Example
Power play	The boss	"Finish this report by month's end or lose your promotion."
Put-down	The boss	"A capable manager would already be done with this report."
Labeling	The boss	"You must be a slow learner. Your report is still not done?"
Raising doubts	The boss	"How can I trust you, Joe, if you can't finish an easy report?"
Misleading information	Joe	"Mary has not gone over with me the information I need from her for the report." (She left him a copy.)
Scapegoating	Joe	"Mary did not give me her input until just today."
Hostile jokes	Joe	"You can't be serious! The report isn't that important."
Deception	Joe	"I gave it to the secretary. Did she lose it?"

Table 7-2
Defensive Tactics

Raising doubts about a person's abilities, values, preferential orientations, or other aspects of his or her life creates confusion and uncertainty. This tactic tends to lack the specificity and clarity present in labeling.

Giving misleading information is the selective presentation of information designed to leave a false and inaccurate impression in the listener's mind. It is not the same as lying or misinforming. Giving misleading information is one form of deception.

Scapegoating and its companion, buck-passing, are methods of shifting responsibility to the wrong person. Blaming other people is another form of scapegoating or buck-passing.

Hostile jokes should not be confused with good humor, which is both therapeutic and nondefensive. Jokes created at the expense of others are destructive and hostile.

Deception may occur through a variety of means, such as lying or creating an impression or image that is at variance with the truth. Deception can be very useful in military operations, but it can be a destructive force in work organizations.

NONDEFENSIVE COMMUNICATION

Nondefensive communication is a constructive, healthy alternative to defensive communication in working relationships. The person who communicates nondefensively may be characterized as centered, assertive, controlled, informative, realistic, and honest. Nondefensive communication is powerful, because the speaker is exhibiting self-control and self-possession without rejecting the listener. Converting defensive patterns of communication to nondefensive ones enhances relationship building at work. Relationship building behaviors and communication help reduce adverse responses, such as blame and anger, following negative events at work.[28]

The subordinately defensive person needs to learn to be more assertive. This can be done in many ways, of which two examples follow. First, instead of asking for permission to do something, report what you intend to do, and invite confirmation. Second, instead of using self-deprecating words, such as "I'm just following orders," drop the *just,* and convert the message into a self-assertive, declarative statement. Nondefensive communication should be self-affirming without being self-aggrandizing. Some people overcompensate for subordinate defensiveness and inadvertently become domineering.

The person prone to be domineering and dominantly defensive needs to learn to be less aggressive. This may be especially difficult because it requires overcoming the person's sense of "I am right." People who are working to overcome dominant defensiveness should be particularly sensitive to feedback from others about their behavior. There are many ways to change this pattern of behavior. Here are two examples. First, instead of giving and denying permission, give people free rein except in situations where permission is essential as a means of clearing approval or ensuring the security of the task. Second, instead of becoming inappropriately angry, provide information about the adverse consequences of a particular course of action.

YOU BE THE JUDGE

If you believe that someone you are working with is lying about the work and deceiving your boss, but you do not have clear proof of it, what should you do?

NONVERBAL COMMUNICATION

Much defensive and nondefensive communication focuses on the language used. However, most of the meaning in a message (an estimated 65 to 90 percent) is conveyed through nonverbal communication.[29] *Nonverbal communication* includes all elements of communication, such as gestures and the use of space, that do not involve words or do not involve language.[30] The four basic kinds of nonverbal communication are proxemics, kinesics, facial and eye behavior, and paralanguage. They are important topics for managers attempting to understand the types and meanings of nonverbal signals from employees. Nonverbal communication is influenced by both psychological and physiological processes.[31]

Some scholars consider this area of communication to be less scientifically rigorous than other areas of communication. In any case, the interpretation of nonverbal communication is specific to the context of the interaction and the actors. That is, nonverbal cues only give meaning in the context of the situation and the interaction of the actors. For example, some federal and state judges attempt to curb nonverbal communication in the courtroom. The judges' primary concern is that nonverbal behavior may unfairly influence jurors' decisions. It is also important to note that nonverbal behavior is culturally bound. Gestures, facial expressions, and body locations have different meanings in different cultures. The globalization of business means managers should be sensitive to the nonverbal customs of other cultures in which they do business.

NONVERBAL COMMUNICATION
All elements of communication that do not involve words.

PROXEMICS

The study of an individual's perception and use of space, including territorial space, is called *proxemics*.[32] *Territorial space* refers to bands of space extending outward from the body. These bands constitute comfort zones. In each comfort zone, different cultures prefer different types of interaction with others. Figure 7-2 (on page 168) presents four zones of territorial space based on U.S. culture.

The first zone, intimate space, extends outward from the body to about 1½ feet. In this zone, we interact with spouses, significant others, family members, and others with whom we have an intimate relationship. The next zone, the personal distance zone, extends from 1½ feet outward to 4 feet. Friends typically interact within this distance. The third zone, the social distance zone, spans the distance from 4 to 12 feet. We prefer that business associates and acquaintances interact with us in this zone. The final zone is the public distance zone, extending 12 feet from the body outward. Most of us prefer that strangers stay at least 12 feet from us, and we become uncomfortable when they move closer.

Territorial space varies greatly across cultures. People often become uncomfortable when operating in territorial spaces different from those in which they are familiar. Edward Hall, a leading proxemics researcher, says Americans working in the Middle East tend to back away to a comfortable conversation distance when interacting with Arabs. Because Arabs' comfortable

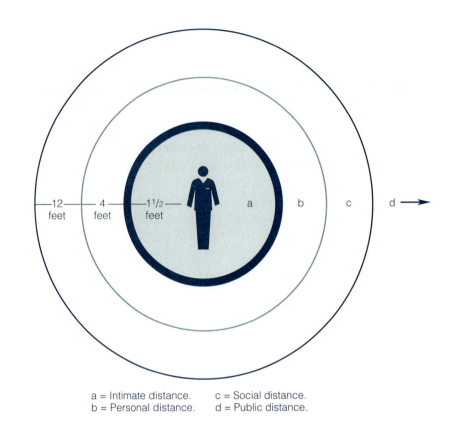

Figure 7-2
Zones of Territorial Space in
U.S. Culture

a = Intimate distance.   c = Social distance.
b = Personal distance.   d = Public distance.

conversation distance is closer than that of Americans, Arabs perceive Americans as cold and aloof. One Arab wondered, "What's the matter? Does he find me somehow offensive?"[33] Personal space tends to be larger in cultures with cool climates, such as the United States, Great Britain, and northern Europe, and smaller in cultures with warm climates, such as southern Europe, the Caribbean, India, or South America.[34]

Our relationships shape our use of territorial space. For example, we hold hands with, or put an arm around, significant others to pull them into intimate space. Conversely, the use of territorial space can shape people's interactions. A 4-foot-wide business desk pushes business interactions into the social distance zone. An exception occurred for one Southwestern Bell manager who met with her seven first-line supervisors around her desk. Being elbow to elbow placed the supervisors in one another's intimate and personal space. They appeared to act more like friends and frequently talked about their children, favorite television shows, and other personal concerns. When the manager moved the staff meeting to a larger room and the spaces around each supervisor were in the social distance zone, the personal exchanges ceased, and they acted more like business associates again.

Seating dynamics, another aspect of proxemics, is the art of seating people in certain positions according to the person's purpose in communication. Figure 7-3 depicts some common seating dynamics. To encourage cooperation, you should seat the other party beside you, facing the same di-

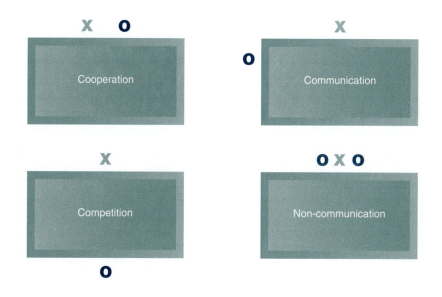

Figure 7-3
Seating Dynamics

rection. To facilitate direct and open communication, seat the other party across a corner of your desk from you or in another place where you will be at right angles. This allows for more honest disclosure. To take a competitive stand with someone, position the person directly across from you. Suppose you hold a meeting around a conference table, and two of the attendees are disrupting your meeting. Where should you seat them? If you place one on each side of yourself, it should stifle the disruptions (unless one is so bold as to lean in front of you to keep chatting).

KINESICS

Kinesics is the study of body movements, including posture.[35] Like proxemics, kinesics is culturally bound; there is no single universal gesture. For example, the U.S. hand signal for "okay" is an insult in other countries. With this in mind, we can interpret some common U.S. gestures. Rubbing one's hands together or exhibiting a sharp intake of breath indicates anticipation. Stress is indicated by a closed hand position (that is, tight fists), hand wringing, or rubbing the temples. Nervousness may be exhibited through drumming fingers, pacing, or jingling coins in the pocket. Perhaps most fun to watch is preening behavior, seen most often in couples on a first date. Preening communicates "I want to look good for you" to the other party and consists of smoothing skirts, straightening the tie, or arranging the hair. No discussion of gestures would be complete without mention of insult gestures—some learned at an early age, much to the anxiety of parents. Sticking out one's tongue and waving fingers with one's thumbs in the ears is a childhood insult gesture.

FACIAL AND EYE BEHAVIOR

The face is a rich source of nonverbal communication. Facial expression and eye behavior are used to add cues for the receiver. The face often gives unintended clues to emotions the sender is trying to hide.

Although smiles have universal meaning, frowns, raised eyebrows, and wrinkled foreheads must all be interpreted in conjunction with the actors, the situation, and the culture. One study of Japanese and U.S. students illustrates the point. The students were shown a stress-inducing film, and their facial expressions were videotaped. When alone, the students had almost identical expressions. However, the Japanese students masked their facial expressions of unpleasant feelings much better than did the American students when another person was present.[36]

As mentioned earlier, eye contact can enhance reflective listening, and it varies by culture. A direct gaze indicates honesty and forthrightness in the United States. This may not be true in other cultures. For example, Barbara Walters was uncomfortable interviewing Muammar al-Qaddafi in Libya because he did not look directly at her. However, in Libya, it is a serious offense to look directly at a woman.[37] In Asian cultures it is considered good behavior to bow the head in deference to a superior rather than to look in the supervisor's eyes.

PARALANGUAGE

Paralanguage consists of variations in speech, such as pitch, loudness, tempo, tone, duration, laughing, and crying.[38] People make attributions about the sender by deciphering paralanguage cues. A high-pitched, breathy voice in a female may contribute to the stereotype of the "dumb blonde." Rapid, loud speech may be taken as a sign of nervousness or anger. Interruptions such as "mmm" and "ah-hah" may be used to speed up the speaker so that the receiver can get in a few words. Clucking of the tongue or the "tsk-tsk" sound is used to shame someone. All these cues relate to how something is said.

HOW ACCURATELY DO WE DECODE NONVERBAL CUES?

Peoples' confidence in their ability to decode nonverbal communication is greater than their accuracy in doing so. Judges with several years' experience in interviewing were asked in one study to watch videotapes of job applicants and to rate the applicants' social skills and motivation levels.[39] The judges were fairly accurate about the social skills, but not about motivation. The judges relied on smiling, gesturing, and speaking as cues to motivation, yet none of these cues are motivation indicators. Thus, incorrectly interpreting nonverbal codes leads to inaccuracy.

Studies of deception emphasize how to use nonverbal cues to interpret whether someone is lying. In one simulation study, customers were asked to detect whether or not automobile salespeople were lying. The customers' ability to detect lies in this study was no better than chance. Does this suggest that salespeople are skilled deceivers who control nonverbal behaviors to prevent detection?[40]

Paul Ekman, a psychologist who has trained judges, Secret Service agents, and polygraphers to detect lies, says that the best way to detect lies is to look for inconsistencies in the nonverbal cues. Rapidly shifting facial

Nonverbal Communication	Signal Received	Reaction from Receiver
Manager looks away when talking to the employee.	Divided attention.	My supervisor is too busy to listen to my problem or simply does not care.
Manager fails to acknowledge greeting from fellow employee.	Unfriendliness.	This person is unapproachable.
Manager glares ominously (i.e., gives the evil eye).	Anger.	Reciprocal anger, fear, or avoidance, depending on who is sending the signal in the organization.
Manager rolls the eyes.	Not taking person seriously.	This person thinks he or she is smarter or better than I am.
Manager sighs deeply.	Disgust or displeasure.	My opinions do not count. I must be stupid or boring to this person.
Manager uses heavy breathing (sometimes accompanied by hand waving).	Anger or heavy stress.	Avoid this person at all costs.
Manager does not maintain eye contact when communicating.	Suspicion or uncertainty.	What does this person have to hide?
Manager crosses arms and leans away.	Apathy or closed-mindedness.	This person already has made up his or her mind; my opinions are not important.
Manager peers over glasses.	Skepticism or distrust.	He or she does not believe what I am saying.
Manager continues to read a report when employee is speaking.	Lack of interest.	My opinions are not important enough to get the supervisor's undivided attention.

Source: From "Steps to Better Listening" by C. Hamilton and B. H. Kleiner. Copyright © February 1987. Reprinted with permission, *Personnel Journal*, all rights reserved.

Table 7-3
Common Nonverbal Cues from Manager to Employee

expressions and discrepancies between the person's words and body, voice, or facial expressions are some clues.[41]

Nonverbal communication is important for managers because of its impact on the meaning of the message. However, a manager must consider the total message and all media of communication. A message can only be given meaning in context, and cues are easy to misinterpret. Table 7-3 presents common nonverbal behaviors exhibited by managers and how employees may interpret them. Nonverbal cues can give others the wrong signal.

COMMUNICATING THROUGH NEW TECHNOLOGIES

Nonverbal behaviors can be important in establishing trust in working relationships, but modern technologies may challenge our ability to maintain trust in relationships. New technologies are an essential feature of modern management. Many organizations around the world are now plugging into the Internet, an electronic and computer-based technology that allows for the easy transfer of information and data across continents.

6. *Describe contemporary information technologies used by managers.*

Managers in today's business world have access to more communication tools than ever before. An understanding of the use of these new technologies influences effective, successful communication. In addition, it is important to understand how these new technologies affect others' communication and behavior. Finally, information technology can encourage or discourage moral dialogue, and moral conversations are central to addressing ethical issues at work.[42]

WRITTEN COMMUNICATION

Many organizations are working toward paperless offices and paperless interfaces with their customers. Some written communication is still required, however. Forms are one category of written communication. Manuals are another. Policy manuals are important in organizations, because they set out guidelines for decision making and rules of actions for organizational members. Operations and procedures manuals explain how to perform various tasks and resolve problems that may occur at work. Reports are a third category of written communication; company annual reports are an example. Reports may summarize the results of a committee's or department's work or provide information on progress toward certain objectives.

Letters and memorandums are briefer, more frequently used categories of written communication in organizations. Letters are a formal means of communication—often with people outside the organization—and may vary substantially in length. Memorandums are another formal means of communication, often to constituencies within the organization. Memos are sometimes used to create a formal, historical record of a specific event or occurrence to which people in the organization may want to refer at some future date. Referring back to Table 7-1, we can conclude that written communication has the advantage of high to moderate data capacity and the possible disadvantage of moderate to low information richness.

COMMUNICATION TECHNOLOGIES

Computer-mediated communication was once used only by technical specialists but now influences virtually all managers' behavior in the work environment. Informational databases are becoming more commonplace. These databases provide a tremendous amount of information with the push of a button. Another example of an informational database is the type of system used in many university libraries, in which books and journals are available through an electronic card catalog.

Electronic mail systems represent another technology; users can leave messages via the computer to be accessed at any time by the receiver. This eliminates the time delay of regular mail and allows for immediate reply. Research comparing e-mail versus face-to-face communication on choices individuals make found that the effects vary with the nature of the decisions and may depend on the complexity and content of what needs to be communicated.[43] Thus, e-mail has strengths and advantages in communication as well as limitations with which to exercise caution. Unfortunately, some people feel much less inhibited when using e-mail, and end up sending caustic messages they would never consider saying in person. The Mood-Watch software system helps guard against "flaming" e-mails. In addition and on a positive note, there are also devices that enable international e-mail users to have their messages translated to and from French, German, Spanish, Portuguese, and English.

Voice mail systems are another widely used communication mode, especially in sales jobs where people are away from the office. Voice behavior influences the quality of the work environment. This has implications for the quality of voice mail as well. Some voice mail systems allow the user to retrieve messages from remote locations. Timely retrieval of messages is important. One manager in the office furniture industry had a problem with her voice mail when first learning to use it. She would forget to check it until late in the day. Employees with problems early in the day felt frustrated with her slow response time. When using voice mail, it is important to remember that the receiver may not retrieve the messages in a timely manner. Urgent messages must be delivered directly.

Facsimile (fax) machine systems allow the immediate transmission of documents. This medium allows the sender to communicate facts, graphs, and illustrations very rapidly. Fax machines are used in cars, as well as offices and remote locations.

Cell phones are also commonplace, permitting communication while away from the office and on the commute to and from work. They are used extensively in sales jobs involving travel. Not all reactions to car phones are positive. For example, one oil producer did not want his thinking time while driving disturbed by a cell phone. Cell phones while driving are also risky, with some estimates suggesting that using a cell phone while driving is as risky as driving while under the influence of alcohol. For this reason, some states have outlawed the use of cell phones while driving a motor vehicle.

How Do Communication Technologies Affect Behavior?

The *new communication technologies* provide faster, more immediate access to information than was available in the past. They provide instant exchange of information in minutes or seconds across geographic boundaries and time zones. Schedules and office hours become irrelevant. The normal considerations of time and distance become less important in the exchange. Hence, these technologies have important influences on people's behavior.

One aspect of computer-mediated communication is its impersonal nature. The sender interacts with a machine, not a person. As mentioned earlier, studies show that using these technologies results in an increase in flaming, or making rude or obscene outbursts by computer.[44] Interpersonal skills like tact and graciousness diminish, and managers are more blunt when using electronic media. People who participate in discussions quietly and politely when face to face may become impolite, more intimate, and uninhibited when they communicate using computer conferencing or electronic mail.[45]

YOU BE THE JUDGE

Should you leave confidential messages on a voice mail system in someone's office because you assume that only that person will listen to the voice mail? Can you be confident about the security of an electronic mail system?

NEW COMMUNICATION TECHNOLOGY
The various new technologies—such as electronic mail, voice mail, and fax machines—which are used for interpersonal communication.

Another effect of the new technologies is that the nonverbal cues we rely on to decipher a message are absent. Gesturing, touching, facial expressions, and eye contact are not available, so the emotional element of the message is difficult to access. In addition, clues to power, such as organizational position and departmental membership, may not be available, so the social context of the exchange is altered.

Communication via technologies also changes group interaction. It tends to equalize participation, because group members participate more equally, and charismatic or higher status members may have less power.[46] Studies of groups that make decisions via computer interaction (computer-mediated groups) have shown that the computer-mediated groups took longer to reach consensus than face-to-face groups. In addition, they were more uninhibited, and there was less influence from any one dominant person. It appears that groups that communicate by computer experience a breakdown of social and organizational barriers.

The potential for overload is particularly great with the new communication technologies. Not only is information available more quickly; the sheer volume of information at the manager's fingertips also is staggering. An individual can easily become overwhelmed by information and must learn to be selective about the information accessed.

A paradox created by the new, modern communication technology lies in the danger it may pose for managers. The danger is that managers cannot get away from the office as much as in the past, because they are more accessible to coworkers, subordinates, and the boss via telecommunications. Interactions are no longer confined to the 8:00 to 5:00 work hours.

In addition, the use of new technologies encourages polyphasic activity (that is, doing more than one thing at a time). Managers can simultaneously make phone calls, send computer messages, and work on memos. Polyphasic activity has its advantages in terms of getting more done—but only up to a point. Paying attention to more than one task at a time splits a person's attention and may reduce effectiveness. Constantly focusing on multiple tasks can become a habit, making it psychologically difficult for a person to let go of work.

Finally, the new technologies may make people less patient with face-to-face communication. The speed advantage of the electronic media may translate into an expectation of greater speed in all forms of communication. However, individuals may miss the social interaction with others and may find their social needs unmet. Communicating via computer means an absence of small talk; people tend to get to the point right away.

With many of these technologies, the potential for immediate feedback is reduced, and the exchange can become one way. Managers can use the new technologies more effectively by keeping the following hints in mind:

1. Strive for completeness in your message.

2. Build in opportunities for feedback.

3. Do not assume you will get an immediate response.

4. Ask yourself if the communication is really necessary.

5. "Disconnect" yourself from the technology at regular intervals.

6. Provide opportunities for social interaction at work.

MANAGERIAL IMPLICATIONS: COMMUNICATE WITH STRENGTH AND CLARITY

Interpersonal communication is important for the quality of working relationships in organizations. Managers who are sensitive and responsive in communicating with employees encourage the development of trusting, loyal relationships. Managers and employees alike benefit from secure working relations. Managers who are directive, dictatorial, or overbearing with employees, in contrast, are likely to find such behavior counterproductive, especially in periods of change.

Encouraging feedback and practicing reflective listening skills at work can open up communication channels in the work environment. Open communication benefits decision-making processes, because managers are better informed and more likely to base decisions on complete information. Open communication encourages nondefensive relationships, as opposed to defensive relationships, among people at work. Defensive relationships create problems because of the use of tactics that create conflict and division among people.

Managers benefit from sensitivity to employees' nonverbal behavior and territorial space, recognizing that understanding individual and cultural diversity is important in interpreting a person's nonverbal behavior. Seeking verbal clarification on nonverbal cues improves the accuracy of the communication and helps build trusting relationships. In addition, managers benefit from an awareness of their own nonverbal behaviors. Seeking employee feedback about their own nonverbal behavior helps managers provide a message consistent with their intentions.

Managers may complement good interpersonal contact with the appropriate use of new information technology. New information technologies' high data capacity is an advantage in a global workplace. The high information richness of interpersonal contacts is an advantage in a culturally diverse work force. Therefore, managers benefit from both interpersonal and technological media by treating them as complementary modes of communication, not as substitutes for each other.

KEY TERMS

barriers to communication	interpersonal communication	one-way communication
communication	language	perceptual screen
communicator	message	receiver
data	new communication technology	reflective listening
defensive communication	nondefensive communication	richness
feedback loop	nonverbal communication	two-way communication
information		

Experiential Exercise

PREPARING FOR AN EMPLOYMENT-SELECTION INTERVIEW

The purpose of this exercise is to help you develop guidelines for an employment-selection interview. Employment-selection interviews are one of the more important settings in which supervisors and job candidates use applied communication skills. There is always the potential for defensiveness and confusion as well as lack of complete information exchange in this interview. This exercise allows you to think through ways to maximize the value of an employment-selection interview, whether you are the supervisor or the candidate, so that it is a productive experience based on effective applied communication.

Your instructor will form your class into groups of students. Each group should work through steps 1 and 2 of the exercise.

Step 1. *Guidelines for the Supervisor*
Develop a set of guidelines for the supervisor in preparing for and then conducting an employment-selection interview. Consider the following questions in developing your guidelines.

   a. What should the supervisor do before the interview?

   b. How should the supervisor act and behave during the interview?

   c. What should the supervisor do after the interview?

Step 2. *Guidelines for the Employee*
Develop another set of guidelines for the employee in preparing for and then being involved in an employment-selection interview. Consider the following questions in developing your guidelines.

   a. What should the employee do before the interview?

   b. How should the employee act and behave during the interview?

   c. What should the employee do after the interview?

Once each group has developed the two sets of guidelines, the instructor will lead the class in a general discussion in which groups share and compare their guidelines. Consider the following questions during this discussion.

1. What similarities are there among the groups for each set of guidelines?

2. What unique or different guidelines have some of the groups developed?

3. What are essential guidelines for conducting an employment-selection interview?

8

Work Teams and Groups

LEARNING OBJECTIVES

After reading this chapter, you should be able to do the following:

1. Define *group* and *work team*.

2. Explain four important aspects of group behavior.

3. Describe group formation, the four stages of a group's development, and the characteristics of a mature group.

4. Explain the task and maintenance functions in teams.

5. Discuss quality circles and quality teams.

6. Identify the social benefits of group and team membership.

7. Discuss empowerment, teamwork, and self-managed teams.

8. Explain the importance of upper echelons and top management teams.

Northrop Grumman was able to achieve teamwork among employees, customers, and partners through knowledge sharing in integrated product teams.[1] Not all teams and groups work face to face. In today's information age, advanced computer and telecommunications technologies enable organizations to be more flexible through the use of virtual teams.[2] Virtual teams also address new workforce demographics, enabling companies to access expertise and the best employees who may be located anywhere in the world. Whether a traditional group or a virtual team, groups and teams continue to play a vital role in organizational behavior and performance at work.

A **group** is two or more people having common interests, objectives, and continuing interaction. Table 8-1 summarizes the characteristics of a well-functioning, effective group.[3] A **work team** is a group of people with complementary skills who are committed to a common mission, performance goals, and approach for which they hold themselves mutually accountable.[4] All work teams are groups, but not all groups are work teams. Groups emphasize individual leadership, individual accountability, and individual work products. Work teams emphasize shared leadership, mutual accountability, and collective work products.

The chapter begins with a traditional discussion of group behavior and group development in the first two sections. The third section discusses teams. The final two sections explore the contemporary team issues of empowerment, self-managed teams, and upper echelon teams.

1. *Define group and work team.*

GROUP
Two or more people with common interests, objectives, and continuing interaction.

WORK TEAM
A group of people with complementary skills who are committed to a common mission, performance goals, and approach for which they hold themselves mutually accountable.

GROUP BEHAVIOR

2. *Explain four important aspects of group behavior.*

Group behavior has been a subject of interest in social psychology for a long time, and many different aspects of group behavior have been studied over the years. We now look at four topics relevant to groups functioning in organizations: norms of behavior, group cohesion, social loafing, and loss of individuality. Group behavior topics related to decision making, such as polarization and groupthink, are addressed in Chapter 9.

Table 8-1
Characteristics of a Well-Functioning, Effective Group

- The atmosphere tends to be relaxed, comfortable, and informal.
- The group's task is well understood and accepted by the members.
- The members listen well to one another; most members participate in a good deal of task-relevant discussion.
- People express both their feelings and their ideas.
- Conflict and disagreement are present and centered around ideas or methods, not personalities or people.
- The group is aware and conscious of its own operation and function.
- Decisions are usually based on consensus, not majority vote.
- When actions are decided, clear assignments are made and accepted by members of the group.

NORMS OF BEHAVIOR

The standards that a work group uses to evaluate the behavior of its members are its *norms of behavior*. These norms may be written or un-written, verbalized or not verbalized, implicit or explicit. As long as individual members of the group understand the norms, the norms can be effective in influencing behavior. Norms may specify what members of a group should do (such as a specified dress code for men and for women), or they may specify what members of a group should not do (such as executives not behaving arrogantly with employees).

Norms may exist in any aspect of work group life. They may evolve informally or unconsciously within a group, or they may arise in response to challenges, such as the norm of disciplined behavior by firefighters in responding to a three-alarm fire to protect the group.[5] Performance norms are among the most important group norms from the organization's perspective, as we discuss in a later section of this chapter. Organizational culture and corporate codes of ethics, such as Johnson & Johnson's credo (see Chapter 2), reflect behavioral norms expected within work groups. Finally, norms that create awareness of emotions and help regulate emotions are critical to groups' effectiveness.[6]

GROUP COHESION

The "interpersonal glue" that makes the members of a group stick together is *group cohesion*. Group cohesion can enhance job satisfaction for members and improve organizational productivity.[7] Highly cohesive groups at work may not have many interpersonal exchanges away from the work-place. Nevertheless, they are able to control and manage their membership better than work groups low in cohesion. This is due to the strong motivation in highly cohesive groups to maintain good, close relationships among the members. We examine group cohesion in further detail, along with factors leading to high levels of group cohesion, when discussing the common characteristics of well-developed groups.

SOCIAL LOAFING

Social loafing occurs when one or more group members rely on the efforts of other group members and fail to contribute their own time, effort, thoughts, or other resources to a group.[8] This may create a real drag on the group's efforts and achievements. Some scholars argue that, from the individual's standpoint, social loafing, or free riding, is rational behavior in response to an experience of inequity or when individual efforts are hard to observe. However, it shortchanges the group, which loses potentially valuable resources possessed by individual members.[9]

A number of methods for countering social loafing exist, such as having identifiable individual contributions to the group product and member self-evaluation systems. For example, if each group member is responsible for a specific input to the group, a member's failure to contribute will be noticed by everyone. If members must formally evaluate their contributions to the group, they are less likely to loaf.

NORMS OF BEHAVIOR
The standards that a work group uses to evaluate the behavior of its members.

GROUP COHESION
The "interpersonal glue" that makes members of a group stick together.

SOCIAL LOAFING
The failure of a group member to contribute personal time, effort, thoughts, or other resources to the group.

YOU BE THE JUDGE

Assume that someone is engaged in social loafing in a group of which you are a member. What should you do? Is this person acting in an unethical manner?

LOSS OF INDIVIDUALITY

Social loafing may be detrimental to group achievement, but it does not have the potentially explosive effects of **loss of individuality**. Loss of individuality, or deindividuation, is a social process in which individual group members lose self-awareness and its accompanying sense of accountability, inhibition, and responsibility for individual behavior.[10]

When individuality is lost, people may engage in morally reprehensible acts and even violent behavior as committed members of their group or organization. For example, loss of individuality was one of several contributing factors in the violent and aggressive acts that led to the riot that destroyed sections of Los Angeles following the Rodney King verdict in the early 1990s. Loss of individuality is not always negative or destructive, however. The loosening of normal ego control mechanisms in the individual may lead to prosocial behavior and heroic acts in dangerous situations.[11] A group that successfully develops into a mature group may not encounter problems with loss of individuality.

GROUP FORMATION AND DEVELOPMENT

3. *Describe group formation, the four stages of a group's development, and the characteristics of a mature group.*

After its formation, a group goes through predictable stages of development. If successful, it emerges as a mature group. One logical group development model proposes four stages following the group's formation.[12] These stages are mutual acceptance, decision making, motivation and commitment, and control and sanctions. To become a mature group, each of the stages in development must be successfully negotiated.

According to this group development model, a group addresses three issues: interpersonal issues, task issues, and authority issues.[13] The interpersonal issues include matters of trust, personal comfort, and security. The task issues include the mission or purpose of the group, the methods the group employs, and the outcomes expected of the group. The authority issues include decisions about who is in charge, how power and influence are managed, and who has the right to tell whom to do what. This section addresses group formation, each stage of group development, and the characteristics of a mature group.

GROUP FORMATION

Formal and informal groups form in organizations for different reasons. Formal groups are sometimes called official or assigned groups, and informal groups may be called unofficial or emergent groups. Formal groups gather to perform various tasks and include an executive and staff, standing committees of the board of directors, project task forces, and temporary committees. An example of a formal group is the task force assembled by The University of Texas at Arlington, whose mission is to design the Goolsby Leadership Academy that will bridge academics and practice. Chaired by the associate dean of business, the task force is composed of seven members with diverse academic expertise and business experience. The task force envisions a five-year developmental plan to create a national center of excellence in preparing Goolsby Fellows for ethical leadership in the twenty-first century.

Diversity is an important consideration in the formation of groups. For example, Monsanto Agricultural Company (MAC—later Monsanto Company) created a task force titled Valuing Diversity to address subtle discrimination resulting from workforce diversity.[14] The original task force was titled Eliminating Subtle Discrimination (ESD) and was composed of fifteen women, minorities, and white males. Subtle discrimination might include the use of gender- or culture-specific language. MAC's and the task force's intent was to build on individual differences—whether in terms of gender, race, or culture—in developing a dominant heterogeneous culture. Diversity can enhance group performance. One study of gender diversity among U.S. workers found that men and women in gender-balanced groups had higher job satisfaction than those in homogeneous groups.[15]

Ethnic diversity has characterized many industrial work groups in the United States since the 1800s. This was especially true during the early years of the 1900s, when waves of immigrant workers arrived from Germany, Yugoslavia, Italy, Poland, Scotland, the Scandinavian countries, and many other nations. Organizations were challenged to blend these culturally and linguistically diverse peoples into effective work groups.

In addition to ethnic, gender, and cultural diversity, there is interpersonal diversity. Chaparral Steel Company (part of Texas Industries) has a team of officers who achieved compatibility through interpersonal diversity. Successful interpersonal relationships are the basis of group effort, a key foundation for business success. In the case of the Chaparral Steel officers, they differed in their needs for inclusion in activities, control of people and events, and interpersonal affection from others. Though diverse in their interpersonal needs, the officers as a group found strength through balance and complementarity.

Informal groups evolve in the work setting to gratify a variety of member needs not met by formal groups. For example, organizational members' inclusion and affection needs might be satisfied through informal athletic or interest groups. Athletic teams representing a department, unit, or company may achieve semiofficial status, such as the American Airlines long-distance running teams that use the corporate logo on their race shirts.

STAGES OF GROUP DEVELOPMENT

All groups, formal and informal, go through four stages of development: mutual acceptance, decision making, motivation and commitment, and control and sanctions. These stages and the emphases in each are shown in Figure 8-1 (on page 182). Demographic diversity and group fault lines (i.e., potential breaking points in a group) are two potential predictors of the sense-making process, subgroup formation patterns, and the nature of group

Stage

Emphasis

Interpersonal Concern and Awareness	Task Planning Authority and Influence	Task Accomplishment Leadership and Performance	Rewards and Punishment

Figure 8-1
Stages of Group Development

conflict at various stages of group development.[16] Hence, group development through these four stages may not always be smooth.

Mutual Acceptance Mutual acceptance is the first stage in a group's development. In this stage, the focus is on the interpersonal relations among the members. Members assess one another with regard to trustworthiness, emotional comfort, and evaluative acceptance. For the Valuing Diversity task force at MAC, trust was one of the early issues to be worked through. The power, influence, and authority issues may also emerge at this point if strong personalities immediately attempt to dominate other group members or dictate the group's agenda. This authority issue is also an interpersonal issue related to trust and acceptance. Once team members establish a comfortable level of mutual trust and acceptance, they can focus their attention on the work of the group.

Decision Making Planning and decision making occur during the second stage of a group's development. The focus turns from interpersonal relations to decision-making activities related to the group's task accomplishment. Specifically, the group must make decisions about what its task is and how to accomplish that task. Wallace Supply Company, an industrial distributor of pipes, valves, and fittings, found employee teams particularly valuable in this aspect of work life.[17] This second stage may be thought of as the planning stage in a group's development. In addition, the issue of authority often begins to surface during this stage of development, if it did not surface during the first stage. The group addresses authority questions like these: Who is responsible for what aspects of the group's work? Does the group need one primary leader and spokesperson?

Motivation and Commitment In the third stage of development, the group has largely resolved the interpersonal and task issues. Member attention is directed to self-motivation and the motivation of other group members for task accomplishment. Some members focus on the task function of initiating activity and ensure that the work of the group really gets moving. Other members contribute to motivation and commitment within the group through maintenance functions such as supporting, encouraging, and recognizing the contributions of their teammates or through establishing the standards that the team may use in evaluating its performance and members.

The latter contribution is illustrated by a twenty-five-member leadership group that monitors "the flow," Eastman Kodak's unique black-and-white film production process named for its layout design. The people who work the flow are called Zebras. With motivation, commitment, and evaluative feedback from the twenty-five-person leadership team, the Zebras substantially enhanced productivity, profitability, and morale.

The emphasis during the motivation and commitment stage of team development is on execution and achievement, whether through a process of questioning and prodding or through facilitation and workload sharing. If key decisions or plans established in the second stage of development need to be revisited, they are, but only in the context of getting work done.

Control and Sanctions   In its final stage of development, a group has become a mature, effective, efficient, and productive unit. The group has successfully worked through necessary interpersonal, task, and authority issues. A mature group is characterized by a clear purpose or mission; a well-understood set of norms of behavior; a high level of cohesion; and a clear, but flexible, status structure of leader–follower relationships. A mature group is able to control its members through the judicious application of specific positive and negative sanctions based on the evaluation of specific member behaviors. Recent research shows that evaluation biases stemming from liking someone operate in face-to-face groups but not in electronic groups, such as virtual teams.[18] If the group's membership changes, either through a loss of an established member or the inclusion of a newcomer, it may well engage in some activities common in earlier stages of development as it accommodates the newcomer or adjusts to the loss.

CHARACTERISTICS OF A MATURE GROUP

The description of a well-functioning, effective group in Table 8-1 characterizes a mature group. Such a group has four distinguishing characteristics: a clear purpose and mission, well-understood norms and standards of conduct, a high level of group cohesion, and a flexible status structure.

Purpose and Mission   The purpose and mission may be assigned to a group (as in the case of The University of Texas at Arlington's mission to design the Goolsby Leadership Academy) or emerge from within the group (as in the case of the American Airlines long-distance running teams). Even in the case of an assigned mission, the group may reexamine, modify, revise, or question the mission. It may also embrace the mission as stated. The importance of mission is exemplified in IBM's Process Quality Management, which requires that a process team of not more than twelve people develop a clear understanding of mission as the first step in the process.[19] The IBM approach demands that all members agree to go in the same direction. The mission statement is converted into a specific agenda, clear goals, and a set of critical success factors. Stating the purpose and mission in the form of specific goals enhances productivity over and above any performance benefits achieved through individual goal setting.[20]

Behavioral Norms Behavioral norms, which evolve over a period of time, are well-understood standards of behavior within a group.[21] They are benchmarks against which team members are evaluated and judged by other team members. Some behavioral norms become written rules, such as an attendance policy or an ethical code for a team. Other norms remain informal, although they are no less well understood by team members. Dress codes and norms about after-hours socializing may fall into this category. Behavioral norms also evolve around performance and productivity.[22] Productivity norms even influence the performance of sports teams.[23] The group's productivity norm may or may not be consistent with, and supportive of, the organization's productivity standards. A high-performance team sets productivity standards above organizational expectations with the intent to excel. Average teams set productivity standards based on, and consistent with, organizational expectations. Noncompliant or counterproductive teams may set productivity standards below organizational expectations with the intent of damaging the organization or creating change.

Group Cohesion Group cohesion was earlier described as the interpersonal attraction binding group members together. It enables a group to exercise effective control over its members in relation to its behavioral norms and standards. Goal conflict in a group, unpleasant experiences, and domination of a subgroup are among the threats to a group's cohesion. Groups with low levels of cohesion have greater difficulty exercising control over their members and enforcing their standards of behavior. A classic study of cohesiveness in 238 industrial work groups found cohesion to be an important factor influencing anxiety, tension, and productivity within the groups.[24] Specifically, work-related tension and anxiety were lower in teams high in cohesion, and they were higher in teams low in cohesion, as depicted in Figure 8-2. This suggests that cohesion has a calming effect on team members, at least concerning work-related tension and anxiety. In addition, actual productivity was found to vary significantly less in highly cohesive teams, making these teams much more predictable with regard to their productivity. The actual productivity levels were primarily determined by the productivity norms within each work group. That is, highly cohesive groups with high production standards are very productive. Similarly, highly cohesive groups with low productivity standards are unproductive. Member satisfaction, commitment, and communication are better in highly cohesive groups. Groupthink may be a problem in highly cohesive groups and is discussed in Chapter 9.

Group cohesion is influenced by a number of factors, most notably time, size, the prestige of the team, external pressure, and internal competition.

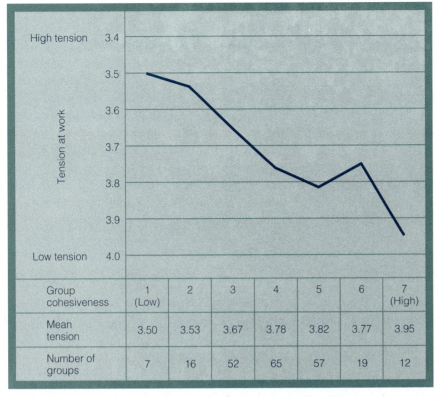

Group cohesiveness	1 (Low)	2	3	4	5	6	7 (High)
Mean tension	3.50	3.53	3.67	3.78	3.82	3.77	3.95
Number of groups	7	16	52	65	57	19	12

Note: Product-moment correlation is .28, and critical ratio is 4.20; p is less than .001.

[a]The measure of tension at work is based on group mean response to the question "Does your work ever make you feel 'jumpy' or nervous?" A low numerical score represents relatively high tension.

Source: From S. E. Seashore, *Group Cohesiveness in the Industrial Work Group*, 1954. Research conducted by Stanley E. Seashore at the Institute for Social Research, University of Michigan. Reprinted by permission.

Figure 8-2
Cohesiveness and Work-Related Tension[a]

Group cohesion evolves gradually over time through a group's normal development. Smaller groups—those of five or seven members, for example—are more cohesive than those of more than twenty-five, although cohesion does not decline much with size after forty or more members. Prestige or social status also influences a group's cohesion, with more prestigious groups, such as the U.S. Air Force Thunderbirds or the U.S. Navy Blue Angels, being highly cohesive. However, even groups of very low prestige may be highly cohesive in how they stick together. Finally, external pressure and internal competition influence group cohesion. Although the mechanics' union, pilots, and other internal constituencies at Eastern Airlines had various differences of opinion, they all pulled together in a cohesive fashion in resisting Frank Lorenzo when he came in to reshape the airline before its demise. Whereas external pressures tend to enhance cohesion, internal competition usually decreases cohesion within a team. However, one study found that company-imposed work pressure disrupted group cohesion by increasing internal competition and reducing cooperative interpersonal activity.[25]

Status Structure **Status structure** is the set of authority and task relations among a group's members. The status structure may be hierarchical or

STATUS STRUCTURE
The set of authority and task relations among a group's members.

egalitarian (i.e., democratic), depending on the group. Successful resolution of the authority issue within a team results in a well-understood status structure of leader–follower relationships. Where leadership problems arise, it is important to find solutions and build team leader effectiveness.[26] Whereas groups tend to have one leader, teams tend to share leadership. For example, one person may be the team's task master, who sets the agenda, initiates much of the work activity, and ensures that the team meets its deadlines. Another team member may take a leadership role in maintaining effective interpersonal relationships in the group. Hence, shared leadership is very feasible in teams. An effective status structure results in role interrelatedness among group members.

Diversity in a group is healthy, and members may contribute to the collective effort through one of four basic styles.[27] These are the contributor, the collaborator, the communicator, and the challenger. The contributor is data driven, supplies necessary information, and adheres to high performance standards. The collaborator sees the big picture and is able to keep a constant focus on the mission and urge other members to join efforts for mission accomplishment. The communicator listens well, facilitates the group's process, and humanizes the collective effort. The challenger is the devil's advocate who questions everything from the group's mission, purpose, and methods to its ethics. Members may exhibit one or more of these four basic styles over a period of time. In addition, an effective group must have an integrator.[28] This can be especially important in cross-functional teams, where different perspectives carry the seeds of conflict. However, cross-functional teams are not necessarily a problem. Effectively managing cross-functional teams of artists, designers, printers, and financial experts enabled Hallmark Cards to cut its new-product development time in half.[29]

Emergent leadership in groups was studied among sixty-two men and sixty women.[30] Groups performed tasks not classified as either masculine or feminine, that is, "sex-neutral" tasks. Men and women both emerged as leaders, and neither gender had significantly more emergent leaders. However, group members who described themselves in masculine terms were significantly more likely to emerge as leaders than group members who described themselves in feminine, androgynous (both masculine and feminine), or undifferentiated (neither masculine nor feminine) terms. Hence, gender stereotypes may play a role in emergent leadership.

TASK AND MAINTENANCE FUNCTIONS

4. *Explain the task and maintenance functions in teams.*

An effective group or team carries out various task functions to perform its work successfully and various maintenance functions to ensure member satisfaction and a sense of team spirit.[31] Teams that successfully fulfill these functions afford their members the potential for psychological intimacy and integrated involvement. Table 8-2 presents nine task and nine maintenance functions in teams or groups.

TASK FUNCTION
An activity directly related to the effective completion of a team's work.

Task functions are those activities directly related to the effective completion of the team's work. For example, the task of initiating activity in-

Task Functions	Maintenance Functions
Initiating activities	Supporting others
Seeking information	Following others' leads
Giving information	Gatekeeping communication
Elaborating concepts	Setting standards
Coordinating activities	Expressing member feelings
Summarizing ideas	Testing group decisions
Testing ideas	Consensus testing
Evaluating effectiveness	Harmonizing conflict
Diagnosing problems	Reducing tension

Table 8-2
Task and Maintenance Functions in Teams or Groups

volves suggesting ideas, defining problems, and proposing approaches and/or solutions to problems. The task of seeking information involves asking for ideas, suggestions, information, or facts. Effective teams have members who fulfill various task functions as they are required.

Some task functions are more important at one time in the life of a group, and other functions are more important at other times. For example, during the engineering test periods for new technologies, the engineering team needs members who focus on testing the practical applications of suggestions and those who diagnose problems and suggest solutions.

The effective use of task functions leads to the success of the group, and the failure to use them may lead to disaster. For example, the successful initiation and coordination of an emergency room (ER) team's activities by the senior resident saved the life of a knife wound victim.[32] The victim was stabbed one-quarter inch below the heart, and the ER team acted quickly to stem the bleeding, begin intravenous fluids, and monitor the victim's vital signs.

Maintenance functions are those activities essential to the effective, satisfying interpersonal relationships within a group or team. For example, following another group member's lead may be as important as leading others. Communication gatekeepers within a group ensure balanced contributions from all members. Because task activities build tension into teams and groups working together, tension-reduction activities are important to drain off negative or destructive feelings. For example, in a study of twenty-five work groups over a five-year period, humor and joking behavior were found to enhance the social relationships in the groups.[33] The researchers concluded that performance improvements in the twenty-five groups indirectly resulted from improved relationships attributable to the humor and joking behaviors. Maintenance functions enhance togetherness, cooperation, and teamwork, enabling members to achieve psychological intimacy while furthering the success of the team. Jody Grant's supportive attitude and comfortable demeanor as chairman and CEO of Texas Capital Bancshares enabled him to build a vibrant bank in the aftermath of the great Texas banking crash. Grant was respected for his expertise *and* his ability to build relationships. Both task and maintenance functions are important for successful groups and teams.

MAINTENANCE FUNCTION
An activity essential to effective, satisfying interpersonal relationships within a team or group.

THE DECISION-MAKING PROCESS

Decision making is a critical activity in the lives of managers. The decisions a manager faces can range from very simple, routine matters for which the manager has an established decision rule (***programmed decisions***) to new and complex decisions that require creative solutions (***nonprogrammed decisions***).[1] Scheduling lunch hours for one's work group is a programmed decision. The manager performs the decision activity on a daily basis, using an established procedure with the same clear goal in mind. In contrast, decisions like buying out another company are nonprogrammed. The decision to acquire a company is unique and unstructured, and requires considerable judgment. Regardless of the type of decision made, it is helpful to understand as much as possible about how individuals and groups make decisions.

Decision making is a process involving a series of steps, as shown in Figure 9-1. The first step is recognition of the problem; that is, the manager realizes that a decision must be made. Identification of the real problem is important; otherwise, the manager may be reacting to symptoms and firefighting rather than dealing with the root cause of the problem. Next, a manager must identify the objective of the decision. In other words, the manager must determine what is to be accomplished by the decision.

The third step in the decision-making process is gathering information relevant to the problem. The manager must pull together sufficient information about why the problem occurred. This involves conducting a thorough diagnosis of the situation and going on a fact-finding mission.

The fourth step is listing and evaluating alternative courses of action. During this step, a thorough "what if" analysis should also be conducted to determine the various factors that could influence the outcome. It is important to generate a wide range of options and creative solutions in order to be able to move on to the fourth step.

Next, the manager selects the alternative that best meets the decision objective. If the problem has been diagnosed correctly and sufficient alternatives have been identified, this step is much easier.

Finally, the solution is implemented. The situation must then be monitored to see whether the decision met its objective. Consistent monitoring and periodic feedback are essential parts of the follow-up process.

Decision making can be stressful. Managers must make decisions with significant risk and uncertainty, and often without full information. They must trust and rely on others in arriving at their decisions, but they are ultimately responsible. Sometimes the decisions are painful and involve exiting businesses, firing people, and admitting wrong. When Raymond V. Gilmartin became CEO of Merck, he relocated the executive and marketing functions 20 miles away from Merck's large complex. Workers hated it, calling it "the mountaintop" and lamenting that executives had isolated themselves from scientists and other employees. Morale sagged, turnover doubled, and Merck struggled to replace its top 5 biggest selling drugs, which had lost their patent protection.[2]

PROGRAMMED DECISION
A simple, routine matter for which a manager has an established decision rule.

NONPROGRAMMED DECISION
A new, complex decision that requires a creative solution.

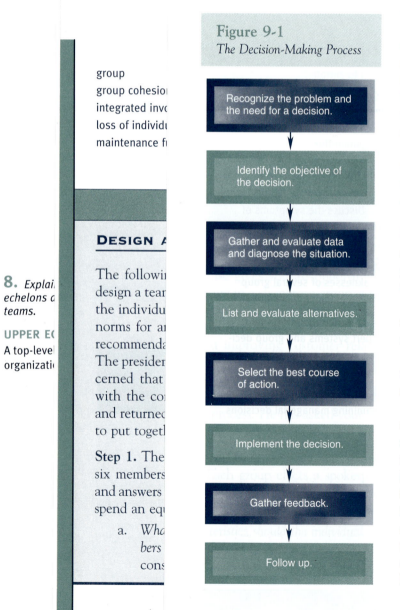

Figure 9-1
The Decision-Making Process

- Recognize the problem and the need for a decision.
- Identify the objective of the decision.
- Gather and evaluate data and diagnose the situation.
- List and evaluate alternatives.
- Select the best course of action.
- Implement the decision.
- Gather feedback.
- Follow up.

group
group cohesion
integrated invo
loss of individu
maintenance fu

DESIGN A

8. *Explai echelons c teams.*

UPPER E(
A top-level
organizatio

The followin
design a tear
the individu
norms for a
recommenda
The presider
cerned that
with the co
and returnec
to put togeth

Step 1. The
six members
and answers
spend an equ
   a. *Wha
   bers
   cons

MODELS OF DECISION MAKING

The success of any organization depends on managers' abilities to make *effective decisions*. An effective decision is timely, is acceptable to the individuals affected by it, and meets the desired objective.[3] This section describes three models of decision making: the rational model, the bounded rationality model, and the garbage can model.

RATIONAL MODEL

Rationality refers to a logical, step-by-step approach to decision making, with a thorough analysis of alternatives and their consequences. The rational model of decision making comes from classic economic theory and contends that the decision maker is completely rational in his or her approach. The rational model has the following important assumptions:

1. The outcome will be completely rational.
2. The decision maker has a consistent system of preferences, which is used to choose the best alternative.
3. The decision maker is aware of all the possible alternatives.
4. The decision maker can calculate the probability of success for each alternative.[4]

In the rational model, the decision maker strives to optimize, that is, to select the best possible alternative.

Given the assumptions of the rational model, it is unrealistic. There are time constraints and limits to human knowledge and information-processing capabilities. In addition, a manager's preferences and needs change often. The rational model is thus an ideal that managers strive for in making decisions. It captures the way a decision should be made but does not reflect the reality of managerial decision making.[5]

BOUNDED RATIONALITY MODEL

Recognizing the deficiencies of the rational model, Herbert Simon suggested that there are limits on how rational a decision maker can actually be. His decision theory, the bounded rationality model, earned a Nobel Prize in 1978.

Simon's model, also referred to as the "administrative man" theory, rests on the idea that there are constraints that force a decision maker to be less than completely rational. The bounded rationality model has four assumptions:

1. Managers select the first alternative that is satisfactory.
2. Managers recognize that their conception of the world is simple.
3. Managers are comfortable making decisions without determining all the alternatives.
4. Managers make decisions by rules of thumb or heuristics.

Bounded rationality assumes that managers *satisfice*; that is, they select the first alternative that is "good enough," because the costs of

EFFECTIVE DECISION
A timely decision that meets a desired objective and is acceptable to those individuals affected by it.

RATIONALITY
A logical, step-by-step approach to decision making, with a thorough analysis of alternatives and their consequences.

1. *Explain the assumptions of bounded rationality.*

BOUNDED RATIONALITY
A theory that suggests that there are limits to how rational a decision maker can actually be.

SATISFICE
To select the first alternative that is "good enough," because the costs in time and effort are too great to optimize.

HEURISTICS
Shortcuts in decision making that save mental activity.

GARBAGE CAN MODEL
A theory that contends that decisions in organizations are random and unsystematic.

Problems
Participants
Solutions
Choice opportunities

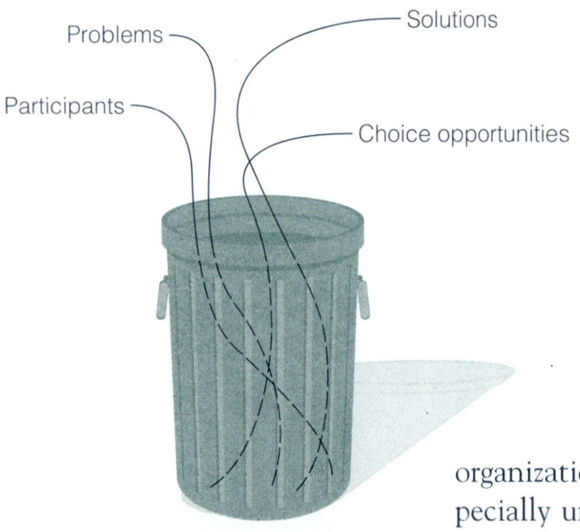

Figure 9-2
The Garbage Can Model

Source: From M. D. Cohen, J. G. March, and J. P. Olsen in *Administrative Science Quarterly* 17 (March 1972): 1–25. Reprinted by permission of the *Administrative Science Quarterly*.

RISK AVERSION
The tendency to choose options that entail fewer risks and less uncertainty.

optimizing in terms of time and effort are too great.[6] Further, the theory assumes that managers develop shortcuts, called *heuristics*, to make decisions in order to save mental activity. Heuristics are rules of thumb that allow managers to make decisions based on what has worked in past experiences.

Does the bounded rationality model more realistically portray the managerial decision process? Research indicates that it does.[7] One of the reasons managers face limits to their rationality is that they must make decisions under risk and time pressure. The situation they find themselves in is highly uncertain, and the probability of success is not known.

GARBAGE CAN MODEL

Sometimes the decision-making process in organizations appears to be haphazard and unpredictable. In the *garbage can model*, decisions are random and unsystematic.[8] Figure 9-2 depicts the garbage can model. In this model, the organization is a garbage can in which problems, solutions, participants, and choice opportunities are floating around randomly. If the four factors happen to connect, a decision is made.[9] The quality of the decision depends on timing. The right participants must find the right solution to the right problem at the right time.

The garbage can model illustrates the idea that not all organizational decisions are made in a step-by-step, systematic fashion. Especially under conditions of high uncertainty, the decision process may be chaotic. Some decisions appear to happen out of sheer luck.

On the high-speed playing field of today's businesses, managers must make critical decisions quickly, with incomplete information, and must also involve employees in the process.

DECISION MAKING AND RISK

Many decisions involve some element of risk. For managers, hiring decisions, promotions, delegation, acquisitions and mergers, overseas expansions, new product development, and other decisions make risk a part of the job.

RISK AND THE MANAGER

Individuals differ in terms of their willingness to take risks. Some people experience *risk aversion*. They choose options that entail fewer risks, preferring familiarity and certainty. Other individuals are risk takers; that is, they accept greater potential for loss in decisions, tolerate greater uncertainty, and in general are more likely to make risky decisions. Risk takers are also more likely to take the lead in group discussions.[10]

Research indicates that women are more averse to risk taking than men and that older, more experienced managers are more risk averse than younger managers. There is also some evidence that successful managers take more risks than unsuccessful managers.[11] However, the tendency to take risks or avoid them is only part of behavior toward risk. Risk taking is influenced not only by an individual's tendency but also by organizational factors. In commercial banks, loan decisions that require the assessment of risk are made every day.

Upper-level managers face a tough task in managing risk-taking behavior. By discouraging lower-level managers from taking risks, they may stifle creativity and innovation. If upper-level managers are going to encourage risk taking, however, they must allow employees to fail without fear of punishment. One way to accomplish this is to consider failure "enlightened trial and error."[12] The key is establishing a consistent attitude toward risk within the organization.

When individuals take risks, losses may occur. Suppose an oil producer thinks there is an opportunity to uncover oil by reentering an old drilling site. She gathers a group of investors and shows them the logs, and they chip in to finance the venture. The reentry is drilled to a certain depth, and nothing is found. Convinced they did not drill deep enough, the producer goes back to the investors and requests additional financial backing to continue drilling. The investors consent, and she drills deeper, only to find nothing. She approaches the investors, and after lengthy discussion, they agree to provide more money to drill deeper. Why do decision makers sometimes throw good money after bad? Why do they continue to provide resources to what looks like a losing venture?

ESCALATION OF COMMITMENT

Continuing to support a failing course of action is known as **escalation of commitment**.[13] In situations characterized by escalation of commitment, individuals who make decisions that turn out to be poor choices tend to hold fast to those choices, even when substantial costs are incurred.[14] An example of escalation is the price wars that often occur between airlines. The airlines reduce their prices in response to competitors until at a certain stage, both airlines are in a "no-win" situation. Yet they continue to compete despite the heavy losses they are incurring. The desire to win is a motivation to continue to escalate, and each airline continues to reduce prices (lose money) based on the belief that the other airline will pull out of the price war. Another example is Motorola, which lost billions of dollars on Iridium, a constellation of sixty-six satellites that would allow subscribers to make phone calls globally. Despite known problems, managers continued to invest in the project, and Iridium eventually had to declare bankruptcy.[15]

Why does escalation of commitment occur? One explanation is offered by cognitive dissonance theory, as we discussed in Chapter 4. This theory assumes that humans dislike inconsistency, and that when there is inconsistency among their attitudes or inconsistency between their attitudes and behavior, they strive to reduce the dissonance.[16]

Other reasons why people may hang on to a losing course of action are optimism and control. Some people are overly optimistic and overestimate

ESCALATION OF COMMITMENT
The tendency to continue to support a failing course of action.

the likelihood that positive things will happen to them. Other people operate under an illusion of control—that they have special skills to control the future that other people don't have.[17] In addition, sunk costs may encourage escalation. Individuals think, "Well, I've already invested this much . . . what's a few dollars more?" And the closer a project is to completion, the more likely escalation is to occur.[18]

Hanging on to a poor decision can be costly to organizations. The Shoreham nuclear power plant, for example, went from a proposed $75 million to a $5 billion project without ever being completed. Organizations can deal with escalation of commitment in several ways. One is to split the responsibility for decisions about projects. One individual can make the initial decision, and another individual can make subsequent decisions on the project. Another suggestion is to provide individuals with a graceful exit from poor decisions so that their images are not threatened. One way of accomplishing this is to reward people who admit to poor decisions before escalating their commitment to them. A study also suggested that having groups, rather than individuals, make an initial investment decision would reduce escalation. Support has been found for this idea. Participants in group decision making may experience a diffusion of responsibility for the failed decision rather than feeling personally responsible; thus, they can pull out of a bad decision without threatening their image.[19]

We have seen that there are limits to how rational a manager can be in making decisions. Most managerial decisions involve considerable risk, and individuals react differently to risk situations.

JUNG'S COGNITIVE STYLES

2. *Describe Jung's cognitive styles and how they affect managerial decision making.*

In Chapter 3 we introduced Jungian theory as a way of understanding and appreciating differences among individuals. This theory is especially useful in pointing out that individuals have different styles of making decisions. Carl Jung's original theory identified two styles of information gathering (sensing and intuiting) and two styles of making judgments (thinking and feeling). You already know what each individual preference means. Jung contended that individuals prefer one style of perceiving and one style of judging.[20] The combination of a perceiving style and a judging style is called a *cognitive style*. There are four cognitive styles: sensing/thinking (ST), sensing/feeling (SF), intuiting/thinking (NT), and intuiting/feeling (NF). Each of the cognitive styles affects managerial decision making.[21]

COGNITIVE STYLE
An individual's preference for gathering information and evaluating alternatives.

STs rely on facts. They conduct an impersonal analysis of the situation and then make an analytical, objective decision. The ST cognitive style is valuable in organizations because it produces a clear, simple solution. STs remember details and seldom make factual errors. Their weakness is that they may alienate others because of their tendency to ignore interpersonal aspects of decisions. In addition, they tend to avoid risks.

SFs also gather factual information, but they make judgments in terms of how they affect people. They place great importance on interpersonal relationships but also take a practical approach to gathering information for problem solving. The SFs' strength in decision making lies in their ability to handle interpersonal problems well and their ability to take calculated risks. SFs may have trouble accepting new ideas that break the rules in the organization.

NTs focus on the alternative possibilities in a situation and then evaluate the possibilities objectively and impersonally. NTs love to initiate ideas, and they like to focus on the long term. They are innovative and will take risks. Weaknesses of NTs include their tendencies to ignore arguments based on facts and to ignore the feelings of others.

NFs also search out alternative possibilities, but they evaluate the possibilities in terms of how they will affect the people involved. They enjoy participative decision making and are committed to developing their employees. However, NFs may be prone to making decisions based on personal preferences rather than on more objective data. They may also become too responsive to the needs of others.

Research tends to support the existence of these four cognitive styles. One study asked managers to describe their ideal organization, and the researchers found strong similarities in the descriptions of managers with the same cognitive style.[22] STs wanted an organization that relied on facts and details and that exercised impersonal methods of control. SFs focused on facts, too, but they did so in terms of the relationships within the organization. NTs emphasized broad issues and described impersonal, idealistic organizations. NFs described an organization that would serve humankind well and focused on general, humanistic values. Other studies have found that MBA students with different cognitive styles exhibited these different styles in making strategic planning decisions and in making production decisions in a computer-simulated manufacturing environment.[23]

All four cognitive styles have much to contribute to organizational decision making.[24] Isabel Briggs Myers, creator of the MBTI, also developed the Z problem-solving model, which capitalizes on the strengths of the four separate preferences (sensing, intuiting, thinking, and feeling). By using the Z problem-solving model, managers can use both their preferences and nonpreferences to make decisions more effectively. The Z model is presented in Figure 9-3 (on page 206).

According to this model, good problem solving has four steps:

1. *Examine the facts and details*. Use sensing to gather information about the problem.
2. *Generate alternatives*. Use intuiting to develop possibilities.
3. *Analyze the alternatives objectively*. Use thinking to logically determine the effects of each alternative.
4. *Weigh the impact*. Use feeling to determine how the people involved will be affected.

Using the Z model can help an individual develop his or her nonpreferences. Another way to use the Z model is to rely on others to perform

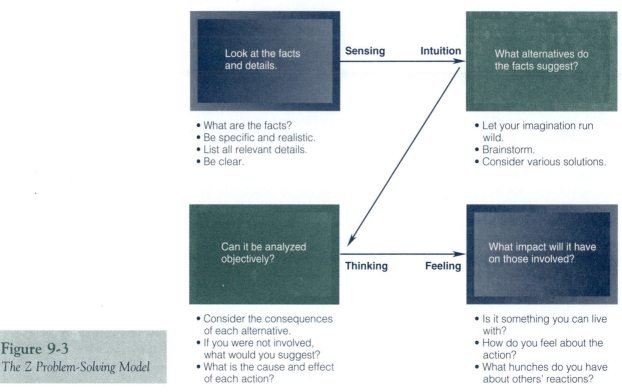

Figure 9-3
The Z Problem-Solving Model

Source: Excerpted from *Type Talk at Work* by Otto Kroeger and Janet M. Thuesen, 1992, Delacorte Press.

the nonpreferred activities. For example, an individual who is an NF might want to turn to a trusted NT for help in analyzing alternatives objectively.

OTHER INDIVIDUAL INFLUENCES ON DECISION MAKING

In addition to the cognitive styles just examined, many other individual differences affect a manager's decision making. Other personality characteristics, attitudes, and values, along with all of the individual differences variables that were discussed in Chapters 3 and 4, have implications for managerial decision making. Managers must use both their logic and their creativity to make effective decisions. Most of us are more comfortable using either logic or creativity, and we show that preference in everyday decision making.

Our brains have two lateral halves (Figure 9-4). The right side is the center for creative functions, while the left side is the center for logic, detail, and planning. There are advantages to both kinds of thinking, so the ideal situation is to be "brain-lateralized" or to be able to use either logic or creativity or both, depending on the situation. There are ways to develop the side of the brain you are not accustomed to using. To develop your right

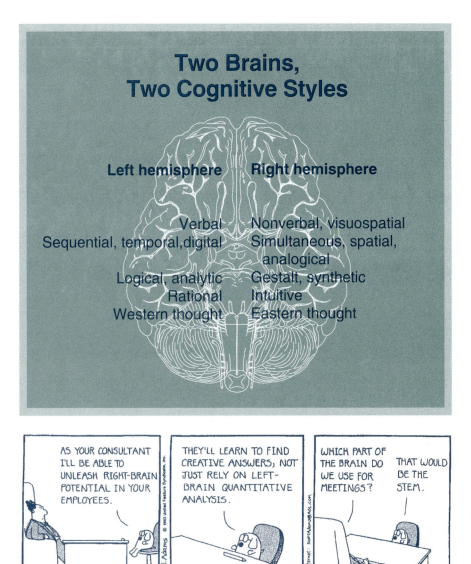

Figure 9-4
Functions of the Left- and Right-Brain Hemispheres

Sources: Based on an idea from *Left Brain, Right Brain* by Springer and Deutsch, p. 272. © 1993 by Sally P. Springer and Georg Deutsch (New York: W. H. Freeman and Company, 1993). DILBERT reprinted by permission of United Features Syndicate, Inc.

side, or creative side, you can ask "what if" questions, engage in play, and follow your intuition. To develop the left side, you can set goals for completing tasks and work to attain these goals. For managers, it is important to see the big picture, craft a vision, and plan strategically—all of which require right-brain skills. It is equally important to be able to understand day-to-day operations and flow chart work processes, which are left-hemisphere brain skills.

Two particular individual influences that can enhance decision-making effectiveness will be highlighted next: intuition and creativity.

THE ROLE OF INTUITION

INTUITION

A fast, positive force in decision making that is utilized at a level below consciousness and involves learned patterns of information.

There is some evidence that managers use their *intuition* to make decisions. Henry Mintzberg, in his work on managerial roles, found that in many cases managers do not appear to use a systematic, step-by-step approach to decision making. Rather, Mintzberg argued, managers make judgments based on "hunches."[25] Daniel Isenberg studied the way senior managers make decisions and found that intuition was used extensively, especially as a mechanism to evaluate decisions made more rationally.[26] Robert Beck studied the way managers at BankAmerica (now Bank of America) made decisions about the future direction of the company following the deregulation of the banking industry. Beck described their use of intuition as an antidote to "analysis paralysis," or the tendency to analyze decisions rather than developing innovative solutions.[27]

Just what is intuition? In Jungian theory, intuiting (N) is one preference used to gather data. This is only one way that the concept of intuition has been applied to managerial decision making, and it is perhaps the most widely researched form of the concept of intuition. There are, however, many definitions of *intuition* in the managerial literature. Chester Barnard, one of the early influential management researchers, argued that intuition's main attributes were speed and the inability of the decision maker to determine how the decision was made.[28] Other researchers have contended that intuition occurs at an unconscious level and that this is why the decision maker cannot verbalize how the decision was made.[29]

Intuition has been variously described as follows:

- The ability to know or recognize quickly and readily the possibilities of a situation.[30]
- Smooth automatic performance of learned behavior sequences.[31]
- Simply analyses frozen into habit and into the capacity for rapid response through recognition.[32]

These definitions share some common assumptions. First, there seems to be a notion that intuition is fast. Second, intuition is utilized at a level below consciousness. Third, there seems to be agreement that intuition involves learned patterns of information. Fourth, intuition appears to be a positive force in decision making.

The use of intuition may lead to more ethical decisions. Intuition allows an individual to take on another's role with ease, and role taking is a fundamental part of developing moral reasoning. You may recall from Chapter 4 the role of cognitive moral development in ethical decision making. One study found a strong link between cognitive moral development and intuition. The development of new perspectives through intuition leads to higher moral growth, and thus to more ethical decisions.[33]

One question that arises is whether managers can be taught to use their intuition. Weston Agor, who has conducted workshops on developing intuitive skills in managers, has attained positive results in organizations such as the former Tenneco and the city of Phoenix. Agor suggests relaxation techniques, using images to guide the mind, and taking creative pauses before making a decision.[34] A review of the research on intuition suggests that although intuition itself cannot be taught, managers can be trained to rely more fully on the promptings of their intuition.[35]

Intuition is an elusive concept, and one with many definitions. There is an interesting paradox regarding intuition. Some researchers view "rational" methods as preferable to intuition, yet satisfaction with a rational decision is usually determined by how the decision feels intuitively.[36] Intuition appears to have a positive effect on managerial decision making, but researchers need to agree on a common definition and conduct further research to increase our knowledge of the role of intuition at work and the influence of experience on our intuitive capabilities.

CREATIVITY AT WORK

Creativity is a process influenced by individual and organizational factors that results in the production of novel and useful ideas, products, or both.[37] The social and technological changes that organizations face require creative decisions.[38] Managers of the future need to develop special competencies to deal with the turbulence of change, and one of these important competencies is the ability to promote creativity in organizations.[39]

CREATIVITY
A process influenced by individual and organizational factors that results in the production of novel and useful ideas, products, or both.

Creativity is a process that is at least in part unconscious. The four stages of the creative process are preparation, incubation, illumination, and verification.[40] Preparation means seeking out new experiences and opportunities to learn, because creativity grows from a base of knowledge. Travel and educational opportunities of all kinds open the individual's mind. Incubation is a process of reflective thought and is often conducted subconsciously. During incubation, the individual engages in other pursuits while the mind considers the problem and works on it. Illumination occurs when the individual senses an insight for solving the problem. Finally, verification is conducted to determine if the solution or idea is valid. This is accomplished by thinking through the implications of the decision, presenting the idea to another person, or trying out the decision. Both individual and organizational influences affect the creative process.

Individual Influences Several individual variables are related to creativity. One group of factors involves the cognitive processes that creative individuals tend to use. One cognitive process is divergent thinking, meaning the individual's ability to generate several potential solutions to a problem.[41] In addition, associational abilities and the use of imagery are associated with creativity.[42] Unconscious processes such as dreams are also essential cognitive processes related to creative thinking.[43]

Personality factors have also been related to creativity in studies of individuals from several different occupations. These characteristics include intellectual and artistic values, breadth of interests, high energy, concern with achievement, independence of judgment, intuition, self-confidence, and a creative self-image.[44] Tolerance of ambiguity, intrinsic motivation, risk taking, and a desire for recognition are also associated with creativity.[45]

There is also evidence that people who are in a good mood are more creative. One study found that individuals who were in a good mood were more successful at creative problem solving than people whose mood was neutral.[46]

Organizational Influences The organizational environment in which people work can either support creativity or impede creative efforts. Creativity killers include focusing on how work is going to be evaluated, being watched while you are working, and competing with other people in win–lose situations. In contrast, creativity facilitators include feelings of autonomy, being part of a team with diverse skills, and having supervisors who are creative role models.[47] High-quality, supportive relationships with supervisors are related to creativity.[48] Flexible organizational structures and participative decision making have also been associated with creativity. An organization can also present impediments to creativity. These barriers include internal political problems, harsh criticism of new ideas, destructive internal competition, and avoidance of risk.[49] The physical environment can also hamper creativity. Companies like Oticon, a Danish hearing-aid manufacturer, and Ethicon Endo-Surgery, a division of Johnson & Johnson, use open-plan offices that eliminate office walls and cubicles so that employees interact more frequently. When people mix, ideas mix as well.[50]

Interestingly, certain kinds of constraints that managers place on employees can actually enhance creativity. These are called variability constraints, and they mean specifying that something must be done differently.

Studies of the role of organizational rewards in encouraging creativity have mixed results. Some studies have shown that monetary incentives improve creative performance, whereas others have found that material rewards do not influence innovative activity.[51] Still other studies have indicated that explicitly contracting to obtain a reward led to lower levels of creativity when compared with contracting for no reward, being presented with just the task, or being presented with the task and receiving the reward later.[52] Organizations can therefore enhance individuals' creative decision making by providing a supportive environment, participative decision making, and a flexible structure.

Individual/Organization Fit Research has indicated that creative performance is highest when there is a match, or fit, between the individual and organizational influences on creativity. For example, when individuals who desire to be creative are matched with an organization that values creative ideas, the result is more creative performance.[53]

A common mistaken assumption regarding creativity is that either you have it or you do not. Research refutes this myth and has shown that individuals can be trained to be more creative.[54] The Disney Institute features a wide range of programs offered to companies, and one of their best-sellers is creativity training. This chapter's Challenge allows you to determine whether you prefer creative or logical problem solving.

Challenge

CREATIVE OR LOGICAL PROBLEM SOLVING: WHAT IS YOUR PREFERENCE?

Try the following creative problem-solving challenge. Each of the following problems is an equation that can be solved by substituting the appropriate words for the letters. Have fun with them!

Examples: 3F = 1Y (3 feet = 1 yard.)
4LC = GL (4 leaf clover = Good luck.)

1. M + M + NH + V + C + RI = NE.
2. "1B in the H = 2 in the B."
3. 8D − 24H = 1W.
4. 3P = 6.
5. HH & MH at 12 = N or M.
6. 4J + 4Q + 4K = All the FC.
7. S & M & T & W & T & F & S are D of W.
8. A + N + AF + MC + CG = AF.
9. T = LS State.
10. 23Y − 3Y = 2D.
11. E − 8 = Z.
12. Y + 2D = T.
13. C + 6D = NYE.
14. Y − S − S − A = W.
15. A & E were in the G of E.
16. My FL and South P are both MC.
17. "NN = GN."
18. N + P + SM = S of C.
19. 1 + 6Z = 1M.
20. "R = R = R."
21. AL & JG & WM & JK were all A.
22. N + V + P + A + A + C + P + I = P of S.
23. S + H of R = USC.

Source: From *A Whack on the Side of the Head* by Roger Von Oech. Copyright © 1983, 1990, 1998 by Roger Von Oech. By permission of Warner Books.

Now try the following logical problem-solving exercise, entitled "Who Owns the Fish?", which is attributed to Albert Einstein.

There are five houses in a row, and in five different colors. In each house lives a person from a different country. Each person drinks a certain drink, plays a certain game, and keeps a certain pet. No two people drink the same drink, play the same game, or keep the same pet.

- The Brit lives in a red house.
- The Swede keeps dogs.
- The Dane drinks tea.
- The green house is on the left of the white house.
- The green house owner drinks coffee.
- The person who plays tennis rears birds.
- The owner of the yellow house plays chess.
- The man living in the house right in the center drinks milk.
- The Norwegian lives in the first house.
- The man who plays poker lives next to the man who keeps cats.
- The man who keeps horses lives next to the one who plays chess.
- The man who plays billiards drinks beer.
- The German plays golf.
- The Norwegian lives next to the blue house.
- The man who plays poker has a neighbor who drinks water.

Question: Who owns the fish?
Answer: Your instructor can provide the solutions to this Challenge.

Source: Adapted from E. O. Welles, "The Billionaire Next Door," *Inc.* (May 2001): p. 80–85.

Part of creativity training involves learning to open up mental locks that keep us from generating creative alternatives to a decision or problem. The following are some mental locks that diminish creativity:

- Searching for the "right" answer.
- Trying to be logical.
- Following the rules.
- Avoiding ambiguity.
- Striving for practicality.
- Being afraid to look foolish.
- Avoiding problems outside our own expertise.
- Fearing failure.
- Believing we are not really creative.
- Not making play a part of work.[55]

3. *Understand the role of creativity in decision making, and practice ways to increase your own creativity.*

Note that many of these mental locks stem from values within organizations. Organizations can facilitate creative decision making in many ways. Rewarding creativity, allowing employees to fail, making work more fun, and providing creativity training are a few suggestions. Also, companies can encourage creativity by exposing employees to new ideas. This can be done in several ways, including job rotation, which moves employees through different jobs and gives them exposure to different information, projects, and teams. Employees can also be assigned to work with groups outside the company, such as suppliers or consultants. Finally, managers can encourage employees to surround themselves with stimuli that they have found to enhance their creative processes. These may be music, artwork, books, or anything else that encourages creative thinking.[56]

We have seen that both individual and organizational factors can produce creativity. Creativity can also mean finding problems as well as fixing them. Recently, four different types of creativity have been proposed, based on the source of the trigger (internal or external) and the source of the problem (presented versus discovered). Responsive creativity means responding to a problem that is presented to you by others because it is part of your job. Expected creativity is discovering problems because you are expected to by the organization. Contributory creativity is responding to problems presented to you because you want to be creative. Proactive creativity is discovering problems because you want to be creative.[57]

3M consistently ranks among the top ten in *Fortune*'s annual list of most admired corporations. It earned this reputation through innovation: More than one-quarter of 3M's sales are from products less than four years old. Post-It Notes, for example, were created by a worker who wanted little adhesive papers to mark hymns for church service. He thought of another worker who had perfected a light adhesive, and the two spent their "free time" developing Post-It Notes. 3M has continued its tradition of innovation with products like Post-It Flags, Nexcare Ease-Off Painless Bandages, and Pop-Up Tape Strips.

Leaders can play key roles in modeling creative behavior. Sir Richard Branson, founder of Virgin Group, believes that if you do not use your employees' creative potential, you are doomed to failure. At Virgin Atlantic Airways, the culture encourages risk taking and rewards innovation. Rules and regulations are not its thing, nor is analyzing ideas to death. Branson says an employee can have an idea in the morning and implement it in the afternoon.[58]

Creativity is a global concern. Poland, for example, is undergoing a major shift from a centrally planned economy and monoparty rule to a market economy and Western-style democracy. One of the major concerns for Polish managers is creativity. Finding ingenious solutions and having the ability to think creatively can be a question of life or death for Polish organizations, which are making the transition to a faster pace of learning and change.[59]

Both intuition and creativity are important influences on managerial decision making. Both concepts require additional research so that managers can better understand how to use intuition and creativity, as well as how to encourage their employees to use them to make more effective decisions.

PARTICIPATION IN DECISION MAKING

Effective management of people can improve a company's economic performance. Firms that capitalize on this fact share several common practices. Chief among them is participation of employees in decision making.[60] Many companies do this through highly empowered self-managed teams like the ones we discussed in Chapter 8. Even in situations where formal teams are not feasible, decision authority can be handed down to front-line employees who have the knowledge and skills to make a difference. At Hampton Inn hotels, for example, guest services personnel are empowered to do whatever is necessary to make guests happy—without consulting their superiors.

THE EFFECTS OF PARTICIPATION

Participative decision making occurs when individuals who are affected by decisions influence the making of those decisions. Participation buffers employees from the negative experiences of organizational politics.[61] In addition, participative management has been found to increase employee creativity, job satisfaction, and productivity.[62]

GE Capital believes in participation. Each year it holds dreaming sessions, and employees from all levels of the company attend strategy and budget meetings to discuss where the company is heading. As a result, young employees came up with e-commerce ideas like http://www.financiallearning.com and http://www.gefn.com, which were highly successful.[63]

As our economy becomes increasingly based on knowledge work, and as new technologies make it easier for decentralized decision makers to connect, participative decision making will undoubtedly increase.[64]

PARTICIPATIVE DECISION MAKING
Decision making in which individuals who are affected by decisions influence the making of those decisions.

FOUNDATIONS FOR PARTICIPATION AND EMPOWERMENT

Organizational and individual foundations underlie empowerment that enhances task motivation and performance. The organizational foundations for empowerment include a participative, supportive organizational culture and a team-oriented work design. A supportive work environment is essential because of the uncertainty that empowerment can cause within the organization. Empowerment requires that lower-level organizational members be able to make decisions and take action on those decisions. As operational employees become empowered to make decisions, real fear, anxiety, or even terror can be created among middle managers in the organization.[65] Senior leadership must create an organizational culture that is supportive and reassuring for these middle managers as the power dynamics of the system change. If not supported and reassured, the middle managers can become a restraining, disruptive force to participative decision-making efforts.

A second organizational foundation for empowerment concerns the design of work. The old factory system relied on work specialization and narrow tasks with the intent of achieving routinized efficiency.[66] This approach to the design of work had some economic advantages, but it also had some distressing disadvantages leading to monotony and fatigue. This approach to the design of work is inconsistent with participation, because the individual feels absolved of much responsibility for a whole piece of work. Team-oriented work designs are a key organizational foundation, because they lead to broader tasks and a greater sense of responsibility. For example, Volvo builds cars using a team-oriented work design in which each person does many different tasks, and each person has direct responsibility for the finished product.[67] These work designs create a context for effective participation so long as the empowered individuals meet necessary individual prerequisites.

The three individual prerequisites for participation and empowerment are (1) the capability to become psychologically involved in participative activities, (2) the motivation to act autonomously, and (3) the capacity to see the relevance of participation for one's own well-being.[68] First, people must be psychologically equipped to become involved in participative activities if they are to be empowered and become effective team members. Not all people are so predisposed. For example, Germany has an authoritarian tradition that runs counter to participation and empowerment at the individual and group level. General Motors encountered significant difficulties implementing quality circles in its German plants, because workers expected to be directed by supervisors, not to engage in participative problem solving. The German initiatives to establish supervisory/worker boards in corporations are intended to change this authoritarian tradition.

A second individual prerequisite is the motivation to act autonomously. People with dependent personalities are predisposed to be told what to do and to rely on external motivation rather than internal, intrinsic motivation.[69] These dependent people are not effective contributors to decision making.

Finally, if participative decision making is to work, people must be able to see how it provides a personal benefit to them. The personal payoff for the individual need not be short term. It may be a long-term benefit that results in people receiving greater rewards through enhanced organizational profitability.

WHAT LEVEL OF PARTICIPATION?

Participative decision making is complex, and one of the things managers must understand is that employees can be involved in some, or all, of the stages of the decision-making process. For example, employees could be variously involved in identifying problems, generating alternatives, selecting solutions, planning implementations, or evaluating results. Research shows that greater involvement in all five of these stages has a cumulative effect. Employees who are involved in all five processes have higher satisfaction and performance levels. And, all decision processes are not created equal. If employees can't be provided with full participation in all stages, the highest payoffs seem to come with involvement in generating alternatives, planning implementations, and evaluating results.[70] Styles of participation in decision making may need to change as the company grows, or as its culture changes.

THE GROUP DECISION-MAKING PROCESS

Managers use groups to make decisions for several reasons. One is *synergy*, which occurs when group members stimulate new solutions to problems through the process of mutual influence and encouragement within the group. Another reason for using a group is to gain commitment to a decision. Groups also bring more knowledge and experience to the problem-solving situation.

Group decisions can sometimes be predicted by comparing the views of the initial group members with the final group decision. These simple relationships are known as *social decision schemes*. One social decision scheme is the majority-wins rule, in which the group supports whatever position is taken by the majority of its members. Another scheme, the truth-wins rule, predicts that the correct decision will emerge as an increasing number of members realize its appropriateness. The two-thirds-majority rule means that the decision favored by two-thirds or more of the members is supported. Finally, the first-shift rule states that members support a decision represented by the first shift in opinion shown by a member.

Research indicates that these social decision schemes can predict a group decision as much as 80 percent of the time.[71] Current research is aimed at discovering which rules are used in particular types of tasks. For example, studies indicate that the majority-wins rule is used most often in judgment tasks (that is, when the decision is a matter of preference or opinion), whereas the truth-wins rule predicts decisions best when the task is an intellective one (that is, when the decision has a correct answer).[72]

SYNERGY
A positive force that occurs in groups when group members stimulate new solutions to problems through the process of mutual influence and encouragement within the group.

SOCIAL DECISION SCHEMES
Simple rules used to determine final group decisions.

ADVANTAGES AND DISADVANTAGES OF GROUP DECISION MAKING

4. *Identify the advantages and disadvantages of group decision making.*

Both advantages and disadvantages are associated with group decision making. The advantages include (1) more knowledge and information through the pooling of group member resources; (2) increased acceptance of, and commitment to, the decision, because the members had a voice in it; and (3) greater understanding of the decision, because members were involved in the various stages of the decision process. The disadvantages of group decision making include (1) pressure within the group to conform and fit in; (2) domination of the group by one forceful member or a dominant clique, who may ramrod the decision; and (3) the amount of time required, because a group makes decisions more slowly than an individual.[73]

Given these advantages and disadvantages, should an individual or a group make a decision? Substantial empirical research indicates that whether a group or an individual should be used depends on the type of task involved. For judgment tasks requiring an estimate or a prediction, groups are usually superior to individuals because of the breadth of experience that multiple individuals bring to the problem.[74] On tasks that have a correct solution, other studies have indicated that the most competent individual outperforms the group.[75] This finding has been called into question, however. Much of the previous research on groups was conducted in the laboratory, where group members interacted only for short periods of time. Researchers wanted to know how a longer experience in the group would affect decisions. Their study showed that groups who worked together for longer periods of time outperformed the most competent member 70 percent of the time. As groups gained experience, the best members became less important to the group's success.[76] This study demonstrated that experience in the group is an important variable to consider when evaluating the individual versus group decision-making question.

Given the emphasis on teams in the workplace, many managers believe that groups produce better decisions than do individuals, yet the evidence is mixed. It is evident that more research needs to be conducted in organizational settings to help answer this question.

Two potential liabilities are found in group decision making: groupthink and group polarization. These problems are discussed in the following sections.

GROUPTHINK

5. *Discuss the symptoms of groupthink and ways to prevent it.*

GROUPTHINK
A deterioration of mental efficiency, reality testing, and moral judgment resulting from pressures within the group.

One liability of a cohesive group is its tendency to develop **groupthink**, a dysfunctional process. Irving Janis, the originator of the groupthink concept, describes groupthink as "a deterioration of mental efficiency, reality testing, and moral judgment" resulting from pressures within the group.[77]

Certain conditions favor the development of groupthink. One of the antecedents is high cohesiveness. Cohesive groups tend to favor solidarity because members identify strongly with the group.[78] High-ranking teams that make decisions without outside help are especially prone to groupthink, because they are likely to have shared mental models; that is, they are more likely to think alike.[79] Two other conditions that encourage group-think are having to make a highly consequential decision and time constraints.[80] A highly consequential decision is one that will have a great impact on the group members and on outside parties. When group members feel that they have a limited time in which to make a decision, they may rush through the process. These antecedents cause members to prefer concurrence in decisions and to fail to evaluate one another's suggestions critically. A group suffering from groupthink shows recognizable symptoms. Table 9-1 presents these symptoms and makes suggestions on how to avoid groupthink.

Symptoms of Groupthink

- *Illusions of invulnerability*. Group members feel they are above criticism. This symptom leads to excessive optimism and risk taking.
- *Illusions of group morality*. Group members feel they are moral in their actions and therefore above reproach. This symptom leads the group to ignore the ethical implications of their decisions.
- *Illusions of unanimity*. Group members believe there is unanimous agreement on the decisions. Silence is misconstrued as consent.
- *Rationalization*. Group members concoct explanations for their decisions to make them appear rational and correct. The results are that other alternatives are not considered, and there is an unwillingness to reconsider the group's assumptions.
- *Stereotyping the enemy*. Competitors are stereotyped as evil or stupid. This leads the group to underestimate its opposition.
- *Self-censorship*. Members do not express their doubts or concerns about the course of action. This prevents critical analysis of the decisions.
- *Peer pressure*. Any members who express doubts or concerns are pressured by other group members, who question their loyalty.
- *Mindguards*. Some members take it upon themselves to protect the group from negative feedback. Group members are thus shielded from information that might lead them to question their actions.

Guidelines for Preventing Groupthink

- Ask each group member to assume the role of the critical evaluator who actively voices objections or doubts.
- Have the leader avoid stating his or her position on the issue prior to the group decision.
- Create several groups that work on the decision simultaneously.
- Bring in outside experts to evaluate the group process.
- Appoint a devil's advocate to question the group's course of action consistently.
- Evaluate the competition carefully, posing as many different motivations and intentions as possible.
- Once consensus is reached, encourage the group to rethink its position by reexamining the alternatives.

Table 9-1
Symptoms of Groupthink and How to Prevent It

Source: Irving L. Janis, *Groupthink: Psychological Studies of Policy Decisions and Fiascoes*, Second Edition. Copyright © 1982 by Houghton Mifflin Company. Used with permission.

An incident that has been examined for these symptoms of groupthink is the space shuttle *Challenger* disaster. On January 28, 1986, seventy-three seconds into its flight, the *Challenger* exploded, killing all seven members of its crew. The evidence pointed toward an O-ring seal that was still cold from nighttime temperatures and failed to do its job. A presidential commission was convened, and its investigation cited flawed decision making as a primary cause of the accident.

An analysis of the *Challenger* incident indicated that the negative symptoms of groupthink increased during the twenty-four hours prior to the decision to launch the spacecraft.[81] National Aeronautics and Space Administration (NASA) management officials were warned by engineers that the launch should be canceled because the O-rings would not withstand the temperatures. The engineers were pressured by their bosses to stifle their dissent, and their opinions were devalued. Further, the decision to launch was made by polling managers—engineers were not polled. The decision makers were overconfident because of NASA's record of success. Some managers knew that a redesign of the rocket casings had been ordered, but this information was withheld from other decision makers.

You Be The Judge

Describe groupthink as an ethical problem.

Consequences of groupthink include an incomplete survey of alternatives, failure to evaluate the risks of the preferred course of action, biased information processing, and a failure to work out contingency plans. The overall result of groupthink is defective decision making. This was evident in the *Challenger* situation. The group considered only two alternatives: launch or no launch. They failed to consider the risks of their decision to launch the shuttle, and they did not develop any contingency plans.

Table 9-1 presents Janis's guidelines for avoiding groupthink. Many of these suggestions center around the notion of ensuring that decisions are evaluated completely, with opportunities for discussion from all group members. This strategy helps encourage members to evaluate one another's ideas critically.

Janis has used the groupthink framework to conduct historical analyses of several political and military fiascoes, including the Bay of Pigs invasion, the Vietnam War, and Watergate. One review of the decision situation in the *Challenger* incident proposed that two variables, time and leadership style, are important to include.[82] When a decision must be made quickly, there is more potential for groupthink. Leadership style can either promote groupthink (if the leader makes his or her opinion known up front) or avoid groupthink (if the leader encourages open and frank discussion).

There are few empirical studies of groupthink, and most of these involved students in a laboratory setting. More applied research may be seen in the future, however, as a questionnaire has been developed to measure the constructs associated with groupthink.[83] Janis's work on groupthink has led to several interdisciplinary efforts at understanding policy decisions.[84] The work underscores the need to examine multiple explanations for failed decisions.

GROUP POLARIZATION

Another group phenomenon was discovered by a graduate student. His study showed that groups made riskier decisions; in fact, the group and each individual accepted greater levels of risk following a group discussion of the issue. Subsequent studies uncovered another shift—toward caution. Thus, group discussion produced shifts both toward more risky positions and toward more cautious positions.[85] Further research revealed that individual group member attitudes simply became more extreme following group discussion. Individuals who were initially against an issue became more radically opposed, and individuals who were in favor of the issue became more strongly supportive following discussion. These shifts came to be known as *group polarization*.[86]

The tendency toward polarization has important implications for group decision making. Groups whose initial views lean a certain way can be expected to adopt more extreme views following interaction.

Several ideas have been proposed to explain why group polarization occurs. One explanation is the social comparison approach. Prior to group discussion, individuals believe they hold better views than the other members. During group discussion, they see that their views are not so far from average, so they shift to more extreme positions.[87] A second explanation is the persuasive arguments view. It contends that group discussion reinforces the initial views of the members, so they take a more extreme position.[88] Both explanations are supported by research. It may be that both processes, along with others, cause the group to develop more polarized attitudes.

Group polarization leads groups to adopt extreme attitudes. In some cases, this can be disastrous. For instance, if individuals are leaning toward a dangerous decision, they are likely to support it more strongly following discussion. Both groupthink and group polarization are potential liabilities of group decision making, but several techniques can be used to help prevent or control these two liabilities.

GROUP POLARIZATION
The tendency for group discussion to produce shifts toward more extreme attitudes among members.

TECHNIQUES FOR GROUP DECISION MAKING

Once a manager has determined that a group decision approach should be used, he or she can determine the technique that is best suited to the decision situation. Seven techniques will be briefly summarized: brainstorming, nominal group technique, Delphi technique, devil's advocacy, dialectical inquiry, quality circles and quality teams, and self-managed teams.

6. *Evaluate the strengths and weaknesses of several group decision-making techniques.*

BRAINSTORMING

Brainstorming is a good technique for generating alternatives. The idea behind **brainstorming** is to generate as many ideas as possible, suspending evaluation until all of the ideas have been suggested. Participants are encouraged to build upon the suggestions of others, and imagination is

BRAINSTORMING
A technique for generating as many ideas as possible on a given subject, while suspending evaluation until all the ideas have been suggested.

emphasized. Evidence suggests, however, that group brainstorming is less effective than a comparable number of individuals working alone. In groups, participants engage in discussions that can make them lose their focus.[89]

One recent trend is the use of electronic brainstorming instead of verbal brainstorming in groups. Electronic brainstorming overcomes two common problems that can produce group brainstorming failure: production blocking and evaluation apprehension. In verbal brainstorming, individuals are exposed to the inputs of others. While listening to others, individuals are distracted from their own ideas. This is referred to as production blocking. When ideas are recorded electronically, participants are free from hearing the interruptions of others; thus, production blocking is reduced. Some individuals suffer from evaluation apprehension in brainstorming groups. They fear that others might respond negatively to their ideas. In electronic brainstorming, input is anonymous, so evaluation apprehension is reduced. Studies indicate that anonymous electronic brainstorming groups outperform face-to-face brainstorming groups in the number of ideas generated.[90]

NOMINAL GROUP TECHNIQUE

NOMINAL GROUP TECHNIQUE (NGT)
A structured approach to group decision making that focuses on generating alternatives and choosing one.

A structured approach to decision making that focuses on generating alternatives and choosing one is called *nominal group technique (NGT)*. NGT involves the following discrete steps:

1. Individuals silently list their ideas.
2. Ideas are written on a chart one at a time until all ideas are listed.
3. Discussion is permitted, but only to clarify the ideas. No criticism is allowed.
4. A written vote is taken.

NGT is a good technique to use in a situation where group members fear criticism from others.[91]

DELPHI TECHNIQUE

DELPHI TECHNIQUE
Gathering the judgments of experts for use in decision making.

The *Delphi technique*, which originated at the Rand Corporation, involves gathering the judgments of experts for use in decision making. Experts at remote locations respond to a questionnaire. A coordinator summarizes the responses to the questionnaire, and the summary is sent back to the experts. The experts then rate the various alternatives generated, and the coordinator tabulates the results. The Delphi technique is valuable in its ability to generate a number of independent judgments without the requirement of a face-to-face meeting.[92]

DEVIL'S ADVOCACY

DEVIL'S ADVOCACY
A technique for preventing group-think in which a group or individual is given the role of critic during decision making.

In the *devil's advocacy* decision method, a group or individual is given the role of critic. This devil's advocate has the task of coming up with the potential problems of a proposed decision. This helps organizations avoid costly mistakes in decision making by identifying potential pitfalls in advance.[93] As we discussed in Chapter 8, a devil's advocate who challenges the CEO and top management team can help sustain the vitality and performance of the upper echelon.

DIALECTICAL INQUIRY

Dialectical inquiry is essentially a debate between two opposing sets of recommendations. Although it sets up a conflict, it is a constructive approach, because it brings out the benefits and limitations of both sets of ideas.[94] When using this technique, it is important to guard against a win–lose attitude and to concentrate on reaching the most effective solution for all concerned. Research has shown that the way a decision is framed (that is, win–win versus win–lose) is very important. A decision's outcome could be viewed as a gain or a loss, depending on the way the decision is framed.[95]

QUALITY CIRCLES AND QUALITY TEAMS

As you recall from Chapter 8, quality circles are small groups that voluntarily meet to provide input for solving quality or production problems. Quality circles are also a way of extending participative decision making into teams. Managers often listen to recommendations from quality circles and implement the suggestions. The rewards for the suggestions are intrinsic—involvement in the decision-making process is the primary reward.

Quality circles are often generated from the bottom up; that is, they provide advice to managers, who still retain decision-making authority. As such, quality circles are not empowered to implement their own recommendations. They operate in parallel fashion to the organization's structure, and they rely on voluntary participation.[96] In Japan, quality circles have been integrated into the organization instead of added on. This may be one reason for Japan's success with this technique. In contrast, the U.S. experience is not as positive. It has been estimated that 60 to 75 percent of the quality circles have failed. Reasons for the failures have included lack of top management support and lack of problem-solving skills among quality circle members.[97]

Quality teams, in contrast, are included in total quality management and other quality improvement efforts as part of a change in the organization's structure. Quality teams are generated from the top down and are empowered to act on their own recommendations. Whereas quality circles emphasize the generation of ideas, quality teams make data-based decisions about improving product and service quality. Various decision-making techniques are employed in quality teams. Brainstorming, flow charts, and cause-and-effect diagrams help pinpoint problems that affect quality.

Some organizations have moved toward quality teams, but Toyota has stuck with quality circles. The company has used them since 1963 and was the second company in the world to do so. Toyota's quality circles constitute a limited form of empowerment—and they like it that way. The members want to participate but don't have the desire to be self-directed. They would rather leave certain decisions to managers, who are trusted to take good care of them. Toyota attributes its success with quality circles to the longevity of their use and to its view of them as true methods of participation.[98]

information technologies to accomplish a task. Virtual teams seldom meet face to face, and membership often shifts according to the project at hand.

How are decisions made in virtual teams? These teams require advanced technologies for communication and decision making. Three basic technologies aid virtual teams in decision making: desktop videoconferencing systems (DVCS); group decision support systems (GDSS), as described in the previous section; and Internet/intranet systems.[112]

Desktop videoconferencing systems are the major technologies that form the basis for other virtual team technologies. DVCS re-create the face-to-face interactions of teams and go one step beyond by supporting more complex levels of communication among virtual team members. Small cameras on top of computer monitors provide video feeds, and voice transmissions are made possible through earpieces and microphones. High-speed data connections are used for communication. All team members can be connected, and outside experts can even be added. A local group can connect with up to fifteen different individuals or groups. Users can simultaneously work on documents, analyze data, or map out ideas.

GDSS make real-time decision making possible in the virtual team. They are ideal systems for brainstorming, focus groups, and group decisions. By using support tools within the GDSS, users can turn off their individual identities and interact with anonymity, and can poll participants and assemble statistical information relevant to the decision being made. GDSS are thus the sophisticated software that makes collaboration possible in virtual teams.

Internal internets, or intranets, are adaptations of Internet technologies for use within a company. For virtual teams, the Internet and intranets can be rich communication and decision-making resources. These tools allow virtual teams to archive text, visual, audio, and data files for use in decision making. They permit virtual teams to inform other organization members about the team's progress and enable the team to monitor other projects within the organization.

By using DVCS, GDSS, and Internet/intranet technologies, virtual teams can capitalize on a rich communications environment for decision making. It is difficult, however, to duplicate the face-to-face environment. The effectiveness of a virtual team's decision making depends on its members' ability to use the tools that are available. Collaborative systems can enhance virtual teams' decision quality if they are used well.[113]

ETHICAL ISSUES IN DECISION MAKING

8. *Utilize an "ethics check" for examining managerial decisions.*

One criterion that should be applied to decision making is the ethical implications of the decision. Ethical decision making in organizations is influenced by many factors, including individual differences and organizational rewards and punishments.

Kenneth Blanchard and Norman Vincent Peale proposed an "ethics check" for decision makers in their book *The Power of Ethical Manage-*

ment.[114] They contend that the decision maker should ponder three questions:

1. Is it legal? (Will I be violating the law or company policy?)

2. Is it balanced? (Is it fair to all concerned in the short term and long term? Does it promote win–win relationships?)

3. How will it make me feel about myself? (Will it make me proud of my actions? How will I feel when others become aware of the decision?)

Groups can also make decisions that are unethical. Beech-Nut, for example, admitted selling millions of jars of "phony" apple juice that contained cheap, adulterated concentrate. Groupthink may have been responsible for this unethical decision. Beech-Nut was losing money, and its managers believed that other companies were selling fake juice. They were convinced that their fake juice was safe for consumers and that no laboratory test could conclusively distinguish real juice from artificial ingredients. Normally a reputable company, Beech-Nut ignored caution and conscience in favor of bottom-line mentality, ignored dissent, and thus suffered damage to its reputation because of unethical practices.[115]

Unethical group decisions like the one at Beech-Nut can be prevented by using the techniques for overcoming groupthink. Appointing a devil's advocate who constantly questions the group's course of action can help bring ethical issues to the surface. Setting up a dialectical inquiry between two subgroups can head off unethical decisions by leading the group to question its course of action.

In summary, all decisions, whether made by individuals or by groups, must be evaluated for their ethics. Organizations should reinforce ethical decision making among employees by encouraging and rewarding it. Socialization processes should convey to newcomers the ethical standards of behavior in the organization. Groups should use devil's advocates and dialectical methods to reduce the potential for groupthink and the unethical decisions that may result. Effective and ethical decisions are not mutually exclusive.

MANAGERIAL IMPLICATIONS: DECISION MAKING IS A CRITICAL ACTIVITY

Decision making is important at all levels of every organization. At times managers may have the luxury of optimizing (selecting the best alternative), but more often they are forced to satisfice (select the alternative that is good enough). And, at times, the decision process can even seem unpredictable and random.

Individuals differ in their preferences for risk, as well as in their styles of gathering information and making judgments. Understanding individual differences can help managers maximize strengths in employee decision

YOU BE THE JUDGE

Using the "ethics check," evaluate the decision to launch the *Challenger*. How could a knowledge of ethical decision making have aided the individuals who made this decision?

styles and build teams that capitalize on strengths. Creativity is one such strength. It can be encouraged by providing employees with a supportive environment that nourishes innovative ideas. Creativity training has been used in some organizations with positive results.

Some decisions are best made by individuals and some by teams or groups. The task of the manager is to diagnose the situation and implement the appropriate level of participation. To do this effectively, managers should know the advantages and disadvantages of various group decision-making techniques and should minimize the potential for groupthink. Finally, decisions made by individuals or groups should be analyzed to see whether they are ethical.

KEY TERMS

bounded rationality	escalation of commitment	participative decision making
brainstorming	garbage can model	programmed decision
cognitive style	group polarization	rationality
creativity	groupthink	risk aversion
Delphi technique	heuristics	satisfice
devil's advocacy	intuition	social decision schemes
dialectical inquiry	nominal group technique (NGT)	synergy
effective decision	nonprogrammed decision	

Experiential Exercise

MAKING A LAYOFF DECISION

Purpose
In this exercise, you will examine how to weigh a set of facts and make a difficult personnel decision about laying off valued employees during a time of financial hardship. You will also examine your own values and criteria used in the decision-making process.

The Problem
Walker Space (WSI) is a medium-sized firm located in Connecticut. The firm essentially has been a subcontractor on many large space contracts that have been acquired by firms like Alliant Techsystems and others.

With the cutback in many of the National Aeronautics and Space Administration programs, Walker has an excess of employees. Stuart Tartaro, the head of one of the sections, has been told by his superior that he must reduce his section of engineers from nine to six. He is looking at the following summaries of their vitae and pondering how he will make this decision:

1. *Roger Allison*, age twenty-six, married, two children. Allison has been with WSI for a year and a half. He is a very good engineer, with a degree from Rensselaer Polytech. He has held two prior jobs and lost both of them because of cutbacks in the space program. He moved to Connecticut from California to take this job. Allison is well liked by his coworkers.

2. *Dave Jones*, age twenty-four, single. Jones is an African American, and the company looked hard to get him because of affirmative action pressure. He is not very popular with his coworkers. Because he has been employed less than a year, not too much is known about his work. On his one evaluation (which was average), Jones accused his supervisor of bias

against African Americans. He is a graduate of the Detroit Institute of Technology.

3. *William Foster*, age fifty-three, married, three children. Foster is a graduate of "the school of hard knocks." After serving in the Vietnam War, he started to go to school but dropped out because of high family expenses. Foster has worked at the company for twenty years. His ratings were excellent for fifteen years. The last five years they have been average. Foster feels his supervisor grades him down because he does not "have sheepskins covering his office walls."

4. *Donald Boyer*, age thirty-two, married, no children. Boyer is well liked by his coworkers. He has been at WSI five years, and he has a B.S. and M.S. in engineering from Purdue University. Boyer's ratings have been mixed. Some supervisors rated him high and some average. Boyer's wife is an M.D.

5. *Ann Shuster*, age twenty-nine, single. Shuster is a real worker, but a loner. She has a B.S. in engineering from the University of California. She is working on her M.S. at night, always trying to improve her technical skills. Her performance ratings have been above average for the three years she has been at WSI.

6. *Sherman Soltis*, age thirty-seven, divorced, two children. He has a B.S. in engineering from Ohio State University. Soltis is very active in community affairs: Scouts, Little League, and United Way. He is a friend of the vice-president through church work. His ratings have been average, although some recent ones indicate that he is out of date. He is well liked and has been employed at WSI for fourteen years.

7. *Warren Fortuna*, age forty-four, married, five children. He has a B.S. in engineering from Georgia Tech. Fortuna headed this section at one time. He worked so hard that he had a heart attack. Under doctor's orders, he resigned from the supervisory position. Since then he has done good work, though because of his health, he is a bit slower than the others. Now and then he must spend extra time on a project, because he did get out of date during the eight years he headed the section. His performance evaluations for the last

two years have been above average. He has been employed at WSI for fourteen years.

8. *Robert Treharne*, age forty-seven, single. He began an engineering degree at MIT but had to drop out for financial reasons. He tries hard to stay current by regular reading of engineering journals and taking all the short courses the company and nearby colleges offer. His performance evaluations have varied, but they tend to be average to slightly above average. He is a loner, and Tartaro thinks this has negatively affected Treharne's performance evaluations. He has been employed at WSI sixteen years.

9. *Sandra Rosen*, age twenty-two, single. She has a B.S. in engineering technology from the Rochester Institute of Technology. Rosen has been employed less than a year. She is enthusiastic, a very good worker, and well liked by her coworkers. She is well regarded by Tartaro.

Tartaro does not quite know what to do. He sees the good points of each of his section members. Most have been good employees. They all can pretty much do one another's work. No one has special training.

He is fearful that the section will hear about the downsizing and morale will drop. Work would fall off. He does not even want to talk to his wife about it, in case she would let something slip. Tartaro has come to you, Edmund Graves, personnel manager at WSI, for some guidelines on this decision—legal, moral, and best personnel practice.

Assignment

You are Edmund Graves. Write a report with your recommendations for termination and a careful analysis of the criteria for the decision. You should also carefully explain to Tartaro how you would go about the terminations and what you would consider reasonable termination pay. You should also advise him about the pension implications of this decision. Generally, fifteen years' service entitles you to at least partial pension.

SOURCE: W. F. Glueck, *Cases and Exercises in Personnel* (Dallas: Business Publications, 1978), 24–26.

10

Power and Political Behavior

LEARNING OBJECTIVES

After reading this chapter, you should be able to do the following:

1. Distinguish between power, influence, and authority.

2. Describe the interpersonal and intergroup sources of power.

3. Understand the ethical use of power.

4. Explain power analysis, an organizational-level theory of power.

5. Identify symbols of power and powerlessness in organizations.

6. Define organizational politics and understand the major influence tactics.

7. Develop a plan for managing employee–boss relationships.

8. Discuss how managers can empower others.

THE CONCEPT OF POWER

Power is the ability to influence someone else. As an exchange relationship, it occurs in transactions between an agent and a target. The agent is the person using the power, and the target is the recipient of the attempt to use power.[1]

Because power is an ability, individuals can learn to use it effectively. *Influence* is the process of affecting the thoughts, behavior, and feelings of another person. *Authority* is the right to influence another person.[2] It is important to understand the subtle differences among these terms. For instance, a manager may have authority but no power. She may have the right, by virtue of her position as boss, to tell someone what to do. But she may not have the skill or ability to influence other people.

In a relationship between the agent and the target, there are many influence attempts that the target considers legitimate. Working forty hours per week, greeting customers, solving problems, and collecting bills are actions that, when requested by the manager, are considered legitimate by a customer service representative. Requests such as these fall within the employee's *zone of indifference*—the range in which attempts to influence the employee are perceived as legitimate and are acted on without a great deal of thought.[3] The employee accepts that the manager has the authority to request such behaviors and complies with the requests. Some requests, however, fall outside the zone of indifference, so the manager must work to enlarge the employee's zone of indifference. Enlarging the zone is accomplished with power (an ability) rather than with authority (a right).

Suppose the manager asks the employee to purchase a birthday gift for the manager's wife or to overcharge a customer for a service call. The employee may think that the manager has no right to ask these things. These requests fall outside the zone of indifference; they're viewed as extraordinary, and the manager has to operate from outside the authority base to induce the employee to fulfill them. In some cases, no power base is enough to induce the employee to comply, especially if the behaviors requested by the manager are considered unethical by the employee.

Failures to understand power and politics can be costly in terms of your career. Managers must learn as much as possible about power and politics to be able to use them effectively and to manage the inevitable political behavior in organizations.

FORMS AND SOURCES OF POWER IN ORGANIZATIONS

Individuals have many forms of power to use in their work settings. Some of them are interpersonal—used in interactions with others. One of the earliest and most influential theories of power comes from French and Raven, who tried to determine the sources of a power a manager uses to influence other people.

1. *Distinguish between power, influence, and authority.*

POWER
The ability to influence another person.

INFLUENCE
The process of affecting the thoughts, behavior, and feelings of another person.

AUTHORITY
The right to influence another person.

ZONE OF INDIFFERENCE
The range in which attempts to influence a person will be perceived as legitimate and will be acted on without a great deal of thought.

2. *Describe the interpersonal and intergroup sources of power.*

INTERPERSONAL FORMS OF POWER

French and Raven identified five forms of interpersonal power that managers use. They are reward, coercive, legitimate, referent, and expert power.[4]

Reward power is power based on the agent's ability to control rewards that a target wants. For example, managers control the rewards of salary increases, bonuses, and promotions. Reward power can lead to better performance, but only as long as the employee sees a clear and strong link between performance and rewards. To use reward power effectively, then, the manager should be explicit about the behavior being rewarded and should make the connection clear between the behavior and the reward.

Coercive power is power that is based on the agent's ability to cause the target to have an unpleasant experience. To coerce someone into doing something means to force the person to do it, often with threats of punishment. Managers using coercive power may verbally abuse employees or withhold support from them.

Legitimate power, which is similar to authority, is power that is based on position and mutual agreement. The agent and target agree that the agent has the right to influence the target. It doesn't matter that a manager thinks he has the right to influence his employees; for legitimate power to be effective, the employees must also believe the manager has the right to tell them what to do. In Native American societies, the chieftain has legitimate power; tribe members believe in his right to influence the decisions in their lives.

Referent power is an elusive power that is based on interpersonal attraction. The agent has referent power over the target because the target identifies with or wants to be like the agent. Charismatic individuals are often thought to have referent power. Interestingly, the agent need not be superior to the target in any way. People who use referent power well are most often individualistic and respected by the target.

Expert power is the power that exists when the agent has specialized knowledge or skills that the target needs. For expert power to work, three conditions must be in place. First, the target must trust that the expertise given is accurate. Second, the knowledge involved must be relevant and useful to the target. Third, the target's perception of the agent as an expert is crucial. Using easy-to-understand language signals the target that the expert has an appreciation for real-world concerns and increases the target's trust in the expert.[5]

Which type of interpersonal power is most effective? Research has focused on this question since French and Raven introduced their five forms of power. Some of the results are surprising. Reward power and coercive power have similar effects.[6] Both lead to compliance. That is, employees will do what the manager asks them to, at least temporarily, if the manager offers a reward or threatens them with punishment. Reliance on these sources of power is dangerous, however, because it may require the manager to be physically present and watchful in order to apply rewards or punishment when the behavior occurs. Constant surveillance creates an uncom-

REWARD POWER
Power based on an agent's ability to control rewards that a target wants.

COERCIVE POWER
Power that is based on an agent's ability to cause an unpleasant experience for a target.

LEGITIMATE POWER
Power that is based on position and mutual agreement; agent and target agree that the agent has the right to influence the target.

REFERENT POWER
An elusive power that is based on interpersonal attraction.

EXPERT POWER
The power that exists when an agent has specialized knowledge or skills that the target needs.

fortable situation for managers and employees and eventually results in a dependency relationship. Employees will not work unless the manager is present.

Legitimate power also leads to compliance. When told "Do this because I'm your boss," most employees will comply. However, the use of legitimate power has not been linked to organizational effectiveness or to employee satisfaction.[7] In organizations where managers rely heavily on legitimate power, organizational goals are not necessarily met.

Referent power is linked with organizational effectiveness. It is the most dangerous power, however, because it can be too extensive and intensive in altering the behavior of others. Charismatic leaders need an accompanying sense of responsibility for others. Magic Johnson's referent power has made him a powerful spokesman for AIDS prevention, especially among young people.

Expert power has been called the power of the future.[8] Of the five forms of power, it has the strongest relationship with performance and satisfaction. It is through expert power that vital skills, abilities, and knowledge are passed on within the organization. Employees internalize what they observe and learn from managers they perceive to be experts.

The results on the effectiveness of these five forms of power pose a challenge in organizations. The least effective power bases—legitimate, reward, and coercive—are the ones most likely to be used by managers.[9] Managers inherit these power bases as part of the position when they take a supervisory job. In contrast, the most effective power bases—referent and expert— are ones that must be developed and strengthened through interpersonal relationships with employees.

USING POWER ETHICALLY

Managers can work at developing all five of these forms of power for future use. The key to using them well is using them ethically, as Table 10-1 (on page 234) shows. Coercive power, for example, requires careful administration if it is to be used in an ethical manner. Employees should be informed of the rules in advance, and any punishment should be used consistently, uniformly, and privately. The key to using all five types of interpersonal power ethically is to be sensitive to employees' concerns and to communicate well.

To French and Raven's five power sources, we can add a source that is very important in today's organizations. *Information power* is access to and control over important information. Consider, for example, the CEO's administrative assistant. He or she has information about the CEO's schedule that people need if they are going to get in to see the CEO. Central to the idea of information power is the person's position in the communication networks in the organization, both formal and informal. Also important is the idea of framing, which is the "spin" that managers put on information. Managers not only pass information on to subordinates; they interpret this information and influence the subordinates' perceptions of it. Information

3. *Understand the ethical use of power.*

INFORMATION POWER
Access to and control over important information.

Form of Power	Guidelines for Use
Reward power	Verify compliance. Make feasible, reasonable requests. Make only ethical requests. Offer rewards desired by subordinates. Offer only credible rewards.
Coercive power	Inform subordinates of rules and penalties. Warn before punishing. Administer punishment consistently and uniformly. Understand the situation before acting. Maintain credibility. Fit punishment to the infraction. Punish in private.
Legitimate power	Be cordial and polite. Be confident. Be clear and follow up to verify understanding. Make sure request is appropriate. Explain reasons for request. Follow proper channels. Exercise power consistently. Enforce compliance. Be sensitive to subordinates' concerns.
Referent power	Treat subordinates fairly. Defend subordinates' interests. Be sensitive to subordinates' needs and feelings. Select subordinates similar to oneself. Engage in role modeling.
Expert power	Maintain credibility. Act confident and decisive. Keep informed. Recognize employee concerns. Avoid threatening subordinates' self-esteem.

Table 10-1
Guidelines for the Ethical Use of Power

Source: Table created from information on pp. 144–152 in *Leadership in Organizations* by Gary A. Yukl. Copyright © 1981. Adapted by permission of Pearson Education, Inc., Upper Saddle River, N.J.

power occurs not only in the downward direction; it may also flow upward from subordinates to managers. In manufacturing plants, database operators often control information about plant metrics and shipping performance that is vital to managerial decision making. Information power can also flow laterally. Salespersons convey information from the outside environment (their customers) that is essential for marketing efforts.

Determining whether a power-related behavior is ethical is complex. Another way to look at the ethics surrounding the use of power is to ask three questions that show the criteria for examining power-related behaviors:[10]

1. *Does the behavior produce a good outcome for people both inside and outside the organization?* This question represents the criterion of *utilitarian outcomes*. The behavior should result in the greatest good for the greatest number of people. If the power-related behavior serves only the individual's self-interest and fails to help the organization reach its goals, it is considered unethical. A salesperson might be tempted to discount a product deeply in order to make a sale that would win a contest. Doing so would be in her self-interest but would not benefit the organization.

2. *Does the behavior respect the rights of all parties?* This question emphasizes the criterion of *individual rights*. Free speech, privacy, and due process are individual rights that are to be respected, and power-related behaviors that violate these rights are considered unethical.

3. *Does the behavior treat all parties equitably and fairly?* This question represents the criterion of *distributive justice*. Power-related behavior that treats one party arbitrarily or benefits one party at the expense of another is unethical. Granting a day of vacation to one employee in a busy week in which coworkers must struggle to cover for him might be considered unethical.

To be considered ethical, power-related behavior must meet all three criteria. If the behavior fails to meet the criteria, then alternative actions should be considered. Unfortunately, most power-related behaviors are not easy to analyze. Conflicts may exist among the criteria; for example, a behavior may maximize the greatest good for the greatest number of people but may not treat all parties equitably. Individual rights may need to be sacrificed for the good of the organization. A CEO may need to be removed from power for the organization to be saved. Still, these criteria can be used on a case-by-case basis to sort through the complex ethical issues surrounding the use of power.

TWO FACES OF POWER: ONE POSITIVE, ONE NEGATIVE

We turn now to a theory of power that takes a strong stand on the "right" versus "wrong" kind of power to use in organizations. David McClelland has spent a great deal of his career studying the need for power and the ways managers use power. As was discussed in Chapter 5, he believes that there are two distinct faces of power, one negative and one positive.[11] The negative face of power is *personal power*—power used for personal gain. Managers who use personal power are commonly described as "power hungry." People who approach relationships with an exchange orientation often use personal power to ensure that they get at least their fair share—and often more—in the relationship. They are most interested in their own needs and interests.

Individuals who rely on personal power at its extreme might be considered Machiavellian—willing to do whatever it takes to get one's own way. Niccolo Machiavelli was an Italian statesman during the sixteenth

PERSONAL POWER
Power used for personal gain.

century who wrote *The Prince*, a guide for acquiring and using power.[12] Among his methods for using power was manipulating others, believing that it was better to be feared than loved. Machiavellians (or high Machs) are willing to manipulate others for personal gain, and are unconcerned with others' opinions or welfare.

SOCIAL POWER
Power used to create motivation or to accomplish group goals.

The positive face of power is *social power*—power used to create motivation or to accomplish group goals. McClelland clearly favors the use of social power by managers. People who approach relationships with a communal orientation focus on the needs and interests of others. They rely on social power.[13] McClelland has found that managers who use power successfully have four power-oriented characteristics:

1. *Belief in the authority system.* They believe that the institution is important and that its authority system is valid. They are comfortable influencing and being influenced. The source of their power is the authority system of which they are a part.

2. *Preference for work and discipline.* They like their work and are very orderly. They have a basic value preference for the Protestant work ethic, believing that work is good for a person over and beyond its income-producing value.

3. *Altruism.* They publicly put the company and its needs before their own needs. They are able to do this because they see their own well-being as integrally tied to the corporate well-being.

4. *Belief in justice.* They believe justice is to be sought above all else. People should receive that to which they are entitled and that which they earn.

McClelland takes a definite stand on the proper use of power by managers. When power is used for the good of the group, rather than for individual gain, it is positive.

INTERGROUP SOURCES OF POWER

Groups or teams within an organization can also use power from several sources. One source of intergroup power is control of *critical resources*.[14] When one group controls an important resource that another group desires, the first group holds power. Controlling resources needed by another group allows the power-holding group to influence the actions of the less powerful group. This process can continue in an upward spiral. Groups seen as powerful tend to be given more resources from top management.[15]

STRATEGIC CONTINGENCIES
Activities that other groups depend on in order to complete their tasks.

Groups also have power to the extent that they control *strategic contingencies*—activities that other groups depend on in order to complete their tasks.[16] The dean's office, for example, may control the number of faculty positions to be filled in each department of a college. The departmental hiring plans are thus contingent on approval from the dean's office. In this case, the dean's office controls the strategic contingency of faculty hiring, and thus has power.

Three factors can give a group control over a strategic contingency.[17] One is the *ability to cope with uncertainty*. If a group can help another group deal with uncertainty, it has power. One organizational group that has gained power in recent years is the legal department. Faced with increasing government regulations and fears of litigation, many other departments seek guidance from the legal department.

Another factor that can give a group control power is a *high degree of centrality* within the organization. If a group's functioning is important to the organization's success, it has high centrality. The sales force in a computer firm, for example, has power because of its immediate effect on the firm's operations and because other groups (accounting and servicing groups, for example) depend on its activities.

The third factor that can give a group power is *nonsubstitutability*—the extent to which a group performs a function that is indispensable to an organization. A team of computer specialists may be powerful because of its expertise with a system. It may have specialized experience that another team cannot provide.

The strategic contingencies model thus shows that groups hold power over other groups when they can reduce uncertainty, when their functioning is central to the organization's success, and when the group's activities are difficult to replace.[18] The key to all three of these factors, as you can see, is dependency. When one group controls something that another group needs, it creates a dependent relationship—and gives one group power over the other.

POWER ANALYSIS: A BROADER VIEW

Amitai Etzioni takes a more sociological orientation to power. Etzioni has developed a theory of power analysis.[19] He says that there are three types of organizational power and three types of organizational involvement, or membership, that will lead to either congruent or incongruent uses of power. The three types of organizational power are the following:

1. *Coercive power*—influencing members by forcing them to do something under threat of punishment, or through fear and intimidation.
2. *Utilitarian power*—influencing members by providing them with rewards and benefits.
3. *Normative power*—influencing members by using the knowledge that they want very much to belong to the organization and by letting them know that what they are expected to do is the "right" thing to do.

Along with these three types of organizational power, Etzioni proposes that we can classify organizations by the type of membership they have:

4. *Explain power analysis, an organizational-level theory of power.*

1. *Alienative membership.* The members have hostile, negative feelings about being in the organization. They don't want to be there. Prisons are a good example of alienative memberships.

2. *Calculative membership.* Members weigh the benefits and limitations of belonging to the organization. Businesses are good examples of organizations with calculative memberships.

3. *Moral membership.* Members have such positive feelings about organizational membership that they are willing to deny their own needs. Organizations with many volunteer workers, such as the American Heart Association, are examples of moral memberships. Religious groups are another example.

Etzioni argues that the type of organizational power should be matched to the type of membership in the organization in order to achieve congruence. Figure 10-1 shows the matches in his power analysis theory.

In an alienative membership, members have hostile feelings. In prisons, for example, Etzioni would contend that coercive power is the appropriate type to use.

A calculative membership is characterized by an analysis of the good and bad aspects of being in the organization. In a business partnership, for example, each partner weighs the benefits from the partnership against the costs entailed in the contractual arrangement. Utilitarian, or reward-based, power is the most appropriate type to use.

In a moral membership, the members have strong positive feelings about the particular cause or goal of the organization. Normative power is the most appropriate to use because it capitalizes on the members' desires to belong.

Etzioni's power analysis is an organizational-level theory. It emphasizes that the characteristics of an organization play a role in determining the type of power appropriate for use in the organization. Etzioni's theory is controversial in its contention that a single type of power is appropriate in any organization.

Figure 10-1
Etzioni's Power Analysis

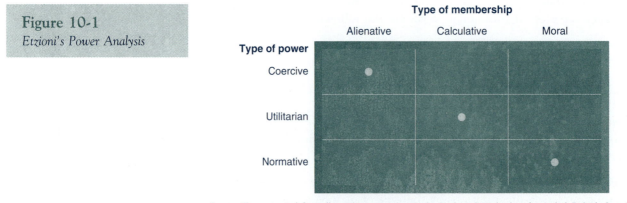

Source: Figure created from discussion on pp. 59–61 in *Modern Organizations* by Amitai Etzioni. Copyright © 1964. Adapted by permission of Pearson Education, Inc., Upper Saddle River, N.J.

SYMBOLS OF POWER

Organization charts show who has authority, but they do not reveal much about who has power. We'll now look at two very different ideas about the symbols of power. The first one comes from Rosabeth Moss Kanter. It is a scholarly approach to determining who has power and who feels powerless. The second is a semiserious look at the tangible symbols of power by Michael Korda.

5. *Identify symbols of power and powerlessness in organizations.*

KANTER'S SYMBOLS OF POWER

Kanter provides several characteristics of powerful people in organizations:[20]

1. *Ability to intercede for someone in trouble.* An individual who can pull someone out of a jam has power.

2. *Ability to get placements for favored employees.* Getting a key promotion for an employee is a sign of power.

3. *Exceeding budget limitations.* A manager who can go above budget limits without being reprimanded has power.

4. *Procuring above-average raises for employees.* One faculty member reported that her department head distributed 10 percent raises to the most productive faculty members although the budget allowed for only 4 percent increases. "I don't know how he did it; he must have pull," she said.

5. *Getting items on the agenda at meetings.* If a manager can raise issues for action at meetings, it's a sign of power.

6. *Access to early information.* Having information before anyone else does is a signal that a manager is plugged in to key sources.

7. *Having top managers seek out their opinion.* When top managers have a problem, they may ask for advice from lower-level managers. The managers they turn to have power.

A theme that runs through Kanter's list is doing things for others: for people in trouble, for employees, for bosses. There is an active, other-directed element in her symbols of power.

You can use Kanter's symbols of power to identify powerful people in organizations. They can be particularly useful in finding a mentor who can effectively use power.

KANTER'S SYMBOLS OF POWERLESSNESS

Kanter also wrote about symptoms of *powerlessness*—a lack of power—in managers at different levels of the organization. First-line supervisors, for example, often display three symptoms of powerlessness: overly close supervision, inflexible adherence to the rules, and a tendency to do the job themselves rather than training their employees to do it. Staff professionals such as accountants and lawyers display different symptoms of powerlessness. When they feel powerless, they tend to resist change and try to protect their turf. Top executives can also feel powerless. They show symptoms such as

POWERLESSNESS
A lack of power.

focusing on budget cutting, punishing others, and using dictatorial, top-down communication. Acting in certain ways can lead employees to believe that a manager is powerless. By making external attributions (blaming others or circumstances) for negative events, a manager looks like he or she has no power.[21]

What can you do when you recognize that employees are feeling powerless? The key to overcoming powerlessness is to share power and delegate decision-making authority to employees.

KORDA'S SYMBOLS OF POWER

Michael Korda takes a different look at symbols of power in organizations.[22] He discusses three unusual symbols: office furnishings, time power, and standing by.

Furniture is not just physically useful; it also conveys a message about power. Locked file cabinets are signs that the manager has important and confidential information in the office. A rectangular (rather than round) conference table enables the most important person to sit at the head of the table. The size of one's desk may convey the amount of power. Most executives prefer large, expensive desks.

Time power means using clocks and watches as power symbols. Korda says that the biggest compliment a busy executive can pay a visitor is to remove his watch and place it face down on the desk, thereby communicating "my time is yours." He also notes that the less powerful the executive, the more intricate the watch; moreover, managers who are really secure in their power wear no watch at all, since they believe nothing important can happen without them. A full calendar is also proof of power. Personal planners are left open on the desk to display busy schedules.

Standing by is a game in which people are obliged to keep their cell phones, pagers, etc., with them at all times so executives can reach them. The idea is that the more you can impose your schedule on other people, the more power you have. In fact, Korda defines *power* as follows: There are more people who inconvenience themselves on your behalf than there are people on whose behalf you would inconvenience yourself. Closely tied to this is the ability to make others perform simple tasks for you, such as getting your coffee or fetching the mail.

While Kanter's symbols focus on the ability to help others, Korda's symbols focus on status—a person's relative standing in a group based on prestige and having other people defer to him or her.[23] By identifying powerful people and learning from their modeled behavior, you can learn the keys to power use in the organization.

6. *Define organizational politics and understand the major influence tactics.*

ORGANIZATIONAL POLITICS
The use of power and influence in organizations.

POLITICAL BEHAVIOR IN ORGANIZATIONS

Like power, the term politics in organizations may conjure up a few negative images. However, **organizational politics** is not necessarily negative; it is the use of power and influence in organizations. As people try to acquire power and expand their power base, they use various tactics and strategies. Some are sanctioned (acceptable to the organization); others are not. ***Political behavior*** refers to actions not officially sanctioned by an organization that are taken to influence others in order to meet one's personal goals.[24]

Politics is a controversial topic among managers. Some managers take a favorable view of political behavior; others see it as detrimental to the organization. In one study of managers, 53 percent reported that politics had a positive impact on the achievement of the organization's goals.[25] In contrast, 44 percent reported that politics distracted organization members from focusing on goal achievement. In a different study, managers displayed conflicting attitudes toward politics in organizations. More than 89 percent agreed that workplace politics was common in most organizations and that successful executives must be good politicians. However, 59 percent indicated that workplaces that were free of politics were more satisfying to work in.[26] These studies point out the controversial nature of political behavior in organizations.

Many organizational conditions encourage political activity. Among them are unclear goals, autocratic decision making, ambiguous lines of authority, scarce resources, and uncertainty.[27] Even supposedly objective activities may involve politics. One such activity is the performance appraisal process. A study of sixty executives who had extensive experience in employee evaluation indicated that political considerations were nearly always part of the performance appraisal process.[28]

The effects of political behavior in organizations can be quite negative when the political behavior is strategically undertaken to maximize self-interest. If people within the organization are competitively pursuing selfish ends, they're unlikely to be attentive to the concerns of others. The workplace can seem less helpful, more threatening, and more unpredictable. People focus on their own concerns rather than on organizational goals. This represents the negative face of power described earlier by David McClelland as personal power. If employees view the organization's political climate as extreme, they experience more anxiety, tension, fatigue, and burnout. They are also dissatisfied with their jobs and are more likely to leave.[29] There are ways to avoid this negative climate, as discussed later in this chapter.

INFLUENCE TACTICS

Influence is the process of affecting the thoughts, behavior, or feelings of another person. That other person could be the boss (upward influence), an employee (downward influence), or a coworker (lateral influence). There are eight basic types of influence tactics. They are listed and described in Table 10-2 (on page 242).[30]

Research has shown that the four tactics used most frequently are consultation, rational persuasion, inspirational appeals, and ingratiation. Upward appeals and coalition tactics are used moderately. Exchange tactics are used least often.

POLITICAL BEHAVIOR
Actions not officially sanctioned by an organization that are taken to influence others in order to meet one's personal goals.

Tactics	Description	Examples
Pressure	The person uses demands, threats, or intimidation to convince you to comply with a request or to support a proposal.	If you don't do this, you're fired. You have until 5:00 to change your mind, or I'm going without you.
Upward appeals	The person seeks to persuade you that the request is approved by higher management, or appeals to higher management for assistance in gaining your compliance with the request.	I'm reporting you to my boss. My boss supports this idea.
Exchange	The person makes an explicit or implicit promise that you will receive rewards or tangible benefits if you comply with a request or support a proposal, or reminds you of a prior favor to be reciprocated.	You owe me a favor. I'll take you to lunch if you'll support me on this.
Coalition	The person seeks the aid of others to persuade you to do something or uses the support of others as an argument for you to agree also.	All the other supervisors agree with me. I'll ask you in front of the whole committee.
Ingratiation	The person seeks to get you in a good mood or to think favorably of him or her before asking you to do something.	Only you can do this job right. I can always count on you, so I have another request.
Rational persuasion	The person uses logical arguments and factual evidence to persuade you that a proposal or request is viable and likely to result in the attainment of task objectives.	This new procedure will save us $150,000 in overhead. It makes sense to hire John; he has the most experience.
Inspirational appeals	The person makes an emotional request or proposal that arouses enthusiasm by appealing to your values and ideals, or by increasing your confidence that you can do it.	Being environmentally conscious is the right thing. Getting that account will be tough, but I know you can do it.
Consultation	The person seeks your participation in making a decision or planning how to implement a proposed policy, strategy, or change.	This new attendance plan is controversial. How can we make it more acceptable? What do you think we can do to make our workers less fearful of the new robots on the production line?

Source: First two columns from G. Yukl and C. M. Falbe, "Influence Tactics and Objectives in Upward, Downward, and Lateral Influence Attempts," *Journal of Applied Psychology* 75 (1990): 132–140. Copyright © 1990 by the American Psychological Association. Reprinted with permission.

Table 10-2
Influence Tactics Used in Organizations

Influence tactics are used for impression management, which was described in Chapter 3. In impression management, individuals use influence tactics to control others' impressions of them. One way in which people engage in impression management is through image building. Another way is to use impression management to get support for important initiatives or projects.

Ingratiation is an example of one tactic often used for impression management. Ingratiation can take many forms, including flattery, opinion conformity, and subservient behavior.[31] Exchange is another influence tactic that may be used for impression management. Offering to do favors for someone in an effort to create a favorable impression is an exchange tactic.

Which influence tactics are most effective? It depends on the target of the influence attempt and the objective. Individuals use different tactics for different purposes, and they use different tactics for different people. Influence attempts with subordinates, for example, usually involve assigning tasks or changing behavior. With peers, the objective is often to request help. With superiors, influence attempts are often made to request approval, resources, political support, or personal benefits. Rational persuasion and coalition tactics are used most often to get support from peers and superiors to change company policy. Consultation and inspirational appeals are particularly effective for gaining support and resources for a new project.[32] Overall, the most effective tactic in terms of achieving objectives is rational persuasion. Pressure is the least effective tactic.

Subordinates often use influence attempts to try to convince their supervisors of their promotability. Rational persuasion works; it has a positive effect on supervisors' assessments of promotability. Ingratiation, a softer tactic, has a negative effect on promotability—supervisors see their subordinate's ingratiation attempts as self-serving attempts to get ahead.[33] When supervisors believe an employee's motive for doing favors for the boss is simply to be a good citizen, they are likely to reward that employee. However, when the motive is seen as brownnosing (ingratiation), supervisors respond negatively.[34] And, as it becomes more obvious that the employee has something to gain by impressing the boss, the likelihood that ingratiation will succeed decreases.

Still, a well-disguised ingratiation is hard to resist. Attempts that are not obvious usually succeed in increasing the target's liking for the ingratiator.[35] Most people have trouble remaining neutral when someone flatters them or agrees with them. However, witnesses to the ingratiation are more likely to question the motive behind the flattery or agreement. Observers are more skeptical than the recipients of the ingratiation.

There is evidence that men and women view politics and influence attempts differently. Men tend to view political behavior more favorably than do women. When both men and women witness political behavior, they view it more positively if the agent is of their gender and the target is of the opposite gender.[36]

Different cultures prefer different influence tactics at work. One study found that American managers dealing with a tardy employee tended to rely on pressure tactics such as "If you don't start reporting on time for work, I will have no choice but to start docking your pay." In contrast, Japanese managers relied on influence tactics that either appealed to the employee's sense of duty ("It is your duty as a responsible employee of this company to begin work on time.") or emphasized a consultative approach ("Is there anything I can do to help you overcome the problems that are preventing you from coming to work on time?").[37]

It is important to note that influence tactics do have some positive effects. When investors form coalitions and put pressure on firms to increase

YOU BE THE JUDGE

What are the most common forms of political behavior that you see in your work or school environment? Are they ethical or unethical? Explain.

their research and development efforts, it works.[38] However, some influence tactics, including pressure, coalition building, and exchange, can have strong ethical implications. There is a fine line between being an impression manager and being seen as a manipulator.

How can a manager use influence tactics well? First, a manager can develop and maintain open lines of communication in all directions: upward, downward, and lateral. Then, the manager can treat the targets of influence attempts—whether managers, employees, or peers—with basic respect. Finally, the manager can understand that influence relationships are reciprocal—they are two-way relationships. As long as the influence attempts are directed toward organizational goals, the process of influence can be advantageous to all involved.

MANAGING POLITICAL BEHAVIOR IN ORGANIZATIONS

Politics cannot and should not be eliminated from organizations. Managers can, however, take a proactive stance and manage the political behavior that inevitably occurs.[39]

Open communication is one key to managing political behavior. Uncertainty tends to increase political behavior, and communication that reduces the uncertainty is important. One form of communication that will help is to clarify the sanctioned and nonsanctioned political behaviors in the organization. For example, you may want to encourage social power as opposed to personal power.[40]

Another key is to clarify expectations regarding performance. This can be accomplished through the use of clear, quantifiable goals and through the establishment of a clear connection between goal accomplishment and rewards.[41]

Participative management is yet another key. Often, people engage in political behavior when they feel excluded from decision-making processes in the organization. By including them, you will encourage positive input and eliminate behind-the-scenes maneuvering.

Encouraging cooperation among work groups is another strategy for managing political behavior. Managers can instill a unity of purpose among work teams by rewarding cooperative behavior and by implementing activities that emphasize the integration of team efforts toward common goals.[42]

Managing scarce resources well is also important. An obvious solution to the problem of scarce resources is to increase the resource pool, but few managers have this luxury. Clarifying the resource allocation process and making the connection between performance and resources explicit can help discourage dysfunctional political behavior.

Providing a supportive organizational climate is another way to manage political behavior effectively. A supportive climate allows employees to discuss controversial issues promptly and openly. This prevents the issue from festering and potentially causing friction among employees.[43]

Managing political behavior at work is important. The perception of dysfunctional political behavior can lead to dissatisfaction.[44] When employees perceive that there are dominant interest groups or cliques at work, they are less satisfied with pay and promotions. When they believe that the organization's reward practices are influenced by who you know rather than how well you perform, they are less satisfied.[45] In addition, when employees believe that their coworkers are exhibiting increased political behavior, they are less satisfied with their coworkers. Open communication, clear expectations about performance and rewards, participative decision-making practices, work group cooperation, effective management of scarce resources, and a supportive organizational climate can help managers prevent the negative consequences of political behavior.

MANAGING UP: MANAGING THE BOSS

One of the least discussed aspects of power and politics is the relationship between you and your boss. This is a crucial relationship, because your boss is your most important link with the rest of the organization.[46] The employee–boss relationship is one of mutual dependence; you depend on your boss to give you performance feedback, provide resources, and supply critical information. She depends on you for performance, information, and support. Because it's a mutual relationship, you should take an active role in managing it. Too often, the management of this relationship is left to the boss; but if the relationship doesn't meet your needs, chances are you haven't taken the responsibility to manage it proactively.

Table 10-3 shows the basic steps to take in managing your relationship with your boss. The first step is to try to understand as much as you can

7. *Develop a plan for managing employee–boss relationships.*

Make Sure You Understand Your Boss and Her Context, Including:
Her goals and objectives.
The pressures on her.
Her strengths, weaknesses, blind spots.
Her preferred work style.
Assess Yourself and Your Needs, Including:
Your own strengths and weaknesses.
Your personal style.
Your predisposition toward dependence on authority figures.
Develop and Maintain a Relationship that:
Fits both your needs and styles.
Is characterized by mutual expectations.
Keeps your boss informed.
Is based on dependability and honesty.
Selectively uses your boss's time and resources.

Table 10-3
Managing Your Relationship with Your Boss

Source: Adapted and reprinted by permission of *Harvard Business Review*. From J. J. Gabarro and J. P. Kotter, "Managing Your Boss," *Harvard Business Review* (May/June 1993): p. 155. Copyright © 1993 by the Harvard Business School Publishing Corporation; all rights reserved.

about your boss. What are the person's goals and objectives? What kind of pressures does the person face in the job? Many individuals naively expect the boss to be perfect and are disappointed when they find that this is not the case. What are the boss's strengths, weaknesses, and blind spots? Because this is an emotionally charged relationship, it is difficult to be objective; but this is a critical step in forging an effective working relationship. What is the boss's preferred work style? Does the person prefer everything in writing or hate detail? Does the boss prefer that you make appointments, or is dropping in at the boss's office acceptable? The point is to gather as much information about your boss as you can and to try to put yourself in that person's shoes.

The second step in managing this important relationship is to assess yourself and your own needs much in the same way you analyzed your boss's. What are your strengths, weaknesses, and blind spots? What is your work style? How do you normally relate to authority figures? Some of us have tendencies toward counterdependence; that is, we rebel against the boss as an authority and view the boss as a hindrance to our performance. Or, in contrast, we might take an overdependent stance, passively accepting the employee–boss relationship and treating the boss as an all-wise, protective parent. What is your tendency? Knowing how you react to authority figures can help you understand your interactions with your boss.

Once you have done a careful self-analysis and tried to understand your boss, the next step is to work to develop an effective relationship. Both parties' needs and styles must be accommodated. A fundraiser for a large volunteer organization related a story about a new boss, describing him as cold, aloof, unorganized, and inept. She made repeated attempts to meet with him and clarify expectations, and his usual reply was that he didn't have the time. Frustrated, she almost looked for a new job. "I just can't reach him!" was her refrain. Then she stepped back to consider her boss's and her own styles. Being an intuitive-feeling type of person, she prefers constant feedback and reinforcement from others. Her boss, an intuitive-thinker, works comfortably without feedback from others and has a tendency to fail to praise or reward others. She sat down with him and cautiously discussed the differences in their needs. This discussion became the basis for working out a comfortable relationship. "I still don't like him, but I understand him better," she said.

Another aspect of managing the relationship involves working out mutual expectations. One key activity is to develop a plan for work objectives and have the boss agree to it.[47] It is important to do things right, but it is also important to do the right things. Neither party to the relationship is a mind reader, and clarifying the goals is a crucial step.

Keeping the boss informed is also a priority. No one likes to be caught off guard, and there are several ways to keep the boss informed. Give the boss a weekly to-do list as a reminder of the progress towards goals. When you read something pertaining to your work, clip it out for the boss. Most busy executives appreciate being given materials they don't have time to find for themselves. Give the boss interim reports, and let the boss know if the work schedule is slipping. Don't wait until it's too late to take action.

The employee–boss relationship must be based on dependability and honesty. This means giving and receiving positive and negative feedback. Most of us are reluctant to give any feedback to the boss, but positive feedback is welcomed at the top. Negative feedback, while tougher to initiate, can clear the air. If given in a problem-solving format, it can even bring about a closer relationship.[48]

One university professor was constantly bombarded by the department head's requests that she serve on committees. When she complained about this to a colleague, she was told, "It's your fault; you need to learn how to say no." She went to the department head, explained that the committee work was keeping her from being an effective researcher and teacher, and asked that he reassign other faculty members to the committees. The department head was astonished that he had relied on her so heavily. "I just didn't realize that you were on so many committees already. Thanks for pointing it out. We need to spread these responsibilities around better."

Another point about negative feedback is that it is better to give it directly, rather than behind the boss's back. If the boss never gets the information, how can the problem be corrected?

Being considerate of the boss's time is important. Before running into the person's office, ask yourself if the meeting is necessary at that particular time. Does the boss need the information right now? Could you supply the information in a note? Is it a matter you could handle yourself? Another good time management technique is to submit an agenda before your meeting with the boss; that way, the boss can select an appropriate time slot and will have time to think about the items.

Finally, remember that the boss is on the same team you are. The golden rule is to make the boss look good, because you expect the boss to do the same for you.

SHARING POWER: EMPOWERMENT

Another positive strategy for managing political behavior is **empowerment**—sharing power within an organization. As modern organizations grow flatter, eliminating layers of management, empowerment becomes more and more important. Jay Conger defines *empowerment* as "creating conditions for heightened motivation through the development of a strong sense of personal self-efficacy."[49] This means sharing power in such a way that individuals learn to believe in their ability to do the job. The driving idea of empowerment is that the individuals closest to the work and to the customers should make the decisions and that this makes the best use of employees' skills and talents. You can empower yourself by developing your sense of self-efficacy. This chapter's Challenge helps you assess your progress in terms of self-empowerment.

Four dimensions comprise the essence of empowerment: meaning, competence, self-determination, and impact.[50] *Meaning* is a fit between the work

8. *Discuss how managers can empower others.*

EMPOWERMENT
Sharing power within an organization.

Challenge

ARE YOU SELF-EMPOWERED?

Check either (a) or (b) to indicate how you usually act in these situations:

1. If someone disagrees with me in a class or a meeting, I
   a. immediately back down
   b. explain my position further
2. When I have an idea for a project, I
   a. typically take a great deal of time to start it
   b. get going on it fairly quickly
3. If my boss or teacher tells me to do something that I think is wrong, I
   a. do it anyway, telling myself he or she is "the boss"
   b. ask for clarification and explain my position
4. When a complicated problem arises, I usually tell myself
   a. I can take care of it
   b. I will not be able to solve it
5. When I am around people of higher authority, I often
   a. feel intimidated and defer to them
   b. enjoy meeting important people
6. As I awake in the morning, I usually feel
   a. alert and ready to conquer almost anything
   b. tired and have a hard time getting myself motivated
7. During an argument I
   a. put a great deal of energy into "winning"
   b. try to listen to the other side and see if we have any points of agreement
8. When I meet new people, I
   a. always wonder what they are "really" up to
   b. try to learn what they are about and give them the benefit of the doubt until they prove otherwise
9. During the day I often
   a. criticize myself on what I am doing or thinking
   b. think positive thoughts about myself
10. When someone else does a great job, I
    a. find myself picking apart that person and looking for faults
    b. often give a sincere compliment
11. When I am working in a group, I try to
    a. do a better job than the others
    b. help the group function more effectively
12. If someone pays me a compliment, I typically
    a. try not to appear boastful and I downplay the compliment
    b. respond with a positive "thank you" or similar response
13. I like to be around people who
    a. challenge me and make me question what I do
    b. give me respect
14. In love relationships I prefer the other person to
    a. have his/her own selected interests
    b. do pretty much what I do
15. During a crisis I try to
    a. resolve the problem
    b. find someone to blame
16. After seeing a movie with friends, I
    a. wait to see what they say before I decide whether I liked it
    b. am ready to talk about my reactions right away
17. When work deadlines are approaching, I typically
    a. get flustered and worry about completion
    b. buckle down and work until the job is done
18. If a job comes up I am interested in, I
    a. go for it and apply
    b. tell myself I am not qualified enough
19. When someone treats me unkindly or unfairly, I
    a. try to rectify the situation
    b. tell other people about the injustice
20. If a difficult conflict situation or problem arises, I
    a. try not to think about it, hoping it will resolve itself
    b. look at various options and may ask others for advice before I figure out what to do

(continued)

Scoring:
Score one point for each of the following circled: 1b, 2b, 3b, 4a, 5b, 6a, 7b, 8b, 9b, 10b, 11b, 12b, 13a, 14a, 15a, 16b, 17b, 18a, 19a, 20b.

Analysis of Scoring:
16–20   You are a take-charge person and generally make the most of opportunities. When others tell you something cannot be done, you may take this as a challenge and do it anyway. You see the world as an oyster with many pearls to harvest.

11–15   You try hard, but sometimes your negative attitude prevents you from getting involved in productive projects. Many times you take responsibility, but there are situations where you look to others to take care of problems.

0–10   You complain too much and are usually focused on the "worst case scenario." To you the world is controlled by fate and no matter what you do it seems to get you nowhere, so you let other people develop opportunities. You need to start seeing the positive qualities in yourself and in others and see yourself as the "master of your fate."

role and the employee's values and beliefs. It is the engine of empowerment through which employees become energized about their jobs. If employees' hearts are not in their work, they cannot feel empowered. *Competence* is the belief that one has the ability to do the job well. Without competence, employees will feel inadequate and lack a sense of empowerment. *Self-determination* is having control over the way one does his or her work. Employees who feel they're just following orders from the boss cannot feel empowered. *Impact* is the belief that one's job makes a difference within the organization. Without a sense of contributing to a goal, employees cannot feel empowered.

Employees need to experience all four of the empowerment dimensions in order to feel truly empowered. Only then will organizations reap the hoped-for rewards from empowerment efforts. The rewards sought are increased effectiveness, higher job satisfaction, and less stress.

Empowerment is easy to advocate but difficult to put into practice. Conger offers some guidelines on how leaders can empower others.

First, managers should express confidence in employees and set high performance expectations. Positive expectations can go a long way toward enabling good performance, as the Pygmalion effect shows (Chapter 3).

Second, managers should create opportunities for employees to participate in decision making. This means participation in the forms of both voice and choice. Employees should not just be asked to contribute their opinions about any issue; they should also have a vote in the decision that is made. One method for increasing participation is using self-managed teams, as we discussed in Chapter 8.

Third, managers should remove bureaucratic constraints that stifle autonomy. Often, companies have antiquated rules and policies that prevent employees from managing themselves. An example is a collection agency where a manager's signature was once required to approve long-term payment arrangements for delinquent customers. Collectors, who spoke directly with customers, were the best judges of whether the payment arrangements were workable, and having to consult a manager made them feel closely supervised and powerless. The rule was dropped, and collections increased.

Fourth, managers should set inspirational or meaningful goals. When individuals feel they "own" a goal, they are more willing to take personal responsibility for it.

Empowerment is a matter of degree. Jobs can be thought of in two dimensions: job content and job context. Job content consists of the tasks and procedures necessary for doing a particular job. Job context is broader. It is the reason the organization needs the job and includes the way the job fits into the organization's mission, goals, and objectives. These two dimensions are depicted in Figure 10-2, the employee empowerment grid.

Both axes of the grid contain the major steps in the decision-making process. As shown on the horizontal axis, decision-making authority over job content increases in terms of greater involvement in the decision-making process. Similarly, the vertical axis shows that authority over job

Figure 10-2
Employee Empowerment Grid

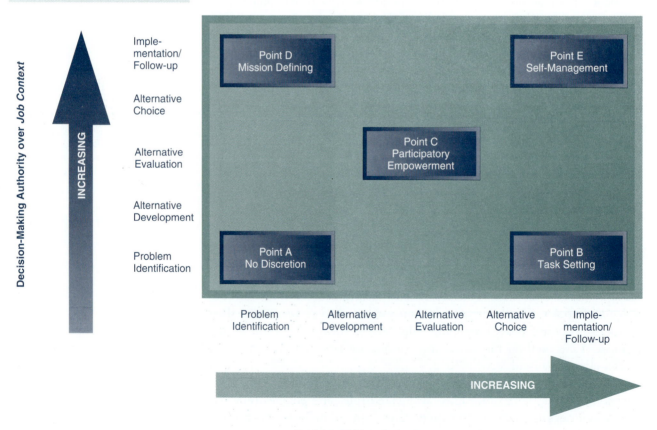

context increases with greater involvement in that decision-making process. Combining job content and job context authority in this way produces five points that vary in terms of the degree of empowerment.[51]

No Discretion (point A) represents the traditional, assembly-line job: highly routine and repetitive, with no decision-making power. If these jobs have a demanding pace and if workers have no discretion, distress will result.

Task Setting (point B) is the essence of most empowerment programs in organizations today. In this case, the worker is empowered to make decisions about the best way to get the job done, but has no decision responsibility for the job context.

Participatory Empowerment (point C) represents a situation that is typical of autonomous work groups that have some decision-making power over both job content and job context. Their involvement is in problem identification, developing alternatives, and evaluating alternatives, but the actual choice of alternatives is often beyond their power. Participatory empowerment can lead to job satisfaction and productivity.

Mission Defining (point D) is an unusual case of empowerment and is seldom seen. Here, employees have power over job context but not job content. An example would be a unionized team that is asked to decide whether their jobs could be better done by an outside vendor. Deciding to outsource would dramatically affect the mission of the company, but would not affect job content, which is specified in the union contract. Assuring these employees of continued employment regardless of their decision would be necessary for this case of empowerment.

Self-Management (point E) represents total decision-making control over both job content and job context. It is the ultimate expression of trust. One example is TXI Chaparral Steel (part of Texas Industries), where employees redesign their own jobs to add value to the organization.

Empowerment should begin with job content and proceed to job context. Because the workforce is so diverse, managers should recognize that some employees are more ready for empowerment than others. Managers must diagnose situations and determine the degree of empowerment to extend to employees.

At Oregon Cutting Systems (a subsidiary of Blount International), empowerment is a key element of the quality process. Oregon Cutting designs and manufactures cutting tools and holds half of the world's market for chains for saws. At Oregon Cutting, machine operators use statistical process control to improve product quality. Operators are empowered to gather their own data, find the causes of problems, make decisions, and act to fix the problems. Managers at Oregon Cutting prefer that employees ask for forgiveness rather than permission. Empowerment is essential to an organizational culture that supports quality.

The empowerment process also carries with it a risk of failure. When you delegate responsibility and authority, you must be prepared to allow employees to fail; and failure is not something most managers tolerate well. At Levi Strauss, an employee failed to order enough fabric to meet a

YOU BE THE JUDGE

Is it possible to have an organization where all power is equally shared, or is the unequal distribution of power a necessary evil in organizations? Explain.

production run on jeans. The manager sat down with the employee and found out what had gone wrong and how to prevent that problem in the future. She did this in a nonthreatening way, without blaming or finger-pointing.[52] Coaching and counseling following a failure can turn it into a learning experience.

MANAGERIAL IMPLICATIONS: USING POWER EFFECTIVELY

Managers must depend on others to get things done. John Kotter argues that managers therefore need to develop power strategies to operate effectively.[53] Kotter offers some guidelines for managing dependence on others and for using power successfully:

- *Use power in ethical ways.* People make certain assumptions about the use of power. One way of using the various forms of power ethically is by applying the criteria of utilitarian outcomes, individual rights, and distributive justice.
- *Understand and use all of the various types of power and influence.* Successful managers diagnose the situation, understand the people involved, and choose a compatible influence method.
- *Seek jobs that allow you to develop your power skills.* Recognize that managerial positions are dependent ones, and look for positions that allow you to focus on a critical issue or problem.
- *Use power tempered by maturity and self-control.* Power for its own sake should not be a goal, nor should power be used for self-aggrandizement.
- *Accept that influencing people is an important part of the management job.* Power means getting things accomplished; it is not a dirty word. Acquiring and using power well is a key to managerial success.

You can use these guidelines to enhance your own power skills. Mastering the power and politics within an organization takes respect and patience. When all people are empowered, the total amount of power within the organization will increase.

KEY TERMS

authority	legitimate power	referent power
coercive power	organizational politics	reward power
empowerment	personal power	social power
expert power	political behavior	strategic contingencies
influence	power	zone of indifference
information power	powerlessness	

Experiential Exercise

SOCIAL POWER ROLE-PLAYS

1. Divide the class into five groups of equal size, each of which is assigned one of the French and Raven types of power.

2. Read the following paragraph and prepare an influence plan using the type of power that has been assigned to your group. When you have finished your planning, select one member to play the role of instructor. Then choose from your own or another group a "student" who is to be the recipient of the "instructor's" efforts.

You are an instructor in a college class and have become aware that a potentially good student has been repeatedly absent from class and sometimes is unprepared when he is there. He seems to be satisfied with the grade he is getting, but you would like to see him attend regularly, be better prepared, and thus do better in the class. You even feel that the student might get really turned on to pursuing a career in this field, which is an exciting one for you. You are respected and liked by your students, and it irritates you that this person treats your dedicated teaching with such a cavalier attitude. You want to influence the student to start attending regularly.

3. Role-playing.
   a. Each group role-plays its influence plan.
   b. During the role-playing, members in other groups should think of themselves as the student being influenced. Fill out the following "Reaction to Influence Questionnaire" for each role-playing episode, including your own.

4. Tabulate the results of the questionnaire within your group. For each role-playing effort, determine how many people thought the power used was reward, coercive, and so on; then add up each member's score for item 2, then for items 3, 4, and 5.

5. Group discussion.
   a. As a class, discuss which influence strategy is the most effective in compliance, long-lasting effect, acceptable attitude, and enhanced relationships.
   b. What are the likely side effects of each type of influence strategy?

Reaction to Influence Questionnaire

Role-Play #1

1. Type of power used (mark one):

   Reward—Ability to influence because of potential reward.

   Coercive—Ability to influence because of capacity to coerce or punish.

   Legitimate—Stems from formal position in organization.

   Referent—Comes from admiration and liking.

   Expert—Comes from superior knowledge or ability to get things done.

Role-Plays				
1	2	3	4	5

(continued)

Think of yourself on the receiving end of the influence attempt just described and record your own reaction with an "X" in the appropriate box.

2. As a result of this influence attempt I will . . .
   definitely not comply   definitely comply
   1   2   3   4   5

3. Any change that does come about will be . . .
   temporary   long-lasting
   1   2   3   4   5

4. My own personal reaction is . . .
   resistant   accepting
   1   2   3   4   5

5. As a result of this influence attempt, my relationship with the instructor will probably be . . .
   worse   better
   1   2   3   4   5

Role-Plays				
1	2	3	4	5

Source: Gib Akin, *Exchange* 3, No. 4 (1978): 38–39. Reprinted by permission of Gib Akin, McIntire School of Commerce, University of Virginia.

11

Leadership and Followership

LEARNING OBJECTIVES

After reading this chapter, you should be able to do the following:

1. Define *leadership* and *followership*.

2. Discuss the differences between leadership and management, and between leaders and managers.

3. Compare autocratic, democratic, and laissez-faire leadership styles.

4. Explain initiating structure and consideration, leader behaviors, and the Leadership Grid.

5. Explain Fiedler's contingency theory of leadership.

6. Distinguish among the path–goal theory, the Vroom-Yetton-Jago theory, and the situational leadership model.

7. Distinguish among transformational, transactional, and charismatic leaders.

8. Discuss the characteristics of effective and dynamic followers.

1. *Define leadership and follower-ship.*

LEADERSHIP
The process of guiding and directing the behavior of people in the work environment.

FORMAL LEADERSHIP
Officially sanctioned leadership based on the authority of a formal position.

INFORMAL LEADERSHIP
Unofficial leadership accorded to a person by other members of the organization.

FOLLOWERSHIP
The process of being guided and directed by a leader in the work environment.

2. *Discuss the differences between leadership and management, and between leaders and managers.*

YOU BE THE JUDGE

Is it ethical for leaders to tell fol-lowers unilaterally what to do without asking their opinions or getting any input from them?

Leadership in organizations is the process of guiding and directing the be-havior of people in the work environment. The first section of the chapter distinguishes leadership from management. *Formal leadership* occurs when an organization officially bestows on a leader the authority to guide and di-rect others in the organization. *Informal leadership* occurs when a person is unofficially accorded power by others in the organization and uses influ-ence to guide and direct their behavior. Leadership is among the most re-searched topics in organizational behavior and one of the least understood social processes in organizations.

Leadership has a long, rich history in organizational behavior. In this chapter, we explore many of the theories and ideas that have emerged along the way in that history. To begin, we examine the differences between lead-ers and managers. Next, we explore the earliest theories of leadership, the trait theories, which tried to identify a set of traits that leaders have in com-mon. Following the trait theories, behavioral theories were developed, proposing that leader behaviors, not traits, are what counts. Contingency theories followed soon after. These theories argue that appropriate leader behavior depends on the situation and the followers. Next, we present some exciting contemporary theories of leadership, followed by the "hot" and exciting new issues that are arising in leadership. We end by discussing *followership*, and providing you with some guidelines for using this leader-ship knowledge.

LEADERSHIP AND MANAGEMENT

John Kotter suggests that leadership and management are two distinct, yet complementary, systems of action in organizations.[1] Specifically, he be-lieves that effective leadership produces useful change in organizations (as exemplified by Lee Iacocca at Chrysler Corporation in the early 1980s) and that good management controls complexity in the organization and its en-vironment (as exemplified by Jack Welch at General Electric). Healthy or-ganizations need both effective leadership and good management.

For Kotter, the management process involves (1) planning and budget-ing, (2) organizing and staffing, and (3) controlling and problem solving. The management process reduces uncertainty and stabilizes an organization. Alfred P. Sloan's integration and stabilization of General Motors after its early growth years are an example of good management.

In contrast, the leadership process involves (1) setting a direction for the organization; (2) aligning people with that direction through communication; and (3) motivating people to action, partly through empowerment and partly through basic need gratification. The leadership process creates uncertainty and change in an organization. Donald Peterson's championing of a quality revolution at Ford Motor Company is an example of effective leadership.

Abraham Zaleznik proposes that leaders have distinct personalities that stand in contrast to the personalities of managers.[2] Zaleznik suggests that both leaders and managers make a valuable contribution to an organization and that each one's contribution is different. Whereas **leaders** agitate for change and new approaches, **managers** advocate stability and the status quo. There is a dynamic tension between leaders and managers that makes it difficult for each to understand the other. Leaders and managers differ along four separate dimensions of personality: attitudes toward goals, conceptions of work, relationships with other people, and sense of self. The differences between these two personality types are summarized in Table 11-1. Zaleznik's distinction between leaders and managers is similar to the distinction made between transactional and transformational leaders, or between leadership and supervision. Transactional leaders use formal rewards and punishment to engage in deal making and contractual obligations, which you will read about later in this chapter.

It has been proposed that some people are strategic leaders, who embody both the stability of managers and the visionary abilities of leaders. Thus, strategic leaders combine the best of both worlds in a synergistic way. The unprecedented success of both Coca-Cola and Microsoft suggests that their leaders, the late Robert Goizueta (of Coke) and Bill Gates, were strategic leaders.[3]

LEADER
An advocate for change and new approaches to problems.

MANAGER
An advocate for stability and the status quo.

EARLY TRAIT THEORIES

The first studies of leadership attempted to identify what physical attributes, personality characteristics, and abilities distinguished leaders from

Personality Dimension	Manager	Leader
Attitudes toward goals	Has an impersonal, passive, functional attitude; believes goals arise out of necessity and reality	Has a personal and active attitude; believes goals arise from desire and imagination
Conceptions of work	Views work as an enabling process that combines people, ideas, and things; seeks moderate risk through coordination and balance	Looks for fresh approaches to old problems; seeks high-risk positions, especially with high payoffs
Relationships with others	Avoids solitary work activity, preferring to work with others; avoids close, intense relationships; avoids conflict	Is comfortable in solitary work activity; encourages close, intense working relationships; is not conflict averse
Sense of self	Is once born; makes a straightforward life adjustment; accepts life as it is	Is twice born; engages in a struggle for a sense of order in life; questions life

Table 11-1
Leaders and Managers

Source: Reprinted by permission of *Harvard Business Review*. From A. Zaleznik, "Managers and Leaders: Are They Different?" *Harvard Business Review* 55 (1977): 67–77. Copyright © 1977 by the Harvard Business School Publishing Corporation; all rights reserved.

other members of a group.[4] The physical attributes considered have been height, weight, physique, energy, health, appearance, and even age. This line of research yielded some interesting findings. However, very few valid generalizations emerged from this line of inquiry. Therefore, there is insufficient evidence to conclude that leaders can be distinguished from followers on the basis of physical attributes.

Leader personality characteristics that have been examined include originality, adaptability, introversion–extroversion, dominance, self-confidence, integrity, conviction, mood optimism, and emotional control. There is some evidence that leaders may be more adaptable and self-confident than the average group member.

With regard to leader abilities, attention has been devoted to such constructs as social skills, intelligence, scholarship, speech fluency, cooperativeness, and insight. In this area, there is some evidence that leaders are more intelligent, verbal, and cooperative and have a higher level of scholarship than the average group member.

These conclusions suggest traits leaders possess, but the findings are neither strong nor uniform. For each attribute or trait claimed to distinguish leaders from followers, there were always at least one or two studies with contradictory findings. For some, the trait theories are invalid, though interesting and intuitively of some relevance. The trait theories have had very limited success in being able to identify the universal, distinguishing attributes of leaders.

BEHAVIORAL THEORIES

3. *Compare autocratic, democratic, and laissez-faire leadership styles.*

Behavioral theories emerged as a response to the deficiencies of the trait theories. Trait theories told us what leaders were like, but didn't address how leaders behaved. Three theories are the foundations of many modern leadership theories: the Lewin, Lippitt, and White studies; the Ohio State studies; and the Michigan studies.

LEWIN STUDIES

The earliest research on leadership style, conducted by Kurt Lewin and his students, identified three basic styles: autocratic, democratic, and laissez-faire.[5] Each leader uses one of these three basic styles when approaching a group of followers in a leadership situation. The specific situation is not an important consideration, because the leader's style does not vary with the situation. The *autocratic style* is directive, strong, and controlling in relationships. Leaders with an autocratic style use rules and regulations to run the work environment. Followers have little discretionary influence over the nature of the work, its accomplishment, or other aspects of the work environment. The leader with a *democratic style* is collaborative, responsive, and interactive in relationships and emphasizes rules and regulations less than the autocratic leader. Followers have a high degree of discretionary influence, although the leader has ultimate authority and responsibility. The

AUTOCRATIC STYLE
A style of leadership in which the leader uses strong, directive, controlling actions to enforce the rules, regulations, activities, and relationships in the work environment.

DEMOCRATIC STYLE
A style of leadership in which the leader takes collaborative, responsive, interactive actions with followers concerning the work and work environment.

leader with a *laissez-faire style* leads through nonleadership. A laissez-faire leader abdicates the authority and responsibility of the position, and this style often results in chaos.

OHIO STATE STUDIES

The leadership research program at The Ohio State University also measured specific leader behaviors. The initial Ohio State research studied aircrews and pilots.[6] The aircrew members, as followers, were asked a wide range of questions about their lead pilots using the Leader Behavior Description Questionnaire (LBDQ). The results using the LBDQ suggested that there were two important underlying dimensions of leader behaviors.[7] These were labeled initiating structure and consideration.

Initiating structure is leader behavior aimed at defining and organizing work relationships and roles, as well as establishing clear patterns of organization, communication, and ways of getting things done. **Consideration** is leader behavior aimed at nurturing friendly, warm working relationships, as well as encouraging mutual trust and interpersonal respect within the work unit. These two leader behaviors are independent of each other. That is, a leader may be high on both, low on both, or high on one while low on the other. The Ohio State studies were intended to describe leader behavior, not to evaluate or judge behavior.[8]

MICHIGAN STUDIES

Another approach to the study of leadership, developed at the University of Michigan, suggests that the leader's style has very important implications for the emotional atmosphere of the work environment and, therefore, for the followers who work under that leader. Two styles of leadership were identified: employee oriented and production oriented.[9]

A production-oriented style leads to a work environment characterized by constant influence attempts on the part of the leader, either through direct, close supervision or through the use of many written and unwritten rules and regulations for behavior. The focus is clearly on getting work done.

In comparison, an employee-oriented leadership style leads to a work environment that focuses on relationships. The leader exhibits less direct or less close supervision and establishes fewer written or unwritten rules and regulations for behavior. Employee-oriented leaders display concern for people and their needs.

These three groups of studies (the Lewin, Lippitt, and White studies; Ohio State studies; and Michigan studies) taken together form the building blocks of many recent leadership theories. What the studies have in common is that two basic leadership styles were identified, with one focusing on tasks (autocratic, production oriented, initiating structure) and one focusing on people (democratic, employee oriented, consideration). You can use this chapter's Challenge (on page 260) to assess your supervisor's task-versus people-oriented styles.

LAISSEZ-FAIRE STYLE
A style of leadership in which the leader fails to accept the responsibilities of the position.

4. *Explain initiating structure and consideration, leader behaviors, and the Leadership Grid.*

INITIATING STRUCTURE
Leader behavior aimed at defining and organizing work relationships and roles, as well as establishing clear patterns of organization, communication, and ways of getting things done.

CONSIDERATION
Leader behavior aimed at nurturing friendly, warm working relationships, as well as encouraging mutual trust and interpersonal respect within the work unit.

Challenge

HOW DOES YOUR SUPERVISOR LEAD?

Answer the following sixteen questions concerning your supervisor's (or professor's) leadership behaviors using the seven-point Likert scale. Then complete the summary to examine your supervisor's behaviors.

	Not at All					Very Much	
1. Is your superior strict about observing regulations?	1	2	3	4	5	(6)	7
2. To what extent does your superior give you instructions and orders?	1	2	3	4	(5)	6	7
3. Is your superior strict about the amount of work you do?	1	2	3	4	(5)	6	7
4. Does your superior urge you to complete your work by the time he or she has specified?	1	2	3	4	5	(6)	7
5. Does your superior try to make you work to your maximum capacity?	1	2	3	4	(5)	6	7
6. When you do an inadequate job, does your superior focus on the inadequate way the job was done instead of on your personality?	1	2	3	4	5	(6)	7
7. Does your superior ask you for reports about the progress of your work?	1	2	(3)	4	5	6	7
8. Does your superior work out precise plans for goal achievement each month?	1	(2)	3	4	5	6	7
9. Can you talk freely with your superior about your work?	1	2	3	4	5	6	(7)
10. Generally, does your superior support you?	1	2	3	4	5	(6)	7
11. Is your superior concerned about your personal problems?	1	2	3	4	5	(6)	7
12. Do you think your superior trusts you?	1	2	3	4	5	6	(7)
13. Does your superior give you recognition when you do your job well?	1	2	3	4	5	(6)	7
14. When a problem arises in your workplace, does your superior ask your opinion about how to solve it?	1	2	3	4	5	(6)	7
15. Is your superior concerned about your future benefits like promotions and pay raises?	1	2	3	4	(5)	6	7
16. Does your superior treat you fairly?	1	2	3	4	5	(6)	7

Add up your answers to Questions 1 through 8. This total indicates your supervisor's performance orientation:

Task orientation = ___38___

Add up your answers to Questions 9 through 16. This total indicates your supervisor's maintenance orientation:

People orientation = ___49___

A score above 40 is high, and a score below 20 is low.

Source: From J. Misumi and M. F. Peterson, "The Performance-Maintenance (PM) Theory of Leadership," *Administrative Science Quarterly* 30 (1985): 207. Reprinted by permission of the Administrative Science Quarterly.

THE LEADERSHIP GRID: A CONTEMPORARY EXTENSION

Robert Blake and Jane Mouton's **Leadership Grid**, originally called the Managerial Grid, was developed with a focus on attitudes.[10] The two underlying dimensions of the grid are labeled Concern for Results and Concern for People. These two attitudinal dimensions are independent of each other and in different combinations form various leadership styles. Blake and Mouton originally identified five distinct managerial styles, and further development of the grid has led to the seven distinct leadership styles shown in Figure 11-1 (on page 262).

The *organization man manager (5,5)* is a middle-of-the-road leader who has a medium concern for people and production. This leader attempts to balance a concern for both people and production without a commitment to either. The *authority-compliance manager (9,1)* has great concern for production and little concern for people. This leader desires tight control in order to get tasks done efficiently and considers creativity and human relations unnecessary. The *country club manager (1,9)* has great concern for people and little concern for production, attempts to avoid conflict, and seeks to be well liked. This leader's goal is to keep people happy through good interpersonal relations, which are more important to him or her than the task. (This style is not a sound human relations approach but rather a soft Theory X approach.)

The *team manager (9,9)* is considered ideal and has great concern for both people and production. This leader works to motivate employees to reach their highest levels of accomplishment, is flexible, responsive to change, and understands the need for change. The *impoverished manager (1,1)* is often referred to as a laissez-faire leader. This leader has little concern for people or production, avoids taking sides, and stays out of conflicts; he or she does just enough to get by. Two new leadership styles have been added to these five original leadership styles within the grid. The *paternalistic "father knows best" manager (9+9)* promises reward for compliance and threatens punishment for non-compliance. The *opportunistic "what's in it for me" manager (Opp)* uses the style that he or she feels will return him or her the greatest self-benefits.

The Leadership Grid is distinguished from the original Ohio State research in two important ways. First, it has attitudinal overtones that are not present in the original research. Whereas the LBDQ aims to describe behavior, the grid addresses both the behavior and the attitude of the leader. Second, the Ohio State approach is fundamentally descriptive and nonevaluative, whereas the grid is normative and prescriptive. Specifically, the grid evaluates the team manager (9,9) as the very best style of managerial behavior. This is the basis on which the grid has been used for team building and leadership training in an organization's development. As an organizational development method, the grid aims to transform the leader in the organization to lead in the "one best way," which according to the grid is

---

LEADERSHIP GRID
An approach to understanding a leader's or manager's concern for results (production) and concern for people.

ORGANIZATION MAN MANAGER (5,5)
A middle-of-the-road leader.

AUTHORITY-COMPLIANCE MANAGER (9,1)
A leader who emphasizes efficient production.

COUNTRY CLUB MANAGER (1,9)
A leader who creates a happy, comfortable work environment.

TEAM MANAGER (9,9)
A leader who builds a highly productive team of committed people.

IMPOVERISHED MANAGER (1,1)
A leader who exerts just enough effort to get by.

PATERNALISTIC "FATHER KNOWS BEST" MANAGER (9+9)
A leader who promises reward and threatens punishment.

OPPORTUNISTIC "WHAT'S IN IT FOR ME" MANAGER (OPP)
A leader whose style aims to maximize self-benefit.

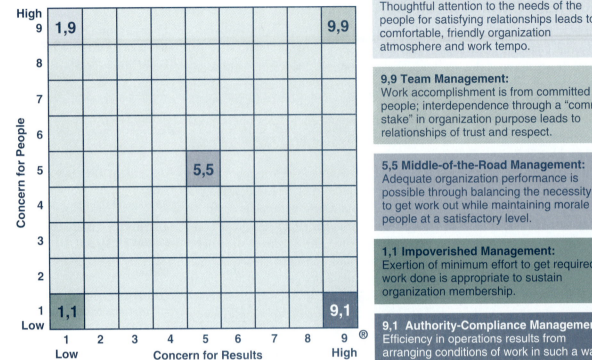

1,9 Country Club Management:
Thoughtful attention to the needs of the people for satisfying relationships leads to a comfortable, friendly organization atmosphere and work tempo.

9,9 Team Management:
Work accomplishment is from committed people; interdependence through a "common stake" in organization purpose leads to relationships of trust and respect.

5,5 Middle-of-the-Road Management:
Adequate organization performance is possible through balancing the necessity to get work out while maintaining morale of people at a satisfactory level.

1,1 Impoverished Management:
Exertion of minimum effort to get required work done is appropriate to sustain organization membership.

9,1 Authority-Compliance Management:
Efficiency in operations results from arranging conditions of work in such a way that human elements interfere to a minimum degree.

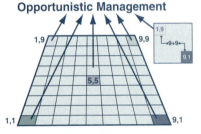

Opportunistic Management

In Opportunisitic Management, people adapt and shift to any grid style needed to gain the maximum advantage. Performance occurs according to a system of selfish gain. Effort is given only for an advantage for personal gain.

9+9: Paternalism/Maternalism Management:
Reward and approval are bestowed to people in return for loyalty and obedience; failure to comply leads to punishment.

Figure 11-1
The Leadership Grid

Source: The Leadership Grid® figure, Paternalism Figure and Opportunism from *Leadership Dilemmas—Grid Solutions*, by Robert R. Blake and Anne Adams McCanse (Formerly the Managerial Grid by Robert R. Blake and Jane S. Mouton). Houston: Gulf Publishing Company (Grid Figure: p. 29, Paternalism Figure: p. 30, Opportunism Figure: p. 31). Copyright 1991 by Blake and Mouton, and Scientific Methods, Inc. Reproduced by permission of the owners.

the team approach. The team style is one that combines optimal concern for people with optimal concern for results.

CONTINGENCY THEORIES

Contingency theories involve the belief that leadership style must be appropriate for the particular situation. By their nature, contingency theories are "if–then" theories: If the situation is _____, then the appropriate leadership behavior is _____. We examine four such theories, including Fiedler's contingency theory, path–goal theory, normative decision theory, and situational leadership theory.

FIEDLER'S CONTINGENCY THEORY

Fiedler's contingency theory of leadership proposes that the fit between the leader's need structure and the favorableness of the leader's situation determine the team's effectiveness in work accomplishment. This theory assumes that leaders are either task oriented or relationship oriented, depending upon how the leaders obtain their primary need gratification.[11] Task-oriented leaders are primarily gratified by accomplishing tasks and getting work done. Relationship-oriented leaders are primarily gratified by developing good, comfortable interpersonal relationships. Accordingly, the effectiveness of both types of leaders depends on the favorableness of their situation. The theory classifies the favorableness of the leader's situation according to the leader's position power, the structure of the team's task, and the quality of the leader–follower relationships.

5. *Explain Fiedler's contingency theory of leadership.*

The Least Preferred Coworker Fiedler classifies leaders using the Least Preferred Coworker (LPC) Scale.[12] The LPC Scale is a projective technique through which a leader is asked to think about the person with whom he or she can work least well (the *least preferred coworker*, or **LPC**).

The leader is asked to describe this least preferred coworker using sixteen eight-point bipolar adjective sets. Two of these bipolar adjective sets follow (the leader marks the blank most descriptive of the least preferred coworker):

Efficient	:	:	:	:	:	:	:	:	Inefficient
Cheerful	:	:	:	:	:	:	:	:	Gloomy

LEAST PREFERRED COWORKER (LPC)
The person a leader has least preferred to work with over his or her career.

Leaders who describe their least preferred coworker in positive terms (that is, pleasant, efficient, cheerful, and so on) are classified as high LPC, or relationship-oriented, leaders. Those who describe their least preferred coworker in negative terms (that is, unpleasant, inefficient, gloomy, and so on) are classified as low LPC, or task-oriented, leaders.

The LPC score is a controversial element in contingency theory.[13] The LPC score has been critiqued conceptually and methodologically because it is a projective technique with low measurement reliability.

TASK STRUCTURE
The degree of clarity, or ambiguity, in the work activities assigned to the group.

POSITION POWER
The authority associated with the leader's formal position in the organization.

LEADER–MEMBER RELATIONS
The quality of interpersonal relationships among a leader and the group members.

Situational Favorableness The leader's situation has three dimensions: task structure, position power, and leader–member relations. Based on these three dimensions, the situation is either favorable or unfavorable for the leader. **Task structure** refers to the number and clarity of rules, regulations, and procedures for getting the work done. **Position power** refers to the leader's legitimate authority to evaluate and reward performance, punish errors, and demote group members.

The quality of **leader–member relations** is measured by the Group-Atmosphere Scale, composed of nine eight-point bipolar adjective sets. Two of these bipolar adjective sets follow:

Friendly :   :   :   :   :   :   :   :   : Unfriendly

Accepting :   :   :   :   :   :   :   :   : Rejecting

A favorable leadership situation is one with a structured task for the work group, strong position power for the leader, and good leader–member relations. In contrast, an unfavorable leadership situation is one with an unstructured task, weak position power for the leader, and moderately poor leader–member relations. Between these two extremes, the leadership situation has varying degrees of moderate favorableness for the leader.

Leadership Effectiveness The contingency theory suggests that low and high LPC leaders are each effective if placed in the right situation.[14] Specifically, low LPC (task-oriented) leaders are most effective in either very favorable or very unfavorable leadership situations. In contrast, high LPC (relationship-oriented) leaders are most effective in situations of intermediate favorableness. Figure 11-2 shows the nature of these relationships and suggests that leadership effectiveness is determined by the degree of fit between the leader and the situation.

What, then, is to be done if there is a misfit? That is, what happens when a low LPC leader is in a moderately favorable situation or when a high LPC leader is in a highly favorable or highly unfavorable situation? It is unlikely that the leader can be changed, according to the theory, because the leader's need structure is an enduring trait that is hard to change. Fiedler recommends that the leader's situation be changed to fit the leader's style.[15] A moderately favorable situation would be reengineered to be more favorable and therefore more suitable for the low LPC leader. A highly favorable or highly unfavorable situation would be changed to one that is moderately favorable and more suitable for the high LPC leader.

Fiedler's theory makes an important contribution in drawing our attention to the leader's situation.

PATH–GOAL THEORY

6. *Distinguish among the path–goal theory, the Vroom-Yetton-Jago theory, and the situational leadership model.*

Robert House developed a path–goal theory of leader effectiveness based on an expectancy theory of motivation.[16] From the perspective of path–goal theory, the basic role of the leader is to clear the follower's path to the goal. The leader uses the most appropriate of four leader behavior styles to help

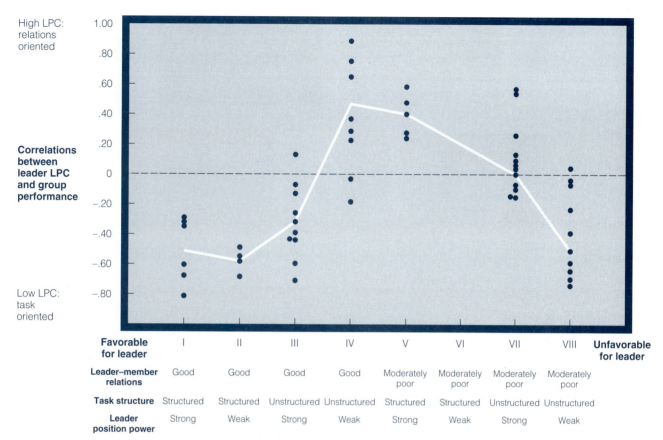

	I	II	III	IV	V	VI	VII	VIII	
Favorable for leader									**Unfavorable for leader**
Leader–member relations	Good	Good	Good	Good	Moderately poor	Moderately poor	Moderately poor	Moderately poor	
Task structure	Structured	Structured	Unstructured	Unstructured	Structured	Structured	Unstructured	Unstructured	
Leader position power	Strong	Weak	Strong	Weak	Strong	Weak	Strong	Weak	

Source: F. E. Fiedler, *A Theory of Leader Effectiveness* (New York: McGraw-Hill, 1964). Reprinted with permission of the author.

Figure 11-2
Leadership Effectiveness in the Contingency Theory

followers clarify the paths that lead them to work and personal goals. The key concepts in the theory are shown in Figure 11-3 (on page 266).

A leader selects from the four leader behavior styles, shown in Figure 11-3, the one that is most helpful to followers at a given time. The directive style is used when the leader must give specific guidance about work tasks, schedule work, and let followers know what is expected. The supportive style is used when the leader needs to express concern for followers' well-being and social status. The participative style is used when the leader must engage in joint decision-making activities with followers. The achievement-oriented style is used when the leader must set challenging goals for followers and show strong confidence in those followers.

In selecting the appropriate leader behavior style, the leader must consider both the followers and the work environment. A few characteristics are included in Figure 11-3. Let us look at two examples. In Example 1, the followers are inexperienced and working on an ambiguous, unstructured task. The leader in this situation might best use a directive style. In Example 2, the followers are highly trained professionals, and the task is a difficult, yet achievable one. The leader in this situation might best use an

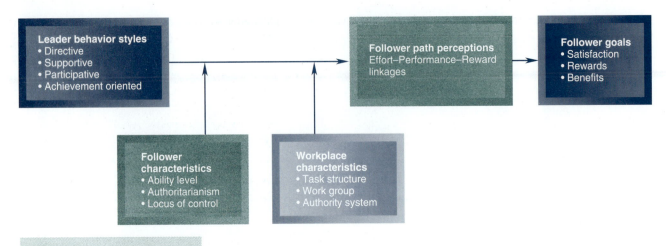

Figure 11-3
The Path–Goal Theory of Leadership

achievement-oriented style. The leader always chooses the leader behavior style that helps followers achieve their goals.

The path–goal theory assumes that leaders adapt their behavior and style to fit the characteristics of the followers and the environment in which they work. Actual tests of the path–goal theory and its propositions provide conflicting evidence.[17] It is premature either to fully accept or fully reject the theory at this point. The path–goal theory does have intuitive appeal and offers a number of constructive ideas for leaders who lead a variety of followers in a variety of work environments.

VROOM-YETTON-JAGO NORMATIVE DECISION MODEL

The Vroom-Yetton-Jago normative decision model helps leaders and managers know when to have employees participate in the decision-making process. Victor Vroom, Phillip Yetton, and Arthur Jago developed and refined the normative decision model, which helps managers determine the appropriate decision-making strategy to use. The model recognizes the benefits of authoritative, democratic, and consultive styles of leader behavior.[18] Five forms of decision making are described in the model:

- *Decide.* The manager makes the decision alone and either announces it or "sells" it to the group.
- *Consult individually.* The manager presents the problem to the group members individually, gets their input, and then makes the decision.
- *Consult group.* The manager presents the problem to the group members in a meeting, gets their inputs, and then makes the decision.
- *Facilitate.* The manager presents the problem to the group in a meeting and acts as a facilitator, defining the problem and the boundaries that surround the decision. The manager's ideas are not given more weight than any other group member's ideas. The objective is to get concurrence.
- *Delegate.* The manager permits the group to make the decision within the prescribed limits, providing needed resources and encouragement.[19]

The key to the normative decision model is that a manager should use the decision method most appropriate for a given decision situation. The manager arrives at the proper method by working through matrices like the one in Figure 11-4. The factors across the top of the model (decision significance, commitment, leader expertise, etc.) are the situational factors in the normative decision model. This matrix is for decisions that must be made under time pressure, but other matrices are also available. For example, there is a different matrix managers can use when their objective is to

Figure 11-4
Time-Driven Model (Reprinted from a Model of Leadership Style by Victor Vroom) 1999

TIME-DRIVEN MODEL

Instructions: The matrix operates like a funnel. You start at the left with a specific decision problem in mind. The column headings denote situational factors which may or may not be present in that problem. You progress by selecting High or Low (H or L) for each relevant situational factor. Proceed down from the funnel, judging only those situational factors for which a judgment is called for, until you reach the recommended process.

Decision Significance	Importance of Commitment	Leader Expertise	Likelihood of Commitment	Group Support	Group Expertise	Team Competence	Process
H	H	H	H	–	–	–	Decide
			L	H	H	H	Delegate
						L	Consult (Group)
					L	–	Consult (Group)
				L	–	–	Consult (Group)
		L	H	H	H	H	Facilitate
						L	Consult (Individually)
					L	–	Consult (Individually)
				L	–	–	Consult (Individually)
			L	H	H	H	Facilitate
						L	Consult (Group)
					L	–	Consult (Group)
				L	–	–	Consult (Group)
	L	H	–	–	–	–	Decide
		L	–	H	H	H	Facilitate
						L	Consult (Individually)
					L	–	Consult (Individually)
				L	–	–	Consult (Individually)
L	H	–	H	–	–	–	Decide
			L	–	–	H	Delegate
						L	Facilitate
	L	–	–	–	–	–	Decide

Source: Reprinted from V. H. Vroom, "Leadership and the Decision-Making Process," *Organizational Dynamics* 28 (2000): 82–94, with permission from Elsevier.

develop subordinates' decision-making skills. Vroom has also developed a Windows-based computer program called Expert System that can be used by managers to determine which style to use.

Although the model offers very explicit predictions, as well as prescriptions, for leaders, its utility is limited to the leader decision-making tasks.

One test of the normative decision model supported it based on leader perceptions of a recent decision process but failed to support the model based on follower perceptions of the same process.[20]

THE SITUATIONAL LEADERSHIP® MODEL

The Situational Leadership® model, developed by Paul Hersey and Kenneth Blanchard, suggests that the leader's behavior should be adjusted to the readiness level of the followers.[21] The model employs two dimensions of leader behavior as used in the Ohio State studies; one dimension is task oriented, and the other is relationship oriented. Follower readiness is categorized into four levels, as shown in Figure 11-5. Follower readiness is determined by the follower's ability and willingness to complete a specific task. Readiness can therefore be low or high depending on the particular task. In addition, readiness varies within a single person according to the task. One person may be willing and able to satisfy simple requests from customers (high readiness), but less able or willing to give highly technical advice to customers (low readiness). It is important that the leader be able to evaluate the readiness level of each follower for each task. The four styles of leader behavior associated with the four readiness levels are depicted in the figure as well.

According to the Situational Leadership® model, a leader should use a telling style (S1) when a follower is unable and unwilling to do a certain task. This style involves providing instructions and closely monitoring performance. As such, the telling style involves considerable task behavior and low relationship behavior. When a follower is unable, but willing and confident to do a task, the leader can use the selling style (S2), in which there is high task behavior and high relationship behavior. In this case, the leader explains decisions and provides opportunities for the employee to seek clarification or help. Sometimes a follower will be able to complete a task, but may seem unwilling or insecure about doing so. In these cases, a participating style (S3) is warranted, which involves high relationship but low task behavior. The leader in this case encourages the follower to participate in decision making. Finally, for tasks in which a follower is able and willing, the leader is able to use a delegating style (S4), characterized by low task behavior and low relationship behavior. In this case, follower readiness is high, and lower levels of leader involvement (task or relationship) are needed.

One key limitation of the Situational Leadership® model is the absence of central hypotheses that could be tested, which would make it a more valid, reliable theory of leadership.[22] However, the theory has intuitive appeal and is widely used for training and development in corporations. In addition, the theory focuses attention on follower readiness as an important determinant of the leadership process.

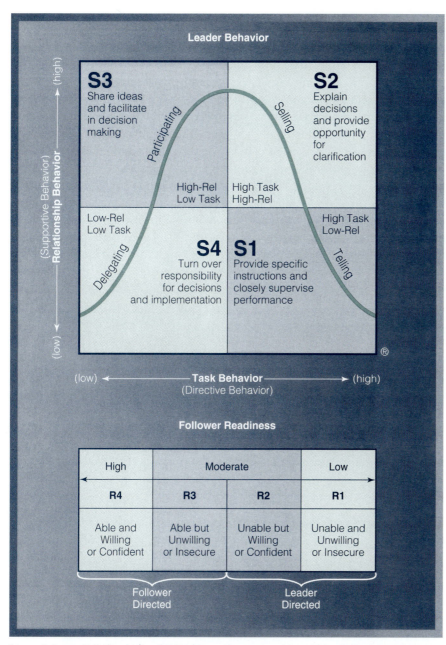

Figure 11-5
The Situational Leadership® Model: The Hersey-Blanchard Model

Source: P. Hersey, K. H. Blanchard, and D. E. Johnson, *Management of Organizational Behavior: Leading Human Resources*, 8rd ed. (Upper Saddle River, N.J.: Pearson Education, Inc., 2001), p. 182. Copyright © 2001, Center for Leadership Studies, Escondido, CA. Used with permission.

RECENT DEVELOPMENTS IN LEADERSHIP THEORY

Leadership is an exciting area of organizational behavior, one in which new research is constantly emerging. Four new developments are important to understand. These are leader–member exchange, substitutes for leadership, transformational leadership, and charismatic leadership.

LEADER–MEMBER EXCHANGE

Leader–member exchange theory, or LMX, recognizes that leaders may form different relationships with followers. The basic idea behind LMX is that leaders form two groups, in-groups and out-groups, of followers. In-group members tend to be similar to the leader, and given greater responsibilities, more rewards, and more attention. They work within the leader's inner circle of communication. As a result, in-group members are more satisfied, have lower turnover, and have higher organizational commitment. In contrast, out-group members are outside the circle and receive less attention and fewer rewards. They are managed by formal rules and policies.[23]

Research on LMX is supportive. In-group members are more likely to engage in organizational citizenship behavior, while out-group members are more likely to retaliate against the organization.[24] And, the type of stress varies by the group to which a subordinate belongs. In-group members' stress comes from the additional responsibilities placed on them by the leader, whereas out-group members' stress comes from being left out of the communication network.[25]

SUBSTITUTES FOR LEADERSHIP

Sometimes situations can neutralize or even replace leader behavior. This is the central idea behind the substitutes for leadership theory.[26] When a task is very satisfying and when employees get feedback about performance, leader behavior is irrelevant, because the employee's satisfaction comes from the interesting work and the feedback. Other things that can substitute for leadership include high skill on the part of the employee, team cohesiveness, and formal controls on the part of the organization. Research on this idea is generally supportive, and other factors that act as substitutes are being identified.[27]

TRANSFORMATIONAL LEADERSHIP

7. *Distinguish among transformational, transactional, and charismatic leaders.*

Transformational leaders inspire and excite followers to high levels of performance.[28] They rely on their personal attributes instead of their official position to manage followers. In contrast, transactional leaders use rewards and punishments to make deals with subordinates. For example, the late Sam Walton may be considered the transformational leader and the visionary heart of Wal-Mart. Certainly, he changed the way the U.S. retailing business operated. As in the case of Wal-Mart, however, it becomes an organizational challenge to figure out a way to institutionalize a transformational leader's style and vision.[29]

There is some evidence that transformational leadership can be learned.[30] As U.S. corporations increasingly operate in a global economy, there is a greater demand for leaders who can practice transformational leadership by converting their visions into reality,[31] and by inspiring followers to perform "above and beyond the call of duty."[32]

Bass, an early writer on transformational leadership, proposed that leaders can be both transformational and transactional. Research on leaders of environmental organizations supports this idea. If the environmental organization is nonprofit, more of a tendency toward transformational leadership is seen.[33] Bass also proposed that transformational leadership adds to the effects of transactional leadership, but exceptional transactional leadership cannot substitute for transformational leadership. Research on leaders from over 200 organizations supports this idea.[34]

CHARISMATIC LEADERSHIP

Anita Roddick (founder of The Body Shop) and Herb Kelleher are charismatic leaders who created a vision and sold it to customers and followers alike, motivating their followers to fulfill the vision. ***Charismatic leadership*** results when a leader uses the force of personal abilities and talents to have profound and extraordinary effects on followers.[35] Some scholars see transformational leadership and charismatic leadership as very similar, but others believe they are different. *Charisma* is a Greek word meaning "gift"; the charismatic leader's unique and powerful gifts are the source of the leader's great influence with followers.[36] In fact, followers often view the charismatic leader as one who possesses superhuman, or even mystical, qualities.[37] Charismatic leaders rely heavily on referent power, discussed in Chapter 10, and charismatic leadership is especially effective in times of uncertainty.[38] Charismatic leadership falls to those who are chosen (are born with the "gift" of charisma) or who cultivate that gift. Some say charismatic leaders are born, and others say they are taught.

Charismatic leadership carries with it not only great potential for high levels of achievement and performance on the part of followers but also shadowy risks of destructive courses of action that might harm followers or other people. Several researchers have attempted to demystify charismatic leadership and distinguish its two faces.[39] The ugly face of charisma is revealed in the personalized power motivations of Adolf Hitler in Nazi Germany and David Koresh of the Branch Davidian cult in Waco, Texas. Both men led their followers into struggle, conflict, and death. The brighter face of charisma is revealed in the socialized power motivations of U.S. President Franklin D. Roosevelt and Sir Richard Branson, founder of Virgin Group, which includes Virgin Atlantic Airways. He is a role model to employees and to many young people because of his energy and creativity, and his ability to lead a balanced happy life. He has achieved success without compromising his ethics.[40]

Despite the warm emotions charismatic leaders can evoke, some charismatic leaders are narcissists who listen only to those who agree with them and do not need advice from those who disagree.[41] Whereas charismatic leaders with socialized power motivation are concerned about the collective well-being of their followers, charismatic leaders with a personalized power motivation are driven by the need for personal gain and glorification.[42]

Charismatic leadership does not address attributes of the situation that may create contingencies for the exercise of leadership.

CHARISMATIC LEADERSHIP
The use, by a leader, of personal abilities and talents in order to have profound and extraordinary effects on followers.

EMERGING ISSUES IN LEADERSHIP

Along with the recent developments in theory, some exciting issues have emerged that leaders must be aware of. These include emotional intelligence, trust, virtual teams, women leaders, and servant leadership.

EMOTIONAL INTELLIGENCE

It has been suggested that effective leaders possess emotional intelligence, which is the ability to recognize and manage emotion in oneself and in others. Emotional intelligence is made up of several competencies, including self-awareness, empathy, adaptability, and self-confidence. These are learned capabilities, and they can be developed.[43] Joe Torre, manager of the New York Yankees, gets the most out of his team, makes his boss happy, and delivers wins. He is a model of emotional intelligence: compassionate, calm under stress, a great motivator. He advocates "managing against the cycle," which means staying calm when situations are tough, but turning up the heat on players when things are going well.[44]

TRUST

Trust has been cited as an essential element in leadership. Trust is the willingness to be vulnerable to the actions of another.[45] This means that followers believe that their leader will act with the followers' welfare in mind. Trustworthiness is also one of the competencies in emotional intelligence. Trust among top management team members facilitates strategy implementation; that means that if team members trust each other, they have a better chance of getting "buy-in" from employees on the direction of the company.[46] And, if employees trust their leaders, they will buy in more readily.

LEADING VIRTUAL TEAMS

How would you go about leading a team of people in different organizations, in different geographic locations around the world, who had never met? They would not have shared understandings of problems, norms, work distribution, roles, or responsibilities. This is a challenge that is becoming more common, and one that Boeing-Rocketdyne faced. This company, which is the major U.S. manufacturer of liquid-fueled rocket engines, put together a virtual team to drive the costs of rocket engines down by 100 times, get the engine to market 10 times faster, and increase the life of a rocket engine by three times—and they did so successfully. What Boeing-Rocketdyne learned is that the leader of such teams needs to be the "spoke in the center of the wheel" in terms of coordination. The leader also needs to help the team create a common language and document results for the entire team.[47] Leading virtual teams requires creativity, because face-to-face interaction that is the hallmark of leadership is not possible.

WOMEN LEADERS

An important, emergent leadership question is this: Do women and men lead differently? Historical stereotypes persist, and people characterize successful managers as having more male-oriented attributes than female-oriented attributes.[48] Although legitimate gender differences may exist, the same leadership traits may be interpreted differently in a man and a woman because of stereotypes. The real issue should be leader behaviors that are not bound by gender stereotypes.

Early evidence shows that women tend to use a more people-oriented style that is inclusive and empowering. Women managers excel in positions that demand strong interpersonal skills.[49] More and more women are assuming positions of leadership in organizations. Donna Dubinsky, CEO of Handspring, cofounded Palm and Handspring, and is known as the mother of the handheld computer. She wants to change the world such that PDAs outsell PCs. Interestingly, much of what we know about leadership is based on studies that were conducted on men. We need to know more about the ways women lead.

SERVANT LEADERSHIP

Robert Greenleaf was director of management research at AT&T for many years. He believed that leaders should serve employees, customers, and the community, and his essays are the basis for today's view called servant leadership. His personal and professional philosophy was that leaders lead by serving others. Other tenets of servant leadership are that work exists for the person as much as the person exists for work, and that servant leaders try to find out the will of the group and lead based on that. Servant leaders are also stewards who consider leadership a trust and desire to leave the organization in better shape for future generations.[50] Although Greenleaf's writings were completed thirty years ago, many have now been published and are becoming more popular.

FOLLOWERSHIP

In contrast to leadership, the topic of followership has not been extensively researched. Much of the leadership literature suggests that leader and follower roles are highly differentiated. The traditional view casts followers as passive, whereas a more contemporary view casts the follower role as an active one with potential for leadership.[51] The follower role has alternatively been cast as one of self-leadership in which the follower assumes responsibility for influencing his or her own performance.[52] This approach emphasizes the follower's individual responsibility and self-control. Self-led followers perform naturally motivating tasks and do work that must be done but that is not naturally motivating. Self-leadership enables followers to be disciplined and effective, essential first steps if one is to become a leader. Organizational programs such as empowerment and self-managed work teams may be used to further activate the follower role.[53]

8. *Discuss the characteristics of effective and dynamic followers.*

TYPES OF FOLLOWERS

Contemporary work environments are ones in which followers recognize their interdependence with leaders and learn to challenge them while at the same time respecting the leaders' authority.[54] Effective followers are active, responsible, and autonomous in their behavior and critical in their thinking without being insubordinate or disrespectful. Effective followers and four other types of followers are identified based on two dimensions: (1) activity versus passivity and (2) independent, critical thinking versus dependent, uncritical thinking.[55] Figure 11-6 shows these follower types.

Alienated followers think independently and critically, yet are very passive in their behavior. As a result, they become psychologically and emotionally distanced from their leaders. Alienated followers are potentially disruptive and a threat to the health of the organization. Sheep are followers who do not think independently or critically and are passive in their behavior. They simply do as they are told by their leaders. Yes people are followers who also do not think independently or critically, yet are very active in their behavior. They uncritically reinforce the thinking and ideas of their leaders with enthusiasm, never questioning or challenging the wisdom of the leaders' ideas and proposals. Yes people are the most dangerous to a leader because they are the most likely to give a false positive reaction and give no warning of potential pitfalls. Survivors are the least disruptive and the lowest risk followers in an organization. They perpetually sample the wind, and their motto is "Better safe than sorry."

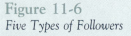

YOU BE THE JUDGE

What should you do if your supervisor acts in an unethical or illegal manner? Talk with the supervisor? Immediately report the action to the company's ethics committee?

Figure 11-6
Five Types of Followers

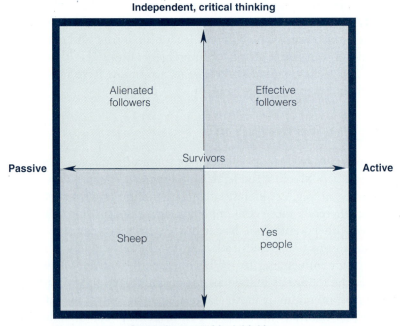

Source: Reprinted by permission of *Harvard Business Review*. From "In Praise of Followers" by R. E. Kelley, Vol. 66, November/December 1988, p. 145. Copyright © 1988 by Harvard Business School Publishing Corporation; all rights reserved.

Effective followers are the most valuable to a leader and an organization because of their active contributions. Effective followers share four essential qualities. First, they practice self-management and self-responsibility. A leader can delegate to an effective follower without anxiety about the outcome. Second, they are committed to both the organization and a purpose, principle, or person outside themselves. Effective followers are not self-centered or self-aggrandizing. Third, effective followers invest in their own competence and professionalism and focus their energy for maximum impact. Effective followers look for challenges and ways in which to add to their talents or abilities. Fourth, they are courageous, honest, and credible.

Effective followers might be thought of as self-leaders who do not require close supervision.[56] The notion of self-leadership, or superleadership, blurs the distinction between leaders and followers. Caring leaders are able to develop dynamic followers.

THE DYNAMIC FOLLOWER

The traditional stereotype of the follower or employee is of someone in a powerless, dependent role rather than in a potent, active, significant role. The latter, in which the follower is dynamic, is a more contemporary, healthy role.[57] The *dynamic follower* is a responsible steward of his or her job, is effective in managing the relationship with the boss, and practices responsible self-management.

DYNAMIC FOLLOWER
A follower who is a responsible steward of his or her job, is effective in managing the relationship with the boss, and practices self-management.

The dynamic follower becomes a trusted adviser to the boss by keeping the supervisor well informed and building trust and dependability into the relationship. He or she is open to constructive criticism and solicits performance feedback. The dynamic follower shares needs and is responsible.

It takes time and patience to nurture a good relationship between a follower and a supervisor. Once this relationship has been developed, it is a valuable resource for both.

CULTURAL DIFFERENCES IN LEADERSHIP

The situational approaches to leadership would lead to the conclusion that a leader must factor in culture as an important situational variable when exercising influence and authority. Thus, global leaders should expect to be flexible enough to alter their approaches when crossing national boundaries and working with people from foreign cultures.[58]

We are beginning to learn more about how perspectives on effective leadership vary across cultures. You might assume that most Europeans view leadership in the same way. Research tells us instead that there are many differences between the European countries. In Nordic countries like Finland, leaders who are direct and close to subordinates are viewed positively, while in Turkey, Poland, and Russia this is not the case. And leaders who give subordinates autonomy are viewed more positively in Germany and Austria than in the Czech Republic and Portugal.[59] There are even differences between the American view of transformational leadership and that found in the United Kingdom. The U.K. approach to transformational leadership is much closer to what we in the United States refer to as servant leadership. It involves more connectedness between leaders and followers, and more vulnerability on the part of the leader.[60]

GUIDELINES FOR LEADERSHIP

Leadership is a key to influencing organizational behavior and achieving organizational effectiveness. When artifacts are eliminated, studies of leadership succession show a moderately strong leader influence on organizational performance.[61] With this said, it is important to recognize that other factors also influence organizational performance. These include environmental factors (such as general economic conditions) and technological factors (such as efficiency).

Corporate leaders play a central role in setting the ethical tone and moral values for their organizations. For example, as chairman and CEO of Johnson & Johnson, James Burke played a pivotal role in modeling ethical leadership at the company in the 1970s and 1980s. Further, Johnson & Johnson ranked No. 1 in the *Fortune* list of most admired corporations in corporate leadership, in part due to the ethical and moral values reflected in the J&J culture and credo.[62]

Five useful guidelines appear to emerge from the extensive leadership research of the past sixty years:

- First, leaders and organizations should appreciate the unique attributes, predispositions, and talents of each leader. No two leaders are the same, and there is value in this diversity.
- Second, although there appears to be no single best style of leadership, there are organizational preferences in terms of style. Leaders should be chosen who challenge the organizational culture, when necessary, without destroying it.
- Third, participative, considerate leader behaviors that demonstrate a concern for people appear to enhance the health and well-being of followers in the work environment. This does not imply, however, that a leader must ignore the team's work tasks.
- Fourth, different leadership situations call for different leadership talents and behaviors. This may result in different individuals taking the leader role, depending on the specific situation in which the team finds itself.
- Fifth, good leaders are likely to be good followers. Although there are distinctions between their social roles, the attributes and behaviors of leaders and followers may not be as distinct as is sometimes thought.

KEY TERMS

authority-compliance manager (9,1)

autocratic style

charismatic leadership

consideration

country club manager (1,9)

democratic style

dynamic follower

followership

formal leadership

impoverished manager (1,1)

informal leadership

initiating structure

laissez-faire style

leader

leadership

Leadership Grid

leader–member relations

least preferred coworker (LPC)

manager

opportunistic "what's in it for me" manager (Opp)

organization man manager (5,5)

paternalist "father knows best" manager (9+9)

position power

task structure

team manager (9,9)

Experiential Exercise

NATIONAL CULTURE AND LEADERSHIP

Effective leadership often varies by national culture, as Hofstede's research has shown. This exercise gives you the opportunity to examine your own and your group's leadership orientation compared to norms from ten countries, including the United States.

Exercise Schedule

1. Preparation (before class)
Complete the 29-item questionnaire.

2. Individual and Group Scoring
Your instructor will lead you through the scoring of the questionnaire, both individually and as a group.

3. Comparison of Effective Leadership Patterns by Nation
Your instructor leads a discussion on Hofstede's value system and presents the culture dimension scores for the ten countries.

In the questionnaire below, indicate the extent to which you agree or disagree with each statement. For example, if you strongly agree with a particular statement, circle the 5 next to the statement.

1 = strongly disagree
2 = disagree
3 = neither agree nor disagree
4 = agree
5 = strongly agree

QUESTIONNAIRE

	STRONGLY DISAGREE				STRONGLY AGREE
1. It is important to have job instructions spelled out in detail so that employees always know what they are expected to do.	1	2	3	4	5
2. Managers expect employees to closely follow instructions and procedures.	1	2	3	4	5
3. Rules and regulations are important because they inform employees what the organization expects of them.	1	2	3	4	5
4. Standard operating procedures are helpful to employees on the job.	1	2	3	4	5
5. Instructions for operations are important for employees on the job.	1	2	3	4	5
6. Group welfare is more important than individual rewards.	1	2	3	4	5

	STRONGLY DISAGREE			STRONGLY AGREE
7. Group success is more important than individual success.	1	2	3	4	5
8. Being accepted by the members of your work group is very important.	1	2	3	4	5
9. Employees should pursue their own goals only after considering the welfare of the group.	1	2	3	4	5
10. Managers should encourage group loyalty even if individual goals suffer.	1	2	3	4	5
11. Individuals may be expected to give up their goals in order to benefit group success.	1	2	3	4	5
12. Managers should make most decisions without consulting subordinates.	1	2	3	4	5
13. Managers should frequently use authority and power when dealing with subordinates.	1	2	3	4	5
14. Managers should seldom ask for the opinions of employees.	1	2	3	4	5
15. Managers should avoid off-the-job social contacts with employees.	1	2	3	4	5
16. Employees should not disagree with management decisions.	1	2	3	4	5
17. Managers should not delegate important tasks to employees.	1	2	3	4	5
18. Managers should help employees with their family problems.	1	2	3	4	5
19. Managers should see to it that employees are adequately clothed and fed.	1	2	3	4	5
20. A manager should help employees solve their personal problems.	1	2	3	4	5
21. Management should see that all employees receive health care.	1	2	3	4	5
22. Management should see that children of employees have an adequate education.	1	2	3	4	5
23. Management should provide legal assistance for employees who get into trouble with the law.	1	2	3	4	5
24. Managers should take care of their employees as they would their children.	1	2	3	4	5
25. Meetings are usually run more effectively when they are chaired by a man.	1	2	3	4	5
26. It is more important for men to have a professional career than it is for women to have a professional career.	1	2	3	4	5
27. Men usually solve problems with logical analysis; women usually solve problems with intuition.	1	2	3	4	5
28. Solving organizational problems usually requires an active, forcible approach, which is typical of men.	1	2	3	4	5
29. It is preferable to have a man, rather than a woman, in a high-level position.	1	2	3	4	5

Source: By Peter Dorfman, *Advances in International Comparative Management*, vol. 3, pages 127–150, 1988. Reprinted by permission of JAI Press Inc. D. Marcic and S. M. Puffer, "Dimensions of National Culture and Effective Leadership Patterns: Hofstede Revisited," *Management International* (Minneapolis/St. Paul: West Publishing, 1994), 10–15. All rights reserved. May not be reproduced without written permission of the publisher.

12

Conflict and Negotiation

LEARNING OBJECTIVES

After reading this chapter, you should be able to do the following:

1. Diagnose functional versus dysfunctional conflict.

2. Identify the causes of conflict in organizations.

3. Identify the different forms of conflict.

4. Understand the defense mechanisms that individuals

exhibit when they engage in interpersonal conflict.

5. Describe ineffective and effective techniques for managing conflict.

6. Understand five styles of conflict management, and diagnose your own preferred style.

THE NATURE OF CONFLICTS IN ORGANIZATIONS

CONFLICT
Any situation in which incompatible goals, attitudes, emotions, or behaviors lead to disagreement or opposition between two or more parties.

All of us have experienced conflict of various types, yet we probably fail to recognize the variety of conflicts that occur in organizations. **Conflict** is defined as any situation in which incompatible goals, attitudes, emotions, or behaviors lead to disagreement or opposition between two or more parties.[1]

Today's organizations may face greater potential for conflict than ever before in history. The marketplace, with its increasing competition and globalization, magnifies differences among people in terms of personality, values, attitudes, perceptions, languages, cultures, and national backgrounds.[2] With the increasing diversity of the workforce, furthermore, comes the potential for incompatibility and conflict.

IMPORTANCE OF CONFLICT MANAGEMENT SKILLS FOR THE MANAGER

Estimates show that managers spend about 21 percent of their time dealing with conflict.[3] That is the equivalent of one day every week. And conflict management skills are a major predictor of managerial success.[4] Emotional intelligence (EQ) relates to the ability to manage conflict. It is the power to control one's emotions and perceive emotions in others, adapt to change, and manage adversity. Conflict management skills may be more a reflection of EQ than of IQ. People who lack emotional intelligence, especially empathy or the ability to see life from another person's perspective, are more likely to be causes of conflict than managers of conflict.[5] EQ seems to be valid across cultures. It is common among successful people not only in North America, but also in Nigeria, India, Argentina, and France.

FUNCTIONAL VERSUS DYSFUNCTIONAL CONFLICT

1. *Diagnose functional versus dysfunctional conflict.*

Not all conflict is bad. In fact, some types of conflict encourage new solutions to problems and enhance creativity in the organization. In these cases, managers will want to encourage the conflicts. Thus, the key to conflict management is to stimulate functional conflict and prevent or resolve dysfunctional conflict. The difficulty, however, is distinguishing between dysfunctional and functional conflicts. The consequences of conflict can be positive or negative, as shown in Table 12-1.

Table 12-1
Consequences of Conflict

Positive Consequences	Negative Consequences
• Leads to new ideas	• Diverts energy from work
• Stimulates creativity	• Threatens psychological well-being
• Motivates change	• Wastes resources
• Promotes organizational vitality	• Creates a negative climate
• Helps individuals and groups establish identities	• Breaks down group cohesion
• Serves as a safety valve to indicate problems	• Can increase hostility and aggressive behaviors

Functional conflict is a healthy, constructive disagreement between two or more people. Functional conflict can produce new ideas, learning, and growth among individuals. When individuals engage in constructive conflict, they develop a better awareness of themselves and others. In addition, functional conflict can improve working relationships: when two parties work through their disagreements, they feel they have accomplished something together. By releasing tensions and solving problems in working together, morale is improved.[6] Functional conflict can lead to innovation and positive change for the organization.[7] Because it tends to encourage creativity among individuals, this positive form of conflict can translate into increased productivity.[8] A key to recognizing functional conflict is that it is often cognitive in origin; that is, it arises from someone challenging old policies or thinking of new ways to approach problems.

Dysfunctional conflict is an unhealthy, destructive disagreement between two or more people. Its danger is that it takes the focus away from the work to be done and places the focus on the conflict itself and the parties involved. Excessive conflict drains energy that could be used more productively. A key to recognizing a dysfunctional conflict is that its origin is often emotional or behavioral. Disagreements that involve personalized anger and resentment directed at specific individuals rather than specific ideas are dysfunctional.[9] Individuals involved in dysfunctional conflict tend to act before thinking, and they often rely on threats, deception, and verbal abuse to communicate. In dysfunctional conflict, the losses to both parties may exceed any potential gain from the conflict.

Diagnosing conflict as good or bad is not easy. The manager must look at the issue, the context of the conflict, and the parties involved. The following questions can be used to diagnose the nature of the conflict a manager faces:

- Are the parties approaching the conflict from a hostile standpoint?
- Is the outcome likely to be a negative one for the organization?
- Do the potential losses of the parties exceed any potential gains?
- Is energy being diverted from goal accomplishment?

If the majority of the answers to these questions are yes, then the conflict is probably dysfunctional. Once the manager has diagnosed the type of conflict, he or she can either work to resolve it (if it is dysfunctional) or to stimulate it (if it is functional).

It is easy to make mistakes in diagnosing conflicts. Sometimes task conflict, which is functional, can be misattributed as being personal, and dysfunctional conflict can follow. Developing trust within the work group can keep this misattribution from occurring.[10]

One occasion when managers should work to stimulate conflict is when they suspect their group is suffering from groupthink, discussed in Chapter 9.[11] When a group fails to consider alternative solutions and becomes stagnant in its thinking, it might benefit from healthy disagreements. Teams exhibiting symptoms of groupthink should be encouraged to consider creative problem solving and should appoint a devil's advocate to point out

FUNCTIONAL CONFLICT
A healthy, constructive disagreement between two or more people.

YOU BE THE JUDGE

How can you stimulate conflict in an ethical manner?

DYSFUNCTIONAL CONFLICT
An unhealthy, destructive disagreement between two or more people.

opposing perspectives. These actions can help stimulate constructive conflict in a group.

CAUSES OF CONFLICT IN ORGANIZATIONS

2. Identify the causes of conflict in organizations.

Conflict is pervasive in organizations. To manage it effectively, managers should understand the many sources of conflict. They can be classified into two broad categories: structural factors, which stem from the nature of the organization and the way in which work is organized, and personal factors, which arise from differences among individuals. Figure 12-1 summarizes the causes of conflict within each category.

STRUCTURAL FACTORS

The causes of conflict related to the organization's structure include specialization, interdependence, common resources, goal differences, authority relationships, status inconsistencies, and jurisdictional ambiguities.

Specialization When jobs are highly specialized, employees become experts at certain tasks. For example, one software company has one specialist for databases, one for statistical packages, and another for expert systems. Highly specialized jobs can lead to conflict, because people have little awareness of the tasks that others perform.

A classic conflict of specialization may occur between salespeople and engineers. Engineers are technical specialists responsible for product design and quality. Salespeople are marketing experts and liaisons with customers. Salespeople are often accused of making delivery promises to customers that engineers cannot keep because the sales force lacks the technical knowledge necessary to develop realistic delivery deadlines.

Interdependence Work that is interdependent requires groups or individuals to depend on one another to accomplish goals.[12] Depending on other people to get work done is fine when the process works smoothly. When there is a problem, however, it becomes very easy to blame the other party, and conflict escalates. In a garment manufacturing plant, for example, when the fabric cutters get behind in their work, the workers who sew the gar-

Figure 12-1
Causes of Conflict in Organizations

Structural Factors
• Specialization
• Interdependence
• Common resources
• Goal differences
• Authority relationships
• Status inconsistencies
• Jurisdictional ambiguities

Conflict

Personal Factors
• Skills and abilities
• Personalities
• Perceptions
• Values and ethics
• Emotions
• Communication barriers
• Cultural differences

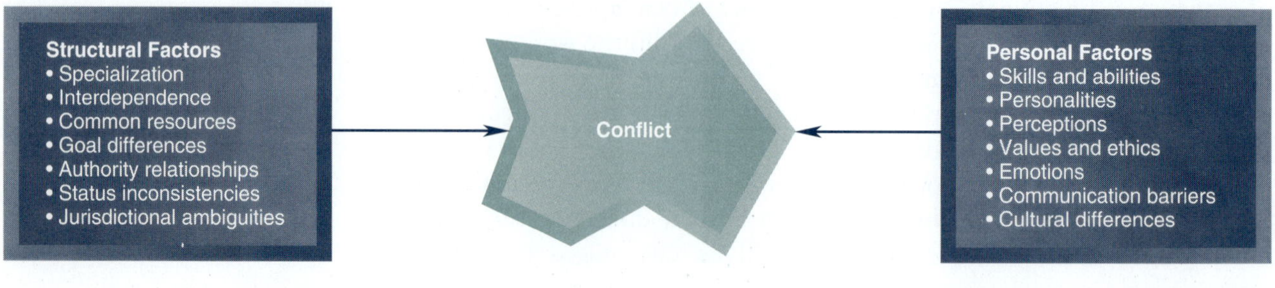

ments are delayed as well. Considerable frustration may result when the workers at the sewing machines feel their efforts are being blocked by the cutters' slow pace.

Common Resources Any time multiple parties must share resources, there is potential for conflict.[13] This potential is enhanced when the shared resources become scarce. For example, managers often share secretarial support. Not uncommonly, one secretary supports ten or more managers, each of whom believes his or her work is most important. This puts pressure on the secretary and leads to potential conflicts in prioritizing and scheduling work.

Goal Differences When work groups have different goals, these goals may be incompatible. For example, in one cable television company, the salesperson's goal was to sell as many new installations as possible. This created problems for the service department, because its goal was timely installations. With increasing sales, the service department's workload became backed up, and orders were delayed. Often these types of conflicts occur because individuals do not have knowledge of another department's objectives.

Authority Relationships A traditional boss–employee relationship is hierarchical in nature with a boss who is superior to the employee. For many employees, such a relationship is not a comfortable one, because another individual has the right to tell them what to do. Some people resent authority more than others, and obviously this creates conflicts. In addition, some bosses are more autocratic than others; this compounds the potential for conflict in the relationship. As organizations move toward the team approach and empowerment, there should be less potential for conflict from authority relationships.

Status Inconsistencies Some organizations have a strong status difference between management and nonmanagement workers. Managers may enjoy privileges—such as flexible schedules, personal telephone calls at work, and longer lunch hours—that are not available to nonmanagement employees. This may result in resentment and conflict.

Jurisdictional Ambiguities Have you ever telephoned a company with a problem and had your call transferred through several different people and departments? This situation illustrates *jurisdictional ambiguity*—that is, unclear lines of responsibility within an organization.[14] When there is no definite source of responsibility for a problem, workers tend to "pass the buck," or avoid dealing with the problem. Conflicts emerge over responsibility for the problem.

JURISDICTIONAL AMBIGUITY
The presence of unclear lines of responsibility within an organization.

   The factors just discussed are structural in that they arise from the ways in which work is organized. Other conflicts come from differences among individuals.

PERSONAL FACTORS

The causes of conflict that arise from individual differences include skills and abilities, personalities, perceptions, values and ethics, emotions, communication barriers, and cultural differences.

Skills and Abilities The workforce is composed of individuals with varying levels of skills and ability. Diversity in skills and abilities may be positive for the organization, but it also holds potential for conflict, especially when jobs are interdependent. Experienced, competent workers may find it difficult to work alongside new and unskilled recruits. Workers can become resentful when their new boss, fresh from college, knows a lot about managing people but is unfamiliar with the technology with which they are working.

Personalities Individuals do not leave their personalities at the doorstep when they enter the workplace. Personality conflicts are realities in organizations. To expect that you will like all of your coworkers may be a naive expectation, as would be the expectation that they will all like you.

One personality trait that many people find difficult to deal with is abrasiveness.[15] An abrasive person ignores the interpersonal aspects of work and the feelings of colleagues. Abrasive individuals are often achievement oriented and hardworking, but their perfectionist, critical style often leaves others feeling unimportant. This style creates stress and strain for those around the abrasive person.[16]

Perceptions Differences in perception can also lead to conflict. For example, managers and workers may not have a shared perception of what motivates people. In this case, the reward system can create conflicts if managers provide what they think employees want rather than what employees really want.

Values and Ethics Differences in values and ethics can be sources of disagreement. Older workers, for example, value company loyalty and probably would not take a sick day when they were not really ill. Younger workers, valuing mobility, like the concept of "mental health days," or calling in sick to get away from work. This may not be true for all workers, but it illustrates that differences in values can lead to conflict.

Most people have their own sets of values and ethics. The extent to which they apply these ethics in the workplace varies. Some people have strong desires for approval from others and will work to meet others' ethical standards. Some people are relatively unconcerned about approval from others and strongly apply their own ethical standards. Still others operate seemingly without regard to ethics or values.[17] When conflicts about values or ethics do arise, heated disagreement is common because of the personal nature of the differences.

Emotions The moods of others can be a source of conflict in the workplace. Problems at home often spill over into the work arena, and the related moods can be hard for others to deal with.

Moods also affect the way we approach conflicts. People in a good mood are more cooperative. People in a negative mood are more concerned for themselves and are more competitive.[18]

Communication Barriers Communication barriers such as physical separation and language can create distortions in messages, and these can lead to conflict. Another communication barrier is value judgment, in which a listener assigns a worth to a message before it is received. For example, suppose a team member is a chronic complainer. When this individual enters the manager's office, the manager is likely to devalue the message before it is even delivered. Conflict can then emerge.

Cultural Differences Although cultural differences are assets in organizations, sometimes they can be seen as sources of conflict. Often, these conflicts stem from a lack of understanding of another culture. In one MBA class, for example, Indian students were horrified when American students challenged the professor. Meanwhile, the American students thought the students from India were too passive. Subsequent discussions revealed that professors in India expected to be treated deferentially and with great respect. While students might challenge an idea vigorously, they would rarely challenge the professor. Diversity training that emphasizes education on cultural differences can make great strides in preventing misunderstandings.

GLOBALIZATION AND CONFLICT

Large transnational corporations employ many different ethnic and cultural groups. In these multiethnic corporations, the widely differing cultures represent vast differences among individuals, so the potential for conflict increases.[19] As indicated in Chapter 2, Hofstede has identified five dimensions along which cultural differences may emerge: individualism/collectivism, power distance, uncertainty avoidance, masculinity/femininity, and long-term/short-term orientation.[20] These cultural differences have many implications for conflict management in organizations.

Individualism means that people believe that their individual interests take priority over society's interests. Collectivism, in contrast, means that people put the good of the group first. For example, the United States is a highly individualistic culture, whereas Japan is a very collectivist culture. The individualism/collectivism dimension of cultural differences strongly influences conflict management behavior. People from collectivist cultures tend to display a more cooperative approach to managing conflict.[21]

Hofstede's second dimension of cultural differences is power distance. In cultures with high power distance, individuals accept that people in organizations have varying levels of power. In contrast, in cultures with low power distance, individuals do not automatically respect those in positions of authority. For example, the United States is a country of low power distance, whereas Brazil is a country with a high power distance. Differences in power distance can lead to conflict. Imagine a U.S. employee managed by a Brazilian supervisor who expects deferential behavior. The supervisor would expect automatic respect based on legitimate power. When this respect was not given, conflict would arise.

Uncertainty avoidance also varies by culture. In the United States, employees can tolerate high levels of uncertainty, whereas employees in Israel tend to prefer certainty in their work settings. A U.S.-based multinational firm might run into conflicts operating in Israel. Suppose such a firm is installing a new technology. Its expatriate workers from the United States would tolerate the uncertainty of the technological transition better than would their Israeli coworkers, and this might lead to conflicts among the employees.

Masculinity versus femininity illustrates the contrast between preferences for assertiveness and material goods versus preferences for human capital and quality of life. The United States is a masculine society, whereas Sweden is considered a feminine society. Adjustment to the assertive interpersonal style of U.S. workers may be difficult for Swedish coworkers.

Conflicts can also arise between cultures that vary in their time orientation of values. China, for example, has a long-term orientation; the Chinese prefer values that focus on the future, such as saving and persistence. The United States and Russia, in contrast, have short-term orientations. These cultures emphasize values in the past and present, such as respect for tradition and fulfillment of social obligations. Conflicts can arise when managers fail to understand the nature of differences in values.

An organization whose workforce consists of multiple ethnicities and cultures holds potential for many types of conflict because of the sheer volume of individual differences among workers. The key to managing conflict in a multicultural workforce is understanding cultural differences and appreciating their value.

FORMS OF CONFLICT IN ORGANIZATIONS

3. *Identify the different forms of conflict.*

Conflict can take on any of several different forms in an organization, including interorganizational, intergroup, intragroup, interpersonal, and intrapersonal conflicts. It is important to note that the prefix *inter* means "between," whereas the prefix *intra* means "within."

INTERORGANIZATIONAL CONFLICT

INTERORGANIZATIONAL CONFLICT
Conflict that occurs between two or more organizations.

Conflict that occurs between two or more organizations is called ***interorganizational conflict***. Competition can heighten interorganizational conflict. Corporate takeovers, mergers, and acquisitions can also produce interorganizational conflict. Conflict between companies and labor unions constitutes interorganizational conflict.

Conflicts between organizations abound. Some of these conflicts can be functional, as when firms improve the quality of their products and services in the spirit of healthy competition. Other interorganizational conflicts can have dysfunctional results.

INTERGROUP CONFLICT

When conflict occurs between groups or teams, it is known as *intergroup conflict*. Conflict between groups can have positive effects within each group, such as increased group cohesiveness, increased focus on tasks, and increased loyalty to the group. There are, however, negative consequences as well. Groups in conflict tend to develop an "us against them" mentality whereby each sees the other team as the enemy, becomes more hostile, and decreases its communication with the other group. Groups are even more competitive and less cooperative than individuals. The inevitable outcome is that one group gains and the other group loses.[22]

Competition between groups must be managed carefully so that it does not escalate into dysfunctional conflict. Research has shown that when groups compete for a goal that only one group can achieve, negative consequences like territoriality, aggression, and prejudice toward the other group can result.[23] Managers should encourage and reward cooperative behaviors across groups. Some effective ways of doing this include modifying performance appraisals to include assessing intergroup behavior and using an external supervisor's evaluation of intergroup behavior. Group members will be more likely to help other groups when they know that the other group's supervisor will be evaluating their behavior, and that they will be rewarded for cooperation.[24] In addition, managers should encourage social interactions across groups so that trust can be developed. Trust allows individuals to exchange ideas and resources with members of other groups and results in innovation when members of different groups co-operate.[25]

INTRAGROUP CONFLICT

Conflict that occurs within groups or teams is called *intragroup conflict*. Some conflict within a group is functional. It can help the group avoid groupthink, as we discussed in Chapter 9. High-performing teams can be distinguished from low-performing teams by the timing and types of conflict they experience.

Even the newest teams, virtual teams, are not immune to conflict. The nuances and subtleties of face-to-face communication are often lacking in these teams, and misunderstandings can result. To avoid dysfunctional conflicts, virtual teams should make sure their tasks fit their methods of interacting. Complex strategic decisions may require face-to-face meetings rather than e-mails or threaded discussions. Face-to-face and telephone interactions early on can eliminate later conflicts, and allow virtual teams to move on to use electronic communication because trust has been developed.[26]

INTERPERSONAL CONFLICT

Conflict between two or more people is *interpersonal conflict*. Conflict between people can arise from many individual differences, including per-

INTERGROUP CONFLICT
Conflict that occurs between groups or teams in an organization.

INTRAGROUP CONFLICT
Conflict that occurs within groups or teams.

INTERPERSONAL CONFLICT
Conflict that occurs between two or more individuals.

sonalities, attitudes, values, perceptions, and the other differences we discussed in Chapters 3 and 4. Later in this chapter, we look at defense mechanisms that individuals exhibit in interpersonal conflict and at ways to cope with difficult people.

INTRAPERSONAL CONFLICT

INTRAPERSONAL CONFLICT
Conflict that occurs within an individual.

When conflict occurs within an individual, it is called *intrapersonal conflict*. There are several types of intrapersonal conflict, including interrole, intrarole, and person–role conflicts. A role is a set of expectations placed on an individual by others.[27] The person occupying the focal role is the role incumbent, and the individuals who place expectations on the person are role senders. Figure 12-2 depicts a set of role relationships.

INTERROLE CONFLICT
A person's experience of conflict among the multiple roles in his or her life.

Interrole conflict occurs when a person experiences conflict among the multiple roles in his or her life. One interrole conflict that many employees experience is work/home conflict, in which their role as worker clashes with their role as spouse or parent.[28] For example, when a child gets sick at school, the parent often must leave work to care for the child.

INTRAROLE CONFLICT
Conflict that occurs within a single role, such as when a person receives conflicting messages from role senders about how to perform a certain role.

Intrarole conflict is conflict within a single role. It often arises when a person receives conflicting messages from role senders about how to perform a certain role. Suppose a manager receives counsel from her department head that she needs to socialize less with the nonmanagement employees. She also is told by her project manager that she needs to be a better team member, and that she can accomplish this by socializing more with the other nonmanagement team members. This situation is one of intrarole conflict.

Figure 12-2
An Organization Member's Role Set

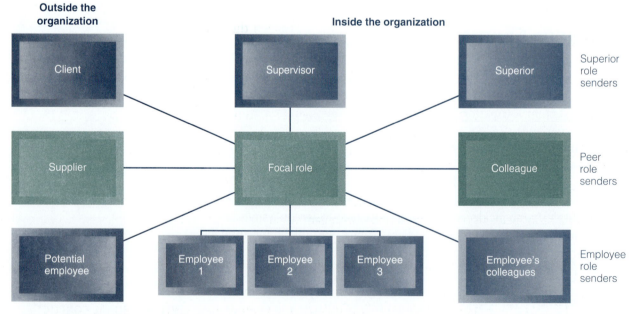

Source: J. C. Quick, J. D. Quick, D. L. Nelson, & J. J. Hurrell, Jr. *Preventive Stress Management in Organizations*, 1997. Copyright © 1997 by the American Psychological Association. Reprinted with permission.

Person–role conflict occurs when an individual in a particular role is expected to perform behaviors that clash with his or her values.[29] Salespeople, for example, may be required to offer the most expensive item in the sales line first to the customer, even when it is apparent that the customer does not want or cannot afford the item. A computer salesman may be required to offer a large, elaborate system to a student he knows is on a tight budget. This may conflict with the salesman's values, and he may experience person–role conflict.

Intrapersonal conflicts can have positive consequences. Often, professional responsibilities clash with deeply held values. A budget shortfall may force you to lay off a loyal, hardworking employee. Your daughter may have a piano recital on the same day your largest client is scheduled to be in town visiting the office. In such conflicts, we often have to choose between right and right; that is, there's no correct response. These may be thought of as *defining moments* that challenge us to choose between two or more things in which we believe.[30] Character is formed in defining moments because they cause us to shape our identities. They help us crystallize our values and serve as opportunities for personal growth.

> **PERSON–ROLE CONFLICT**
> Conflict that occurs when an individual is expected to perform behaviors in a certain role that conflict with his or her personal values.

INTRAPERSONAL CONFLICT

Intrapersonal conflict can be managed with careful self-analysis and diagnosis of the situation. Two actions in particular can help prevent or resolve intrapersonal conflicts.

First, when seeking a new job, you should find out as much as possible about the values of the organization.[31] Many person–role conflicts center around differences between the organization's values and the individual's values. Research has shown that when there is a good fit between the values of the individual and the organization, the individual is more satisfied and committed and is less likely to leave the organization.[32]

Second, to manage intrarole or interrole conflicts, role analysis is a good tool.[33] In role analysis, the individual asks the various role senders what they expect of him or her. The outcomes are clearer work roles and the reduction of conflict and ambiguity.[34] Role analysis is a simple tool that clarifies the expectations of both parties in a relationship and reduces the potential for conflict within a role or between roles.

All these forms of conflict can be managed. An understanding of the many forms is a first step. The next section focuses more extensively on interpersonal conflict because of its pervasiveness in organizations.

INTERPERSONAL CONFLICT

When a conflict occurs between two or more people, it is known as interpersonal conflict. To manage interpersonal conflict, it is helpful to understand power networks in organizations, defense mechanisms exhibited by individuals, and ways to cope with difficult people.

POWER NETWORKS

According to Mastenbroek, individuals in organizations are organized in three basic types of power networks.[35] Based on these power relationships, certain kinds of conflict tend to emerge. Figure 12-3 illustrates three basic kinds of power relationships in organizations.

The first relationship is equal versus equal, in which there is a horizontal balance of power among the parties. An example of this type of relationship would be a conflict between individuals from two different project teams. The behavioral tendency is toward suboptimization; that is, the focus is on a win–lose approach to problems, and each party tries to maximize its power at the expense of the other party. Conflict within this type of network can lead to depression, low self-esteem, and other distress symptoms. Interventions like improving coordination between the parties and working toward common interests can help manage these conflicts.

The second power network is high versus low, or a powerful versus a less powerful relationship. Conflicts that emerge here take the basic form of the powerful individuals trying to control others, with the less powerful people trying to become more autonomous. Conflict in this network can lead to job dissatisfaction, low organizational commitment, and turnover.[36]

Figure 12-3

Power Relationships in Organizations

Types of power relationships	Behavioral tendencies and problems	Interventions
Equal vs. equal 	Suboptimization • Tendency to compete with one another • Covert fighting for positions • Constant friction in border areas	• Defining demarcation lines • Improving coordination procedures • Integrating units • Teaching negotiating skills • Clarifying common interest • Activating central authority
High vs. low 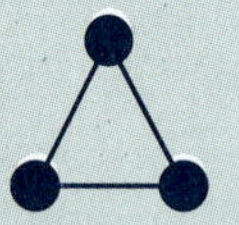	Control vs. autonomy • Resistance to change • Motivation problems	• Bureaucratizing power through rules • Using a different style of leadership • Structural and cultural interventions
High vs. middle vs. low 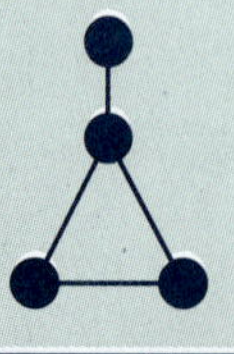	Role conflict, role ambiguity, stress • Concessions, double-talk, and use of sanctions and rewards to strengthen the position	• Improving communication • Clarifying tasks • Horizontalization, vertical task expansion • Teaching power strategies

Source: W. F. G. Mastenbroek, *Conflict Management and Organization Development*, 1987. Copyright John Wiley & Sons Limited. This material is used by permission of John Wiley & Sons, Inc.

Organizations typically respond to these conflicts by tightening the rules. However, the more successful ways of managing these conflicts are to try a different style of leadership, such as a coaching and counseling style, or to change the structure to a more decentralized one.

The third power network is high versus middle versus low. This power network illustrates the classic conflicts felt by middle managers. Two particular conflicts are evident for middle managers: role conflict, in which conflicting expectations are placed on the manager from bosses and employees, and role ambiguity, in which the expectations of the boss are unclear. Improved communication among all parties can reduce role conflict and ambiguity. In addition, middle managers can benefit from training in positive ways to influence others.

Knowing the typical kinds of conflicts that arise in various kinds of relationships can help a manager diagnose conflicts and devise appropriate ways to manage them.

DEFENSE MECHANISMS

When individuals are involved in conflict with another human being, frustration often results.[37] Conflicts can often arise within the context of a performance appraisal session. Most people do not react well to negative feedback, as was illustrated in a classic study.[38] In this study, when employees were given criticism about their work, over 50 percent of their responses were defensive.

When individuals are frustrated, as they often are in interpersonal conflict, they respond by exhibiting defense mechanisms.[39] Defense mechanisms are common reactions to the frustration that accompanies conflict. Table 12-2 (on page 292) describes several defense mechanisms seen in organizations.

Aggressive mechanisms, such as fixation, displacement, and negativism, are aimed at attacking the source of the conflict. In *fixation*, an individual fixates on the conflict, or keeps up a dysfunctional behavior that obviously will not solve the conflict. An example of fixation occurred in a university, where a faculty member became embroiled in a battle with the dean because the faculty member felt he had not received a large enough salary increase. He persisted in writing angry letters to the dean, whose hands were tied because of a low budget allocation to the college. *Displacement* means directing anger toward someone who is not the source of the conflict. For example, a manager may respond harshly to an employee after a telephone confrontation with an angry customer. Another aggressive defense mechanism is *negativism*, which is active or passive resistance. Negativism is illustrated by a manager who, when appointed to a committee on which she did not want to serve, made negative comments throughout the meeting.

Compromise mechanisms, such as compensation, identification, and rationalization, are used by individuals to make the best of a conflict situation. *Compensation* occurs when an individual tries to make up for an inadequacy by putting increased energy into another activity. Compensation can be seen when a person makes up for a bad relationship at home by

4. *Understand the defense mechanisms that individuals exhibit when they engage in interpersonal conflict.*

FIXATION
An aggressive mechanism in which an individual keeps up a dysfunctional behavior that obviously will not solve the conflict.

DISPLACEMENT
An aggressive mechanism in which an individual directs his or her anger toward someone who is not the source of the conflict.

NEGATIVISM
An aggressive mechanism in which a person responds with pessimism to any attempt at solving a problem.

COMPENSATION
A compromise mechanism in which an individual attempts to make up for a negative situation by devoting himself or herself to another pursuit with increased vigor.

Defense Mechanism	Psychological Process
Aggressive Mechanisms	
• Fixation	Person maintains a persistent, nonadjustive reaction even though all the cues indicate the behavior will not cope with the problem.
• Displacement	Individual redirects pent-up emotions toward persons, ideas, or objects other than the primary source of the emotion.
• Negativism	Person uses active or passive resistance, operating unconsciously.
Compromise Mechanisms	
• Compensation	Individual devotes himself or herself to a pursuit with increased vigor to make up for some feeling of real or imagined inadequacy.
• Identification	Individual enhances own self-esteem by patterning behavior after another's, frequently also internalizing the values and beliefs of the other person; also vicariously shares the glories or suffering in the disappointments of other individuals or groups.
• Rationalization	Person justifies inconsistent or undesirable behavior, beliefs, statements, and motivations by providing acceptable explanations for them.
Withdrawal Mechanisms	
• Flight or withdrawal	Through either physical or psychological means, person leaves the field in which frustration, anxiety, or conflict is experienced.
• Conversion	Emotional conflicts are expressed in muscular, sensory, or bodily symptoms of disability, malfunctioning, or pain.
• Fantasy	Person daydreams or uses other forms of imaginative activity to obtain an escape from reality and obtain imagined satisfactions.

Table 12-2
Common Defense Mechanisms

Source: Timothy W. Costello and Sheldon S. Zalkind, adapted table from "Psychology in Administration: A Research Orientation" from *Journal of Conflict Resolution* III 1959, pp. 148–149. Reprinted by permission of Sage Publications, Inc.

IDENTIFICATION
A compromise mechanism whereby an individual patterns his or her behavior after another's.

RATIONALIZATION
A compromise mechanism characterized by trying to justify one's behavior by constructing bogus reasons for it.

spending more time at the office. *Identification* occurs when one individual patterns his or her behavior after another's. One supervisor at a construction firm, not wanting to acknowledge consciously that she was not likely to be promoted, mimicked the behavior of her boss, even going so far as to buy a car just like the boss's. *Rationalization* is trying to justify one's behavior by constructing bogus reasons for it. Employees may rationalize unethical behavior like padding their expense accounts because "everyone else does it."

Withdrawal mechanisms are exhibited when frustrated individuals try to flee from a conflict using either physical or psychological means. Flight, conversion, and fantasy are examples of withdrawal mechanisms. Physically escaping a conflict is *flight*. An employee who takes a day off after a blowup with the boss is an example. *Withdrawal* may take the form of emotionally leaving a conflict, such as exhibiting an "I don't care anymore" attitude. *Conversion* is a process whereby emotional conflicts become expressed in physical symptoms. Most of us have experienced the conversion reaction of a headache following an emotional exchange with another person. *Fantasy* is an escape by daydreaming. Workers may daydream about exotic vacations while stuck in a boring job, or about getting even with a colleague with whom they had a conflict.

Knowledge of these defense mechanisms can be extremely beneficial to a manager. By understanding the ways in which people typically react to interpersonal conflict, managers can be prepared for employees' reactions and help them uncover their feelings about a conflict.

FLIGHT / WITHDRAWAL
A withdrawal mechanism that entails physically escaping a conflict (flight) or psychologically escaping (withdrawal).

CONVERSION
A withdrawal mechanism in which emotional conflicts are expressed in physical symptoms.

FANTASY
A withdrawal mechanism that provides an escape from a conflict through daydreaming.

CONFLICT MANAGEMENT STRATEGIES AND TECHNIQUES

The overall approach (or strategy) you use in a conflict is important in determining whether the conflict will have a positive or negative outcome.

These overall strategies are competitive versus cooperative strategies. Table 12-3 depicts the two strategies and four different conflict scenarios. The competitive strategy is founded on assumptions of win–lose and entails dishonest communication, mistrust, and a rigid position from both parties.[40] The cooperative strategy is founded on different assumptions: the potential for win–win outcomes, honest communication, trust, openness to risk and vulnerability, and the notion that the whole may be greater than the sum of the parts.

To illustrate the importance of the overall strategy, consider the case of two groups competing for scarce resources. Suppose budget cuts have to be made at an insurance company. The claims manager argues that the sales training staff should be cut, because agents are fully trained. The sales training manager argues that claims personnel should be cut, because the company is processing fewer claims. This could turn into a dysfunctional brawl, with both sides refusing to give ground. This would constitute a win–lose, lose–win, or lose–lose scenario. Personnel cuts could be made in only one

Strategy	Department A	Department B	Organization
Competitive	Lose	Lose	Lose
	Lose	Win	Lose
	Win	Lose	Lose
Cooperative	Win–	Win–	Win

Table 12-3
Win–Lose versus Win–Win Strategies

department, or in both departments. In all three cases, with the competitive approach the organization winds up in a losing position.

Even in such intense conflicts as those over scarce resources, a win–win strategy can lead to an overall win for the organization. In fact, conflicts over scarce resources can be productive if the parties have cooperative goals—a strategy that seeks a winning solution for both parties. To achieve a win–win outcome, the conflict must be approached with open-minded discussion of opposing views. Through open-minded discussion, both parties integrate views and create new solutions that facilitate productivity and strengthen their relationship; the result is feelings of unity rather than separation.[41]

In the example of the conflict between the claims manager and sales training manager, open-minded discussion might reveal that there are ways to achieve budget cuts without cutting personnel. Sales support might surrender part of its travel budget, and claims might cut out overtime. This represents a win–win situation for the company. The budget has been reduced, and relationships between the two departments have been preserved. Both parties have given up something (note the "win–" in Table 12-3), but the conflict has been resolved with a positive outcome.

You can see the importance of the broad strategy used to approach a conflict. We now move from broad strategies to more specific techniques.

INEFFECTIVE TECHNIQUES

5. *Describe ineffective and effective techniques for managing conflict.*

There are many specific techniques for dealing with conflict. Before turning to techniques that work, it should be recognized that some actions commonly taken in organizations to deal with conflict are not effective.[42]

Nonaction is doing nothing in hopes that the conflict will disappear. Generally, this is not a good technique, because most conflicts do not go away, and the individuals involved in the conflict react with frustration.

NONACTION
Doing nothing in hopes that a conflict will disappear.

Secrecy, or trying to keep a conflict out of view of most people, only creates suspicion. An example is an organizational policy of pay secrecy. In some organizations, discussion of salary is grounds for dismissal. When this is the case, employees suspect that the company has something to hide.

SECRECY
Attempting to hide a conflict or an issue that has the potential to create conflict.

Administrative orbiting is delaying action on a conflict by buying time, usually by telling the individuals involved that the problem is being worked on or that the boss is still thinking about the issue. Like nonaction, this technique leads to frustration and resentment.

ADMINISTRATIVE ORBITING
Delaying action on a conflict by buying time.

Due process nonaction is a procedure set up to address conflicts that is so costly, time consuming, or personally risky that no one will use it. Some companies' sexual harassment policies are examples of this technique. To file a sexual harassment complaint, detailed paperwork is required, the accuser must go through appropriate channels, and the accuser risks being branded a troublemaker. Thus, the company has a procedure for handling complaints (due process), but no one uses it (nonaction).

DUE PROCESS NONACTION
A procedure set up to address conflicts that is so costly, time consuming, or personally risky that no one will use it.

Character assassination is an attempt to label or discredit an opponent. Character assassination can backfire and make the individual who uses it appear dishonest and cruel. It often leads to name-calling and accu-

CHARACTER ASSASSINATION
An attempt to label or discredit an opponent.

sations by both parties, and both parties end up losers in the eyes of those who witness the conflict.

EFFECTIVE TECHNIQUES

Fortunately, there are effective conflict management techniques. These include appealing to superordinate goals, expanding resources, changing personnel, changing structure, and confronting and negotiating.

Superordinate Goals   An organizational goal that is more important to both parties in a conflict than their individual or group goals is a ***superordinate goal***.[43] Superordinate goals cannot be achieved by an individual or by one group alone. The achievement of these goals requires cooperation by both parties.

One effective technique for resolving conflict is to appeal to a superordinate goal—in effect, to focus the parties on a larger issue on which they both agree. This helps them realize their similarities rather than their differences.

In the conflict between service representatives and cable television installers that was discussed earlier, appealing to a superordinate goal would be an effective technique for resolving the conflict. Both departments can agree that superior customer service is a goal worthy of pursuit and that this goal cannot be achieved unless cables are installed properly and in a timely manner, and customer complaints are handled effectively. Quality service requires that both departments cooperate to achieve the goal.

Expanding Resources   One conflict resolution technique is so simple that it may be overlooked. If the conflict's source is common or scarce resources, providing more resources may be a solution. Of course, managers working with tight budgets may not have the luxury of obtaining additional resources. Nevertheless, it is a technique to be considered. In the example earlier in this chapter, one solution to the conflict among managers over secretarial support would be to hire more secretaries.

Changing Personnel   Sometimes a conflict is prolonged and severe, and efforts at resolution fail. In such cases, it may be appropriate to change personnel. Transferring or firing an individual may be the best solution, but only after due process.

Changing Structure   Another way to resolve a conflict is to change the structure of the organization. One way of accomplishing this is to create an integrator role. An integrator is a liaison between groups with very different interests. In severe conflicts, it may be best that the integrator be a neutral third party.[44] Creating the integrator role is a way of opening dialogue between groups that have difficulty communicating.

Using cross-functional teams is another way of changing the organization's structure to manage conflict. In the old methods of designing new products in organizations, many departments had to contribute, and delays

SUPERORDINATE GOAL
An organizational goal that is more important to both parties in a conflict than their individual or group goals.

resulted from difficulties in coordinating the activities of the various departments. Using a cross-functional team made up of members from different departments improves coordination and reduces delays by allowing many activities to be performed at the same time rather than sequentially.[45] The team approach allows members from different departments to work together and reduces the potential for conflict.

Confronting and Negotiating Some conflicts require confrontation and negotiation between the parties. Both these strategies require skill on the part of the negotiator and careful planning before engaging in negotiations. The process of negotiating involves an open discussion of problem solutions, and the outcome often is an exchange in which both parties work toward a mutually beneficial solution.

Negotiation is a joint process of finding a mutually acceptable solution to a complex conflict. Negotiating is a useful strategy under the following conditions:

- There are two or more parties. Negotiation is primarily an interpersonal or intergroup process.
- There is a conflict of interest between the parties such that what one party wants is not what the other party wants.
- The parties are willing to negotiate because each believes it can use its influence to obtain a better outcome than by simply taking the side of the other party.
- The parties prefer to work together rather than to fight openly, give in, break off contact, or take the dispute to a higher authority.

DISTRIBUTIVE BARGAINING
A negotiation approach in which the goals of the parties are in conflict, and each party seeks to maximize its resources.

There are two major negotiating approaches: distributive bargaining and integrative negotiation.[46] **Distributive bargaining** is an approach in which the goals of one party are in direct conflict with the goals of the other party. Resources are limited, and each party wants to maximize its share of the resources (get its part of the pie). It is a competitive or win–lose approach to negotiations. Sometimes distributive bargaining causes negotiators to focus so much on their differences that they ignore their common ground. In these cases, distributive bargaining can become counterproductive. The reality is, however, that some situations are distributive in nature, particularly when the parties are interdependent. If a negotiator wants to maximize the value of a single deal and is not worried about maintaining a good relationship with the other party, distributive bargaining may be an option.

INTEGRATIVE NEGOTIATION
A negotiation approach that focuses on the merits of the issues and seeks a win–win solution.

In contrast, **integrative negotiation** is an approach in which the parties' goals are not seen as mutually exclusive and in which the focus is on making it possible for both sides to achieve their objectives. Integrative negotiation focuses on the merits of the issues and is a win–win approach. (How can we make the pie bigger?) For integrative negotiation to be successful, certain preconditions must be present. These include having a common goal, faith in one's own problem-solving abilities, a belief in the validity of the other party's position, motivation to work together, mutual trust, and clear communication.[47]

Cultural differences in negotiation must be acknowledged. Japanese negotiators, for example, when working with American negotiators, tend to see their power as coming from their role (buyer versus seller). Americans, in contrast, view their power as their ability to walk away from the negotiations.[48] Neither culture understands the other very well, and the negotiations can resemble a dance in which one person is waltzing and the other doing a samba. The collectivism-individualism dimension (discussed in Chapter 2) has a great bearing on negotiations. Americans, with their individualism, negotiate from a position of self-interest; Japanese focus on the good of the group. How can cross-cultural negotiations be more effective? One action you can take is to learn as much about other cultures as possible.

Gender may also play a role in negotiation. There appears to be no evidence that men are better negotiators that women or vice versa. The differences lie in how negotiators are treated. Women are blatantly discriminated against in terms of the offers made to them in negotiations.[49] Gender stereotypes also affect the negotiating process. Women may be seen as accommodating, conciliatory, and emotional (negatives in negotiations) and men may be seen as assertive, powerful, and convincing (positive for negotiations) in accordance with traditional stereotypes. Sometimes, when women feel they're being stereotyped, they exhibit stereotype reactance, which is a tendency to display behavior inconsistent with (or opposite of) the stereotype. This means they become more assertive and convincing. Alternatively, men may choke when they're expected to fulfill the stereotype, fearing that they might not be able to live up to the stereotype.

One way to help men and women avoid stereotyping each other is to promote shared, positive identities between the negotiators. This means recognizing similarities between the two parties; for example, recognizing each other as highly successful professionals. This results in more cooperation because of shared and equal status, as opposed to more competition because of gender stereotypes.[50]

CONFLICT MANAGEMENT STYLES

Managers have at their disposal a variety of conflict management styles: avoiding, accommodating, competing, compromising, and collaborating. One way of classifying styles of conflict management is to examine the styles' assertiveness (the extent to which you want your goals met) and cooperativeness (the extent to which you want to see the other party's concerns met).[51] Figure 12-4 (on page 298) graphs the five conflict management styles using these two dimensions. Table 12-4 (on page 299) lists appropriate situations for using each conflict management style.

6. *Understand five styles of conflict management, and diagnose your own preferred style.*

AVOIDING

Avoiding is a style low on both assertiveness and cooperativeness. Avoiding is a deliberate decision to take no action on a conflict or to stay out of a conflict situation. Some relationship conflicts, such as those

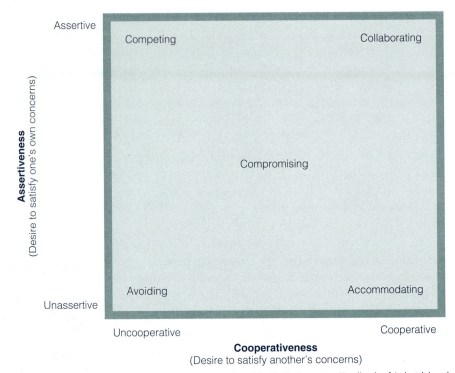

Assertive

Competing

Collaborating

Assertiveness
(Desire to satisfy one's own concerns)

Compromising

Avoiding

Accommodating

Unassertive

Uncooperative

Cooperative

Cooperativeness
(Desire to satisfy another's concerns)

Figure 12-4
Conflict Management Styles

Source: K. W. Thomas, "Conflict and Conflict Management," in M. D. Dunnette, *Handbook of Industrial and Organizational Psychology* (New York: Wiley, 1976), 900. Used with permission of John Wiley & Sons, Inc.

involving political norms and personal tastes, may distract team members from their tasks and avoiding may be an appropriate strategy.[52] When the parties are angry and need time to cool down, it may be best to use avoidance. There is a potential danger in using an avoiding style too often, however. Research shows that overuse of this style results in negative evaluations from others in the workplace.[53]

ACCOMMODATING

A style in which you are concerned that the other party's goals be met but relatively unconcerned with getting your own way is called accommodating. It is cooperative but unassertive. Appropriate situations for accommodating include times when you find you are wrong, when you want to let the other party have his or her way so that that individual will owe you similar treatment later, or when the relationship is important. Overreliance on accommodating has its dangers. Managers who constantly defer to others may find that others lose respect for them. In addition, accommodating managers may become frustrated because their own needs are never met, and they may lose self-esteem.[54]

COMPETING

Competing is a style that is very assertive and uncooperative. You want to satisfy your own interests and are willing to do so at the other party's

YOU BE THE JUDGE

In what situations is the competing style of conflict management appropriate? What unethical behaviors might be associated with this style? How can these behaviors be avoided?

Conflict-Handling Style	Appropriate Situation
Competing	1. When quick, decisive action is vital (e.g., emergencies). 2. On important issues where unpopular actions need implementing (e.g., cost cutting, enforcing unpopular rules, discipline). 3. On issues vital to company welfare when you know you are right. 4. Against people who take advantage of noncompetitive behavior.
Collaborating	1. To find an integrative solution when both sets of concerns are too important to be compromised. 2. When your objective is to learn. 3. To merge insights from people with different perspectives. 4. To gain commitment by incorporating concerns into a consensus. 5. To work through feelings that have interfered with a relationship.
Compromising	1. When goals are important, but not worth the effort or potential disruption of more assertive modes. 2. When opponents with equal power are committed to mutually exclusive goals. 3. To achieve temporary settlements to complex issues. 4. To arrive at expedient solutions under time pressure. 5. As a backup when collaboration or competition is unsuccessful.
Avoiding	1. When an issue is trivial, or more important issues are pressing. 2. When you perceive no chance of satisfying your concerns. 3. When potential disruption outweighs the benefits of resolution. 4. To let people cool down and regain perspective. 5. When gathering information supersedes immediate decision. 6. When others can resolve the conflict more effectively. 7. When issues seem tangential or symptomatic of other issues.
Accommodating	1. When you find you are wrong—to allow a better position to be heard, to learn, and to show your reasonableness. 2. When issues are more important to others than to yourself—to satisfy others and maintain cooperation. 3. To build social credits for later issues. 4. To minimize loss when you are outmatched and losing. 5. When harmony and stability are especially important. 6. To allow employees to develop by learning from mistakes.

Source: *The Conflict Positive Organization*, by D. Tjosvold, © 1991. Reprinted by permission of Pearson Education, Inc., Upper Saddle River, N.J.

Table 12-4
Uses of Five Styles of Conflict Management

expense. In an emergency or in situations where you know you are right, it may be appropriate to put your foot down. For example, environmentalists forced Shell Oil Company (part of Royal Dutch/Shell Group) to scrap its plans to build a refinery in Delaware after a bitter "To Hell with Shell" campaign.[55] Relying solely on competing strategies is dangerous, though. Managers who do so may become reluctant to admit when they are wrong and may find themselves surrounded by people who are afraid to disagree with them.

COMPROMISING

The compromising style is intermediate in both assertiveness and cooperativeness, because each party must give up something to reach a solution to the conflict. Compromises are often made in the final hours of union–management negotiations, when time is of the essence. Compromise may be an effective backup style when efforts toward collaboration are not successful.[56]

It is important to recognize that compromises are not optimal solutions. Compromise means partially surrendering one's position for the sake of coming to terms. Often, when people compromise, they inflate their demands to begin with. The solutions reached may only be temporary, and often compromises do nothing to improve relationships between the parties in the conflict.

COLLABORATING

A win–win style that is high on both assertiveness and cooperativeness is known as collaborating. Working toward collaborating involves an open and thorough discussion of the conflict and arriving at a solution that is satisfactory to both parties. Situations where collaboration may be effective include times when both parties need to be committed to a final solution or when a combination of different perspectives can be formed into a solution. Collaborating requires open, trusting behavior and sharing information for the benefit of both parties. Long term, it leads to improved relationships and effective performance.[57]

Research on the five styles of conflict management indicates that although most managers favor a certain style, they have the capacity to change styles as the situation demands.[58] A study of project managers found that managers who used a combination of competing and avoiding styles were seen as ineffective by the engineers who worked on their project teams.[59] In another study of conflicts between R&D project managers and technical staff, competing and avoiding styles resulted in more frequent conflict and lower performance, whereas the collaborating style resulted in less frequent conflict and better performance.[60] Use this chapter's Challenge to assess your dominant conflict management style.

Cultural differences also influence the use of different styles of conflict management. For example, one study compared Turkish and Jordanian managers with U.S. managers. All three groups preferred the collaborating style. Turkish managers also reported frequent use of the competing style, whereas Jordanian and U.S. managers reported that it was one of their least used styles.[61]

The human resources manager of one U.S. telecommunications company's office in Singapore engaged a consultant to investigate the conflict in the office.[62] Twenty-two expatriates from the United States and Canada and thirty-eight Singaporeans worked in the office. The consultant used the Thomas model (Figure 12-4) and distributed questionnaires to all managers

Challenge

WHAT IS YOUR CONFLICT-HANDLING STYLE?

Instructions:

For each of the fifteen items, indicate how often you rely on that tactic by circling the appropriate number.

	Rarely Always
1. I argue my case with my coworkers to show the merits of my position.	1—2—3—④—5
2. I negotiate with my coworkers so that a compromise can be reached.	1—2—3—4—⑤
3. I try to satisfy the expectations of my coworkers.	1—2—3—4—⑤
4. I try to investigate an issue with my coworkers to find a solution acceptable to us.	1—2—3—4—⑤
5. I am firm in pursuing my side of the issue.	1—2—3—④—5
6. I attempt to avoid being "put on the spot" and try to keep my conflict with my coworkers to myself.	1—②—3—4—5
7. I hold on to my solution to a problem.	1—②—3—4—5
8. I use "give and take" so that a compromise can be made.	1—2—③—4—5
9. I exchange accurate information with my coworkers to solve a problem together.	1—2—3—④—5
10. I avoid open discussion of my differences with my coworkers.	1—②—3—4—5
11. I accommodate the wishes of my coworkers.	1—2—3—④—5
12. I try to bring all our concerns out in the open so that the issues can be resolved in the best possible way.	1—2—3—4—⑤
13. I propose a middle ground for breaking deadlocks.	1—2—3—④—5
14. I go along with the suggestions of my coworkers.	1—2—3—④—5
15. I try to keep my disagreements with my coworkers to myself in order to avoid hard feelings.	1—②—3—4—5

Scoring Key:

Collaborating		Accommodating		Competing		Avoiding		Compromising	
Item	Score	Item	Score	Item	Score	Item	Score	Item	Score
4.	5	3.	5	1.	4	6.	2	2.	5
9.	4	11.	4	5.	4	10.	2	8.	3
12.	5	14.	4	7.	2	15.	2	13.	4
Total = 14		Total = 13		Total = 10		Total = 6		Total = 12	

Your primary conflict-handling style is: _Collaborating_   Your backup conflict-handling style is: _Accommodating_
(The category with the highest total.)   (The category with the second highest total.)

Source: Reprinted with permission of Academy of Management, PO Box 3020, Briar Cliff Manor, NY 10510-8020. *A Measure of Styles of Handling Interpersonal Conflict* (Adaptation), M. A. Rahim, Academy of Management Journal, June 1983. Reproduced by permission of the publisher via Copyright Clearance Center, Inc.

to determine their conflict management styles. The results were not surprising: The expatriate managers preferred the competing, collaborating, and compromising styles, while the Asians preferred the avoiding and accommodating styles.

Workshops were conducted within the firm to develop an understanding of the differences and how they negatively affected the firm. The Asians interpreted the results as reflecting the tendency of Americans to "shout first and ask questions later." They felt that the Americans had an arrogant attitude and could not handle having their ideas rejected. The Asians attributed their own styles to their cultural background. The Americans attributed the results to the stereotypical view of Asians as unassertive and timid, and they viewed their own results as reflecting their desire to "get things out in the open."

The process opened a dialogue between the two groups, who began to work on the idea of harmony through conflict. They began to discard the traditional stereotypes in favor of shared meanings and mutual understanding.

It is important to remember that preventing and resolving dysfunctional conflict is only half the task of effective conflict management. Stimulating functional conflict is the other half.

MANAGERIAL IMPLICATIONS: CREATING A CONFLICT-POSITIVE ORGANIZATION

Dean Tjosvold argues that well-managed conflict adds to an organization's innovation and productivity.[63] He discusses procedures for making conflict positive. Too many organizations take a win–lose, competitive approach to conflict or avoid conflict altogether. These two approaches view conflict as negative. A positive view of conflict, in contrast, leads to win–win solutions. Figure 12-5 illustrates these three approaches to conflict management.

Four interrelated steps are involved in creating a conflict-positive organization:

1. *Value diversity and confront differences.* Differences should be seen as opportunities for innovation, and diversity should be celebrated. Open and honest confrontations bring out differences, and they are essential for positive conflict.

Figure 12-5
Three Organization Views of Conflict

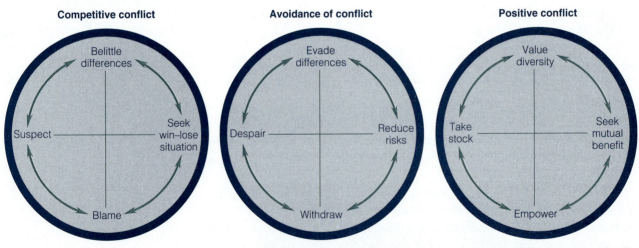

Source: *The Conflict Positive Organization*, by D. Tjosvold, © 1991. Reprinted by permission of Pearson Education, Inc., Upper Saddle River, N.J.

2. *Seek mutual benefits, and unite behind cooperative goals.* Conflicts have to be managed together. Through conflict, individuals learn how much they depend on one another. Even when employees share goals, they may differ on how to accomplish the goals. The important point is that they are moving toward the same objectives. Joint rewards should be given to the whole team for cooperative behavior.

3. *Empower employees to feel confident and skillful.* People must be made to feel that they control their conflicts and that they can deal with their differences productively. When they do so, they should be recognized.

4. *Take stock to reward success and learn from mistakes.* Employees should be encouraged to appreciate one another's strengths and weaknesses and to talk directly about them. They should celebrate their conflict managment successes and work out plans for ways they can improve in the future.

Tjosvold believes that a conflict-positive organization has competitive advantages for the future.

KEY TERMS

administrative orbiting	fixation	intrapersonal conflict
character assassination	flight/withdrawal	intrarole conflict
compensation	functional conflict	jurisdictional ambiguity
conflict	identification	negativism
conversion	integrative negotiation	nonaction
displacement	intergroup conflict	person–role conflict
distributive bargaining	interorganizational conflict	rationalization
due process nonaction	interpersonal conflict	secrecy
dysfunctional conflict	interrole conflict	superordinate goal
fantasy	intragroup conflict	

Experiential Exercise

THE WORLD BANK GAME: AN INTERGROUP NEGOTIATION

The purposes of this exercise are to learn about conflict and trust between groups and to practice negotiation skills. In the course of the exercise, money will be won or lost. Your team's objective is to win as much money as it can. Your team will be paired with another team, and both teams will receive identical instructions. After reading these instructions, each team will have ten minutes to plan its strategy.

Each team is assumed to have contributed $50 million to the World Bank. Teams may have to pay more or may receive money from the World Bank, depending on the outcome.

Each team will receive twenty cards. These cards are the weapons. Each card has a marked side (X) and an unmarked side. The marked side signifies that the weapon is armed; the unmarked side signifies that the weapon is unarmed.

At the beginning, each team will place ten of its twenty weapons in their armed position (marked side up) and the remaining ten in their unarmed position (marked side down). The weapons will remain in the team's possession and out of sight of the other team at all times.

The game will consist of *rounds* and *moves*. Each round will be composed of seven moves by each team. There will be two or more rounds in the game, depending on the time available. Payoffs will be determined and recorded after each round. The rules are as follows:

1. A move consists of turning two, one, or none of the team's weapons from armed to unarmed status, or vice versa.

2. Each team has one and a half minutes for each move. There is a thirty-second period between each move. At the end of the one and a half minutes, the team must have turned two, one, or none of its weapons from armed to unarmed status or from unarmed to armed status. If the team fails to move in the allotted time, no change can be made in weapon status until the next move.

3. The two-minute length of the period between the beginning of one move and the beginning of the next is unalterable.

Finances

The funds each team has contributed to the World Bank are to be allocated in the following manner: $30 million will be returned to each team to be used as the team's treasury during the course of the game, and $20 million will be retained for the operation of the World Bank.

Payoffs

1. If there is an attack:

    a. Each team may announce an attack on the other team by notifying the banker during the thirty seconds following any minute-and-a-half period used to decide upon the move (including the seventh, or final, decision period in any round). The choice of each team during the decision period just ended counts as a move. An attack may not be made during negotiations.

    b. If there is an attack by one or both teams, two things happen: (1) the round ends, and (2)

the World Bank assesses a penalty of $2.5 million on each team.

    c. The team with the greater number of armed weapons wins $1.5 million for each armed weapon it has over and above the number of armed weapons of the other team. These funds are paid directly from the treasury of the losing team to the treasury of the winning team. The banker will manage the transfer of funds.

2. If there is no attack:

    At the end of each round (seven moves), each team's treasury will receive from the World Bank $1 million for each of its weapons that is at that point unarmed; and each team's treasury will pay to the World Bank $1 million for each of its weapons remaining armed.

Negotiations

Between moves, each team will have the opportunity to communicate with the other team through its negotiations. Either team may call for negotiations by notifying the banker during any of the thirty-second periods between decisions. A team is free to accept or reject any invitation to negotiate.

Negotiators from both teams are required to meet after the third and sixth moves (after the thirty-second period following the move, if there is no attack).

Negotiations can last no longer than three minutes. When the two negotiators return to their teams, the minute-and-a-half decision period for the next move will begin once again.

Negotiators are bound only by (a) the three-minute time limit for negotiations and (b) their required appearance after the third and sixth moves. They are always free to say whatever is necessary to benefit themselves or their teams. The teams are not bound by agreements made by their negotiators, even when those agreements are made in good faith.

Special Roles

Each team has ten minutes to organize itself and plan team strategy. During this period, before the first round begins, each team must choose persons to fill the following roles:

- A *negotiator*—activities stated above.
- A *representative*—to communicate the team's decisions to the banker.
- A *recorder*—to record the moves of the team and to keep a running balance of the team's treasury.
- A *treasurer*—to execute all financial transactions with the banker.

The instructor will serve as the banker for the World Bank and will signal the beginning of each of the rounds.

At the end of the game, each participant should complete the following questionnaire, which assesses reactions to the World Bank Game.

World Bank Questionnaire

1. To what extent are you satisfied with your team's strategy?

   Highly   1 2 3 4 5 6 7   Highly
   dissatisfied   satisfied

2. To what extent do you believe the other team is trustworthy?

   Highly   1 2 3 4 5 6 7   Highly
   untrustworthy   trustworthy

3. To what extent are you satisfied with the performance of your negotiator?

   Highly   1 2 3 4 5 6 7   Highly
   dissatisfied   satisfied

4. To what extent was there a consensus on your team regarding its moves?

   Very little   1 2 3 4 5 6 7   A great deal

5. To what extent do you trust the other members of your team?

   Very little   1 2 3 4 5 6 7   A great deal

6. Select one word that describes how you feel about your team: _____ .

7. Select one word that describes how you feel about the other team: _____ .

Negotiators only:
How did you see the other team's negotiator?

Phony and   1 2 3 4 5 6 7   Authentic
insincere   and sincere

At the end of the game, the class will reconvene and discuss team members' responses to the World Bank Questionnaire. In addition, the following questions are to be addressed:

1. What was each team's strategy for winning? What strategy was most effective?

2. Contrast the outcomes in terms of win–win solutions to conflict versus win–lose solutions.

Source: Adapted by permission from N. H. Berkowitz and H. A. Hornstein, "World Bank: An Intergroup Negotiation," in J. W. Pfeiffer and J. E. Jones, eds., *The 1975 Handbook for Group Facilitators* (San Diego: Pfeiffer), 58–62. Copyright © 1975. Pfeiffer/Jossey-Bass. This material is used by permission of John Wiley & Sons, Inc.

(continued)

WORLD BANK RECORD SHEET

		Round One		Round Two		Round Three		Round Four	
		Armed	Unarmed	Armed	Unarmed	Armed	Unarmed	Armed	Unarmed
Move		10	10	10	10	10	10	10	10
	1								
	2								
	3								
Required Negotiation	4								
	5								
	6								
Required Negotiation	7								

	Round One	Round Two	Round Three	Round Four
Funds in Team Treasury	$30 million			
Funds of Other Treasury	$30 million			
Funds in World Bank	$40 million			

PART 4

Organizational Processes and Structure

13

Jobs and the Design of Work

LEARNING OBJECTIVES

After reading this chapter, you should be able to do the following:

1. Define the term *job*, and identify six patterns of defining *work*.

2. Discuss the four traditional approaches to job design.

3. Describe the job characteristics model.

4. Compare the social information-processing (SIP) model with traditional job design approaches.

5. Explain the interdisciplinary approach to job design.

6. Compare Japanese, German, and Scandinavian approaches to work.

7. Explain how job control, uncertainty, and conflict can be managed for employee well-being.

8. Discuss five contemporary issues in the design of work.

Overly structured, inflexible jobs can cause unwanted turnover, while flexible work design policies can have the reverse effect. A *job* is defined as an employee's specific work and task activities in an organization. A job is not the same as an organizational position or a career. *Organizational position* identifies a job in relation to other parts of the organization; *career* refers to a sequence of job experiences over time.

This chapter focuses on jobs and the design of work as elements of the organization's structure. Jobs help people define their work and become integrated into the organization. The first section in the chapter examines the meaning of work in organizations. The second major section addresses four traditional approaches to job design developed between the late 1800s and the 1970s. The third major section examines four alternative approaches to job design developed over the past couple of decades. The final section addresses emerging issues in job design.

JOB
A set of specified work and task activities that engage an individual in an organization.

1. *Define the term* job, *and identify six patterns of defining* work.

WORK IN ORGANIZATIONS

Work is effortful, productive activity resulting in a product or a service. Work is one important reason why organizations exist. A job is composed of a set of specific tasks, each of which is an assigned piece of work to be done in a specific time period. Work is an especially important human endeavor because it has a powerful effect in binding a person to reality. Through work, people become securely attached to reality and securely connected in human relationships.

Work has different meanings for different people. For all people, work is organized into jobs, and jobs fit into the larger structure of an organization. The structure of jobs is the concern of this chapter, and the structure of the organization is the concern of the next chapter. Both chapters emphasize organizations as sets of task and authority relationships through which people get work done.

WORK
Mental or physical activity that has productive results.

THE MEANING OF WORK

The *meaning of work* differs from person to person, and from culture to culture. In an increasingly global workplace, it is important to understand and appreciate differences among individuals and between cultures with regard to the meaning of work. One study found six patterns people follow in defining *work*, and these help explain the cultural differences in people's motivation to work.[1]

MEANING OF WORK
The way a person interprets and understands the value of work as part of life.

- Pattern A people define *work* as an activity in which value comes from performance and for which a person is accountable. It is generally self-directed and devoid of negative affect.
- Pattern B people define *work* as an activity that provides a person with positive personal affect and identity. Work contributes to society and is not unpleasant.
- Pattern C people define *work* as an activity from which profit accrues to others by its performance and that may be done in various settings

other than a working place. Work is usually physically strenuous and somewhat compulsive.

- Pattern D people define *work* as primarily a physical activity a person must do that is directed by others and generally performed in a working place. Work is usually devoid of positive affect and is unpleasantly connected to performance.
- Pattern E people define *work* as a physically and mentally strenuous activity. It is generally unpleasant and devoid of positive affect.
- Pattern F people define *work* as an activity constrained to specific time periods that does not bring positive affect through its performance.

These six patterns were studied in six different countries: Belgium, Germany, Israel, Japan, the Netherlands, and the United States. Table 13-1 summarizes the percentage of workers in each country who defined *work* according to each of the six patterns. An examination of the table shows that a small percentage of workers in all six countries used either Pattern E or Pattern F to define *work*. Furthermore, there are significant differences among countries in how *work* is defined. In the Netherlands, *work* is defined most positively and with the most balanced personal and collective reasons for doing it. *Work* is defined least positively and with the most collective reason for doing it in Germany and Japan. Belgium, Israel, and the United States represent a middle position between these two. Future international studies should include Middle Eastern countries, India, Central and South American countries, and other Asian countries to better represent the world's cultures.

In another international study, 5,550 people across ten occupational groups in twenty different countries completed the Work Value Scales

Table 13-1

Work Definition Patterns by Nation

Sample	Pattern[a]					
	A	B	C	D	E	F
Total Sample (N = 4,950)	11%	28%	18%	22%	11%	12%
Nation						
Belgium	8%	40%	13%	19%	11%	9%
Germany	8	26	13	28	11	14
Israel	4	22	33	23	9	9
Japan	21	11	13	29	10	17
The Netherlands	15	43	12	11	9	9
United States	8	30	19	19	12	11

Note: $X^2 = 680.98$ (25 degrees of freedom). $P<.0001$ Significance level

[a]In Pattern A, work is valued for its performance. The person is accountable and generally self-directed. In Pattern B, work provides a person with positive affect and identity. It contributes to society. In Pattern C, work provides profit to others by its performance. It is physical and not confined to a working place. In Pattern D, work is a required physical activity directed by others and generally unpleasant. In Pattern E, work is physically and mentally strenuous. It is generally unpleasant. In Pattern F, work is constrained to specific time periods. It does not bring positive affect through performance.

Source: From G. W. England and I. Harpaz, "How Working Is Defined: National Contexts and Demographic and Organizational Role Influences," from *Journal of Organizational Behavior*, 11, 1990. Copyright John Wiley & Sons, Limited. Reproduced with permission.

(WVS).[2] The WVS is composed of thirteen items measuring various aspects of the work environment, such as responsibility and job security. The study found two common basic work dimensions across cultures. Work content is one dimension, measured by items such as "the amount of responsibility on the job." Job context is the other dimension, measured by items such as "the policies of my company." This finding suggests that people in many cultures distinguish between the nature of the work itself and elements of the context in which work is done. This supports Herzberg's two-factor theory of motivation (see Chapter 5) and his job enrichment method discussed later in this chapter. Although the meaning of *work* differs among countries, new theorizing about crafting a job also suggests that individual employees can alter work meaning and work identity by changing task and relationship configurations in their work.[3]

JOBS IN ORGANIZATIONS

Task and authority relationships define an organization's structure. Jobs are the basic building blocks of this task–authority structure and are considered the micro-structural element to which employees most directly relate. Jobs are usually designed to complement and support other jobs in the organization. Isolated jobs are rare.

Jobs in organizations are interdependent and designed to make a contribution to the organization's overall mission and goals. For salespeople to be successful, the production people must be effective. For production people to be effective, the material department must be effective. These interdependencies require careful planning and design so that all of the "pieces of work" fit together into a whole. For example, an envelope salesperson who wants to take an order for 1 million envelopes from John Hancock Financial Services must coordinate with the production department to establish an achievable delivery date. The failure to incorporate this interdependence into his planning could create conflict and doom the company to failure in meeting John Hancock's expectations. The central concerns of this chapter are designing work and structuring jobs to prevent such problems and to ensure employee well-being. Inflexible jobs that are rigidly structured have an adverse effect and lead to stressed-out employees.

Chapter 14 addresses the larger issues in the design of organizations. In particular, it examines the competing processes of differentiation and integration in organizations. Differentiation is the process of subdividing and departmentalizing the work of an organization. Jobs result from differentiation, which is necessary because no one can do it all (contrary to the famous statement made by Harold Geneen, former chairman of ITT: "If I had enough arms and legs and time, I'd do it all myself"). Even small organizations must divide work so that each person is able to accomplish a manageable piece of the whole. At the same time the organization divides up the work, it must also integrate those pieces back into a whole. Integration is the process of connecting jobs and departments into a coordinated, cohesive whole. For example, if the envelope salesperson had coordinated with the production manager before finalizing the order with John Hancock, the company could have met the customer's expectations, and integration would have occurred.

TRADITIONAL APPROACHES TO JOB DESIGN

2. Discuss the four traditional approaches to job design.

Failure to differentiate, integrate, or both may result in badly designed jobs, which in turn cause a variety of performance problems in organizations. Good job design helps avoid these problems, improves productivity, and enhances employee well-being. Four approaches to job design that were developed during the twentieth century are scientific management, job enlargement/job rotation, job enrichment, and the job characteristics theory. Each approach offers unique benefits to the organization, the employee, or both, but each also has limitations and drawbacks. Furthermore, an unthinking reliance on a traditional approach can be a serious problem in any company. The later job design approaches were developed to overcome the limitations of traditional job design approaches. For example, job enlargement was intended to overcome the problem of boredom associated with scientific management's narrowly defined approach to jobs.

SCIENTIFIC MANAGEMENT

WORK SIMPLIFICATION
Standardization and the narrow, explicit specification of task activities for workers.

Scientific management, an approach to work design first advocated by Frederick Taylor, emphasized work simplification. **Work simplification** is the standardization and the narrow, explicit specification of task activities for workers.[4] Jobs designed through scientific management have a limited number of tasks, and each task is scientifically specified so that the worker is not required to think or deliberate. According to Taylor, the role of management and the industrial engineer is to calibrate and define each task carefully. The role of the worker is to execute the task. The elements of scientific management, such as time and motion studies, differential piece rate systems of pay, and the scientific selection of workers, all focus on the efficient use of labor to the economic benefit of the corporation. Employees who are satisfied with various aspects of repetitive work may like scientifically designed jobs.

Two arguments supported the efficient and standardized job design approach of scientific management in the early days of the American industrial revolution. The first argument was that work simplification allowed workers of diverse ethnic and skill backgrounds to work together in a systematic way. This was important during the first great period of globalization in the late 1800s during which Germans, Scots, Hungarians, Poles, and other immigrants came to work in America.[5] Taylor's unique approach to work standardization allowed diverse individuals to be blended into a functional workforce.

The second argument for scientific management was that work simplification led to production efficiency in the organization and, therefore, to higher profits. This economic argument for work simplification tended to treat labor as a means of production and dehumanized it. This is a problem in some modern service jobs, such as flipping hamburgers.

A fundamental limitation of scientific management is that it undervalues the human capacity for thought and ingenuity. Jobs designed through scientific management use only a portion of a person's capabilities. This underutilization makes work boring, monotonous, and understimulating. The failure to fully utilize the workers' capacity in a constructive fashion may cause a variety of work problems. Contemporary approaches to enhancing motivation through pay and compensation work to overcome these problems through modern job designs that retain talent and reduce turnover.[6]

JOB ENLARGEMENT/JOB ROTATION

Job enlargement is a traditional approach to overcome the limitations of overspecialized work, such as boredom.[7] *Job enlargement* is a method of job design that increases the number of tasks in a job. *Job rotation*, a variation of job enlargement, exposes a worker to a variety of specialized job tasks over time. The reasoning behind these approaches to the problems of overspecialization is as follows. First, the core problem with overspecialized work was believed to be lack of variety. That is, jobs designed by scientific management were too narrow and limited in the number of tasks and activities assigned to each worker. Second, a lack of variety led to understimulation and underutilization of the worker. Third, the worker would be more stimulated and better utilized by increasing the variety in the job. Variety could be increased by increasing the number of activities or by rotating the worker through different jobs. For example, job enlargement for a lathe operator in a steel plant might include selecting the steel pieces to be turned and performing all of the maintenance work on the lathe. As an example of job rotation, an employee at a small bank might take new accounts one day, serve as a cashier another day, and process loan applications on a third day.

One of the first studies of the problem of repetitive work was conducted at IBM after World War II. The company implemented a job enlargement program during the war and evaluated the effort after six years.[8] The two most important results were a significant increase in product quality and a reduction in idle time, both for people and for machines. Less obvious and measurable are the benefits of job enlargement to IBM through enhanced worker status and improved manager–worker communication. Thus, job enlargement does counter the problems of work specialization.

A later study examined the effects of mass production jobs on assembly-line workers in the automotive industry.[9] Mass production jobs have six characteristics: mechanically controlled work pace, repetitiveness, minimum skill requirements, predetermined tools and techniques, minute division of the production process, and a requirement for surface mental attention, rather than thoughtful concentration. The researchers conducted 180 private interviews with assembly-line workers and found generally positive attitudes toward pay, security, and supervision. They concluded that job

JOB ENLARGEMENT
A method of job design that increases the number of activities in a job to overcome the boredom of overspecialized work.

JOB ROTATION
A variation of job enlargement in which workers are exposed to a variety of specialized jobs over time.

enlargement and job rotation would improve other job aspects, such as repetition and a mechanical work pace.

Job rotation and **cross-training** programs are variations of job enlargement. Pharmaceutical company Eli Lilly has found that job rotation can be a proactive means for enhancing work experiences for career development and can have tangible benefits for employees in the form of salary increases and promotions.[10] In cross-training, workers are trained in different specialized tasks or activities. All three kinds of programs horizontally enlarge jobs; that is, the number and variety of an employee's tasks and activities are increased. Graphic Controls Corporation (now a subsidiary of Tyco International) used cross-training to develop a flexible workforce that enabled the company to maintain high levels of production.[11]

JOB ENRICHMENT

Whereas job enlargement increases the number of job activities through horizontal loading, job enrichment increases the amount of job responsibility through vertical loading. Both approaches to job design are intended, in part, to increase job satisfaction for employees. A study to test whether job satisfaction results from characteristics of the job or of the person found that an interactionist approach is most accurate and that job redesign can contribute to increased job satisfaction for some employees. Another two-year study found that intrinsic job satisfaction and job perceptions are reciprocally related to each other.[12]

Job enrichment is a job design or redesign method aimed at increasing the motivational factors in a job. Job enrichment builds on Herzberg's two-factor theory of motivation, which distinguished between motivational and hygiene factors for people at work. Whereas job enlargement recommends increasing and varying the number of activities a person does, job enrichment recommends increasing the recognition, responsibility, and opportunity for achievement. For example, enlarging the lathe operator's job means adding maintenance activities, and enriching the job means having the operator meet with customers who buy the products.

Herzberg believes that only certain jobs should be enriched and that the first step is to select the jobs appropriate for job enrichment.[13] He recognizes that some people prefer simple jobs. Once jobs are selected for enrichment, management should brainstorm about possible changes, revise the list to include only specific changes related to motivational factors, and screen out generalities and suggestions that would simply increase activities or numbers of tasks. Those whose jobs are to be enriched should not participate in this process because of a conflict of interest. Two key problems can arise in the implementation of job enrichment. First, an initial drop in performance can be expected as workers accommodate to the change. Second, first-line supervisors may experience some anxiety or hostility as a result of employees' increased responsibility.

A seven-year implementation study of job enrichment at AT&T found the approach beneficial.[14] Job enrichment required a big change in man-

CROSS-TRAINING
A variation of job enlargement in which workers are trained in different specialized tasks or activities.

JOB ENRICHMENT
Designing or redesigning jobs by incorporating motivational factors into them.

agement style, and AT&T found that it could not ignore hygiene factors in the work environment just because it was enriching existing jobs. Although the AT&T experience with job enrichment was positive, a critical review of job enrichment did not find that to be the case generally.[15] One problem with job enrichment as a strategy for work design is that it is based on an oversimplified motivational theory. Another problem is the lack of consideration for individual differences among employees. Job enrichment, like scientific management's work specialization and job enlargement/job rotation, is a universal approach to the design of work and thus does not differentiate among individuals.

JOB CHARACTERISTICS THEORY

The job characteristics theory, which was initiated during the mid-1960s, is a traditional approach to the design of work that makes a significant departure from the three earlier approaches. It emphasizes the interaction between the individual and specific attributes of the job; therefore, it is a person–job fit model rather than a universal job design model. It originated in a research study of 470 workers in forty-seven different jobs across eleven industries.[16] The study measured and classified relevant task characteristics for these forty-seven jobs and found four core job characteristics: job variety, autonomy, responsibility, and interpersonal interaction. The study also found that core job characteristics did not affect all workers in the same way. A worker's values, religious beliefs, and ethnic background influenced how the worker responded to the job. Specifically, workers with rural values and strong religious beliefs preferred jobs high in core characteristics, and workers with urban values and weaker religious beliefs preferred jobs low in core characteristics.

Richard Hackman and his colleagues modified the original model by including three critical psychological states of the individual and refining the measurement of core job characteristics. The result is the **Job Characteristics Model** shown in Figure 13-1 (on page 316).[17] The **Job Diagnostic Survey (JDS)** was developed to diagnose jobs by measuring the five core job characteristics and three critical psychological states shown in the model. The core job characteristics stimulate the critical psychological states in the manner shown in Figure 13-1. This results in varying personal and work outcomes, as identified in the figure.

The five core job characteristics are defined as follows:

1. *Skill variety.* The degree to which a job includes different activities and involves the use of multiple skills and talents of the employee.

2. *Task identity.* The degree to which the job requires completion of a whole and identifiable piece of work—that is, doing a job from beginning to end with a tangible outcome.

3. *Task significance.* The degree to which the job has a substantial impact on the lives or work of other people, whether in the immediate organization or in the external environment.

3. *Describe the job characteristics model.*

JOB CHARACTERISTICS MODEL
A framework for understanding person–job fit through the interaction of core job dimensions with critical psychological states within a person.

JOB DIAGNOSTIC SURVEY (JDS)
The survey instrument designed to measure the elements in the Job Characteristics Model.

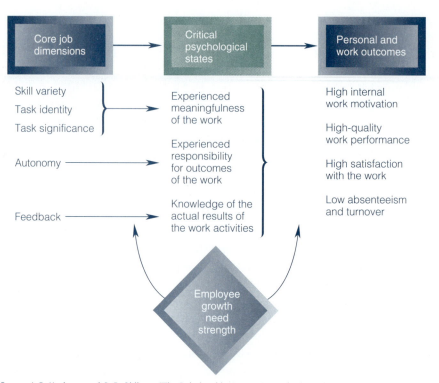

Figure 13-1
The Job Characteristics Model

Source: J. R. Hackman and G. R. Oldham, "The Relationship Among Core Job Dimensions, the Critical Psychological States, and On-the-Job Outcomes," *The Job Diagnostic Survey: An Instrument for the Diagnosis of Jobs and the Evaluation of Job Redesign Projects*, 1974. Reprinted by permission of Greg R. Oldham.

4. *Autonomy.* The degree to which the job provides the employee with substantial freedom, independence, and discretion in scheduling the work and in determining the procedures to be used in carrying it out.

5. *Feedback from the job itself.* The degree to which carrying out the work activities results in the employee's obtaining direct and clear information about the effectiveness of his or her performance.

Hackman and his colleagues say that the five core job characteristics interact to determine an overall Motivating Potential Score (MPS) for a specific job. The MPS indicates a job's potential for motivating incumbents. An individual's MPS is determined by the following equation:

$$\text{MPS} = \frac{\left[\begin{array}{c}\text{Skill}\\\text{variety}\end{array}\right] + \left[\begin{array}{c}\text{Task}\\\text{identity}\end{array}\right] + \left[\begin{array}{c}\text{Task}\\\text{significance}\end{array}\right]}{3} \times [\text{Autonomy}] \times [\text{Feedback}].$$

The Job Characteristics Model includes *growth need strength* (the desire to grow and fully develop one's abilities) as a moderator. People with a high growth need strength respond favorably to jobs with high MPSs, and individuals with low growth need strength respond less favorably to such jobs. The job characteristics theory further suggests that core job dimensions stimulate three critical psychological states according to the relationships specified in the model. These critical psychological states are defined as follows:

1. *Experienced meaningfulness of the work*, or the degree to which the employee experiences the job as one that is generally meaningful, valuable, and worthwhile.

2. *Experienced responsibility for work outcomes*, or the degree to which the employee feels personally accountable and responsible for the results of the work he or she does.

3. *Knowledge of results*, or the degree to which the employee knows and understands, on a continuous basis, how effectively he or she is performing the job.

In one early study, Hackman and Oldham administered the JDS to 658 employees working on sixty-two different jobs in seven business organizations.[18] The JDS was useful for job redesign efforts through one or more of five implementing concepts: (1) combining tasks into larger jobs, (2) forming natural work teams to increase task identity and task significance, (3) establishing relationships with customers, (4) loading jobs vertically with more responsibility, and/or (5) opening feedback channels for the job incumbent. For example, if an automotive mechanic received little feedback on the quality of repair work performed, one redesign strategy would be to solicit customer feedback one month after each repair.

In an international study, the Job Characteristics Model was tested in a sample of fifty-seven jobs from thirty-seven organizations in Hong Kong.[19] Job incumbents and their supervisors both completed questionnaires about the incumbents' jobs.[20] The supervisory version asked the supervisor to rate the employee's job. The study supported the model in general. However, task significance was not a reliable core job dimension in Hong Kong, which suggests either national differences in the measurement of important job dimensions or cultural biases about work. This result also suggests that value differences may exist between American and Asian people with regard to jobs.

An alternative to the Job Characteristics Model is the Job Characteristics Inventory (JCI) developed by Henry Sims and Andrew Szilagyi.[21] The JCI primarily measures core job characteristics. It is not as comprehensive as the JDS, because it does not incorporate critical psychological states, personal and work outcomes, or employee needs. The JCI does give some consideration to structural and individual variables that affect the relationship between core job characteristics and the individual.[22] One comparative analysis of the two models found similarities in the measures and in the models' predictions.[23] The comparative analysis also found two differences. First, the variety scales in the two models appear to have different effects on performance. Second, the autonomy scales in the two models appear to have different effects on employee satisfaction. Overall, the two models together support the usefulness of a person–job fit approach to the design of work over the earlier, universal theories.

ALTERNATIVE APPROACHES TO JOB DESIGN

Because each of the traditional job design approaches has limitations, several alternative approaches to job design have emerged over the past couple of decades. This section examines four of these alternatives that are in the process of being tried and tested. First, it examines the social information-processing model. Second, it reviews the interdisciplinary approach of Michael Campion and Paul Thayer. Their approach builds on the traditional job design approaches. Third, this section examines the international perspectives of the Japanese, the Germans, and the Scandinavians. Finally, it focuses on the health and well-being aspects of work design. Healthy work enables individuals to adapt, function well, and balance work with private life activities.[24] An emerging fifth approach to the design of work through teams and autonomous work groups was addressed in Chapter 8.

SOCIAL INFORMATION PROCESSING

4. *Compare the social information-processing (SIP) model with traditional job design approaches.*

SOCIAL INFORMATION-PROCESSING (SIP) MODEL
A model that suggests that the important job factors depend in part on what others tell a person about the job.

The traditional approaches to the design of work emphasize objective core job characteristics. In contrast, the ***social information-processing (SIP) model*** emphasizes the interpersonal aspects of work design. Specifically, the SIP model says that what others tell us about our jobs is important.[25] The SIP model has four basic premises about the work environment.[26] First, other people provide cues we use to understand the work environment. Second, other people help us judge what is important in our jobs. Third, other people tell us how they see our jobs. Fourth, other people's positive and negative feedback helps us understand our feelings about our jobs.

People's perceptions and reactions to their jobs are shaped by information from other people in the work environment.[27] In other words, what others believe about a person's job may be important to understanding the person's perceptions of, and reactions to, the job. This does not mean that objective job characteristics are unimportant; rather, it means that others can modify the way these characteristics affect us. For example, one study of task complexity found that the objective complexity of a task must be distinguished from the subjective task complexity experienced by the employee.[28] While objective task complexity may be a motivator, the presence of others in the work environment, social interaction, or even daydreaming may be important additional sources of motivation. The SIP model makes an important contribution to the design of work by emphasizing the importance of other people and the social context of work. In some cases, these aspects of the work environment may be more important than objective core job characteristics. For example, the subjective feedback of other people about how difficult a particular task is may be more important to a person's motivation to perform than an objective probability estimate of the task's difficulty.

INTERDISCIPLINARY APPROACH

5. *Explain the interdisciplinary approach to job design.*

The interdisciplinary approach to job design of Michael Campion and Paul Thayer builds on the traditional job design approaches and does not emphasize the social aspects of the work environment. Four approaches—the mechanistic, motivational, biological, and perceptual/motor approaches—are necessary, they say, because no one approach can solve all performance problems caused by poorly designed jobs. Each approach has its benefits, as well as its limitations.

The interdisciplinary approach allows the job designer or manager to consider trade-offs and alternatives among the approaches based on desired outcomes. If a manager finds poor performance a problem, for example, the manager should analyze the job to ensure a design aimed at improving performance. The interdisciplinary approach is important because badly designed jobs cause far more performance problems than managers realize.[29]

Table 13-2 summarizes the positive and negative outcomes of each job design approach. The mechanistic and motivational approaches to job design are very similar to scientific management's work simplification and to the Job Characteristics Model, respectively. Because these were discussed earlier in the chapter, they are not further elaborated here.

The biological approach to job design emphasizes the person's interaction with physical aspects of the work environment and is concerned with the amount of physical exertion, such as lifting and muscular effort, required by the position. For example, an analysis of medical claims at Chaparral

Table 13-2
Summary of Outcomes from Various Job Design Approaches

Job Design Approach (Discipline)	Positive Outcomes	Negative Outcomes
Mechanistic Approach (mechanical engineering)	Decreased training time Higher personnel utilization levels Lower likelihood of error Less chance of mental overload Lower stress levels	Lower job satisfaction Lower motivation Higher absenteeism
Motivational Approach (industrial psychology)	Higher job satisfaction Higher motivation Greater job involvement Higher job performance Lower absenteeism	Increased training time Lower personnel utilization levels Greater chance of errors Greater chance of mental overload and stress
Biological Approach (biology)	Less physical effort Less physical fatigue Fewer health complaints Fewer medical incidents Lower absenteeism Higher job satisfaction	Higher financial costs because of changes in equipment or job environment
Perceptual Motor Approach (experimental psychology)	Lower likelihood of error Lower likelihood of accidents Less chance of mental stress Decreased training time Higher personnel utilization levels	Lower job satisfaction Lower motivation

Steel Company (part of TXI, formerly Texas Industries) identified lower back problems as the most common physical problem experienced by steel workers and managers alike. As a result, the company instituted an education and exercise program under expert guidance to improve care of the lower back. Program graduates received back cushions for their chairs with "Chaparral Steel Company" embossed on them. Herman Miller designed an office chair to support the lower back and other parts of the human body.[30] The chair was tested in several offices including that of the director of human resources for Valero Energy Corporation prior to large-scale production. Lower back problems associated with improper lifting may be costly, but they are not fatal. Campion describes the potentially catastrophic problem that occurred at Three Mile Island, when nuclear materials contaminated the surrounding area and threatened disaster. Campion concluded that poor design of the control room operator's job caused the problem.

The perceptual/motor approach to job design also emphasizes the person's interaction with physical aspects of the work environment and is based on engineering that considers human factors such as strength or coordination, ergonomics, and experimental psychology. It places an important emphasis on human interaction with computers, information, and other operational systems. This approach addresses how people mentally process information acquired from the physical work environment through perceptual and motor skills. The approach emphasizes perception and fine motor skills, as opposed to the gross motor skills and muscle strength emphasized in the mechanistic approach. The perceptual/motor approach is more likely to be relevant to operational and technical work, such as keyboard operations and data entry jobs, which may tax a person's concentration and attention, than to managerial, administrative, and custodial jobs, which are less likely to strain concentration and attention.

One study using the interdisciplinary approach to improve jobs evaluated 377 clerical, 80 managerial, and 90 analytical positions.[31] The jobs were improved by combining tasks and adding ancillary duties. The improved jobs provided greater motivation for the incumbents and were better from a perceptual/motor standpoint. The jobs were poorly designed from a mechanical engineering standpoint, however, and they were unaffected from a biological standpoint. Again, the interdisciplinary approach considers trade-offs and alternatives when evaluating job redesign efforts.

INTERNATIONAL PERSPECTIVES ON THE DESIGN OF WORK

6. *Compare Japanese, German, and Scandinavian approaches to work.*

Each nation or ethnic group has a unique way of understanding and designing work.[32] As organizations become more global and international, an appreciation of the perspectives of other nations is increasingly important. The Japanese, Germans, and Scandinavians in particular have distinctive perspectives on the design and organization of work.[33] Each country's perspective is forged within its unique cultural and economic system, and each is distinct from the approaches used in North America.

The Japanese Approach The Japanese began harnessing their productive energies during the 1950s by drawing on the product quality ideas of W. Edwards Deming.[34] In addition, the central government became actively involved in the economic resurgence of Japan, and it encouraged companies to conquer industries rather than to maximize profits.[35] Such an industrial policy, which built on the Japanese cultural ethic of collectivism, has implications for how work is done. Whereas Frederick Taylor and his successors in the United States emphasized the job of an individual worker, the Japanese work system emphasizes the strategic level and encourages collective and cooperative working arrangements.[36] As Table 13-1 shows, the Japanese emphasize performance, accountability, and other- or self-directedness in defining work, whereas Americans emphasize the positive affect, personal identity, and social benefits of work.

The Japanese success with lean production has drawn the attention of managers. **Lean production** methods are similar to the production concept of **sociotechnical systems (STS)**, although there are some differences.[37] In particular, STS gives greater emphasis to teamwork and self-managed and autonomous work groups, to the ongoing nature of the design process, and to human values in the work process. The approaches are similar, however, in that both differ from Taylor's scientific management and both emphasize job variety, feedback to work groups and teams, support of human resources, and control of production variance close to the point of origin. Hence, the Japanese emphasis on lean production has led to a renewed consideration of the STS concept.

The German Approach The German approach to work has been shaped by Germany's unique educational system, cultural values, and economic system. The Germans are a highly educated and well-organized people. For example, their educational system has a multitrack design with technical and university alternatives. The German economic system puts a strong emphasis on free enterprise, private property rights, and management–labor cooperation. A comparison of voluntary and mandated management–labor cooperation in Germany found that productivity was superior under voluntary cooperation.[38] The Germans value hierarchy and authority relationships and, as a result, are generally disciplined.[39] Germany's workers are highly unionized, and their discipline and efficiency have enabled Germany to be highly productive while its workers labor substantially fewer hours than do Americans.

The traditional German approach to work design was **technocentric**, an approach that placed technology and engineering at the center of job design decisions. Recently, German industrial engineers have moved to a more **anthropocentric** approach, which places human considerations at the center of job design decisions. The former approach uses a natural scientific process in the design of work, whereas the latter relies on a more humanistic process, as shown in Figure 13-2 (on page 322). In the anthropocentric approach, work is evaluated using the criteria of practicability and

LEAN PRODUCTION
Using committed employees with ever-expanding responsibilities to achieve zero waste, 100 percent good product, delivered on time, every time.

SOCIOTECHNICAL SYSTEMS (STS)
Giving equal attention to technical and social considerations in job design.

TECHNOCENTRIC
Placing technology and engineering at the center of job design decisions.

ANTHROPOCENTRIC
Placing human considerations at the center of job design decisions.

worker satisfaction at the individual level and the criteria of endurability and acceptability at the group level. Figure 13-2 also identifies problem areas and disciplines concerned with each aspect of the work design.

The Scandinavian Approach The Scandinavian cultural values and economic system stand in contrast to the German system. The social democratic tradition in Scandinavia has emphasized social concern rather than industrial efficiency. The Scandinavians place great emphasis on a work design model that encourages a high degree of worker control and good social support systems for workers.[40] Lennart Levi believes that circumstantial and inferential scientific evidence provides a sufficiently strong basis for legislative and policy actions for redesigns aimed at enhancing worker well-being. An example of such an action for promoting good working environments and occupational health was Swedish Government Bill 1976/77:149, which stated, "Work should be safe both physically and mentally, *but also* provide opportunities for involvement, job satisfaction, and personal development." In 1991, the Swedish Parliament set up the Swedish Working Life Fund to fund research, intervention programs, and demonstration projects in work design. For example, a study of Stockholm police on shift schedules found that going from a daily, counterclockwise rotation to a clockwise rotation was more compatible with human biology and resulted in improved sleep, less fatigue, lower systolic blood pressure, and lower blood levels of triglycerides and glucose.[41] Hence, the work redesign improved the police officers' health.

Figure 13-2
Hierarchical Model of Criteria for the Evaluation of Human Work

Scientific approaches of labor sciences	Levels of evaluation of human work	Problem areas and assignment to disciplines
View from natural science → Primarily oriented to individuals ← Primarily oriented to groups ← View from cultural studies ←	Practicability	Technical, anthropometric, and psychophysical problems (ergonomics)
	Endurability	Technical, physiological, and medical problems (ergonomics and occupational health)
	Acceptability	Economical and sociological problems (occupational psychology and sociology, personnel management)
	Satisfaction	Sociopsychological and economic problems (occupational psychology and sociology, personnel management)

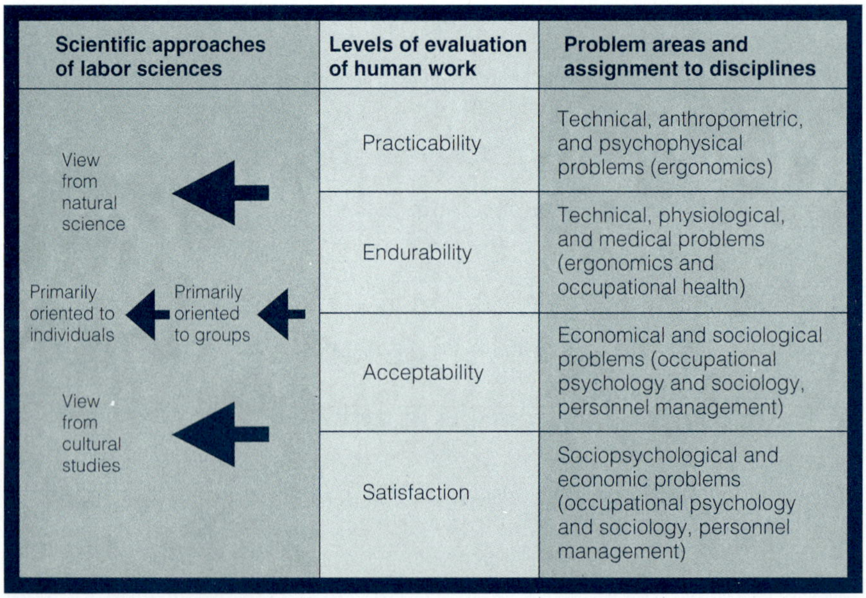

Source: H. Luczak, "'Good Work' Design: An Ergonomic, Industrial Engineering Perspective," in J. C. Quick, L. R. Murphy, and J. J. Hurrell, eds., *Stress and Well-Being at Work* (Washington, D.C.: American Psychological Association). Reprinted by permission.

WORK DESIGN AND WELL-BEING

An international group of scholars, including American social scientists, has been concerned about designing work and jobs that are both healthy and productive.[42] Economic and industry-specific upheavals in the United States during the 1990s led to job loss and unemployment, and the adverse health impact of these factors has received attention.[43] Attention has also been devoted to the effects of specific work design parameters on psychological health.[44] Frank Landy believes that organizations should redesign jobs to increase worker control and reduce worker uncertainty, while at the same time managing conflict and task/job demands. These objectives can be achieved in several ways.

Control in work organizations can be increased by (1) giving workers the opportunity to control several aspects of the work and the workplace; (2) designing machines and tasks with optimal response times and/or ranges; and (3) implementing performance-monitoring systems as a source of relevant feedback to workers. Uncertainty can be reduced by (1) providing employees with timely and complete information needed for their work; (2) making clear and unambiguous work assignments; (3) improving communication at shift change time; and (4) increasing employee access to information sources. Conflict at work can be managed through (1) participative decision making to reduce conflict; (2) using supportive supervisory styles to resolve conflict; and (3) having sufficient resources available to meet work demands, thus preventing conflict. Task/job design can be improved by enhancing core job characteristics and not patterning service work after assembly-line work.

Task uncertainty was shown to have an adverse effect on morale in a study of 629 employment security work units in California and Wisconsin.[45] More important, the study showed that morale was better predicted by considering both the overall design of the work unit and the task uncertainty. This study suggests that if one work design parameter, such as task uncertainty, is a problem in a job, its adverse effects on people may be mitigated by other work design parameters. For example, higher pay may offset an employee's frustration with a difficult coworker, or a friendly, supportive working environment may offset frustration with low pay. This chapter's Challenge (on page 324) provides you with an opportunity to evaluate how psychologically healthy your work environment is.

CONTEMPORARY ISSUES IN THE DESIGN OF WORK

A number of contemporary issues related to specific aspects of the design of work have an effect on increasing numbers of employees. Rather than addressing job design or worker well-being in a comprehensive way, these issues address one or another aspect of a job. The issues include telecommuting, alternative work patterns, technostress, task revision, and

7. *Explain how job control, uncertainty, and conflict can be managed for employee well-being.*

YOU BE THE JUDGE

Suppose that the design of a particular job exposes employees to a health or safety risk and that redesigning the job would cost the company more than paying the medical claims if an employee is injured or hurt. Should the company tell employees doing the job about its decision not to redesign the job to make it safer? Is it ethical for the company not to redesign the job?

8. *Discuss five contemporary issues in the design of work.*

Challenge

Is Your Work Environment a Healthy One?

To determine whether your work environment is a healthy one, read the text section on "Work Design and Well-Being," then complete the following four steps. Answer each question in the four steps "yes" or "no."

Step 1. Control and Influence
- _Y_ Do you have influence over the pace of your work?
- _Y_ Are system response times neither too fast nor too slow?
- _N_ Do you have a say in your work assignments and goals?
- _Y_ Is there an opportunity for you to comment on your performance appraisal?

Step 2. Information and Uncertainty
- _Y_ Do you receive timely information to complete your work?
- _Y_ Do you receive complete information for your work assignments?
- _Y_ Is there adequate planning for changes that affect you at work?
- _N_ Do you have access to all the information you need at work?

Step 3. Conflict at Work
- _N_ Does the company apply policies clearly and consistently?
- _Y_ Are job descriptions and task assignments clear and unambiguous?
- _N_ Are there adequate policies and procedures for the resolution of conflicts?
- _Y_ Is your work environment an open, participative one?

Step 4. Job Scope and Task Design
- _Y_ Is there adequate variety in your work activities and/or assignments?
- _Y_ Do you receive timely, constructive feedback on your work?
- _Y_ Is your work important to the overall mission of the company?
- _Y_ Do you work on more than one small piece of a big project?

Scoring:
Count the number of "yes" answers in Steps 1 through 4: ___12___

If you have 10 to 16 "yes" answers, this suggests that your work environment is a psychologically healthy one.

If you have 7 or fewer "yes" answers, this may suggest that your work environment is not as psychologically healthy as it could be.

---

skill development. Telecommuting and alternative work patterns such as job sharing can increase flexibility for employees. Companies use these and other approaches to the design of work as ways to manage a growing business while contributing to a better balance of work and family life for employees.

TELECOMMUTING

Telecommuting, as noted in Chapter 2, is when employees work at home or in other locations geographically separate from their company's main location. Telecommuting may entail working in a combination of home, satellite office, and main office locations. This flexible arrangement is designed to achieve a better fit between the needs of the individual employee and the organization's task demands.

Telecommuting has been around since the 1970s but was slower to catch on than some expected.[46] This was due to the inherent paradoxes associated with telecommuting.[47] Actually, with a greater emphasis on managing the work rather than the worker, managers can enhance control, effectively decentralize, and even encourage teamwork through telecommuting. A number of companies, such as AT&T in Phoenix and Bell Atlantic (now part of Verizon Communications), have programs in telecommuting for a wide range of employees. These flexible arrangements help some companies respond to changing demographics and a shrinking labor pool. The Travelers Group (now part of Citigroup) was one of the first companies to try telecommuting and was considered an industry leader in telecommuting. Because of its confidence in its employees, Travelers reaped rewards from telecommuting, including higher productivity, reduced absenteeism, expanded opportunities for workers with disabilities, and an increased ability to attract and retain talent.[48]

Since the September 11, 2001, attacks, concerns for employee safety have led to a renewed interest in telecommuting.[49] Telecommuting enables employees to avoid both the risks and hassles associated with air travel in particular, which has become somewhat more troublesome since 9/11.

Telecommuting is neither a cure-all nor a universally feasible alternative. Many telecommuters feel a sense of social isolation. Furthermore, not all forms of work are amenable to telecommuting. For example, firefighters and police officers must be at their duty stations to be successful in their work. Employees for whom telecommuting is not a viable option within a company may feel jealous of those able to telecommute. In addition, telecommuting may have the potential to create the sweatshops of the twenty-first century. Thus, telecommuting is a novel, emerging issue.

ALTERNATIVE WORK PATTERNS

Job sharing is an alternative work pattern in which more than one person occupies a single job. Job sharing may be an alternative to telecommuting for addressing demographic and labor pool concerns. Job sharing is found throughout a wide range of managerial and professional jobs, as well as in production and service jobs. It is not common among senior executives.

The four-day workweek is a second type of alternative work schedule. Information systems personnel at the United Services Automobile Association (USAA) in San Antonio, Texas, work four ten-hour days and enjoy a three-day weekend. This arrangement provides the benefit of more time for those who want to balance work and family life through weekend travel. However, the longer workdays may be a drawback for employees with many family or social activities on weekday evenings. Hence, the four-day workweek has both benefits and limitations.

Flextime is a third alternative work pattern. Flextime, in which employees can set their own daily work schedules, has been applied in

JOB SHARING
An alternative work pattern in which more than one person occupies a single job.

FLEXTIME
An alternative work pattern that enables employees to set their own daily work schedules.

numerous ways in work organizations. For example, many companies in highly concentrated urban areas, like Houston, Los Angeles, and New York City, allow employees to set their own daily work schedules as long as they start their eight hours at any thirty-minute interval from 6:00 A.M. to 9:00 A.M. This arrangement is designed to ease traffic and commuting pressures. It also is somewhat responsive to individual biorhythms, allowing early risers to go to work early and nighthawks to work late. Typically, 9:00 A.M. to 3:00 P.M. is the required core working time for everyone in the company. Flextime options take many forms in organizations, depending on the nature of the work and the coordination requirements in various jobs. Even in companies without formal flextime programs, flextime may be an individual option arranged between supervisor and subordinate. For example, a first-line supervisor who wants to complete a college degree may negotiate a work schedule accommodating both job requirements and course schedules at the university. Flextime options may be more likely for high performers who assure their bosses that work quality and productivity will not suffer.[50]

TECHNOLOGY AT WORK

New technologies and electronic commerce are here to stay and are changing the face of work environments, dramatically in some cases. As forces for change, new technologies are a double-edged sword that can be used to improve job performance, or to create stress. On the positive side, modern technologies are helping to revolutionize the way jobs are designed and the way work gets done. The *virtual office* is a mobile platform of computer, telecommunication, and information technology and services that allows mobile workforce members to conduct business virtually anywhere, anytime, globally. While virtual offices have benefits, they may also lead to a lack of social connection or to technostress.

Technostress is stress caused by new and advancing technologies in the workplace, most often information technologies.[51] For example, the widespread use of electronic bulletin boards as a forum for rumors of layoffs may cause feelings of uncertainty and anxiety (technostress). However, the same electronic bulletin boards can be an important source of information and thus reduce uncertainty for workers.

New information technologies enable organizations to monitor employee work performance, even when the employee is not aware of the monitoring.[52] These new technologies also allow organizations to tie pay to performance because performance is electronically monitored.[53] Three guidelines can help make electronic workplace monitoring, especially of performance, less distressful. First, workers should participate in the introduction of the monitoring system. Second, performance standards should be seen as fair. Third, performance records should be used to improve performance, not to punish the performer. In the extreme, new technologies that allow for virtual work in remote locations take employees beyond such monitoring.[54]

VIRTUAL OFFICE
A mobile platform of computer, telecommunication, and information technology and services.

TECHNOSTRESS
The stress caused by new and advancing technologies in the workplace.

TASK REVISION

A new concept in the design of work is **task revision**.[55] Task revision is an innovative way to modify an incorrectly specified role or job. Task revision assumes that organizational roles and job expectations may be correctly or incorrectly defined. Furthermore, a person's behavior in a work role has very different performance consequences depending on whether the role is correctly or incorrectly defined. Table 13-3 sets out the performance consequences of three categories of role behaviors based on the definition of the role or job. As indicated in the table, standard role behavior leads to good performance if the role is correctly defined, and it leads to poor performance if the role is incorrectly defined. These performances go to the extreme when incumbents exhibit extreme behavior in their jobs.[56] Going to extremes leads one to exceed expectations and display extraordinary behavior (extrarole behavior); this results in either excellent performance or very poor performance, depending on the accuracy of the defined role.

Counter-role behavior is when the incumbent acts contrary to the expectations of the role or exhibits deviant behavior. This is a problem if the role is correctly defined. For example, poor performance occurred on a hospital ward when the nursing supervisor failed to check the administration of all medications for the nurses she was supervising, resulting in one near fatality because a patient was not given required medication by a charge nurse. The nursing supervisor exhibited counter-role behavior in believing she could simply trust the nurses and did not have to double-check their actions. The omission was caught on the next shift. When a role or task is correctly defined (for example, double-checking medication administration), counter-role behavior leads to poor performance.

Task revision is counter-role behavior in an incorrectly specified role and is a useful way to correct for the problem in the role specification (see Table 13-3). Task revision is a form of role innovation that modifies the job to achieve a better performance. Task revision is the basis for long-term adaptation when the current specifications of a job are no longer

TASK REVISION
The modification of incorrectly specified roles or jobs.

COUNTER-ROLE BEHAVIOR
Deviant behavior in either a correctly or incorrectly defined job or role.

Table 13-3
Performance Consequences of Role Behaviors

Role Characteristics	Standard Role Behavior (Meets Expectations)	Extra Role Behavior (Goes beyond Expectations)	Counter-Role Behavior (Differs from Expected)
Correctly specified role	Ordinary good performance	Excellent performance (organizational citizenship and prosocial behavior)	Poor performance (deviance, dissent, and grievance)
Incorrectly specified role	Poor performance (bureaucratic behavior)	Very poor performance (bureaucratic zeal)	Excellent performance (task revision and redirection, role innovation)

Source: Republished with permission of Academy of Management, PO Box 3020, Briar Cliff Manor, NY 10510-8020. "Task Revision: A Neglected Form of Work Performance," (Table), R. M. Staw & R. D. Boettger, *Academy of Management Journal*, 1990, Vol. 33. Reproduced by permission of the publisher via Copyright Clearance Center, Inc.

applicable.[57] For example, the traditional role for a surgeon is to complete surgical procedures in an accurate and efficient manner. Based on this definition, socio-emotional caregiving is counter-role behavior on the part of the surgeon. However, if the traditional role were to be labeled incorrect, the surgeon's task revision through socio-emotional caregiving would be viewed as leading to much better medical care for patients.

SKILL DEVELOPMENT

Problems in work system design are often seen as the source of frustration for those dealing with technostress.[58] However, system and technical problems are not the only sources of technostress in new information technologies. Some experts see a growing gap between the skills demanded by new technologies and the skills possessed by employees in jobs using these technologies.[59] Although technical skills are important and are emphasized in many training programs, the largest sector of the economy is actually service-oriented, and service jobs require interpersonal skills. Managers also need a wide range of nontechnical skills to be effective in their work.[60] Therefore, any discussion of jobs and the design of work must recognize the importance of incumbent skills and abilities to meet the demands of the work. Organizations must consider the talents and skills of their employees when they engage in job design efforts. The two issues of employee skill development and job design are interrelated. The knowledge and information requirements for jobs of the future are especially high.

MANAGERIAL IMPLICATIONS: THE CHANGING NATURE OF WORK

Work is an important aspect of a healthy life. The two central needs in human nature are to engage in productive work and to form healthy relationships with others. Work means different things to different ethnic and national groups. Therefore, job design efforts must be sensitive to cultural values and beliefs.

In crafting work tasks and assignments, managers should make an effort to fit the jobs to the people who are doing them. There are no universally accepted ways to design work, and early efforts to find them have been replaced by a number of alternatives. Early approaches to job design were valuable for manufacturing and administrative jobs of the mid-1900s. Now, however, the changing nature of work in the United States and the Americans with Disabilities Act (ADA) challenge managers to find new ways to define work and design jobs.

The distinguishing feature of job design in the foreseeable future is flexibility. Dramatic global, economic, and organizational changes dictate that managers be flexible in the design of work in their organizations. Jobs must be designed to fit the larger organizational structures discussed in Chapter 14. Organizations must ask, does the job support the organization's mission? Employees must ask, does the job meet my short- and long-term needs?

Technology is one of the distinguishing features of the modern workplace. Advances in information, mechanical, and computer technology are transforming work into a highly scientific endeavor demanding employees who are highly educated, knowledgeable workers. American workers can expect these technological advances to continue during their lifetimes and should expect to meet the challenge through continuous skill development and enhancement.

KEY TERMS

anthropocentric	job enrichment	task revision
counter-role behavior	job rotation	technocentric
cross-training	job sharing	technostress
flextime	lean production	virtual office
job	meaning of work	work
Job Characteristics Model	social information-processing (SIP) model	work simplification
Job Diagnostic Survey (JDS)		
job enlargement	sociotechnical systems (STS)	

Experiential Exercise

CHAOS AND THE MANAGER'S JOB

Managers' jobs are increasingly chaotic as a result of high rates of change, uncertainty, and turbulence. Some managers thrive on change and chaos, but others have a difficult time responding to high rates of change and uncertainty in a positive manner. This questionnaire gives you an opportunity to evaluate how you would react to a manager's job that is rather chaotic.

Exercise Schedule

1. Preparation (preclass)
   Complete the questionnaire.

2. Individual Scoring
   Give yourself 4 points for each A, 3 points for each B, 2 points for each C, 1 point for each D, and 0 points for each E. Compute the total, divide by 24, and round to one decimal place.

3. Group Discussion
   Your instructor may have you discuss your scores in groups of six students. The higher your score, the more you respond positively to change and chaos; the lower your score, the more difficulty you would have responding to this manager's job in a positive manner. In addition, answer the following questions.

   a. If you could redesign this manager's job, what are the two or three aspects of the job that you would change first?

   b. What are the two or three aspects of the job that you would feel no need to change?

Source: "Chaos and the Manager's Job" in D. Marcic, "Option B. Quality and the New Management Paradigm," *Organizational Behavior: Experiences and Cases*, 4th ed. (Minneapolis/St. Paul: West Publishing, 1995): 296–297. Reprinted by permission.

A Manager's Job[a]

Listed below are some statements a thirty-seven-year-old manager made about his job at a large and successful corporation. If your job had these characteristics, how would you react to them? After each statement are five letters, A–E. Circle the letter that best describes how you would react according to the following scale:

A.   I would enjoy this very much; it's completely acceptable.

B.   This would be enjoyable and acceptable most of the time.

C.   I'd have no reaction one way or another, or it would be about equally enjoyable and unpleasant.

D.   This feature would be somewhat unpleasant for me.

E.   This feature would be very unpleasant for me.

1. I regularly spend 30–40 percent of my time in meetings.	A B C D E
2. A year and a half ago, my job did not exist, and I have been essentially inventing it as I go along.	A B C D E
3. The responsibilities I either assume or am assigned consistently exceed the authority I have for discharging them.	A B C D E
4. At any given moment in my job, I average about a dozen phone calls to be returned.	A B C D E
5. There seems to be very little relation in my job between the quality of my performance and my actual pay and fringe benefits.	A B C D E
6. I need about two weeks of management training a year to stay current in my job.	A B C D E
7. Because we have very effective equal employment opportunity in my company and because it is thoroughly multinational, my job consistently brings me into close contact at a professional level with people of many races, ethnic groups, and nationalities and of both sexes.	A B C D E
8. There is no objective way to measure my effectiveness.	A B C D E
9. I report to three different bosses for different aspects of my job, and each has an equal say in my performance appraisal.	A B C D E
10. On average, about a third of my time is spent dealing with unexpected emergencies that force all scheduled work to be postponed.	A B C D E
11. When I need to meet with the people who report to me, it takes my secretary most of a day to find a time when we are all available, and even then I have yet to have a meeting where everyone is present for the entire meeting.	A B C D E
12. The college degree I earned in preparation for this type of work is now obsolete, and I probably should return for another degree.	A B C D E
13. My job requires that I absorb about 100–200 pages a week of technical material.	A B C D E
14. I am out of town overnight at least one night a week.	A B C D E
15. My department is so interdependent with several other departments in the company that all distinctions about which department is responsible for which tasks are quite arbitrary.	A B C D E
16. I will probably get a promotion in about a year to a job in another division that has most of these same characteristics.	A B C D E
17. During the period of my employment here, either the entire company or the division I worked in has been reorganized every year or so.	A B C D E
18. While I face several possible promotions, I have no real career path.	A B C D E
19. While there are several possible promotions I can see ahead of me, I think I have no realistic chance of getting to the top levels of the company.	A B C D E
20. While I have many ideas about how to make things work better, I have no direct influence on either the business policies or the personnel policies that govern my division.	A B C D E
21. My company has recently put in an "assessment center" where I and other managers must go through an extensive battery of psychological tests to assess our potential.	A B C D E

22. My company is a defendant in an antitrust suit, and if the case comes to trial, I will probably have to testify about some decisions that were made a few years ago.   A B C D E

23. Advanced computer and other electronic office technology is continually being introduced into my division, necessitating constant learning on my part.   A B C D E

24. The computer terminal and screen I have in my office can be monitored in my boss's office without my knowledge.   A B C D E

14

Organizational Design and Structure

LEARNING OBJECTIVES

After reading this chapter, you should be able to do the following:

1. Define *differentiation* and *integration* as organizational design processes.

2. Discuss six basic design dimensions of an organization.

3. Briefly describe five structural configurations for organizations.

4. Describe four contextual variables for an organization.

5. Explain the four forces reshaping organizations.

6. Discuss emerging organizational structures.

7. Identify two cautions about the effect of organizational structures on people.

Organizational design is the process of constructing and adjusting an organization's structure to achieve its goals. The design process begins with the organization's goals, which are broken into tasks as the basis for jobs, as discussed in Chapter 13. Jobs are grouped into departments, and departments are linked to form the *organizational structure*. Chapter 14 builds on Chapter 13 by examining the macro structure of the organization in a parallel fashion to how Chapter 13 examines the micro structure of the organization.

The first section of the chapter examines the design processes of differentiation and integration. The second section addresses the six basic design dimensions of an organization's structure. The organization's structure gives it the form to fulfill its function in the environment. As Louis Sullivan, the father of the skyscraper, said, "Form ever follows function." The third section of the chapter presents five structural configurations for organizations. Based on its mission and purpose, an organization determines the best structural configuration for its unique situation. The fourth section examines size, technology, environment, and strategy and goals as *contextual variables* influencing organizational design. When the organization's contextual variables change, the organization must redesign itself to meet new demands and functions. The fifth section examines four forces shaping organizations today. The final section notes several areas where managers should be cautious with regard to structural weaknesses and dysfunctional structural constellations.

ORGANIZATIONAL DESIGN
The process of constructing and adjusting an organization's structure to achieve its goals.

ORGANIZATIONAL STRUCTURE
The linking of departments and jobs within an organization.

CONTEXTUAL VARIABLES
A set of characteristics that influence the organization's design processes.

KEY ORGANIZATIONAL DESIGN PROCESSES

Differentiation is the design process of breaking the organizational goals into tasks. Integration is the design process of linking the tasks together to form a structure that supports goal accomplishment. These two processes are the keys to successful organizational design. The organizational structure is designed to prevent chaos through an orderly set of reporting relationships and communication channels. Understanding the key design processes and organizational structure helps a person understand the larger working environment and may prevent confusion in the organization.

The organization chart is the most visible representation of the organization's structure and underlying components. Figure 14-1 (on pages 334 and 335) is the organizational chart for the American Heart Association's National Center. Most organizations have a series of organization charts showing reporting relationships throughout the system. The underlying components are (1) formal lines of authority and responsibility (the organizational structure designates reporting relationships by the way jobs and departments are grouped) and (2) formal systems of communication, coordination, and integration (the organizational structure designates the expected patterns of formal interaction among employees).[1]

1. *Define differentiation and integration as organizational design processes.*

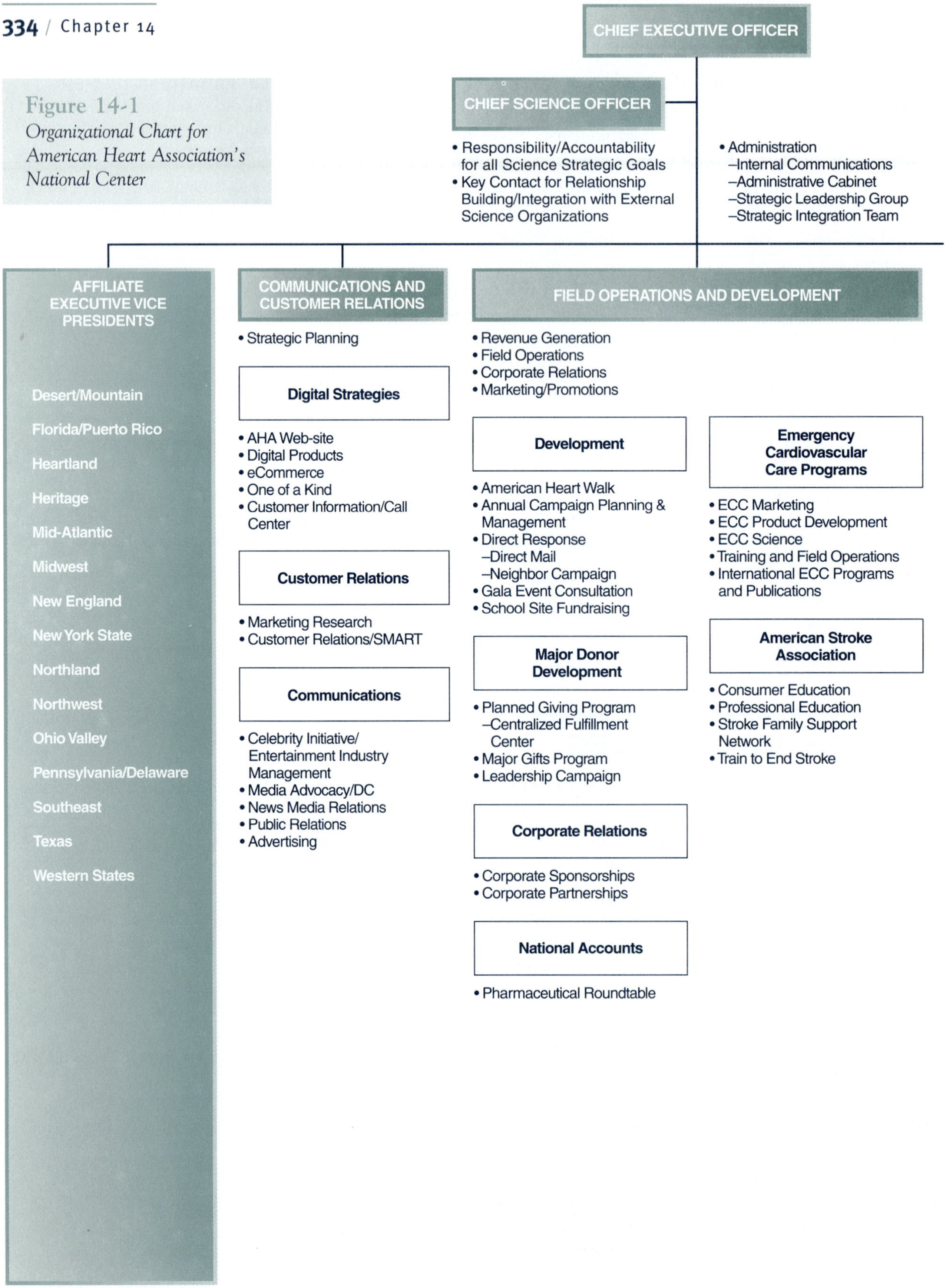

Figure 14-1
Organizational Chart for
American Heart Association's
National Center

CHIEF EXECUTIVE OFFICER

CHIEF SCIENCE OFFICER

- Responsibility/Accountability
  for all Science Strategic Goals
- Key Contact for Relationship
  Building/Integration with External
  Science Organizations

- Administration
  –Internal Communications
  –Administrative Cabinet
  –Strategic Leadership Group
  –Strategic Integration Team

**AFFILIATE
EXECUTIVE VICE
PRESIDENTS**

Desert/Mountain

Florida/Puerto Rico

Heartland

Heritage

Mid-Atlantic

Midwest

New England

New York State

Northland

Northwest

Ohio Valley

Pennsylvania/Delaware

Southeast

Texas

Western States

**COMMUNICATIONS AND
CUSTOMER RELATIONS**

- Strategic Planning

Digital Strategies

- AHA Web-site
- Digital Products
- eCommerce
- One of a Kind
- Customer Information/Call
  Center

Customer Relations

- Marketing Research
- Customer Relations/SMART

Communications

- Celebrity Initiative/
  Entertainment Industry
  Management
- Media Advocacy/DC
- News Media Relations
- Public Relations
- Advertising

FIELD OPERATIONS AND DEVELOPMENT

- Revenue Generation
- Field Operations
- Corporate Relations
- Marketing/Promotions

Development

- American Heart Walk
- Annual Campaign Planning &
  Management
- Direct Response
  –Direct Mail
  –Neighbor Campaign
- Gala Event Consultation
- School Site Fundraising

**Major Donor
Development**

- Planned Giving Program
  –Centralized Fulfillment
  Center
- Major Gifts Program
- Leadership Campaign

Corporate Relations

- Corporate Sponsorships
- Corporate Partnerships

National Accounts

- Pharmaceutical Roundtable

**Emergency
Cardiovascular
Care Programs**

- ECC Marketing
- ECC Product Development
- ECC Science
- Training and Field Operations
- International ECC Programs
  and Publications

**American Stroke
Association**

- Consumer Education
- Professional Education
- Stroke Family Support
  Network
- Train to End Stroke

Figure 14-1
Concluded

ADVOCACY

- Strategic Public Policy
- Affiliate Advocacy Consultation
- Public Health
- Government Relations

Public Advocacy (Washington D.C.)

- Federal Public Policy
- Grassroots

Health Initiatives and Field Advocacy

- Operation Heartbeat
- Operation Stroke
- State/Local Public Policy

Minority Initiatives

- Minority Health Integration

SCIENCE OPERATIONS

- Strategic Integration with All Other KWPs
- Administrative Oversight for Science Key Work Process Functions
- Strategic Direction for Professional/Patient Initiatives
- Science Strategic Planning

Research Administration and Scientific Publishing

- Research Policy
- Peer Review Services
- National Center Research Programs
- AHA Journals

Science and Medicine

- Science Content Review
- Science Consultation
- Councils Administration
- Biostatistics and Research Services

Professional Education

- Get with the Guidelines/Quality Improvement Initiatives
- Continuing Medical Education Initiatives
- Professional Education Virtual Team

Meetings and Science Marketing

- Logistics Management for all Association Wide Meetings
- Scientific Meeting Program Coordination
- Science KWP Marketing and Corporate Development

Patient Education

- Strategic Direction and Implementation of Patient Education Initiatives

CORPORATE OPERATIONS AND CFO

- Audit and Consulting Services

Finance

- Affiliate Financial Services
- Financial Systems and Training Support

Human Resources

- Personnel
- Training/Organizational Development
- HRIS

Information Technology

- Infrastructure Solutions
- Affiliate Operations
- Business Solutions
- Network Systems
- Strategic Consulting
- Support Services
- Telecommunications

Production and Distribution

- Design and Media Services
- Facilities and Office Services
- Editorial Services
- Purchasing
- Distribution and Printing

CORPORATE SECRETARY AND COUNSEL

- Administration
  - Board of Directors
  - CRRC/ERC
  - Delegate Assembly
  - Nominating & Awards
  - Committee Appointments
- Legal
  - Licensing and Records Management
  - Legal Services
  - Conflict of Interest Review Committee
  - Copyright Permissions
- Food Certification
- Consumer Publications

DIFFERENTIATION

DIFFERENTIATION
The process of deciding how to divide the work in an organization.

Differentiation is the process of deciding how to divide the work in an organization.[2] Differentiation ensures that all essential organizational tasks are assigned to one or more jobs and that the tasks receive the attention they need. Many dimensions of differentiation have been considered in organizations. Lawrence and Lorsch found four dimensions of differentiation in one study: (1) manager's goal orientation, (2) time orientation, (3) interpersonal orientation, and (4) formality of structure.[3] Table 14-1 shows some typical differences in orientation for various functional areas of an organization. Three different forms of differentiation are horizontal, vertical, and spatial.

Horizontal differentiation is the degree of differentiation between organizational subunits and is based on employees' specialized knowledge, education, or training. For example, two university professors who teach specialized subjects in different academic departments are subject to horizontal differentiation. Horizontal differentiation increases with specialization and departmentation.

Specialization refers to the particular grouping of activities performed by an individual.[4] The degree of specialization or the division of labor in the organization gives an indication of how much training is needed, what the scope of a job is, and what individual characteristics are needed for job holders. Specialization can also lead to the development of a specialized vocabulary, as well as other behavioral norms. As the two college professors specialize in their subjects, abbreviations or acronyms take on unique meanings. For example, OB means "organizational behavior" to a professor of management but "obstetrics" to a professor of medicine.

Usually, the more specialized the jobs within an organization, the more departments are differentiated within that organization (the greater the departmentation). Departmentation can be by function, product, service, client, geography, process, or some combination of these. A large organization may departmentalize its structure using all or most of these methods at different levels of the organization.

Vertical differentiation is the difference in authority and responsibility in the organizational hierarchy. Vertical differentiation occurs, for example, between a chief executive and a maintenance supervisor. Tall, narrow organizations have greater vertical differentiation, and flat, wide organizations have less vertical differentiation. The height of the organization is also influenced by level of horizontal differentiation and span of control. The

Table 14-1

Differentiation between Marketing and Engineering

Basis for Difference	Marketing	Engineering
Goal orientation	Sales volume	Design
Time orientation	Long run	Medium run
Interpersonal orientation	People oriented	Task oriented
Structure	Less formal	More formal

span of control refers to and defines the number of subordinates a manager can and should supervise.[5]

Tall structures—those with narrow spans of control—tend to be characterized by closer supervision and tighter controls. In addition, the communication becomes more burdensome, since directives and information must be passed through more layers. The banking industry has often had tall structures. Flat structures—those with wider spans of control—have simpler communication chains and reduced promotion opportunities due to fewer levels of management. Sears is an example of an organization that has gone to a flat structure. With the loss of more than a million middle management positions in organizations, many organizations are now flatter. The degree of vertical differentiation affects organizational effectiveness, but there is no consistent finding that flatter or taller organizations are better.[6] Organizational size, type of jobs, skills and personal characteristics of employees, and degree of freedom must all be considered in determining organizational effectiveness.[7]

Spatial differentiation is the geographic dispersion of an organization's offices, plants, and personnel. A salesperson in New York and one in Portland experience spatial differentiation. An increase in the number of locations increases the complexity of organizational design but may be necessary for organizational goal achievement or organizational protection. For example, if an organization wants to expand into a different country, it may be best to form a separate subsidiary that is partially owned and managed by citizens of that country. Few U.S. citizens think of Shell Oil Company as being a subsidiary of Royal Dutch/Shell Group, a company whose international headquarters is in the Netherlands.

Spatial differentiation may give an organization political and legal advantages in a country because it is identified as a local company. Distance is as important as political and legal issues in making spatial differentiation decisions. For example, a salesperson in Lubbock, Texas, would have a hard time servicing accounts in Beaumont, Texas (over 500 miles away), whereas a salesperson in Delaware might be able to cover all of that state, as well as parts of one or two others.

Horizontal, vertical, and spatial differentiation indicate the amount of width, height, and breadth an organizational structure needs. Just because an organization is highly differentiated along one of these dimensions does not mean it must be highly differentiated along the others. The university environment, for example, is generally characterized by great horizontal differentiation but relatively little vertical and spatial differentiation. A company such as Coca-Cola is characterized by a great deal of all three types of differentiation. The more structurally differentiated an organization is, the more complex it is.[8]

Complexity refers to the number of activities, subunits, or subsystems within the organization. Lawrence and Lorsch suggest that an organization's complexity should mirror the complexity of its environment. As the complexity of an organization increases, its need for mechanisms to link and coordinate the differentiated parts also increases. If these links do not exist, the departments or differentiated parts of the organization can lose sight of the organization's larger mission, and the organization runs the risk of chaos. Designing and building linkage and coordination mechanisms is known as *integration*.

INTEGRATION

INTEGRATION
The process of coordinating the different parts of an organization.

Integration is the process of coordinating the different parts of an organization. Integration mechanisms are designed to achieve unity among individuals and groups in various jobs, departments, and divisions in the accomplishment of organizational goals and tasks.[9] Integration helps keep the organization in a state of dynamic equilibrium, a condition in which all the parts of the organization are interrelated and balanced.

Vertical linkages are used to integrate activities up and down the organizational chain of command. A variety of structural devices can be used to achieve vertical linkage. These include hierarchical referral, rules and procedures, plans and schedules, positions added to the structure of the organization, and management information systems.[10]

The vertical lines on an organization chart indicate the lines of hierarchical referral up and down the organization. When employees do not know how to solve a problem, they can refer it up the organization for consideration and resolution. Work that needs to be assigned is usually delegated down the chain of command as indicated by the vertical lines.

Rules and procedures, as well as plans and schedules, provide standing information for employees without direct communication. These vertical integrators, such as an employee handbook, communicate to employees standard information or information that they can understand on their own. These integrators allow managers to have wider spans of control, because the managers do not have to inform each employee of what is expected and when it is expected. Vertical integrators encourage managers to use management by exception—to make decisions when employees bring problems up the hierarchy. Military organizations depend heavily on vertical linkages. The army, for example, has a well-defined chain of command. Certain duties are expected to be carried out, and proper paperwork is to be in place. In times of crisis, however, much more information is processed, and the proper paperwork becomes secondary to "getting the job done." Vertical linkages help individuals understand their roles in the organization, especially in times of crisis.

Adding positions to the hierarchy is used as a vertical integrator when a manager becomes overloaded by hierarchical referral or problems arise in the chain of command. Positions such as "assistant to" may be added or another level may be added. Adding levels to the hierarchy often reflects growth and increasing complexity. This action tends to reduce the span of control, thus allowing more communication and closer supervision.

Management information systems that are designed to process information up and down the organization also serve as a vertical linkage mechanism. With the advent of computers and network technology, it has become easier for managers and employees to communicate through written reports that are entered into a network and then electronically compiled for managers in the hierarchy. Electronic mail systems allow managers and employees greater access to one another without having to be in the same place at the same time or even attached by telephone. These types of systems make information processing up and down the organization more efficient.

Generally, the taller the organization, the more vertical integration mechanisms are needed. This is because the chains of command and communication are longer. Additional length requires more linkages to minimize the potential for misunderstandings and miscommunications.

Horizontal integration mechanisms provide the communication and coordination that are necessary for links across jobs and departments in the organization. The need for horizontal integration mechanisms increases as the complexity of the organization increases. The horizontal linkages are built into the design of the organization by including liaison roles, task forces, integrator positions, and teams.

A liaison role is created when a person in one department or area of the organization has the responsibility for coordinating with another department (for example, a liaison between the engineering and production departments). Task forces are temporary committees composed of representatives from multiple departments who assemble to address a specific problem affecting these departments.[11]

A stronger device for integration is to develop a person or department designed to be an integrator. In most organizations, the integrator has a good deal of responsibility, but not much authority. Such an individual must have the ability to get people together to resolve differences within the perspective of organizational goals.[12]

The strongest method of horizontal integration is through teams. Horizontal teams cut across existing lines of organizational structure to create new entities that make organizational decisions. An example of this may occur in product development with the formation of a team that includes marketing, research, design, and production personnel. Ford used such a cross-functional team to develop the Taurus automobile, which was designed to regain market share in the United States. The information exchanged by such a product development team should lead to a product that is acceptable to a wider range of organizational groups, as well as to customers.[13]

The use of these linkage mechanisms varies from organization to organization, as well as within areas of the same organization. In general, the flatter the organization, the more necessary are horizontal integration mechanisms.

BASIC DESIGN DIMENSIONS

Differentiation, then, is the process of dividing work in the organization, and integration is the process of coordinating work in the organization. From a structural perspective, every manager and organization look for the best combination of differentiation and integration for accomplishing the goals of the organization. There are many ways to approach this process. One way

2. *Discuss six basic design dimensions of an organization.*

is to establish a desired level of each structural dimension on a high to low continuum and then develop a structure that meets the desired configuration. These structural dimensions include the following[14]:

1. *Formalization*: The degree to which an employee's role is defined by formal documentation (procedures, job descriptions, manuals, and regulations).

2. *Centralization*: The extent to which decision-making authority has been delegated to lower levels of an organization. An organization is centralized if the decisions are made at the top of the organization and decentralized if decision making is pushed down to lower levels in the organization.

3. *Specialization*: The degree to which organizational tasks are subdivided into separate jobs. The division of labor and the degree to which formal job descriptions spell out job requirements indicate the level of specialization in the organization.

4. *Standardization*: The extent to which work activities are described and performed routinely in the same way. Highly standardized organizations have little variation in the defining of jobs.

5. *Complexity*: The number of activities within the organization and the amount of differentiation needed within the organization.

6. *Hierarchy of authority*: The degree of vertical differentiation through reporting relationships and the span of control within the structure of the organization.

An organization that is high on formalization, centralization, specialization, standardization, and complexity and has a tall hierarchy of authority is said to be highly bureaucratic. Bureaucracies are not in and of themselves bad; however, they are often tainted by abuse and red tape. The Internal Revenue Service was often described as bureaucratic and went through a major reorganization to become more responsive and flexible.

An organization that is on the opposite end of each of these continua is very flexible and loose. Control is very hard to implement and maintain in such an organization, but at certain times such an organization is appropriate. The research and development departments in many organizations are often more flexible than other departments in order to stimulate creativity. An important organizational variable, which is not included in the structural dimensions, is trust.

Another approach to the process of accomplishing organizational goals is to describe what is and is not important to the success of the organization rather than worry about specific characteristics. Henry Mintzberg feels that the following questions can guide managers in designing formal structures that fit each organization's unique set of circumstances[15]:

1. How many tasks should a given position in the organization contain, and how specialized should each task be?

2. How standardized should the work content of each position be?

FORMALIZATION
The degree to which the organization has official rules, regulations, and procedures.

CENTRALIZATION
The degree to which decisions are made at the top of the organization.

SPECIALIZATION
The degree to which jobs are narrowly defined and depend on unique expertise.

STANDARDIZATION
The degree to which work activities are accomplished in a routine fashion.

COMPLEXITY
The degree to which many different types of activities occur in the organization.

HIERARCHY OF AUTHORITY
The degree of vertical differentiation across levels of management.

3. What skills, abilities, knowledge, and training should be required for each position?

4. What should be the basis for the grouping of positions within the organization into units, departments, divisions, and so on?

5. How large should each unit be, and what should the span of control be (that is, how many individuals should report to each manager)?

6. How much standardization should be required in the output of each position?

7. What mechanisms should be established to help individuals in different positions and units to adjust to the needs of other individuals?

8. How centralized or decentralized should decision-making power be in the chain of authority? Should most of the decisions be made at the top of the organization (centralized) or be made down in the chain of authority (decentralized)?

The manager who can answer these questions has a good understanding of how the organization should implement the basic structural dimensions. These basic design dimensions act in combination with one another and are not entirely independent characteristics of an organization. This chapter's Challenge (on page 342) gives you (or a friend) an opportunity to consider how decentralized your company is.

FIVE STRUCTURAL CONFIGURATIONS

Differentiation, integration, and the basic design dimensions combine to yield various structural configurations. Mintzberg proposes five structural configurations: the simple structure, the machine bureaucracy, the professional bureaucracy, the divisionalized form, and the adhocracy.[16] Table 14-2 (on page 343) summarizes the prime coordinating mechanism, the key part of the organization, and the type of decentralization for each of these structural configurations. The five basic parts of the organization, for Mintzberg, are the upper echelon or strategic apex; the middle level; the operating core, where work is accomplished; the technical staff; and the support staff. Figure 14-2 (on page 343) depicts these five basic parts with a small strategic apex, connected by a flaring middle line to a large, flat operating core. Each configuration affects people in the organization somewhat differently.

3. *Briefly describe five structural configurations for organizations.*

SIMPLE STRUCTURE

The *simple structure* is an organization with little technical and support staff, strong centralization of decision making in the upper echelon, and a minimal middle level. This structure has a minimum of vertical differentiation of authority and minimal formalization. It achieves coordination through direct supervision, often by the chief executive in the upper echelon. An example of a simple structure is a small, independent landscape practice in which

SIMPLE STRUCTURE
A centralized form of organization that emphasizes the upper echelon and direct supervision.

Challenge

HOW DECENTRALIZED IS YOUR COMPANY?

Decentralization is one of the key design dimensions in an organization. It is closely related to several behavioral dimensions of an organization, such as leadership style, degree of participative decision making, and the nature of power and politics within the organization.

The following questionnaire allows you to get an idea about how decentralized your organization is. (If you do not have a job, have a friend who does work complete the questionnaire to see how decentralized his or her organization is.) Which level in your organization has the authority to make each of the following eleven decisions? Answer the questionnaire by circling one of the following:

0 = The board of directors makes the decision. *cc*
1 = The CEO makes the decision. *c*
2 = The division/functional manager makes the decision. *R*
3 = A subdepartment head makes the decision.
4 = The first-level supervisor makes the decision. *ME*
5 = Operators on the shop floor make the decision. *Me2*

Decision Concerning: Circle Appropriate Level

		0	1	2	3	4	5
a.	The number of workers required.	0	(1)	2	3	4	5
b.	Whether to employ a worker.	0	1	(2)	3	4	5
c.	Internal labor disputes.	0	1	(2)	3	4	5
d.	Overtime worked at shop level.	0	(1)	2	3	4	5
e.	Delivery dates and order priority.	0	1	(2)	3	4	5
f.	Production planning.	0	1	(2)	3	4	5
g.	Dismissal of a worker.	0	(1)	2	3	4	5
h.	Methods of personnel selection.	0	(1)	2	3	4	5
i.	Method of work to be used.	0	1	(2)	3	4	5
j.	Machinery or equipment to be used.	0	1	2	(3)	4	5
k.	Allocation of work among workers.	0	1	(2)	3	4	5

Scoring

Add up all your circled numbers.
Total = _19_.
The higher your number (for example, 45 or more), the more decentralized your organization. The lower your number (for example, 25 or less), the more centralized your organization.

Source: From D. Miller and C. Droge, "Psychological and Traditional Determinants of Structure," *Administrative Science Quarterly* 31 (1986): 558. Reprinted by permission of the Administrative Science Quarterly.

one or two landscape architects supervise the vast majority of work with no middle-level managers. Even an organization with as few as thirty people can become dysfunctional as a simple structure after an extended period.

MACHINE BUREAUCRACY

MACHINE BUREAUCRACY
A moderately decentralized form of organization that emphasizes the technical staff and standardization of work processes.

The **machine bureaucracy** is an organization with a well-defined technical and support staff differentiated from the line operations of the organi-

Structural Configuration	Prime Coordinating Mechanism	Key Part of Organization	Type of Decentralization
Simple structure	Direct supervision	Upper echelon	Centralization
Machine bureaucracy	Standardization of work processes	Technical staff	Limited horizontal decentralization
Professional bureaucracy	Standardization of skills	Operating level	Vertical and horizontal decentralization
Divisionalized form	Standardization of outputs	Middle level	Limited vertical decentralization
Adhocracy	Mutual adjustment	Support staff	Selective decentralization

Source: H. Mintzberg, *The Structuring of Organizations*, © 1979, p. 301. Adapted by permission of Pearson Education, Inc., Upper Saddle River, N.J.

Table 14-2
Five Structural Configurations of Organizations

zation, limited horizontal decentralization of decision making, and a well-defined hierarchy of authority. The technical staff is powerful in a machine bureaucracy. There is strong formalization through policies, procedures, rules, and regulations. Coordination is achieved through the standardization of work processes. An example of a machine bureaucracy is an automobile assembly plant, with routinized operating tasks. The strength of the machine bureaucracy is efficiency of operation in stable, unchanging environments. The weakness of the machine bureaucracy is its slow responsiveness to external changes and to individual employee preferences and ideas.

Figure 14-2
Mintzberg's Five Basic Parts of an Organization

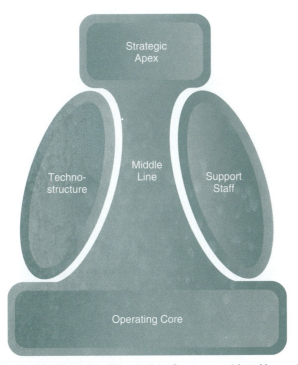

Source: From H. Mintzberg, *The Structuring of Organizations*, © 1979, p. 20. Adapted by permission of Pearson Education, Inc., Upper Saddle River, N.J.

PROFESSIONAL BUREAUCRACY

The *professional bureaucracy* emphasizes the expertise of the professionals in the operating core of the organization. The technical and support staffs serve the professionals. There is both vertical and horizontal differentiation in the professional bureaucracy. Coordination is achieved through the standardization of the professionals' skills. Examples of professional bureaucracies are hospitals and universities. The doctors, nurses, and professors are given wide latitude to pursue their work based on professional training and indoctrination through professional training programs. Large accounting firms may fall into the category of professional bureaucracies.

DIVISIONALIZED FORM

The *divisionalized form* is a loosely coupled, composite structural configuration.[17] It is a configuration composed of divisions, each of which may have its own structural configuration. Each division is designed to respond to the market in which it operates. There is vertical decentralization from the upper echelon to the middle of the organization, and the middle level of management is the key part of the organization. This form of organization may have one division that is a machine bureaucracy, one that is an adhocracy, and one that is a simple structure. An example of this form of organization is Valero Energy Corporation, headquartered in San Antonio, Texas, with oil refining operations throughout the country. The divisionalized organization uses standardization of outputs as its coordinating mechanism.

ADHOCRACY

The *adhocracy* is a highly open and decentralized, rather than highly structured, configuration with minimal formalization and order. It is designed to fuse interdisciplinary experts into smoothly functioning ad hoc project teams. Liaison devices are the primary mechanism for integrating the project teams through a process of mutual adjustment. There is a high degree of horizontal specialization based on formal training and expertise. Selective decentralization of the project teams occurs within the adhocracy. An example of this form of organization is the National Aeronautics and Space Administration (NASA), which is composed of many talented experts who work in small teams on a wide range of projects related to America's space agenda. New high-technology businesses also often select an adhocracy design. Paradoxically, though, some new high-tech ventures choose bureaucratic design strategies as antidotes for the uncertainty, anxiety, and stress of their typically turbulent operating environments.

CONTEXTUAL VARIABLES

4. Describe four contextual variables for an organization.

The basic design dimensions and the resulting structural configurations play out in the context of the organization's internal and external environments. Four contextual variables influence the success of an organization's design: size, technology, environment, and strategy and goals. These variables provide a manager with challenges in considering an organizational design, although they are not necessarily determinants of structure. As the content of the organization changes, so should the structural design. Also, the amount of change in the contextual variables throughout the life of the organization influences the amount of change needed in the basic dimensions of the organization's structure.[18]

SIZE

The total number of employees is the appropriate definition of size when discussing the design of organizational structure. This is logical, because people and their interactions are the building blocks of structure. Other measures, such as net assets, production rates, and total sales, are usually highly correlated with the total number of employees but may not reflect the actual number of interpersonal relationships that are necessary to effectively structure an organization.

Electronic Data Systems (EDS) began as an entrepreneurial venture of H. Ross Perot and had grown into an internationally prominent provider of information technology services when it was bought by General Motors Corporation (GM) in the early 1980s. Nearly half of EDS's revenues came from GM at the time of the buyout. The early culture of EDS placed a premium on technical competence, high achievement drive, an entrepreneurial attitude, and a maverick spirit. EDS continued to grow and to change. In 1996, it was spun off by GM and became an autonomous company once again.[19] However, following the spin-off, the company has struggled to find a clear focus and identity, and has lost two chairmen (Les Aberthal and Dick Brown) in the process.

Although there is some argument over the degree of influence that size has on organizational structure, there is no argument that it does influence design options. In one study, Meyer found size of the organization to be the most important of all variables considered in influencing the organization's structure and design, whereas other researchers argue that the decision to expand the organization's business causes an increase in size as the structure is adjusted to accommodate the planned growth.[20] Downsizing is a planned strategy to reduce the size of an organization, and is often accompanied by related restructuring and revitalization activities.[21]

How much influence size exerts on the organization's structure is not as important as the relationship between size and the design dimensions of structure. In other words, when exploring structural alternatives, what should the manager know about designing structures for large and small organizations?

Table 14-3 (on page 346) illustrates the relationships among each of the design dimensions and organizational size. Formalization, specialization, and standardization all tend to be greater in larger organizations, because they are necessary to control activities within the organization. For example, larger organizations are more likely to use documentation, rules, written policies and procedures, and detailed job descriptions than to rely on personal

YOU BE THE JUDGE

Should legal limits be set to prevent large companies from engaging in very competitive behavior to drive small companies out of business?

Basic Design Dimensions	Small Organizations	Large Organizations
Formalization	Less	More
Centralization	High	Low
Specialization	Low	High
Standardization	Low	High
Complexity	Low	High
Hierarchy of authority	Flat	Tall

Table 14-3

Relationship between Organizational Size and Basic Design Dimensions

observation by the manager. The more relationships that have to be managed by the structure, the more formalized and standardized the processes need to be. McDonald's has several volumes that describe how to make all its products, how to greet customers, how to maintain the facilities, and so on. This level of standardization, formalization, and specialization helps McDonald's maintain the same quality of product no matter where a restaurant is located. In contrast, at a small, locally owned café, your hamburger and french fries may taste a little different every time you visit. This is evidence of a lack of standardization.

Formalization and specialization also help a large organization decentralize decision making. Because of the complexity and number of decisions in a large organization, formalization and specialization are used to set parameters for decision making at lower levels. Can you imagine the chaos if George W. Bush, commander-in-chief of all U.S. military forces, had to make operational-level decisions in the war on terrorism? By decentralizing decision making, the larger organization adds horizontal and vertical complexity, but not necessarily spatial complexity. However, it is more common for a large organization to have more geographic dispersion.

Another dimension of design, hierarchy of authority, is related to complexity. As size increases, complexity increases; thus, more levels are added to the hierarchy of authority. This keeps the span of control from getting too large. However, there is a balancing force, because formalization and specialization are added. The more formalized, standardized, and specialized the roles within the organization, the wider the span of control can be.

Although some have argued that the future belongs to small, agile organizations, others argue that size continues to be an advantage. To take advantage of size, organizations must become centerless corporations with a global core.[22] These concepts are pioneered by Booz Allen Hamilton based on their worldwide technology and management consulting. The global core provides strategic leadership, helps distribute and provide access to the company's capabilities and knowledge, creates the corporate identity, ensures access to low cost capital, and exerts control over the enterprise as a whole.

TECHNOLOGY

An organization's technology is an important contextual variable in determining the organization's structure, as noted in Chapter 2.[23] Technology is defined as the tools, techniques, and actions used by an organization to transform inputs into outputs.[24] The inputs of the organization include human resources, machines, materials, information, and money. The outputs are the products and services that the organization offers to the external environment. Determining the relationship between technology and structure is complicated, because different departments may employ very different technologies. As organizations become larger, there is greater variation in technologies across units in the organization. Joan Woodward, Charles Perrow, and James Thompson have developed ways to understand traditional organizational technologies. More work is needed to better understand the contemporary engineering, research and development, and knowledge-based technologies of the information age.

Woodward introduced one of the best-known classification schemes for technology, identifying three types: unit, mass, or process production. Unit technology is small-batch manufacturing technology and, sometimes, made-to-order production. Examples include Smith & Wesson's arms manufacture and the manufacture of fine furniture. Mass technology is large-batch manufacturing technology. Examples include American automotive assembly lines and latex glove production. Process production is continuous-production processes. Examples include oil refining and beer making. Woodward classified unit technology as the least complex, mass technology as more complex, and process technology as the most complex. The more complex the organization's technology, the more complex the administrative component or structure of the organization needs to be.

Perrow proposed an alternative to Woodward's scheme based on two variables: task variability and problem analyzability. Task variability considers the number of exceptions encountered in doing the tasks within a job. Problem analyzability examines the types of search procedures followed to find ways to respond to task exceptions. For example, for some exceptions encountered while doing a task, the appropriate response is easy to find. If you are driving down a street and see a sign that says, "Detour—Bridge Out," it is very easy to respond to the task variability. When Thomas Edison was designing the first electric light bulb, however, the problem analyzability was very high for his task.

Perrow went on further to identify the four key aspects of structure that could be modified to the technology. These structural elements are (1) the amount of discretion that an individual can exercise to complete a task, (2) the power of groups to control the unit's goals and strategies, (3) the level of interdependence among groups, and (4) the extent to which organizational units coordinate work using either feedback or planning. Figure 14-3 (on page 348) summarizes Perrow's findings about types of technology and basic design dimensions.[25]

Thompson offered yet another view of technology and its relationship to organizational design. This view is based on the concept of **technological interdependence** (i.e., the degree of interrelatedness of the organization's various technological elements) and the pattern of an organization's

TECHNOLOGICAL INTERDEPENDENCE
The degree of interrelatedness of the organization's various technological elements.

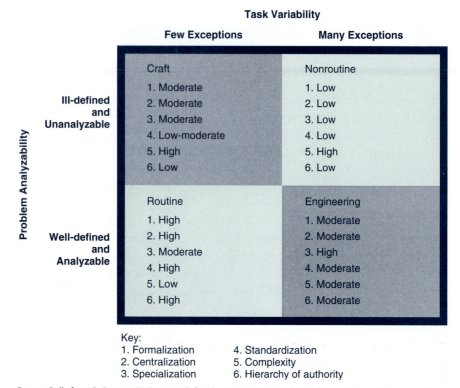

Source: Built from C. Perrow, "A Framework for the Comparative Analysis of Organizations," *American Sociological Review* (April 1967): 194–208.

Figure 14-3
Summary of Perrow's Findings about the Relationship between Technology and Basic Design Dimensions

work flows. Thompson's research suggests that greater technological interdependence leads to greater organizational complexity and that the problems of this greater complexity may be offset by decentralized decision making.[26]

The research of these three early scholars on the influence of technology on organizational design can be combined into one integrating concept—routineness in the process of changing inputs into outputs in an organization. This routineness has a very strong relationship with organizational structure. The more routine and repetitive the tasks of the organization, the higher the degree of formalization that is possible; the more centralized, specialized, and standardized the organization can be; and the more hierarchical levels with wider spans of control that are possible.

Since the work of Woodward, Perrow, and Thompson, however, an important caveat to the discussion of technology has emerged: the advance of information technology has influenced how organizations transform inputs into outputs. The introduction of computer-integrated networks, CAD/CAM systems, and computer-integrated manufacturing has broadened the span of control, flattened the organizational hierarchy, decentralized decision making, and lowered the amount of specialization and standardization.[27] Advances in information technology have allowed for other advances in manufacturing, such as mass customization. Hewlett-Packard has found a key to mass customization in postponing the task of differentiating a product for a specific customer until the latest possible time.[28]

ENVIRONMENT

The third contextual variable for organizational design is *environment*. The environment of an organization is most easily defined as anything outside the boundaries of that organization. Different aspects of the environment have varying degrees of influence on the organization's structure. The general environment includes all conditions that may have an impact on the organization. These conditions could include economic factors, political considerations, ecological changes, sociocultural demands, and governmental regulation.

When aspects of the general environment become more focused in areas of direct interest to the organization, those aspects become part of the *task environment*, or specific environment. The task environment is that part of the environment that is directly relevant to the organization. Typically, this level of environment includes stakeholders such as unions, customers, suppliers, competitors, government regulatory agencies, and trade associations.

The domain of the organization refers to the area the organization claims for itself with respect to how it fits into its relevant environments. The domain is particularly important because it is defined by the organization, and it influences how the organization perceives and acts within its environments.[29] For example, Wal-Mart and Neiman Marcus both sell clothing apparel, but their domains are very different.

The organization's perceptions of its environment and the actual environment may not be the same. The environment that the manager perceives is the environment that the organization responds to and organizes for.[30] Therefore, two organizations may be in relatively the same environment from an objective standpoint, but if the managers perceive differences, the organizations may enact very different structures to deal with this same environment.

The perception of *environmental uncertainty* or the perception of the lack of environmental uncertainty is how the contextual variable of environment most influences organizational design. Some organizations have relatively static environments with little uncertainty, whereas others are so dynamic that no one is sure what tomorrow may bring. Binney & Smith, for example, has made relatively the same product for more than fifty years with very few changes in the product design or packaging. The environment for its Crayola products is relatively static. In fact, customers rebelled when the company tried to get rid of some old colors and add new ones. In contrast, in the last two decades, competitors in the airline industry have encountered deregulation, mergers, bankruptcies, safety changes, changes in cost and price structures, changes in customer and employee demographics, and changes in global competition. The uncertainty of the environment of the major airlines has been relatively high during this period.

ENVIRONMENT
Anything outside the boundaries of an organization.

TASK ENVIRONMENT
The elements of an organization's environment that are related to its goal attainment.

ENVIRONMENTAL UNCERTAINTY
The amount and rate of change in the organization's environment.

Basic Design Dimensions	Mechanistic	Organic
Formalization	High	Low
Centralization	High	Low
Specialization	High	Low
Standardization	High	Low
Complexity	Low	High
Hierarchy of authority	Strong, tall	Weak, flat

Table 14-4
Mechanistic and Organic Organizational Forms

MECHANISTIC STRUCTURE
An organizational design that emphasizes structured activities, specialized tasks, and centralized decision making.

ORGANIC STRUCTURE
An organizational design that emphasizes teamwork, open communication, and decentralized decision making.

The amount of uncertainty in the environment influences the structural dimensions. Burns and Stalker labeled two structural extremes that are appropriate for the extremes of environmental uncertainty—*mechanistic structure* and *organic structure*.[31] Table 14-4 compares the structural dimensions of these two extremes. The mechanistic and organic structures are opposite ends of a continuum of organizational design possibilities. Although the general premise of environmental uncertainty and structural dimensions has been upheld by research, the organization must make adjustments for the realities of its perceived environment when designing its structure.[32]

The question for those trying to design organizational structures is how to determine environmental uncertainty. Dess and Beard defined three dimensions of environment that should be measured in assessing the degree of uncertainty: capacity, volatility, and complexity.[33] The capacity of the environment reflects the abundance or scarcity of resources. If resources abound, the environment supports expansion, mistakes, or both. In contrast, in times of scarcity, the environment demands survival of the fittest. Volatility is the degree of instability. The airline industry is in a volatile environment. This makes it difficult for managers to know what needs to be done. The complexity of the environment refers to the differences and variability among environmental elements.

If the organization's environment is uncertain, dynamic, and complex and resources are scarce, the manager needs an organic structure that is better able to adapt to its environment. Such a structure allows the manager to monitor the environment from a number of internal perspectives, thus helping the organization maintain flexibility in responding to environmental changes.[34]

STRATEGY AND GOALS

The fourth contextual variable that influences how the design dimensions of structure should be enacted is the strategies and goals of the organization. Strategies and goals provide legitimacy to the organization, as well as employee direction, decision guidelines, and criteria for performance.[35] In addition, strategies and goals help the organization fit into its environment.

As more understanding of the contextual influence of strategies and goals has developed, several strategic dimensions that influence structure have been defined. One of these definitions was put forth by Danny Miller.[36]

His framework for these strategic dimensions and their implications for organizational structure is shown in Table 14-5.

For example, when Apple Computer introduced personal computers to the market, its strategies were very innovative. The structure of the organization was relatively flat and very informal. Apple had Friday afternoon beer and popcorn discussion sessions, and eccentric behavior was easily accepted. As the personal computer market became more competitive, however, the structure of Apple changed to help it differentiate its products and to help control costs. The innovative strategies and structures devised by Steve Jobs, one of Apple's founders, were no longer appropriate. The board of directors recruited John Scully, a marketing expert from PepsiCo, to help Apple better compete in the market it had created. In 1996 and 1997, Apple reinvented itself again and brought back Jobs to try to restore its innovative edge. Since his return, Apple has become a major player in the digital music market with its introduction of the iPod, selling over 300,000 units in one quarter.

Limitations exist, however, on how much strategies and goals influence structure. Because the structure of the organization includes the formal information-processing channels in the organization, it stands to reason that the need to change strategies may not be communicated throughout the organization. In such a case, the organization's structure influences its strategic choice.

The inefficiency of the structure to perceive environmental changes may even lead to organizational failure. In the airline industry, several carriers failed to adjust quickly enough to deregulation and the highly competitive marketplace. Only those airlines that were generally viewed as lean structures with good information-processing systems have flourished in the turbulent years since deregulation. Examples of how different design dimensions can affect the strategic decision process are listed in Table 14-6 (on page 352).

Strategic Dimension	Predicted Structural Characteristics
Innovation—to understand and manage new processes and technologies	Low formalization Decentralization Flat hierarchy
Market differentiation—to specialize in customer preferences	Moderate to high complexity Moderate to high formalization Moderate centralization
Cost control—to produce standardized products efficiently	High formalization High centralization High standardization Low complexity

Table 14-5

Miller's Integrative Framework of Structural and Strategic Dimensions

Source: D. Miller, "The Structural and Environmental Correlates of Business Strategy," *Strategic Management Journal* 8 (1987): 55–76. Copyright © 1987 John Wiley & Sons Limited. Reproduced with permission.

Formalization
As the level of formalization increases, so does the probability of the following:
1. The strategic decision process will become reactive to crisis rather than proactive through opportunities.
2. Strategic moves will be incremental and precise.
3. Differentiation in the organization will not be balanced with integrative mechanisms.
4. Only environmental crises that are in areas monitored by the formal organizational systems will be acted upon.
Centralization
As the level of centralization increases, so does the probability of the following:
1. The strategic decision process will be initiated by only a few dominant individuals.
2. The decision process will be goal-oriented and rational.
3. The strategic process will be constrained by the limitations of top managers.
Complexity
As the level of complexity increases, so does the probability of the following:
1. The strategic decision process will become more politicized.
2. The organization will find it more difficult to recognize environmental opportunities and threats.
3. The constraints on good decision processes will be multiplied by the limitations of each individual within the organization.

Table 14-6
Examples of How Structure Affects the Strategic Decision Process

Source: Republished with permission of Academy of Management, PO Box 3020, Briar Cliff Manor, N.J. 10510-8020. "The Strategic Decision Process and Organizational Structure" (Table), J. Fredrickson, *Academy of Management Review* (1986): 284. Reproduced by permission of the publisher via Copyright Clearance Center, Inc.

The four contextual variables—size, technology, environment, and strategy and goals—combine to influence the design process. However, the existing structure of the organization influences how the organization interprets and reacts to information about each of the variables. Each of the contextual variables has management researchers who claim that it is the most important variable in determining the best structural design. Because of the difficulty in studying the interactions of the four contextual dimensions and the complexity of organizational structures, the argument about which variable is most important continues.

What is apparent is that there must be some level of fit between the structure and the contextual dimensions of the organization. The better the fit, the more likely the organization will achieve its short-run goals. In addition, the better the fit, the more likely the organization will process information and design appropriate organizational roles for long-term prosperity, as indicated in Figure 14-4.

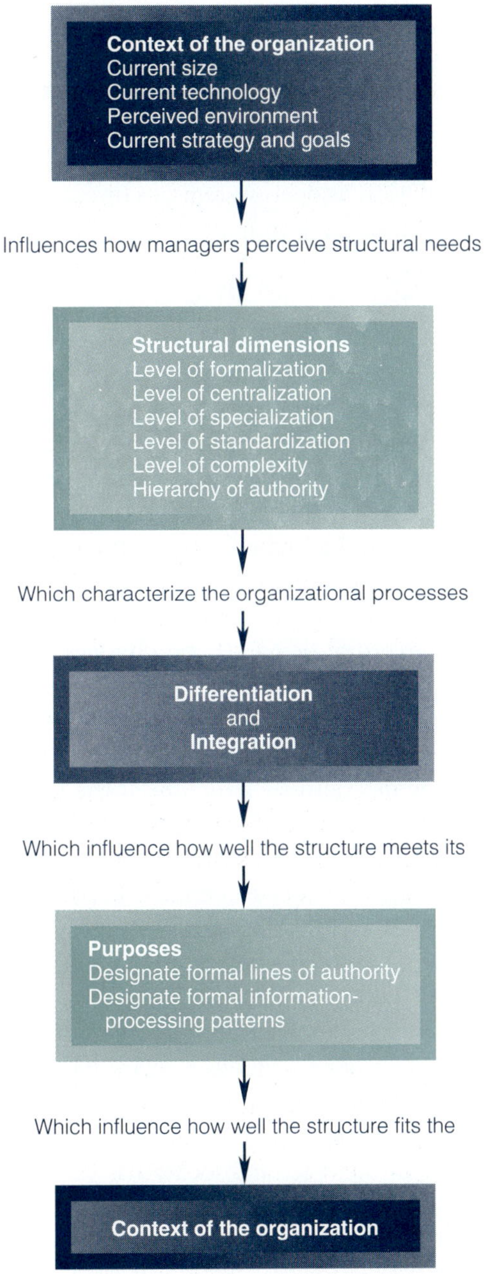

Context of the organization
Current size
Current technology
Perceived environment
Current strategy and goals

Influences how managers perceive structural needs

Structural dimensions
Level of formalization
Level of centralization
Level of specialization
Level of standardization
Level of complexity
Hierarchy of authority

Which characterize the organizational processes

Differentiation
and
Integration

Which influence how well the structure meets its

Purposes
Designate formal lines of authority
Designate formal information-
processing patterns

Which influence how well the structure fits the

Context of the organization

Figure 14-4
The Relationship among Key Organizational Design Elements

FORCES RESHAPING ORGANIZATIONS

Managers and researchers traditionally examine organizational design and structure within the framework of basic design dimensions and contextual variables. Several forces reshaping organizations are causing managers to go beyond the traditional frameworks and to examine ways to make

5. *Explain the four forces reshaping organizations.*

organizations more responsive to customer needs. Some of these forces include shorter life cycles within the organization, globalization, and rapid changes in information technology. These forces together increase the demands on process capabilities within the organization and emerging organizational structures. To successfully retain their health and vitality, organizations must function as open systems, as discussed in Chapter 1, that are responsive to their task environment.[37]

LIFE CYCLES IN ORGANIZATIONS

Organizations are dynamic entities. As such, they ebb and flow through different stages. Usually, researchers think of these stages as *organizational life cycles*. The total organization has a life cycle that begins at birth, moves through growth and maturity to decline, and possibly experiences revival.[38]

Organizational subunits may have very similar life cycles. Because of changes in technology and product design, many organizational subunits, especially those that are product based, are experiencing shorter life cycles. Hence, the subunits that compose the organization are changing more rapidly than in the past. These shorter life cycles enable the organization to respond quickly to external demands and changes.

When a new organization or subunit is born, the structure is organic and informal. If the organization or subunit is successful, it grows and matures. This usually leads to formalization, specialization, standardization, complexity, and a more mechanistic structure. If the environment changes, however, the organization must be able to respond. A mechanistic structure is not able to respond to a dynamic environment as well as an organic one. If the organization or subunit does respond, it becomes more organic and revives; if not, it declines and possibly dies.

Shorter life cycles put more pressure on the organization to be both flexible and efficient at the same time. Further, as flexible organizations use design to their competitive advantage, discrete organizational life cycles may give way to a kaleidoscope of continuously emerging, efficiency-seeking organizational designs.[39] The manager's challenge in this context becomes one of creating congruency among various organizational design dimensions to fit continuously changing markets and locations.

GLOBALIZATION

Another force that is reshaping organizations is the process of globalization. In other words, organizations operate worldwide rather than in just one country or region. Globalization makes spatial differentiation even more of a reality for organizations. Besides the obvious geographic differences, there may be deep cultural and value system differences. This adds another type of complexity to the structural design process and necessitates the creation of integrating mechanisms so that people are able to understand and interpret one another, as well as coordinate with one another.

The choice of structure for managing an international business is generally based on choices concerning the following three factors:

ORGANIZATIONAL LIFE CYCLE
The differing stages of an organization's life from birth to death.

1. *The level of vertical differentiation.* A hierarchy of authority must be created that clarifies the responsibilities of both domestic and foreign managers.

2. *The level of horizontal differentiation.* Foreign and domestic operations should be grouped in such a way that the company effectively serves the needs of all customers.

3. *The degree of formalization, specialization, standardization, and centralization.* The global structure must allow decisions to be made in the most appropriate area of the organization. However, controls must be in place that reflect the strategies and goals of the parent firm.[40]

CHANGES IN INFORMATION-PROCESSING TECHNOLOGIES

Many of the changes in information-processing technologies have allowed organizations to move into new product and market areas more quickly. However, just as shorter life cycles and globalization have caused new concerns for designing organizational structures, so has the increased availability of advanced information-processing technologies.

Organizational structures are already feeling the impact of advanced information-processing technologies. More integration and coordination are evident, because managers worldwide can be connected through computerized networks. The basic design dimensions have also been affected as follows:

1. The hierarchy of authority has been flattened.

2. The basis of centralization has been changed. Now managers can use technology to acquire more information and make more decisions, or they can use technology to push information and decision making lower in the hierarchy and thus decrease centralization.

3. Less specialization and standardization are needed, because people using advanced information-processing technologies have more sophisticated jobs that require a broader understanding of how the organization gets work done.[41]

Advances in information processing are leading to knowledge-based organizations, the outlines of which are now only seen dimly. Some of the hallmarks of these new organizational forms are virtual enterprising, dynamic teaming, and knowledge networking.[42] This fifth generation of management thought and practice leads to co-creation of products and services. Future organizations may well be defined by networks of overlapping teams.

DEMANDS ON ORGANIZATIONAL PROCESSES

Because of the forces reshaping organizations, managers find themselves trying to meet what seem to be conflicting goals: an efficiency orientation that results in on-time delivery *and* a quality orientation that results in customized, high-quality goods or services.[43] Traditionally, managers have seen efficiency and customization as conflicting demands.

Roles of Managers Today
1. Strictly adhering to boss–employee relationships.
2. Getting things done by giving orders.
3. Carrying messages up and down the hierarchy.
4. Performing a prescribed set of tasks according to a job description.
5. Having a narrow functional focus.
6. Going through channels, one by one by one.
7. Controlling subordinates.

Roles of Future Managers
1. Having hierarchical relationships subordinated to functional and peer relationships.
2. Getting things done by negotiating.
3. Solving problems and making decisions.
4. Creating the job by developing entrepreneurial projects.
5. Having broad cross-functional collaboration.
6. Emphasizing speed and flexibility.
7. Coaching their workers.

Table 14-7
Structural Roles of Managers Today versus Managers of the Future

Source: Reprinted by permission of the publisher, from *Management Review*, January 1991 © 1991. Thomas R. Horton. American Management Association, New York. All rights reserved.

To meet these conflicting demands, organizations need to become "dynamically stable."[44] To do so, an organization must have managers who see their roles as architects who clearly understand the "how" of the organizing process. Managers must combine long-term thinking with flexible and quick responses that help improve process and know-how. The organizational structure must help define, at least to some degree, roles for managers who hope to successfully address the conflicting demands of dynamic stability. The differences between the structural roles of managers today and managers of the future are illustrated in Table 14-7.

EMERGING ORGANIZATIONAL STRUCTURES

6. *Discuss emerging organizational structures.*

The demands on managers and on process capabilities place demands on structures. The emphasis in organizations is shifting to organizing around processes, a key tenet of total quality management (TQM). This process orientation emerges from the combination of three streams of applied organizational design: high-performance, self-managed teams; managing processes rather than functions; and the evolution of information technology. Three emerging organizational structures associated with these changes are network organizations, virtual organizations, and the circle organization.

Network organizations are weblike structures that contract some or all of their operating functions to other organizations and then coordinate their activities through managers and other employees at their headquarters. Information technology is the basis for building the weblike structure of the network organization and business unit managers that are essential to the success of these systems. This type of organization has arisen in the age of electronic commerce and brought into practice transaction cost economics, interorganizational collaborations, and strategic alliances. Network organizations can be global in scope.[45]

Virtual organizations are temporary network organizations consisting of independent enterprises. Many dot.coms were virtual organizations designed to come together swiftly to exploit an apparent market opportunity. They may function much like a theatrical troupe that comes together for a "performance."[46] Trust can be a challenge for virtual organizations because it is a complex phenomenon involving ethics, morals, emotions, values, and natural attitudes. However, trust and trustworthiness are important connective issues in virtual environments.

The circle organization is a third emerging structure crafted by Harley-Davidson in its drive to achieve teamwork without teams.[47] The company evolved the circle form of organization shown in Figure 14-5. The three organizational parts are those that (1) create demand, (2) produce product, and (3) provide support. As the figure indicates, these three parts are linked by the leadership and strategy council (LSC). The circle organization is a more open system, organic structure for customer responsiveness. One innovation in this organizational scheme is the "circle coach," who possesses acute communication, listening, and influencing skills so as to be highly respected by circle members and the company's president.

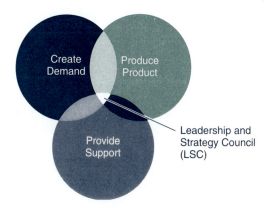

Figure 14-5
Harley-Davidson's Circle Organization

CAUTIONARY NOTES ABOUT STRUCTURE

This chapter has identified the purposes of structure, the processes of organizational design, and the dimensions and contexts that must be considered in structure. In addition, it has looked at forces and trends in organizational design. Two cautionary notes are important for the student of organizational behavior. First, an organizational structure may be weak or deficient. In general, if the structure is out of alignment with its contextual variables, one or more of the following four symptoms appears. First, decision making is delayed because the hierarchy is overloaded and too much information is being funneled through one or two channels. Second, decision making lacks quality, because information linkages are not providing the correct information to the right person in the right format. Third, the organization does not respond innovatively to a changing environment, especially when coordinated effort is lacking across departments. Fourth, a great deal of conflict is evident when departments are working against one another rather than working for the strategies and goals of the organization as a whole; the structure is often at fault.

The second caution is that the personality of the chief executive may adversely affect the structure of the organization.[48] Managers' personal, cognitive biases and political ideologies affect their good judgment and decision making.[49] Five dysfunctional combinations of personality and organization have been identified: the paranoid, the depressive, the dramatic, the compulsive,

7. *Identify two cautions about the effect of organizational structures on people.*

and the schizoid.[50] Each of these personality–organization constellations can create problems for the people who work in the organization. For example, in a paranoid constellation, people are suspicious of each other, and distrust in working relationships may interfere with effective communication and task accomplishment. For another example, in a depressive constellation, people feel depressed and inhibited in their work activities, which can lead to low levels of productivity and task accomplishment.

MANAGERIAL IMPLICATIONS: FITTING PEOPLE AND STRUCTURES TOGETHER

Organizations are complex social systems composed of numerous interrelated components. They can be complicated to understand. Managers who design, develop, and improve organizations must have a mastery of the basic concepts related to the anatomy and processes of organizational functioning. It is essential for executives at the top to have a clear concept of how the organization can be differentiated and then integrated into a cohesive whole.

People can work better in organizations if they understand how their jobs and departments relate to other jobs and teams in the organization. An understanding of the whole organization enables people to better relate their contribution to the overall mission of the organization and to compensate for structural deficiencies that may exist in the organization.

Different structural configurations place unique demands on the people who work within them. The diversity of people in work organizations suggests that some people are better suited for a simple structure, others are better suited to a professional bureaucracy, and still others are most productive in an adhocracy. Organizational structures are not independent of the people who work within them. This is especially true for organizations operating in a global work environment.

Managers must pay attention to the technology of the organization's work, the amount of change occurring in the organization's environment, and the regulatory pressures created by governmental agencies as the managers design effective organizations and subunits to meet emerging international demands and a diverse, multicultural workforce.

YOU BE THE JUDGE

Suppose an employee complains about organizational design problems and suggests a solution. The organization is redesigned accordingly, but that employee's department is eliminated. Is it ethical for the company to terminate the employee? Should the company always make room for a person who has a beneficial idea for the organization?

KEY TERMS

adhocracy	formalization	organizational structure
centralization	hierarchy of authority	professional bureaucracy
complexity	integration	simple structure
contextual variables	machine bureaucracy	specialization
differentiation	mechanistic structure	standardization
divisionalized form	organic structure	task environment
environment	organizational design	technological interdependence
environmental uncertainty	organizational life cycle	

Experiential Exercise

WORDS-IN-SENTENCES COMPANY

Purpose: To design an organization for a particular task and carry through to production; to compare design elements with effectiveness.

Group Size: Any number of groups of six to fourteen persons.

Time Required: Fifty to ninety minutes.

Related Topics: Dynamics within groups, work motivation.

Background

You are a small company that manufactures words and then packages them in meaningful English-language sentences. Market research has established that sentences of at least three words but not more than six words are in demand. Therefore, packaging, distribution, and sales should be set up for three- to six-word sentences.

The "words-in-sentences" (WIS) industry is highly competitive; several new firms have recently entered what appears to be an expanding market. Since raw materials, technology, and pricing are all standard for the industry, your ability to compete depends on two factors: (1) volume and (2) quality.

Your Task

Your group must design and participate in running a WIS company. You should design your organization to be as efficient as possible during each ten-minute production run. After the first production run, you will have an opportunity to reorganize your company if you want.

Raw Materials

For each production you will be given a "raw material word or phrase." The letters found in the word or phrase serve as raw materials available to produce new words in sentences. For example, if the raw material word is "organization," you could produce the words and sentence: "Nat ran to a zoo."

Production Standards

Several rules must be followed in producing "words-in-sentences." If these rules are not followed, your output will not meet production specifications and will not pass quality-control inspection.

1. The same letter may appear only as often in a manufactured word as it appears in the raw material word or phrase; for example, "organization" has two o's. Thus, "zoo" is legitimate, but not "zoonosis." It has too many o's and s's.

2. Raw material letters can be used again in different manufactured words.

3. A manufactured word may be used only once in a sentence and in only one sentence during a production run; if a word—for example, "a"—is used once in a sentence, it is out of stock.

4. A new word may not be made by adding "s" to form the plural of an already manufactured word.

5. A word is defined by its spelling, not its meaning.

6. Nonsense words or nonsense sentences are unacceptable.

7. All words must be in the English language.

8. Names and places are acceptable.

9. Slang is not acceptable.

Measuring Performance

The output of your WIS company is measured by the total number of acceptable words that are packaged in sentences. The sentences must be legible, listed on no more than two sheets of paper, and handed to the Quality Control Review Board at the completion of each production run.

Delivery

Delivery must be made to the Quality Control Review Board thirty seconds after the end of each production run, or else all points are lost.

Quality Control

If any word in a sentence does not meet the standards set forth above, all the words in the sentence will be rejected. The Quality Control Review Board (composed of one member from each company) is the final arbiter of acceptability. In the event of a tie on the Review Board, a coin toss will determine the outcome.

Exercise Schedule	Unit Time	Total Time
1. **Form groups, organizations, and assign workplaces** Groups should have between six and fourteen members (if there are more than eleven or twelve persons in a group, assign one or two observers). Each group is a company.	2–5 min.	2–5 min.
2. **Read "Background"** Ask the instructor about any points that need clarification.	5 min.	10 min.
3. **Design organizations** Design your organizations using as many members as you see fit to produce your "words-in-sentences." You may want to consider the following. a. What is your objective? b. What technology would work here? c. What type of division of labor is effective? Assign one member of your group to serve on the Quality Review Board. This person may also take part in production runs.	7–15 min.	14–25 min.
4. **Production Run #1** The instructor will hand each WIS company a sheet with a raw material word or phrase. When the instructor announces "Begin production," you are to manufacture as many words as possible and package them in sentences for delivery to the Quality Control Review Board. You will have ten minutes. When the instructor announces "Stop production," you will have thirty seconds to deliver your output to the Quality Control Review Board. Output received after thirty seconds does not meet the delivery schedule and will not be counted.	7–10 min.	21–35 min.
5. **Quality Review Board meets, evaluates output** While that is going on, groups discuss what happened during the previous production run.	5–10 min.	26–45 min.
6. **Companies evaluate performance and type of organization** Groups may choose to restructure and reorganize for the next production run.	5–10 min	31–55 min
7. **Production Run #2 (same as Production Run #1)**	7–10 min.	38–65 min.
8. **Quality Review Board meets** Quality Review Board evaluates output while groups draw their organization charts (for Runs #1 and #2) on the board.	5–10 min.	43–75 min.
9. **Class discussion** Instructor leads discussion of exercise as a whole. Discuss the following questions: a. What were the companies' scores for Runs #1 and #2? b. What type of structure did the "winning" company have? Did it reorganize for Run #2? c. What type of task was there? Technology? Environment? d. What would Joan Woodward, Henry Mintzberg, Frederick Taylor, Lawrence and Lorsch, or Burns and Stalker say about WIS company organization?	7–15 min.	50–90 min.

Source: "Words-in-Sentences Company" in Dorothy Marcic, *Organizational Behavior: Experiences and Cases*, 4th ed. (St. Paul: West, 1995), 303–305. Reprinted by permission.

15

Organizational Culture

LEARNING OBJECTIVES

After reading this chapter, you should be able to do the following:

1. Define *organizational culture* and explain its three levels.

2. Identify the four functions of culture within an organization.

3. Explain the relationship between organizational culture and performance.

4. Contrast the characteristics of adaptive and nonadaptive cultures.

5. Describe five ways leaders reinforce organizational culture.

6. Describe the three stages of organizational socialization and the ways culture is communicated in each step.

7. Identify ways of assessing organizational culture.

8. Explain actions managers can take to change organizational culture.

THE KEY ROLE OF ORGANIZATIONAL CULTURE

1. *Define organizational culture and explain its three levels.*

The concept of organizational culture has its roots in cultural anthropology. Just as there are cultures in larger human society, there seem to be cultures within organizations. These cultures are similar to societal cultures. They are shared, communicated through symbols, and passed down from generation to generation of employees.

The concept of cultures in organizations was alluded to as early as the Hawthorne studies, which described work group culture. The topic came into its own during the early 1970s, when managers and researchers alike began to search for keys to survival for organizations in a competitive and turbulent environment. Then, in the early 1980s, several books on corporate culture were published, including Deal and Kennedy's *Corporate Cultures,*[1] Ouchi's *Theory Z,*[2] and Peters and Waterman's *In Search of Excellence.*[3] These books found wide audiences, and research began in earnest on the elusive topic of organizational cultures. Executives indicated that these cultures were real and could be managed.[4]

CULTURE AND ITS LEVELS

Many definitions of *organizational culture* have been proposed. Most of them agree that there are several levels of culture and that these levels differ in terms of their visibility and their ability to be changed. The definition adopted in this chapter is that **organizational (corporate) culture** is a pattern of basic assumptions that are considered valid and that are taught to new members as the way to perceive, think, and feel in the organization.[5]

Edgar Schein, in his comprehensive book on organizational culture and leadership, suggests that organizational culture has three levels. His view of culture is presented in Figure 15-1. The levels range from visible artifacts and creations to testable values to invisible and even preconscious basic assumptions. To achieve a complete understanding of an organization's culture, all three levels must be studied.

ARTIFACTS

Symbols of culture in the physical and social work environment are called **artifacts**. They are the most visible and accessible level of culture. The key to understanding culture through artifacts lies in figuring out what they mean. Artifacts are also the most frequently studied manifestation of organizational culture, perhaps because of their accessibility. Among the artifacts of culture are personal enactment, ceremonies and rites, stories, rituals, and symbols.[6]

Personal Enactment Culture can be understood, in part, through an examination of the behavior of organization members. Personal enactment is behavior that reflects the organization's values. In particular, personal enactment by the top managers provides insight into these values. If, for example, customer service is highly valued, then the CEO may be seen going

---

ORGANIZATIONAL (CORPORATE) CULTURE
A pattern of basic assumptions that are considered valid and that are taught to new members as the way to perceive, think, and feel in the organization.

ARTIFACTS
Symbols of culture in the physical and social work environment.

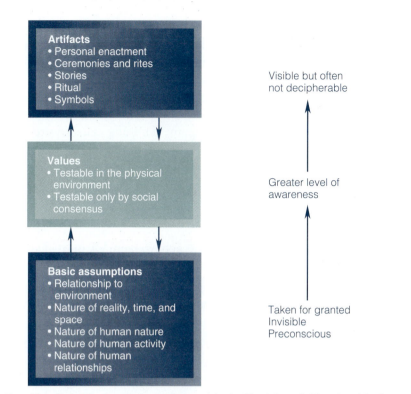

Visible but often not decipherable

Greater level of awareness

Taken for granted
Invisible
Preconscious

Figure 15-1
Levels of Organizational Culture

Source: From Edgar H. Schein, *Organizational Culture and Leadership: A Dynamic View.* Copyright © 1985 Jossey-Bass, Inc. This material is used by permission of John Wiley & Sons, Inc.

the extra mile for the customer, as did the late Sam Walton of Wal-Mart. He reinforced quality service by visiting stores often and recognizing individual employees. The CEO transmits values to others in the organization through modeling appropriate behavior.

Steve Irby is the founder and CEO of Stillwater Designs, the company that created Kicker audio speakers. He values good relationships and believes that people are the most important part of his company. Irby builds trust with his employees by sharing the financial results of the business each month. The employees know that if monthly sales are higher than the sales in the same month of the previous year, Irby will hold a cookout for the employees on the following Friday. Irby and the general manager always do the cooking. Another entrepreneur, David Neeleman, who founded JetBlue Airways, enacts customer service values by playing flight attendant occasionally.

Modeled behavior is a powerful learning tool for employees, as Bandura's social learning theory demonstrated.[7] As we saw in Chapter 5, individuals learn vicariously by observing others' behavior and patterning their own behavior similarly. The values reflected in that behavior can permeate the entire employee population.

Ceremonies and Rites Relatively elaborate sets of activities that are enacted time and again on important occasions are known as organizational ceremonies and rites.[8] These occasions provide opportunities to reward and recognize employees whose behavior is congruent with the values of the company. Ceremonies and rites send a message that individuals who both espouse and exhibit corporate values are heroes to be admired.

The ceremonies also bond organization members together. Southwestern Bell (now part of SBC Communications) emphasized the importance of management training to the company. Training classes were kicked off by a high-ranking executive (a rite of renewal), and completion of the classes was signaled by a graduation ceremony (a rite of passage). Six kinds of rites in organizations have been identified[9]:

1. *Rites of passage* show that an individual's status has changed. Retirement dinners are an example.

2. *Rites of enhancement* reinforce the achievement of individuals. An example is the awarding of certificates to sales contest winners.

3. *Rites of renewal* emphasize change in the organization and commitment to learning and growth. An example is the opening of a new corporate training center.

4. *Rites of integration* unite diverse groups or teams within the organization and renew commitment to the larger organization. Company functions such as annual picnics fall into this category.

5. *Rites of conflict reduction* focus on dealing with conflicts or disagreements that arise naturally in organizations. Examples are grievance hearings and the negotiation of union contracts.

6. *Rites of degradation* are used by some organizations to visibly punish persons who fail to adhere to values and norms of behavior. Some CEOs, for example, are replaced quite publicly for unethical conduct or for failure to achieve organizational goals. In some Japanese organizations, employees who perform poorly are given ribbons of shame as punishment.

Wal-Mart's annual meeting is an important cultural ceremony. Almost 20,000 shareholders, associates (the company's preferred term for employees), and analysts attend the Wal-Mart annual meeting. Celebrities such as Nolan Ryan, Trisha Yearwood, and Amy Grant are featured. Although the meeting doesn't begin until 10 A.M., people start arriving at 7 A.M. for the extravaganza held for the benefit of the associates. Because it is the primary vehicle for perpetuating Wal-Mart's culture, videos of the meeting are played in Wal-Mart stores to motivate associates who are unable to attend.

The annual meeting is like a big family reunion. Patriotism is a common theme. The associates hear stories and watch videos about Wal-Mart's "Buy American" program, which has rescued jobs in small towns and created new ones. Associates who go the "extra mile" for customers are recognized and rewarded. One associate delivered a Sega Genesis on his own time on Christmas Eve, and another group of employees replaced presents for a family whose home was burglarized. Each example points to the generosity and compassion of Wal-Mart associates.[10]

Stories Some researchers have argued that the most effective way to reinforce organizational values is through stories.[11] As they are told and retold, stories give meaning and identity to organizations and are especially helpful in orienting new employees. Part of the strength of organizational stories is that the listeners are left to draw their own conclusions—a powerful communication tool.[12]

Sometimes stories are about organizational heroes and their quests. Jack Stack was sent to Springfield Remanufacturing because its owner, International Harvester, wanted to close the plant. When Stack got there, he found that the problem was the plant's existing management. He found motivated and willing workers, and instead of closing the plant, turned it around and then purchased the plant.[13]

Research by Joanne Martin and her colleagues has indicated that certain themes appear in stories across different types of organizations[14]:

1. *Stories about the boss.* These stories may reflect whether the boss is "human" or how the boss reacts to mistakes.

2. *Stories about getting fired.* Events leading to employee firings are recounted.

3. *Stories about how the company deals with employees who have to relocate.* These stories relate to the company's actions toward employees who have to move—whether the company is helpful and takes family and other personal concerns into account.

4. *Stories about whether lower-level employees can rise to the top.* Often, these stories describe a person who started out at the bottom and eventually became the CEO.

5. *Stories about how the company deals with crisis situations.* The example of the client crisis at IBM shows how the company overcomes obstacles.

6. *Stories about how status considerations work when rules are broken.* When Tom Watson, Sr., was CEO of IBM, he was once confronted by a security guard because he was not wearing an ID badge.

These are the themes that can emerge when stories are passed down. The information from these stories serves to guide the behavior of organization members.

To be effective cultural tools, stories must be credible. You can't tell a story about your flat corporate hierarchy and then have reserved parking spaces for managers. Stories that aren't backed by reality can lead to cynicism and mistrust.

Effective stories, however, can reinforce culture and create renewed energy. Lucasfilm is the home of director and producer George Lucas and the birthplace of such blockbusters as *Star Wars* and *Forrest Gump*. Stories of the company's legendary accomplishments are used to reinforce the creative culture and to rally the troops. When Gail Currey, former head of the company's digital division, found her 300 designers were grumbling, she reminded them of how they did *Gump* when everyone else said it was impossible and what a hit the film was. The geniuses would then head back to their computers to add to the company's success.[15]

Rituals   Everyday organizational practices that are repeated over and over are rituals. They are usually unwritten, but they send a clear message about "the way we do things around here." While some companies insist that people address each other by their titles (Mr., Mrs., Ms., Miss) and surnames to reinforce a professional image, others prefer that employees operate on a first-name basis—from the top manager on down. Hewlett-Packard values open communication, so its employees address one another by first names only.

The Charles Machine Works, producer of Ditch Witch underground excavation equipment, values informality, teamwork, and a flat organizational structure. One ritual practiced in the company is that workers are referred to as employees or team members, not subordinates. The idea is that implying that one person is lower than others is in opposition to the value placed on teamwork.

As everyday practices, rituals reinforce the organizational culture. Insiders who commonly practice the rituals may be unaware of their subtle influence, but outsiders recognize it easily.

Symbols   Symbols communicate organizational culture by unspoken messages. Southwest Airlines has used symbols in several ways. During its early years, the airline emphasized its customer service value by using the heart symbol (the "Love" airline) and love bites (peanuts). More recently, the airline has taken on the theme of fun. Flight attendants wear casual sports clothes in corporate colors. Low fares are "fun fares," and weekend getaways are "fun packs." Some aircraft are painted to resemble Shamu the whale, underscoring the fun image.

Symbols are representative of organizational identity and membership to employees. Nike's trademark "swoosh" is proudly tattooed above the ankles of some Nike employees. Apple Computer employees readily identify themselves as "Apple People." Symbols are used to build solidarity in the organizational culture.[16]

Symbols may be only mental images. At Southwestern Bell, company loyalty was valued. Longtime company employees were referred to as "bleeding blue and gold" (company colors).

Personal enactment, rites and ceremonies, stories, rituals, and symbols serve to reinforce the values that are the next level of culture.

VALUES

ESPOUSED VALUES
What members of an organization say they value.

Values are the second, and deeper, level of culture. They reflect a person's underlying beliefs of what should be or should not be. Values are often consciously articulated, both in conversation and in a company's mission statement or annual report. However, there may be a difference between a company's *espoused values* (what the members say they value) and its *enacted values* (values reflected in the way the members actually be-have).[17] Values also may be reflected in the behavior of individuals, which is an artifact of culture.

ENACTED VALUES
Values reflected in the way individuals actually behave.

Unwanted sexual behavior is a problem in some companies. It is not often a problem, however, for companies that value equal treatment of women and men at work. This value guides individuals' behavior.[18]

Values underlie the adaptable and innovative culture at Levi Strauss. As guides for behavior, they are reinforced in the aspirations statement and in the reward system of the organization. Workforce diversity is valued at Levi Strauss. A former strong supporter of the Boy Scouts of America, the company discontinued its funding after the Scouts were shown to dis-criminate on the basis of sexual orientation. Mary Gross, a Levi Strauss spokesperson, expressed the company's position on valuing diversity: "One of the family values of this company is treating people who are different from you the same as you'd like to be treated. Tolerance is a pretty impor-tant family value."[19]

Some organizational cultures are characterized by values that support healthy lifestyle behaviors. When the workplace culture values worker health and psychological needs, there is enhanced potential for high per-formance and improved well-being.[20] One such culture is that of Clif Bar, Inc., a maker of energy bars. Clif Bar's culture may represent the extreme in terms of promoting fitness. It attracts and hires individuals who are sports enthusiasts, and provides them with a culture that shares those values. There is a twenty-two-foot rock climbing wall in the office, along with a corpo-rate gym.

YOU BE THE JUDGE

Is it ethical to influence an indi-vidual's values through the orga-nizational culture? If culture shapes behavior, is managing cul-ture a manipulative tactic? Explain.

ASSUMPTIONS

Assumptions are the deeply held beliefs that guide behavior and tell members of an organization how to perceive and think about things. As the deepest and most fundamental level of an organization's culture, according to Edgar Schein, they are the essence of culture. They are so strongly held that a member behaving in any fashion that would vio-late them would be unthinkable. Another characteristic of assumptions is that they are often unconscious. Organization members may not be aware of their assumptions and may be reluctant or unable to discuss them or change them.

ASSUMPTIONS
Deeply held beliefs that guide behavior and tell members of an organization how to perceive and think about things.

TXI Chaparral Steel is a small steel manufacturer that outperforms all other domestic and foreign steel companies in amount of steel produced per person. Located in Midlothian, Texas, the company has fewer than 1,300 employees. Its success is due, in large part, to its assumptions about people. Chaparral Steel's values reflect three basic assumptions: (1) that people are basically good, which is reflected in the company's emphasis on trust; (2) that people want opportunities to learn and grow, which is seen in the value placed on education and training; and (3) that people are motivated by op-portunities to learn and by work that is challenging and enjoyable, which is reflected in Chaparral's goal-setting program.

FUNCTIONS AND EFFECTS OF ORGANIZATIONAL CULTURE

2. *Identify the four functions of culture within an organization.*

In an organization, culture serves four basic functions. First, culture provides a sense of identity to members and increases their commitment to the organization.[21] When employees internalize the values of the company, they find their work intrinsically rewarding and identify with their fellow workers. Motivation is enhanced, and employees are more committed.[22]

Second, culture is a sense-making device for organization members. It provides a way for employees to interpret the meaning of organizational events.[23]

Third, culture reinforces the values in the organization. The culture at SSM Health Care emphasizes patient care and continuous improvement. The St. Louis-based company, which owns and manages 21 acute care hospitals in four states, values compassionate, holistic, high-quality care. SSM was the first health care organization ever to win the Baldrige Quality Award.[24]

Finally, culture serves as a control mechanism for shaping behavior. Norms that guide behavior are part of culture. At Westinghouse, employee suggestions increased fivefold following the emphasis on total quality. It became a norm to think of ways to improve processes at the division.

The effects of organizational culture are hotly debated by organizational behaviorists and researchers. It seems that managers attest strongly to the positive effects of culture in organizations, but it is difficult to quantify these effects. John Kotter and James Heskett have reviewed three theories about the relationship between organizational culture and performance and the evidence that either supports or refutes these theories.[25] The three are the strong culture perspective, the fit perspective, and the adaptation perspective.

THE STRONG CULTURE PERSPECTIVE

STRONG CULTURE
An organizational culture with a consensus on the values that drive the company and with an intensity that is recognizable even to outsiders.

The strong culture perspective states that organizations with "strong" cultures perform better than other organizations.[26] A *strong culture* is an organizational culture with a consensus on the values that drive the company and with an intensity that is recognizable even to outsiders. Thus, a strong culture is deeply held and widely shared. It also is highly resistant to change. One example of a strong culture is IBM's. Its culture is one we are all familiar with: conservative, with a loyal workforce and an emphasis on customer service.

3. *Explain the relationship between organizational culture and performance.*

Strong cultures are thought to facilitate performance for three reasons. First, these cultures are characterized by goal alignment; that is, all employees share common goals. Second, strong cultures create a high level of motivation because of the values shared by the members. Third, strong cultures provide control without the oppressive effects of a bureaucracy.

To test the strong culture hypothesis, Kotter and Heskett selected 207 firms from a wide variety of industries. They used a questionnaire to calculate a culture strength index for each firm, and they correlated that index with the firm's economic performance over a twelve-year period. They concluded that strong cultures were associated with positive long-term economic performance, but only modestly.

There are also two perplexing questions about the strong culture perspectives. First, what can be said about evidence showing that strong economic performance can create strong cultures, rather than the reverse? Second, what if the strong culture leads the firm down the wrong path? Sears, for example, is an organization with a strong culture, but in the 1980s, it focused inward, ignoring competition and consumer preferences and damaging its performance. Changing Sears' strong but stodgy culture has been a tough task, with financial performance only recently showing an upward trend.[27]

THE FIT PERSPECTIVE

The "fit" perspective argues that a culture is good only if it fits the industry or the firm's strategy. For example, a culture that values a traditional hierarchical structure and stability would not work well in the computer manufacturing industry, which demands fast response and a lean, flat organization. Three particular characteristics of an industry may affect culture: the competitive environment, customer requirements, and societal expectations.[28] In the computer industry, firms face a highly competitive environment, customers who require highly reliable products, and a society that expects state-of-the-art technology and high-quality service.

Sometimes there is a wide range of cultures within the same industry, with big differences in performance.[29] Nokia, the Finnish maker of wireless phones, has a young, sophisticated, hip culture, and it controls 56 percent of the market. Ericsson's culture is austere and conservative, more like a middle-aged Swedish engineer, and it has 5 percent of the market.[30, 31] Both companies are tying their future success to the mobile Internet market, but the fit perspective would predict that the more agile Nokia will perform better in the future.

A study of twelve large U.S. firms indicated that cultures consistent with industry conditions help managers make better decisions. It also indicated that cultures need not change as long as the industry doesn't change. If the industry does change, however, many cultures change too slowly to avoid negative effects on firms' performance.[32]

The fit perspective is useful in explaining short-term performance but not long-term performance. It also indicates that it is difficult to change culture quickly, especially if the culture is widely shared and deeply held. But it doesn't explain how firms can adapt to environmental change.

THE ADAPTATION PERSPECTIVE

The third theory about culture and performance is the adaptation perspective. Its theme is that only cultures that help organizations adapt to environmental change are associated with excellent performance. An

ADAPTIVE CULTURE
An organizational culture that encourages confidence and risk taking among employees, has leadership that produces change, and focuses on the changing needs of customers.

4. *Contrast the characteristics of adaptive and nonadaptive cultures.*

adaptive culture is a culture that encourages confidence and risk taking among employees,[33] has leadership that produces change,[34] and focuses on the changing needs of customers.[35] 3M is a company with an adaptive culture, in that it encourages new product ideas from all levels within the company.

To test the adaptation perspective, Kotter and Heskett interviewed industry analysts about the cultures of twenty-two firms. The contrast between adaptive cultures and nonadaptive cultures was striking. The results of the study are summarized in Table 15-1.

Adaptive cultures facilitate change to meet the needs of three groups of constituents: stockholders, customers, and employees. Nonadaptive cultures are characterized by cautious management that tries to protect its own interests. Adaptive firms showed significantly better long-term economic performance in Kotter and Heskett's study. One contrast that can be made is between Hewlett-Packard (HP), a high performer, and Xerox, a lower performer. The industry analysts viewed HP as valuing excellent leadership more than Xerox did and as valuing all three key constituencies more than Xerox did. Economic performance from 1977 through 1988 suported this difference: HP's index of annual net income growth was 40.2, as compared to Xerox's 13.1. Kotter and Heskett concluded that the cultures that promote long-term performance are those that are most adaptive.

Given that high-performing cultures are adaptive ones, it is important to know how managers can develop adaptive cultures. In the next section, we will examine the leader's role in managing organizational culture.

Table 15-1
Adaptive versus Nonadaptive Organizational Cultures

	Adaptive Organizational Cultures	Nonadaptive Organizational Cultures
Core values	Most managers care deeply about customers, stockholders, and employees. They also strongly value people and processes that can create useful change (e.g., leadership up and down the management hierarchy).	Most managers care mainly about themselves, their immediate work group, or some product (or technology) associated with that work group. They value the orderly and risk-reducing management process much more highly than leadership initiatives.
Common behavior	Managers pay close attention to all their constituencies, especially customers, and initiate change when needed to serve their legitimate interests, even if that entails taking some risks.	Managers tend to behave somewhat insularly, politically, and bureaucratically. As a result, they do not change their strategies quickly to adjust to or take advantage of changes in their business environments.

THE LEADER'S ROLE IN SHAPING AND REINFORCING CULTURE

According to Edgar Schein, leaders play crucial roles in shaping and reinforcing culture.[36] The five most important elements in managing culture are (1) what leaders pay attention to; (2) how leaders react to crises; (3) how leaders behave; (4) how leaders allocate rewards; and (5) how leaders hire and fire individuals.

5. *Describe five ways leaders reinforce organizational culture.*

WHAT LEADERS PAY ATTENTION TO

Leaders in an organization communicate their priorities, values, and beliefs through the themes that consistently emerge from what they focus on. These themes are reflected in what they notice, comment on, measure, and control. The late Ray Kroc, founder of McDonald's, paid attention to detail. He built the company on the basis of a vision of providing identical, high-quality hamburgers at low cost.[37] Through careful training, quality control, and even special measuring cups, he honed his company's expertise so that the Big Mac in Miami would be the same as the Big Mac in Moscow.

If leaders are consistent in what they pay attention to, measure, and control, employees receive clear signals about what is important in the organization. If, however, leaders are inconsistent, employees spend a lot of time trying to decipher and find meaning in the inconsistent signals.

HOW LEADERS REACT TO CRISES

The way leaders deal with crises communicates a powerful message about culture. Emotions are heightened during a crisis, and learning is intense. Salomon Brothers' history is marked as "before crisis" and "after crisis" following its bond trading scandal. When Warren Buffett took over as acting CEO, he immediately began to craft a more ethical culture. He sent a memo making ethical behavior the top priority and demanding that executives report instantaneously, directly to him, any legal violations or moral failures of any Salomon employee. Buffett sent letters of apology to Salomon's customers promising to do future business with honesty and candor. He provided full disclosure of the company's wrongdoing rather than covering it up. His management of the crisis showed that ethical misconduct would not be tolerated or hidden from the authorities, and his actions helped Salomon earn back its integrity.[38]

Difficult economic times present crises for many companies and illustrate their different values. Some organizations do everything possible to prevent laying off workers. Others may claim that employees are important but quickly institute major layoffs at the first signal of an economic downturn. Employees may perceive that the company shows its true colors in a crisis and thus may pay careful attention to the reactions of their leaders.

HOW LEADERS BEHAVE

Through role modeling, teaching, and coaching, leaders reinforce the values that support the organizational culture. Employees often emulate leaders' behavior and look to the leaders for cues to appropriate behavior. Many companies are encouraging employees to be more entrepreneurial—to take more initiative and be more innovative in their jobs. A study showed that if managers want employees to be more entrepreneurial, they must demonstrate such behaviors themselves.[39] This is the case with any cultural value. Employees observe the behavior of leaders to find out what the organization values.

How Leaders Allocate Rewards

To ensure that values are accepted, leaders should reward behavior that is consistent with the values. Some companies, for example, may claim that they use a pay-for-performance system that distributes rewards on the basis of performance. When the time comes for raises, however, the increases are awarded according to length of service with the company. Imagine the feelings of a high-performing newcomer who has heard leaders espouse the value of rewarding individual performance and then receives only a tiny raise.

Some companies may value teamwork. They form cross-functional teams and empower these teams to make important decisions. However, when performance is appraised, the criteria for rating employees focus on individual performance. This sends a confusing signal to employees about the company's culture: Is individual performance valued, or is teamwork the key?

How Leaders Hire and Fire Individuals

A powerful way that leaders reinforce culture is through the selection of newcomers to the organization. Leaders often unconsciously look for individuals who are similar to current organizational members in terms of values and assumptions. Some companies hire individuals on the recommendation of a current employee; this tends to perpetuate the culture because the new employees typically hold similar values. Promotion-from-within policies also serve to reinforce organizational culture.

The way a company fires an employee and the rationale behind the firing also communicate the culture. Some companies deal with poor performers by trying to find a place within the organization where they can perform better and make a contribution. Other companies seem to operate under the philosophy that those who cannot perform are out quickly.

The reasons for terminations may not be directly communicated to other employees, but curiosity leads to speculation. An employee who displays unethical behavior and is caught may simply be reprimanded even though such behavior is clearly against the organization's values. Other employees may view this as a failure to reinforce the values within the organization.

One executive who has won awards for his leadership is Hatim Tyabji, founder and CEO of Bytemobile. He has a history of founding successful businesses, such as VeriFone and Saraide. As Saraide's CEO, Tyabji created and reinforced a values-based culture and reinforces it daily. One of his darkest hours occurred when the company's values were severely challenged. One year, in mid-August, it looked like Saraide's numbers for the quarter were going to be pleasing to Wall Street. One particular unit was over-achieving. But Tyabji was informed by his HR manager that the head of that overproducing unit was engaged in malfeasance—getting orders in ways that were totally unethical. Some managers suggested that he wait to deal with the problem until after the numbers were reported for the quarter. Tyabji felt he had to do something; he got on a plane to confront the in-dividual. The individual said, ". . . I'll help you bring home the quarter." Tyabji said, "I cannot let you stay—not one day, not one minute."[40] Exec-utive commitment to ethical behavior is an important way of sustaining an ethical organizational culture.[41]

ORGANIZATIONAL SOCIALIZATION

We have seen that leaders play key roles in shaping an organization's culture. Another process that perpetuates culture is the way it is handed down from generation to generation of employees. Newcomers learn the culture through *organizational socialization*—the process by which new-comers are transformed from outsiders to participating, effective members of the organization.[42] The process is also a vehicle for bringing newcomers into the organizational culture. As we saw earlier, cultural socialization be-gins with the careful selection of newcomers who are likely to reinforce the organizational culture.[43] Once selected, newcomers pass through the so-cialization process.

THE STAGES OF THE SOCIALIZATION PROCESS

The organizational socialization process is generally described as having three stages: anticipatory socialization, encounter, and change and acquisi-tion. Figure 15-2 (on page 374) presents a model of the process and the key concerns at each stage of it.[44] It also describes the outcomes of the process, which will be discussed in the next section of the chapter.

Anticipatory Socialization *Anticipatory socialization*, the first stage, en-compasses all of the learning that takes place prior to the newcomer's first day on the job. It includes the newcomer's expectations. The two key con-cerns at this stage are realism and congruence.

Realism is the degree to which a newcomer holds realistic expectations about the job and about the organization. One thing newcomers should re-ceive information about during entry into the organization is the culture. Information about values at this stage can help newcomers begin to con-struct a scheme for interpreting their organizational experiences. A deeper understanding of the organization's culture will be possible through time and experience in the organization.

There are two types of *congruence* between an individual and an orga-nization: congruence between the individual's abilities and the demands of the job, and the fit between the organization's values and the individual's values. Organizations disseminate information about their values through

6. *Describe the three stages of organizational socialization and the ways culture is communicated in each step.*

ORGANIZATIONAL SOCIALIZATION
The process by which newcomers are transformed from outsiders to participating, effective members of the organization.

ANTICIPATORY SOCIALIZATION
The first socialization stage, which encompasses all of the learning that takes place prior to the newcomer's first day on the job.

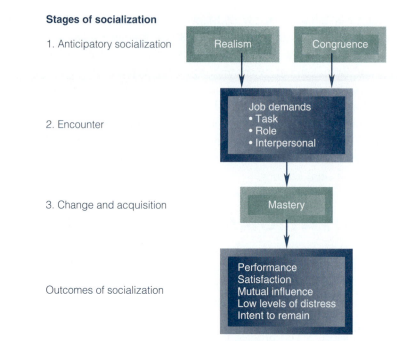

Stages of socialization

1. Anticipatory socialization — Realism | Congruence

2. Encounter — Job demands
• Task
• Role
• Interpersonal

3. Change and acquisition — Mastery

Outcomes of socialization — Performance
Satisfaction
Mutual influence
Low levels of distress
Intent to remain

Figure 15-2

The Organizational Socialization Process: Stages and Outcomes

Source: From "An Ethical Weather Report: Assessing the Organization's Ethical Climate" by John B. Cullen, et al. in "Organizational Dynamics," Autumn 1989. Copyright © 1989, with permission from Elsevier.

their Web pages, annual reports, and recruitment brochures.[45] Value congruence is particularly important for organizational culture. It is also important in terms of newcomer adjustment. Newcomers whose values match the company's values are more satisfied with their new jobs, adjust more quickly, and say they intend to remain with the firm longer.[46]

One of the concerns for both the individual and the organization is whether or not there is a good fit. Some companies use extensive testing of job candidates to improve person–organization fit.

Encounter The second stage of socialization, **encounter**, is when newcomers learn the tasks associated with the job, clarify their roles, and establish new relationships at work. This stage commences on the first day at work and is thought to encompass the first six to nine months on the new job. Newcomers face task demands, role demands, and interpersonal demands during this period.

Task demands involve the actual work performed. Learning to perform tasks is related to the organization's culture. In some organizations, newcomers are given considerable latitude to experiment with new ways to do the job, and creativity is valued. In others, newcomers are expected to learn the established procedures for their tasks. Newcomers may also need guidance from the culture about work hours. Is a value placed on putting in long hours, or is leaving work at 5 P.M. to spend time with family more the norm?

Role demands involve the expectations placed on newcomers. Newcomers may not know exactly what is expected of them (role ambiguity) or

ENCOUNTER
The second socialization stage, in which the newcomer learns the tasks associated with the job, clarifies roles, and establishes new relationships at work.

may receive conflicting expectations from other individuals (role conflict). The way newcomers approach these demands depends in part on the culture of the organization. Are newcomers expected to operate with considerable uncertainty, or is the manager expected to clarify the newcomers' roles? Some cultures even put newcomers through considerable stress in the socialization process, including humility-inducing experiences, so newcomers will be more open to accepting the firm's values and norms. Long hours, tiring travel schedules, and an overload of work are part of some socialization practices.

Interpersonal demands arise from relationships at work. Politics, leadership style, and group pressure are interpersonal demands. All of them reflect the values and assumptions that operate within the organization. Most organizations have basic assumptions about the nature of human relationships. The Korean chaebol LG Group strongly values harmony in relationships and in society, and its decision-making policy emphasizes unanimity.

In the encounter stage, the expectations formed in anticipatory socialization may clash with the realities of the job. It is a time of facing the task, role, and interpersonal demands of the new job.

Change and Acquisition   In the third and final stage of socialization, **change and acquisition**, newcomers begin to master the demands of the job. They become proficient at managing their tasks, clarifying and negotiating their roles, and engaging in relationships at work. The time when the socialization process is completed varies widely, depending on the individual, the job, and the organization. The end of the process is signaled by newcomers being considered by themselves and others as organizational insiders.

CHANGE AND ACQUISITION
The third socialization stage, in which the newcomer begins to master the demands of the job.

OUTCOMES OF SOCIALIZATION

Newcomers who are successfully socialized should exhibit good performance, high job satisfaction, and the intention to stay with the organization. In addition, they should exhibit low levels of distress symptoms.[47] High levels of organizational commitment are also marks of successful socialization.[48] This commitment is facilitated throughout the socialization process by the communication of values that newcomers can buy into. Successful socialization is also signaled by mutual influence; that is, the newcomers have made adjustments in the job and organization to accommodate their knowledge and personalities. Newcomers are expected to leave their mark on the organization and not be completely conforming.

When socialization is effective, newcomers understand and adopt the organization's values and norms. This ensures that the company's culture, including its central values, survives. It also provides employees a context for interpreting and responding to things that happen at work, and it ensures a shared framework of understanding among employees.[49]

Newcomers adopt the company's norms and values more quickly when they receive positive support from organizational insiders. Sometimes this is accomplished through informal social gatherings.[50]

SOCIALIZATION AS CULTURAL COMMUNICATION

Socialization is a powerful cultural communication tool. While the transmission of information about cultural artifacts is relatively easy, the transmission of values is more difficult. The communication of organizational assumptions is almost impossible, since organization members themselves may not be consciously aware of them.

The primary purpose of socialization is the transmission of core values to new organization members.[51] Newcomers are exposed to these values through the role models they interact with, the training they receive, and the behavior they observe being rewarded and punished. Newcomers are vigilant observers, seeking clues to the organization's culture and consistency in the cultural messages they receive. If they are expected to adopt these values, it is essential that the message reflect the underlying values of the organization.

One company known for its culture is the Walt Disney Company. Disney transmits its culture to employees though careful selection, socialization, and training. The Disney culture is built around customer service, and its image serves as a filtering process for applicants. Peer interviews are used to learn how applicants interact with each other. Disney tries to secure a good fit between employee values and the organization's culture. To remind employees of the image they are trying to project, employees are referred to as "cast members" and they occupy a "role." They work either "on stage" or "backstage" and wear "costumes," rather than uniforms. Disney operates its own "universities," which are attended by all new employees. Once trained at a Disney university, cast members are paired with role models to continue their learning on-site.

Companies such as Disney use the socialization process to communicate messages about organizational culture. Both individuals and organizations can take certain actions to ensure the success of the socialization process.

ASSESSING ORGANIZATIONAL CULTURE

7. *Identify ways of assessing organizational culture.*

Although some organizational scientists argue for assessing organizational culture with quantitative methods, others say that organizational culture must be assessed with qualitative methods.[52] Quantitative methods, such as questionnaires, are valuable because of their precision, comparability, and objectivity. Qualitative methods, such as interviews and observations, are valuable because of their detail, descriptiveness, and uniqueness.

Two widely used quantitative assessment instruments are the Organizational Culture Inventory (OCI) and the Kilmann-Saxton Culture-Gap Survey. Both assess the behavioral norms of organizational cultures, as opposed to the artifacts, values, or assumptions of the organization.

ORGANIZATIONAL CULTURE INVENTORY

The OCI focuses on behaviors that help employees fit into the organization and meet the expectations of coworkers. Using Maslow's motivational need hierarchy as its basis, it measures twelve cultural styles. The two underlying dimensions of the OCI are task/people and security/satisfaction. There are four satisfaction cultural styles and eight security cultural styles.

A self-report instrument, the OCI contains 120 questions. It provides an individual assessment of culture and may be aggregated to the work group and to the organizational level.[53] It has been used in firms throughout North America, Western Europe, New Zealand, and Thailand, as well as in U.S. military units, the Federal Aviation Administration, and nonprofit organizations.

KILMANN-SAXTON CULTURE-GAP SURVEY

The Kilmann-Saxton Culture-Gap Survey focuses on what actually happens and on the expectations of others in the organization.[54] Its two underlying dimensions are technical/human and time (the short term versus the long term). With these two dimensions, the actual operating norms and the ideal norms in four areas are assessed. The areas are task support (short-term technical norms), task innovation (long-term technical norms), social relationships (short-term human orientation norms), and personal freedom (long-term human orientation norms). Significant gaps in any of the four areas are used as a point of departure for cultural change to improve performance, job satisfaction, and morale.

A self-report instrument, the Gap Survey provides an individual assessment of culture and may be aggregated to the work group. It has been used in firms throughout the United States and in nonprofit organizations.

TRIANGULATION

A study of a rehabilitation center in a 400-bed hospital incorporated *triangulation* (the use of multiple methods to measure organizational culture) to improve inclusiveness and accuracy in measuring the organizational culture.[55] Triangulation has been used by anthropologists, sociologists, and other behavioral scientists to study organizational culture. Its name comes from the navigational technique of using multiple reference points to locate an object. In the rehabilitation center study, the three methods used to triangulate on the culture were (1) obtrusive observations by eight trained observers, which provided an outsider perspective; (2) self-administered questionnaires, which provided quantitative insider information; and (3) personal interviews with the center's staff, which provided qualitative contextual information.

TRIANGULATION
The use of multiple methods to measure organizational culture.

The study showed that each of the three methods made unique contributions toward the discovery of the rehabilitation center's culture. The complete picture could not have been drawn with just a single technique. Triangulation can lead to a better understanding of the phenomenon of culture and is the best approach to assessing organizational culture.

CHANGING ORGANIZATIONAL CULTURE

Changing situations may require changes in the existing culture of an organization. With rapid environmental changes such as globalization, workforce diversity, and technological innovation, the fundamental assumptions and basic values that drive the organization may need to be altered. One particular situation that may require cultural change is a merger or acquisition. The blending of two distinct organizational cultures may prove difficult.

Despite good-faith efforts, combining cultures is difficult, especially if organizational culture differences are supplemented by national culture differences. InFocus, the world leader in multimedia projection products, based in Oregon, merged with Proxima ASA, headquartered in Norway. These two cultures were difficult to align. InFocus was a culture of collaboration and empowerment, whereas Proxima was a more conservative culture, without stock options or profit sharing. InFocus tended to overcommunicate with employees; Proxima communicated selectively. Attempts to impose InFocus ways on Proxima employees met with much resistance. "You're just being an American," was a common refrain.[56]

Alterations in culture may also be required when an organization employs people from different countries. Research indicates that some organizational cultures actually enhance differences in national cultures.[57] One study compared foreign employees working in a multinational organization with employees working in different organizations within their own countries. The assumption was that the employees from various countries working for the same multinational organization would be more similar than employees working in diverse organizations in their native countries. The results were surprising, in that there were significantly greater differences between the employees of the multinational than between managers working for different companies within their native countries. In the multinational, Swedes became more Swedish, Americans became more American, and so forth. It appears that employees enhance their national culture traditions even when working within a single organizational culture.[58] This is more likely to occur when diversity is moderate. When diversity is very high, employees are more likely to develop a shared identity in the organization's culture instead of relying on their own national culture.[59]

8. *Explain actions managers can take to change organizational culture.*

Changing an organization's culture is feasible but difficult.[60] One reason for the difficulty is that assumptions—the deepest level of culture—are often unconscious. As such, they are often nonconfrontable and nondebatable. Another reason for the difficulty is that culture is deeply ingrained and behavioral norms and rewards are well learned.[61] In a sense, employees must unlearn the old norms before they can learn new ones. Managers who want to change the culture should look first to the ways culture is maintained.

A model for cultural change that summarizes the interventions managers can use is presented in Figure 15-3. In this model, the numbers represent the actions managers can take. There are two basic approaches to changing the existing culture: (1) helping current members buy into a new set of values (actions 1, 2, and 3); or (2) adding newcomers and socializing them into the organization, and removing current members as appropriate (actions 4 and 5).[62]

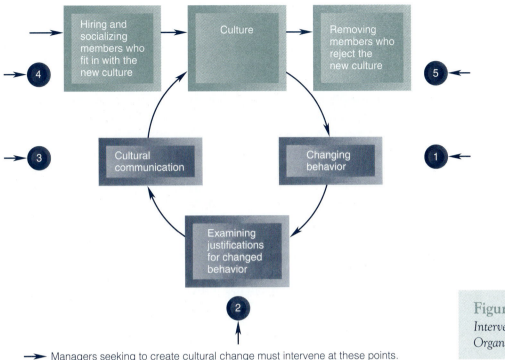

Managers seeking to create cultural change must intervene at these points.

Source: From Vijay Sathe "How to Decipher and Change Corporate Culture," Chap. 13 in *Gaining Control of the Corporate Culture* (R. H. Kilmann et al., eds.) Fig. 1, p. 245. Copyright © 1985 Jossey-Bass, Inc. This material is used by permission of John Wiley & Sons, Inc.

Figure 15-3
Interventions for Changing Organizational Culture

The first action is to change behavior in the organization. Even if behavior does change, however, this change is not sufficient for cultural change to occur. Behavior is an artifact (level 1) of culture. Individuals may change their behavior but not the values that drive it. They may rationalize, "I'm only doing this because my manager wants me to."

Therefore, managers must use action 2, which is to examine the justifications for the changed behavior. Are employees buying into the new set of values, or are they just complying?

The third action, cultural communication, is extremely important. All of the artifacts (personal enactment, stories, rites and ceremonies, rituals, and symbols) must send a consistent message about the new values and beliefs. It is crucial that the communication be credible; that is, managers must live the new values and not just talk about them. The communication must also be persuasive. Individuals may resist cultural change and may have to be persuaded to try the new behavior by someone they respect and can identify with.

The two remaining actions (4 and 5) involve shaping the workforce to fit the intended culture. First, the organization can revise its selection strategies to more accurately reflect the new culture. Second, the organization can identify individuals who resist the cultural change or who are no longer comfortable with the values in the organization. Reshaping the workforce should not involve a ruthless pursuit of nonconforming employees; it should

YOU BE THE JUDGE

One way of changing culture is to remove members who do not change with the culture. How can this be done ethically?

be a gradual and subtle change that takes considerable time. Changing personnel in the organization is a lengthy process; it cannot be done effectively in a short period of time without considerable problems.

Evaluating the success of cultural change may be best done by looking at behavior. Cultural change can be assumed to be successful if the behavior is intrinisically motivated—on "automatic pilot." If the new behavior would persist even if rewards were not present, and if the employees have internalized the new value system, then the behavior is probably intrinisically motivated. If employees automatically respond to a crisis in ways consistent with the corporate culture, then the cultural change effort can be deemed successful.

One organization that has changed its culture is AT&T. In 1984, the courts ordered the breakup of AT&T. Prior to the breakup, the company operated in a stable environment with low levels of uncertainty. The organization was a highly structured bureaucracy. The culture emphasized lifetime employment, promotion from within, and loyalty. AT&T faced minimal competition, and it offered individual security. When the courts ordered AT&T to divest its Bell operating companies, the old culture was no longer effective. The company had to move toward a culture that holds individuals accountable for their performance. Change at AT&T was painful and slow, but it was necessary for the company to be able to operate in the new competitive environment.[63] Changing environments may bring about changes in organizational culture.

Given the current business environment, managers may want to focus on three particular cultural modifications: (1) support for a global view of business, (2) reinforcement of ethical behavior, and (3) empowerment of employees to excel in product and service quality.

DEVELOPING A GLOBAL ORGANIZATIONAL CULTURE

The values that drive the organizational culture should support a global view of the company and its efforts. To do so, the values should be clear to everyone involved so that everyone understands them. The values should also be strongly supported at the top. Management should embody the shared values and reward employees who support the global view. Finally, the values should be consistent over time. Consistent values give an organization a unifying theme that competitors may be unable to emulate.[64]

Global corporations suffer from the conflicting pressures of centralization and decentralization. An overarching corporate culture that integrates the decentralized subsidiaries in locations around the world can be an asset in the increasingly competitive global marketplace.

Following are six specific guidelines for managers who want to create a global culture[65]:

1. Create a clear and simple mission statement. A shared mission can unite individuals from diverse cultural backgrounds.
2. Create systems that ensure an effective flow of information. Coordination councils and global task forces can be used to ensure that informa-

tion flows throughout the geographically dispersed organization are consistent.

3. Create "matrix minds" among managers; that is, broaden managers' minds to allow them to think globally. IBM does this through temporary overseas assignments. Managers with international experience share that experience when they return to the home organization.

4. Develop global career paths. This means ensuring not only that home country executives go overseas but also that executives from other countries rotate into service in the home office.

5. Use cultural differences as a major asset. The former Digital Equipment Corporation (now part of Hewlett-Packard), for example, transferred its research and development functions to Italy to take advantage of the free-flowing Italian management style that encouraged creativity. Its manufacturing operations went to Germany, which offered a more systematic management style.

6. Implement worldwide management education and team development programs. Unified training efforts that emphasize corporate values can help establish a shared identity among employees.

These guidelines are specifically aimed at multinational organizations that want to create a global corporate culture, but other organizations can also benefit from them. Companies that want to broaden employees' views or to use the diversity of their workforce as a resource will find several of these recommendations advantageous.

DEVELOPING AN ETHICAL ORGANIZATIONAL CULTURE

The organizational culture can have profound effects on the ethical behavior of organization members.[66] When a company's culture promotes ethical norms, individuals behave accordingly. Managers can encourage ethical behavior by being good role models for employees. They can institute the philosophy that ethical behavior makes good business sense and puts the company in congruence with the larger values of the society.[67] Managers can also communicate that rationalizations for unethical behavior are not tolerated. For example, some salespersons justify padding their expense accounts because everyone else does it. Declaring these justifications illegitimate sends a clear message about the lack of tolerance for such behavior.

Trust is another key to effectively managing ethical behavior, especially in cultures that encourage whistle-blowing (as we saw in Chapter 2). Employees must trust that whistle-blowers will be protected, that procedures used to investigate ethical problems will be fair, and that management will take action to solve problems that are uncovered.

Cummins, Inc., is proud of its values-driven culture and its emphasis on ethics. One summer, a Cummins engineer received an innocuous looking package in the mail from Illinois. When he opened it, he realized that it contained partial plans for a new engine that was being designed by Cummins's arch rival, Caterpillar. The plans were vital corporate intelligence slipped to the engineer by an obviously disgruntled Caterpillar employee. (At that time, Caterpillar was facing long and difficult strikes by employees.) The engineer reported the package to Cummins's legal department, who rewrapped the package and sent it back to Caterpillar. Three more packages arrived, which were sent back to Illinois. Caterpillar's legal counsel got wind of the event and sent a note of thanks to Cummins. "I find it gratifying," the Caterpillar executive wrote, "when ethical behavior overshadows the temptation for a competitive edge."[68]

The reasons most often cited for unethical corporate conduct are interesting.[69] They include the belief that a behavior is not really unethical, that it is in the organization's best interest, that it will not be discovered, and that the organization will support it because it offers a good outcome for the organization. An ethical corporate culture can eliminate the viability of these excuses by clearly communicating the boundaries of ethical conduct, selecting employees who support the ethical culture, rewarding organization members who exhibit ethical behavior, and conspicuously punishing members who engage in unethical behavior.

Organizations that seek to encourage ethical behavior can do so by using their organizational culture. By completing this chapter's Challenge, you can assess the ethical culture of an organization with which you're familiar.

DEVELOPING A CULTURE OF EMPOWERMENT AND QUALITY

Throughout this book, we have seen that successful organizations promote a culture that empowers employees and excels in product and service quality. Empowerment serves to unleash employees' creativity and productivity. It requires eliminating traditional hierarchical notions of power. Cultures that emphasize empowerment and quality are preferred by employees. Companies that value empowerment and continuous improvement have cultures that promote high product and service quality.[70]

General Motors' Cadillac division experienced a massive cultural change. The company installed state-of-the-art robotics technology at its Hamtramck Assembly Center.[71] The idea was to use tomorrow's technology to build the Cadillac of the future. The plant, intended to be a technology showcase, turned into a technology disaster. Robots went haywire, spray-painting one another, smashing windshields, and destroying cars. Computer systems had bugs that led to body parts being installed on the wrong cars.

The new technology was considered a total failure, and the reason cited for the failure was that "people issues" had not been addressed. The technology was yanked. The plant was redesigned to develop a balance between technology and people. Extensive employee involvement and a teamwork approach to design were used to empower employees throughout the Cadillac division.

Managers decided to incorporate input from assemblers in the product design process.[72] Designers, product development engineers, and assembly workers came together in teams to design the new car models. Once the

Challenge

ORGANIZATIONAL CULTURE AND ETHICS

Think about the organization you currently work for or one you know something about and complete the following Ethical Climate Questionnaire.

Use the scale below and write the number that best represents your answer in the space next to each item.

To what extent are the following statements true about your company?

Completely false	Mostly false	Somewhat false	Somewhat true	Mostly true	Completely true
0	1	2	3	4	5

____ 1. In this company, people are expected to follow their own personal and moral beliefs.

____ 2. People are expected to do anything to further the company's interests.

____ 3. In this company, people look out for each other's good.

____ 4. It is very important here to follow the company's rules and procedures strictly.

____ 5. In this company, people protect their own interests above other considerations.

____ 6. The first consideration is whether a decision violates any law.

____ 7. Everyone is expected to stick by company rules and procedures.

____ 8. The most efficient way is always the right way in this company.

____ 9. Our major consideration is what is best for everyone in the company.

___ 10. In this company, the law or ethical code of the profession is the major consideration.

___ 11. It is expected at this company that employees will always do what is right for the customer and the public.

To score the questionnaire, first add up your responses to questions 1, 3, 6, 9, 10, and 11. This is subtotal number 1. Next, reverse the scores on questions 2, 4, 5, 7, and 8 (5 = 0, 4 = 1, 3 = 2, 2 = 3, 1 = 4, 0 = 5). Add the reverse scores to form subtotal number 2. Add subtotal number 1 to subtotal number 2 for an overall score.

Subtotal 1 _____ + Subtotal 2 _____ = Overall Score _____.

Overall scores can range from 0 to 55. The higher the score, the more the organization's culture encourages ethical behavior.

Source: Reprinted from *Organizational Dynamics*, Autumn 1989, "An Ethical Weather Report: Assessing the Organization's Ethical Climate" by J. B. Cullen, B. Victor, and C. Stephens. Copyright © 1989 with permission from Elsevier.

cars were designed, the rest of the assembly workers were consulted a year and a half prior to the scheduled date of production. The designs were then revised to improve the cars' quality. More than 300 modifications were made on the Seville and El Dorado models alone.

Teams were also used to improve quality once a model went into production. A team made up of engineers, assemblers, and supervisors worked on a continuous quality improvement process that targeted electrical system problems. The team effort reduced defects by 90 percent. Employee involvement was the key to the turnaround of Cadillac's culture. The original culture, emphasizing technology as the means for success, was replaced with a culture that emphasizes empowerment and product quality. One of the results was the Malcolm Baldrige National Quality Award.

Small companies can also have cultures that support quality. Texas Nameplate makes metal product identification tags that are found on computers, refrigerators, and military equipment. Employees entered the Baldrige award competition never dreaming they would win; they just wanted to get feedback from the Baldrige judges on how to make their product and service quality better. On the third time, they won—the smallest company (fifty-seven employees) ever to win the award. The judges noted that Texas Nameplate employees visit customers to identify opportunities to improve products. In addition, employees are empowered to make decisions, and as a result, product rejects were reduced to less than 1 percent. Because of its culture, Texas Nameplate was able to eliminate its quality control department.[73]

Managers can learn from the experience of Cadillac that employee empowerment is a key to achieving quality. Involving employees in decision making, removing obstacles to their performance, and communicating the value of product and service quality reinforce the values of empowerment and quality in the organizational culture.

MANAGERIAL IMPLICATIONS: THE ORGANIZATIONAL CULTURE CHALLENGE

Managing organizational culture is a key challenge for leaders in today's organizations. With the trend toward downsizing and restructuring, maintaining an organizational culture in the face of change is difficult. In addition, such challenges as globalization, workforce diversity, technology, and managing ethical behavior often require that an organization change its culture. Adaptive cultures that can respond to changes in the environment can lead the way in terms of organizational performance.

Managers have at their disposal many techniques for managing organizational culture. These techniques range from manipulating the artifacts of culture, such as ceremonies and symbols, to communicating the values that guide the organization. The socialization process is a powerful cultural communication process. Managers are models who communicate the organizational culture to employees through personal enactment. Their modeled behavior sets the norms for the other employees to follow. Their leadership is essential for developing a culture that values diversity, supports empowerment, fosters innovations in product and service quality, and promotes ethical behavior.

KEY TERMS

adaptive culture	change and acquisition	organizational (corporate) culture
anticipatory socialization	enacted values	organizational socialization
artifacts	encounter	strong culture
assumptions	espoused values	triangulation

Experiential Exercise

CONTRASTING ORGANIZATIONAL CULTURES

To complete this exercise, groups of four or five students should be formed. Each group should select one of the following pairs of organizations:

American Airlines and Northwest Airlines
Anheuser-Busch and Coors
Hewlett-Packard and Xerox
Albertsons and Winn-Dixie
Target and J. C. Penney

Use your university library's resources to gather information about the companies' cultures.

Contrast the cultures of the two organizations using the following dimensions:

- Strength of the culture.
- Fit of the culture with the industry's environment.
- Adaptiveness of the culture.

Which of the two is the better performer? On what did you base your conclusion? How does the performance of each relate to its organizational culture?

Source: Adapted with the permission of The Free Press, a Division of Simon & Schuster, Inc. from *Corporate Culture and Performance* by John P. Kotter and James L. Heskett. Copyright © 1992 by Kotter Associates, Inc. and James L. Heskett. All rights reserved.

16

Managing Change

LEARNING OBJECTIVES

After reading this chapter, you should be able to do the following:

1. Identify the major external and internal forces for change in organizations.

2. Define the terms *incremental change*, *strategic change*, *transformational change*, and *change agent*.

3. Describe the major reasons individuals resist change, and discuss methods organizations can use to manage resistance.

4. Apply force field analysis to a problem.

5. Explain Lewin's organizational change model.

6. Describe the use of organizational diagnosis and needs analysis as a first step in organizational development.

7. Discuss the major organization development interventions.

8. Identify the ethical issues that must be considered in organization development efforts.

FORCES FOR CHANGE IN ORGANIZATIONS

Change has become the norm in most organizations. Plant closings, business failures, mergers and acquisitions, and downsizing have become experiences common to American companies. *Adaptiveness, flexibility,* and *responsiveness* are characteristics of the organizations that will succeed in meeting the competitive challenges that businesses face.[1] In the past, organizations could succeed by claiming excellence in one area—quality, reliability, or cost, for example—but this is not the case today. The current environment demands excellence in all areas.

As we saw in Chapter 1, change is what's on managers' minds. The pursuit of organizational effectiveness through downsizing, restructuring, reengineering, productivity management, cycle-time reduction, and other efforts is paramount. Organizations are in a state of tremendous turmoil and transition, and all members are affected. Continued downsizings may have left firms leaner but not necessarily richer. Though downsizing can increase shareholder value by better aligning costs with revenues, firms may suffer from public criticism for their actions. Laying off employees may be accompanied by increases in CEO pay and stock options, linking the misery of employees with the financial success of owners and management.[2]

Organizations must also deal with ethical, environmental, and other social issues. Competition is fierce, and companies can no longer afford to rest on their laurels. American Airlines has developed a series of programs to constantly reevaluate and change its operating methods to prevent the company from stagnating. General Electric holds off-site WorkOut sessions with groups of managers and employees whose goal is to make GE a faster, less complex organization that can respond effectively to change. In the Work-Out sessions, employees recommend specific changes, explain why they are needed, and propose ways the changes can be implemented. Top management must make an immediate response: an approval, a disapproval (with an explanation), or a request for more information. The GE WorkOut sessions eliminate the barriers that keep employees from contributing to change.

There are two basic forms of change in organizations. ***Planned change*** is change resulting from a deliberate decision to alter the organization. Companies that wish to move from a traditional hierarchical structure to one that facilitates self-managed teams must use a proactive, carefully orchestrated approach. Not all change is planned, however. ***Unplanned change*** is imposed on the organization and is often unforeseen. Changes in government regulations and changes in the economy, for example, are often unplanned. Responsiveness to unplanned change requires tremendous flexibility and adaptability on the part of organizations. Managers must be prepared to handle both planned and unplanned forms of change in organizations.

Forces for change can come from many sources. Some of these are external, arising from outside the company, whereas others are internal, arising from sources within the organization.

1. *Identify the major external and internal forces for change in organizations.*

PLANNED CHANGE
Change resulting from a deliberate decision to alter the organization.

UNPLANNED CHANGE
Change that is imposed on the organization and is often unforeseen.

EXTERNAL FORCES

The four major managerial challenges we have described throughout the book are major external forces for change. Globalization, workforce diversity, technological change, and managing ethical behavior are challenges that precipitate change in organizations.

Globalization The power players in the global market are the multinational and transnational organizations. Conoco, for example, formed a joint venture with Arkhangelskgeoldobycha, a Russian firm, to develop a new oil field in Russia. This partnership, named Polar Lights, was the first Russian–American joint venture to develop an oil field in Russia. The project has been successful, and the production from Polar Lights has now passed the 75 million barrel production milestone.[3]

New opportunities are not limited to the former Soviet Union, however, and the United States is but one nation in the drive to open new markets. Japan and Germany are responding to global competition in powerful ways, and the emergence of the European Union as a powerful trading group will have a profound impact on world markets. By joining with their European neighbors, companies in smaller countries will begin to make major progress in world markets, thus increasing the fierce competition that already exists.

All of these changes, along with others, have led companies to rethink the borders of their markets and to encourage their employees to think globally. Jack Welch, former CEO of GE, was among the first to call for a boundaryless company, in which there are no mental distinctions between domestic and foreign operations or between managers and employees.[4] The thought that drives the boundaryless company is that barriers that get in the way of people's working together should be removed. Globalizing an organization means rethinking the most efficient ways to use resources, disseminate and gather information, and develop people. It requires not only structural changes but also changes in the minds of employees.

The Hartford Financial Services Group is globalizing but finding some challenges along the way. When the company attempted to enter the lucrative British and Dutch insurance markets by acquiring British and Dutch companies, the overseas staff resisted changes suggested by Hartford, such as using laptops and introducing new financial products. The introduction of such U.S. business practices is often referred to as "economic imperialism" by employees who feel they are being forced to substitute corporate values for personal or national values.

Hartford needed its European staff to understand that they were part of a transnational company. Its solution was to offer a stock ownership plan that tied the personal fortunes of the staff to the company. This gave employees a considerable interest in Hartford's success and helped them identify with the company.[5]

Workforce Diversity Related to globalization is the challenge of workforce diversity. As we have seen throughout this book, workforce diversity is a powerful force for change in organizations. Let us recap the demographic trends contributing to workforce diversity that we discussed at length in Chapter 2. First, the workforce will see increased participation from females, because the majority of new workers will be female.[6] Second, the workforce will be more culturally diverse than ever. Part of this is attributable to globalization, but in addition, U.S. demographics are changing. The participation of African Americans and Hispanic Americans is increasing in record numbers. Third, the workforce is aging. There will be fewer young workers and more middle-aged Americans working.[7]

A few years ago, Denny's, the restaurant chain, was a name synonymous with racism. In 1994, the company paid $54.4 million to settle two lawsuits brought by African American customers who claimed some restaurants refused to seat or serve them. Denny's undertook radical changes led by a blunt-talking CEO and a determined diversity officer in 1995. Because Denny's responded quickly, decisively, and sincerely, it weathered the crisis. Performance appraisals are now based on valuing diversity. A top manager who doesn't do so can have up to 25 percent of his or her bonus withheld. Minorities now own 42 percent of the Denny's franchises. Minorities hold 32 percent of management positions in Advantica, Denny's parent company. The commitment to diversity has moved the company to the top of *Fortune*'s list of the 50 Best Companies for Asians, African Americans, and Hispanics for 2 years running.[8]

Technological Change Rapid technological innovation is another force for change in organizations, and those that fail to keep pace can quickly fall behind. *Smart tags*, for example, are replacing bar codes for tracking and scanning products. Bar codes are passive identification markers whose stripes are unchangeable, and items must be lined up individually for scanning (like in a grocery store checkout line). Manufacturers are starting to use radio-frequency identification (RFID) tags that are as small as two matches laid side by side, and hold digital memory chips the size of a pinhead. RFIDs are also used in show dogs and cats. The tags are injected under a pet's skin with a syringe.

RFIDs contain a lot more information than bar codes, and users can alter the information on them. As many as fifty tags per second can be read—forty times faster than bar-code scanners. Ford uses RFIDs to track parts. Data such as a unique ID, part type, plant location, and time/date stamps are included on the tag. Because RFIDs are reusable, the long-term costs are about the same as bar codes.[9]

Technological innovations bring about profound change because they are not just changes in the way work is performed. Instead, the innovation process promotes associated changes in work relationships and organizational structures.[10] The team approach adopted by many organizations leads to flatter structures, decentralized decision making, and more open communication between leaders and team members.

Managing Ethical Behavior Recent ethical scandals have brought ethical behavior in organizations to the forefront of public consciousness.

Ethical issues, however, are not always public and monumental. Employees face ethical dilemmas in their daily work lives. The need to manage ethical behavior has brought about several changes in organizations. Most center around the idea that an organization must create a culture that encourages ethical behavior.

One company that undertook a massive campaign to move to a more ethical organizational culture was Hamilton Sundstrand Corporation, which was a major defense contractor in the aerospace industry until 1999 when it was acquired by United Technologies. Earlier, however, Hamilton Sundstrand had faced charges of ethical violations by Pentagon officials that resulted in a $227 million penalty. The company's stock dropped substantially as well.

Hamilton Sundstrand took immediate steps to emphasize ethical conduct in its culture, including encouraging whistle-blowing by employees. A corporate director of business conduct and ethics was hired. A code of conduct was written. Employees were given thirty days to read it and sign a card obligating them to follow the code. Extensive ethics training sessions were conducted with all 8,000 aerospace division employees. Hotlines were established for employees to report ethical violations or to simply ask questions. Each hotline call was answered within twenty-four hours. The most critical ingredient in Hamilton Sundstrand's change was encouraging whistle-blowing. Employees were made aware that appropriate action would be taken and that whistle-blowers would be protected. Extensive follow-up by the company indicated that the program worked. The company committed no more ethical violations, employees reported satisfaction with the program, and hotline calls resulted in actions against those who violated Hamilton Sundstrand's ethics policy.[11]

Society expects organizations to maintain ethical behavior both internally and in relationships with other organizations. Ethical behavior is expected in relationships with customers, the environment, and society. These expectations may be informal, or they may come in the form of increased legal requirements.

These four challenges are forces that place pressures to change on organizations. There are other forces as well. Legal developments, changing stakeholder expectations, and shifting consumer demands can also lead to change.[12] And some companies change simply because others are changing.[13] Other powerful forces for change originate from within the organization.

INTERNAL FORCES

Pressures for change that originate inside the organization are generally recognizable in the form of signals indicating that something needs to be altered. Employers hope that employees will recognize and report problems that must be addressed. In some organizations, however, there is a norm of organizational silence in which employees avoid bringing up certain issues, even when everyone is aware that a problem exists.

Declining effectiveness is a pressure to change. A company that experiences its third quarterly loss within a fiscal year is undoubtedly motivated to do something about it. Some companies react by instituting layoffs and massive cost-cutting programs, whereas others look at the bigger picture, view the loss as symptomatic of an underlying problem, and seek the cause of the problem.

A crisis may also stimulate change in an organization. Strikes or walkouts may lead management to change the wage structure. The resignation of a key decision maker may cause the company to rethink the composition of its management team and its role in the organization. A much-publicized crisis that led to change at Exxon (now ExxonMobil) was the oil spill caused by the *Exxon Valdez* oil tanker. The accident brought about many changes in Exxon's environmental policies.

Changes in employee expectations can also trigger change in organizations. A company that hires a group of young newcomers may find that their expectations are very different from those expressed by older workers. The workforce is more educated than ever before. Although this has its advantages, workers with more education demand more of employers. Today's workers are also concerned with career and family balance issues, such as dependent care. The many sources of workforce diversity hold potential for a host of differing expectations among employees.

Changes in the work climate at an organization can also stimulate change. A workforce that seems lethargic, unmotivated, and dissatisfied is a symptom that must be addressed. This symptom is common in organizations that have experienced layoffs. Workers who have escaped a layoff may grieve for those who have lost their jobs and may find it hard to continue to be productive. They may fear that they will be laid off as well, and many feel insecure in their jobs.

CHANGE IS INEVITABLE

We have seen that organizations face substantial pressures to change from both external and internal sources. Change in organizations is inevitable, but change is a process that can be managed. The scope of change can vary from small to quantum.

THE SCOPE OF CHANGE

Change can be of a relatively small scope, such as a modification in a work procedure (an *incremental change*). Such changes, in essence, are a fine-tuning of the organization, or the making of small improvements. Change can also be of a larger scale, such as the restructuring of an organization (a *strategic change*).[14] In strategic change, the organization moves from an old state to a known new state during a controlled period of time. Strategic change usually involves a series of transition steps.

The most massive scope of change is *transformational change*, in which the organization moves to a radically different, and sometimes unknown,

2. *Define the terms incremental change, strategic change, transformational change, and change agent.*

INCREMENTAL CHANGE
Change of a relatively small scope, such as making small improvements.

STRATEGIC CHANGE
Change of a larger scale, such as organizational restructuring.

TRANSFORMATIONAL CHANGE
Change in which the organization moves to a radically different, and sometimes unknown, future state.

future state.[15] In transformational change, the organization's mission, culture, goals, structure, and leadership may all change dramatically.[16]

THE CHANGE AGENT'S ROLE

CHANGE AGENT
The individual or group that undertakes the task of introducing and managing a change in an organization.

The individual or group that undertakes the task of introducing and managing a change in an organization is known as a *change agent*. Change agents can be internal, such as managers or employees who are appointed to oversee the change process. In her book *The Change Masters*, Rosabeth Moss Kanter notes that at companies like Hewlett-Packard and Polaroid, managers and employees alike are developing the needed skills to produce change and innovation in the organization.[17] Change agents can also be external, such as outside consultants.

Internal change agents have certain advantages in managing the change process. They know the organization's past history, its political system, and its culture. Because they must live with the results of their change efforts, internal change agents are likely to be very careful about managing change. There are disadvantages, however, to using internal change agents. They may be associated with certain factions within the organization and may easily be accused of favoritism. Furthermore, internal change agents may be too close to the situation to have an objective view of what needs to be done.

In a recent study, interviews were conducted with 150 internal change agents at thirty organizations. The researchers focused on middle managers as change agents because to make large-scale changes, organizations need a critical mass of change leaders in the middle of the company. Change leaders, as the researchers call them, tend to be young, in the twenty-five to forty age range. They are more flexible than ordinary general managers and much more people oriented. A high number of change leaders are women. The change leaders have a balance of technical and interpersonal skills. They are tough decision makers who focus on performance results. They also know how to energize people and get them aligned in the same direction. They get more out of people than ordinary managers can. In addition, they have the ability to operate in more than one leadership style and can shift from a team mode to command and control, depending on the situation. They are also comfortable with uncertainty.[18]

If change is large scale or strategic in nature, it may take a team of leaders to make change happen. A team assembling leaders with a variety of skills, expertise, and influence that can work together harmoniously may be needed to accomplish change of large scope.[19]

External change agents bring an outsider's objective view to the organization. They may be preferred by employees because of their impartiality. External change agents face certain problems, however; not only is their knowledge of the organization's history limited, but they may also be viewed with suspicion by organization members. External change agents have more power in directing changes if employees perceive the change agents as being trustworthy, possessing important expertise, having a track record that establishes credibility, and being similar to them.[20]

THE PROCESS OF CHANGE IN ORGANIZATIONS

Organizations tend to respond to change by continuing to do what they are good at. After all, these strategies have been successful in the past. After periods of success, organizations can lose the ability to recognize when it is necessary to give up past strategies and try something new. Once an organization has made the decision to change, careful planning and analysis must take place. Change processes such as business process reengineering cannot ensure the success of the change. The people aspects of change are the most critically important for successful transformations.[21] Even Michael Hammer, who launched the reengineering movement, admits that he forgot about the "oeioke aspects" of change. "I was reflecting on my engineering background and was insufficiently appreciative of the human dimension. I've learned that it's critical."[22] If people are not taken into account, a change process will be negatively affected or may even fail. Like organizations, people tend to cling to what has worked in the past, especially if they have been successful and they see no need for change.[23]

The challenge of managing the change process involves harnessing the energy of diverse individuals who hold a variety of views of change. It is important to recognize that most changes will be met with varying degrees of resistance and to understand the basis of resistance to change.

RESISTANCE TO CHANGE

People often resist change in a rational response based on self-interest. However, there are countless other reasons people resist change. Many of these center around the notion of reactance—that is, a negative reaction that occurs when individuals feel that their personal freedom is threatened.[24] Some of the major reasons for resisting change follow.

Fear of the Unknown Change often brings with it substantial uncertainty. Employees facing a technological change, such as the introduction of a new computer system, may resist the change simply because it introduces ambiguity into what was once a comfortable situation for them. This is especially a problem when there has been little communication about the change.

Fear of Loss When a change is impending, some employees may fear losing their jobs; this fear is particularly acute when an advanced technology like robotics is introduced. Employees may also fear losing their status because of a change.[25] Computer systems experts, for example, may feel threatened when they feel their expertise is eroded by the installation of a more user-friendly networked information system. Another common fear is that changes may diminish the positive qualities the individual enjoys in the job. Computerizing the customer service positions at Southwestern Bell (now part of SBC Communications), for example, threatened the autonomy that representatives previously enjoyed.

3. *Describe the major reasons individuals resist change, and discuss methods organizations can use to manage resistance.*

YOU BE THE JUDGE

Is it ethical for an organization to coerce individuals to change?

Fear of Failure Some employees fear changes because they fear their own failure. Employees may fear that changes will result in increased workloads or increased task difficulty, and they may question their own competencies for handling these. They may also fear that performance expectations will be elevated following the change, and that they may not measure up.[26] Resistance can also stem from a fear that the change itself will not really take place. In one large library that was undergoing a major automation effort, employees were doubtful that the vendor could really deliver the state-of-the-art system that was promised. In this case, the implementation never became a reality—the employees' fears were well founded.[27]

Disruption of Interpersonal Relationships Employees may resist change that threatens to limit meaningful interpersonal relationships on the job. Librarians facing the automation effort described previously feared that once the computerized system was implemented, they would not be able to interact as they did when they had to go to another floor of the library to get help finding a resource. In the new system, with the touch of a few buttons on the computer, they would get their information without consulting another librarian.

Personality Conflicts When the change agent's personality engenders negative reactions, employees may resist the change. A change agent who appears insensitive to employee concerns and feelings may meet considerable resistance, because employees perceive that their needs are not being taken into account.

Politics Organizational change may also shift the existing balance of power in the organization. Individuals or groups who hold power under the current arrangement may be threatened with losing these political advantages in the advent of change.

Cultural Assumptions and Values Sometimes cultural assumptions and values can be impediments to change, particularly if the assumptions underlying the change are alien to employees. This form of resistance can be very difficult to overcome, because some cultural assumptions are unconscious. As we discussed in Chapter 2, some cultures tend to avoid uncertainty. In Mexican and Greek cultures, for example, change that creates a great deal of uncertainty may be met with great resistance.

We have described several sources of resistance to change. The reasons for resistance are as diverse as the workforce itself and vary with different individuals and organizations. The challenge for managers is introducing change in a positive manner and managing employee resistance.

MANAGING RESISTANCE TO CHANGE

The traditional view of resistance to change treated it as something to be overcome, and many organizational attempts to reduce the resistance have only served to intensify it. The contemporary view holds that resistance is simply a form of feedback and that this feedback can be used very productively to manage the change process.[28] One key to managing resistance is to plan for it and to be ready with a variety of strategies for using the resistance as feedback and helping employees negotiate the transition. Three key strategies for managing resistance to change are communication, participation, and empathy and support.[29]

Communication about impending change is essential if employees are to adjust effectively. The details of the change should be provided, but equally important is the rationale behind the change. Employees want to know why change is needed. If there is no good reason for it, why should they favor the change? Providing accurate and timely information about the change can help prevent unfounded fears and potentially damaging rumors from developing. Delaying the announcement of a change and handling information in a secretive fashion can serve to fuel the rumor mill. Open communication in a culture of trust is a key ingredient for successful change.[30] It is also beneficial to inform people about the potential consequences of the change. Educating employees on new work procedures is often helpful. Studies on the introduction of computers in the workplace indicate that providing employees with opportunities for hands-on practice helps alleviate fears about the new technology. Employees who have experience with computers display more positive attitudes and greater efficacy—a sense that they can master their new tasks.[31]

There is substantial research support underscoring the importance of participation in the change process. Employees must be engaged and involved in order for change to work—as supported by the notion "That which we create, we support." GE's WorkOut process, which was mentioned earlier in this chapter, is a good illustration of how to get a large group together in a free-form, open-ended meeting. The outcome is a change to which everyone is committed. The group comes together later, after the change is implemented, to see what has been learned and to look for what is happening on the horizon. Participation by a large group can move change further along.[32] Participation helps employees become involved in the change and establish a feeling of ownership in the process. When employees are allowed to participate, they are more committed to the change.

Another strategy for managing resistance is providing empathy and support to employees who have trouble dealing with the change. Active listening is an excellent tool for identifying the reasons behind resistance and for uncovering fears. An expression of concerns about the change can provide important feedback that managers can use to improve the change process. Emotional support and encouragement can help an employee deal with the anxiety that is a natural response to change. Employees who experience severe reactions to change can benefit from talking with a counselor. Some companies provide counseling through their employee assistance plans.

Open communication, participation, and emotional support can go a long way toward managing resistance to change. Managers must realize that some resistance is inevitable, however, and should plan ways to deal with resistance early in the change process.

Managing resistance to change is a long and often arduous process. GTE Mobilnet (later GTE Wireless and now part of Verizon Communications) faced substantial resistance to change when it implemented its customer connection initiative, with the goal of building a cellular-phone network that ranked first in customer service. The change agent, Ben Powell, and his teammates tried to persuade staffers at Mobilnet's 350 service centers to send new cellular phones out the door with fully charged batteries in them. The salespeople liked the idea—they could tell customers that their phones were ready to use immediately. Service workers, however, balked at the idea because they were the ones who had to install the batteries.

Powell and his team essentially repeated the following dialogue 350 times: "You can't see why you need to bother with installing the batteries? Here are sales figures showing how much revenue we lose by making customers wait to use their phones. The average customer calls everybody he knows when he first gets the thing, like a kid with a new toy—but only if it has a charged battery in it. Don't have room to stock all those batteries? We'll help you redesign your workspace to accommodate them. Can't predict how many of which battery you'll need on hand at any given time? We'll provide data to help you with those projections. Can't afford any of this to come out of your operating budget? We'll fund it for you."

As Powell said, "When you meet this kind of resistance, the only thing you can do is keep plugging away. . . . Finally, in the last six months or so we have been getting to the point where we're really changing how we do business. But it's taken years. Not weeks. Not months. On a day-to-day basis, it feels like bowling in sand."[33]

BEHAVIORAL REACTIONS TO CHANGE

In spite of attempts to minimize the resistance to change in an organization, some reactions to change are inevitable. Negative reactions may be manifested in overt behavior or through more passive resistance to change. People show four basic, identifiable reactions to change: disengagement, disidentification, disenchantment, and disorientation.[34] Managers can use interventions to deal with these reactions, as shown in Table 16-1.

Disengagement is psychological withdrawal from change. The employee may appear to lose initiative and interest in the job. Employees who disengage may fear the change but approach it by doing nothing and simply hoping for the best. Disengaged employees are physically present but mentally absent. They lack drive and commitment, and they simply comply without real psychological investment in their work. Disengagement can be recognized by behaviors such as being hard to find or doing only the basics to get the job done. Typical disengagement statements include "No problem" or "This won't affect me."

One oil and gas company that started ventures in Russia found that the very idea of change was alien to Russian managers. They felt that the man-

DISENGAGEMENT
Psychological withdrawal from change.

Reaction	Expression	Managerial Intervention
Disengagement	Withdrawal	Confront, identify
Disidentification	Sadness, worry	Explore, transfer
Disenchantment	Anger	Neutralize, acknowledge
Disorientation	Confusion	Explain, plan

Table 16-1
Reactions to Change and Managerial Interventions

Source: Table adapted from H. Woodward and S. Buchholz, *Aftershock: Helping People through Corporate Change*, p. 15. Copyright © 1987 John Wiley & Sons, Inc. This material is used by permission of John Wiley & Sons, Inc.

ager's task was to establish procedures and ensure continuity. When Western managers tried to institute change, the Russian managers disengaged, believing that their job was to secure stability rather than change.[35]

The basic managerial strategy for dealing with disengaged individuals is to confront them with their reaction and draw them out so that they can identify the concerns that need to be addressed. Disengaged employees may not be aware of the change in their behavior, and they need to be assured of your intentions. Drawing them out and helping them air their feelings can lead to productive discussions. Disengaged people seldom become cheerleaders for the change, but they can be brought closer to accepting and working with a change by open communication with an empathetic manager who is willing to listen.

Another reaction to change is *disidentification*. Individuals reacting in this way feel that their identity has been threatened by the change, and they feel very vulnerable. Many times they cling to a past procedure because they had a sense of mastery over it, and it gave them a sense of security. "My job is completely changed" and "I used to . . ." are verbal indications of disidentification. Disidentified employees often display sadness and worry. They may appear to be sulking and dwelling on the past by reminiscing about the old ways of doing things.

Because disidentified employees are so vulnerable, they often feel like victims in the change process. Managers can help them through the transition by encouraging them to explore their feelings and helping them transfer their positive feelings into the new situation. One way to do this is to help them identify what they liked in the old situation and then show them how it is possible to have the same positive experience in the new situation. Disidentified employees need to see that work itself and emotion are separable—that is, that they can let go of old ways and experience positive reactions to new ways of performing their jobs.

Disenchantment is also a common reaction to change. It is usually expressed as negativity or anger. Disenchanted employees realize that the past is gone, and they are mad about it. They may try to enlist the support of other employees by forming coalitions. Destructive behaviors like sabotage and backstabbing may result. Typical verbal signs of disenchantment are "This will never work" and "I'm getting out of this company as soon as I can." The anger of a disenchanted person may be directly expressed in

DISIDENTIFICATION
Feeling that one's identity is being threatened by a change.

DISENCHANTMENT
Feeling negativity or anger toward a change.

organizational cultures where it is permissible to do so. This behavior tends to get the issues out in the open. More often, however, cultures view the expression of emotion at work as improper and unbusinesslike. In these cultures, the anger is suppressed and emerges in more passive-aggressive ways, such as badmouthing and starting rumors. One of the particular dangers of disenchantment is that it is quite contagious in the workplace.

It is often difficult to reason with disenchanted employees. Thus, the first step in managing this reaction is to bring these employees from their highly negative, emotionally charged state to a more neutral state. To neutralize the reaction does not mean to dismiss it; rather, it means to allow the individuals to let off the necessary steam so that they can come to terms with their anger. The second part of the strategy for dealing with disenchanted employees is to acknowledge that their anger is normal and that you do not hold it against them. Sometimes disenchantment is a mask for one of the other three reactions, and it must be worked through to get to the core of the employee's reaction. Employees may also become cynical about change and lose faith in the leaders of change.

DISORIENTATION
Feelings of loss and confusion due to a change.

A final reaction to change is ***disorientation***. Disoriented employees are lost and confused, and often they are unsure of their feelings. They waste energy trying to figure out what to do instead of how to do things. Disoriented individuals ask a lot of questions and become very detail oriented. They may appear to need a good deal of guidance and may leave their work undone until all of their questions have been answered. "Analysis paralysis" is characteristic of disoriented employees. They feel that they have lost touch with the priorities of the company, and they may want to analyze the change to death before acting on it. Disoriented employees may ask questions like "Now what do I do?" or "What do I do first?"

Disorientation is a common reaction among people who are used to clear goals and unambiguous directions. When change is introduced, it creates uncertainty and a lack of clarity. The managerial strategy for dealing with this reaction is to explain the change in a way that minimizes the ambiguity that is present. The information about the change needs to be put into a framework or an overall vision so that the disoriented individual can see where he or she fits into the grand scheme of things. Once the disoriented employee sees the broader context of the change, you can plan a series of steps to help this employee adjust. The employee needs a sense of priorities to work on.

Managers need to be able to diagnose these four reactions to change. Because each reaction brings with it significant and different concerns, no single universal strategy can help all employees adjust. By recognizing each reaction and applying the appropriate strategy, it is possible to help even strong resisters work through a transition successfully.

LEWIN'S CHANGE MODEL

4. *Apply force field analysis to a problem.*

Kurt Lewin developed a model of the change process that has stood the test of time and continues to influence the way organizations manage

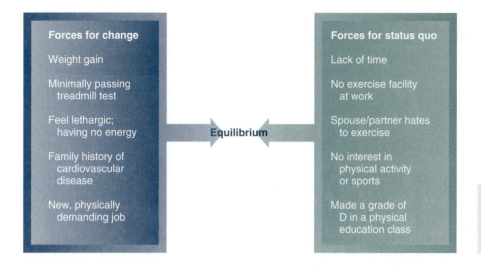

Figure 16-1
*Force Field Analysis of a
Decision to Engage in Exercise*

planned change. Lewin's model is based on the idea of force field analysis.[36] Figure 16-1 shows a force field analysis of a decision to engage in exercise behavior.

This model contends that a person's behavior is the product of two opposing forces; one force pushes toward preserving the status quo, and the other force pushes for change. When the two opposing forces are approximately equal, current behavior is maintained. For behavioral change to occur, the forces maintaining the status quo must be overcome. This can be accomplished by increasing the forces for change, by weakening the forces for the status quo, or by a combination of these actions. This chapter's Challenge, (on page 400) asks you to apply force field analysis to a problem in your life.

Lewin's change model is a three-step process, as shown in Figure 16-2. The process begins with **unfreezing**, which is a crucial first hurdle in the change process. Unfreezing involves encouraging individuals to discard old behaviors by shaking up the equilibrium state that maintains the status quo. Organizations often accomplish unfreezing by eliminating the rewards for current behavior and showing that current behavior is not valued. By unfreezing, individuals accept that change needs to occur. In essence, individuals surrender by allowing the boundaries of their status quo to be opened in preparation for change.[37]

The second step in the change process is **moving**. In the moving stage, new attitudes, values, and behaviors are substituted for old ones. Organizations accomplish moving by initiating new options and explaining the rationale for the change, as well as by providing training to help employees

5. *Explain Lewin's organizational change model.*

UNFREEZING
The first step in Lewin's change model, in which individuals are encouraged to discard old behaviors by shaking up the equilibrium state that maintains the status quo.

MOVING
The second step in Lewin's change model, in which new attitudes, values, and behaviors are substituted for old ones.

Unfreezing	Moving	Refreezing
Reducing forces for status quo	Developing new attitudes, values, and behaviors	Reinforcing new attitudes, values, and behaviors

Figure 16-2
Lewin's Change Model

Challenge

APPLYING FORCE FIELD ANALYSIS

Think of a problem you are currently facing. An example would be trying to increase the amount of study time you devote to a particular class.

1. Describe the problem, as specifically as possible.
2. List the forces driving change on the arrows at the left side of the diagram.
3. List the forces restraining change on the arrows at the right side of the diagram.
4. What can you do, specifically, to remove the obstacles to change?

5. What can you do to increase the forces driving change?
6. What benefits can be derived from breaking a problem down into forces driving change and forces restraining change?

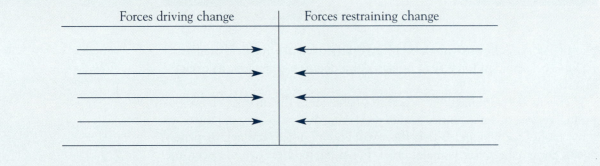

Forces driving change	Forces restraining change

REFREEZING

The final step in Lewin's change model, in which new attitudes, values, and behaviors are established as the new status quo.

---

develop the new skills they need. Employees should be given the overarching vision for the change so that they can establish their roles within the new organizational structure and processes.[38]

Refreezing is the final step in the change process. In this step, new attitudes, values, and behaviors are established as the new status quo. The new ways of operating are cemented in and reinforced. Managers should ensure that the organizational culture and formal reward systems encourage the new behaviors and avoid rewarding the old ways of operating. Changes in the reward structure may be needed to ensure that the organization is not rewarding the old behaviors and merely hoping for the new behaviors. A study by Exxon Research and Engineering showed that framing and displaying a mission statement in managers' offices may eventually change the behavior of 2 percent of the managers. In contrast, changing managers' evaluation and reward systems will change the behavior of 55 percent of the managers almost overnight.[39]

The approach used by Monsanto to increase opportunities for women within the company is an illustration of how to use Lewin's model effectively. First, Monsanto emphasized unfreezing by helping employees debunk negative stereotypes about women in business. This also helped overcome resistance to change. Second, Monsanto moved employees' attitudes and behaviors by diversity training in which differences were emphasized as positive, and supervisors learned ways of training and developing female employees. Third, Monsanto changed its reward system so that managers were evaluated and paid according to how they coached and promoted women, which helped refreeze the new attitudes and behaviors.

Lewin's model proposes that for change efforts to be successful, the three-stage process must be completed. Failures in efforts to change can be traced back to one of the three stages. Successful change thus requires that old behaviors be discarded, new behaviors be introduced, and these new behaviors be institutionalized and rewarded. This is a learning process, and the learning theories discussed in Chapter 6 certainly apply. Skinner's work helps us understand how to encourage new behaviors and extinguish old ones by using reinforcers. Bandura's social learning theory points out the importance of modeling. Managers should model appropriate behavior, because employees look to them to pattern their own behavior.

Organizations that wish to change can select from a variety of methods to make a change become reality. Organization development is a method that consists of various programs for making organizations more effective.

ORGANIZATION DEVELOPMENT INTERVENTIONS

Organization development (OD) is a systematic approach to organizational improvement that applies behavioral science theory and research in order to increase individual and organizational well-being and effectiveness.[40] This definition implies certain characteristics. First, OD is a systematic approach to planned change. It is a structured cycle of diagnosing organizational problems and opportunities and then applying expertise to them. Second, OD is grounded in solid research and theory. It involves the application of our knowledge of behavioral science to the challenges that organizations face. Third, OD recognizes the reciprocal relationship between individuals and organizations. It acknowledges that for organizations to change, individuals must change. Finally, OD is goal oriented. It is a process that seeks to improve both individual and organizational well-being and effectiveness.

Organization development has a rich history. Some of the early work in OD was conducted by Kurt Lewin and his associates during the 1940s. This work was continued by Rensis Likert, who pioneered the use of attitude surveys in OD. During the 1950s, Eric Trist and his colleagues at the Tavistock Institute in London focused on the technical and social aspects of organizations and how they affect the quality of work life. These programs on the quality of work life migrated to the United States during the 1960s. During this time, a 200-member OD network was established, and it has grown to more than 4,100 members today. As the number of practitioners has increased, so has the number of different OD methods. One compendium of organizational change methods estimates that more than 300 different methods have been used.[41]

ORGANIZATION DEVELOPMENT (OD)
A systematic approach to organizational improvement that applies behavioral science theory and research in order to increase individual and organizational well-being and effectiveness.

Organization development is also being used internationally. OD has been applied in Canada, Sweden, Norway, Germany, Japan, Australia, Israel, and Mexico, among others. Some OD methods are difficult to implement in other cultures. As OD becomes more internationally widespread, we will increase our knowledge of how culture affects the success of different OD approaches.

Prior to deciding on a method of intervention, managers must carefully diagnose the problem they are attempting to address. Diagnosis and needs analysis is a critical first step in any OD intervention. Following this, an intervention method is chosen and applied. Finally, a thorough follow-up of the OD process is conducted. Figure 16-3 presents the OD cycle, a continuous process of moving the organization and its employees toward effective functioning.

DIAGNOSIS AND NEEDS ANALYSIS

6. *Describe the use of organizational diagnosis and needs analysis as a first step in organizational development.*

Before any intervention is planned, a thorough organizational diagnosis should be conducted. Diagnosis is an essential first step for any organization development intervention.[42] The term *diagnosis* comes from *dia* (through) and *gnosis* (knowledge of). Thus, the diagnosis should pinpoint specific problems and areas in need of improvement. Problems can arise in any part of the organization. Six areas to examine carefully are the organization's purpose, structure, reward system, support systems, relationships, and leadership.[43]

Harry Levinson's diagnostic approach asserts that the process should begin by identifying where the pain (the problem) in the organization is, what it is like, how long it has been happening, and what has already been done about it.[44] Then a four-part, comprehensive diagnosis can begin. The first part of the diagnosis involves achieving an understanding of the organization's history. In the second part, the organization as a whole is analyzed to obtain data about its structure and processes. In the third part, interpretive data about attitudes, relationships, and current organizational functioning are gathered. In the fourth part of the diagnosis, the data are analyzed and conclusions are reached. In each stage of the diagnosis, the data can be gathered using a variety of methods, including observation, interviews, questionnaires, and archival records.

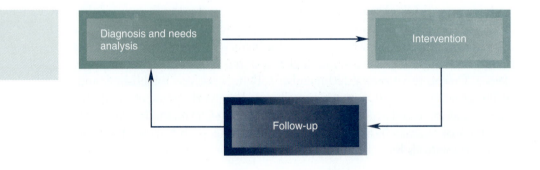

Figure 16-3
The Organization Development Cycle

Diagnosis and needs analysis → Intervention

Follow-up

The diagnostic process may yield the conclusion that change is necessary. As part of the diagnosis, it is important to address the following issues:

- What are the forces for change?
- What are the forces preserving the status quo?
- What are the most likely sources of resistance to change?
- What are the goals to be accomplished by the change?

This information constitutes a force field analysis, as discussed earlier in the chapter.

A needs analysis is another crucial step in managing change. This is an analysis of the skills and competencies that employees must have to achieve the goals of the change. A needs analysis is essential because interventions such as training programs must target these skills and competencies.

Hundreds of alternative OD intervention methods exist. One way of classifying these methods is by the target of change. The target of change may be the organization, groups within the organization, or individuals.

Organization- and Group-Focused Techniques

Some OD intervention methods emphasize changing the organization itself or changing the work groups within the organization. Intervention methods in this category include survey feedback, management by objectives, product and service quality programs, team building, and process consultation.

7. *Discuss the major organization development interventions.*

Survey Feedback **Survey feedback** is a widely used intervention method whereby employee attitudes are solicited using a questionnaire. Once the data are collected, they are analyzed and fed back to the employees to diagnose problems and plan other interventions. Survey feedback is often used as an exploratory tool and then is combined with some other intervention. The effectiveness of survey feedback in actually improving outcomes (absenteeism or productivity, for example) increases substantially when this method is combined with other interventions.[45]

Some surveys are developed by managers within the organization and tailored to a specific problem or issue. Well-established and widely used surveys also are available for use. Two such surveys are the Survey of Organizations and the Michigan Organizational Assessment Questionnaire, both of which were developed at the University of Michigan's Institute for Social Research.[46] A large body of research indicates that these surveys have good reliability and validity, and they are useful tools for gathering employees' perceptions of their work environments.

For survey feedback to be an effective method, certain guidelines should be used. Employees must be assured that their responses to the questionnaire will be confidential and anonymous. Unless this assurance is given, the responses may not be honest. Feedback should be reported in a group format; that is, no individual responses should be identified. Employees must be able to trust that there will be no negative repercussions from their

SURVEY FEEDBACK
A widely used method of intervention whereby employee attitudes are solicited using a questionnaire.

responses. Employees should be informed of the purpose of the survey. Failing to do this can set up unrealistic expectations about the changes that might come from the surveys.

In addition, management must be prepared to follow up on the survey results. If some things cannot be changed, the rationale (for example, prohibitive cost) must be explained to the employees. Without appropriate follow-through, employees will not take the survey process seriously the next time.

MANAGEMENT BY OBJECTIVES (MBO)

An organization-wide intervention technique that involves joint goal setting between employees and managers.

Management by Objectives   As an organization-wide technique, **management by objectives (MBO)** involves joint goal setting between employees and managers. The MBO process includes the setting of initial objectives, periodic progress reviews, and problem solving to remove any obstacles to goal achievement.[47] All these steps are joint efforts between managers and employees.

MBO is a valuable intervention because it meets three needs. First, it clarifies what is expected of employees. This reduces role conflict and ambiguity. Second, MBO provides knowledge of results, an essential ingredient in effective job performance. Finally, MBO provides an opportunity for coaching and counseling by the manager. The problem-solving approach encourages open communication and discussion of obstacles to goal achievement.[48]

Companies that have used MBO successfully include the former Tenneco, Mobil (now part of ExxonMobil), and General Electric. The success of MBO in effecting organizational results hinges on the linking of individual goals to the goals of the organization. MBO is usually tailored to the organization; as such, MBO programs may appear to differ widely across organizations.[49] Nevertheless, the programs all focus on joint goal setting and evaluation. MBO programs should be used with caution, however. An excessive emphasis on goal achievement can result in cutthroat competition among employees, falsification of results, and striving for results at any cost. In addition, top management support is essential if the program aspires to be more than just an exercise in red tape.

QUALITY PROGRAM

A program that embeds product and service quality excellence in the organizational culture.

Product and Service Quality Programs   **Quality programs**—programs that embed product and service quality excellence in the organizational culture—are assuming key roles in the organization development efforts of many companies. For example, the success or failure of a service company may depend on the quality of customer service it provides.[50] The quality revolution consists of programs that entail two steps. The first step is to raise aspirations about the product and service quality, both within the company and among its customers. If the organization is to improve, employees must be committed to product and service quality excellence, and customers must expect it. The second step is to embed product and service quality excellence in the organizational culture, using continual improvement tools such as benchmarking to change habits, attitudes, skills, and knowledge. Benchmarking involves comparing products and processes with those of other companies in order to imitate and improve on them. Xerox uses benchmarking to improve the product quality of its copiers. Service quality improvement programs can lead to competitive advantage, increased productivity, enhanced employee morale, and word-of-mouth advertising from satisfied customers. Gateway, Inc., provides toll-free technical support for the life of the customer's Gateway computer system, and it is reputed to have the best qualified technical support staff in the industry.

The Ritz-Carlton Hotel Company (now part of Marriott International) integrated its comprehensive service quality program into marketing and business objectives. The Atlanta-based company, which managed twenty-eight luxury hotels, won the Malcolm Baldrige Award for service quality. Key elements of Ritz-Carlton's quality program included participatory executive leadership, thorough information gathering, coordinated execution, and employees who were empowered to "move heaven and earth" to satisfy customers.[51]

At Ritz-Carlton, the company president and thirteen senior executives made up the senior quality management team, which met weekly to focus on service quality. Quality goals were established at all levels of the company. The crucial product and service requirements of travel consumers were translated into Ritz-Carlton Gold Standards, which included a credo, a motto, three steps of service, and twenty Ritz-Carlton Basics. These standards guided service quality throughout the organization.

Employees were required to act on a customer complaint at once and were empowered to provide "instant pacification," no matter what it took. Quality teams set action plans at all levels of the company. Each hotel had a quality leader, who served as a resource to the quality teams. Daily quality production reports provided an early warning system for identifying areas that needed quality improvement.

The Ritz-Carlton program had all of the hallmarks of an excellent service quality program: committed leadership, empowered teams and employees, carefully researched standards and goals, and constant monitoring. The company reaped rewards from its excellent service; it received hundreds of quality-related awards, along with best-in-industry rankings from all three major hotel-ranking organizations.

After celebrating an award as the best hotel in the world, Ritz-Carlton did not stop its quality improvement process. At one hotel, the chief complaint was that room service was always late. A quality team was put together, including a cook, a waiter, and a room service order taker. They studied how the process flowed. When they discovered that the service elevator was slow, they added an engineer and a representative from the elevator company to the team. They found the elevators worked well. Next they posted a team member in the elevator twenty-four hours a day for a week. Every time the door opened, the team member had to find out why. Finally, a team member noticed that housemen who helped the maids got on the elevator a lot. It turned out that the housemen were stealing towels from other floors because their maids needed more. The problem with room service was that the hotel didn't own enough towels. Ritz-Carlton bought more towels, and room service complaints fell 50 percent.[52]

TEAM BUILDING
An intervention designed to improve the effectiveness of a work group.

Team Building As an organization development intervention, **team building** can improve the effectiveness of work groups. Team building usually begins with a diagnostic process through which team members identify problems, and it continues with the team's planning actions to take in order to resolve those problems. The OD practitioner in team building serves as a facilitator, and the work itself is completed by team members.[53]

Team building is a very popular OD method. A survey of Fortune 500 companies indicated that human resource managers considered team building the most successful OD technique.[54] Managers are particularly interested in building teams that can learn. To build learning teams, members must be encouraged to seek feedback, discuss errors, reflect on successes and failures, and experiment with new ways of performing. Mistakes should be analyzed for ways to improve, and a climate of mutual support should be developed. Leaders of learning teams are good coaches who promote a climate of psychological safety so that team members feel comfortable discussing problems.[55]

YOU BE THE JUDGE

Suppose you are a consultant, and an organization asks you to deliver a team-building intervention. You know a little about team building, but not a lot. You do know that a competitor will probably get the job if you do not do it. What should you do?

One popular technique for team building is the use of outdoor challenges. Participants go through a series of outdoor activities, such as climbing a fourteen-foot wall. Similar physical challenges require the participants to work as a team and focus on trust, communication, decision making, and leadership. GE and Weyerhaeuser use outdoor challenges at the beginning of their team-building courses, and later in the training, team members apply what they have learned to actual business situations.[56] A more recent innovation in team building is the use of improvisational comedy.

Because team building is a relatively new intervention, it is difficult to assess its effectiveness. Preliminary studies, however, indicate that team building can improve group processes.[57]

Large Group Interventions Among the newer techniques on the horizon for managing change are large group interventions, which bring all of the key members of a group together in one room for an extended period of time. Prior to the event, consultants work with the organization to determine who will participate and what the goal of the event should be. Large group interventions are intended to create a critical mass of people within an organization to support a change. These individuals then become internal change agents who implement the changes that are designed by the large group. One such intervention is FutureSearch, which uses a set format. It works with self-managed teams, lasts three days, and includes forty to eighty participants. The advantage of large group interventions is that they can quickly have an impact because they involve many people at once.[58]

PROCESS CONSULTATION
An OD method that helps managers and employees improve the processes that are used in organizations.

Process Consultation Pioneered by Edgar Schein, **process consultation** is an OD method that helps managers and employees improve the processes that are used in organizations.[59] The processes most often targeted are communication, conflict resolution, decision making, group interaction, and leadership.

One of the distinguishing features of the process consultation approach is that an outside consultant is used. The role of the consultant is to help employees help themselves. In this way, the ownership of a successful outcome rests with the employees.[60] The consultant guides the organization members in examining the processes in the organization and in refining them. The steps in process consultation are entering the organization, defining the relationship, choosing an approach, gathering data and diagnosing problems, intervening, and gradually leaving the organization.

Process consultation is an interactive technique between employees and an outside consultant, so it is seldom used as a sole OD method. Most often, it is used in combination with other OD interventions.

All the preceding OD methods focus on changing the organization or the work group. Other OD methods are aimed at facilitating change within individuals.

INDIVIDUAL-FOCUSED TECHNIQUES

Organization development efforts that are targeted toward individuals include skills training, sensitivity training, management development training, role negotiation, job redesign, stress management programs, and career planning.

Skills Training The key question addressed by **skills training** is "What knowledge, skills, and abilities are necessary to do this job effectively?" Skills training is accomplished either in formal classroom settings or on the job. The challenge of integrating skills training into organization development is the rapid change that most organizations face. The job knowledge in most positions requires continual updates to keep pace with rapid change.

FedEx depends on more than 214,000 full- and part-time employees in more than 210 countries to deliver 100 percent customer satisfaction. The company is constantly changing its products and services, sometimes at the rate of 1,700 changes per year. FedEx decided to accomplish its mission using Web-based training and job skills testing. Employees find the training easy to use, convenient, and individualized. FedEx has found it to be economical as well because it eliminates travel expenses and the need for instructors. In job skills testing, every customer service employee takes a test every six months via computer. The test generates a unique prescription that informs employees what they do well and how they need to improve.[61]

Sensitivity Training Also called T-group training, **sensitivity training** is designed to help individuals understand how their behavior affects others. In a typical session, groups of ten to twelve strangers (T-groups) are formed. Participants from the same organization are placed in different T-groups. The trainer serves as a resource person but does not engage in structuring behaviors. The members are left on their own to work out the interaction

SKILLS TRAINING
Increasing the job knowledge, skills, and abilities that are necessary to do a job effectively.

SENSITIVITY TRAINING
An intervention designed to help individuals understand how their behavior affects others.

in the group, and they are encouraged to concentrate on the "here and now" of the experience and on openness with other group members. It is important that the trainer be well qualified to monitor the group's progress. The trainer intervenes only to help move the group forward.[62]

The outcome of sensitivity training should be an increased sensitivity to others, and in some cases this has been demonstrated. In other cases, however, the new and better ways of dealing with others did not persist on the job. When people returned to their jobs, which rewarded the old behaviors, the new behavior patterns were quickly extinguished. There are also side effects from T-groups. Because they result in emotional exposure, some participants feel vulnerable and react negatively to the extreme personal nature of the interactions.

Sensitivity training is less popular today than it was in the early 1980s.[63] It can still be used, however, to help managers deal with current challenges like cultural, gender, age, and ability diversity. T-groups can help employees understand others better, become aware of their own feelings and perceptions, and improve communication.

MANAGEMENT DEVELOPMENT
A host of techniques for enhancing managers' skills in an organization.

Management Development Training **Management development** encompasses a host of techniques designed to enhance a manager's skills on the job. Management development training generally focuses on four types of learning: verbal information, intellectual skills, attitudes, and development.[64]

Development as a manager requires an integration of classroom learning with on-the-job experiences. One way of accomplishing development is through the use of action learning, a technique that was pioneered in Europe.[65] In action learning, managers take on unfamiliar problems or familiar problems in unfamiliar settings. The managers work on the problems and meet weekly in small groups made up of individuals from different organizations. The outcome of action learning is that managers learn about themselves through the challenges of their comrades. Other techniques that provide active learning for participants are simulation, business games, role-playing, and case studies.[66]

Management development is also used, especially in transnational firms, as a way of transmitting organizational culture. Trainees are given strong messages about what constitutes desired managerial behavior. Shared values are promoted, and these are tied to managers' career aspirations.[67]

ROLE NEGOTIATION
A technique whereby individuals meet and clarify their psychological contract.

Role Negotiation Individuals who work together sometimes have differing expectations of one another within the working relationship. **Role negotiation** is a simple technique whereby individuals meet and clarify their psychological contract. In doing this, the expectations of each party are clarified and negotiated. The outcome of role negotiation is a better understanding between the two parties of what each can be expected to give and receive in the reciprocal relationship. When both parties have a mutual agreement on expectations, there is less ambiguity in the process of working together.

Job Redesign As an OD intervention method, **job redesign** emphasizes the fit between individual skills and the demands of the job. Chapter 13 outlined several approaches to job design. Many of these methods are used as OD techniques for realigning task demands and individual capabilities, or for redesigning jobs to fit new techniques or organizational structures better.

One company that has undergone tremendous change is Harley-Davidson. The motorcycle manufacturer was close to financial disaster when it engaged in a radical restructuring effort. The company essentially threw out the old hierarchies and traditional jobs, opted for a leaner organization, and redesigned jobs to allow employees more participation and control. The company credits its renewed success, in part, to its redesign efforts.[68]

Steelcase, the world's leading designer and manufacturer of office furniture, used job redesign as a key component of its comprehensive change from a traditional manufacturing system to a "factory within a factory" design. In the old system, jobs were designed around the principle of task simplicity and specialization. In the new design, operations are arranged by products, with each factory run by a self-managed team. Employees' jobs are now flexible, team oriented, and characterized by high levels of empowerment.

Health Promotion Programs As organizations have become increasingly concerned with the costs of distress in the workplace, health promotion programs have become a part of larger organization development efforts. Companies that have successfully integrated health promotion programs into their organizations include AT&T, Caterpillar, Kimberly-Clark, and Johnson & Johnson.

The components of health promotion and stress management programs vary widely. They can include education about stress and coping, diagnosis of the causes of stress, relaxation training, company-provided exercise programs, and employee assistance programs. These efforts all focus on helping employees manage stress before it becomes a problem.

Career Planning Matching an individual's career aspirations with the opportunities in the organization is career planning. This proactive approach to career management is often part of an organization's development efforts. Career planning is a joint responsibility of organizations and individuals. Companies like IBM, Travelers Insurance (part of Citigroup), and 3M have implemented career-planning programs.

Career-planning activities benefit the organization, as well as its individuals. Through counseling sessions, employees identify their skills and skill deficiencies. The organization then can plan its training and development efforts based on this information. In addition, the process can be used to identify and nurture talented employees for potential promotion.

Managers can choose from a host of organization development techniques to facilitate organizational change. Some of these techniques are aimed toward organizations or groups, and others focus on individuals. Large-scale changes in organizations require the use of multiple techniques. For

JOB REDESIGN
An OD intervention method that alters jobs to improve the fit between individual skills and the demands of the job.

example, implementing a new technology like robotics may require simultaneous changes in the structure of the organization, the configuration of work groups, and individual attitudes.

We should recognize at this point that the organization development methods just described are means to an end. Programs do not drive change; business needs do. The OD methods are merely vehicles for moving the organization and its employees in a more effective direction.

ETHICAL CONSIDERATIONS IN ORGANIZATION DEVELOPMENT

8. *Identify the ethical issues that must be considered in organization development efforts.*

Organization development is a process of helping organizations improve. It may involve resistance to change, shifts in power, losses of control, and redefinition of tasks.[69] These are all sensitive issues. Further, the change agent, whether a manager from within the organization or a consultant from outside, is in a position of directing the change. Such a position carries the potential for misuse of power. The ethical concerns surrounding the use of organization development center around four issues.[70]

The first issue is the selection of the OD method to be used. Every change agent has inherent biases about particular methods, but these biases must not enter into the decision process. The OD method used must be carefully chosen in accordance with the problem as diagnosed, the organization's culture, and the employees concerned. All alternatives should be given fair consideration in the choice of a method. In addition, the OD practitioner should never use a method he or she is not skilled in delivering. Using a method you are not an expert in is unethical, because the client assumes you are.

The second ethical issue is voluntary participation. No employee should be forced to participate in any OD intervention.[71] To make an informed decision about participation, employees should be given information about the nature of the intervention and what will be expected of them. They should also be afforded the option to discontinue their participation at any time they so choose.

The third issue of ethical concern is confidentiality. Change agents gather a wealth of information during organizational diagnoses and interventions. Successful change agents develop a trusting relationship with employees. They may receive privileged information, sometimes unknowingly. It is unethical for a change agent to reveal information in order to give some group or individual political advantage or to enhance the change agent's own standing. Consultants should not reveal information about an organization to its competitors. The use of information gathered from OD efforts is a sensitive issue and presents ethical dilemmas.

A final ethical concern in OD is the potential for manipulation by the change agent. Because any change process involves influence, some individuals may feel manipulated. The key to alleviating the potential for manipulation is open communication. Participants should be given complete knowledge of the rationale for change, what they can expect of the change process, and what the intervention will entail. No actions should be taken that limit the participants' freedom of choice.[72]

ARE ORGANIZATION DEVELOPMENT EFFORTS EFFECTIVE?

Because organization development is designed to help organizations manage change, it is important to evaluate the effectiveness of these efforts. The success of any OD intervention depends on a host of factors, including the technique used, the competence of the change agent, the organization's readiness for change, and top management commitment. No single method of OD is effective in every instance. Instead, multiple-method OD approaches are recommended, because they allow organizations to capitalize on the benefits of several approaches.[73]

Efforts to evaluate OD efforts have focused on outcomes such as productivity. One review of more than 200 interventions indicated that worker productivity improved in 87 percent of the cases.[74] A separate analysis of 98 of these interventions revealed impressive productivity increases.[75] We can conclude that when properly applied and managed, organization development programs have positive effects on performance.[76]

MANAGERIAL IMPLICATIONS: MANAGING CHANGE

Several guidelines can be used to facilitate the success of management change efforts.[77] First, managers should recognize the forces for change. These forces can come from a combination of sources both internal and external to the organization.

A shared vision of the change should be developed that includes participation by all employees in the planning process. Top management must be committed to the change and should visibly demonstrate support, because employees look to these leaders to model appropriate behavior. A comprehensive diagnosis and needs analysis should be conducted. The company then must ensure that there are adequate resources for carrying out the change.

Resistance to change should be planned for and managed. Communication, participation, and empathetic support are ways of helping employees adjust. The reward system within the organization must be carefully evaluated to ensure that new behaviors, rather than old ones, are being reinforced. Participation in the change process should also be recognized and rewarded.

The organization development technique used should be carefully selected to meet the goals of the change. Finally, organization development efforts should be managed in an ethical manner and should preserve employees' privacy and freedom of choice. By using these guidelines, managers can meet the challenges of managing change while enhancing productivity in their organizations.

KEY TERMS

change agent	management development	sensitivity training
disenchantment	moving	skills training
disengagement	organization development (OD)	strategic change
disidentification	planned change	survey feedback
disorientation	process consultation	team building
incremental change	quality program	transformational change
job redesign	refreezing	unfreezing
management by objectives (MBO)	role negotiation	unplanned change

Experiential Exercise

ORGANIZATIONAL DIAGNOSIS OF THE UNIVERSITY

The purpose of this exercise is to give you experience in organizational diagnosis. Assume that your team has been hired to conduct a diagnosis of problem areas in your university and to make preliminary recommendations for organization development interventions.

Each team member should complete the following University Profile. Then, as a team, evaluate the strengths and weaknesses within each area (academics, teaching, social, cultural, and administrative) using the accompanying University Diagnosis form. Finally, make recommendations concerning organization development interventions for each area. Be as specific as possible in both your diagnosis and your recommendations. Each team should then present its diagnosis to the class.

University Profile

Not True	1	2	3	4	5	Very True

I. Academics

1 2 3 4 5   1. There is a wide range of courses to choose from.

1 2 3 4 5   2. Classroom standards are too easy.

1 2 3 4 5   3. The library is adequate.

1 2 3 4 5   4. Textbooks are helpful.

II. Teachers

1 2 3 4 5   1. Teachers here are committed to quality instruction.

1 2 3 4 5   2. We have a high-quality faculty.

III. Social

1 2 3 4 5   1. Students are friendly to one another.

1 2 3 4 5   2. It is difficult to make friends.

1 2 3 4 5   3. Faculty get involved in student activities.

1 2 3 4 5   4. Too much energy goes into drinking and goofing off.

IV. Cultural Events

1 2 3 4 5   1. There are ample activities on campus.

1 2 3 4 5   2. Student activities are boring.

1 2 3 4 5   3. The administration places a high value on student activities.

1 2 3 4 5   4. Too much emphasis is placed on sports.

1 2 3 4 5   5. We need more "cultural" activities.

V. Organizational/Management

1 2 3 4 5   1. Decision making is shared at all levels of the organization.

1 2 3 4 5   2. There is unity and cohesiveness among departments and units.

1 2 3 4 5   3. Too many departmental clashes hamper the organization's effectiveness.

1 2 3 4 5   4. Students have a say in many decisions.

1 2 3 4 5   5. The budgeting process seems fair.

1 2 3 4 5   6. Recruiting and staffing are handled thoughtfully, with student needs in mind.

University Diagnosis

	STRENGTH	WEAKNESS	INTERVENTION
1. Academic			
2. Teaching			
3. Social			
4. Cultural			
5. Administrative			

Source: "Organizational Diagnosis of the University" by D. Marcic, *Organizational Behavior: Experiences and Cases* (St. Paul, Minn.: West Publishing Company, 1989), 326–329. Reprinted by permission.

Chapter 1

1. H. Schwartz, "The Clockwork or the Snakepit: An Essay on the Meaning of Teaching Organizational Behavior," *Organizational Behavior Teaching Review* 11, No. 2 (1987): 19–26.

2. K. Lewin, "Field Theory in Social Science," selected theoretical papers (edited by Dorin Cartwright) (New York: Harper, 1951).

3. N. Schmitt, ed., Industrial/Organizational Section in *Encyclopedia of Psychology* (Washington, D.C.: American Psychological Association, and New York: Oxford University Press, 2000).

4. R. M. Yerkes, "The Relation of Psychology to Military Activities," *Mental Hygiene* 1 (1917): 371–376.

5. N. Gross, W. Mason, and A. McEachen, *Explorations in Role Analysis: Studies of the School Superintendent Role* (New York: Wiley, 1958).

6. J. S. Adams, A. Tashchian, and T. H. Stone. "Codes of Ethics as Signals for Ethical Behavior," *Journal of Business Ethics* 29 (2001): 199–211.

7. F. W. Taylor, *The Principles of Scientific Management* (New York: Norton, 1911).

8. E. A. Locke and G. P. Latham, *A Theory of Goal Setting and Task Performance* (Englewood Cliffs, N.J.: Prentice-Hall, 1990).

9. A. L. Wilkins and W. G. Ouchi, "Efficient Cultures: Exploring the Relationship between Culture and Organizational Performance," *Administrative Science Quarterly* 28 (1983): 468–481.

10. M. F. R. Kets de Vries and D. Miller, "Personality, Culture, and Organization," *Academy of Management Review* 11 (1986): 266–279.

11. H. Schwartz, *Narcissistic Process and Corporate Decay: The Theory of the Organizational Ideal* (New York: NYU Press, 1990).

12. J. G. March and H. A. Simon, *Organizations* (New York: Wiley, 1958).

13. H. B. Elkind, *Preventive Management: Mental Hygiene in Industry* (New York: B. C. Forbes, 1931).

14. J. C. Quick, "Occupational Health Psychology: Historical Roots and Future Directions," *Health Psychology* 18 (1999).

15. K. R. Pelletier, *Mind as Healer, Mind as Slayer: A Holistic Approach to Preventing Stress Disorders* (New York: Delacorte, 1977).

16. D. R. Ilgen, "Health Issues at Work," *American Psychologist* 45 (1990): 273–283.

17. R. L. A. Sterba, "The Organization and Management of the Temple Corporations in Ancient Mesopotamia," *Academy of Management Review* 1 (1976): 16–26; S. P. Dorsey, *Early English Churches in America* (New York: Oxford University Press, 1952).

18. Sir I. Moncreiffe of That Ilk, *The Highland Clans: The Dynastic Origins, Chiefs, and Background of the Clans and of Some Other Families Connected to Highland History*, rev. ed. (New York: C. N. Potter, 1982).

19. D. Shambaugh, "The Soldier and the State in China: The Political Work System in the People's Liberation Army," *Chinese Quarterly* 127 (1991): 527–568.

20. L. L'Abate, ed., *Handbook of Developmental Family Psychology and Psychopathology* (New York: Wiley, 1993).

21. J. A. Hostetler, *Communitarian Societies* (New York: Holt, Rinehart & Winston, 1974).

22. J. M. Lewis, "The Family System and Physical Illness," in *No Single Thread: Psychological Health in Family Systems* (New York: Brunner/Mazel, 1976).

23. D. Katz and R. L. Kahn, *The Social Psychology of Organizations*, 2nd ed. (New York: John Wiley & Sons, 1978); H. J. Leavitt, "Applied Organizational Change in Industry: Structural, Technological, and Humanistic Approaches," in J. G. March, ed., *Handbook of Organizations* (Chicago: Rand McNally, 1965): 1144–1170.

24. J. D. Thompson, *Organizations in Action* (New York: McGraw-Hill, 1967).

25. F. J. Roethlisberger and W. J. Dickson, *Management and the Worker* (Cambridge, Mass.: Harvard University Press, 1939).

26. W. L. French and C. H. Bell, *Organization Development*, 4th ed. (Englewood Cliffs, N.J.: Prentice-Hall, 1990).

27. J. P. Kotter, "Managing External Dependence," *Academy of Management Review* 4 (1979): 87–92.

28. H. K. Steensma and D. G. Corley, "Organizational Context as a Moderator of Theories on Firm Boundaries for Technology Sourcing," *Academy of Management Journal* 44 (2001): 271–291.

29. N. Brinker and D. T. Phillips, *On the Brink: The Life and Leadership of Norman Brinker* (Arlington, Tex.: The Summit Publishing Group, 1996).

30. R. Teerlink and L. Ozley, *More Than a Motorcycle: The Leadership Journey at Harley-Davidson* (Boston: Harvard Business School Publishing, 2000).

31. D. Packard, K. R. Lewis, and D. Kirby, *The HP Way: How Bill Hewlett and I Built Our Company* (New York: Harper Business, 1996).

32. H. Morgan, *Companies That Care: The Most Family-Friendly Companies in America, What They Offer, and How They Got That Way* (New York: Simon & Schuster, 1991).

33. American Heart Association, *Your Heart: An Owner's Manual* (Englewood Cliffs, N.J.: Prentice-Hall, 1995).

34. M. K. Gowing, J. D. Kraft, and J. C. Quick, *The New Organizational Reality: Downsizing, Restructuring and Revitalization* (Washington, D.C.: American Psychological Association, 1998); T. Tang and R. M. Fuller, "Corporate Downsizing: What Managers Can Do to Lessen the Negative Effects of Layoffs," *SAM Advanced Management Journal*, 60 (1995): 12–15, 31.

35. L. E. Thurow, *Head to Head: The Coming Economic Battle among Japan, Europe, and America* (New York: William Morrow, 1992).

36. J. E. Patterson, *Acquiring the Future: America's Survival and Success in the Global Economy* (Homewood, Ill.: Dow Jones-Irwin, 1990); H. B. Stewart, *Recollecting the Future: A View of Business, Technology, and Innovation in the Next 30 Years* (Homewood, Ill.: Dow Jones-Irwin, 1989).

37. L. R. Offermann and M. K. Gowing, "Organizations of the Future," *American Psychologist* 45 (1990): 95–108.

38. R. S. Fosler, W. Alonso, J. A. Meyer, and R. Kern, *Demographic Change and the American Future* (Pittsburgh, Pa.: University of Pittsburgh Press, 1990).

39. D. Ciampa, *Total Quality* (Reading, Mass.: Addison-Wesley, 1992).

40. American Management Association, *Blueprints for Service Quality: The Federal Express Approach* (New York: American Management Association, 1991); P. R. Thomas, L. J. Gallace, and K. R. Martin, *Quality Alone Is Not Enough* (New York: American Management Association, 1992).

41. J. A. Edosomwan, "Six Commandments to Empower Employees for Quality Improvement," *Industrial Engineering* 24 (1992): 14–15.

42. See also the five articles in the Special Research Forum on Teaching Effectiveness in the Organizational Sciences, *The Academy of Management Journal* 40 (1997): 1265–1398.

43. R. M. Steers, L. W. Porter, and G. A. Bigley, *Motivation and Leadership at Work* (New York: McGraw-Hill, 1996).

44. H. Levinson, *Executive Stress* (New York: New American Library, 1975).

45. D. L. Whetzel, "The Department of Labor Identifies Workplace Skills," *Industrial/Organizational Psychologist* 29 (1991): 89–90.

46. D. A. Whetton and K. S. Cameron, *Developing Management Skills*, 3rd ed. (New York: HarperCollins, 1995).

47. C. Argyris and D. A. Schon, *Organizational Learning: A Theory of Action Perspective* (Reading, Mass.: Addison-Wesley, 1978).

48. E. E. Lawler III, "From Job-Based to Competency-Based Organizations," *Journal of Organizational Behavior* 15 (1994): 3–15.

Chapter 2

1. M. A. Hitt, R. E. Hoskisson, and J. S. Harrison, "Strategic Competitiveness in the 1990s: Challenges and Opportunities for U.S.

Executives," *Academy of Management Executive* 5 (1991): 7–22.

2. S. C. Harper, "The Challenges Facing CEOs: Past, Present, and Future," *Academy of Management Executive* 6 (1992): 7–25.

3. T. R. Mitchell and W. G. Scott, "America's Problems and Needed Reforms: Confronting the Ethic of Personal Advantage," *Academy of Management Executive* 4 (1990): 23–25.

4. B. Spindle, "Sinking in Sync—The Global Slowdown Surprises Economists and Many Companies," *The Wall Street Journal* (December 21, 2000): A1–A10.

5. D. Jamieson and J. O'Mara, *Managing Workforce 2000* (San Francisco: Jossey-Bass, 1991).

6. K. Sera, "Corporate Globalization: A New Trend," *Academy of Management Executive* 6 (1992): 89–96.

7. K. Ohmae, *Borderless World: Power and Strategies in the Interlinked Economy* (New York: Harper & Row, 1990).

8. C. A. Bartlett and S. Ghoshal, *Managing across Borders: The Transnational Solution* (Boston: Harvard Business School Press, 1989).

9. K. R. Xin and J. L. Pearce, "Guanxi: Connections as Substitutes for Formal Institutional Support," *Academy of Management Journal* 39 (1996): 1641–1658.

10. P. S. Chan, "Franchise Management in East Asia," *Academy of Management Executive* 4 (1990): 75–85.

11. H. Weihrich, "Europe 1992: What the Future May Hold," *Academy of Management Executive* 4 (1990): 7–18.

12. R. Sharpe, "Hi-Tech Taboos," *The Wall Street Journal* (October 31, 1995): A1.

13. G. Hofstede, *Culture's Consequences: International Differences in Work-Related Values* (Beverly Hills, Calif.: Sage Publications, 1980).

14. G. Hofstede, "Motivation, Leadership, and Organization: Do American Theories Apply Abroad?" *Organizational Dynamics* (Summer 1980): 42–63.

15. R. Buda and S. M. Elsayed-Elkhouly, "Cultural Differences between Arabs and Americans," *Journal of Cross-Cultural Psychology* 29 (1998): 487–492.

16. G. Hofstede, "Gender Stereotypes and Partner Preferences of Asian Women in Masculine and Feminine Countries," *Journal of Cross-Cultural Psychology* 27 (1996): 533–546.

17. G. Hofstede, "Cultural Constraints in Management Theories," *Academy of Management Executive* 7 (1993): 81–94.

18. *Inc. Magazine*, Goldhirsh Group, Inc., 38 Commercial Wharf, Boston, MA 02110 (http://www.inc.com). Opening a Foreign Office: A Five-Country Comparison (Table), *Inc. Magazine*, April 1992.

19. A. J. Michel, "Goodbyes Can Cost Plenty in Europe," *Fortune* (April 6, 1992): 16.

20. M. Adams, "Building a Rainbow One Stripe at a Time," *HR Magazine* 9 (August 1999): 72–79.

21. E. Brandt, "Global HR," *Personnel Journal* 70 (1991): 38–44.

22. J. A. Gilbert and J. M. Ivancevich, "Valuing Diversity: A Tale of Two Organizations," *Academy of Management Executive* 4 (2000): 93–105.

23. R. W. Judy and C. D'Amico, *Workforce 2020* (Indianapolis, Ind.: Hudson Institute, 1997).

24. L. S. Gottfredson, "Dilemmas in Developing Diversity Programs," in S. E. Jackson, ed., *Diversity in the Workplace: Human Resources Initiatives* (New York: Guilford Press, 1992), 279–305.

25. U.S. Census Bureau, 2000.

26. Catalyst, *Catalyst Census of Women Corporate Officers and Top Earners*, 2000.

27. S. W. Wellington, *Women in Corporate Leadership: Progress and Prospects* (New York: Catalyst, 1996).

28. U.S. Department of Labor, "Usual Weekly Earnings Summary," *Labor Force Statistics from the Current Population Survey* (Washington, D.C.: U.S. Government, 2001).

29. A. M. Morrison, R. P. White, E. Van Velsor, and the Center for Creative Leadership, *Breaking the Glass Ceiling: Can Women Reach the Top of America's Largest Corporations?* (Reading, Mass.: Addison-Wesley, 1987).

30. N. J. Adler, "Global Leadership: Women Leaders," *Management International Review* 37 (1997): 171–196.

31. A. Eyring and B. A. Stead, "Shattering the Glass Ceiling: Some Successful Corporate Practices," *Journal of Business Ethics* 17 (1998): 245–251.

32. Catalyst, *Advancing Women in Business: The Catalyst Guide* (San Francisco: Jossey-Bass, 1998).

33. U.S. Department of Health and Human Services, *Profile of Older Americans* (Washington, D.C.: U.S. Government, 1997).

34. W. B. Johnston, "Global Workforce 2000: The New World Labor Market," *Harvard Business Review* 69 (1991): 115–127.

35. S. E. Jackson and E. B. Alvarez, "Working through Diversity as a Strategic Imperative," in S. E. Jackson, ed., *Diversity in the Workplace: Human Resources Initiatives* (New York: Guilford Press, 1992): 13–36.

36. "Managing Generational Diversity," *HR Magazine* 36 (1991): 91–92.

37. U.S. Bureau of the Census, *Population Profile of the United States, 1997* (Washington, D.C.: U.S. Government Printing Office, 1997).

38. W. J. Rothwell, "HRD and the Americans with Disabilities Act," *Training and Development Journal* (August 1991): 45–47.

39. J. Waldrop, "The Cost of Hiring the Disabled," *American Demographics* (March 1991): 12.

40. J. J. Laabs, "The Golden Arches Provide Golden Opportunities," *Personnel Journal* (July 1991): 52–57.

41. L. Winfield and S. Spielman, "Making Sexual Orientation Part of Diversity," *Training and Development* (April 1995): 50–51.

42. N. E. Day and P. Schoenrade, "Staying in the Closet versus Coming Out: Relationships between Communication about Sexual Orientation and Work Attitudes," *Personnel Psychology* 50 (1997): 147–163.

43. J. Landau, "The Relationship of Race and Gender to Managers' Ratings of Promotion Potential," *Journal of Organizational Behavior* 16 (1995): 391–400.

44. P. Barnum, "Double Jeopardy for Women and Minorities: Pay Differences with Age," *Academy of Management Journal* 38 (1995): 863–880.

45. P. A. Galagan, "Tapping the Power of a Diverse Workforce," *Training and Development Journal* 26 (1991): 38–44.

46. R. Thomas, "From Affirmative Action to Affirming Diversity," *Harvard Business Review* 68 (1990): 107–117.

47. T. H. Cox, Jr., *Cultural Diversity in Organizations: Theory, Research and Practice* (San Francisco: Berrett-Koehler, 1994).

48. Task Force on Management of Innovation, *Technology and Employment: Innovation and Growth in the U.S. Economy* (Washington, D.C.: U.S. Government Research Council, 1987).

49. C. H. Ferguson, "Computers and the Coming of the U.S. Keiretsu," *Harvard Business Review* 68 (1990): 55–70.

50. C. Arnst, "The Networked Corporation," *Business Week* (June 26, 1995): 86–89.

51. J. A. Senn, *Information Systems in Management*, 4th ed. (Belmont, Calif.: Wadsworth, 1990).

52. D. K. Sorenson and O. Bouhaddou, and H. R. Warner, *Knowledge Engineering in Health Informatics* (New York: Springer, 1999).

53. M. T. Damore, "A Presentation and Examination of the Integration of Unlawful Discrimination Practices in the Private Business Sector with Artificial Intelligence" (Thesis, Oklahoma State University, 1992).

54. A. Tanzer and R. Simon, "Why Japan Loves Robots and We Don't," *Forbes* (April 16, 1990): 148–153.

55. E. Fingleton, "Jobs for Life: Why Japan Won't Give Them Up," *Fortune* (March 20, 1995): 119–125.

56. M. Iansiti, "How the Incumbent Can Win: Managing Technological Transitions in the Semiconductor Industry," *Management Science* 46 (2000): 169–185.

57. M. B. W. Fritz, S. Narasimhan, and H. Rhee, "Communication and Coordination in the Virtual Office," *Journal of Management Information Systems* 14 (1998): 7–28.

58. M. Apgar IV, "The Alternative Workplace: Changing Where and How People Work," *Harvard Business Review* (May–June 1998): 121–136.

59. D. L. Nelson, "Individual Adjustment to Information-Driven Technologies: A Critical Review," *MIS Quarterly* 14 (1990): 79–98.

60. M. Allen, "Legislation Could Restrict Bosses from Snooping on Their Workers," *The Wall Street Journal* (September 24, 1991): B1–B8.

61. K. D. Hill and S. Kerr, "The Impact of Computer-Integrated Manufacturing Systems on the First Line Supervisor," *Journal of Organizational Behavior Management* 6 (1984): 81–87.

62. J. Anderson, "How Technology Brings Blind People into the Workplace," *Harvard Business Review* 67 (1989): 36–39.

63. D. L. Nelson and M. G. Kletke, "Individual Adjustment during Technological Innovation: A Research Framework," *Behaviour and Information Technology* 9 (1990): 257–271.

64. D. Mankin, T. Bikson, B. Gutek, and C. Stasz, "Managing Technological Change: The Process Is the Key," *Datamation* 34 (1988): 69–80.

65. M. R. Fusilier, C. D. Aby, Jr., J. K. Worley, and S. Elliott, "Perceived Seriousness of Business Ethics Issues," *Business and Professional Ethics Journal* 15 (1996): 67–78.

66. J. S. Mill, *Utilitarianism, Liberty, and Representative Government* (London: Dent, 1910).

67. K. H. Blanchard and N. V. Peale, *The Power of Ethical Management* (New York: Morrow, 1988).

68. C. Fried, *Right and Wrong* (Cambridge, Mass.: Harvard University Press, 1978).

69. I. Kant, *Groundwork of the Metaphysics of Morals*, trans. H. J. Paton (New York: Harper & Row, 1964).

70. A. Smith, *An Inquiry into the Nature and Causes of the Wealth of Nations*, vol. 10 of The Harvard Classics, ed. C. J. Bullock (New York: P. F. Collier & Son, 1909).

71. R. C. Solomon, "Corporate Roles, Personal Virtues: Aristotelean Approach to Business Ethics," *Business Ethics Quarterly* 2 (1992): 317–339; R. C. Solomon, *A Better Way to Think about Business: How Personal Integrity Leads to Corporate Success* (New York: Oxford University Press, 1999).

72. L. R. Smeltzer and M. M. Jennings, "Why an International Code of Business Ethics Would Be Good for Business," *Journal of Business Ethics* 17 (1998): 57–66.

73. J. J. Koch, "Wells Fargo's and IBM's HIV Policies Help Protect Employees' Rights," *Personnel Journal* (April 1990): 40–48.

74. A. Arkin, "Positive HIV and AIDS Policies at Work," *Personnel Management* (December 1994): 34–37.

75. U.S. EEOC. 1980. Discrimination because of Sex under Title VII of the 1964 Civil Rights Act as amended: Adoption of interim guidelines—sexual harassment. *Federal Register* 45: 25024–25025; S. J. Adler, "Lawyers Advise Concerns to Provide Precise Written Policy to Employees," *The Wall Street Journal* (October 9, 1991): B1.

76. L. F. Fitzgerald, F. Drasgow, C. L. Hulin, M. J. Gelfand, and V. J. Magley, "Antecedents and Consequences of Sexual Harassment in Organizations: A Test of an Integrated Model," *Journal of Applied Psychology* 82 (1997): 578–589.

77. E. Felsenthal, "Rulings Open Way for Sex-Harass Cases," *The Wall Street Journal* (June 29, 1998): A10.

78. K. T. Schneider, S. Swan, and L. F. Fitzgerald, "Job-Related and Psychological Effects of Sexual Harassment in the Workplace: Empirical Evidence from Two Organiza-tions," *Journal of Applied Psychology* 82 (1997): 401–415.

79. A. M. O'Leary-Kelly, R. L. Paetzold, and R. W. Griffin, "Sexual Harassment as Aggressive Behavior: An Actor-Based Perspective," *Academy of Management Review* 25 (2000): 372–388.

80. L. M. Goldenhar, N. G. Swanson, J. J. Hurrell, Jr., A. Ruder, and J. Deddens, "Stressors and Adverse Outcomes for Female Construction Workers," *Journal of Occupational Health Psychology* 3 (1998): 19–32; C. S. Piotrkowski, "Gender Harassment, Job Satisfaction and Distress Among Employed White and Minority Women," *Journal of Occupational Health Psychology* 3 (1998): 33–42.

81. G. N. Powell and S. Foley, "Something to Talk About: Romantic Relationships in Organizational Settings," *Journal of Management* 24 (1998): 421–448.

82. D. Fields, M. Pang, and C. Chio, "Distributive and Procedural Justice as Predictors of Employee Outcomes in Hong Kong," *Journal of Organizational Behavior* 21 (2000): 547–562.

83. H. L. Laframboise, "Vile Wretches and Public Heroes: The Ethics of Whistleblowing in Government," *Canadian Public Administration* (Spring 1991): 73–78.

84. D. B. Turban and D. W. Greening, "Corporate Social Performance and Organizational Attractiveness to Prospective Employees," *Academy of Management Journal* 40 (1996): 658–672.

Chapter 3

1. K. Lewin, "Formalization and Progress in Psychology," in D. Cartwright, ed., *Field Theory in Social Science* (New York: Harper, 1951).

2. N. S. Endler and D. Magnusson, "Toward an Interactional Psychology of Personality," *Psychological Bulletin* 83 (1976): 956–974.

3. J. R. Terborg, "Interactional Psychology and Research on Human Behavior in Organizations," *Academy of Management Review* 6 (1981): 561–576.

4. T. J. Bouchard, Jr., "Twins Reared Together and Apart: What They Tell Us about Human Diversity," in S. W. Fox, ed., *Individuality and Determinism* (New York: Plenum Press, 1984).

5. R. D. Arvey, T. J. Bouchard, Jr., N. L. Segal, and L. M. Abraham, "Job Satisfaction: Environmental and Genetic Components," *Journal of Applied Psychology* 74 (1989): 235–248.

6. G. Allport, *Pattern and Growth in Personality* (New York: Holt, 1961).

7. R. B. Cattell, *Personality and Mood by Questionnaire* (San Francisco: Jossey-Bass, 1973).

8. J. M. Digman, "Personality Structure: Emergence of a Five-Factor Model," *Annual Review of Psychology* 41 (1990): 417–440.

9. T. A. Judge, J. J. Martocchio, and C. J. Thoresen, "Five-Factor Model of Personality and Employee Absence," *Journal of Applied Psychology* 82 (1997): 745–755.

10. H. J. Bernardin, D. K. Cooke, and P. Villanova, "Conscientiousness and Agreeableness as Predictors of Rating Leniency," *Journal of Applied Psychology* 85 (2000): 232–234.

11. S. E. Seibert and M. L. Kraimer, "The Five-Factor Model of Personality and Career Success," *Journal of Vocational Behavior* 58 (2001): 1–21.

12. G. M. Hurtz and J. J. Donovan, "Personality and Job Performance: The Big Five Revisited," *Journal of Applied Psychology* 85 (2000): 869–879.

13. M. R. Barrick and M. K. Mount, "The Big Five Personality Dimensions and Job Performance: A Meta-Analysis," *Personnel Psychology* 44 (1991): 1–26.

14. S. Freud, *An Outline of Psychoanalysis* (New York: Norton, 1949).

15. C. Rogers, *On Becoming a Person: A Therapist's View of Psychotherapy*, 2nd ed. (Boston: Houghton Mifflin, 1970).

16. D. D. Clark and R. Hoyle, "A Theoretical Solution to the Problem of Personality-Situational Interaction," *Personality and Individual Differences* 9 (1988): 133–138.

17. D. Byrne and L. J. Schulte, "Personality Dimensions as Predictors of Sexual Behavior," in J. Bancroft, ed., *Annual Review of Sexual Research*, vol. 1 (Philadelphia: Society for the Scientific Study of Sex, 1990).

18. J. B. Rotter, "Generalized Expectancies for Internal vs. External Control of Reinforcement," *Psychological Monographs* 80, whole No. 609 (1966).

19. T. A. Judge and J. E. Bono, "Relationship of Core Self-Evaluations Traits—Self-Esteem, Generalized Self-Efficacy, Locus of Control, and Emotional Stability—with Job Satisfaction and Job Performance: A Meta-Analysis," *Journal of Applied Psychology* 86 (2001); 80–92.

20. S. S. K. Lam and J. Shaubroeck, "The Role of Locus of Control in Reactions to Being Promoted and to Being Passed Over: A Quasi Experiment," *Academy of Management Journal* 43 (2000): 66–78.

21. A. Bandura, *Self-Efficacy: The Exercise of Control* (San Francisco: Freeman, 1997).

22. J. Shaubroeck, J. R. Jones, and J. L. Xie, "Individual Differences in Utilizing Control to Cope with Job Demands: Effects on Susceptibility to Infectious Disease," *Journal of Applied Psychology* 86 (2001): 265–278.

23. B. W. Pelham and W. B. Swann, Jr., "From Self-Conceptions to Self-Worth: On the Sources and Structure of Global Self-Esteem," *Journal of Personality and Social Psychology* 57 (1989): 672–680.

24. A. H. Baumgardner, C. M. Kaufman, and P. E. Levy, "Regulating Affect Interpersonally: When Low Esteem Leads to Greater Enhancement," *Journal of Personality and Social Psychology* 56 (1989): 907–921.

25. J. Schimel, T. Pyszczynski, J. Arndt, and J. Greenberg, "Being Accepted for Who We Are: Evidence that Social Validation of the Intrinsic Self Reduces General Defensiveness," *Journal of Personality and Social Psychology* 80 (2001): 35–52.

26. P. Tharenou and P. Harker, "Moderating Influences of Self-Esteem on Relationships between Job Complexity, Performance, and Satisfaction," *Journal of Applied Psychology* 69 (1984): 623–632.

27. R. A. Ellis and M. S. Taylor, "Role of Self-Esteem within the Job Search Process," *Journal of Applied Psychology* 68 (1983): 632–640.

28. J. Brockner and T. Hess, "Self-Esteem and Task Performance in Quality Circles," *Academy of Management Journal* 29 (1986): 617–623.

29. B. R. Schlenker, M. F. Weingold, and J. R. Hallam, "Self-Serving Attributions in Social Context: Effects of Self-Esteem and Social Pressure," *Journal of Personality and Social Psychology* 57 (1990): 855–863.

30. M. K. Duffy, J. D. Shaw, and E. M. Stark, "Performance and Satisfaction in Conflicted Interdependent Groups: When and How Does Self-Esteem Make a Difference?" *Academy of Management Journal* 43 (2000): 772–782.

31. T. Mussweiler, S. Gabriel, and G. V. Bodenhausen, "Shifting Social Identities as a Strategy for Deflecting Threatening Social Comparisons," *Journal of Personality and Social Psychology* 79 (2000): 398–409.

32. M. Snyder and S. Gangestad, "On the Nature of Self-Monitoring: Matters of Assessment, Matters of Validity," *Journal of Personality and Social Psychology* 51 (1986): 123–139.

33. A. Mehra, M. Kilduff, and D. J. Brass, "The Social Networks of High and Low Self-Monitors: Implications for Workplace Performance," *Administrative Science Quarterly* 46 (2001): 121–146.

34. W. H. Turnley and M. C. Bolino, "Achieving Desired Images While Avoiding Undesired Images: Exploring the Role of Self-Monitoring in Impression Management," *Journal of Applied Psychology* 86 (2001): 351–360.

35. M. Kilduff and D. V. Day, "Do Chameleons Get Ahead? The Effects of Self-Monitoring on Managerial Careers," *Academy of Management Journal* 37 (1994): 1047–1060.

36. A. H. Church, "Managerial Self-Awareness in High-Performing Individuals in Organizations," *Journal of Applied Psychology* 82 (1997): 281–292.

37. A. M. Isen and R. A. Baron, "Positive Affect and Organizational Behavior," in B. M. Staw and L. L. Cummings, eds., *Research in Organizational Behavior*, vol. 12 (Greenwich, Conn.: JAI Press, 1990).

38. D. Watson and L. A. Clark, "Negative Affectivity: The Disposition to Experience Aversive Emotional States," *Psychological Bulletin* 96 (1984): 465–490.

39. R. A. Baron, "Interviewer's Moods and Reactions to Job Applicants: The Influence of Affective States on Applied Social Judgments," *Journal of Applied Social Psychology* 16 (1987): 16–28.

40. J. M. George, "Mood and Absence," *Journal of Applied Psychology* 74 (1989): 287–324.

41. M. J. Burke, A. P. Brief, and J. M. George, "The Role of Negative Affectivity in Understanding Relations between Self-Reports of Stressors and Strains: A Comment on the Applied Psychology Literature," *Journal of Applied Psychology* 78 (1993): 402–412.

42. S. Barsade, A. Ward, J. Turner, and J. Sonnenfeld, "To Your Heart's Content: A Model of Affective Diversity in Top Management Teams," *Administrative Science Quarterly* 45 (2000): 802–836.

43. W. Mischel, "The Interaction of Person and Situation," in D. Magnusson and N. S. Endler, eds., *Personality at the Crossroads: Current Issues in Interactional Psychology* (Hillsdale, N.J.: Erlbaum, 1977).

44. H. Rorschach, *Psychodiagnostics* (Bern: Hans Huber, 1921).

45. C. G. Jung, *Psychological Types* (New York: Harcourt & Brace, 1923).

46. Consulting Psychologists Press.

47. R. Benfari and J. Knox, *Understanding Your Management Style* (Lexington, Mass.: Lexington Books, 1991).

48. O. Kroeger and J. M. Thuesen, *Type Talk* (New York: Delacorte Press, 1988).

49. S. Hirsch and J. Kummerow, *Life Types* (New York: Warner Books, 1989).

50. I. B. Myers and M. H. McCaulley, *Manual: A Guide to the Development and Use of the Myers-Briggs Type Indicator* (Palo Alto, Calif.: Consulting Psychologists Press, 1990).

51. G. P. Macdaid, M. H. McCaulley, and R. I. Kainz, *Myers-Briggs Type Indicator: Atlas of Type Tables* (Gainesville, Fla.: Center for Application of Psychological Type, 1987).

52. J. B. Murray, "Review of Research on the Myers-Briggs Type Indicator," *Perceptual and Motor Skills* 70 (1990): 1187–1202.

53. J. G. Carlson, "Recent Assessment of the Myers-Briggs Type Indicator," *Journal of Personality Assessment* 49 (1985): 356–365.

54. A. Thomas, M. Benne, M. Marr, E. Thomas, and R. Hume, "The Evidence Remains Stable: The MBTI Predicts Attraction and Attrition in an Engineering Program," *Journal of Psychological Type* 55 (2000): 35–42.

55. C. Walck, "Training for Participative Management: Implications for Psychological Type," *Journal of Psychological Type* 21 (1991): 3–12.

56. E. C. Webster, *The Employment Interview: A Social Judgment Process* (Schomberg, Canada: SIP, 1982).

57. N. Adler, *International Dimensions of Organizational Behavior*, 2nd ed. (Boston: PWS-Kent, 1991).

58. L. R. Offerman and M. K. Gowing, "Personnel Selection in the Future: The Impact of Changing Demographics and the Nature of Work," in Schmitt, Borman & Associates, eds., *Personnel Selection in Organizations* (San Francisco: Jossey-Bass, 1993).

59. J. Park and M. R. Banaji, "Mood and Heuristics: The Influence of Happy and Sad States on Sensitivity and Bias in Stereotyping," *Journal of Personality and Social Psychology* 78 (2000): 1005–1023.

60. M. W. Levine and J. M. Shefner, *Fundamentals of Sensation and Perception* (Reading, Mass.: Addison-Wesley, 1981).

61. R. L. Dipboye, H. L. Fromkin, and K. Willback, "Relative Importance of Applicant Sex, Attractiveness, and Scholastic Standing in Evaluations of Job Applicant Resumes," *Journal of Applied Psychology* 60 (1975): 39–43.

62. I. H. Frieze, J. E. Olson, and J. Russell, "Attractiveness and Income for Men and Women in Management," *Journal of Applied Social Psychology* 21 (1991): 1039–1057.

63. P. Ekman and W. Friesen, *Unmasking the Face* (Englewood Cliffs, N.J.: Prentice-Hall, 1975).

64. J. E. Rehfeld, "What Working for a Japanese Company Taught Me," *Harvard Business Review* (November–December 1990): 167–176.

65. M. W. Morris and R. P. Larrick, "When One Cause Casts Doubt on Another: A Normative Analysis of Discounting in Causal Attribution," *Psychological Review* 102 (1995): 331–355.

66. G. B. Sechrist and C. Stangor, "Perceived Consensus Influences Intergroup Behavior and Stereotype Accessibility," *Journal of Personality and Psychology* 80 (2001): 645–654.

67. L. Copeland, "Learning to Manage a Multicultural Workforce," *Training* (May 1988): 48–56.

68. S. Ferrari, "Human Behavior in International Groups," *Management International Review* 7 (1972): 31–35.

69. A. Feingold, "Gender Differences in Effects of Physical Attractiveness on Romantic Attraction: A Comparison across Five Research Paradigms," *Journal of Personality and Social Psychology* 59 (1990): 981–993.

70. M. Snyder, "When Belief Creates Reality," *Advances in Experimental Social Psychology* 18 (1984): 247–305.

71. E. Burnstein and Y. Schul, "The Informational Basis of Social Judgments: Operations in Forming an Impression of Another Person," *Journal of Experimental Social Psychology* 18 (1982): 217–234.

72. R. L. Gross and S. E. Brodt, "How Assumptions of Consensus Undermine Decision Making," *MIT Sloan Management Review* 42 (Winter 2001): 86–94.

73. R. Rosenthal and L. Jacobson, *Pygmalion in the Classroom: Teacher Expectations and Pupils' Intellectual Development* (New York: Holt, Rinehart & Winston, 1968).

74. D. Eden and Y. Zuk, "Seasickness as a Self-Fulfilling Prophecy: Raising Self-Efficacy to Boost Performance at Sea," *Journal of Applied Psychology* 80 (1995): 628–635.

75. N. M. Kierein and M. A. Gold, "Pygmalion in Work Organizations: A Meta-Analysis," *Journal of Organizational Behavior* 21 (2000): 913–928.

76. D. Eden, "Pygmalion without Interpersonal Contrast Effects: Whole Groups Gain from Raising Manager Expectations," *Journal of Applied Psychology* 75 (1990): 394–398.

77. R. A. Giacolone and P. Rosenfeld, eds., *Impression Management in Organizations* (Hillsdale, N.J.: Erlbaum, 1990); J. Tedeschi and V. Melburg, "Impression Management and Influence in the Organization," in S. Bacharach and E. Lawler, eds., *Research in the Sociology of Organizations* (Greenwich, Conn.: JAI Press, 1984), 31–58.

78. A. Colella and A. Varma, "The Impact of Subordinate Disability on Leader–Member Exchange Relationships," *Academy of Management Journal* 44 (2001): 304–315.

79. D. C. Gilmore and G. R. Ferris, "The Effects of Applicant Impression Management Tactics on Interviewer Judgments," *Journal of Management* (December 1989): 557–564.

80. C. K. Stevens and A. L. Kristof, "Making the Right Impression: A Field Study of Applicant Impressions Management during Job Interviews," *Journal of Applied Psychology* 80 (1995): 587–606.

81. S. J. Wayne and R. C. Liden, "Effects of Impression Management on Performance Ratings: A Longitudinal Study," *Academy of Management Journal* 38 (1995): 232–260.

82. R. A. Baron, "Impression Management by Applicants during Employment Interviews: The 'Too Much of a Good Thing' Effect," in R. W. Eder and G. R. Ferris, eds., *The Employment Interview: Theory, Research, and Practice* (Newbury Park, Calif.: Sage Publications, 1989).

83. F. Heider, *The Psychology of Interpersonal Relations* (New York: Wiley, 1958).

84. B. Weiner, "An Attributional Theory of Achievement Motivation and Emotion," *Psychological Review* (October 1985): 548–573.

85. P. D. Sweeney, K. Anderson, and S. Bailey, "Attributional Style in Depression: A Meta-Analytic Review," *Journal of Personality and Social Psychology* 51 (1986): 974–991.

86. P. Rosenthal, D. Guest, and R. Peccei, "Gender Differences in Managers' Causal Explanations for Their Work Performance," *Journal of Occupational and Organizational Psychology* 69 (1996): 145–151.

87. J. Silvester, "Spoken Attributions and Candidate Success in Graduate Recruitment Interviews," *Journal of Occupational and Organizational Psychology* 70 (1997): 61–71.

88. L. Ross, "The Intuitive Psychologist and His Shortcomings: Distortions in the Attribution Process," in L. Berkowitz, ed., *Advances in Experimental Social Psychology* (New York: Academic Press, 1977).

89. D. T. Miller and M. Ross, "Self-Serving Biases in the Attribution of Causality: Fact or Fiction?" *Psychological Bulletin* 82 (1975): 313–325.

90. J. R. Schermerhorn, Jr., "Team Development for High-Performance Management," *Training and Development Journal* 40 (1986): 38–41.

91. J. G. Miller, "Culture and the Development of Everyday Causal Explanation," *Journal of Personality and Social Psychology* 46 (1984): 961–978.

92. G. Si, S. Rethorst, and K. Willimczik, "Causal Attribution Perception in Sports Achievement: A Cross-Cultural Study on Attributional Concepts in Germany and China," *Journal of Cross-Cultural Psychology* 26 (1995): 537–553.

Chapter 4

1. A. H. Eagly and S. Chaiken, *The Psychology of Attitudes* (Orlando, Fla.: Harcourt Brace Jovanovich, 1993).

2. M. J. Rosenberg, C. I. Hovland, W. J. McGuire, R. P. Abelson, and J. H. Brehm, *Attitude Organization and Change* (New Haven, Conn.: Yale University Press, 1960).

3. L. Festinger, *A Theory of Cognitive Dissonance* (Evanston, Ill.: Row, Peterson, 1957).

4. R. H. Fazio and M. P. Zanna, "On the Predictive Validity of Attitudes: The Roles of Direct Experience and Confidence," *Journal of Personality* 46 (1978): 228–243.

5. A. Tversky and D. Kahneman, "Judgment under Uncertainty: Heuristics and Biases," in D. Kahneman, P. Slovic, and A. Tversky, eds., *Judgment under Uncertainty* (New York: Cambridge University Press, 1982): 3–20.

6. D. Rajecki, *Attitudes*, 2nd ed. (Sunderland, Mass.: Sinauer Associates, 1989).

7. I. Ajzen and M. Fishbein, "Attitude–Behavior Relations: A Theoretical Analysis and Review of Empirical Research," *Psychological Bulletin* 84 (1977): 888–918.

8. B. T. Johnson and A. H. Eagly, "Effects of Involvement on Persuasion: A Meta-Analysis," *Psychological Bulletin* 106 (1989): 290–314.

9. K. G. DeBono and M. Snyder, "Acting on One's Attitudes: The Role of History of Choosing Situations," *Personality and Social Psychology Bulletin* 21 (1995): 629–636.

10. I. Ajzen and M. Fishbein, *Understanding Attitudes and Predicting Social Behavior* (Englewood Cliffs, N.J.: Prentice-Hall, 1980).

11. I. Ajzen, "From Intentions to Action: A Theory of Planned Behavior," in J. Kuhl and J. Beckmann, eds., *Action-Control: From Cognition to Behavior* (Heidelberg: Springer, 1985).

12. I. Ajzen, "The Theory of Planned Behavior," *Organizational Behavior and Human Decision Processes* 50 (1991): 1–33.

13. D. A. Garvin, "Quality Problems, Policies, and Attitudes in the United States and Japan: An Exploratory Study," *Academy of Management Journal* 29 (1986): 653–673.

14. E. A. Locke, "The Nature and Causes of Job Satisfaction," in M. Dunnette, ed., *Handbook of Industrial and Organizational Psychology* (Chicago: Rand McNally, 1976).

15. P. C. Smith, L. M. Kendall, and C. L. Hulin, *The Measurement of Satisfaction in Work and Retirement* (Skokie, Ill.: Rand McNally, 1969).

16. D. J. Weiss, R. V. Davis, G. W. England, and L. H. Lofquist, *Manual for the Minnesota Satisfaction Questionnaire* (Minneapolis: Industrial Relations Center, University of Minnesota, 1967).

17. M. T. Iaffaldano and P. M. Muchinsky, "Job Satisfaction and Job Performance: A Meta-Analysis," *Psychological Bulletin* 97 (1985): 251–273.

18. L. A. Bettencourt, K. P. Gwinner, and M. L. Meuter, "A Comparison of Attitude, Personality, and Knowledge Predictors of Service-Oriented Organizational Citizenship Behaviors," *Journal of Applied Psychology* 86 (2001): 29–41.

19. D. W. Organ, *Organizational Citizenship Behavior: The Good Soldier Syndrome* (Lexington, Mass.: Lexington Books, 1988).

20. P. M. Podsakoff, S. B. Mackenzie, and C. Hui, "Organizational Citizenship Behaviors and Managerial Evaluations of Employee Performance: A Review and Suggestions for Future Research," in G. Ferris, ed., *Research in Personnel and Human Resources Management* (Greenwich, Conn.: JAI Press, 1993), 1–40.

21. S. L. Wagner and M. C. Rush, "Altruistic Organizational Citizenship Behavior: Context, Disposition, and Age," *Journal of Social Psychology* 140 (2000): 379–391.

22. C. Ostroff, "The Relationship between Satisfaction, Attitudes and Performance: An Organizational Level Analysis," *Journal of Applied Psychology* 77 (1992): 963–974.

23. R. Griffin and T. Bateman, "Job Satisfaction and Organizational Commitment," in C. Cooper and I. Robertson, eds., *International Review of Industrial and Organizational Psychology* (New York: Wiley, 1986).

24. J. R. Lincoln, "Employee Work Attitudes and Management Practice in the U.S. and Japan: Evidence from a Large Comparative Survey," *California Management Review* (Fall 1989): 89–106.

25. I. A. McCormick and C. L. Cooper, "Executive Stress: Extending the International Comparison," *Human Relations* 41 (1988): 65–72.

26. A. Krishnan and R. Krishnan, "Organizational Variables and Job Satisfaction," *Psychological Research Journal* 8 (1984): 1–11.

27. R. T. Mowday, L. W. Porter, and R. M. Steers, *Employee–Organization Linkages: The Psychology of Commitment* (New York: Academic Press, 1982).

28. H. S. Becker, "Notes on the Concept of Commitment," *American Journal of Sociology* 66 (1960): 32–40.

29. J. P. Meyer, N. J. Allen, and C. A. Smith, "Commitment to Organizations and Occupations: Extension and Test of a Three-Component Model," *Journal of Applied Psychology* 78 (1993): 538–551.

30. J. P. Curry, D. S. Wakefield, J. L. Price, and C. W. Mueller, "On the Causal Ordering of Job Satisfaction and Organizational Commitment," *Academy of Management Journal* 29 (1986): 847–858.

31. B. Benkhoff, "Ignoring Commitment Is Costly: New Approaches Establish the Missing Link between Commitment and Performance," *Human Relations* 50 (1997): 701–726; N. J. Allen and J. P. Meyer, "Affective, Continuance and Normative Commitment to the Organization: An Examination of Construct Validity," *Journal of Vocational Behavior* 49 (1996): 252–276.

32. M. J. Somers, "Organizational Commitment, Turnover, and Absenteeism: An Examination of Direct and Interaction Effects," *Journal of Organizational Behavior* 16 (1995): 49–58; L. Lum, J. Kervin, K. Clark, F. Reid, and W. Sirola, "Explaining Nursing Turnover Intent: Job Satisfaction, Pay Satisfaction, or Organizational Commitment?" *Journal of Organizational Behavior* 19 (1998): 305–320.

33. R. Eisenberger *et al.*, "Reciprocation of Perceived Organizational Support," *Journal of Applied Psychology* 86 (2001): 42–51; J. E. Finegan, "The Impact of Person and Organizational Values on Organizational Commitment," *Journal of Occupational and Organizational Psychology* 73 (2000): 149–169.

34. A. al-Meer, "Organizational Commitment: A Comparison of Westerners, Asians, and Saudis," *International Studies of Management and Organization* 19 (1989): 74–84.

35. F. Luthans, H. S. McCaul, and N. C. Dodd, "Organizational Commitment: A Comparison of American, Japanese, and Korean Employees," *Academy of Management Journal* 28 (1985): 213–219.

36. D. J. Koys, "The Effects of Employee Satisfaction, Organizational Citizenship Behavior, and Turnover on Organizational Effectiveness: A Unit-Level, Longitudinal Study," *Personnel Psychology* 54 (2001): 101–114.

37. J. Cooper and R. T. Croyle, "Attitudes and Attitude Change," *Annual Review of Psychology* 35 (1984): 395–426.

38. R. Abelson, "A Push from the Top Shatters a Glass Ceiling," *The New York Times* (August 22, 1999): 1 and 33.

39. D. M. Mackie and L. T. Worth, "Processing Deficits and the Mediation of Positive Affect in Persuasion," *Journal of Personality and Social Psychology* 57 (1989): 27–40.

40. J. W. Brehm, *Responses to Loss of Freedom: A Theory of Psychological Reactance* (New York: General Learning Press, 1972).

41. R. Petty, D. T. Wegener, and L. R. Fabrigar, "Attitudes and Attitude Change," *Annual Review of Psychology* 48 (1997): 609–647.

42. W. Wood, "Attitude Change: Persuasion and Social Influence," *Annual Review of Psychology* 51 (2000): 539–570.

43. M. Rokeach, *The Nature of Human Values* (New York: Free Press, 1973).

44. C. Anderson, "Values-Based Management," *The Academy of Management Executive* 11 (1997): 25–46.

45. M. Rokeach and S. J. Ball-Rokeach, "Stability and Change in American Value Priorities, 1968–1981," *American Psychologist* 44 (1989): 775–784.

46. G. W. England, "Organizational Goals and Expected Behavior of American Managers," *Academy of Management Journal* 10 (1967): 107–117.

47. E. C. Ravlin and B. M. Meglino, "Effects of Values on Perception and Decision Making: A Study of Alternative Work Values Measures," *Journal of Applied Psychology* 72 (1987): 666–673.

48. E. C. Ravlin and B. M. Meglino, "The Transitivity of Work Values: Hierarchical Preference Ordering of Socially Desirable Stimuli," *Organizational Behavior and Human Decision Processes* 44 (1989): 494–508.

49. B. M. Meglino, E. C. Ravlin, and C. L. Adkins, "A Work Values Approach to Corporate Culture: A Field Test of the Value Congruence Process and Its Relationship to Individual Outcomes," *Journal of Applied Psychology* 74 (1989): 424–432.

50. T. A. Judge and R. D. Bretz, Jr., "Effects of Work Values on Job Choice Decisions," *Journal of Applied Psychology* 77 (1992): 261–271.

51. A. Weiss, "The Value System," *Personnel Administrator* (July 1989): 40–41.

52. R. H. Doktor, "Asian and American CEOs: A Comparative Study," *Organizational Dynamics* 18 (1990): 46–56.

53. R. L. Tung, "Handshakes across the Sea: Cross-Cultural Negotiating for Business Success," *Organizational Dynamics* (Winter 1991): 30–40.

54. C. Gomez, B. L. Kirkman, and D. L. Shapiro, "The Impact of Collectivism and In-Group/Out-Group Membership on the Evaluation Generosity of Team Members," *Academy of Management Journal* 43 (2000): 1097–1106; J. Zhou and J. J. Martocchio, "Chinese and American Managers' Compensation Award Decisions: A Comparative Policy-Capturing Study," *Personnel Psychology* 54 (2001): 115–145.

55. R. Neale and R. Mindel, "Rigging Up Multicultural Teamworking," *Personnel Management* (January 1992): 27–30.

56. P. F. Buller, J. J. Kohls, and K. S. Anderson, "When Ethics Collide: Managing Conflicts across Cultures," *Organizational Dynamics* 28 (2000): 52–66.

57. K. Hodgson, "Adapting Ethical Decisions to a Global Marketplace," *Management Review* 81 (1992): 53–57.

58. J. Bae and J. J. Lawler, "Organizational and HRM Strategies in Korea: Impact on Firm Performance in an Emerging Economy," *Academy of Management Journal* 43 (2000): 502–517.

59. F. Navran, "Your Role in Shaping Ethics," *Executive Excellence* 9 (1992): 11–12.

60. K. Labich, "The New Crisis in Business Ethics," *Fortune* (April 20, 1992): 167–176.

61. E. A. Lind, J. Greenberg, K. S. Scott, and T. D. Welchans, "The Winding Road from Employee to Complainant: Situational and Psychological Determinants of Wrongful-Termination Claims," *Administrative Science Quarterly* 45 (2000): 557–590.

62. W. H. Wagel, "A New Focus on Business Ethics at General Dynamics," *Personnel* (August 1987): 4–8.

63. G. Flynn, "Make Employee Ethics Your Business," *Personnel Journal* (June 1995): 30–40.

64. M. S. Baucus and D. A. Baucus, "Paying the Piper: An Empirical Examination of Longer-Term Financial Consequences of Illegal Corporate Behavior," *Academy of Management Journal* 40 (1997): 129–151.

65. J. O. Cherrington and D. J. Cherrington, "A Menu of Moral Issues: One Week in the Life of *The Wall Street Journal*," *Journal of Business Ethics* 11 (1992): 255–265.

66. B. L. Flannery and D. R. May, "Environmental Ethical Decision Making in the U.S. Metal-Finishing Industry," *Academy of Management Journal* 43 (2000): 642–662.

67. K. R. Andrews, "Ethics in Practice," *Harvard Business Review* (September–October 1989): 99–104.

68. A. Bhide and H. H. Stevens, "Why Be Honest if Honesty Doesn't Pay?" *Harvard Business Review* (September–October 1990): 121–129.

69. R. Levering, M. Moskowitz, J. Sung, C. Daniels, and T. Spencer, "The 100 Best Companies to Work For," *Fortune* 143 (January 8, 2001): 148–160; C. Williamson, "Best Workplaces Are Revealed," *Pensions & Investments* 28 (February 7, 2000): 2 and 46.

70. J. B. Rotter, "Generalized Expectancies for Internal versus External Control of Reinforcement," *Psychological Monographs* 80 (1966): 1–28.

71. L. K. Trevino and S. A. Youngblood, "Bad Apples in Bad Barrels: A Causal Analysis of Ethical Decision-Making Behavior," *Journal of Applied Psychology* 75 (1990): 378–385.

72. H. M. Lefcourt, *Locus of Control: Current Trends in Theory and Research*, 2nd ed. (Hillsdale, N.J.: Erlbaum, 1982).

73. N. Machiavelli, *The Prince*, trans. George Bull (Middlesex, England: Penguin Books, 1961).

74. R. Christie and F. L. Geis, *Studies in Machiavellianism* (New York: Academic Press, 1970).

75. R. A. Giacalone and S. B. Knouse, "Justifying Wrongful Employee Behavior: The Role of Personality in Organizational Sabotage," *Journal of Business Ethics* 9 (1990): 55–61.

76. S. B. Knouse and R. A. Giacalone, "Ethical Decision-Making in Business: Behavioral Issues and Concerns," *Journal of Business Ethics* 11 (1992): 369–377.

77. L. Kohlberg, "Stage and Sequence: The Cognitive Developmental Approach to Socialization," in D. A. Goslin, ed., *Handbook of Socialization Theory and Research* (Chicago: Rand McNally, 1969): 347–480.

78. C. I. Malinowski and C. P. Smith, "Moral Reasoning and Moral Conduct: An Investigation Prompted by Kohlberg's Theory," *Journal of Personality and Social Psychology* 49 (1985): 1016–1027.

79. M. Brabeck, "Ethical Characteristics of Whistleblowers," *Journal of Research in Personality* 18 (1984): 41–53.

80. W. Y. Penn and B. D. Collier, "Current Research in Moral Development as a Decision Support System," *Journal of Business Ethics* 4 (1985): 131–136.

81. Trevino and Youngblood, "Bad Apples in Bad Barrels."

82. C. Gilligan, *In a Different Voice: Psychological Theory and Women's Development* (Cambridge, Mass.: Harvard University Press, 1982).

83. S. Jaffee and J. S. Hyde, "Gender Differences in Moral Orientation: A Meta-Analysis," *Psychological Bulletin* 126 (2000): 703–726.

84. G. R. Franke, D. F. Crown, and D. F. Spake, "Gender Differences in Ethical Perceptions of Business Practices: A Social Role Theory Perspective," *Journal of Applied Psychology* 82 (1997): 920–934.

85. S. A. Goldman and J. Arbuthnot, "Teaching Medical Ethics: The Cognitive-Developmental Approach," *Journal of Medical Ethics* 5 (1979): 171–181.

Chapter 5

1. R. M. Steers, L. W. Porter, and G. Bigley, *Motivation and Leadership at Work*, 6th ed. (New York: McGraw-Hill, 1996).

2. J. P. Campbell and R. D. Pritchard, "Motivation Theory in Industrial and Organizational Psychology," in M. D. Dunnette, ed., *Handbook of Industrial and Organizational Psychology* (Chicago: Rand McNally, 1976), 63–130.

3. M. Weber, *The Protestant Ethic and the Spirit of Capitalism* (London: Talcott Parson, tr., 1930).

4. S. Freud, *Civilization and Its Discontents*, trans. and ed. J. Strachey (New York: Norton, 1961).

5. K. J. Sweetman, "Employee Loyalty around the Globe," *Sloan Management Review* 42 (2001): 16.

6. B. S. Frey, *Not Just for the Money: An Economic Theory of Personal Motivation* (Brookfield, Vt.: Edgar Elger, 1997).

7. F. J. Roethlisberger, *Management and Morale* (Cambridge, Mass.: Harvard University Press, 1941).

8. A. Smith, *An Inquiry into the Nature and Causes of the Wealth of Nations*, vol. 10 of *The Harvard Classics*, C. J. Bullock, ed. (New York: Collier, 1909).

9. F. W. Taylor, *The Principles of Scientific Management* (New York: Norton, 1911).

10. Hearings before Special Committee of the House of Representatives to Investigate the Taylor and Other Systems of Shop Management under Authority of House Resolution 90, vol. 3, 1377–1508 contains Taylor's testimony before the committee from Thursday, January 25, through Tuesday, January 30, 1912.

11. A. H. Maslow, "A Theory of Human Motivation," *Psychological Review* 50 (1943): 370–396.

12. W. James, *The Principles of Psychology* (New York: H. Holt & Co., 1890; Cambridge, Mass.: Harvard University Press, 1983).

13. J. Dewey, *Human Nature and Conduct: An Introduction to Social Psychology* (New York: Holt, 1922).

14. S. Freud, *A General Introduction to Psycho-Analysis: A Course of Twenty-Eight Lectures Delivered at the University of Vienna* (New York: Liveright, 1963); A. Adler, *Understanding Human Nature* (Greenwich, Conn.: Fawcett, 1927).

15. L. W. Porter, "A Study of Perceived Need Satisfactions in Bottom and Middle Management Jobs," *Journal of Applied Psychology* 45 (1961): 1–10.

16. E. E. Lawler III and J. L. Suttle, "A Causal Correlational Test of the Need Hierarchy Concept," *Organizational Behavior and Human Performance* 7 (1973): 265–287.

17. D. M. McGregor, *The Human Side of Enterprise* (New York: McGraw-Hill, 1960).

18. D. M. McGregor, "The Human Side of Enterprise," *Management Review* (November 1957): 22–28, 88–92.

19. D. E. Petersen and J. Hillkirk, *A Better Idea: Redefining the Way Americans Work* (Boston: Houghton Mifflin, 1991).

20. G. E. Forward, D. E. Beach, D. A. Gray, and J. C. Quick, "Mentofacturing: A Vision for American Industrial Excellence," *Academy of Management Executive* 5 (1991): 32–44.

21. C. P. Alderfer, *Human Needs in Organizational Settings* (New York: Free Press, 1972).

22. B. Schneider and C. P. Alderfer, "Three Studies of Need Satisfactions in Organizations," *Administrative Science Quarterly* 18 (1973): 489–505.

23. H. A. Murray, *Explorations in Personality: A Clinical and Experimental Study of Fifty Men of College Age* (New York: Oxford University Press, 1938).

24. D. C. McClelland, *Motivational Trends in Society* (Morristown, N.J.: General Learning Press, 1971).

25. J. P. Chaplin and T. S. Krawiec, *Systems and Theories of Psychology* (New York: Holt, Rinehart & Winston, 1960).

26. D. C. McClelland, "Achievement Motivation Can Be Learned," *Harvard Business Review* 43 (1965): 6–24.

27. E. A. Ward, "Multidimensionality of Achievement Motivation among Employed Adults," *Journal of Social Psychology* 134 (1997): 542–544.

28. A. Sagie, D. Elizur, and H. Yamauchi, "The Structure and Strength of Achievement Motivation: A Cross-Cultural Comparison," *Journal of Organizational Behavior* 17 (1996): 431–444.

29. D. C. McClelland and D. Burnham, "Power Is the Great Motivator," *Harvard Business Review* 54 (1976): 100–111; J. Hall and J. Hawker, *Power Management Inventory* (The Woodlands, Tex.: Teleometrics International, 1988).

30. F. Luthans, "Successful versus Effective Real Managers," *Academy of Management Executive* 2 (1988): 127–131.

31. S. Schachter, *The Psychology of Affiliation* (Stanford, Calif.: Stanford University Press, 1959).

32. F. Herzberg, B. Mausner, and B. Snyderman, *The Motivation to Work* (New York: Wiley, 1959).

33. F. Herzberg, *Work and the Nature of Man* (Cleveland: World, 1966).

34. F. J. Leach and J. D. Westbrook, "Motivation and Job Satisfaction in One Government Research and Development Environment," *Engineering Management Journal* 12 (2000): 3–8.

35. P. M. Blau, *Exchange and Power in Social Life* (New York: Wiley, 1964).

36. A. Etzioni, "A Basis for Comparative Analysis of Complex Organizations," in A. Etzioni, ed., *A Sociological Reader on Complex Organizations*, 2nd ed. (New York: Holt, Rinehart & Winston, 1969): 59–76.

37. O. Janssen, "Job Demands, Perceptions of Effort–Reward Fairness and Innovative Work Behavior," *Journal of Occupational & Organizational Psychology* 73 (2000): 287–302.

38. J. P. Campbell, M. D. Dunnette, E. E. Lawler III, and K. E. Weick, Jr., *Managerial Behavior, Performance and Effectiveness* (New York: McGraw-Hill, 1970).

39. J. S. Adams, "Inequity in Social Exchange," in L. Berkowitz, ed., *Advances in Experimental Social Psychology*, vol. 2 (New York: Academic Press, 1965): 267–299; J. S. Adams, "Toward an Understanding of Inequity," *Journal of Abnormal and Social Psychology* 67 (1963): 422–436.

40. J. Nelson-Horchler, "The Best Man for the Job Is a Man," *Industry Week* (January 7, 1991): 50–52.

41. P. D. Sweeney, D. B. McFarlin, and E. J. Inderrieden, "Using Relative Deprivation Theory to Explain Satisfaction with Income and Pay Level: A Multistudy Examination," *Academy of Management Journal* 33 (1990): 423–436.

42. R. C. Huseman, J. D. Hatfield, and E. A. Miles, "A New Perspective on Equity Theory: The Equity Sensitivity Construct," *Academy of Management Review* 12 (1987): 222–234.

43. D. McLoughlin and S. C. Carr, "Equity and Sensitivity and Double Demotivation," *Journal of Social Psychology* 137 (1997): 668–670.

44. K. E. Weick, M. G. Bougon, and G. Maruyama, "The Equity Context," *Organizational Behavior and Human Performance* 15 (1976): 32–65.

45. R. Coles, *Privileged Ones* (Boston: Little, Brown, 1977).

46. J. Greenberg, "Equity and Workplace Status: A Field Experiment," *Journal of Applied Psychology* 73 (1988): 606–613.

47. R. A. Cosier and D. R. Dalton, "Equity Theory and Time: A Reformulation," *Academy of Management Review* 8 (1983): 311–319.

48. J. E. Martin and M. W. Peterson, "Two-Tier Wage Structures: Implications for Equity Theory," *Academy of Management Journal* 30 (1987): 297–315.

49. V. H. Vroom, *Work and Motivation* (New York: Wiley, 1964/1970).

50. U. R. Larson, "Supervisor's Performance Feedback to Subordinates: The Effect of Performance Valence and Outcome Dependence," *Organizational Behavior and Human Decision Processes* 37 (1986): 391–409.

51. M. C. Kernan and R. G. Lord, "Effects of Valence, Expectancies, and Goal-Performance Discrepancies in Single and Multiple Goal Environments," *Journal of Applied Psychology* 75 (1990): 194–203.

52. R. J. Sanchez, D. M. Truxillo, and T. N. Bauer, "Development and Examination of an Expectancy-Based Measure of Test-Taking Motivation," *Journal of Applied Psychology* 85 (2000): 739–750.

53. W. VanEerde and H. Thierry, "Vroom's Expectancy Models and Work-Related Criteria: A Meta-Analysis," *Journal of Applied Psychology* 81 (1996): 575–586.

54. E. D. Pulakos and N. Schmitt, "A Longitudinal Study of a Valence Model Approach for the Prediction of Job Satisfaction of New Employees," *Journal of Applied Psychology* 68 (1983): 307–312.

55. F. J. Landy and W. S. Becker, "Motivation Theory Reconsidered," in L. L. Cummings and B. M. Staw, eds., *Research in Organizational Behavior* 9 (Greenwich, Conn.: JAI Press, 1987): 1–38.

56. L. Kohlberg, "The Cognitive-Developmental Approach to Socialization," in D. A. Goslin, ed., *Handbook of Socialization Theory and Research* (Chicago: Rand McNally, 1969).

57. N. J. Adler, *International Dimensions of Organizational Behavior* (Boston: PWS-Kent, 1991).

58. G. Hofstede, "Motivation, Leadership, and Organization: Do American Theories Apply Abroad?" *Organizational Dynamics* 9 (1980): 42–63.

59. G. H. Hines, "Cross-Cultural Differences in Two-Factor Theory," *Journal of Applied Psychology* 58 (1981): 313–317.

Chapter 6

1. I. P. Pavlov, *Conditioned Reflexes* (New York: Oxford University Press, 1927).

2. B. Cannon, "Walter B. Cannon: Reflections on the Man and His Contributions," *Centennial Session*, American Psychological Association Centennial Convention, Washington, D.C., 1992.

3. B. F. Skinner, *The Behavior of Organisms: An Experimental Analysis* (New York: Appleton-Century-Crofts, 1938).

4. B. F. Skinner, *Science and Human Behavior* (New York: Free Press, 1953).

5. F. Luthans and R. Kreitner, *Organizational Behavior Modification and Beyond* (Glenview, Ill.: Scott, Foresman, 1985).

6. A. D. Stajkovic and F. Luthans, "A Meta-Analysis of the Effects of Organizational Behavior Modification on Task Performance, 1975–95," *Academy of Management Journal* 40 (1997): 1122–1149.

7. A. D. Stajkovic and F. Luthans, "Differential Effects of Incentive Motivators on Work," *Academy of Management Journal* 44 (2001): 580–591.

8. J. Hale, "Strategic Rewards: Keeping Your Best Talent from Walking Out the Door," *Compensation & Benefits Management* 14 (1998): 39–50.

9. B. F. Skinner, *Contingencies of Reinforcement: A Theoretical Analysis* (New York: Appleton-Century-Crofts, 1969).

10. J. P. Chaplin and T. S. Krawiec, *Systems and Theories of Psychology* (New York: Holt, Rinehart & Winston, 1960).

11. A. Bandura, *Social Learning Theory* (Englewood Cliffs, N.J.: Prentice-Hall, 1977); A. Bandura, "Self-Efficacy: Toward a Unifying Theory of Behavioral Change," *Psychological Review* 84 (1977): 191–215.

12. A. Bandura, "Regulation of Cognitive Processes through Perceived Self-Efficacy," *Developmental Psychology* (September 1989): 729–735.

13. J. M. Phillips and S. M. Gully, "Role of Goal Orientation, Ability, Need for Achievement, and Locus of Control in the Self-Efficacy and Goal-Setting Process," *Journal of Applied Psychology* 82 (1997): 792–802.

14. J. C. Weitlauf, R. E. Smith, and D. Cervone, "Generalization Effects of Coping-Skills Training: Influence of Self-Defense Training on Women's Efficacy Beliefs, Assertiveness, and Aggression," *Journal of Applied Psychology* 85 (2000): 625–633.

15. A. D. Stajkovic and F. Luthans, "Social Cognitive Theory and Self-Efficacy: Going Beyond Traditional Motivational and Behavioral Approaches," *Organizational Dynamics* (Spring 1998): 62–74.

16. A. D. Stajkovic and F. Luthans, "Self-Efficacy and Work-Related Performance: A Meta-Analysis," *Psychological Bulletin* 124 (1998): 240–261.

17. V. Gecas, "The Social Psychology of Self-Efficacy," *Annual Review of Sociology* 15 (1989): 291–316.

18. O. Isachsen and L. V. Berens, *Working Together: A Personality Centered Approach to Management* (Coronado, Calif.: Neworld Management Press, 1988); O. Krueger and J. M. Thuesen, *Type Talk* (New York: Tilden Press, 1988).

19. E. A. Locke and G. P. Latham, *A Theory of Goal Setting and Task Performance* (Englewood Cliffs, N.J.: Prentice-Hall, 1990).

20. T. O. Murray, *Management by Objectives: A Systems Approach to Management* (Fort Worth, Tex.: Western Company, n.d.).

21. W. T. Brooks and T. W. Mullins, *High Impact Time Management* (Englewood Cliffs, N.J.: Prentice-Hall, 1989).

22. E. A. Locke, "Toward a Theory of Task Motivation and Incentives," *Organizational Behavior and Human Performance* 3 (1968): 157–189.

23. J. C. Quick, "Dyadic Goal Setting within Organizations: Role Making and Motivational Considerations," *Academy of Management Review* 4 (1979): 369–380.

24. D. McGregor, "An Uneasy Look at Performance Appraisal," *Harvard Business Review* 35 (1957): 89–94.

25. J. R. Hollenbeck, C. R. Williams, and H. J. Klein, "An Empirical Examination of the Antecedents of Commitment to Difficult Goals," *Journal of Applied Psychology* 74 (1989): 18–23.

26. R. C. Rodgers and J. E. Hunter, "The Impact of Management by Objectives on Organizational Productivity," unpublished paper (Lexington: University of Kentucky, 1989).

27. E. A. Locke, K. N. Shaw, L. M. Saari, and G. P. Latham, "Goal Setting and Task Performance: 1969–1980," *Psychological Bulletin* 90 (1981): 125–152.

28. D. B. Fedora, W. D. Davis, J. M. Maslync, and K. Mathiesond, "Performance Improvement Efforts in Response to Negative Feedback: The Roles of Source Power and Recipient Self-Esteem," *Journal of Management* 27 (2001): 79–98.

29. J. C. Quick, "Dyadic Goal Setting and Role Stress," *Academy of Management Journal* 22 (1979): 241–252.

30. G. S. Odiorne, *Management by Objectives: A System of Managerial Leadership* (New York: Pitman, 1965).

31. American Management Association, *Blueprints for Service Quality: The Federal Express Approach* (New York: American Management Association, 1991).

32. G. P. Latham and G. A. Yukl, "A Review of Research on the Application of Goal Setting in Organizations," *Academy of Management Journal* 18 (1975): 824–845.

33. P. F. Drucker, *The Practice of Management* (New York: Harper & Bros., 1954).

34. R. D. Prichard, P. L. Roth, S. D. Jones, P. J. Galgay, and M. D. Watson, "Designing a Goal-Setting System to Enhance Performance: A Practical Guide," *Organizational Dynamics* 17 (1988): 69–78.

35. C. L. Hughes, *Goal Setting: Key to Individual and Organizational Effectiveness* (New York: American Management Association, 1965).

36. M. E. Tubbs and S. E. Ekeberg, "The Role of Intentions in Work Motivation: Implications for Goal-Setting Theory and Research," *Academy of Management Review* 16 (1991): 180–199.

37. J. M. Ivancevich, J. T. McMahon, J. W. Streidl, and A. D. Szilagyi, "Goal Setting: The Tenneco Approach to Personnel Development and Management Effectiveness," *Organizational Dynamics* 7 (1978): 58–80.

38. J. R. Hollenbeck and A. P. Brief, "The Effects of Individual Differences and Goal Origin on Goal Setting and Performance," *Organizational Behavior and Human Decision Processes* 40 (1987): 392–414.

39. R. A. Katzell and D. E. Thompson, "Work Motivation: Theory and Practice," *American Psychologist* 45 (1990): 144–153; M. W. McPherson, "Is Psychology the Science of Behavior?" *American Psychologist* 47 (1992): 329–335.

40. E. A. Locke, "The Ideas of Frederick W. Taylor: An Evaluation," *Academy of Management Review* 7 (1982): 15–16; R. M. Yerkes and J. D. Dodson, "The Relation of Strength of Stimulus to Rapidity of Habit-Formation," *Journal of Comparative Neurology and Psychology* 18 (1908): 459–482.

41. P. Cappelli and N. Rogovsky, "Employee Involvement and Organizational Citizenship: Implications for Labor Law Reform and 'Lean Production,'" *Industrial & Labor Relations Review* 51 (1998): 633–653.

42. I. M. Jawahar and C. R. Williams, "Where All the Children Are Above Average: The Performance Appraisal Purpose Effect," *Personnel Psychology* 50 (1997): 905–925.

43. M. E. Tubbs and M. L. Trusty, "Direct Reports of Motivation for Task Performance Levels: Some Construct-Related Evidence," *Journal of Psychology* 135 (2001): 185–205.

44. R. R. Kilburg, *Executive Coaching: Developing Managerial Wisdom in a World of Chaos* (Washington, D.C.: American Psychological Association, 2000).

45. H. H. Meyer, E. Kay, and J. R. P. French, "Split Roles in Performance Appraisal," *Harvard Business Review* 43 (1965): 123–129.

46. W. A. Fisher, J. C. Quick, L. L. Schkade, and G. W. Ayers, "Developing Administrative Personnel through the Assessment Center Technique," *Personnel Administrator* 25 (1980): 44–46, 62.

47. M. B. DeGregorio and C. D. Fisher, "Providing Performance Feedback: Reactions to Alternative Methods," *Journal of Management* 14 (1988): 605–616.

48. G. C. Thornton, "The Relationship between Supervisory and Self-Appraisals of Executive Performance," *Personnel Psychology* 21 (1968): 441–455.

49. A. S. DeNisi and A. N. Kluger, "Feedback Effectiveness: Can 360-Degree Appraisals Be Improved?" *Academy of Management Executive* 14 (2000): 129–140.

50. L. Hirschhorn, "Leaders and Followers in a Postindustrial Age: A Psychodynamic View," *Journal of Applied Behavioral Science* 26 (1990): 529–542.

51. F. M Jablin, "Superior–Subordinate Communication: The State of the Art," *Psychological Bulletin* 86 (1979): 1201–1222.

52. J. Pfeffer, "Six Dangerous Myths about Pay," *Harvard Business Review* 76 (1998): 108–119.

53. M. Erez, "Work Motivation from a Cross-Cultural Perspective," in A. M. Bouvy, F. J. R. Van de Vijver, P. Boski, and P. G. Schmitz, eds., *Journeys into Cross-Cultural Psychology* (Amsterdam, Netherlands: Swets & Zeitlinger, 1994), 386–403.

54. George T. Milkovich and Jerry M. Newman, *Compensation*, 4th ed. (Homewood, Ill.: Irwin, 1993).

55. S. Kerr, "On the Folly of Rewarding A, While Hoping for B," *Academy of Management Journal* 18 (1975): 769–783.

56. J. M. Bardwick, *Danger in the Comfort Zone* (New York: American Management Association, 1991).

57. M. J. Martinko and W. L. Gardner, "The Leader/Member Attributional Process," *Academy of Management Review* 12 (1987): 235–249.

58. K. N. Wexley, R. A. Alexander, J. P. Greenawalt, and M. A. Couch, "Attitudinal Congruence and Similarity as Related to Interpersonal Evaluations in Manager–Subordinate Dyads," *Academy of Management Journal* 23 (1980): 320–330.

59. H. H. Kelley, *Attribution in Social Interaction* (New York: General Learning Press, 1971).

60. H. H. Kelley, "The Processes of Causal Attribution," *American Psychologist* 28 (1973): 107–128.

61. A. M. Young and P. L. Perrewe, "What Did You Expect? An Examination of Career-Related Support and Social Support among Mentors and Proteges," *Journal of Management* 26 (2000): 611–633.

62. K. Doherty, "The Good News about Depression," *Business and Health* 3 (1989): 1–4.

63. K. E. Kram, "Phases of the Mentor Relationship," *Academy of Management Journal* 26 (1983): 608–625.

64. T. N. Bauer and S. G. Green, "Development of Leader–Member Exchange: A Longitudinal Test," *Academy of Management Journal* 39 (1996): 1538–1567.

65. K. E. Kram and L. A. Isabella, "Mentoring Alternatives: The Role of Peer Relationships in Career Development," *Academy of Management Journal* 28 (1985): 110–132.

66. J. Greco, "Hey, Coach!" *Journal of Business Strategy* 22 (2001): 28–32.

Chapter 7

1. D. L. Whetzel, "The Department of Labor Identifies Workplace Skills," *The Industrial/Organizational Psychologist* (July 1991): 89–90.

2. *Richness* is a term originally coined by W. D. Bodensteiner, "Information Channel Utilization under Varying Research and Development Project Conditions" (Ph.D. diss., University of Texas at Austin, 1970).

3. R. Reik, *Listen with the Third Ear* (New York: Pyramid, 1972).

4. A. G. Athos and J. J. Gabarro, *Interpersonal Behavior: Communication and Understanding in Relationships* (Englewood Cliffs, N.J.: Prentice-Hall, 1978).

5. A. D. Mangelsdorff, "Lessons Learned from the Military: Implications for Management" (Distinguished Visiting Lecture, University of Texas at Arlington, 29 January 1993).

6. J. J. Lynch, *A Cry Unheard: New Insights into the Medical Consequences of Loneliness* (Baltimore, Md.: Bancroft Press, 2000).

7. D. A. Morand, "Language and Power: An Empirical Analysis of Linguistic Strategies Used in Superior–Subordinate Communication," *Journal of Organizational Behavior* 21 (2000): 235–249.

8. F. Luthans, "Successful versus Effective Real Managers," *Academy of Management Executive* 2 (1988): 127–132.

9. L. E. Penley, E. R. Alexander, I. E. Jernigan, and C. I. Henwood, "Communication Abilities of Managers: The Relationship of Performance," *Journal of Management* 17 (1991): 57–76.

10. F. M. Jablin, "Superior–Subordinate Communication: The State of the Art," *Psychological Bulletin* 86 (1979): 1201–1222; W. C. Reddin, *Communication within the Organization: An Interpretive Review of Theory and Research* (New York: Industrial Communication Council, 1972).

11. B. Barry and J. M. Crant, "Dyadic Communication Relationships in Organizations: An Attribution Expectancy Approach," *Organization Science* 11 (2000): 648–665.

12. J. C. Quick, D. L. Nelson, and J. D. Quick, *Stress and Challenge at the Top: The Paradox of the Successful Executive* (Chichester, England: Wiley, 1990).

13. A. Furhham and P. Stringfield, "Congruence in Job-Performance Ratings: A Study of 360 Degree Feedback Examining Self, Manager, Peers, and Consultant Ratings," *Human Relations* 51 (1998): 517–530.

14. J. W. Gilsdorf, "Organizational Rules on Communicating: How Employees Are—and Are Not—Learning the Ropes," *Journal of Business Communication* 35 (1998): 173–201.

15. E. A. Gerloff and J. C. Quick, "Task Role Ambiguity and Conflict in Supervision–Subordinate Relationships," *Journal of Applied Communication Research* 12 (1984): 90–102.

16. E. H. Schein, "Reassessing the 'Divine Rights' of Managers," *Sloan Management Review* 30 (1989): 63–68.

17. D. Tannen, *That's Not What I Mean! How Conversational Style Makes or Breaks Your Relations with Others* (New York: Morrow, 1986); D. Tannen, *You Just Don't Understand* (New York: Ballentine, 1990).

18. D. G. Allen and R. W. Griffeth, "A Vertical and Lateral Information Processing: The Effects of Gender, Employee Classification Level, and Media Richness on Communication and Work Outcomes," *Human Relations* 50 (1997): 1239–1260.

19. K. L. Ashcraft, "Empowering 'Professional' Relationships," *Management Communication Quarterly* 13 (2000): 347–393.

20. G. Hofstede, *Culture's Consequences: International Differences in Work-Related Values* (Beverly Hills, Calif.: Sage Publications, 1980).

21. G. Hofstede, "Motivation, Leadership, and Organization: Do American Theories Apply Abroad?" *Organizational Dynamics* 9 (1980): 42–63.

22. H. Levinson, *Executive* (Cambridge, Mass.: Harvard University Press, 1981).

23. P. Benimadhu, "Adding Value through Diversity: An Interview with Bernard F. Isautier," *Canadian Business Review* 22 (1995): 6–11.

24. M. J. Gannon and Associates, *Understanding Global Cultures: Metaphorical Journeys through 17 Countries* (Thousand Oaks, Calif.: Sage Publications, 1994).

25. T. Wells, *Keeping Your Cool under Fire: Communicating Nondefensively* (New York: McGraw-Hill, 1980).

26. R. D. Laing, *The Politics of the Family and Other Essays* (New York: Pantheon, 1971).

27. H. S. Schwartz, *Narcissistic Process and Corporate Decay: The Theory of the Organizational Ideal* (New York: New York University Press, 1990).

28. W. R. Forrester and M. F. Maute, "The Impact of Relationship Satisfaction on Attribution, Emotions, and Behaviors Following Service Failure," *Journal of Applied Business Research* (2000): 1–45.

29. M. L. Knapp, *Nonverbal Communication in Human Interaction* (New York: Holt, Rinehart & Winston, 1978); J. McCroskey and L. Wheeless, *Introduction to Human Communication* (New York: Allyn & Bacon, 1976).

30. A. M. Katz and V. T. Katz, eds., *Foundations of Nonverbal Communication* (Carbondale, Ill.: Southern Illinois University Press, 1983).

31. M. D. Lieberman, "Intuition: A Social Cognitive Neuroscience Approach," *Psychological Bulletin* (2000): 109–138.

32. E. T. Hall, *The Hidden Dimension* (Garden City, N.Y.: Doubleday Anchor, 1966).

33. E. T. Hall, "Proxemics," in A. M. Katz and V. T. Katz, eds., *Foundations of Nonverbal Communication* (Carbondale, Ill.: Southern Illinois University Press, 1983).

34. R. T. Barker and C. G. Pearce, "The Importance of Proxemics at Work," *Supervisory Management* 35 (1990): 10–11.

35. R. L. Birdwhistell, *Kinesics and Context* (Philadelphia: University of Pennsylvania Press, 1970).

36. P. Ekman and W. V. Friesen, "Research on Facial Expressions of Emotion," in A. M. Katz and V. T. Katz, eds., *Foundations of Nonverbal Communication* (Carbondale, Ill.: Southern Illinois University Press, 1983).

37. C. Barnum and N. Wolniansky, "Taking Cues from Body Language," *Management Review* 78 (1989): 59.

38. Katz and Katz, *Foundations of Nonverbal Communication*, 181.

39. R. Gifford, C. F. Ng, and M. Wilkinson, "Nonverbal Cues in the Employment Interview: Links between Applicant Qualities and Interviewer Judgments," *Journal of Applied Psychology* 70 (1985): 729–736.

40. P. J. DePaulo and B. M. DePaulo, "Can Deception by Salespersons and Customers Be Detected through Nonverbal Behavioral Cues?" *Journal of Applied Social Psychology* 19 (1989): 1552–1577.

41. P. Ekman, *Telling Lies* (New York: Norton, 1985); D. Goleman, "Nonverbal Cues Are Easy to Misinterpret," *New York Times* (September 17, 1991): B5.

42. B. Drake and K. Yuthas, "It's Only Words—Impacts of Information Technology on Moral Dialogue," *Journal of Business Ethics* 23 (2000): 41–60.

43. N. Frohlich and J. Oppenheimer, "Some Consequences of E-Mail vs. Face-to-Face Communication in Experiment," *Journal of Economic Behavior & Organization* 35 (1998): 389–403.

44. C. Brod, *Technostress: The Human Cost of the Computer Revolution* (Reading, Mass.: Addison-Wesley, 1984).

45. S. Kiesler, "Technology and the Development of Creative Environments," in Y. Ijiri and R. L. Kuhn, eds., *New Directions in Creative and Innovative Management* (Cambridge, Mass.: Ballinger Press, 1988).

46. S. Kiesler, J. Siegel, and T. W. McGuire, "Social Psychological Aspects of Computer-Mediated Communication," *American Psychologist* 39 (1984): 1123–1134.

Chapter 8

1. G. Garcia, "Measuring Performance at Northrop Grumman," *Knowledge Management Review* 3 (2001): 22–25.

2. A. M. Towsend, S. M. DeMarie, and A. R. Hendrickson, "Virtual Teams: Technology and the Workplace of the Future," *Academy of Management Executive* 12 (1998): 17–29.

3. D. M. McGregor, *The Human Side of Enterprise* (New York: McGraw-Hill, 1960).

4. J. R. Katzenbach and D. K. Smith, "The Discipline of Teams," *Harvard Business Review* 71 (1993): 111–120.

5. K. L. Bettenhausen and J. K. Murnighan, "The Development and Stability of Norms in Groups Facing Interpersonal and Structural Challenge," *Administrative Science Quarterly* 36 (1991): 20–35.

6. V. U. Druskat and S. B. Wolff, "Building the Emotional Intelligence of Groups," *Harvard Business Review* 79 (2001): 80–90.

7. I. Summers, T. Coffelt, and R. E. Horton, "Work-Group Cohesion," *Psychological Reports* 63 (1988): 627–636.

8. K. H. Price, "Working Hard to Get People to Loaf," *Basic and Applied Social Psychology* 14 (1993): 329–344.

9. R. Albanese and D. D. Van Fleet, "Rational Behavior in Groups: The Free-Riding Tendency," *Academy of Management Review* 10 (1985): 244–255.

10. E. Diener, "Deindividuation, Self-Awareness, and Disinhibition," *Journal of Personality and Social Psychology* 37 (1979): 1160–1171.

11. S. Prentice-Dunn and R. W. Rogers, "Deindividuation and the Self-Regulation of Behavior," in P. Paulus, ed., *Psychology of Group Influence* (Hillsdale, N.J.: Erlbaum, 1989), 87–109.

12. B. M. Bass and E. C. Ryterband, *Organizational Psychology*, 2nd ed. (Boston: Allyn & Bacon, 1979); B. W. Tuckman, "Developmental Sequences in Small Groups," *Psychological Bulletin* 63 (1963): 384–399.

13. W. G. Bennis and H. A. Shepard, "A Theory of Group Development," *Human Relations* 9 (1956): 415–438.

14. S. Caudron, "Monsanto Responds to Diversity," *Personnel Journal* (November 1990): 72–80.

15. D. L. Fields and T. C. Bloom, "Employee Satisfaction in Work Groups with Different Gender Composition," *Journal of Organizational Behavior* 18 (1997): 181–196.

16. D. C. Lau and J. K. Murnighan, "Demographic Diversity and Faultlines: The Compositional Dynamics of Organizational Groups," *Academy of Management Review* 23 (1998): 325–340.

17. D. Nichols, "Quality Program Sparked Company Turnaround," *Personnel* (October 1991): 24. For a commentary on Wallace's hard times and subsequent emergence from Chapter 11 bankruptcy, see R. C. Hill, "When the Going Gets Tough: A Baldrige Award Winner on the Line," *Academy of Management Executive* 7 (1993): 75–79.

18. S. Weisband and L. Atwater, "Evaluating Self and Others in Electronic and Face-to-Face Groups," *Journal of Applied Psychology* 84 (1999): 632–639.

19. M. Hardaker and B. K. Ward, "How to Make a Team Work," *Harvard Business Review* 65 (1987): 112–120.

20. C. R. Gowen, "Managing Work Group Performance by Individual Goals and Group Goals for an Interdependent Group Task," *Journal of Organizational Behavior Management* 7 (1986): 5–27.

21. K. L. Bettenhausen and J. K. Murnighan, "The Emergence of Norms in Competitive Decision-Making Groups," *Administrative Science Quarterly* 30 (1985): 350–372; K. L. Bettenhausen, "Five Years of Groups Research: What We Have Learned and What Needs to Be Addressed," *Journal of Management* 17 (1991): 345–381.

22. J. E. McGrath, *Groups: Interaction and Performance* (Englewood Cliffs, N.J.: Prentice-Hall, 1984).

23. K. L. Gammage, A. V. Carron, and P. A. Estabrooks, "Team Cohesion and Individual Productivity," *Small Group Research* 32 (2001): 3–18.

24. S. E. Seashore, *Group Cohesiveness in the Industrial Work Group* (Ann Arbor, Mich.: University of Michigan, 1954).

25. S. M. Klein, "A Longitudinal Study of the Impact of Work Pressure on Group Cohesive Behaviors," *International Journal of Management* 12 (1996): 68–75.

26. N. Steckler and N. Fondas, "Building Team Leader Effectiveness: A Diagnostic Tool," *Organizational Dynamics* 23 (1995): 20–35.

27. G. Parker, *Team Players and Teamwork* (San Francisco: Jossey-Bass, 1990).

28. N. R. F. Maier, "Assets and Liabilities in Group Problem Solving: The Need for an Integrative Function," *Psychological Review* 74 (1967): 239–249.

29. T. A. Stewart, "The Search for the Organization of Tomorrow," *Fortune* (May 18, 1992): 92–98.

30. J. R. Goktepe and C. E. Schneier, "Role of Sex, Gender Roles, and Attraction in Predicting Emergent Leaders," *Journal of Applied Psychology* 74 (1989): 165–167.

31. W. R. Lassey, "Dimensions of Leadership," in W. R. Lassey and R. R. Fernandez, eds., *Leadership and Social Change* (La Jolla, Calif.: University Associates, 1976), 10–15.

32. J. D. Quick, G. Moorhead, J. C. Quick, E. A. Gerloff, K. L. Mattox, and C. Mullins, "Decision Making among Emergency Room Residents: Preliminary Observations and a Decision Model," *Journal of Medical Education* 58 (1983): 117–125.

33. W. J. Duncan and J. P. Feisal, "No Laughing Matter: Patterns of Humor in the Workplace," *Organizational Dynamics* 17 (1989): 18–30.

34. A. Hunter, "Best Practice Club," *Personnel Today* (April 15, 2003): 8.

35. P. F. Drucker, "There's More Than One Kind of Team," *The Wall Street Journal* (February 11, 1992): A16.

36. B. L. Kirkman, C. B. Gibson, and D. L. Shapiro, "'Exporting' Teams: Enhancing the Implementation and Effectiveness of Work Teams in Global Affiliates," *Organizational Dynamics* 30 (2001): 12–29.

37. P. M. Podsakoff, M. Ahearne, and S. B. MacKenzie, "Organizational Citizenship Behavior and the Quantity and Quality of Work Group Performance," *Journal of Applied Psychology* 82 (1997): 262–270.

38. L. Hirschhorn, *Managing in the New Team Environment* (Upper Saddle River, N.J.: Prentice-Hall), 521A.

39. W. L. Mohr and H. Mohr, *Quality Circles: Changing Images of People at Work* (Reading, Mass.: Addison-Wesley, 1983).

40. R. W. Griffin, "A Longitudinal Assessment of the Consequences of Quality Circles in an Industrial Setting," *Academy of Management Journal* 31 (1988): 338–358.

41. P. Shaver and D. Buhrmester, "Loneliness, Sex-Role Orientation, and Group Life: A Social Needs Perspective," in P. Paulus, ed., *Basic Group Processes* (New York: Springer-Verlag, 1985), 259–288.

42. K. W. Thomas and B. A. Velthouse, "Cognitive Elements of Empowerment: An 'Interpretive' Model of Intrinsic Task Motivation," *Academy of Management Review* 15 (1990): 666–681.

43. R. R. Blake, J. S. Mouton, and R. L. Allen, *Spectacular Teamwork: How to Develop the Leadership Skills for Team Success* (New York: Wiley, 1987).

44. American Management Association, *Blueprints for Service Quality: The Federal Express Approach*, AMA Management Briefing (New York: AMA, 1991).

45. W. C. Byham, *ZAPP! The Human Lightning of Empowerment* (Pittsburgh, Pa.: Developmental Dimensions, 1989).

46. F. Shipper and C. C. Manz, "Employee Self-Management without Formally Designated Teams: An Alternative Road to Empowerment," *Organizational Dynamics* (Winter 1992): 48–62.

47. P. Block, *The Empowered Manager: Positive Political Skills at Work* (San Francisco: Jossey-Bass, 1987).

48. V. J. Derlega and J. Grzelak, eds., *Cooperation and Helping Behavior: Theories and Research* (New York: Academic Press, 1982).

49. A. G. Athos and J. J. Gabarro, *Interpersonal Behavior: Communication and Understanding in Relationships* (Englewood Cliffs, N.J.: Prentice-Hall, 1978).

50. J. L. Cordery, W. S. Mueller, and L. M. Smith, "Attitudinal and Behavioral Effects of Autonomous Group Working: A Longitudinal Field Study," *Academy of Management Journal* 34 (1991): 464–476.

51. G. Moorhead, C. P. Neck, and M. S. West, "The Tendency Toward Defective Decision Making within Self-Managing Teams: The Relevance of Groupthink for the 21st Century," *Organizational Behavior & Human Decision Processes* 73 (1998): 327–351.

52. B. M. Staw and L. D. Epstein, "What Bandwagons Bring: Effects of Popular Management Techniques on Corporate Performance, Reputation, and CEO Pay," *Administrative Science Quarterly* 45 (2000): 523–556.

53. R. M. Robinson, S. L. Oswald, K. S. Swinehart, and J. Thomas, "Southwest Industries: Creating High-Performance Teams for High-Technology Production," *Planning Review* 19, published by the Planning Forum (November–December 1991): 10–47.

54. A. Lienert, "Forging a New Partnership," *Management Review* 83 (1994): 39–43.

55. S. Thiagaraian, "A Game for Cooperative Learning," *Training and Development* (May 1992): 35–41.

56. D. C. Hambrick and P. Mason, "Upper Echelons: The Organization as a Reflection of Its Top Managers," *Academy of Management Review* 9 (1984): 193–206.

57. D. C. Hambrick, "The Top Management Team: Key to Strategic Success," *California Management Review* 30 (1987): 88–108.

58. A. D. Henderson and J. W. Fredrickson, "Top Management Team Coordination Needs and the CEO Pay Gap: A Competitive Test of Economic and Behavioral Views," *Academy of Management Journal* 44 (2001): 96–117.

59. D. C. Hambrick and G. D. S. Fukutomi, "The Seasons of a CEO's Tenure," *Academy of Management Review* 16 (1991): 719–742.

60. J. C. Quick, D. L. Nelson, and J. D. Quick, "Successful Executives: How Independent?" *Academy of Management Executive* 1 (1987): 139–145.

61. L. Love, *The Evolving Pinnacle of the Corporation: An Exploratory Study of the Antecedents, Processes, and Consequences of Co-CEOs*, (Arlington, Texas: The University of Texas at Arlington, 2003): unpublished dissertation.

62. N. J. Adler, *International Dimensions of Organizational Behavior* (Mason, Ohio: South-Western, 2001).

63. I. D. Steiner, *Group Process and Productivity* (New York: Academic Press, 1972).

64. A. Taylor III, "The Gentlemen at Ford Are Kicking Butt," *Fortune* (June 22, 1998): 70–75.

65. U. Glunk, M. G. Heijltjes, and R. Olie, "Design Characteristics and Functioning of Top Management Teams in Europe," *European Management Journal* 19 (2001): 291–300.

66. J. W. Pfeiffer and C. Nolde, eds., *The Encyclopedia of Team-Development Activities* (San Diego: University Associates, 1991).

Chapter 9

1. H. A. Simon, *The New Science of Management Decision* (New York: Harper & Row, 1960).

2. F. Hawthorne, "Merck at Risk," *Chief Executive*, June 2003: 54.

3. G. Huber, *Managerial Decision Making* (Glenview, Ill.: Scott, Foresman, 1980).

4. H. A. Simon, *Administrative Behavior* (New York: Macmillan, 1957).

5. E. F. Harrison, *The Managerial Decision-Making Process* (Boston: Houghton Mifflin, 1981).

6. R. L. Ackoff, "The Art and Science of Mess Management," *Interfaces* (February 1981): 20–26.

7. R. M. Cyert and J. G. March, eds., *A Behavioral Theory of the Firm* (Englewood Cliffs, N.J.: Prentice-Hall, 1963).

8. M. D. Cohen, J. G. March, and J. P. Olsen, "A Garbage Can Model of Organizational Choice," *Administrative Science Quarterly* 17 (1972): 1–25.

9. J. G. March and J. P. Olsen, "Garbage Can Models of Decision Making in Organizations," in J. G. March and R. Weissinger-Baylon, eds., *Ambiguity and Command* (Marshfield, Mass.: Pitman, 1986), 11–53.

10. D. van Knippenberg, B. van Knippenberg, and E. van Dijk, "Who Takes the Lead in Risky Decision Making? Effects of Group Members' Risk Preferences and Prototypicality," *Organizational Behavior and Human Decision Processes* 83 (2000): 213–234.

11. K. R. MacCrimmon and D. Wehrung, *Taking Risks* (New York: Free Press, 1986).

12. T. S. Perry, "How Small Firms Innovate: Designing a Culture for Creativity," *Research Technology Management* 28 (1995): 14–17.

13. B. M. Staw, "Knee-Deep in the Big Muddy: A Study of Escalating Commitment to

a Chosen Course of Action," *Organizational Behavior and Human Performance* 16 (1976): 27–44; B. M. Staw, "The Escalation of Commitment to a Course of Action," *Academy of Management Review* 6 (1981): 577–587.

14. B. M. Staw and J. Ross, "Understanding Behavior in Escalation Situations," *Science* 246 (1989): 216–220.

15. S. Finkelstein and S. H. Sanford, "Learning from Corporate Mistakes: The Rise and Fall of Iridium," *Organizational Dynamics* 29 (2000): 138–148.

16. L. Festinger, *A Theory of Cognitive Dissonance* (Evanston, Ill.: Row, Peterson, 1957).

17. B. M. Staw, "The Escalation of Commitment: An Update and Appraisal," in Z. Shapira, ed., *Organizational Decision Making* (Cambridge, England: Cambridge University Press, 1997).

18. D. M. Boehne and P. W. Paese, "Deciding Whether to Complete or Terminate an Unfinished Project: A Strong Test of the Project Completion Hypothesis," *Organizational Behavior and Human Decision Processes* 81 (2000): 178–194; H. Moon, "Looking Forward and Looking Back: Integrating Completion and Sunk Cost Effects within an Escalation-of-Commitment Progress Decision," *Journal of Applied Psychology* 86 (2000): 104–113.

19. G. Whyte, "Diffusion of Responsibility: Effects on the Escalation Tendency," *Journal of Applied Psychology* 76 (1991): 408–415.

20. C. G. Jung, *Psychological Types* (London: Routledge & Kegan Paul, 1923).

21. W. Taggart and D. Robey, "Minds and Managers: On the Dual Nature of Human Information Processing and Management," *Academy of Management Review* 6 (1981): 187–195; D. Hellriegel and J. W. Slocum, Jr., "Managerial Problem-Solving Styles," *Business Horizons* 18 (1975): 29–37.

22. I. I. Mitroff and R. H. Kilmann, "On Organization Stories: An Approach to the Design and Analysis of Organization through Myths and Stories," in R. H. Killman, L. R. Pondy, and D. P. Slevin, eds., *The Management of Organization Design* (New York: Elsevier–North Holland, 1976).

23. B. K. Blaylock and L. P. Rees, "Cognitive Style and the Usefulness of Information," *Decision Sciences* 15 (1984): 74–91; D. L. Davis, S. J. Grove, and P. A. Knowles, "An Experimental Application of Personality Type as an Analogue for Decision-Making Style," *Psychological Reports* 66 (1990): 167–175.

24. I. B. Myers, *Gifts Differing* (Palo Alto, Calif.: Consulting Psychologists Press, 1980).

25. H. Mintzberg, "Planning on the Left Side and Managing on the Right," *Harvard Business Review* 54 (1976): 51–63.

26. D. J. Isenberg, "How Senior Managers Think," *Harvard Business Review* 62 (1984): 81–90.

27. R. N. Beck, "Visions, Values, and Strategies: Changing Attitudes and Culture," *Academy of Managment Executive* 1 (1987): 33–41.

28. C. I. Barnard, *The Functions of the Executive* (Cambridge, Mass.: Harvard University Press, 1938).

29. R. Rowan, *The Intuitive Manager* (New York: Little, Brown, 1986).

30. W. H. Agor, *Intuition in Organizations* (Newbury Park, Calif.: Sage, 1989).

31. Isenberg, "How Senior Managers Think," 81–90.

32. H. A. Simon, "Making Management Decisions: The Role of Intuition and Emotion," *Academy of Management Executive* 1 (1987): 57–64.

33. J. L. Redford, R. H. McPhierson, R. G. Frankiewicz, and J. Gaa, "Intuition and Moral Development," *Journal of Psychology* 129 (1994): 91–101.

34. W. H. Agor, "How Top Executives Use Their Intuition to Make Important Decisions," *Business Horizons* 29 (1986): 49–53.

35. O. Behling and N. L. Eckel, "Making Sense Out of Intuition," *Academy of Management Executive* 5 (1991): 46–54.

36. L. R. Beach, *Image Theory: Decision Making in Personal and Organizational Contexts* (Chichester, England: Wiley, 1990).

37. L. Livingstone, "Person–Environment Fit on the Dimension of Creativity: Relationships with Strain, Job Satisfaction, and Performance" (Ph.D. diss., Oklahoma State University, 1992).

38. M. A. West and J. L. Farr, "Innovation at Work," in M. A. West and J. L. Farr, eds., *Innovation and Creativity at Work: Psychological and Organizational Strategies* (New York: Wiley, 1990): 3–13.

39. G. Morgan, *Riding the Waves of Change* (San Francisco: Jossey-Bass, 1988).

40. G. Wallas, *The Art of Thought* (New York: Harcourt Brace, 1926).

41. M. D. Mumford and S. B. Gustafson, "Creativity Syndrome: Integration, Application, and Innovation," *Psychological Bulletin* 103 (1988): 27–43.

42. T. Poze, "Analogical Connections—The Essence of Creativity," *Journal of Creative Behavior* 17 (1983): 240–241.

43. I. Sladeczek and G. Domino, "Creativity, Sleep, and Primary Process Thinking in Dreams," *Journal of Creative Behavior* 19 (1985): 38–46.

44. F. Barron and D. M. Harrington, "Creativity, Intelligence, and Personality," *Annual Review of Psychology* 32 (1981): 439–476.

45. R. J. Sternberg, "A Three-Faced Model of Creativity," in R. J. Sternberg, ed., *The Nature of Creativity* (Cambridge, England: Cambridge University Press, 1988), 125–147.

46. A. M. Isen, "Positive Affect and Decision Making," in W. M. Goldstein and R. M. Hogarth, eds., *Research on Judgment and Decision Making* (Cambridge, England: Cambridge University Press, 1997).

47. T. Stevens, "Creativity Killers," *Industry Week* (January 23, 1995): 63.

48. C. Axtell, D. Holman, K. Unsworth, T. Wall, and P. Waterson, "Shopfloor Innovation:

Facilitating the Suggestion and Implementation of Ideas," *Journal of Occupational Psychology* 73 (2000): 265–285.

49. T. M. Amabile, R. Conti, H. Coon, J. Lazenby, and M. Herron, "Assessing the Work Environment for Creativity," *Academy of Management Journal* 39 (1996): 1154–1184.

50. T. Tetenbaum and H. Tetenbaum, "Office 2000: Tear Down the Wall," *Training* (February 2000): 58–64.

51. D. M. Harrington, "Creativity, Analogical Thinking, and Muscular Metaphors," *Journal of Mental Imagery* 6 (1981): 121–126; R. M. Kanter, *The Change Masters* (New York: Simon & Schuster, 1983).

52. T. M. Amabile, B. A. Hennessey, and B. S. Grossman, "Social Influences on Creativity: The Effects of Contracted-for Reward," *Journal of Personality and Social Psychology* 50 (1986): 14–23.

53. Livingstone, "Person–Environment Fit."

54. R. L. Firestein, "Effects of Creative Problem-Solving Training on Communication Behaviors in Small Groups," *Small Group Research* (November 1989): 507–521.

55. R. Von Oech, *A Whack on the Side of the Head* (New York: Warner, 1983).

56. A. G. Robinson and S. Stern, *How Innovation and Improvement Actually Happen* (San Francisco: Berrett Koehler, 1997).

57. K. Unsworth, "Unpacking Creativity," *Academy of Management Review* 26 (2001): 289–297.

58. M. F. R. Kets de Vries, R. Branson, and P. Barnevik, "Charisma in Action: The Transformational Abilities of Virgin's Richard Branson and ABBS's Percy Barnevik," *Organizational Dynamics* 26 (1998): 7–21.

59. M. Kostera, M. Proppe, and M. Szatkowski, "Staging the New Romantic Hero in the Old Cynical Theatre: On Managers, Roles, and Change in Poland," *Journal of Organizational Behavior* 16 (1995): 631–646.

60. J. Pfeffer, "Seven Practices of Successful Organizations," *California Management Review* 40 (1998): 96–124.

61. L. A. Witt, M. C. Andrews, and K. M. Kacmar, "The Role of Participation in Decision-Making in the Organizational Politics–Job Satisfaction Relationship," *Human Relations* 53 (2000): 341–358.

62. C. R. Leana, E. A. Locke, and D. M. Schweiger, "Fact and Fiction in Analyzing Research on Participative Decision Making: A Critique of Cotton, Vollrath, Froggatt, Lengnick-Hall, and Jennings," *Academy of Management Review* 15 (1990): 137–146; J. L. Cotton, D. A. Vollrath, M. L. Lengnick-Hall, and K. L. Froggatt, "Fact: The Form of Participation Does Matter—A Rebuttal to Leana, Locke, and Schweiger," *Academy of Management Review* 15 (1990): 147–153.

63. G. Hamel, "Reinvent Your Company," *Fortune* 141 (June 12, 2000): 98–118.

64. T. W. Malone, "Is Empowerment Just a Fad? Control, Decision Making, and Informa-

tion Technology," *Sloan Management Review* 38 (1997): 23–35.

65. T. L. Brown, "Fearful of 'Empowerment': Should Managers Be Terrified?" *Industry Week* (June 18, 1990): 12.

66. L. Hirschhorn, "Stresses and Patterns of Adjustment in the Postindustrial Factory," in G. M. Green and F. Baker, eds., *Work, Health, and Productivity* (New York: Oxford University Press, 1991), 115–126.

67. P. G. Gyllenhammar, *People at Work* (Reading, Mass.: Addison-Wesley, 1977).

68. R. Tannenbaum and F. Massarik, "Participation by Subordinates in the Managerial Decision-Making Process," *Canadian Journal of Economics and Political Science* 16 (1950): 408–418.

69. H. Levinson, *Executive* (Cambridge, Mass.: Harvard University Press, 1981).

70. J. S. Black and H. B. Gregersen, "Participative Decision Making: An Integration of Multiple Dimensions," *Human Relations* 50 (1997): 859–878.

71. G. Stasser, L. A. Taylor, and C. Hanna, "Information Sampling in Structured and Unstructured Discussion of Three- and Six-Person Groups," *Journal of Personality and Social Psychology* 57 (1989): 67–78.

72. E. Kirchler and J. H. Davis, "The Influence of Member Status Differences and Task Type on Group Consensus and Member Position Change," *Journal of Personality and Social Psychology* 51 (1986): 83–91.

73. R. F. Maier, "Assets and Liabilities in Group Problem Solving," *Psychological Review* 74 (1967): 239–249.

74. M. E. Shaw, *Group Dynamics: The Psychology of Small Group Behavior*, 3rd ed. (New York: McGraw-Hill, 1981).

75. P. W. Yetton and P. C. Bottger, "Individual versus Group Problem Solving: An Empirical Test of a Best Member Strategy," *Organizational Behavior and Human Performance* 29 (1982): 307–321.

76. W. Watson, L. Michaelson, and W. Sharp, "Member Competence, Group Interaction, and Group Decision Making: A Longitudinal Study," *Journal of Applied Psychology* 76 (1991): 803–809.

77. I. Janis, *Victims of Groupthink* (Boston: Houghton Mifflin, 1972).

78. M. A. Hogg and S. C. Hains, "Friendship and Group Identification: A New Look at the Role of Cohesiveness in Groupthink," *European Journal of Social Psychology* 28 (1998): 323–341.

79. P. E. Jones and H. M. P. Roelofsma, "The Potential for Social Contextual and Group Biases in Team Decision-Making: Biases, Conditions, and Psychological Mechanisms," *Ergonomics* 43 (2000): 1129–1152; J. M. Levine, E. T. Higgins, and H. Choi, "Development of Strategic Norms in Groups," *Organizational Behavior and Human Decision Processes* 82 (2000): 88-101.

80. C. P. Neck and G. Moorhead, "Groupthink Remodeled: The Importance of Leadership, Time Pressure, and Methodical Decision Making Procedures," *Human Relations* 48 (1995): 537–557.

81. J. K. Esser and J. S. Lindoerfer, "Groupthink and the Space Shuttle *Challenger* Accident: Toward a Quantitative Case Analysis," *Journal of Behavioral Decision Making* 2 (1989): 167–177.

82. G. Moorhead, R. Ference, and C. P. Neck, "Group Decision Fiascoes Continue: Space Shuttle *Challenger* and a Revised Groupthink Framework," *Human Relations* 44 (1991): 539–550.

83. J. R. Montanari and G. Moorhead, "Development of the Groupthink Assessment Inventory," *Educational and Psychological Measurement* 49 (1989): 209–219.

84. P. t'Hart, "Irving L. Janis' Victims of Groupthink," *Political Psychology* 12 (1991): 247–278.

85. J. A. F. Stoner, "Risky and Cautious Shifts in Group Decisions: The Influence of Widely Held Values," *Journal of Experimental Social Psychology* 4 (1968): 442–459.

86. S. Moscovici and M. Zavalloni, "The Group as a Polarizer of Attitudes," *Journal of Personality and Social Psychology* 12 (1969): 125–135.

87. G. R. Goethals and M. P. Zanna, "The Role of Social Comparison in Choice of Shifts," *Journal of Personality and Social Psychology* 37 (1979): 1469–1476.

88. A. Vinokur and E. Burnstein, "Effects of Partially Shared Persuasive Arguments on Group-Induced Shifts: A Problem-Solving Approach," *Journal of Personality and Social Psychology* 29 (1974): 305–315.

89. K. Dugosh, P. Paulus, E. Roland, and H. Yang, "Cognitive Stimulation in Brainstorming," *Journal of Personality and Social Psychology* 79 (2000): 722–735.

90. W. H. Cooper, R. B. Gallupe, S. Pollard, and J. Cadsby, "Some Liberating Effects of Anonymous Electronic Brainstorming," *Small Group Research* 29 (1998): 147–178.

91. A. Van de Ven and A. Delbecq, "The Effectiveness of Nominal, Delphi and Interacting Group Decision-Making Processes," *Academy of Management Journal* 17 (1974): 605–621.

92. A. L. Delbecq, A. H. Van de Ven, and D. H. Gustafson, *Group Techniques for Program Planning: A Guide to Nominal, Group, and Delphi Processes* (Glenview, Ill.: Scott, Foresman, 1975).

93. R. A. Cosier and C. R. Schwenk, "Agreement and Thinking Alike: Ingredients for Poor Decisions," *Academy of Management Executive* 4 (1990): 69–74.

94. D. M. Schweiger, W. R. Sandburg, and J. W. Ragan, "Group Approaches for Improving Strategic Decision Making: A Comparative Analysis of Dialectical Inquiry, Devil's Advocacy, and Consensus," *Academy of Management Journal* 29 (1986): 149–159.

95. G. Whyte, "Decision Failures: Why They Occur and How to Prevent Them," *Academy of Management Executive* 5 (1991): 23–31.

96. E. E. Lawler III and S. A. Mohrman, "Quality Circles: After the Honeymoon," *Organizational Dynamics* (Spring 1987): 42–54.

97. T. L. Tang and E. A. Butler, "Attributions of Quality Circles' Problem-Solving Failure: Differences among Management, Supporting Staff, and Quality Circle Members," *Public Personnel Management* 26 (1997): 203–225.

98. S. R. Olberding, "Toyota on Competition and Quality Circles," *The Journal for Quality and Participation* 21 (1998): 52–54.

99. J. Schilder, "Work Teams Boost Productivity," *Personnel Journal* 71 (1992): 67–72.

100. P. S. Goodman, R. Devadas, and T. L. Griffith-Hughson, "Groups and Productivity: Analyzing the Effectiveness of Self-Managed Teams," in J. P. Campbell, R. J. Campbell, and Associates, eds., *Productivity in Organizations* (San Francisco: Jossey-Bass, 1988), 295–327.

101. C. J. Nemeth, "Managing Innovation: When Less Is More," *California Management Review* 40 (1997): 59–68.

102. N. Adler, *International Dimensions of Organizational Behavior*, 3rd ed. (Cincinnati, Ohio: South-Western, 1997).

103. G. K. Stephens and C. R. Greer, "Doing Business in Mexico: Understanding Cultural Differences," *Organization Dynamics* 24 (1995): 39–55.

104. C. R. Greer and G. K. Stephens, "Escalation of Commitment: A Comparison of Differences between Mexican and U. S. Decision-Makers," *Journal of Management* 27 (2001): 51–78.

105. "How Organizations Are Becoming More Efficient Using Expert Systems," *I/S Analyzer Case Studies* 36 (1995): 2–6.

106. J. Wybo, "FMIS: A Decision Support System for Forest Fire Prevention and Fighting," *IEEE Transactions on Engineering Management* 45 (1998): 127–131.

107. M. S. Poole, M. Holmes, and G. DeSanctis, "Conflict Management in a Computer-Supported Meeting Environment," *Management Science* 37 (1991): 926–953.

108. S. S. K. Lam and J. Schaubroeck, "Improving Group Decisions by Better Pooling Information: A Comparative Advantage of Groups Decision Support Systems," *Journal of Applied Psychology* 85 (2000): 565–573.

109. D. Kirkpatrick, "Here Comes the Payoff from PCs," *Fortune* (March 23, 1992): 93–102.

110. A. T. McCartt and J. Rohrbaugh, "Managerial Openness to Change and the Introduction of GDSS: Explaining Initial Success and Failure in Decision Conferencing," *Organization Science* 6 (1995): 569–584.

111. P. L. McLeod, R. S. Baron, M. W. Marti, and K. Yoon, "The Eyes Have It: Minority Influence in Face-to-Face and Computer-Mediated Group Discussion," *Journal of Applied Psychology* 82 (1997): 706–718.

112. A. M. Townsend, S. M. DeMarie, and A. R. Hendrickson, "Virtual Teams: Technology and the Workplace of the Future," *Academy of Management Executive* 12 (1998): 17–29.

113. L. M. Jessup and J. F. George, "Theoretical and Methodological Issues in Group Support Systems," *Small Group Research* 28 (1997): 394–413.

114. K. Blanchard and N. V. Peale, *The Power of Ethical Management* (New York: Fawcett Crest, 1988).

115. R. R. Sims, "Linking Groupthink to Unethical Behavior in Organizations," *Journal of Business Ethics* 11 (1992): 651–662.

Chapter 10

1. G. C. Homans, "Social Behavior as Exchange," *American Journal of Sociology* 63 (1958): 597–606.

2. R. D. Middlemist and M. A. Hitt, *Organizational Behavior: Managerial Strategies for Performance* (St. Paul, Minn.: West Publishing, 1988).

3. C. Barnard, *The Functions of the Executive* (Cambridge, Mass.: Harvard University Press, 1938).

4. J. R. P. French and B. Raven, "The Bases of Social Power," in D. Cartwright, ed., *Group Dynamics: Research and Theory* (Evanston, Ill.: Row, Peterson, 1962); T. R. Hinkin and C. A. Schriesheim, "Development and Application of New Scales to Measure the French and Raven (1959) Bases of Social Power," *Journal of Applied Psychology* 74 (1989): 561–567.

5. K. D. Elsbach and G. Elofson, "How the Packaging of Decision Explanations Affects Perceptions of Trustworthiness," *Academy of Management Journal* 43, No. 1 (2000): 80–89.

6. P. M. Podsakoff and C. A. Schriesheim, "Field Studies of French and Raven's Bases of Power: Critique, Reanalysis, and Suggestions for Future Research," *Psychological Bulletin* 97 (1985): 387–411.

7. M. A. Rahim, "Relationships of Leader Power to Compliance and Satisfaction with Supervision: Evidence from a National Sample of Managers," *Journal of Management* 15 (1989): 545–556.

8. C. Argyris, "Management Information Systems: The Challenge to Rationality and Emotionality," *Management Science* 17 (1971): 275–292; J. Naisbitt and P. Aburdene, *Megatrends 2000* (New York: Morrow, 1990).

9. P. P. Carson, K. D. Carson, E. L. Knight, and C. W. Roe, "Power in Organizations: A Look through the TQM Lens," *Quality Progress* (November 1995): 73–78.

10. M. Velasquez, D. J. Moberg, and G. F. Cavanaugh, "Organizational Statesmanship and Dirty Politics: Ethical Guidelines for the Organizational Politician," *Organizational Dynamics* 11 (1982): 65–79.

11. D. E. McClelland, *Power: The Inner Experience* (New York: Irvington, 1975).

12. N. Machiavelli, *The Prince*, trans. by G. Bull (Middlesex, England: Penguin Books, 1961).

13. S. Chen, A. Y. Lee-Chai, and J. A. Bargh, "Relationship Orientation as a Moderator of the Effects of Social Power," *Journal of Personality and Social Psychology* 80, No. 2 (2001): 173–187.

14. J. Pfeffer and G. Salancik, *The External Control of Organizations* (New York: Harper & Row, 1978).

15. T. M. Welbourne and C. O. Trevor, "The Roles of Departmental and Position Power in Job Evaluation," *Academy of Management Journal* 43, No. 4 (2000): 761–771.

16. R. H. Miles, *Macro Organizational Behavior* (Glenview, Ill.: Scott, Foresman, 1980).

17. D. Hickson, C. Hinings, C. Lee, R. E. Schneck, and J. M. Pennings, "A Strategic Contingencies Theory of Intraorganizational Power," *Administrative Science Quarterly* 14 (1971): 219–220.

18. C. R. Hinings, D. J. Hickson, J. M. Pennings, and R. E. Schneck, "Structural Conditions of Intraorganizational Power," *Administrative Science Quarterly* 19 (1974): 22–44.

19. A. Etzioni, *Modern Organizations* (Upper Saddle River, N.J.: Prentice-Hall, 1964).

20. R. Kanter, "Power Failure in Management Circuits," *Harvard Business Review* (July–August 1979): 31–54.

21. F. Lee and L. Z. Tiedens, "Who's Being Served? 'Self-Serving' Attributions in Social Hierarchies," *Organizational Behavior and Human Decision Processes* 84, No. 2 (March 2001): 254–287.

22. M. Korda, *Power: How to Get It, How to Use It* (New York: Random House, 1975).

23. S. R. Thye, "A Status Value Theory of Power in Exchange Relations," *American Sociological Review* (2000): 407–432.

24. B. T. Mayes and R. T. Allen, "Toward a Definition of Organizational Politics," *Academy of Management Review* 2 (1977): 672–678.

25. D. L. Madison, R. W. Allen, L. W. Porter, and B. T. Mayes, "Organizational Politics: An Exploration of Managers' Perceptions," *Human Relations* 33 (1980): 92–107.

26. J. Gandz and V. Murray, "The Experience of Workplace Politics," *Academy of Management Journal* 23 (1980): 237–251.

27. D. A. Ralston, "Employee Ingratiation: The Role of Management," *Academy of Management Review* 10 (1985): 477–487; D. R. Beeman and T. W. Sharkey, "The Use and Abuse of Corporate Politics," *Business Horizons* (March–April 1987): 25–35.

28. C. O. Longnecker, H. P. Sims, and D. A. Gioia, "Behind the Mask: The Politics of Employee Appraisal," *Academy of Management Executive* 1 (1987): 183–193.

29. M. Valle and P. L. Perrewe, "Do Politics Perceptions Relate to Political Behaviors? Tests of an Implicit Assumption and Expanded Model," *Human Relations* 53, No. 3 (2000): 359–386.

30. D. Kipnis, S. M. Schmidt, and I. Wilkinson, "Intraorganizational Influence Tactics: Explorations in Getting One's Way," *Journal of Applied Psychology* 65 (1980): 440–452; D. Kipnis, S. Schmidt, C. Swaffin-Smith, and I. Wilkinson, "Patterns of Managerial Influence: Shotgun Managers, Tacticians, and Bystanders," *Organizational Dynamics* (Winter 1984): 60–67; G. Yukl and C. M. Falbe, "Influence Tactics and Objectives in Upward, Downward, and Lateral Influence Attempts," *Journal of Applied Psychology* 75 (1990): 132–140.

31. G. R. Ferris and T. A. Judge, "Personnel/Human Resources Management: A Political Influence Perspective," *Journal of Management* 17 (1991): 447–488.

32. G. Yukl, P. J. Guinan, and D. Sottolano, "Influence Tactics Used for Different Objectives with Subordinates, Peers, and Superiors," *Groups & Organization Management* 20 (1995): 272–296.

33. R. A. Thacker and S. J. Wayne, "An Examination of the Relationship between Upward Influence Tactics and Assessments of Promotability," *Journal of Management* 21 (1995): 739–756.

34. K. K. Eastman, "In the Eyes of the Beholder: An Attributional Approach to Ingratiation and Organizational Citizenship Behavior," *Academy of Management Journal* 37 (1994): 1379–1391.

35. R. A. Gordon, "Impact of Ingratiation on Judgments and Evaluations: A Meta-Analytic Investigation," *Journal of Personality and Social Psychology* 71 (1996): 54–70.

36. A. Drory and D. Beaty, "Gender Differences in the Perception of Organizational Influence Tactics," *Journal of Organizational Behavior* 12 (1991): 249–258.

37. R. Y. Hirokawa and A. Miyahara, "A Comparison of Influence Strategies Utilized by Managers in American and Japanese Organizations," *Communication Quarterly* 34 (1986): 250–265.

38. P. David, M. A. Hitt, and J. Gimeno, "The Influence of Activism by Institutional Investors on R&D," *Academy of Management Journal* 44, No. 1 (2001): 144–157.

39. K. Kumar and M. S. Thibodeaux, "Organizational Politics and Planned Organizational Change," *Group and Organization Studies* 15 (1990): 354–365.

40. McClelland, *Power*.

41. Beeman and Sharkey, "Use and Abuse of Corporate Politics," 37.

42. C. P. Parker, R. L. Dipboye, and S. L. Jackson, "Perceptions of Organizational Politics: An Investigation of Antecedents and Consequences," *Journal of Management* 21 (1995): 891–912.

43. S. J. Ashford, N. P. Rothbard, S. K. Piderit, and J. E. Dutton, "Out on a Limb: The Role of Context and Impression Management in Selling Gender-Equity Issues," *Administrative Science Quarterly* 43 (1998): 23–57.

44. J. Zhou and G. R. Ferris, "The Dimensions and Consequences of Organizational Politics Perceptions: A Confirmatory Analysis," *Journal of Applied Social Psychology* 25 (1995): 1747–1764.

45. M. L. Seidal, J. T. Polzer, and K. J. Stewart, "Friends in High Places: The Effects of Social

Networks on Discrimination in Salary Negotiations," *Administrative Science Quarterly* 45 (2000): 1–24.

46. J. J. Gabarro and J. P. Kotter, "Managing Your Boss," *Harvard Business Review* (January–February 1980): 92–100.

47. P. Newman, "How to Manage Your Boss," Peat, Marwick, Mitchell & Company's *Management Focus* (May–June 1980): 36–37.

48. F. Bertolome, "When You Think the Boss Is Wrong," *Personnel Journal* 69 (1990): 66–73.

49. J. Conger and R. Kanungo, *Charismatic Leadership: The Elusive Factor in Organizational Effectiveness* (New York: Jossey-Bass, 1988).

50. G. M. Spreitzer, M. A. Kizilos, and S. W. Nason, "A Dimensional Analysis of the Relationship between Psychological Empowerment and Effectiveness, Satisfaction, and Strain," *Journal of Management* 23 (1997): 679–704.

51. R. C. Ford and M. D. Fottler, "Empowerment: A Matter of Degree," *Academy of Management Executive* 9 (1995): 21–31.

52. B. Dumaine, "The Bureaucracy Busters," *Fortune* (June 17, 1991): 36–50.

53. J. P. Kotter, "Power, Dependence, and Effective Management," *Harvard Business Review* 55 (1977): 125–136; J. P. Kotter, *Power and Influence* (New York: Free Press, 1985).

Chapter 11

1. J. P. Kotter, "What Leaders Really Do," *Harvard Business Review* 68 (1990): 103–111.

2. A. Zaleznik, "HBR Classic—Managers and Leaders: Are They Different?" *Harvard Business Review* 70 (1992): 126–135.

3. W. G. Rowe, "Creating Wealth in Organizations: The Role of Strategic Leadership," *Academy of Management Executive* 15 (2001): 81–94.

4. R. M. Stogdill, "Personal Factors Associated with Leadership: A Survey of the Literature," *Journal of Psychology* 25 (1948): 35–71.

5. K. Lewin, R. Lippitt, and R. K. White, "Patterns of Aggressive Behavior in Experimentally Created 'Social Climates,'" *Journal of Social Psychology* 10 (1939): 271–299.

6. R. M. Stogdill and A. E. Coons, eds., *Leader Behavior: Its Description and Measurement*, research monograph no. 88 (Columbus, Ohio: Bureau of Business Research, The Ohio State University, 1957).

7. A. W. Halpin and J. Winer, "A Factorial Study of the Leader Behavior Description Questionnaire," in R. M. Stogdill and A. E. Coons, eds., *Leader Behavior: Its Description and Measurement*, research monograph no. 88 (Columbus, Ohio: Bureau of Business Research, The Ohio State University, 1957), 39–51.

8. E. A. Fleishman, "Leadership Climate, Human Relations Training, and Supervisory Behavior," *Personnel Psychology* 6 (1953): 205–222.

9. R. Kahn and D. Katz, "Leadership Practices in Relation to Productivity and Morale," in D. Cartwright and A. Zander, eds., *Group Dynamics, Research and Theory* (Elmsford, NY: Row, Paterson, 1960).

10. R. R. Blake and J. S. Mouton, *The Managerial Grid III: The Key to Leadership Excellence* (Houston: Gulf, 1985).

11. F. E. Fiedler, *A Theory of Leader Effectiveness* (New York: McGraw-Hill, 1964).

12. F. E. Fiedler, *Personality, Motivational Systems, and Behavior of High and Low LPC Persons*, tech. rep. no. 70-12 (Seattle: University of Washington, 1970).

13. J. T. McMahon, "The Contingency Theory: Logic and Method Revisited," *Personnel Psychology* 25 (1972): 697–710; L. H. Peters, D. D. Hartke, and J. T. Pohlman, "Fiedler's Contingency Theory of Leadership: An Application of the Meta-Analysis Procedures of Schmidt and Hunter," *Psychological Bulletin* 97 (1985): 224–285.

14. F. E. Fiedler, "The Contingency Model and the Dynamics of the Leadership Process," in L. Berkowitz, ed., *Advances in Experimental and Social Psychology*, vol. 11 (New York: Academic Press, 1978).

15. F. E. Fiedler, "Engineering the Job to Fit the Manager," *Harvard Business Review* 43 (1965): 115–122.

16. R. J. House, "A Path–Goal Theory of Leader Effectiveness," *Administrative Science Quarterly* 16 (1971): 321–338; R. J. House and T. R. Mitchell, "Path–Goal Theory of Leadership," *Journal of Contemporary Business* 3 (1974): 81–97.

17. C. A. Schriesheim and V. M. Von Glinow, "The Path–Goal Theory of Leadership: A Theoretical and Empirical Analysis," *Academy of Management Journal* 20 (1977): 398–405; E. Valenzi and G. Dessler, "Relationships of Leader Behavior, Subordinate Role Ambiguity, and Subordinate Job Satisfaction," *Academy of Management Journal* 21 (1978): 671–678; N. R. F. Maier, *Leadership Methods and Skills* (New York: McGraw-Hill, 1963).

18. V. H. Vroom and P. W. Yetton, *Leadership and Decision Making* (Pittsburgh: University of Pittsburgh, 1973).

19. V. H. Vroom, "Leadership and the Decision-Making Process," *Organizational Dynamics* 28 (2000): 82–94.

20. R. H. G. Field and R. J. House, "A Test of the Vroom-Yetton Model Using Manager and Subordinate Reports," *Journal of Applied Psychology* 75 (1990): 362–366.

21. P. Hersey and K. H. Blanchard, "Life Cycle Theory of Leadership," *Training and Development Journal* 23 (1969): 26–34; P. Hersey, K. H. Blanchard, and D. E. Johnson, *Management of Organizational Behavior: Leading Human Resources*, 8th ed. (Upper Saddle River, N.J.: Prentice-Hall, 2001).

22. B. M. Bass, *Bass and Stogdill's Handbook of Leadership: Theory, Research, and Managerial Applications*, 3rd ed. (New York: Free Press, 1990).

23. G. B. Graen and M. Uhl-Bien, "Relationship-Based Approach to Leadership: Development of Leader–Member Exchange (LMX) Theory of Leadership over 25 Years," *Leadership Quarterly* 6 (1995): 219–247; C. R. Gerstner and D. V. Day, "Meta-Analytic Review of Leader–Member Exchange Theory: Correlates and Construct Issues," *Journal of Applied Psychology* 82 (1997): 827–844; R. C. Liden, S. J. Wayne, and R. T. Sparrowe, "An Examination of the Mediating Role of Psychological Empowerment on the Relations between the Job, Interpersonal Relationships, and Work Outcomes," *Journal of Applied Psychology* 85 (2001): 407–416.

24. J. Townsend, J. S. Phillips, and T. J. Elkins, "Employee Retaliation: The Neglected Consequence of Poor Leader–Member Exchange Relations," *Journal of Occupational Health Psychology* 5 (2000): 457–463.

25. D. Nelson, R. Basu, and R. Purdie, "An Examination of Exchange Quality and Work Stressors in Leader–Follower Dyads," *International Journal of Stress Management* 5 (1998): 103–112.

26. S. Kerr and J. M. Jermier, "Substitutes for Leadership: Their Meaning and Measurement," *Organizational Behavior and Human Performance* 22 (1978): 375–403.

27. P. M. Podsakoff, S. B. MacKenzie, and W. H. Bommer, "Meta-Analysis of the Relationships between Kerr and Jermier's Substitutes for Leadership and Employee Job Attitudes, Role Perceptions, and Performance," *Journal of Applied Psychology* 81 (1996): 380–399.

28. J. M. Burns, *Leadership* (New York: Harper & Row, 1978); T. O. Jacobs, *Leadership and Exchange in Formal Organizations* (Alexandria, Va.: Human Resources Research Organization, 1971).

29. N. Tichy and M. A. DeVanna, *The Transformational Leader* (New York: Wiley, 1986).

30. B. M. Bass, "From Transactional to Transformational Leadership: Learning to Share the Vision," *Organizational Dynamics* 19 (1990): 19–31; B. M. Bass, *Leadership and Performance beyond Expectations* (New York: Free Press, 1985).

31. W. Bennis, "Managing the Dream: Leadership in the 21st Century," *Training* 27 (1990): 43–48.

32. P. M. Podsakoff, S. B. MacKenzie, R. H. Moorman, and R. Fetter, "Transformational Leader Behaviors and Their Effects on Followers' Trust in Leader, Satisfaction, and Organizational Citizenship Behaviors," *Leadership Quarterly* 1 (1990): 107–142.

33. C. P. Egri and S. Herman, "Leadership in the North American Environmental Sector: Values, Leadership Styles, and Contexts of Environmental Leaders and Their Organizations," *Academy of Management Journal* 43 (2000): 571–604.

34. T. A. Judge and J. E. Bono, "Five-Factor Model of Personality and Transformational Leadership," *Journal of Applied Psychology* 85 (2001): 751–765.

35. R. J. House and M. L. Baetz, "Leadership: Some Empirical Generalizations and New Research Directions," in B. M. Staw, ed., *Research in Organizational Behavior*, vol. 1 (Greenwood, Conn.: JAI Press, 1979), 399–401.

36. J. A. Conger and R. N. Kanungo, "Toward a Behavioral Theory of Charismatic Leadership in Organizational Settings," *Academy of Management Review* 12 (1987): 637–647.

37. A. R. Willner, *The Spellbinders: Charismatic Political Leadership* (New Haven, Conn.: Yale University Press, 1984).

38. D. Waldman, G. G. Ramirez, R. J. House, and P. Puranam, "Does Leadership Matter? CEO Leadership Attributes and Profitability under Conditions of Perceived Environmental Uncertainty," *Academy of Management Journal* 44 (2001): 134–143.

39. J. M. Howell, "Two Faces of Charisma: Socialized and Personalized Leadership in Organizations," in J. A. Conger, ed., *Charismatic Leadership: Behind the Mystique of Exceptional Leadership* (San Francisco: Jossey-Bass, 1988).

40. F. J. Yammarino, F. Dansereau, and C. J. Kennedy, "A Multiple-Level Multidimensional Approach to Leadership: Viewing Leadership through an Elephant's Eye," *Organizational Dynamics* 29 (2001): 149–163.

41. M. Maccoby, "Narcissistic Leaders: The Incredible Pros, the Inevitable Cons," *Harvard Business Review* 78 (2000): 68–77.

42. D. Sankowsky, "The Charismatic Leader as Narcissist: Understanding the Abuse of Power," *Organizational Dynamics* 23 (1995): 57–71.

43. D. Goleman, *Emotional Intelligence* (New York: Bantam Books, 1995).

44. J. Useem, "A Manager for All Seasons," *Fortune* (April 30, 2001): 66–72.

45. R. C. Mayer, J. H. Davis, and F. D. Schoorman, "An Integrative Model of Organizational Trust," *Academy of Management Review* 20 (1995): 709–734.

46. R. S. Dooley and G. E. Fryxell, "Attaining Decision Quality and Commitment from Dissent: The Moderating Effects of Loyalty and Competence in Strategic Decision-Making Teams," *Academy of Management Journal* 42 (1999): 389–402.

47. A. Malhotra, A. Majchrzak, R. Carman, and V. Lott, "Radical Innovation without Collocation: A Case Study at Boeing-Rocketdyne," *MIS Quarterly* 25 (2001): 229–249.

48. M. E. Heilman, C. J. Block, R. F. Martell, and M. C. Simon, "Has Anything Changed? Current Characteristics of Men, Women, and Managers," *Journal of Applied Psychology* 74 (1989): 935–942.

49. A. H. Eagly, S. J. Darau, and M. Makhijani, "Gender and the Effectiveness of Leaders: A Meta-Analysis," *Psychological Bulletin* 117 (1995): 125–145.

50. R. K. Greenleaf, L. C. Spears, and D. T. Frick, eds., *On Becoming a Servant-Leader* (San Francisco: Jossey-Bass, 1996).

51. E. P. Hollander and L. R. Offerman, "Power and Leadership in Organizations: Relationships in Transition," *American Psychologist* 45 (1990): 179–189.

52. H. P. Sims, Jr., and C. C. Manz, *Company of Heros: Unleashing the Power of Self-Leadership* (New York: John Wiley & Sons, 1996).

53. C. C. Manz and H. P. Sims, "Leading Workers to Lead Themselves: The External Leadership of Self-Managing Work Teams," *Administrative Science Quarterly* 32 (1987): 106–128.

54. L. Hirschhorn, "Leaders and Followers in a Postindustrial Age: A Psychodynamic View," *Journal of Applied Behavioral Science* 26 (1990): 529–542.

55. R. E. Kelley, "In Praise of Followers," *Harvard Business Review* 66 (1988): 142–148.

56. C. C. Manz and H. P. Sims, "SuperLeadership: Beyond the Myth of Heroic Leadership," *Organizational Dynamics* 20 (1991): 18–35.

57. W. J. Crockett, "Dynamic Subordinancy," *Training and Development Journal* (May 1981): 155–164.

58. N. J. Adler, *International Dimensions in Organizational Behavior* (Boston: PWS-Kent, 1991).

59. F. C. Brodback *et al.*, "Cultural Variation of Leadership Prototypes across 22 European Countries," *Journal of Occupational and Organizational Psychology* 73 (2000): 1–29.

60. B. Alimo-Metcalfe and R. J. Alban-Metcalfe, "The Development of a New Transformational Leadership Questionnaire," *Journal of Occupational and Organizational Psychology* 74 (2001): 1–27.

61. G. A. Yukl, *Leadership in Organizations*, 2nd ed. (Upper Saddle River, N.J.: Prentice-Hall, 1989).

62. P. B. Murphy and G. Enderle, "Managerial Ethical Leadership: Examples Do Matter," *Business Ethics Quarterly* 5 (1995): 117–128.

Chapter 12

1. Definition adapted from D. Hellriegel, J. W. Slocum, Jr., and R. W. Woodman, *Organizational Behavior* (St. Paul: West, 1992); R. D. Middlemist and M. A. Hitt, *Organizational Behavior* (St. Paul: West, 1988).

2. D. Tjosvold, *The Conflict-Positive Organization* (Reading, Mass.: Addison-Wesley, 1991).

3. K. Thomas and W. Schmidt, "A Survey of Managerial Interests with Respect to Conflict," *Academy of Management Journal* 19 (1976): 315–318; G. L. Lippitt, "Managing Conflict in Today's Organizations," *Training and Development Journal* 36 (1982): 66–74.

4. M. Rajim, "A Measure of Styles of Handling Interpersonal Conflict," *Academy of Management Journal* 26 (1983): 368–376.

5. D. Goleman, *Emotional Intelligence* (New York: Bantam Books, 1995); J. Stuller, "Unconventional Smarts," *Across the Board* 35 (1998): 22–23.

6. Tjosvold, *The Conflict-Positive Organization*, 4.

7. R. A. Cosier and D. R. Dalton, "Positive Effects of Conflict: A Field Experiment," *International Journal of Conflict Management* 1 (1990): 81–92.

8. D. Tjosvold, "Making Conflict Productive," *Personnel Administrator* 29 (1984): 121–130.

9. A. C. Amason, W. A. Hochwarter, K. R. Thompson, and A. W. Harrison, "Conflict: An Important Dimension in Successful Management Teams," *Organizational Dynamics* 24 (1995): 25–35.

10. T. L. Simons and R. S. Peterson, "Task Conflict and Relationship Conflict in Top Management Teams: The Pivotal Role of Intergroup Trust," *Journal of Applied Psychology* 85 (2000): 102–111.

11. I. Janis, *Groupthink*, 2nd ed. (Boston: Houghton Mifflin, 1982).

12. J. D. Thompson, *Organizations in Action* (New York: McGraw-Hill, 1967).

13. G. Walker and L. Poppo, "Profit Centers, Single-Source Suppliers, and Transaction Costs," *Administrative Science Quarterly* 36 (1991): 66–87.

14. R. Miles, *Macro Organizational Behavior* (Glenview, Ill.: Scott, Foresman, 1980).

15. H. Levinson, "The Abrasive Personality," *Harvard Business Review* 56 (1978): 86–94.

16. J. C. Quick and J. D. Quick, *Organizational Stress and Preventive Management* (New York: McGraw-Hill, 1984).

17. F. N. Brady, "Aesthetic Components of Management Ethics," *Academy of Management Review* 11 (1986): 337–344.

18. J. A. Rhoades, J. Arnold, and C. Jay, "The Role of Affective Traits and Affective States in Disputants' Motivation and Behavior During Episodes of Organizational Conflict," *Journal of Organizational Behavior* 22 (2001): 329–345.

19. V. K. Raizada, "Multi-Ethnic Corporations and Inter-Ethnic Conflict," *Human Resource Management* 20 (1981): 24–27; T. Cox, Jr., "The Multicultural Organization," *Academy of Management Executive* 5 (1991): 34–47.

20. G. Hofstede, *Culture's Consequences: International Differences in Work-Related Values* (Beverly Hills, Calif.: Sage, 1980); G. Hofstede and M. H. Bond, "The Confucius Connection: From Cultural Roots to Economic Growth," *Organizational Dynamics* (Spring 1988): 4–21; G. Hofstede, "Cultural Constraints in Management Theories," *Academy of Management Executive* 7 (1993): 81–94.

21. T. H. Cox, S. A. Lobel, and P. L. McLead, "Effects of Ethnic Group Cultural Differences on Cooperative and Competitive Behavior in a Group Task," *Academy of Management Journal* 34 (1991): 827–847.

22. J. Schopler, C. A. Insko, J. Wieselquist, *et al.*, "When Groups Are More Competitive than Individuals: The Domain of the Discontinuity Effect," *Journal of Personality and Social Psychology* 80 (2001): 632–644.

23. M. Sherif and C. W. Sherif, *Social Psychology* (New York: Harper & Row, 1969).

24. C. Song, S. M. Sommer, and A. E. Hartman, "The Impact of Adding an External Rater on Interdepartmental Cooperative Behaviors of Workers," *International Journal of Conflict Management* 9 (1998): 117–138.

25. W. Tsai and S. Ghoshal, "Social Capital and Value Creation: The Role of Intrafirm

Networks," *Academy of Management Journal* 41 (1998): 464–476.

26. M. L. Maznevski and K. M. Chudoba, "Bridging Space over Time: Global Virtual-Team Dynamics and Effectiveness," *Organization Science* 11 (2000): 473–492.

27. D. Katz and R. Kahn, *The Social Psychology of Organizations*, 2nd ed. (New York: Wiley, 1978).

28. D. L. Nelson and J. C. Quick, "Professional Women: Are Distress and Disease Inevitable?" *Academy of Management Review* 10 (1985): 206–218; D. L. Nelson and M. A. Hitt, "Employed Women and Stress: Implications for Enhancing Women's Mental Health in the Workplace," in J. C. Quick, J. Hurrell, and L. A. Murphy, eds., *Stress and Well-being at Work: Assessments and Interventions for Occupational Mental Health* (Washington, D.C.: American Psychological Association, 1992).

29. R. L. Kahn, *et al.*, *Organizational Stress: Studies in Role Conflict and Ambiguity* (New York: Wiley, 1964).

30. J. L. Badaracco, Jr., "The Discipline of Building Character," *Harvard Business Review* (March–April 1998): 115–124.

31. B. Schneider, "The People Make the Place," *Personnel Psychology* 40 (1987): 437–453.

32. C. A. O'Reilly, J. Chatman, and D. F. Caldwell, "People and Organizational Culture: A Profile Comparison Approach to Assessing Person-Organization Fit," *Academy of Management Journal* 34 (1991): 487–516.

33. I. Dayal and J. M. Thomas, "Operation KPE: Developing a New Organization," *Journal of Applied Behavioral Science* 4 (1968): 473–506.

34. R. H. Miles, "Role Requirements as Sources of Organizational Stress," *Journal of Applied Psychology* 61 (1976): 172–179.

35. W. F. G. Mastenbroek, *Conflict Management and Organization Development* (Chichester, England: Wiley, 1987).

36. M. R. Frone, "Interpersonal Conflict at Work and Psychological Outcomes: Testing a Model among Young Workers," *Journal of Occupational Health Psychology* 5 (2000): 246–255.

37. K. Thomas, "Conflict and Conflict Management," in M. D. Dunnette, ed., *Handbook of Industrial and Organizational Psychology* (New York: Wiley, 1976).

38. H. H. Meyer, E. Kay, and J. R. P. French, "Split Roles in Performance Appraisal," *Harvard Business Review* 43 (1965): 123–129.

39. T. W. Costello and S. S. Zalkind, *Psychology in Administration: A Research Orientation* (Englewood Cliffs, N.J.: Prentice-Hall, 1963).

40. C. A. Insko, J. Scholper, L. Gaertner, *et al.*, "Interindividual–Intergroup Discontinuity Reduction through the Anticipation of Future Interaction," *Journal of Personality and Social Psychology* 80 (2001): 95–111.

41. D. Tjosvold and M. Poon, "Dealing with Scarce Resources: Open-Minded Interaction for Resolving Budget Conflicts," *Group and Organization Management* 23 (1998): 237–255.

42. Miles, *Macro Organizational Behavior; R. Steers, Introduction to Organizational Behavior*, 4th ed. (Glenview, Ill.: Harper-Collins, 1991).

43. A. Tyerman and C. Spencer, "A Critical Text of the Sherrif's Robber's Cave Experiments: Intergroup Competition and Cooperation between Groups of Well-Acquainted Individuals," *Small Group Behavior* 14 (1983): 515–531; R. M. Kramer, "Intergroup Relations and Organizational Dilemmas: The Role of Categorization Processes," in B. Staw and L. Cummings, eds., *Research in Organizational Behavior* 13 (Greenwich, Conn.: JAI Press, 1991), 191–228.

44. R. Blake and J. Mouton, "Overcoming Group Warfare," *Harvard Business Review* 64 (1984): 98–108.

45. D. G. Ancona and D. Caldwell, "Improving the Performance of New Product Teams," *Research Technology Management* 33 (1990): 25–29.

46. R. J. Lewicki, J. A. Litterer, J. W. Minton, and D. M. Saunders, *Negotiation*, 2nd ed. (Burr Ridge, Ill.: Irwin, 1994).

47. C. K. W. De Dreu, S. L. Koole, and W. Steinel, "Unfixing the Fixed Pie: A Motivated Information-Processing Approach to Integrative Negotiation," *Journal of Personality and Social Psychology* 79 (2000): 975–987.

48. M. H. Bazerman, J. R. Curhan, D. A. Moore, and K. L. Valley, "Negotiation," *Annual Review of Psychology* 51 (2000): 279–314.

49. I. Ayers and P. Siegelman, "Race and Gender Discrimination in Bargaining for a New Car," *American Economic Review* 85 (1995): 304–321.

50. L. J. Kray, L. Thompson, and A. Galinsky, "Battle of the Sexes: Gender Stereotype Confirmation and Reactance in Organizations," *Journal of Personality and Social Psychology* 80 (2001): 942–958.

51. K. W. Thomas, "Conflict and Conflict Management," in M. D. Dunnette, ed., *Handbook of Industrial and Organizational Psychology* (New York: Wiley, 1976), 900.

52. C. K. W. De Dreu and A. E. M. Van Vianen, "Managing Relationship Conflict and the Effectiveness of Organizational Teams," *Journal of Organizational Behavior* 22 (2001): 309–328.

53. R. A. Baron, S. P. Fortin, R. L. Frei, L. A. Hauver, and M. L. Shack, "Reducing Organizational Conflict: The Role of Socially Induced Positive Affect," *International Journal of Conflict Management* 1 (1990): 133–152.

54. S. L. Phillips and R. L. Elledge, *The Team Building Source Book* (San Diego: University Associates, 1989).

55. Gladwin and Walter, "How Multinationals Can Manage," 228.

56. K. W. Thomas, "Toward Multidimensional Values in Teaching: The Example of Conflict Behaviors," *Academy of Management Review* 2 (1977): 484–490.

57. S. Alper, D. Tjosvold, and K. S. Law, "Conflict Management, Efficacy, and Performance in Organizational Teams," *Personnel Psychology* 53 (2000): 625–642.

58. W. King and E. Miles, "What We Know and Don't Know about Measuring Conflict," *Management Communication Quarterly* 4 (1990): 222–243.

59. J. Barker, D. Tjosvold, and I. R. Andrews, "Conflict Approaches of Effective and Ineffective Project Managers: A Field Study in a Matrix Organization," *Journal of Management Studies* 25 (1988): 167–178.

60. M. Chan, "Intergroup Conflict and Conflict Management in the R&D Divisions of Four Aerospace Companies," *IEEE Transactions on Engineering Management* 36 (1989): 95–104.

61. M. K. Kozan, "Cultural Influences on Styles of Handling Interpersonal Conflicts: Comparisons among Jordanian, Turkish, and U.S. Managers," *Human Relations* 42 (1989): 787–799.

62. S. McKenna, "The Business Impact of Management Attitudes towards Dealing with Conflict: A Cross-Cultural Assessment," *Journal of Managerial Psychology* 10 (1995): 22–27.

63. Tjosvold, *The Conflict-Positive Organization*.

Chapter 13

1. G. W. England and I. Harpaz, "How Working Is Defined: National Contexts and Demographic and Organizational Role Influences," *Journal of Organizational Behavior* 11 (1990): 253–266.

2. L. R. Gomez-Mejia, "The Cross-Cultural Structure of Task-Related and Contextual Constructs," *Journal of Psychology* 120 (1986): 5–19.

3. A. Wrzesniewski and J. E. Dutton, "Crafting a Job: Revisioning Employees as Active Crafters of Their Work," *Academy of Management Review* 26 (2001): 179–201.

4. F. W. Taylor, *The Principles of Scientific Management* (New York: Norton, 1911).

5. T. Bell, *Out of This Furnace* (Pittsburgh: University of Pittsburgh Press, 1941).

6. P. Cappelli, "A Market-Driven Approach to Retaining Talent," *Harvard Business Review* 78 (2000): 103–111.

7. N. D. Warren, "Job Simplification versus Job Enlargement," *Journal of Industrial Engineering* 9 (1958): 435–439.

8. C. R. Walker, "The Problem of the Repetitive Job," *Harvard Business Review* 28 (1950): 54–58.

9. C. R. Walker and R. H. Guest, *The Man on the Assembly Line* (Cambridge, Mass.: Harvard University Press, 1952).

10. M. A. Campion, L. Cheraskin, and M. J. Stevens, "Career-Related Antecedents and Outcomes of Job Rotation," *Academy of Management Journal* 37 (1994): 1518–1542.

11. E. Santora, "Keep Up Production Through Cross-Training," *Personnel Journal* (June 1992): 162–166.

12. R. P. Steel and J. R. Rentsch, "The Dispositional Model of Job Attitudes Revisited: Findings of a 10-Year Study," *Journal of Applied*

Psychology 82 (1997): 873–879; C. S. Wong, C. Hui, and K. S. Law, "A Longitudinal Study of the Job Perception–Job Satisfaction Relationship: A Text of the Three Alternative Specifications," *Journal of Occupational & Organizational Psychology* 71 (Part 2, 1998): 127–146.

13. F. Herzberg, "One More Time: How Do You Motivate Employees?" *Harvard Business Review* 46 (1968): 53–62.

14. R. N. Ford, "Job Enrichment Lessons from AT&T," *Harvard Business Review* 51 (1973): 96–106.

15. R. J. House and L. A. Wigdor, "Herzberg's Dual-Factor Theory of Job Satisfaction and Motivation: A Review of the Evidence and a Criticism," *Personnel Psychology* 20 (1967): 369–389.

16. A. N. Turner and P. R. Lawrence, *Industrial Jobs and the Worker* (Cambridge, Mass.: Harvard University Press, 1965).

17. J. R. Hackman and G. R. Oldham, "The Job Diagnostic Survey: An Instrument for the Diagnosis of Jobs and the Evaluation of Job Redesign Projects," *Technical Report No. 4* (New Haven, Conn.: Department of Administrative Sciences, Yale University, 1974).

18. J. R. Hackman and G. R. Oldham, "Development of the Job Diagnostic Survey," *Journal of Applied Psychology* 60 (1975): 159–170.

19. P. H. Birnbaum, J. L. Farh, and G. Y. Y. Wong, "The Job Characteristics Model in Hong Kong," *Journal of Applied Psychology* 71 (1986): 598–605.

20. J. R. Hackman and G. R. Oldham, *Work Design* (Reading, Mass.: Addison-Wesley, 1980).

21. H. P. Sims, A. D. Szilagyi, and R. T. Keller, "The Measurement of Job Characteristics," *Academy of Management Journal* 19 (1976): 195–212.

22. H. P. Sims and A. D. Szilagyi, "Job Characteristic Relationships: Individual and Structural Moderators," *Organizational Behavior and Human Performance* 17 (1976): 211–230.

23. Y. Fried, "Meta-Analytic Comparison of the Job Diagnostic Survey and Job Characteristic Inventory as Correlates of Work Satisfaction and Performance," *Journal of Applied Psychology* 76 (1991): 690–698.

24. M. F. R. Kets de Vries, "Creating Authentizotic Organizations: Well-Functioning Individuals in Vibrant Companies," *Human Relations* 54 (2001): 101–111.

25. G. R. Salancik and J. Pfeffer, "A Social Information Processing Approach to Job Attitudes and Task Design," *Administrative Science Quarterly* 23 (1978): 224–253.

26. J. Pfeffer, "Management as Symbolic Action: The Creation and Maintenance of Organizational Paradigms," in L. L. Cummings and B. M. Staw, eds., *Research in Organizational Behavior*, vol. 3 (Greenwich, Conn.: JAI Press, 1981), 1–52.

27. J. Thomas and R. Griffin, "The Social Information Processing Model of Task Design: A Review of the Literature," *Academy of Management Review* 8 (1983): 672–682.

28. D. J. Campbell, "Task Complexity: A Review and Analysis," *Academy of Management Review* 13 (1988): 40–52.

29. M. A. Campion and P. W. Thayer, "Job Design: Approaches, Outcomes, and Trade-offs," *Organizational Dynamics* 16 (1987): 66–79.

30. J. Teresko, "Emerging Technologies," *Industry Week* (February 27, 1995): 1–2.

31. M. A. Campion and C. L. McClelland, "Interdisciplinary Examination of the Costs and Benefits of Enlarged Jobs: A Job Design Quasi-Experiment," *Journal of Applied Psychology* 76 (1991): 186–199.

32. B. Kohut, *Country Competitiveness: Organizing of Work* (New York: Oxford University Press, 1993).

33. J. C. Quick and L. E. Tetrick, eds., *Handbook of Occupational Health Psychology* (Washington, D.C.: American Psychological Association, 2002).

34. W. E. Deming, *Out of the Crisis* (Cambridge, Mass.: MIT Press, 1986).

35. L. Thurow, *Head to Head: The Coming Economic Battle among Japan, Europe, and America* (New York: Morrow, 1992).

36. M. A. Fruin, *The Japanese Enterprise System—Competitive Strategies and Cooperative Structures* (New York: Oxford University Press, 1992).

37. W. Niepce and E. Molleman, "Work Design Issue in Lean Production from a Sociotechnical System Perspective: Neo-Taylorism or the Next Step in Sociotechnical Design?" *Human Relations* 51 (1998): 259–287.

38. E. Furubotn, "Codetermination and the Modern Theory of the Firm: A Property-Rights Analysis," *Journal of Business* 61 (1988): 165–181.

39. H. Levinson, *Executive: The Guide to Responsive Management* (Cambridge, Mass.: Harvard University Press, 1981).

40. B. Gardell, "Scandinavian Research on Stress in Working Life" (Paper presented at the IRRA Symposium on Stress in Working Life, Denver, September 1980).

41. L. Levi, "Psychosocial, Occupational, Environmental, and Health Concepts; Research Results; and Applications," in G. P. Keita and S. L. Sauter, eds., *Work and Well-Being: An Agenda for the 1990s* (Washington, D.C.: American Psychological Association, 1992), 199–211.

42. L. R. Murphy and C. L. Cooper, eds., *Healthy and Productive Work: An International Perspective* (London and New York: Taylor & Francis, 2000).

43. R. L. Kahn, *Work and Health* (New York: Wiley, 1981); M. Gowing, J. Kraft, and J. C. Quick, *The New Organizational Reality: Downsizing, Restructuring, and Revitalization* (Washington, D.C.: American Psychological Association, 1998).

44. F. J. Landy, "Work Design and Stress," in G. P. Keita and S. L. Sauter, eds., *Work and Well-Being: An Agenda for the 1990s* (Washington, D.C.: American Psychological Association, 1992), 119–158.

45. C. Gresov, R. Drazin, and A. H. Van de Ven, "Work-Unit Task Uncertainty, Design, and Morale," *Organizational Studies* 10 (1989): 45–62.

46. Y. Baruch, "The Status of Research on Teleworking and an Agenda for Future Research," *International Journal of Management Review* 3 (2000): 113–129.

47. K. E. Pearlson and C. S. Saunders, "There's No Place Like Home: Managing Telecommuting Paradoxes," *Academy of Management Executive* 15 (2001): 117–128.

48. S. Caudron, "Working at Home Pays Off," *Personnel Journal* (November 1992): 40–47.

49. E. E. Potter, "Telecommuting: The Future of Work, Corporate Culture, and American Society," *Journal of Labor Research*, 01953613, Winter 2003, Vol. 24, Issue 1.

50. S. M. Pollan and M. Levine, "Asking for Flextime," *Working Women* (February 1994): 48.

51. S. Zuboff, *In the Age of the Smart Machine: The Future of Work and Power* (New York: Basic Books, 1988).

52. B. A. Gutek and S. J. Winter, "Computer Use, Control over Computers, and Job Satisfaction," in S. Oskamp and S. Spacapan, eds., *People's Reactions to Technology in Factories, Offices, and Aerospace: The Claremont Symposium on Applied Social Psychology* (Newbury Park, Calif.: Sage, 1990), 121–144.

53. L. M. Schleifer and B. C. Amick III, "System Response Time and Method of Pay: Stress Effects in Computer-Based Tasks," *International Journal of Human-Computer Interaction* 1 (1989): 23–39.

54. K. Voight, "Virtual Work: Some Telecommuters Take Remote Work to the Extreme," *The Wall Street Journal Europe* (Feburary 1, 2001): 1.

55. B. M. Staw and R. D. Boettger, "Task Revision: A Neglected Form of Work Performance," *Academy of Management Journal* 33 (1990): 534–559.

56. H. S. Schwartz, "Job Involvement as Obsession Compulsion," *Academy of Management Review* 7 (1982): 429–432.

57. C. J. Nemeth and B. M. Staw, "The Trade-offs of Social Control and Innovation in Groups and Organizations," in L. Berkowitz, ed., *Advances in Experimental Social Psychology*, vol. 22 (New York: Academic Press, 1989), 175–210.

58. G. Salvendy, *Handbook of Industrial Engineering: Technology and Operations Management* (New York: John Wiley & Sons, 2001).

59. D. M. Herold, "Using Technology to Improve Our Management of Labor Market Trends," in M. Greller, ed., "Managing Careers with a Changing Workforce," *Journal of Organizational Change Management* 3 (1990): 44–57.

60. D. A. Whetten and K. S. Cameron, *Developing Management Skills* (Upper Saddle River, N.J.: Prentice Hall, 2001).

Chapter 14

1. J. Child, *Organization* (New York: Harper & Row, 1984).

2. P. Lawrence and J. Lorsch, "Differentiation and Integration in Complex Organizations," *Administrative Science Quarterly* 12 (1967): 1–47.

3. P. Lawrence and J. Lorsch, *Organization and Environment: Managing Differentiation and Integration*, rev. ed. (Cambridge, Mass.: Harvard University Press, 1986).

4. J. Hage, "An Axiomatic Theory of Organizations," *Administrative Science Quarterly* 10 (1965): 289–320.

5. W. Ouchi and J. Dowling, "Defining the Span of Control," *Administrative Science Quarterly* 19 (1974): 357–365.

6. L. Porter and E. Lawler III, "Properties of Organization Structure in Relation to Job Attitudes and Job Behavior," *Psychological Bulletin* 65 (1965): 23–51.

7. J. Ivancevich and J. Donnelly, Jr., "Relation of Organization and Structure to Job Satisfaction, Anxiety-Stress, and Performance," *Administrative Science Quarterly* 20 (1975): 272–280.

8. R. Dewar and J. Hage, "Size, Technology, Complexity, and Structural Differentiation: Toward a Theoretical Synthesis," *Administrative Science Quarterly* 23 (1978): 111–136.

9. Lawrence and Lorsch, "Differentiation and Integration," 1–47.

10. J. R. R. Galbraith, *Designing Complex Organizations* (Reading, Mass.: Addison-Wesley-Longman, 1973).

11. W. Altier, "Task Forces: An Effective Management Tool," *Management Review* 76 (1987): 26–32.

12. P. Lawrence and J. Lorsch, "New Managerial Job: The Integrator," *Harvard Business Review* 45 (1967): 142–151.

13. J. Lorsch and P. Lawrence, "Organizing for Product Innovation," *Harvard Business Review* 43 (1965): 110–111.

14. D. Pugh, D. Hickson, C. Hinnings, and C. Turner, "Dimensions of Organization Structure," *Administrative Science Quarterly* 13 (1968): 65–91; B. Reimann, "Dimensions of Structure in Effective Organizations: Some Empirical Evidence," *Academy of Management Journal* 17 (1974): 693–708; S. Robbins, *Organization Theory: The Structure and Design of Organizations*, 3rd ed. (Englewood Cliffs, N.J.: Prentice-Hall, 1990).

15. H. Mintzberg, *The Structuring of Organizations* (Englewood Cliffs, N.J.: Prentice-Hall, 1979).

16. Mintzberg, *The Structuring of Organizations*.

17. K. Weick, "Educational Institutions as Loosely Coupled Systems," *Administrative Science Quarterly* (1976): 1–19.

18. D. Miller and C. Droge, "Psychological and Traditional Determinants of Structure," *Administrative Science Quarterly* 31 (1986): 540; H. Tosi, Jr., and J. Slocum, Jr., "Contingency Theory: Some Suggested Directions," *Journal of Management* 10 (1984): 9–26.

19. D. Mack and J. C. Quick, "EDS: An Inside View of a Corporate Life Cycle Transition," *Organizational Dynamics* 30(3) (2002): 282–293.

20. M. Meyer, "Size and the Structure of Organizations: A Causal Analysis," *American Sociological Review* 37 (1972): 434–441; J. Beyer and H. Trice, "A Reexamination of the Relations between Size and Various Components of Organizational Complexity," *Administrative Science Quarterly* 24 (1979): 48–64; B. Mayhew, R. Levinger, J. McPherson, and T. James, "Systems Size and Structural Differentiation in Formal Organizations: A Baseline Generator for Two Major Theoretical Propositions," *American Sociological Review* 37 (1972): 26–43.

21. M. Gowing, J. Kraft, and J. C. Quick, *The New Organizational Reality: Downsizing, Restructuring, and Revitalization* (Washington, D.C.: American Psychological Association, 1998).

22. B. A. Pasternack and A. J. Viscio, *The Centerless Corporation: A New Model for Transforming Your Organization for Growth and Prosperity* (New York: Simon & Schuster, 1999).

23. J. Woodward, *Industrial Organization: Theory and Practices* (London: Oxford University Press, 1965).

24. C. Perrow, "A Framework for the Comparative Analysis of Organizations," *American Sociological Review* 32 (1967): 194–208; D. Rosseau, "Assessment of Technology in Organizations: Closed versus Open Systems Approaches," *Academy of Management Review* 4 (1979): 531–542.

25. Perrow, "A Framework for the Comparative Analysis of Organizations," 194–208.

26. J. D. Thompson, *Organizations in Action* (New York: McGraw-Hill, 1967).

27. P. Nemetz and L. Fry, "Flexible Manufacturing Organizations: Implication for Strategy Formulation and Organization Design," *Academy of Management Review* 13 (1988): 627–638; G. Huber, "The Nature and Design of Post-Industrial Organizations," *Management Science* 30 (1984): 934.

28. E. Feitzinger and H. L. Lee, "Mass Customization at Hewlett-Packard: The Power of Postponement," *Harvard Business Review* 75 (1997): 116–121.

29. Thompson, *Organizations in Action*.

30. H. Downey, D. Hellriegel, and J. Slocum, Jr., "Environmental Uncertainty: The Construct and Its Application," *Administrative Science Quarterly* 20 (1975): 613–629.

31. T. Burns and G. Stalker, *The Management of Innovation* (London: Tavistock, 1961); Mintzberg, *The Structuring of Organizations*.

32. M. Chandler and L. Sayles, *Managing Large Systems* (New York: Harper & Row, 1971).

33. G. Dess and D. Beard, "Dimensions of Organizational Task Environments," *Administrative Science Quarterly* 29 (1984): 52–73.

34. J. Courtright, G. Fairhurst, and L. Rogers, "Interaction Patterns in Organic and Mechanistic Systems," *Academy of Management Journal* 32 (1989): 773–802.

35. R. Daft, *Organization Theory and Design*, 8th ed. (Mason, OH: South-Western/Thomson Learning, 2004).

36. D. Miller, "The Structural and Environmental Correlates of Business Strategy," *Strategic Management Journal* 8 (1987): 55–76.

37. W. R. Scott, *Organizations: Rational, Natural, and Open Systems*, 4th ed. (Upper Saddle River, N.J.: Prentice-Hall, 1997).

38. D. Miller and P. Friesen, "A Longitudinal Study of the Corporate Life Cycle," *Management Science* 30 (1984): 1161–1183.

39. M. H. Overholt, "Flexible Organizations: Using Organizational Design as a Competitive Advantage," *Human Resource Planning* 20 (1997): 22–32; P. W. Roberts and R. Greenwood, "Integrating Transaction Cost and Institutional Theories: Toward a Constrained-Efficiency Framework for Understanding Organizational Design Adoption," *Academy of Management Review* 22 (1997): 346–373.

40. C. W. L. Hill and G. R. Jones, *Strategic Management Theory*, 5th ed. (Boston: Houghton Mifflin, 2000).

41. Daft, *Organization Theory and Design*.

42. C. M. Savage, *5th Generation Management, Revised Edition: Co-Creating through Virtual Enterprising, Dynamic Teaming, and Knowledge Networking* (Boston: Butterworth-Heinemann, 1996).

43. S. M. Davis, *Future Perfect* (Perseus Publishing, 1997).

44. A. Boynton and B. Victor, "Beyond Flexibility: Building and Managing a Dynamically Stable Organization," *California Management Review* 8 (Fall 1991): 53–66.

45. J. Fulk, "Global Network Organizations: Emergence and Future Prospects," *Human Relations* 54 (2001): 91–100.

46. The use of the theatrical troupe as an analogy for virtual organizations was first used by David Mack circa 1995.

47. R. Teerlink and L. Ozley, *More than a Motorcycle: The Leadership Journey at Harley-Davidson* (Boston: Harvard Business School Press, 2000).

48. W. A. Cohen and N. Cohen, *The Paranoid Organization and 8 Other Ways Your Company Can Be Crazy: Advice from an Organizational Shrink* (New York: American Management Association, 1993).

49. P. E. Tetlock, "Cognitive Biases and Organizational Correctives: Do Both Disease and Cure Depend on the Politics of the Beholder?" *Administrative Science Quarterly* 45 (2000): 293–326.

50. M. F. R. Kets de Vries and D. Miller, "Personality, Culture, and Organization," *Academy of Management Review* 11 (1986): 266–279.

Chapter 15

1. T. E. Deal and A. A. Kennedy, *Corporate Cultures* (Reading, Mass.: Addison-Wesley, 1982).

2. W. Ouchi, *Theory Z* (Reading, Mass.: Addison-Wesley, 1981).

3. T. J. Peters and R. H. Waterman, *In Search of Excellence* (New York: Harper & Row, 1982).

4. M. Gardner, "Creating a Corporate Culture for the Eighties," *Business Horizons* (January–February 1985): 59–63.

5. Definition adapted from E. H. Schein, *Organizational Culture and Leadership* (San Francisco: Jossey-Bass, 1985), 9.

6. C. D. Sutton and D. L. Nelson, "Elements of the Cultural Network: The Communicators of Corporate Values," *Leadership and Organization Development* 11 (1990): 3–10.

7. A. Bandura, *Social Learning Theory* (Englewood Cliffs, N.J.: Prentice-Hall, 1977).

8. J. M. Beyer and H. M. Trice, "How an Organization's Rites Reveal Its Culture," *Organizational Dynamics* 16 (1987): 5–24.

9. H. M. Trice and J. M. Beyer, "Studying Organizational Cultures through Rites and Ceremonials," *Academy of Management Review* 9 (1984): 653–669.

10. M. J. Schneider, "The Wal-Mart Annual Meeting: From Small-Town America to a Global Corporate Culture," *Human Organization* 57 (1998): 292–299.

11. H. Levinson and S. Rosenthal, *CEO: Corporate Leadership in Action* (New York: Basic Books, 1984).

12. V. Sathe, "Implications of Corporate Culture: A Manager's Guide to Action," *Organizational Dynamics* 12 (1987): 5–23.

13. R. J. Holder and R. McKinney, "Corporate Change and the Hero's Quest," *Journal for Quality and Participation* 15 (1992): 34–36; E. Schein and W. Bennis, *Corporate Culture Survival Guide* (San Francisco: Jossey-Bass, 1999).

14. J. Martin, M. S. Feldman, M. J. Hatch, and S. B. Sitkin, "The Uniqueness Paradox in Organizational Stories," *Administrative Science Quarterly* 28 (1983): 438–453.

15. B. Durrance, "Stories at Work," *Training and Development* (February 1997): 25–29.

16. R. Goffee and G. Jones, "What Holds the Modern Company Together?" *Harvard Business Review* (November–December 1996): 133–143.

17. C. Argyris and D. A. Schon, *Organizational Learning* (Reading, Mass.: Addison-Wesley, 1978).

18. G. Timmerman and C. Bajema, "The Impact of Organizational Culture on Perceptions and Experiences of Sexual Harassment," *Journal of Vocational Behavior* 57 (2000): 188–205.

19. "Sounds Like a New Woman," *New Woman* (February 1993): 144.

20. M. Peterson, "Work, Corporate Culture, and Stress: Implications for Worksite Health Promotion," *American Journal of Health Behavior* 21 (1997): 243–252.

21. L. Smircich, "Concepts of Culture and Organizational Analysis," *Administrative Science Quarterly* (1983): 339–358.

22. Y. Weiner and Y. Vardi, "Relationships between Organizational Culture and Individual Motivation: A Conceptual Integration," *Psychological Reports* 67 (1990): 295–306.

23. M. R. Louis, "Surprise and Sense Making: What Newcomers Experience in Entering Unfamiliar Organizational Settings," *Administrative Science Quarterly* 25 (1980): 209–264.

24. L. Adams, "Security High as Baldrige Awards Presented," *Quality* 24 (2003): 8. Also see http://www.ssmhc.com.

25. J. P. Kotter and J. L. Heskett, *Corporate Culture and Performance* (New York: Free Press, 1992).

26. Deal and Kennedy, *Corporate Cultures.*

27. D. R. Katz, *The Big Store* (New York: Viking, 1987).

28. G. G. Gordon, "Industry Determinants of Organizational Culture," *Academy of Management Review* 16 (1991): 396–415.

29. T. Noda and D. J. Collis, "The Evolution of Intraindustry Firm Heterogeneity: Insights from a Process Study," *Academy of Management Journal* 44 (2001): 897–925.

30. D. Rynecki and L. Clifford, "Ten Stocks to Last the Decade," *Fortune* 142 (2000): 114–122.

31. T. Harbert, "A Tale of Two Mobile Telephone Makers," *Company Business and Marketing* 26 (2000): 88; C. P. Wallace, "Ericsson's Wake-Up Call," *Time Europe* (May 12, 2003): 19.

32. G. Donaldson and J. Lorsch, *Decision Making at the Top* (New York: Basic Books, 1983).

33. R. H. Kilman, M. J. Saxton, and R. Serpa, eds., *Gaining Control of the Corporate Culture* (San Francisco: Jossey-Bass, 1986).

34. J. P. Kotter, *A Force for Change: How Leadership Differs from Management* (New York: Free Press, 1990); R. M. Kanter, *The Change Masters* (New York: Simon & Schuster, 1983).

35. T. Peters and N. Austin, *A Passion for Excellence: The Leadership Difference* (New York: Random House, 1985).

36. Schein, *Organizational Culture and Leadership.*

37. W. A. Cohen, *The Art of the Leader* (Englewood Cliffs, N.J.: Prentice-Hall, 1990).

38. R. R. Sims, "Changing an Organization's Culture under New Leadership," *Journal of Business Ethics* 25 (2000): 65–78.

39. J. A. Pearce II, T. R. Kramer, and D. K. Robbins, "Effects of Managers' Entrepreneurial Behavior on Subordinates," *Journal of Business Venturing* 12 (1997): 147–160.

40. D. A. Whetten, "Saraide's Chairman Hatim Tyabji on Creating and Sustaining a Values-Based Organizational Culture," *Academy of Management Executive* 14 (2000): 32–40.

41. G. R. Weaver, L. K. Trevino, and P. L. Cochran, "Corporate Ethics Programs as Control Systems: Influences of Executive Commitment and Environmental Factors," *Academy of Management Journal* 42 (1999): 41–57.

42. D. C. Feldman, "The Multiple Socialization of Organization Members," *Academy of Management Review* 6 (1981): 309–318.

43. R. Pascale, "The Paradox of Corporate Culture: Reconciling Ourselves to Socialization," *California Management Review* 27 (1985): 26–41.

44. D. L. Nelson, "Organizational Socialization: A Stress Perspective," *Journal of Occupational Behavior* 8 (1987): 311–324.

45. D. M. Cable, L. Aiman-Smith, P. W. Mulvey, and J. R. Edwards, "The Sources and Accuracy of Job Applicants' Beliefs about Organizational Culture," *Academy of Management Journal* 43 (2000): 1076–1085.

46. J. Chatman, "Matching People and Organizations: Selection and Socialization in Public Accounting Firms," *Administrative Science Quarterly* 36 (1991): 459–484.

47. D. L. Nelson, J. C. Quick, and M. E. Eakin, "A Longitudinal Study of Newcomer Role Adjustment in U.S. Organizations," *Work and Stress* 2 (1988): 239–253.

48. N. J. Allen and J. P. Meyer, "Organizational Socialization Tactics: A Longitudinal Analysis of Links to Newcomers' Commitment and Role Orientation," *Academy of Management Journal* 33 (1990): 847–858.

49. T. N. Bauer, E. W. Morrison, and R. R. Callister, "Organizational Socialization: A Review and Directions for Future Research," *Research in Personnel and Human Resources Management* 16 (1998): 149–214.

50. D. M. Cable and C. K. Parsons, "Socialization Tactics and Person–Organization Fit," *Personnel Psychology* 54 (2001): 1–23.

51. M. R. Louis, "Acculturation in the Workplace: Newcomers as Lay Ethnographers," in B. Schneider, ed., *Organizational Climate and Culture* (San Francisco: Jossey-Bass, 1990), 85–129.

52. D. M. Rousseau, "Assessing Organizational Culture: The Case for Multiple Methods," in B. Schneider, ed., *Organizational Climate and Culture* (San Francisco: Jossey-Bass, 1990).

53. R. A. Cooke and D. M. Rousseau, "Behavioral Norms and Expectations: A Quantitative Approach to the Assessment of Organizational Culture," *Group and Organizational Studies* 12 (1988): 245–273.

54. R. H. Kilmann and M. J. Saxton, *Kilmann-Saxton Culture-Gap Survey* (Pittsburgh: Organizational Design Consultants, 1983).

55. W. J. Duncan, "Organizational Culture: 'Getting a Fix' on an Elusive Concept," *Academy of Management Executive* 3 (1989): 229–236.

56. B. Woods, "Caution: Merging Cultures," *Chief Executive* (July 2001): 28.

57. N. J. Adler, *International Dimensions of Organizational Behavior*, 2nd ed. (Boston: PWS Kent, 1991).

58. A. Laurent, "The Cultural Diversity of Western Conceptions of Management," *International Studies of Management and Organization* 13 (1983): 75–96.

59. P. C. Earley and E. Mosakowski, "Creating Hybrid Team Cultures: An Empirical Test of Transnational Team Functioning," *Academy of Management Journal* 43 (2000): 26–49.

60. P. Bate, "Using the Culture Concept in an Organization Development Setting," *Journal of Applied Behavior Science* 26 (1990): 83–106.

61. K. R. Thompson and F. Luthans, "Organizational Culture: A Behavioral Perspective," in B. Schneider, ed., *Organizational Climate and Culture* (San Francisco: Jossey-Bass, 1990).

62. V. Sathe, "How to Decipher and Change Corporate Culture," in R. H. Kilman et al., *Managing Corporate Cultures* (San Francisco: Jossey-Bass, 1985).

63. J. B. Shaw, C. D. Fisher, and W. A. Randolph, "From Maternalism to Accountability: The Changing Cultures of Ma Bell and Mother Russia," *Academy of Management Executive* 5 (1991): 7–20.

64. D. Lei, J. W. Slocum, Jr., and R. W. Slater, "Global Strategy and Reward Systems: The Key Roles of Management Development and Corporate Culture," *Organizational Dynamics* 19 (1990): 27–41.

65. S. H. Rhinesmith, "Going Global from the Inside Out," *Training and Development Journal* 45 (1991): 42–47.

66. L. K. Trevino and K. A. Nelson, *Managing Business Ethics: Straight Talk about How to Do It Right* (New York: John Wiley & Sons, 1995).

67. A. Bhide and H. H. Stevenson, "Why Be Honest if Honesty Doesn't Pay?" *Harvard Business Review* (September–October 1990): 121–129.

68. J. L. Cruikshank and D. B. Sicilia, *The Engine That Could* (Boston: Harvard Business School Press, 1997).

69. S. W. Gellerman, "Why Good Managers Make Bad Ethical Choices," *Harvard Business Review* 64 (1986): 85–90.

70. J. R. Detert, R. G. Schroeder, and J. J. Mauriel, "A Framework for Linking Culture and Improvement Initiatives in Organizations," *Academy of Management Review* 25 (2000): 850–863.

71. J. Teresko, "Best Plants: Cadillac," *Industry Week* (October 21, 1991): 29–32.

72. M. Krebs, "Cadillac Starts Down a New Road," *Industry Week* (August 5, 1991): 18–23.

73. K. L. Alexander, "Texas Nameplate: Company Commitment Pays Off," *USA Today* (November 18, 1998): 5B.

Chapter 16

1. M. A. Verespej, "When Change Becomes the Norm," *Industry Week* (March 16, 1992): 35–38.

2. H. J. Van Buren III, "The Bindingness of Social and Psychological Contracts: Toward a Theory of Social Responsibility in Downsizing," *Journal of Business Ethics* 25 (2000): 205–219.

3. "Conoco Plans to Develop Oil Fields in Russia: Cost of Up to $3 Billion," *Journal Record* (June 19, 1992): 16.

4. L. Hirschhorn and T. Gilmore, "The New Boundaries of the 'Boundaryless' Company," *Harvard Business Review* (May–June 1992): 104–115.

5. M. Hickins, "Reconcilable Differences," *Management Review* 87 (1998): 54–58.

6. L. R. Offerman and M. Gowing, "Organizations of the Future: Changes and Challenges," *American Psychologist* (February 1990): 95–108.

7. W. B. Johnston, "Global Work Force 2000: The New World Labor Market," *Harvard Business Review*, (March–April 1991): 115–127.

8. A. Faircloth, "Guess Who's Coming to Denny's," *Fortune* (August 3, 1998) 108–110.

9. G. Bylinsky, "Hot New Technologies for American Factories," *Fortune* (June 26, 2000): 288A–288K.

10. R. M. Kanter, "Improving the Development, Acceptance, and Use of New Technology: Organizational and Interorganizational Challenges," in *People and Technology in the Workplace* (Washington, D.C.: National Academy Press, 1991), 15–56.

11. J. A. Benson and D. L. Ross, "Sundstrand: A Case Study in Transformation of Cultural Ethics," *Journal of Business Ethics* 17 (1998): 1517–1527.

12. S. A. Mohrman and A. M. Mohrman, Jr., "The Environment as an Agent of Change," in A. M. Mohrman, Jr., et al., eds., *Large-Scale Organizational Change* (San Francisco: Jossey-Bass, 1989), 35–47.

13. T. D'Aunno, M. Succi, and J. A. Alexander, "The Role of Institutional and Market Forces in Divergent Organizational Change," *Administrative Science Quarterly* 45 (2000): 679–703.

14. D. Nadler, "Organizational Frame-Bending: Types of Change in the Complex Organization," in R. Kilmann and T. Covin, eds., *Corporate Transformation* (San Francisco: Jossey-Bass, 1988), 66–83.

15. L. Ackerman, "Development, Transition, or Transformation: The Question of Change in Organizations," *OD Practitioner* (December 1986): 1–8.

16. T. D. Jick, *Managing Change* (Homewood, Ill.: Irwin, 1993), 3.

17. R. M. Kanter, *The Change Masters* (New York: Simon & Schuster, 1983).

18. J. R. Katzenbach, *Real Change Leaders* (New York: Times Business, 1995).

19. J. L. Denis, L. Lamothe, and A. Langley, "The Dynamics of Collective Leadership and Strategic Change in Pluralistic Organizations," *Academy of Management Journal* 44 (2001): 809–837.

20. M. Beer, *Organization Change and Development: A Systems View* (Santa Monica, Calif.: Goodyear, 1980), 78.

21. F. Cheyunski and J. Millard, "Accelerated Business Transformation and the Role of the Organizational Architect," *Journal of Applied Behavioral Science* 34 (1998): 268–285.

22. N. A. M. Worren, K. Ruddle, and K. Moore, "From Organizational Development to Change Management: The Emergence of a New Profession," *Journal of Applied Behavioral Science* 35 (1999): 273–286.

23. P. G. Audia, E. A. Locke, and K. G. Smith, "The Paradox of Success: An Archival and a Laboratory Study of Strategic Persistence Following Radical Environmental Change," *Academy of Management Journal* 43 (2000): 837–853.

24. J. W. Brehm, *A Theory of Psychological Reactance* (New York: Academic Press, 1966).

25. J. A. Klein, "Why Supervisors Resist Employee Involvement," *Harvard Business Review* 62 (1984): 87–95.

26. B. L. Kirkman, R. G. Jones, and D. L. Shapiro, "Why Do Employees Resist Teams? Examining the 'Resistance Barrier' to Work Team Effectiveness," *International Journal of Conflict Management* 11 (2000): 74–92.

27. D. L. Nelson and M. A. White, "Management of Technological Innovation: Individual Attitudes, Stress, and Work Group Attributes," *Journal of High Technology Management Research* 1 (1990): 137–148.

28. D. Klein, "Some Notes on the Dynamics of Resistance to Change: The Defender Role," in W. G. Bennis, K. D. Benne, R. Chin, and K. E. Corey, eds., *The Planning of Change*, 3rd ed. (New York: Holt, Rinehart & Winston, 1969), 117–124.

29. T. G. Cummings and E. F. Huse, *Organizational Development and Change* (St. Paul, Minn.: West, 1989).

30. N. DiFonzo and P. Bordia, "A Tale of Two Corporations: Managing Uncertainty during Organizational Change," *Human Resource Management* 37 (1998): 295–303.

31. L. P. Livingstone, M. A. White, D. L. Nelson, and F. Tabak. "Delays in Technological Innovation Implementations: Some Preliminary Results on a Common but Understudied Occurrence," working paper, Oklahoma State University.

32. D. T. Jaffe and C. D. Scott, "Reengineering in Practice: Where Are the People? Where Is the Learning?" *Journal of Applied Behavioral Science* 34 (1998): 250–267.

33. A. B. Fisher, "Making Change Stick," *Fortune* (April 17, 1995): 121–131.

34. J. P. Kotter and L. A. Schlesinger, "Choosing Strategies for Change," *Harvard Business Review* 57 (1979): 109–112; W. Bridges, *Transitions: Making Sense of Life's Changes* (Reading, Mass.: Addison-Wesley, 1980); H. Woodward and S. Buchholz, *Aftershock: Helping People through Corporate Change* (New York: Wiley, 1987).

35. S. Michailova, "Contrasts in Culture: Russian and Western Perspectives on Organizational Change," *Academy of Management Executive* 14 (2000): 99–112.

36. K. Lewin, "Frontiers in Group Dynamics," *Human Relations* 1 (1947): 5–41.

37. W. McWhinney, "Meta-Praxis: A Framework for Making Complex Changes," in A. M. Mohrman, Jr., et al., eds., *Large-Scale Organizational Change* (San Francisco: Jossey-Bass, 1989), 154–199.

38. M. Beer and E. Walton, "Developing the Competitive Organization: Interventions and Strategies," *American Psychologist* 45 (1990): 154–161.

39. B. Bertsch and R. Williams, "How Multinational CEOs Make Change Programs Stick," *Long Range Planning* 27 (1994): 12–24.

40. W. L. French and C. H. Bell, *Organization Development: Behavioral Science Interventions for Organization Improvement*, 4th ed. (Englewood Cliffs, N.J.: Prentice-Hall, 1990); W. W. Burke, *Organization Development: A Normative View* (Reading, Mass.: Addison-Wesley, 1987).

41. A. Huczynski, *Encyclopedia of Organizational Change Methods* (Brookfield, Vt.: Gower, 1987).

42. A. O. Manzini, *Organizational Diagnosis* (New York: AMACOM, 1988).

43. M. R. Weisbord, "Organizational Diagnosis: Six Places to Look for Trouble with or without a Theory," *Group and Organization Studies* (December 1976): 430–444.

44. H. Levinson, *Organizational Diagnosis* (Cambridge, Mass.: Harvard University Press, 1972).

45. J. Nicholas, "The Comparative Impact of Organization Development Interventions," *Academy of Management Review* 7 (1982): 531–542.

46. C. Cammann, M. Fichman, G. D. Jenkins, and J. Klesh, "Assessing the Attitudes and Perceptions of Organization Members," in S. Seashore, E. Lawler III, P. Mirvis, and C. Cammann, eds., *Assessing Organizational Change: A Guide to Methods, Measures, and Practices* (New York: Wiley, 1983), 71–138.

47. G. Odiorne, *Management by Objectives* (Marshfield, Mass.: Pitman, 1965).

48. E. Huse, "Putting in a Management Development Program That Works," *California Management Review* 9 (1966): 73–80.

49. J. P. Muczyk and B. C. Reimann, "MBO as a Complement to Effective Leadership," *Academy of Management Executive* (May 1989): 131–138.

50. L. L. Berry and A. Parasuraman, "Prescriptions for a Service Quality Revolution in America," *Organizational Dynamics* 20 (1992): 5–15.

51. "Five Companies Win 1992 Baldrige Quality Awards," *Business America* (November 2, 1992): 7–16.

52. D. M. Anderson, "Hidden Forces," *Success* (April 1995): 12.

53. W. G. Dyer, *Team Building: Issues and Alternatives*, 2nd ed. (Reading, Mass.: Addison-Wesley, 1987).

54. E. Stephan, G. Mills, R. W. Pace, and L. Ralphs, "HRD in the Fortune 500: A Survey," *Training and Development Journal* (January 1988): 26–32.

55. A. Edmondson, "Psychological Safety and Learning Behavior in Work Teams," *Administrative Science Quarterly* 44 (1999): 350–383.

56. M. Whitmire and P. R. Nienstedt, "Lead Leaders into the '90s," *Personnel Journal* (May 1991): 80–85.

57. E. Salas, T. L. Dickinson, S. I. Tannenbaum, and S. A. Converse, *A Meta-Analysis of Team Performance and Training*, Naval Training System Center Technical Reports (Orlando, Fla.: U.S. Government, 1991).

58. B. B. Bunker and B. T. Alban, *Large Group Interventions* (San Francisco: Jossey-Bass, 1997).

59. E. Schein, *Its Role in Organization Development*, vol. 1 of Process Consultation (Reading, Mass.: Addison-Wesley, 1988).

60. H. Hornstein, "Organizational Development and Change Management: Don't Throw the Baby Out with the Bath Water," *Journal of Applied Behavioral Science* 37 (2001): 223–226.

61. Anon., "A History of Constant Innovation," *Workforce* 82 (March 2003): S4–S8.

62. J. Campbell and M. Dunnette, "Effectiveness of T-Group Experiences in Managerial Training and Development," *Psychological Bulletin* 70 (1968): 73–103.

63. R. T. Golembiewski, *Organization Development* (New Brunswick, N.J.: Transaction Publishers, 1989).

64. N. M. Dixon, "Evaluation and Management Development," in J. Pfeiffer, ed., *The 1991 Annual: Developing Human Resources* (San Diego: University Associates, 1991), 287–296.

65. R. W. Revans, *Action Learning* (London: Blonde & Briggs, 1980).

66. I. L. Goldstein, *Training in Organizations*, 3rd ed. (Pacific Grove, Calif.: Brooks/Cole, 1993).

67. K. Kamoche, "Developing Managers: The Functional, the Symbolic, the Sacred, and the Profane," *Organization Studies* 21 (2000): 747–774.

68. C. Steinburg, "Taking Charge of Change," *Training and Development* (March 1992): 26–32.

69. D. A. Nadler, "Concepts for the Management of Organizational Change," in J. R. Hackman, E. E. Lawler III, and L. W. Porter, eds., *Perspectives on Organizational Behavior* (New York: McGraw-Hill, 1983).

70. Cummings and Huse, *Organizational Development*; P. E. Connor and L. K. Lake, *Managing Organizational Change* (New York: Praeger, 1988).

71. R. L. Lowman, "Ethical Human Resource Practice in Organizational Settings," in D. W. Bray, ed., *Working with Organizations* (New York: Guilford Press, 1991).

72. H. Kelman, "Manipulation of Human Behavior: An Ethical Dilemma for the Social Scientist," in W. Bennis, K. Benne, and R. Chin, eds., *The Planning of Change* (New York: Holt, Rinehart, & Winston, 1969).

73. A. M. Pettigrew, R. W. Woodman, and K. S. Cameron, "Studying Organizational Change and Development: Challenges for Future Research," *Academy of Management Journal* 44 (2001): 697–713.

74. R. A. Katzell and R. A. Guzzo, "Psychological Approaches to Worker Productivity," *American Psychologist* 38 (1983): 468–472.

75. R. A. Guzzo, R. D. Jette, and R. A. Katzell, "The Effects of Psychologically Based Intervention Programs on Worker Productivity," *Personnel Psychology* 38 (1985): 275–291.

76. Goldstein, *Training in Organizations*.

77. T. Covin and R. H. Kilmann, "Participant Perceptions of Positive and Negative Influences on Large-Scale Change," *Group and Organization Studies* 15 (1990): 233–248.

A

adaptive culture An organizational culture that encourages confidence and risk taking among employees, has leadership that produces change, and focuses on the changing needs of customers.

adhocracy A selectively decentralized form of organization that emphasizes the support staff and mutual adjustment among people.

administrative orbiting Delaying action on a conflict by buying time.

affect The emotional component of an attitude.

affective commitment The type of organizational commitment that is based on an individual's desire to remain in an organization.

anthropocentric Placing human considerations at the center of job design decisions.

anthropology The science of the learned behavior of human beings.

anticipatory socialization The first socialization stage, which encompasses all of the learning that takes place prior to the newcomer's first day on the job.

artifacts Symbols of culture in the physical and social work environment.

assumptions Deeply held beliefs that guide behavior and tell members of an organization how to perceive and think about things.

attitude A psychological tendency expressed by evaluating an entity with some degree of favor or disfavor.

attribution theory A theory that explains how individuals pinpoint the causes of the behavior of themselves and others.

authority The right to influence another person.

authority-compliance manager (9,1) A leader who emphasizes efficient production.

authority-obedience manager (9,1) A manager who emphasizes efficient production.

autocratic style A style of leadership in which the leader uses strong, directive, controlling actions to enforce the rules, regulations, activities, and relationships in the work environment.

B

barriers to communication Aspects such as physical separation, status differences, gender differences, cultural diversity, and language that can impair effective communication in a workplace.

behavioral measures Personality assessments that involve observing an individual's behavior in a controlled situation.

benevolent An individual who is comfortable with an equity ratio less than that of his or her comparison other.

bounded rationality A theory that suggests that there are limits upon how rational a decision maker can actually be.

brainstorming A technique for generating as many ideas as possible on a given subject, while suspending evaluation until all the ideas have been suggested.

C

centralization The degree to which decisions are made at the top of the organization.

challenge The call to competition, contest, or battle.

change The transportation or modification of an organization and/or its stakeholders.

change agent The individual or group that undertakes the task of introducing and managing a change in an organization.

change and acquisition The third socialization stage, in which the newcomer begins to master the demands of the job.

character assassination An attempt to label or discredit an opponent.

character theory An ethical theory that emphasizes the character, personal virtues, and integrity of the individual.

charismatic leadership The use, by a leader, of personal abilities and talents in order to have profound and extraordinary effects on followers.

classical conditioning Modifying behavior so that a conditioned stimulus is paired with an unconditioned stimulus and elicits an unconditioned response.

coercive power Power that is based on an agent's ability to cause an unpleasant experience for a target.

cognitive dissonance A state of tension that is produced when an individual experiences conflict between attitudes and behavior.

cognitive moral development The process of moving through stages of maturity in terms of making ethical decisions.

cognitive style An individual's preference for gathering information and evaluating alternatives.

collectivism A cultural orientation in which individuals belong to tightly knit social frameworks, and they depend strongly on large extended families or clans.

communication The evoking of a shared or common meaning in another person.

communicator The person originating a message.

compensation A compromise mechanism in which an individual attempts to make up for a negative situation by devoting himself or herself to another pursuit with increased vigor.

complexity The degree to which many different types of activities occur in the organization.

conflict Any situation in which incompatible goals, attitudes, emotions, or behaviors lead to disagreement or opposition between two or more parties.

consensus An informational cue indicating the extent to which peers in the same situation behave in a similar fashion.

consequential theory An ethical theory that emphasizes the consequences or results of behavior.

consideration Leader behavior aimed at nurturing friendly, warm working relationships, as well as encouraging mutual trust and interpersonal respect within the work unit.

consistency An informational cue indicating the frequency of behavior over time.

contextual variables A set of characteristics that influences the organization's design processes.

continuance commitment The type of organizational commitment that is based on the fact that an individual cannot afford to leave.

conversion A withdrawal mechanism in which emotional conflicts are expressed in physical symptoms.

counter-role behavior Deviant behavior in either a correctly or incorrectly defined job or role.

country club manager (1,9) A manager who creates a happy, comfortable work environment.

creativity A process influenced by individual and organizational factors that results in the production of novel and useful ideas, products, or both.

cross-training A variation of job enlargement in which workers are trained in different specialized tasks or activities.

cultural theory An ethical theory that emphasizes respect for different cultural values.

D

data Uninterpreted and unanalyzed facts.

defensive communication Communication that can be aggressive, attacking and angry, or passive and withdrawing.

Delphi technique Gathering the judgments of experts for use in decision making.

democratic style A style of leadership in which the leader takes collaborative, reciprocal, interactive actions with followers concerning the work and work environment.

devil's advocacy A technique for preventing groupthink in which a group or individual is given the role of critic during decision making.

dialectical inquiry A debate between two opposing sets of recommendations.

differentiation The process of deciding how to divide the work in an organization.

discounting principle The assumption that an individual's behavior is accounted for by the situation.

disenchantment Feeling negativity or anger toward a change.

disengagement Psychological withdrawal from change.

disidentification Feeling that one's identity is being threatened by a change.

disorientation Feelings of loss and confusion due to a change.

displacement An aggressive mechanism in which an individual directs his or her anger toward someone who is not the source of the conflict.

distinctiveness An informational cue indicating the degree to which an individual behaves the same way in other situations.

distributive bargaining A negotiation approach in which the goals of the parties are in conflict, and each party seeks to maximize its resources.

distributive justice The fairness of the outcomes that individuals receive in an organization.

diversity All forms of individual differences, including culture, gender, age, ability, personality, religious affiliation, economic class, social status, military attachment, and sexual orientation.

divisionalized form A moderately decentralized form of organization that emphasizes the middle level and standardization of outputs.

due process nonaction A procedure set up to address conflicts that is so costly, time-consuming, or personally risky that no one will use it.

dynamic follower A follower who is a responsible steward of his or her job, is effective in managing the relationship with the boss, and practices self-management.

dysfunctional conflict An unhealthy, destructive disagreement between two or more people.

E

effective decision A timely decision that meets a desired objective and is acceptable to those individuals affected by it.

empowerment Sharing power within an organization.

enacted values Values reflected in the way individuals actually behave.

encounter The second socialization stage, in which the newcomer learns the tasks associated with the job, clarifies roles, and establishes new relationships at work.

engineering The applied science of energy and matter.

entitled An individual who is comfortable with an equity ratio greater than that of his or her comparison other.

environment Anything outside the boundaries of an organization.

environmental uncertainty The amount and rate of change in the organization's environment.

equity sensitive An individual who prefers an equity ratio equal to that of his or her comparison other.

escalation of commitment The tendency to continue to commit resources to a losing course of action.

espoused values What members of an organization say they value.

ethical behavior Acting in ways consistent with one's personal values and the commonly held values of the organization and society.

expatriate manager A manager who works in a country other than his or her home country.

expectancy The belief that effort leads to performance.

expert power The power that exists when an agent has information or knowledge that the target needs.

expert system A computer-based application that uses a representation of human expertise in a specialized field of knowledge to solve problems.

extinction The attempt to weaken a behavior by attaching no consequences to it.

extraversion A preference indicating that an individual is energized by interaction with other people.

F

fantasy A withdrawal mechanism that provides an escape from a conflict through daydreaming.

feedback loop The pathway that completes two-way communication.

feeling Making decisions in a personal, value-oriented way.

femininity The cultural orientation in which relationships and concern for others are valued.

first-impression error The tendency to form lasting opinions about an individual based on initial perceptions.

fixation An aggressive mechanism in which an individual keeps up a dysfunctional behavior that obviously will not solve the conflict.

flextime An alternative work pattern through which employees can set their own daily work schedules.

flight/withdrawal A withdrawal mechanism that entails physically escaping a conflict (flight) or psychologically escaping (withdrawal).

followership The process of being guided and directed by a leader in the work environment.

formal leadership Officially sanctioned leadership based on the authority of a formal position.

formal organization The official, legitimate, and most visible part of the system.

formalization The degree to which the organization has official rules, regulations, and procedures.

functional conflict A healthy, constructive disagreement between two or more people.

fundamental attribution error The tendency to make attributions to internal causes when focusing on someone else's behavior.

G

garbage can model A theory that contends that decisions in organizations are random and unsystematic.

generalized self-efficacy An individual's beliefs and expectancies about his or her ability to accomplish a specific task effectively.

glass ceiling A transparent barrier that keeps women from rising above a certain level in organizations.

goal setting The process of establishing desired results that guide and direct behavior.

group Two or more people with common interests or objectives.

group cohesion The "interpersonal glue" that makes members of a group stick together.

group polarization The tendency for group discussion to produce shifts toward more extreme attitudes among members.

groupthink A deterioration of mental efficiency, reality testing, and moral judgment resulting from in-group pressures.

guanxi The Chinese practice of building networks for social exchange.

H

Hawthorne studies Studies conducted during the 1920s and 1930s that discovered the existence of the informal organization.

heuristics Shortcuts in decision making that save mental activity.

hierarchy of authority The degree of vertical differentiation across levels of management.

humanistic theory The personality theory that emphasizes individual growth and improvement.

hygiene factor A work condition related to dissatisfaction caused by discomfort or pain.

I

identification A compromise mechanism whereby an individual patterns his or her behavior after another's.

implicit personality theory Opinions formed about other people that are based on our own mini-theories about how people behave.

impoverished manager (1,1) A manager who exerts just enough effort to avoid being fired.

impression management The process by which individuals try to control the impression others have of them.

incremental change Change of a relatively small scope, such as making small improvements.

individual differences The way in which factors such as skills, abilities, personalities, perceptions, attitudes, values, and ethics differ from one individual to another.

individualism A cultural orientation in which people belong to loose social frameworks, and their primary concern is for themselves and their families.

inequity The situation in which a person perceives he or she is receiving less than he or she is giving, or is giving less than he or she is receiving.

influence The process of affecting the thoughts, behavior, and feelings of another person.

informal leadership Unofficial leadership accorded to a person by other members of the organization.

informal organization The unofficial and less visible part of the system.

information Data that have been interpreted, analyzed, and have meaning to some user.

information power Access to and control over important information.

initiating structure Leader behavior aimed at defining and organizing work relationships and roles, as well as establishing clear patterns of organization, communication, and ways of getting things done.

instrumental values Values that represent the acceptable behaviors to be used in achieving some end state.

instrumentality The belief that performance is related to rewards.

integrated involvement Closeness achieved through tasks and activities.

integration The process of coordinating the different parts of an organization.

integrative approach The broad theory that describes personality as a composite of an individual's psychological processes.

integrative negotiation A negotiation approach that focuses on the merits of the issues and seeks a win-win solution.

interactional psychology The psychological approach that emphasizes that in order to understand human behavior, we must know something about the person and about the situation.

intergroup conflict Conflict that occurs between groups or teams in an organization.

interorganizational conflict Conflict that occurs between two or more organizations.

interpersonal communication Communication between two or more people in an organization.

interpersonal conflict Conflict that occurs between two or more individuals.

interrole conflict A person's experience of conflict among the multiple roles in his or her life.

intrapersonal conflict Conflict that occurs within an individual.

intrarole conflict Conflict that occurs within a single role, such as when a person receives conflicting messages from role senders about how to perform a certain role.

introversion A preference indicating that an individual is energized by time alone.

intuiting Gathering information through "sixth sense" and focusing on what could be rather than what actually exists.

intuition A fast, positive force in decision making utilized at a level below consciousness that involves learned patterns of information.

J

job A set of specified work and task activities that engage an individual in an organization.

Job Characteristics Model A framework for understanding person-job fit through the interaction of core job dimensions with critical psychological states within a person.

Job Diagnostic Survey (JDS) The survey instrument designed to measure the elements in the Job Characteristics Model.

job enlargement A method of job design that increases the number of activities in a job to overcome the boredom of overspecialized work.

job enrichment Designing or redesigning jobs by incorporating motivational factors into them.

job redesign An OD intervention method that alters jobs to improve the fit between individual skills and the demands of the job.

job rotation A variation of job enlargement in which workers are exposed to a variety of specialized jobs over time.

job satisfaction A pleasurable or positive emotional state resulting from the appraisal of one's job or job experiences.

job sharing An alternative work pattern in which there is more than one person occupying a single job.

judging Preferring closure and completion in making decisions.

jurisdictional ambiguity The presence of unclear lines of responsibility within an organization.

L

laissez-faire style A style of leadership in which the leader fails to accept the responsibilities of the position.

language The words, their pronunciation, and the methods of combining them used and understood by a group of people.

leader An advocate for change and new approaches to problems.

leader–member relations The quality of interpersonal relationships among a leader and the group members.

leadership The process of guiding and directing the behavior of people in the work environment.

Leadership Grid An approach to understanding a leader's or manager's concern for results (production) and concern for people.

lean production Using committed employees with ever-expanding responsibilities to achieve zero waste, 100 percent good product, delivered on time, every time.

learning A change in behavior acquired through experience.

least preferred coworker (LPC) The person a leader has least preferred to work with over his or her career.

legitimate power Power that is based on position and mutual agreement; agent and target agree that the agent has the right to influence the target.

locus of control An individual's generalized belief about internal control (self-control) versus external control (control by the situation or by others).

loss of individuality A social process in which individual group members lose self-awareness and its accompanying sense of accountability, inhibition, and responsibility for individual behavior.

M

M-oriented behavior Leader behavior that is sensitive to employees' feelings, emphasizes comfort in the work environment, works to reduce stress levels, and demonstrates appreciation for follower contributions.

Machiavellianism A personality characteristic indicating one's willingness to do whatever it takes to get one's own way.

machine bureaucracy A moderately decentralized form of organization that emphasizes the technical staff and standardization of work processes.

maintenance function An activity essential to effective, satisfying interpersonal relationships within a team or group.

management The study of overseeing activities and supervising people in organizations.

management by objectives (MBO) A goal-setting program based on interaction and negotiation between employees and managers.

management development A host of techniques for enhancing managers' skills in an organization.

manager An advocate for stability and the status quo.

Managerial Grid An approach to understanding a manager's concern for production and concern for people.

masculinity The cultural orientation in which assertiveness and materialism are valued.

meaning of work The way a person interprets and understands the value of work as part of life.

mechanistic structure An organizational design that emphasizes structured activities, specialized tasks, and centralized decision making.

medicine The applied science of healing or treatment of diseases to enhance an individual's health and well-being.

mentoring A work relationship that encourages development and career enhancement for people moving through the career cycle.

message The thoughts and feelings that the communicator is attempting to elicit in the receiver.

moral maturity The measure of a person's cognitive moral development.

motivation The process of arousing and sustaining goal-directed behavior.

motivation factor A work condition related to satisfaction of the need for psychological growth.

moving The second step in Lewin's change model, in which new attitudes, values, and behaviors are substituted for old ones.

Myers-Briggs Type Indicator (MBTI) An instrument developed to measure Carl Jung's theory of individual differences.

N

need for achievement A manifest (easily perceived) need that concerns individuals' issues of excellence, competition, challenging goals, persistence, and overcoming difficulties.

need for affiliation A manifest (easily perceived) need that concerns an individual's need to establish and maintain warm, close, intimate relationships with other people.

need for power A manifest (easily perceived) need that concerns an individual's need to make an impact on others, influence others, change people or events, and make a difference in life.

need hierarchy The theory that behavior is determined by a progression of physical, social, and psychological needs.

negative affect An individual's tendency to accentuate the negative aspects of himself or herself, other people, and the world in general.

negative consequences Results of a behavior that a person finds unattractive or aversive.

negativism An aggressive mechanism in which a person responds with pessimism to any attempt at solving a problem.

new communication technology The various new technologies—such as electronic mail, voice mail, and fax machines—which are used for interpersonal communication.

nominal group technique (NGT) A structured approach to group decision making that focuses on generating alternatives and choosing one.

nonaction Doing nothing in hopes that a conflict with disappear.

nondefensive communication Communication that is assertive, direct, and powerful.

nonprogrammed decision A new, complex decision that requires a creative solution.

nonverbal communication All elements of communication that do not involve words.

normative commitment A perceived obligation to remain with the organization.

norms of behavior The standards that a work group uses to evaluate the behavior of its members.

O

objective knowledge Knowledge that results from research and scholarly activities.

one-way communication Communication in which a person sends a message to another person and no questions, feedback, or interaction follow.

operant conditioning Modifying behavior through the use of positive or negative consequences following specific behaviors.

opportunistic "what's in it for me" manager (Opp) A leader whose style aims to maximize self-benefit.

organic structure An organizational design that emphasizes teamwork, open communication, and decentralized decision making.

organization development (OD) A systematic approach to organizational improvement that applies behavioral science theory and research in order to increase individual and organizational well-being and effectiveness.

organization man manager (5,5) A manager who maintains the status quo.

organizational behavior The study of individual behavior and group dynamics in organizational settings.

organizational citizenship behavior Behavior that is above and beyond the call of duty.

organizational commitment The strength of an individual's identification with an organization.

organizational (corporate) culture A pattern of basic assumptions that are considered valid and that are taught to new members as the way to perceive, think, and feel in the organization.

organizational design The process of constructing and adjusting an organization's structure to achieve its goals.

organizational life cycle The differing stages of an organization's life from birth to death.

organizational politics The use of power and influence in organizations.

organizational socialization The process by which newcomers are transformed from outsiders to participating, effective members of the organization.

organizational structure The linking of departments and jobs within an organization.

P

P-oriented behavior Leader behavior that encourages a fast work pace, emphasizes good quality and high accuracy, works toward high-quantity production, and demonstrates concern for rules and regulations.

participative decision making Decision making in which individuals who are affected by decisions influence the making of those decisions.

paternalistic "father knows best" manager (9+9) A leader who promises reward and threatens punishment.

people The human resources of the organization.

perceiving Preferring to explore many alternatives and flexibility.

perceptual screen A window through which we interact with people that influences the quality, accuracy, and clarity of the communication.

performance appraisal The evaluation of a person's performance.

person–role conflict Conflict that occurs when an individual is expected to perform behaviors in a certain role that conflict with his or her personal values.

personal power Power used for personal gain.

personality A relatively stable set of characteristics that influences an individual's behavior.

planned change Change resulting from a deliberate decision to alter the organization.

political behavior Actions not officially sanctioned by an organization that are taken to influence others in order to meet one's personal goals.

position power The authority associated with the leader's formal position in the organization.

positive affect An individual's tendency to accentuate the positive aspects of himself or herself, other people, and the world in general.

positive consequences Results of a behavior that a person finds attractive or pleasurable.

power The ability to influence another person.

power distance The degree to which a culture accepts unequal distribution of power.

powerlessness A lack of power.

procedural justice The fairness of the process by which outcomes are allocated in an organization.

process consultation An OD method that helps managers and employers improve the processes that are used in organizations.

professional bureaucracy A decentralized form of organization that emphasizes the operating level and standardization of skills.

programmed decision A simple, routine matter for which a manager has an established decision rule.

projection Overestimating the number of people who share our own beliefs, values, and behaviors.

projective test A personality test that elicits an individual's response to abstract stimuli.

psychoanalysis Sigmund Freud's method for delving into the unconscious mind to understand better a person's motives and needs.

psychodynamic theory The personality theory that emphasizes the unconscious determinants of behavior.

psychological intimacy Emotional and psychological closeness to other teams or group members.

psychology The science of human behavior.

punishment The attempt to eliminate or weaken undesirable behavior by either bestowing negative consequences or withholding positive consequences.

Q

quality circle (QC) A small group of employees who work voluntarily on company time, typically one hour per week, to address work-related problems such as quality control, cost reduction, production planning and techniques, and even product design.

quality program A program that embeds product and service quality excellence into the organizational culture.

quality team A team that is part of an organization's structure and is empowered to act on its decisions regarding product and service quality.

R

rationality A logical, step-by-step approach to decision making, with a thorough analysis of alternatives and their consequences.

rationalization A compromise mechanism characterized by trying to justify one's behavior by constructing bogus reasons for it.

receiver The person receiving a message.

referent power An elusive power that is based on interpersonal attraction.

reflective listening A skill intended to help the receiver and communicator clearly and fully understand the message sent.

refreezing The final step in Lewin's change model, which involves the establishment of new attitudes, values, and behaviors as the new status quo.

reinforcement The attempt to develop or strengthen desirable behavior by either bestowing positive consequences or withholding negative consequences.

reinvention The creative application of new technology.

reward power Power based on an agent's ability to control rewards that a target wants.

richness The ability of a medium or channel to elicit or evoke meaning in the receiver.

risk aversion The tendency to choose options that entail fewer risks and less uncertainty.

robotics The use of robots in organizations.

role negotiation A technique whereby individuals meet and clarify their psychological contract.

rule-based theory An ethical theory that emphasizes the character of the act itself rather than its effects.

S

satisfice To select the first alternative that is "good enough," because the costs in time and effort are too great to optimize.

secrecy Attempting to hide a conflict or an issue that has the potential to create conflict.

selective perception The process of selecting information that supports our individual viewpoints while discounting information that threatens our viewpoints.

self-esteem An individual's general feeling of self-worth.

self-fulfilling prophecy The situation in which our expectations about people affect our interaction with them in such a way that our expectations are fulfilled.

self-interest What is in the best interest and benefit to an individual.

self-managed team A team that makes decisions that were once reserved for managers.

self-monitoring The extent to which people base their behavior on cues from other people and situations.

self-report questionnaire A common personality assessment that involves an individual's responses to a series of questions.

self-serving bias The tendency to attribute one's own successes to internal causes and one's failures to external causes.

sensing Gathering information through the five senses.

sensitivity training An intervention designed to help individuals understand how their behavior affects others.

simple structure A centralized form of organization that emphasizes the upper echelon and direct supervision.

skill development The mastery of abilities essential to successful functioning in organizations.

skills training Increasing the job knowledge, skills, and abilities that are necessary to do a job effectively.

social decision schemes Simple rules used to determine final group decisions.

social information-processing (SIP) model A model that suggests that the important job factors depend in part on what others tell a person about the job.

social learning The process of deriving attitudes from family, peer groups, religious organizations, and culture.

social loafing The failure of a group member to contribute personal time, effort, thoughts, or other resources to the group.

social perception The process of interpreting information about another person.

social power Power used to create motivation or to accomplish group goals.

social responsibility The obligation of an organization to behave in ethical ways.

sociology The science of society.

sociotechnical systems (STS) Giving equal attention to technical and social considerations in job design.

specialization The degree to which jobs are narrowly defined and depend on unique expertise.

standardization The degree to which work activities are accomplished in a routine fashion.

status structure The set of authority and task relations among a group's members.

stereotype A generalization about a group of people.

strategic change Change of a larger scale, such as organizational restructuring.

strategic contingencies Activities that other groups depend on in order to complete their tasks.

strong culture An organizational culture with a consensus on the values that drive the company and with an intensity that is recognizable even to outsiders.

strong situation A situation that overwhelms the effects of individual personalities by providing strong cues for appropriate behavior.

structure The manner in which an organization's work is designed at the micro level, as well as how departments, divisions, and the overall organization are designed at the macro level.

superordinate goal An organizational goal that is more important to both parties in a conflict than their individual or group goals.

survey feedback A widely used method of intervention whereby employee attitudes are solicited using a questionnaire.

synergy A positive force in groups that occurs when group members stimulate new solutions to problems through the process of mutual influence and encouragement in the group.

T

task An organization's mission, purpose, or goal for existing.

task environment The elements of an organization's environment that are related to its goal attainment.

task function An activity directly related to the effective completion of a team's work.

task revision The modification of incorrectly specified roles or jobs.

task structure The degree of clarity, or ambiguity, in the work activity assigned to the group.

task-specific self-efficacy An individual's beliefs and expectancies about his or her ability to perform a specific task effectively.

team A small number of people with complementary skills who are committed to a common mission, performance goals, and approach for which they hold themselves mutually accountable.

team building An intervention designed to improve the effectiveness of a work group.

team manager (9,9) A manager who builds a highly productive team of committed people.

technocentric Placing technology and engineering at the center of job design decisions.

technological interdependence The degree of interrelatedness of the organization's various technological elements.

technology The intellectual and mechanical processes used by an organization to transform inputs into products or services that meet organizational goals.

technostress The stress caused by new and advancing technologies in the workplace.

telecommuting Transmitting work from a home computer to the office using a modem.

terminal values Values that represent the goals to be achieved, or the end states of existence.

Theory X A set of assumptions of how to manage individuals who are motivated by lower-order needs.

Theory Y A set of assumptions of how to manage individuals who are motivated by higher-order needs.

thinking Making decisions in a logical, objective fashion.

time orientation Whether a culture's values are oriented toward the future (long-term orientation) or toward the past and present (short-term orientation).

total quality management (TQM) The total dedication to continuous improvement and to customers so that the customers' needs are met and their expectations exceeded.

trait theory The personality theory that states that in order to understand individuals, we must break down behavior patterns into a series of observable traits.

transformational change Change in which the organization moves to a radically different, and sometimes unknown, future state.

transnational organization An organization in which the global viewpoint supersedes national issues.

triangulation The use of multiple methods to measure organizational culture.

two-way communication A form of communication in which the communicator and receiver interact.

U

uncertainty avoidance The degree to which a culture tolerates ambiguity and uncertainty.

unfreezing The first step in Lewin's change model, which involves encouraging individuals to discard old behaviors by shaking up the equilibrium state that maintains the status quo.

unplanned change Change that is imposed on the organization and is often unforeseen.

upper echelon A top-level executive team in an organization.

V

valence The value or importance one places on a particular reward.

values Enduring beliefs that a specific mode of conduct or end state of existence is personally or socially preferable to an opposite or converse mode of conduct or end state of existence.

virtual office A mobile platform of computer, telecommunication, and information technology and services.

W

whistle-blower An employee who informs authorities of the wrongdoings of his or her company or co-workers.

work Mental or physical activity that has productive results.

work simplification Standardization and the narrow, explicit specification of task activities for workers.

work team A group of people with complementary skills who are committed to a common mission, performance goals, and approach for which they hold themselves mutually accountable.

Z

zone of indifference The range in which attempts to influence a person will be perceived as legitimate and will be acted on without a great deal of thought.